THE
RESTLESS
GENERATION

THE RESTLESS GENERATION

How rock music changed the face of 1950s Britain

PETE FRAME

ROGAN
HOUSE

Exclusive distributors:
Music Sales Ltd, 14–15 Berners Street, London W1T 3LJ
Order number: JR 400180

First edition: October 2007
ISBN 978-0-95295-407-1
A catalogue record for this book is available from the British Library

Cover by Phil Smee at Waldo's Design & Dream Emporium
Printed and bound in the EU
Published by Rogan House

TO
GEORGE BAXTER SMITH
sage of the hills

A thousand men, say, go searching for gold.
After six months, one of 'em is lucky – one out of a thousand.
His find represents not only his own labour but that of the
nine hundred and ninety-nine others to boot.

Howard, the old prospector, in the 1948 film
The Treasure of the Sierra Madre

UBI SEMEN — IBI MESSIS

Introduction

Ubi semen, ibi messis. Our school motto proved prophetic. Often with good reason, we used to think it meant 'where the semen, there the mess is', but the accurate translation was 'where the seed, there the harvest'.

I became a teenager in November 1955, the month that *Rock Around The Clock* by Bill Haley & his Comets went to number one, the month *The Blackboard Jungle* burst onto the screen, the month rock 'n' roll got a grip on Britain, certainly on me. I must have known that I was destined to become a griot for my tribe. Would that I had been as passionately interested in medicine or architecture or banking or anything equally useful – but rock 'n' roll became the focus of my life. Accordingly, I have written this book from the perspective of both rabid fan and (as some have generously described me) historian, having lived with rock 'n' roll as the soundtrack of my schooldays and then, after many years of writing about more recent rock history, having gone back to re-examine the whole topsy-turvy fifties decade, in microscopic detail. These days, it seems, the past is not just a foreign country – it's a different planet.

I remember my headmaster at Luton Grammar School saying "sometimes, we might weaken and listen to a pop record", as though it were a sin on a par with wanking or telling lies or bullying. God, it was all I ever thought about! (Further distractions, the twin temptations of girls and motorbikes, had yet to materialize.) I made it my business to hear and evaluate every new record that came out. Grammar-grubs were supposed to be above all that; finding sustenance in popular music was a pursuit reserved for the hoi-polloi, we were told. Discussing the latest Jerry Lee Lewis record or passing round the music weeklies was a clandestine activity, frowned upon if discovered. It was beyond our control, of course: no book on the syllabus, no chemistry experiment, no athletic endeavour was anywhere near as vital or interesting as hearing the new Little Richard record for the first time. And then a hundred times after that.

As my mates and I suspected, we were not alone: there were a handful of terminal rock 'n' roll maniacs in every town and, moving in the circles I did, I was able to meet up with quite a few of them over the years.

I began collecting interviews for this book in 1989 but could never find the time to set everything out and start assembling what was a colossal jigsaw until four years ago, when I moved to a remote outpost in the Scottish Highlands. So much easier to work when there are no distractions and you're snowed in.

Although most of it was written wearing my historian's hat, some of my teenage prejudices have inevitably surfaced – but only in the cause of providing a clearer, more authentic picture of the times. A few bêtes noires (Jack Payne and Billy Cotton, for instance) get a bit of a roasting and I have been fairly scathing about the BBC. With ample justification. Listening to BBC Radio during the 1950s was like driving along a beautiful country lane with one's view obscured, all but obliterated, by an enormous, slow-moving lorry – not just for a few miles but for many years. I grew to love the BBC, of course. It is tempting to think that I mellowed with age, but it was the Beeb that changed, not me. They eventually took the blinds from their windows and grew into their boast as the greatest broadcasting organisation in the world. (A bit of creeping there; I don't want to bite the hand that feeds me.)

Of course, I realised long before I started this project that it would have even less commercial appeal than the other books in my esoteric catalogue, but there are things that a chap needs to do. I've never been in step with current trends and so, rather than embark on the fatiguing and probably fruitless task of trying to find a publisher who had even heard of Lonnie Donegan or Jack Good, I decided to knock the book out on my own independent label as a limited edition for friends and other interested parties. Book publishing? Why not? Let's have a go! I had got as far as getting the cover designed, obtaining quotes for a modest print run and finding a noble rock star acquaintance to pay for it when, at around seven minutes to midnight, who should come tripping back into my life but Johnny Rogan?

Since I first got to know him in the golden age of *Zigzag*, he had not only become the acclaimed author of more than 20 books but had also unlocked the secret codes of publishing. A man with a keen interest in political and social history as well as rock music, he was eager to read the manuscript and, even though he winced at some of my rampant self-indulgence and schoolboy enthusiasm, he offered a deal and a distribution network which I could not refuse.

After much conjecture we settled on The Restless Generation as the most apposite title after rejecting a long list including Move It, The Last Minutes Of Innocence, Solid Gone, The Boy Can't Help It, Turn It Down, Cool For Cats, Night Bus To Soho, Blue Jean Bop, The End Of Winter, Dream Chasers, Shake It Baby, Coffee Bar Cowboys, The Midnight Special, Looking For The Magic, The First Hurrah, The Noisy Revolution, The Siege Of Tin Pan Alley, Trouble Boys, Smoke Gets In Your Eyes, Playing For Keeps, Whole Lotta Shakin', Before The Beatles, Lend Me Your Comb, The Origin Of The Species and It Came From Outer Space. Was it a restless generation? Yes, of course ... and thanks to having been liberated from war and austerity by the previous generation, youngsters were now ready, willing and able to indulge themselves, to reject conformity in the shape of institution haircuts and regulation grey, and express themselves as teenagers – the first bunch of kids to do so. No longer little adults waiting to become big adults, we luxuriated in a world of our own, a teenage world from which uncomprehending, carping oldies were excluded. New youth and musical movements fused together in celebration as a generation gap opened.

The photograph of Tommy Steele on the cover has long been one of my favourites, seeming to catch not just that tick of time in November 1956 but the spirit of the whole innocent and optimistic decade. My thanks to Phil Smee for adapting it to include my old school colours – rhubarb and custard, as we called it.

I would like to thank the many people who allowed me to delve into their memories, interrogate them remorselessly and then phone at all hours to dig even deeper – including John Allison, Chris Barber, Lionel Bart, Rory Blackwell, Ron Bowden, Joe Brown, Denny Carter, Bill Colyer, Vince Cooze, Tony Crombie, Brian Daley, Karl Dallas, John RT Davies, Julian Davies, Diz Disley, Lonnie Donegan, Angela and Derek Duffy, Vince Eager, Jack and June Elliott, Mick Eve, Adam Faith, Georgie Fame, Sheila Finn, Vic Flick, Eric Ford,

Johnny Gentle, Jack Good, Benny Green, Colin Green, Brian Gregg, John Gustafson, Freddie Harper, Wee Willie Harris, John Hasted, Pat Hawes, John Jack, George Jennings, Bob Kelly, Tony Kohn, Alexis Korner, Bert Lankester, Freddy Lloyd, Chas McDevitt, Ian McLean, Tex Makins, Ben Marshall, Hank Marvin, Sonny Morris, Mickie Most, Alex Murray, Pete Newman, Mike O'Neill, Ken Orpen, Larry Page, John Paul, John Pilgrim, Roy Powell, Duffy Power, Rick Richards, Ian Samwell, Peggy Seeger, Tony Sheridan, Hylda Sims, Big Jim Sullivan, Redd Sullivan, David Sutch, Roger Van-Engel, Bill Varley, Bob Watson, Alan Weighall, Bruce Welch, Nancy Whiskey, Wally Whyton, Marty Wilde, Rory Wilde, Don Wilson, Martin Winsor, Eric Winter, Bobby Woodman and Johnny Worth. To those who have died in the interim, I apologise for taking so long to pull the book together.

Also of considerable help, whether they knew it or not, were Chloe Alexander, Sharon Anderson, Graham Andrews, Ray Baisden, Barry Ballard, Paul Barber, Ellie Barker, Stephanie Barnes, Stuart Batsford, John Beecher, Will Birch, Stuart Booth, John Braley, Holger Bunte, Laurence Canty, Anny Chettleborough, Andy Childs, Alan Clayson, Jeff Cloves, Stuart Colman, Nigel Cross, Susan Currie, Fred Dellar, Jeff Dexter, Roger Dopson, Bill Drummond, Todd Everett, Art Fein, Rob Finnis, John Firminger, Darren Fogden, Josie Frame, Eddie Garden, Vic Gibbons, Charlie Gillett, Lucy Grant, Jeff Griffin, Phil Guidal, Rob Gurney, Colin Hill, Richard Hoare, Dorothy Howe, Kevin Howlett, Ken Hunt, Dave Laing, Colin Larkin, Pete Latham, Barry Lazell, Spencer Leigh, Mark Lewisohn, Mark Leviton, Ian Luck, Dave McAleer, Brian McGarry, Phil McMullen, George Melly, Bill Millar, Peter Moody, Jonathan Morrish, Christian Nauwelaers, Roger Nunn, Peter O'Brien, Betty Osment, Carole Pallister, John Peel, Chris Petit, Deborah Philips, Robert Plant, John Platt, Tony Poole, Rocky Prior, Suzi Quatro, Donna Reed, Paul Reno, Rosie Russell, Neil Scaplehorn, Gene Sculatti, Phil Shaw, Tom Sheehan, Keith Smith, Porgie Smith, Primrose Smith, Paul Stanley, Mark Stanton, Christine Stotesbury, David Suff, Alan Taylor, John Taylor, Bruce Thompson, John Tobler, Lynda Tolmie, Ray Topping, Judy Totton, Steve Turner, John Walters, Ed Ward, Garry Whannel, Cliff White, Phil White, Joyce Wilde, Paul Woodcraft, everybody at Ace Records.

Hopefully, somebody will invent a time machine before I do the final mambo.   Pete Frame, May 2007

One

Its origins were as obscure as they were strange. Essentially, American rock 'n' roll was created by fusing rhythm and blues, as played by black musicians, with country and western, as played by whites. In Britain, home-grown rock 'n' roll evolved from skiffle, the bastard offspring of traditional, New Orleans-style jazz – and if skiffle has a source, it's twelve miles out of London, up a tributary of the Thames called the River Crane.

If you're one of those people who like to put exact dates on seminal events, then it has to be October 1949. It was in a corrugated iron hut, round the side of the White Hart public house in Bath Road, Cranford, that Ken Colyer and his mates introduced a handful of curious punters to a primitive musical diversion, a style they had devised themselves, based on whatever appropriate instruments were at hand, and whatever songs they felt like singing.

Colyer was the first musician in Britain to say "look, I know I was born in Norfolk, the son of a chauffeur, and that I earn my crust working as a cleaner on the Underground but, for the next few minutes, we are all going to believe that I'm a slave's son stumbling from town to town in the Mississippi delta, or else a black criminal incarcerated in the prison farm at Angola." And no one was going to believe it more than Ken himself, because, above anything else in this world, that's what he would like to have been. Others on the nascent trad-jazz scene might have tried their best to duplicate southern blacks in a mixture of celebration and tribute, but none went as far as Colyer. He lived with them, played with them, suffered with them – and, more importantly for the province of this book, reinvented and stylised a musical form which had never previously been defined, plucking from jazz folklore the word 'skiffle' as a convenient catch-all description to hang up over it.

It took more than five years to catch on, years Colyer spent in a whirlpool of drinking, carousing, travelling, exploring, grafting, gambling, working, playing and generally immersing himself in the broke and busted, earthy, scuffling lifestyle of his heroes. He was resolute and stubborn: anything he saw as a threat to his integrity, any hint of commercial compromise, was not on the schedule. It might not have suited his pocket, but it suited his nature perfectly that financial success should elude him. As he wrote in his autobiography *When Dreams Are In The Dust*, published after his death by friends and admirers: "I have had to pay heavily for being the keeper of the flame".

In early 1956, when Lonnie Donegan was being fêted as a star and skiffle was beginning to take off nationally, *Melody Maker* canvassed Colyer for his comments. By then, he was already feeling somewhat prickly and embittered, like a bloke who'd discovered a goldmine, only to be swindled out of the rights to it – so who couldn't forgive him for injecting a tart note into his overview? "Skiffle came about in Chicago in the rent parties of the prohibition era," he explained. "When I was with the Crane River Jazzmen, we started the first skiffle in this country, playing it chiefly for our own amusement."

"Personally, I don't give a damn if the craze for skiffle doesn't last," he concluded. "The style has not produced any worthwhile talent. There is no originality. One good thing has come out of it, however: we have built up a market which at least encourages the record companies to issue the genuine material."

The traditional jazz world, as it got a toehold in London during the late forties, mirrored that of cricket, in that it was made up of gentlemen and players. The gentlemen benefited from a public school education and family wealth; for the players, it was shit or bust. They shared the same dressing room and the same pitch, but the cricketers' status was always highlighted on the scorecard and in tables of statistics, where the gentlemen's initials appeared as well as their surnames. It was surnames only for the players, underlining their social inferiority, but if there was any resentment, it was never mentioned in the press.

One thing was certain: Ken Colyer was a player – as was his brother Bill, who not only has the deepest roots of anyone in this book, but was born and raised less than a quarter of a mile from the 2Is Coffee Bar, the cradle of Britain's rock 'n' roll revolution. Not that he would ever have set foot in the place, not for all the tea in China.

Born in April 1922, Bill Colyer spent his whole childhood in Soho. "The old man was a chauffeur for Doria Leventhal's, a gown factory in Poland Street, and the whole family lived in a couple of bug-infested, flea-ridden rooms on the third floor of a crumbling tenement in Broadwick Street. The building was straight out of *Oliver Twist* and should really have been demolished decades earlier. We were very poor, way down the scale."

It was his schoolchum George Daniels, a year older, who got him interested in jazz. "By the time I was 10 or 11, we were bunking into Leicester Square cinemas to see Bing Crosby films like *Forty Second Street* and *Gold Diggers Of 1933*, and *Pennies From Heaven*, which also starred Louis Armstrong. They made a very powerful impression on me, along with Paul Muni films like *Scarface* and *I Am A Fugitive From A Chain Gang*. We saw them all three or four times each – streetwise kids, getting Americanised very fast."

Bill left school at 14, getting a job as a trainee electrician at Horsfields, based at 16 St Anne's Court, an alley connecting Dean Street with Wardour Street. "It couldn't have been better situated, because it was literally yards away from a jazz club called Jig's. We used to go up there at night and listen through the grating. The resident band was made up of West Indians like Cyril Blake and Brylo Ford, but sometimes they would have American stars on there too, like Fats Waller. It was one of several places on the patch where visiting musicians could go for after-hour jam sessions or to meet kindred spirits. This was the late thirties, of course, when jazz was still a dirty word as far as most people were concerned."

To feed a deepening jazz addiction, he and George would cycle over to Levy's in Whitechapel – the only shop selling the kind of records they were interested in hearing. "They were already importing American 78s, which they let us listen to, even though we didn't have enough money to buy more than one a month. I was one of those kids who needed to read and memorise every scrap of information about jazz that I could find – so I would pore through *Melody Maker* and *Down Beat* (also available at Levy's) and the one or two enthusiasts' publications that you could subscribe to, even then, in the years leading up to the war. And, of course, I meticulously catalogued and annotated all my 78s, which I stored in a converted orange box, lined with oil cloth, to keep them safe."

"When I got indoors at night, I was allowed to have an hour with my gramophone, which was a wind-up thing with a tiddly little sound horn and steel needles. Then it was a case of 'Stop that stupid row!' Those records were my pride and joy, and woe betide anyone who tampered with them, especially Ken. He was under very strict instructions: never, ever touch Bill's records."

Younger brother Ken had been born in Great Yarmouth, where their mother's family lived, on 18 April 1928 – but, except for his first couple of weeks, had lived with Bill, middle brother Bob, sister Val, their father and mother, in the Broadwick Street tenement. "When I was 16, he was 10," says Bill, "and I firmly believed that little boys should be seen and not heard, so we weren't particularly close at that point."

"In those days, buying a record was a special event; you couldn't wait for your mum and dad to go out so that you could play it and play it and play it until you knew every note and nuance. George and I would get together as often as we could, either to play records or just talk about them."

"In 1939, it became obvious that London was going to be bombed sooner or later," Bill continues. "Chamberlain was doing his best to deny it but as soon as the first air-raid sirens went off – false alarms, as it turned out – the old man moved us out to the suburbs. He managed to get enough money to put down on a house in Cranford, on one of the many jerry-built estates that were going up around the London perimeter. Starting price, two hundred and fifty quid." Where he got the money was something of a mystery to the family. He had come out of the Navy in 1919 and secured a job as driver for his lieutenant, Sir William Cory, whose family just happened to own a shipping line. "That became his trade, chauffeur and butler, but he talked his way out of most jobs he had. He'd be working for the upper classes, yet reviling them." Naturally enough, it was an attitude that rubbed off on his sons.

They escaped the bombs but not the noise and pollution of Heathrow, which planners were determined to expand from a bumpy runway and a bunch of pre-fab huts and sheds into the busiest airport in the world.

"I'd commute to work on my bike but when the war started I used to stay up in Soho, more often than not, crashing with friends. Then, during the blitz, I was on fire duty. I slept on a camp bed in the basement of Ganton House in Ganton Street, going out on call whenever I was needed – either helping with rescue work or putting out incendiaries with the stirrup pump and bucket I had to lug around. I also changed my job: I quit the electrician's when I found I could earn more working for the bomb-damage repair squad, putting tarpaulins across collapsed roofs."

"I was working on a roof in Wood Lane, out in Shepherds Bush, the day I got the buff envelope. My call-up had been deferred for a while, because I was on the bomb squad, but now I had to report for training at Prestatyn in North Wales."

"Whenever I was near a radio, I was tuned in to Ambrose, Lew Stone, Henry Hall – always listening out for hot solos or that occasional drummer who really knew how to lay down a beat. A tremendous number of those dance band guys were jazzers, starting to play 'hot' as they called it. By this time jazz had become a way of life to me. Half my conversation was about jazz and I was forever poring through magazines, usually printed on paper thinner than bog-paper because of wartime shortages, learning the names of every musician in every band."

The first record Bill Colyer ever bought was *E Flat Blues* by Nat Gonella, an early English Louis Armstrong devotee who made dance band records, but by the time he was called up he was familiar with many of the songs that subsequently found their way into the repertoires of skiffle groups. These included *Alabamy Bound* and *When The Saints Go Marching In* in various versions, *Salty Dog* by Clara Smith, *Matchbox Blues* by Blind Lemon Jefferson, *How Long How Long Blues* by Leroy Carr, *It's Tight Like That* and *Mama Don't Allow* by Tampa Red and Georgia Tom, *KC Moan* by the Memphis Jug Band, *Bucket's Got A Hole In It* and *Digging My Potatoes* by Washboard Sam, and *Bottle It Up And Go* by Tommy McClellan. A frustrated drummer, he was intrigued by the possibilities of the washboard as a rhythm instrument – especially after hearing the Washboard Rhythm Kings' rip-roaring version of *Tiger Rag*, cut for RCA Victor in 1932.

Bill spent four years in khaki. He was out in the Middle East when he eventually got demobbed and went home to Cranford. "With my gratuity, I bought a Ferguson wireless and replaced my wind-up gramophone with an electrical turntable, which was quite an innovation at the time. So now I could use the radio as an amplifier and actually hear my records for the first time electronically! Now it was twice as magical – you were really hearing the music in all its glory!"

Meanwhile, despite vain attempts to lie about his age and join the Merchant Navy, Ken Colyer had spent the war in Cranford, looking after his mother and sister. The man of the house. However, the minute his dad and brother returned from fighting the Hun, Ken took off. He was 17, with a head full of dreams.

"Unknown to me," says Bill, "he'd been playing my records while I was away. In 1944, I'd been on the Normandy landings, and when we got as far inland as Brussels, we were due for a medal ribbon or two and a spot of leave. I wrote to my mum saying I would soon be home for a while – and she wrote back saying 'now don't be angry, but Ken's been playing your records . . . but he's been treating them with great respect, wiping them clean and using new needles'. She also told me that my other brother Bob had been using my bike, which I'd carefully greased and hung up on the wall of the shed. So I was seething!"

"I'd calmed down by the time I got home – and I found that Ken hadn't merely been playing my records, he'd absorbed them and become just as besotted as I was. I had about fifty 78s, I suppose, everyone from Sleepy John Estes to Duke Ellington, and what excited him most was the deep blues stuff and the jazz of New Orleans. He just picked up on it and was off in dreamland."

Since leaving school, Ken Colyer had toiled in two different iron foundries in Slough, then as a builder's labourer, a stable boy, and finally a milkman, doing a horse and cart round for the Co-op. Like Hopalong Cassidy, he worked with a horse called Topper. Together they toured the streets of Whitton, inured to the occasional throb of doodle-bug flying bombs.

He'd just turned 17 when he got his place at Merchant Navy training school and it was on VE day that he reported to Glasgow pool for his ten-quid-a-month assignment as a cabin boy on the *British Hussar*, a 22-year-old rotten tub of a tanker, imbued from prow to stern with the grime and stench of crude oil. Shore gangs knew her as a bad luck ship. With a piss-artist captain and a keel weakened by age and accident, every journey was perilous, but over the next year, Ken managed to set foot in Venice, Trieste, Abadan, Port Said, Haifa, Aden and Copenhagen. The supercilious officers – their attitudes little changed since the days of Nelson, according to

Ken – strengthened his distrust of those in power: "All my life, I have resented authority," he wrote in his autobiography. Accordingly, he compensated for being "treated like scum" by filching food and blankets to barter with dockside scavengers, trading them for local currency.

He was also learning to play the trumpet he'd saved up for. Had he investigated pawn-shops and street markets, he could have picked up a cheaper model but he went to Selmer's in Charing Cross Road and shelled out twenty quid. With assistance from the ship's electrician and constant reference to his Nat Gonella tutor, he picked up the rudiments – practising in the poky washhouse to cause minimum aggravation to his workmates – but he soon abandoned scales and notation in favour of playing by ear and instinct. He had little interest in anything that could be presented as sheet music; all he wanted to do was play 'hot horn'.

On foreign shores, Ken gave scant attention to architectural splendour or classic ruins but sometimes on deck he was entranced by the sheer beauty all around him: "The Arabian Sea in the quiet still of the night is what dreams are made of," he wrote, "when the sea is like velvet in the moonlight and the deepest blue you have ever seen, and the bow wave creams away with a gentle hiss." Other times, the sea was so rough that waves crashed down the funnel, twisting the railings and ripping the wooden superstructure from the bridge.

When the wheel-man steering the *Hussar* inadvertently rammed a Swedish ore carrier in the Suez in April 1946, she was dry-docked locally for repairs, leaving the crew to enjoy a spate of wild bar parties with other Brits stranded in the area. At the climax of these, everybody was obliged to do a turn or sing a couple of songs: "sing, you bastard, sing – or show us your fucking ring!" was the cry. Too far gone to know or care if he was singing in tune, Ken would always attempt the songs he knew inside out from listening to his brother's records – *I Gotta Right To Sing The Blues*, *Beale Street Blues* or *See See Rider*.

Once back in Blighty, Ken had no intention of returning to the miseries of skivvying on the *Hussar*. Instead, he enrolled at the Merchant Navy's cookery school in the basement of the Seaman's Mission in Dock Street, hoping to improve his prospects. No chance. His next position was that of a scullion, "the lowest of the low", peeling spuds and scouring pots and pans on the *Waimana*, a coal-burner built in Belfast in 1911.

In the bars of Durban, Fremantle and Sydney, he learned to drink prodigious quantities of beer – up to 15 pints of Guinness and bitter, half and half, a night – but even that was nowhere near as much as some of his workmates consumed. They were often too sozzled to return to the ship unaided, sometimes too stewed to get back before she sailed.

Ken's problem wasn't so much drinking excessively as working excessively. As a result of humping 145lb sacks of potatoes up and down ladders and gangways, he spent a month in a Sydney hospital recuperating from emergency surgery on a bilateral hernia. He was eventually shipped home on the same cargo-cruiser as the England cricket team, disconsolate after losing the Ashes. Don Bradman had thrashed the England bowling to rack up a series average of 97 – almost twice that of our top scorer, Len Hutton.

Colyer's final ship was a refrigerated meat carrier, the *Port Sydney*, another 30-year-old rustbucket which had somehow survived the war and just managed to scrape through its Lloyds certificate each year. Again Ken was a galley lackey but on this trip he would be going to the New World for the first time. "We went to Montreal; a glorious, breathtaking trip down the St Lawrence River," he wrote. "The Middle East had been a glimpse of hell, but this was a glimpse of heaven."

Whereas he had nothing but contempt for most citizens of the Middle East – "every wog is a born thief" was a favourite epigram – he had nothing but admiration for the descendants of slaves in the Americas, especially those who played jazz or sang the blues. In Montreal, he felt he was getting close: he could sit in cafés whose jukeboxes were loaded with records by Albert Ammons and Pete Johnson. One night, while seeking out some live jazz, he chanced upon a club where Oscar Peterson – a local lad, then unknown outside Montreal – strolled in, took the stage, and played the best piano he'd heard in all his life.

He was still fluttering from that experience when he learned that the next voyage would take him to New York. First chance he got, he was off to Eddie Condon's club on West Third Street, where he was enchanted by jazz in its finest flower – just as it said on the menu.

"They were playing with a power, swing and tonal quality I would not have believed possible," he wrote. "It struck me for the first time that the gramophone record is badly misleading when it comes to jazz. No recording could ever capture completely the greatness of this music." He couldn't wait to write to brother Bill and tell him about the relentless power and dazzling virtuosity of Wild Bill Davison's cornet playing.

In New York, he bought snazzy shirts for his brothers, a first edition of Mezz Mezzrow's *Really The Blues* and a copy of the album Leadbelly cut for Moses Asch. To his eternal regret, he had missed seeing Leadbelly in concert at the Town Hall by one hour.

Next trip, en route to New Brunswick, they sailed into the teeth of a hurricane. On top of that, it was 36 degrees below zero, the worst weather any of the crew had ever known. The *Sydney* eventually limped into St John with ice two feet thick frozen to the hull, the shaking crew well aware that several ships had gone down in the storms.

Ken's brother Bill refused to be put off by such trifles. "As soon as I got a letter from Ken saying that he was in New York, spending his nights in jazz clubs, listening to the most scintillating music he had ever known, I made up my mind to join the Merchant Navy too. I joined as soon as was practical and ended up, after a lot of argy-bargy, on the same boat as Ken, the *Port Sydney*. I was even lower than the lowest of the low, shovelling coal in the very bowels of the ship – four hours on, eight hours off, every day we were at sea."

"Ironically, when I joined her, the damned thing went to South America. The schedule had been changed and we went to Rio Grande, Montevideo and Buenos Aires on the corned beef run. I joined the Merch specifically to get to New York and hear some jazz and I never got anywhere near the place."

It was a slow plodding ship, steaming at seven or eight knots and breaking down frequently, leaving them to drift around in the fog until things got fixed. Trips would last three to four months, with 10-day stopovers in each port, taking on cargo and cleaning the boilers and fireboxes.

Meanwhile, Ken's trumpet playing was coming along, though he still lived in fear of some disgruntled crewman throwing it over the side. Out on deck, weather permitting, silhouetted against the night sky, he would blow it at the moon in imitation, near as he could get it, of his heroes. He and the ship's carpenter were also learning to play guitars they'd acquired on their travels; a Scouse shipmate called Hank, something of a Jimmie Rodgers fan, was teaching them chords.

"The second cook had a banjo too and the three of them used to play together, with Ken alternating between guitar and trumpet," recalls Bill. "Not wanting to be left out, I started playing wire brushes on a suitcase or a tin bucket. That became our routine: I would come off watch, have a shower and join the others, playing a couple of hours a night, seven nights a week, month after month."

Halfway through a second South American trip, Ken suddenly said "bugger this for a lark, I want to play jazz" – and the Colyer brothers swallowed the anchor as soon as they reached King George V Dock in November 1948.

During time ashore in London, they had seen the British jazz movement gathering momentum, though at little more than snail's pace. In their search for the meagre supply of hot music, they had visited the Leicester Square Jazz Club, above the Cafe de L'Europe, where they saw Graeme Bell's band, jazz nutters who had optimistically and recklessly dumped their day jobs in Australia to try and make a living in Europe. They also saw George Webb's Dixielanders, featuring youthful Guards officer cum bohemian Humphrey Lyttelton as the new boy of the band.

The details of this music's incubation and emergence should not concern us overmuch but, in a nutshell, what would eventually climax as the ghastly 'Trad Boom', started as a handful of madly enthusiastic white British amateurs, some of whom had only just acquired instruments, trying their best to emulate the cornucopian music of their heroes, the black musicians who started and developed jazz in New Orleans and whose records they had recently been able to acquire.

The first bunch to do this were pianist George Webb and sundry pals, who initially got together for their own amusement but then organised the Bexleyheath & District Rhythm Club, in the back bar of the Red Barn, opposite Barnehurst railway station, so that others could share their elation. This was sometime during 1943. The music they played was of a style never previously heard in Britain, an homage to King Oliver's Creole Jazz Band, Jelly Roll Morton's Red Hot Peppers and Louis Armstrong's Hot Five and Hot Seven. They played where they could until the end of 1947, when Humph, taking several of Webb's men, formed his own band and carried on where the Dixielanders left off. They took over Monday nights at the Leicester Square club when the Graeme Bell Band went on tour, and presided over some of the most frenetic dancing ever seen in the West End. When the noise and yahoo got out of hand, they moved on to the infinitely grubbier basement premises of Mac's Rehearsal Rooms ('good pianos' was their proud boast) at 41 Great Windmill Street, which for a few months became the headquarters of the London Jazz Club.

A handful of other bands were going, or trying to get going, and in June 1948, the grandiloquently named National Federation of Jazz Organisations of Great Britain set up shop. That October, the London Jazz Club moved to a long-term home in the basement of 100 Oxford Street, which functioned as Mack's Restaurant during the day. (Obviously a lot of entrepreneurs called Mac were hanging around the fringes of Soho in the late 1940s.) And that was the state of play.

The only time Ken Colyer had played in public was when, while waiting for a ship at Victoria Docks, he had gone to the Bridge House in Canning Town and sat in with the resident band for a couple of numbers. He had written to George Webb from some foreign clime, expressing an interest in joining a band and seeking some guidance, but received no reply. He didn't know a soul amongst the jazz élite.

When a band called the Jelly Roll Kings auditioned to replace John Haim, who had mysteriously died in his sleep at only 19 – there was no suggestion of misadventure, even though he was by all accounts 'a bit of a lad' – Ken went along, but sparks flew immediately. They said he was too loud, though friends suspect that he might have been too good, running rings round the others.

Christmas 1948 came and went. Nothing happening. Bill was working on a building site; Ken had taken a job cleaning tube train carriages at the Ealing Common depot. He hated every minute.

Two

From a chap who lived a few doors down, Ken Colyer got wind of three local lads reputed not only to like jazz but to be playing it too. On cornet, guitar and drums, respectively, Sonny Morris, Ben Marshall and Ron Bowden had been trying to get something going with pianist Ralph Dollimore, but he faded out of the picture as Ken edged in. "Ken turned up on my doorstep one day saying he wanted to get a band together playing New Orleans music," says Marshall. "As I asked him in, I was thinking 'I wonder what New Orleans music is?' – it was completely foreign to us at the time. We had been thinking more in terms of straightforward dance band stuff with a little swing influence – our favourites were Artie Shaw, Harry James' small group, and a bit of Muggsy Spanier – but Ken was so effusive and enthusiastic the first time we got together that we just had to give it a go." As soon as he played them a selection of records by his idols, they were hooked.

During the first two decades of the century, the more turbulent and unfettered parts of New Orleans were peaking as a melting pot of sex and drugs and booze and jazz. Jazz! Who knows where it came from or how it surfaced from the steaming, heady brew swirled up by prisoners and slaves singing work-songs and hymns, by blacks experimenting with military band instruments left around after the Civil War, by Hispanics and Creoles introducing strains of their cultural heritage, by whorehouse pianists and funeral bands, by minstrels, ragtime ticklers and blues singers but the quintessential New Orleans style was being defined towards the end of that period, when Kid Ory's Creole Jazz Band ruled the roost.

By this time, Jelly Roll Morton had already wrought all the innovations he was going to make and was now watching younger guys develop them. The pioneering cornettists Buddy Bolden, King Oliver and Bunk Johnson had already fired up the imaginations of a new generation of players, like teenage prodigy Louis Armstrong, who graduated from the Waifs' Home Band to the bars of Storyville in 1916, just as the authorities were moving in to clean up what had been an open, fully sanctioned red-light district. When, two years later, King Oliver went looking for better times in Chicago, on a road to salvation which would see dramatically increasing traffic over the coming decades, Armstrong replaced him in Ory's band and was soon acclaimed as the hottest, coolest cornettist in the ghetto. On paddlewheel riverboats, in clubs and dens and dives, he honed his skills and refined his style – until 1922, when he jumped at Oliver's invitation to join him in Chicago.

They played and made records together for two years but Armstrong was anxious to climb and left to begin a pissed and stoned odyssey that led to the 1925-28 Hot Five and Hot Seven recording sessions which sealed his reputation as the genius of his genre.

During this period, Armstrong phased out his cornet in favour of the more sophisticated trumpet, until then associated with classical and symphonic music. Purists (they were around even then) threw their hands up in horror, in much the same silly way as they would when Dylan went electric.

In 1929, Armstrong moved to New York and eventually to global stardom. Meanwhile, his departure from New Orleans had been a slow-motion pre-play of what would happen when the Beatles left Liverpool: the 'New Orleans Sound' was buoyant for a while but was then stunted by tourism and show-biz.

However, as jazz and swing swept through the body of America during the thirties, adopted and gentrified by white musicians, more than one influential school of thought concluded that the only genuine, authentic jazz was that played by black men from New Orleans. What were now re-evaluated as seminal recordings were reissued and languishing pioneers were 'rediscovered'. Jelly Roll Morton and Sidney Bechet were pulled from the backwaters and encouraged to record music that was now seen as representing the very essence of the black experience (though, interestingly, both were Creoles). Thus began, in the early forties, the New Orleans Revival: the dusting off and re-creation of styles which had been state-of-the-art 15 years or more earlier.

The traditional New Orleans jazz band was idealised as a front line of cornet, trombone and clarinet weaving polyphonic melody over all or most of a bass/banjo/piano/drums rhythm section – and various units sprang up in this format, some white and some black.

In the vanguard of the former was the San Francisco based Yerba Buena Jazz Band, led by cornettist Lu Watters. (Like the Armstrong-Oliver union, they featured two cornets.) Leading the latter was the most authentic of the revival bands, named after and fronted by Bunk Johnson, a bona fide, certified original whose heyday performances had been scrutinised and studied by a wide-eyed Louis Armstrong, 20 years his junior. Johnson had quit the sporting life and retired to the rural hinterlands in 1931, but eight years later, two ethnomusicologists, William Russell and Frederic Ramsey Jr, dug him out of seclusion and summoned up a second wind, after a set of dentures had been furnished to facilitate his embouchure. At the age of 60, Bunk enthusiastically recreated a world that had once exhausted him. That the edges of his music were rough only added to his cachet; to many New Orleans adherents, the records he and his band cut in the mid-forties, after they had peppered the original stew with a slew of idiosyncratic tastes and flavours and nuances, were as important as any recorded by Armstrong. To Ken Colyer, they were the most glorious and inspirational pieces of music in the history of mankind. If there was a God, his name was Bunk Johnson, and heaven was New Orleans.

What Ken had in mind was an English version of the kind of music Bunk Johnson was making on those records. It seemed like a tall order, but they could have a blast trying. Barrelling enthusiasm carried the day.

Ben Marshall and Ron Bowden had not long returned from National Service. Schoolfriends, they had been called up together, working on the post-war wind-down at RAF Sopley, near Bournemouth. "We were RT operators with a lot of spare time," says Bowden, "so we started a quartet to play in the Sergeants' Mess. When we got out, towards the end of 1948, we were hanging around with Sonny Morris and, not wanting to be left out of it, he bought himself a cornet."

When Colyer came on the scene, Morris still had a month or so to go with the Household Cavalry, but he was only stationed at Windsor and could get a bus home for rehearsals any time he liked. Despite his inexperience, Marshall had made it clear to Colyer that there could be no question of off-loading their mate; any band would have to feature two cornets. It wasn't what Colyer had envisaged –

but what was? He had intended to join an established band, and here he was trying to build one from scratch.

Rehearsals went surprisingly well; they just tried to put themselves into a New Orleans frame of mind, and battered their way through any shortcomings. Starting on the second day of spring 1949, they forked out a few bob to landlord Clarrie Brinsden to hire the hut beside their local, the White Hart in Cranford, where they could make as much noise as they wanted. Every Tuesday (and later every Friday) evening, Sonny learned to improvise around Ken's lead, while Ron and Ben thrummed out a rhythm.

When, in May, Colyer learned that a member of Mick Mulligan's Band, John R.T. Davies, lived only three miles away at Longford, he was round there like a shot. By the end of the evening, John had forgotten about the Mulligan Band, wild and eccentric and loveable though they were, and avowed allegiance to the Colyer philosophy. His 17-year-old brother Julian, who had just that Easter left Stowe, remembers the visit like a scene from his favourite film.

"Ken came round to the house and asked to speak to John. After a few words, they trooped upstairs to his room, got their horns out and started tootling away – and it struck me immediately that I was hearing, for the first time, somebody who actually meant what he was playing. Ken was actually saying something, rather than just playing tunes. I was absolutely bowled over. When they took a breather, I blurted out to Ken 'Blimey, you sound just like Mutt Carey!' – to which he replied 'Do you want to join the band too?'" Instinctively and intuitively, Julian said yes. What else was he going to do?

"It was something completely different, and both my brother and I became dedicated to it straight away," says Julian. "At that time, I hadn't made up my mind that I wanted to play New Orleans music as such – I just wanted to play jazz in very general terms – but as soon as Ken entered my life, that's all I wanted to play . . . and it's never been any different."

The brothers Davies duly turned up at the White Hart in John's Austin Ruby, crammed to the roof with instruments. Julian played the sousaphone and John played every instrument that had ever been invented: although he'd played banjo with Mulligan, he would now concentrate on trombone. Ben Marshall switched from guitar to banjo after experimenting with the one that John had brought along, and discovering how much better it cut through and blended in.

"We used to spend a lot of time together," says Sonny Morris, "seven nights a week, in fact. None of us were married and when we weren't playing, we were listening to records, drinking, or just talking." Often they would congregate at Sonny's house in Waye Avenue; he was looking after Bill Colyer's records and gramophone, since Bill was living in digs in town. "We couldn't get enough of Bunk Johnson or Mutt Carey: they were Ken's favourites, and they became ours too."

On occasion, indeed on many occasions that summer, they would take up their instruments, walk down Sonny's back garden, out of the gate, into the fields, and rehearse on the banks of the River Crane. Sometimes they would stand, other times sit in a circle on the grass. "Serenading the cows" they used to call it. Overcoats and gloves helped them stay out past dusk, getting to grips with numbers they'd been listening to on record, or working on band originals like John R. T.'s (wait for it) *After Dark*.

Vigorously opposed to pecking orders, Colyer had suggested that the band be run on democratic lines, with all members having equal input. "A good New Orleans band has no stars," he would tell the others, "it's the ensemble sound that is all important." No one objected to this ideal, even though they obviously looked to Ken for guidance. Calling it Ken Colyer's Jazz Band would have implied leadership, so they settled on the Crane River Jazz Band. It was an appropriate but whimsical name, which allowed them to adopt the old spiritual *Down By The Riverside* as their signature tune. The traffic on the Great West Road might have been increasing, but in the late forties Cranford still had the ambience of a country village, surrounded by flat agricultural land. A hefty stream in the days when it needed a ford, the Crane had been reduced to little more than a drainage ditch, fast flowing after winter storms but almost dry by the end of summer. It wasn't exactly the Mississippi, but what the heck? They could dream, couldn't they? The Crane River Jazz Band. They liked the name, thought it had a good ring to it.

Inevitably, the weekly White Hart hut rehearsals began to attract attention. Unless you wanted to get on a bus and go to the pictures, there wasn't that much to do in Cranford and despite the chill, pub customers and local lads soon started to hover outside, listening to skeletal, barely recognisable versions of *Lowdown Blues* and *Creole Love Call*. It wasn't long before they began to poke their heads round the door and ask if they could come in to watch and listen.

It was a friend called Ted Swift who thought of putting a table by the door and extracting an entrance fee of sixpence per head. With the band's approval, he organised membership cards and the Crane River Jazz Club formally opened its doors some time during that summer of 1949. "Essentially, people were paying to watch us rehearse, often going over the same numbers several times each, but no one seemed to mind," says Sonny Morris. Almost by accident, they had created their own scene, with more punters coming along every week. Most of them had never heard or seen anything like it before.

"We were certainly swimming against the tide," says Julian Davies. "Most of the other bands on the scene at that time were revivalist bands, content to repeat what the legendary historical figures had played – but Ken's ambition was for us to play the current, contemporary New Orleans style, whose boundaries were still being determined by Bunk Johnson and George Lewis and the other players working in the city. We were playing in the idiom, rather than slavishly copying old 78s, and that's what made the Cranes different from the rest."

Since Bunk Johnson – "the greatest teacher I ever had" – had seen fit to bring into his repertoire such unlikely numbers as Irving Berlin's *When I Leave The World Behind*, Ken was happy to incorporate very offbeat, very English tunes like the folk song *Bobby Shaftoe* and the 1930s music hall favourite *A Miner's Dream Of Home* into their fast expanding set.

Answering the call for a clarinet player, Cy Laurie came to Cranford to see what was going on but the vibe wasn't entirely to his taste and he decided to work on his own band. He did, however, recommend a friend: Monty Sunshine. With a name like that, he had to be perfect for the job. He had also been born in 1928, the same year as Ken, Sonny, Ben and Ron. If you believe in fate, such coincidences are unusually attractive. As soon as he got out of the RAF, Monty joined – but living in Dalston and going to art college in Camberwell, he wasn't able to make the Cranes the focal point of his life, like the others seemed to be doing.

By the start of the new decade, the Crane River Jazz Band was a flourishing, reasonably proficient sextet comprising trumpet, second trumpet, clarinet, trombone, double bass (recently added in favour of sousaphone), and banjo. No drums, however; Bowden had walked. Their club membership was growing, with most of the punters around their age, 21-ish, between school and marriage. "Ken was interested in nothing but playing music," says Sonny Morris, "and that suited the rest of us just fine: we never wanted to stop, just couldn't get enough of it."

The weekly White Hart meetings acquired a growing sense of occasion, with audience and band sharing an exclusive, esoteric ritual as arcane as Freemasonry. A hep square dance. For the band it had already become more than just fun. When they got on stage, playing in front of enthusiastic, appreciative faces, it was like soaring into a different dimension, even though they were in a scruffy little timber-framed, corrugated-tin shack-cum-dancehall with a stage about six inches off the floor. "At times, it got so full that you could hardly move," recalls Sonny. "We had to string a rope across the front of the stage to prevent ourselves being forced backwards by milling punters."

To save them blowing their lungs out, they would play two sets with a breather in between – which Bill Colyer, now functioning as their manager, thought to fill by playing records. Record recitals had for some time been a feature of the jazz world, but not in conjunction with a live band . . . so here was Bill, originating a blueprint for the tour disc-jockey who seeks 'to turn the audience on to great sounds' they might not have heard before. "I took my electric turntable and radio up there," says Bill, "and all the devouts would listen to my precious 78s of Jelly Roll Morton and King Oliver and Leadbelly, which I introduced with a bit of rabbit about their historical background and context. In some ways, it was a strange and privileged feeling – like preaching the gospel, giving a sermon in the middle of a spiritualist church service. Meanwhile, the band would be over in the pub, smashing back the pints, getting ready to take the stage again." Food was still rationed, but beer wasn't...and bitter was only a shilling a pint.

It wasn't only New Orleans jazz the Cranes listened to when they got together; they were equally passionate about country blues and spasm music – so why not have a bash at playing that too? John Davies, who like the original core had just broken free from National Service, not only had an impressive record collection, he also had his own recording equipment set up at home. He had picked up a cutting lathe from somewhere and connected that to an amplifier, which Julian (by now an apprentice at EMI) had put together from bits and pieces. Thus was the band able to experiment with their own brand of spasm music and, wonder of wonders, record it!

Still in existence is an acetate, cut direct to disc in John's bedroom, of a bluesy, jug-bandy 12-bar they called *Greenline Stomp,* in honour of the bus stop down the road. Julian, who always had ambitions to play a jug, played his newly acquired double bass (after he'd had it for about three weeks, Ken said 'Can't you play that thing yet?'); John and Ken played guitars; Sonny played cornet; Bill played washboard; and Ben played a kazoo with a horn stuck into the end of it to make it a bit louder. The acetate whirled, the groove was cut. Gus Cannon scenes in the Middlesex suburbs.

Soon, in October 1949, varying combinations of this group replaced the record recital as interval entertainment at the White Hart. Since it was performed by a breakdown group, it was never described as anything but 'breakdown music'. The word 'skiffle' was still some years away from being introduced into the traditional jazz lexicon, but that is in effect what it was: prototypical skiffle . . . and the Crane River Jazz Band were the first to be playing it on a regular basis.

In their pursuit of breakdown music, they were unabashed revivalists, drawing from three decades of American race records. Originally cut for regional distribution in the South, records by blues singers and jug bands began to sell in Northern cities too – and thankfully the big record companies weren't slow to recognise a money spinner. Their involvement guaranteed that literally hundreds of rural folk artists had at least a couple of their songs preserved for posterity. In chasing the dollar, they inadvertently created a library of black culture, the roots of rhythm 'n' blues and rock 'n' roll.

Among the numbers the Cranes performed were several from the Leadbelly catalogue, including *Midnight Special, Take This Hammer* and *John Henry; How Long Blues* and *Midnight Hour Blues* from recordings by Leroy Carr; and *Trouble In Mind, Sporting Life* and

Careless Love, sourced from Big Bill Broonzy, Brownie McGhee and Lonnie Johnson, respectively. Their most audacious adaptation was *Crane River Woman*, on which Bill took lead vocal. He merely replaced the recurring title of the Mississippi Sheiks' *Corrine Corrina* with the more apposite "Crane River Woman, where you been so long?"

"We were trapped in a way because people always wanted to hear the same numbers," says Bill. "The jazz band could never get away without playing *Eh La Bas, Tiger Rag* and *Snag It*, while the breakdown group was always being pressed to play the songs that had become most familiar, though we tried to introduce at least one new one every week."

Throughout the band's two-year lifespan, they always struggled an inch away from equilibrium. Ron Bowden had left at the end of the first year, to involve himself in the bebop scene centred on the El Cino Club in Hounslow, and finding an adequate replacement proved impossible. Several drummers came and went, each either unsuitable or unable to commit to the workload, and it was often down to Bill Colyer playing washboard with the band as well as the breakdown group.

In May 1950, they were joined by pianist Pat Hawes, a former Humph sideman freshly released from the RAF, and his zest added immeasurably to the strange and potent cocktail: five ex-National Servicemen cutting loose after two years of routine, repression and spit 'n' polish discipline; a teenager recoiling from the constraints of public school; and the crusading Colyer brothers making up for lost time. "We were a bunch of roughnecks playing a purposely primitive music," wrote Ken. When a job went particularly well, they went home bristling like revolutionaries.

"I had no hesitation in joining them," says Pat Hawes. "They were a hard-drinking lot, they knew how to have a good time, and I enjoyed the music they played. They were a bit mad, of course, but everybody was entitled to go a bit mad. About a week after I got out of the RAF, the Korean War started and things began to look very hostile. I got a telegram saying I was liable to be recalled at any time, so nobody was looking too far ahead. We'd just had the Berlin airlift, and the whole world seemed to be teetering on the brink of something very nasty. Can you wonder that we used to get pissed-up now and then?"

During the first half of 1950, they were star attraction at a second Crane River Jazz Club, a floating affair run by jazz fanatic Jimmy Bryning in whatever location he could hire for the evening, be it the Cumbrae Club in Uxbridge Road, Ealing, the West Ealing Club in Mervyn Road, Boston Manor, or the White Hart in Acton. They also played the odd art school and club job, including the ambitiously named Greenwich Village, the latest in a long line of clubs operating in Mac's Rehearsal Rooms (at the same time as Bruce Forsyth was trying to make a name for himself as a 'juvenile lead' at the Windmill Theatre across the road).

Perhaps their greatest coup was finding their way onto the television show *Picture Page*, hosted by the exquisitely gowned Sylvia Peters, the first British jazz band to secure such exposure – not that more than a handful of the population had television sets at the time. They shared the programme with yet to be knighted Mortimer Wheeler, who expounded on a tray of fossils, after which John R.T. Davies explained the basic rudiments of the band and its repertoire, his impeccable Stowe accent perfect for the BBC sensibilities. Sylvia listened intently, betraying no curiosity about his fez.

In July 1950, they set up a permanent Crane River Jazz Club in the West End, in the cellar of 11 Great Newport Street. Described in advertisements as 'New Orleans in London', it ran every Monday until the following July, by which time the premises had just undergone a name change from the London Studio to Studio 51. Compère James Asman, later the *Record Mirror*'s traditional jazz expert, was a great fan of the Cranes. "They were rough and incredibly crude," he wrote, "but their music was virile and alive with the spirit which had activated the pioneers in the streets of Storyville."

These were qualities which *Melody Maker*'s Maurice Burman missed when the band made their one and only appearance on the BBC Light Programme's *Jazz Club* in February 1951. He could detect nothing but "a primordial sense of jazz" buried in a deluge of "extremely bad intonation, very poor tone and lack of technique." Why certain elements within the audience had gone bananas, he was at a loss to understand.

As an extension of its dance band coverage, the *Melody Maker*, then eight pages for fourpence, had become a weekly *Sporting Life* for jazz musicians. Jazz-mad journalists like Max Jones and Sinclair

Traill wrote scholarly reviews of the latest American record releases and comprehensive profiles of all the greats, from Leadbelly to Bird, but over the years, the paper was increasingly constrained by a high-handed, stuffed-shirt reactionary faction who could never come to terms with rock 'n' roll, or any of its primitive predecessors.

A man who advertised himself as 'vocal coach to the stars', Maurice Burman winced when swashbucklers, untrained amateurs, ignored the basic disciplines. He was a knuckle-rapper of the type that used to force left-handed people to write with their right; conventional standards must be observed. Of course, the Cranes were Young Turks and didn't give a tinker's cuss what old farts thought; in fact, Ken freely admitted that his entire style was based on trial and error, and that he didn't even realise that he was switching keys mid-stream until the classically trained John Davies put him straight. Nevertheless, as the band's manager, Bill Colyer felt obliged to mark Burman's card. "One of the main troubles in the jazz world today," he wrote in *Melody Maker*'s letters column, "is that there are too many listening with their heads rather than their emotions."

Young, committed guys having a go, playing on their own terms, sticking to their guns and waving their flag in the face of old-fogey criticism. Imbued with rock 'n' roll spirit before anyone knew such a thing existed. "I went to see them and thought they were dreadful," wrote George Melly in *Owning Up*. "There were no solos. Every number was ensemble throughout, and to my ears monotonous ensemble at that. Like most people, I thought Ken was joking – but slowly and reluctantly, we began to appreciate the qualities of his approach. It was primitive but serious. It was also patently sincere."

The Cranes got to play as far afield as Sheffield, Nottingham, Liverpool and even Newcastle (a serious safari for a band in 1950), but their appearance in a 13-band Festival of Britain extravaganza at the Royal Festival Hall in July 1951 was to be their last. 'A Landmark in British Jazz' was the billing. Six months away from becoming Queen, Princess Elizabeth was guest of honour, "thus bestowing on jazz some of the grace and dignity already symbolic of the Festival of Britain," noted *Melody Maker*. Grace and dignity? Neither state had any relevance to the Cranes' *raison d'être* but they were far from fazed by the occasion. "We weren't impressed," says Sonny Morris. "We thought we were doing *them* a favour."

Of the many recordings they made, their Festival Hall performance of *I'm Travelling*, preserved for posterity on a Parlophone single, catches most accurately and succinctly the character of the band. Colyer at 23, soul-deep, trying to make sure the Cranes went out on a high note.

His first band had been a two-year apprenticeship of shared discovery, frustration, elation, gloom and all the other emotional extremes that any novice band feels, but his next was riven almost from the outset by divergent interests.

"Money had reared its head that summer," says Ben Marshall. Ian and Keith Christie, the clarinet player and trombonist in Humphrey Lyttelton's band, had for some time been experimenting with their own part-time offshoot, the Christie Brothers Stompers, on whose records Ken Colyer, Ben Marshall and Pat Hawes had guested. When the Christies decided to leave Humph and go for it, they invited the Crane trio to join them. "There was a lot of heart searching, but the temptation was more than we could resist," admits Marshall. "The two nights a week the Christies had lined up at the London Jazz Club paid me more than I was getting for a week's work – and the idea of dumping our day jobs and becoming professional musicians was just too compelling."

Left with the name and a handful of contracted gigs, Sonny Morris and Monty Sunshine recruited replacements and tried to put on a happy face with a refurbished Crane River Band, which stumbled on in one form or another, for several years – "but it was never the same," according to Morris.

A cult supergroup, the Christie Brothers Stompers made an immediate impact on the bubbling scene, but any unanimity quickly dissolved. "We joined the band hoping to play in the style of the records we'd made, which had a sort of Kid Ory/Mutt Carey sound," says Marshall, "and everything was fine for a month or so, but then other influences began to cloud the original vision. Pat was happy to play New Orleans piano and played it extremely well, but he felt the need to stretch himself more, I think – and Keith Christie certainly did…so suggestions for other tunes were coming in and taking us away from New Orleans."

This was more than Colyer could endure. Soaring on *Saratoga Moan* was one thing, but swanning on *S'Wonderful* was another.

Having played his first gig with the Christies on 11 August 1951, he played his last on 27 October. Eleven weeks. Not much of a dream. "I'll take so much shit from anybody and no more," he wrote. "Then my expression changes and there are dangerous warning signs that a volcano is about to erupt. Once made, I am an implacable enemy."

"Ken was an ignorant bastard, not to put too fine a point on it," reckons Pat Hawes. "Basically, he was a kind-hearted bloke who didn't find it easy to get on with people, but there was definitely a nasty side to his temperament as well."

"He could never suffer fools gladly," says Sonny Morris. "A lot of people thought he was moody, but I don't remember him that way – far from it: we used to laugh all the time. He was certainly very shy, especially with women, but he could still talk the hind leg off a donkey if he wanted to. There again, I've seen him travel 250 miles in a car and not say a word."

Keith Christie thought the initials KC were the best that a jazz musician could have, but not Ken Colyer. He would have preferred to have been born Nigel Osborn or Norman Oliver…and one thing was certain: neither his ideals nor his musical integrity were up for sale, hire or compromise. If the music he was contributing to wasn't exactly to his taste, he didn't want to know. Bye bye Christie brothers. What's life all about if your dreams are being smothered?

In November 1951, Colyer went back to sea . . . with only one aim: to reach New Orleans.

Three

In official notes for the guidance of servicemen, the British government considered four American cities to be "unhealthy for the purpose of leaves of absence": Jacksonville, St Louis, Savannah and, top of the list, New Orleans. One can only sit and wonder what kind of pen-pushing civil servant could have reached such arbitrary conclusions. Presumably one who didn't get off on corruption, crime, gambling, prostitution, booze, Creole food, the Mississippi, riverboats, cotton bales on the quayside, the Vieux Carré, streets with names like Bourbon and Rampart, wrought iron balconies, levees, Mardi Gras, and the very idea that you could leave town on various dream-laden radial roads, including both Highway 51 and Highway 61. Somebody who didn't get off on jazz, obviously.

New Orleans! Just to walk those streets. Just to soak in that history. Just to sense the ghostly presence of Buddy Bolden and Jelly Roll Morton. Just to look out across Lake Pontchartrain and breathe the air.

Ken Colyer's prime inspiration and influence, Bunk Johnson, had died at the age of 70, after a long illness, back home in New Iberia, in July 1949, just as the Cranes were getting to grips with his music. But his band was still working under the leadership of his long-time clarinet companion George Lewis, and several of the other guys who played on the records were hanging in there too. Ken was desperate to see and hear them.

There was only one slight problem, of course . . . how to get there. Somehow, he must manage to get assigned to a ship that was heading for New Orleans – which, as he knew only too well, was easier said than done.

Inauspiciously, he began his quest in Newcastle, where – after he and a mate had literally drunk a pub's entire stock of Carlsberg lager – he found himself on a ship "that should have been in the scrapyard", the *Llandovery Castle*, bound for South Africa. Stopping off at Ascension Island, St Helena, Cape Town and various ports around the African coast, he was able to stock up on potent local brews, the effects of which led to the locker-room in which he prepared vegetables becoming known as Hangover Square. For the first time, he was working on a passenger ship, an experience which reinforced his contempt for the gentry: "I was to become convinced that those snobs in First Class would have eaten shit if it was well cooked and presented on a silver serving dish, and they damn near did at times, if they did but know it."

In a whorehouse in Mombasa, he got stuck into not only local hooch but weed too. "The madam was an olive-skinned woman with a look of breeding about her. She turned on the gramophone and danced naked: the most erotic dance I've ever seen. A joint and a drink and life was perfect."

Back home via the Suez and onto another ship, the *Tamoroa*, taking emigrants to New Zealand. The wrong direction again. But plenty of time to practise Leadbelly's cascading bass lines on his guitar and to keep his lip in on trumpet. Home through the Panama Canal. At least now he could truthfully say that his expeditions had taken him around the world.

The next trip looked more promising. He was flown out to Mobile, Alabama, to work on the *Empire Patria*, carrying trucks and mining equipment up the Orinoco River, to Puerto Ordaz in Venezuela. Colyer radiated when he heard black stevedores singing and hollering as they loaded the cargo. The ship eased out across the Caribbean, where "sunset was the best part of the day; a glorious panorama of colour every evening. I always found time to lean on the rail and drink it in."

Other than the scenery, it was no picnic. A drunk and brawling crew, an engine incapacitated by a broken piston, hurricanes, food supplies running short, knackered steering, no clean linen, and temperatures that kept him in a permanent state of discomfort, were no inducement to remain in the Merchant Navy a day longer than necessary. It took no time at all to convince himself of this. On returning to Mobile, after the first round trip, he hopped on a bus for a quick in-and-out reconnaissance visit to New Orleans, only 150 miles away. In the land of his dreams, with all senses overloading, he was hot-wired by an intense but all-too-short infusion of native jazz and a swift guided tour. A few weeks later, when the *Empire Patria* docked in Mobile after a second voyage to Puerto Ordaz, he jumped ship.

In the Mobile immigration office, Colyer had been given a 31-day visa, but he intended to stay indefinitely. Two conspirators lowered his suitcase, guitar and trumpet to the quay and he legged it to the Greyhound bus station for a one-way ticket to the fountainhead of jazz. That was the end of his maritime career. The big kiss-off of 1952.

"The instincts that had driven me to get there had been right," he wrote later. "I was to hear music that would soon be gone forever. I was just in time." To his utter astonishment and delight, he found that George Lewis was playing at Manny's Tavern, a couple of doors down from the bar he'd fallen into. The pot of gold at the rainbow's end.

He made friends, found a room as near to heaven as he would get – above the Mardi Gras Club – and began to sit in with the Lewis Band on a regular basis. "At times, I could actually see colours, besides hear their harmonic sense and interplay. They had the master touch and made it sound effortless."

To detail Colyer's New Orleans sojourn adequately would need a book, and since such a book already exists, it would be duplicating information that is available elsewhere and goings-on that have only peripheral relevance to the study in hand. Basically, the dream continued until Christmas; music, beer, Southern fried chicken, King Bee roll-ups and the hospitality of good people sustaining and charging his mind, body and soul. When the money he'd saved ran out, he got a roofing job. Out on the tiles day and night, with two or three hours kip in between.

A few days before his visa expired, he was given a quiet word of warning: it was going round that he was a 'nigger lover' and it was suggested that he sit in with white musicians more. Ken ignored the advice: he wanted the consummate buzz and an education of maximum profundity. That was, after all, the reason he'd come to New Orleans. "Sitting in with the Lewis Band," he wrote, "I had a big warm cavern of sunshine in my belly and not a worry in the world." He certainly found no time to worry about the Louisiana State law which forbade white and coloured musicians to share the same stage.

Had he not been walking on air, he might have noticed the trap door. The Monday after Christmas, when he went to try and extend his visa – claiming to be waiting in frustration for the arrival of a suitable ship to join – he was arrested and unceremoniously carted off to the Parish Prison on Broad Street.

Twelve hours a day banged up with three other 'criminals', the other twelve hours in the day-pen. The bed was spartan, the food atrocious, the noise intolerable, and the guards unqualified, mouthy meat-heads who had greased the Sheriff's palm to get the job. "Anything you might read about corruption in the penal system is perfectly true," he wrote. "Life suddenly didn't look so rosy. I wonder what Little Lord Fauntleroy would have done."

From his cell window, he could see across the yard to the wing reserved for coloured inmates. Racial segregation, even in prison. "It was good to hear their voices, and their singing, sometimes at dead of night. The best singer would start up a song and maybe a hundred voices would chant the chorus, all in perfect harmony. Sometimes during the day, something stompy would start, and they would get it going until the whole place would be rocking. It would be so joyous that even hardened men would stop and listen. 'Them goddam niggers sure can sing,' you would hear them say. But at night, it was always the wailing blues and *You'll Be A Long Time Dead*."

The Warden debilitated and demoralised his prisoners by serving food with any protein, nourishment or taste filtered out. Fury over this reached fever pitch on the lifers' and long-term wing while Colyer was there: had not the Sheriff interceded with wide-handed promises to improve conditions, he would have been able to witness a real-life rehearsal for Riot In Cell Block 11.

Running with the jazz intelligentsia that had befriended Colyer was one Aaron Kahn, who was so mortified by his description of prison conditions that he instigated an enquiry which resulted in the Sheriff being convicted of graft and incarcerated in his own jail. Ken was tickled pink by this, and who can blame him?

When he'd gone back to sea in November 1951, hardly anyone in Britain had ever heard of Ken Colyer, let alone seen him play – a few hundred, a few thousand at most. Traditional jazz was still in its infancy. While he was away, however, the music began to gather momentum and when, at the end of 1952, *Melody Maker* started printing news items about his New Orleans adventures and fascinating reports from the man himself, he quickly acquired, among the traditional jazz cognoscenti, a respect and reverence only two steps down from Marco Polo and Captain Cook. He had actually done things like attend a funeral across the river in Gretna, "a pretty rugged coloured quarter", just so he could see John Casimir's Young Tuxedo Band leading the parade. He was forced to negotiate dirt and gravel roads, through dangerous territory, but Colyer didn't care. "I'd walk my legs off to hear these men playing," he wrote. "That's my music." He had sat in, many times, with his idols, the black pioneers, "sitting back, blowing easy, taking part in the greatest music of my life."

To some *Melody Maker* readers, this was comparable to Dr Livingstone exploring the most inaccessible stretches of the Zambesi, or Henry Miller getting smashed in the whorehouses of Paris. When he was arrested, it was front-page headline news: 'British Jazzman Held In New Orleans Gaol.'

Technically, he was only an immigration detainee, but the authorities still treated him like a criminal. Like an innocent James Cagney figure, in stripes behind bars in some heroic Hollywood black and whiter, Ken actually had to smuggle out his letters to brother Bill, who passed them on to the *Melody Maker*. "A bribe in the right quarter" was all it took.

"In your replies, don't ever mention anything about my letters," he warned. "All written mail in and out is censored and I've already been tipped off by a trusty that if there is ever a shakedown and I'm caught with any written reports about this place, I'll be taken up to Number Five and worked over." He was starting to sound like the Birdman of Alkatraz.

Bail had apparently been set at $500, but when three of his acquaintances from the New Orleans Jazz Club turned up with the money, it was refused. As soon as the arrangements could be made, Ken was informed, he would be sent to New York for deportation.

After holding him for 38 days, the authorities relented and released him on bail. On getting out, he was astonished to learn that George Lewis and Jim Robinson wanted him to go on tour with them. A stunned and tearful Colyer, fearful of ending his days on the chain gang, had to refuse the offer to wear the shoes of his hero Bunk Johnson in the band of his dreams.

His release had been timely: in mid-February, just before leaving New Orleans, he was able to immerse himself in the Mardi Gras.

With his new friends from the city, he partied all day and into the night. "I stayed on my feet till daybreak," he wrote in his last *Melody Maker* bulletin.

After his prison ordeal, it seemed only fitting to Colyer that he should cock a snook at those Immigration bastards by leaving America in the finest possible style. For reasons of speed and efficiency, he was shipped back to England on the fastest liner in history, the *United States*, which had, on her maiden voyage the previous summer, captured the Blue Ribband trophy, held by the *Queen Mary* since 1938.

Enjoying the very zenith of the passenger liner era, he stood on deck looking at the shooting New York skyline knowing that, with his name on the undesirable aliens file, it was unlikely that he would ever set foot on American soil again. But he'd seen and felt more of it, the real grass roots of America, than any other English musician would for many years.

In less than four days, Ken was strolling nonchalantly up the platform at Waterloo Station, looking out for his brother Bill, who had gone to meet him. Along for the ride, equally eager to welcome him home, were two old confreres, Monty Sunshine and Chris Barber. They already had a band waiting for him, primed and itching to go.

Four

A precocious 22-year-old, Chris Barber had recently devised his career plan – in a field where no careers existed. "I came to the conclusion that if you want to play jazz as though your life depends on it, then make your life depend on it!"

His interest had first been aroused eight years earlier, when a BBC radio announcer said "this is jazz", and played *Oasis* by Eric Winstone's Orchestra. "I wrote to my father, the only letter I ever wrote to him during my three years at boarding school, saying 'I like this jazz stuff, will you send me some?' He played classical violin, a very good amateur, but knew nothing about jazz, so he bought the current issue of *The Gramophone*, in which there were a couple of five-star reviews by Edgar Jackson: one of *Body And Soul* by Coleman Hawkins and one of *Old Man River* by Harry James, both of which he bought and sent up to me. That was my introduction . . . and from that moment, I was hooked."

"There was almost no jazz on the market in those days. Records weren't being pressed because they didn't have the raw materials and they couldn't afford convoy space to bring any more in. It was obviously more important to fill the ships up with food and other wartime essentials. So finding old 78s became my principal interest."

Barber had been born in Welwyn Garden City on 17 April 1930 and from age six to nine, until war broke out, had lived in Colindale and gone to King Alfred School in Hampstead, an informal, student-friendly establishment founded by late-Victorian radicals. "My mother, a very modern lady, a flapper and a science teacher with a degree from Girton, taught me at home for a year. Then I went to a couple of schools in Malvern, where we'd been evacuated, until King Alfred finally got organised and moved itself to the country, to some cowsheds in Royston, owned by one of the teachers."

He seems to have been one of those kids who absorbed and understood schoolwork with the least expenditure of time and effort. Taking full advantage of an ultra-progressive regime that encouraged pupils to specialise in subjects they found interesting,

13-year-old Barber was bumped up to the sixth form mathematics class for the duration. For light relief, he would listen to BBC radio, which had been broadcasting music since the outbreak of war, but soon he discovered the American Forces Network station, AFN, where he heard such exotica as Duke Ellington, Tampa Red, Lester Young, Slim Gaillard, the Golden Gate Quartet and Louis Jordan. He began to request records on a regular basis, hearing his name on the radio for the first time.

At weekends, he and school friends would cycle the two miles to Bassingbourn, headquarters of the 91st Bomber Group of the US Eighth Air Force, and lie on the grass verge, watching the B17s – almost low enough to touch – coming in to land after bombing raids, some of them badly shot up, their front gunners slumped and bloody. It was during this time, summer 1943, that the airfield's most famous resident, the Memphis Belle, went into the history books as the first American bomber to complete 25 missions over occupied Europe. A year and a half later, just before Christmas 1944, Glenn Miller played his last concert at Bassingbourn, before flying off to eternity.

Once a week, Barber travelled the 14 miles into Cambridge for a violin lesson. "I saved the bus fare by cycling, hanging onto the back of any passing lorries with the violin strapped across my back. Not only did I get there a damned sight quicker but also I was able to add the money to my gramophone records pot. During the war, just about the only shops selling jazz records were in London, Oxford and Cambridge. By sheer chance, I was within easy access of one of the few jazz outlets in Britain. So at Miller's, I was able to find 78s by Jelly Roll Morton, Fats Waller and Benny Moten. No new jazz records were coming off the presses, but a lot of their stock, such as it was, was made up of pre-war English pressings originally intended for France, Europe's principal jazz market." The young school-kid, filling those precious half hours listening to as many records as possible, grilling the staff for information about who played on what, and usually buying one – carefully packing it into the stout cardboard carrying-case he'd made for the bike-rides back.

"When the war finished and I moved back to my mother's house in Golders Green, I had maybe fifty or sixty 78s – not bad for a 15-year-old." King Alfred (now reinstated in Hampstead) didn't have anyone qualified to teach higher mathematics, so he transferred to St

Paul's, enduring the "diabolically long" bus ride from Golders Green to Hammersmith every morning. He enlarged his record collection by wheeling and dealing, making expeditions to the West End. "I was very lucky, because my next door neighbours had American relations, who were happy to buy records for me – current releases on jazz and race labels like Blue Note and Bluebird. For a couple of years, I spent all my spare time listening to great music by everyone from Big Maceo to Erskine Tate, Jimmy Yancey to Cow Cow Davenport. That's all I was interested in: jazz and blues – music that has preoccupied me ever since."

Some time in 1947, on a visit to Dobell's Record Shop, he saw an advertisement for a concert by George Webb's Dixielanders, to be held at King George's Hall, in the YMCA building round the corner from the Dominion Theatre in Tottenham Court Road. It was the latest of a series in which evangelistic promoters, grooving amateur jazzmen and ardent punters transformed the normally staid venue into the Hot Club of London for the evening. Naturally, he went along.

"That was the most exciting sound I'd ever heard in my life," says Barber, "even though the band wasn't very good! And I still think it was the most exciting thing I've ever heard in my life – because there was no progression. I went from never hearing any live jazz to hearing that!"

By summer 1948, his days were spent scratching away at a desk in the actuarial department of the Clerical and Medical Insurance Company, his evenings playing records at home or hanging out in basement clubs on the edges of Soho. New Orleans-inspired jazz was now attracting a cult following but, partly due to the exuberance of fans, was having difficulty establishing a permanent central London venue. The series of Hot Club of London concerts had finished earlier in the year and the landlords had expelled the organisers of the Leicester Square Jazz Club from the Café de l'Europe. The hottest band in town, led by Humphrey Lyttelton, had been playing regularly at Mac's Rehearsal Rooms in Great Windmill Street but they moved to the 100 Club (Mack's Restaurant by day) at 100 Oxford Street in October 1948. For the foreseeable future, on Mondays and Saturdays, it was Mecca for enthusiasts from all corners of the capital and beyond.

It was during this time that Barber bought his first trombone, an unplanned purchase, the way he tells it. "One evening, Harry Brown tapped me on the shoulder and asked me if I wanted to buy a trombone. It hadn't occurred to me; I had been thinking more of a trumpet, captivated as I was by the image of Louis Armstrong tooting up at the stars. Well, why not, I thought, and as soon as I could scrape up the money I handed over £6.10.0 for this trombone. I'd seen him playing it in Humph's band and imagined it must be all right, but it was a terrible thing, probably not worth more than a couple of quid. Nevertheless, it started me off. I began learning how to play it at home, applying the music theory I'd picked up from violin lessons at school."

Of course, finding other novice musicians to play with was not easy and attempts to get something going foundered until he met Alex Revell in 1949. "We got talking at the 100 Club," Revell remembers. "Chris was working by then, but still looked like an earnest schoolboy, with his thick grey-flannel trousers and a pile of records under his arm, noticeably different from the art students and Hooray Henrys who made up the bulk of the audience and used to leap around all the time. We discovered that we had similar interests." Barber had found a soul mate. As indeed had Alex.

Five months older than Chris, Alex Revell had grown up to a soundtrack of his father's records, "lots of Ethel Waters and Ruth Etting, with musicians like Joe Venuti and Eddie Lang playing on them", and was further intrigued by his cousin's collection of Duke Ellington 78s. "Then I heard Louis Armstrong's Hot Seven and Bix Beiderbecke and I was never the same again. I wanted to buy a trumpet but my father vetoed that idea, saying it would be too loud (he didn't know about muting), so I got a clarinet instead."

With other boys from the Ilford area, most of whom attended a youth club at Gearies Junior School in Gants Hill, Revell enjoyed his first tentative experiments with ensemble jazz. They played there every week, and occasionally on the deserted airfield at Hornchurch, in the underground shelters, where the acoustics made it all sound so much better. Most of the players – including Hugh Middleton, Tony Taylor, Howard Daniels, Ollie Howlett and Fred Curtis – were dabblers who came and went, but Revell formed a lifelong bond with two lads from Ilford County High School: Ferdy Favager and Ben Cohen.

"When I first knew him, Ferdy was unfamiliar with jazz but, living only a few streets apart, we used to bump into each other," recalls Revell. "As soon as I found out that he had a banjo, I invited him round and put Louis Armstrong's *Willie The Weeper* on the gramophone. I went into the kitchen to get some orangeade and came back to find him playing along to the record. First time he'd ever heard it! I was amazed! After that, he and I used to talk about jazz for hours on end." Ben Cohen turned out to be a dedicated cornet player, but though the trio felt they could become the core of a decent band, they never played beyond Gearies School or each other's front rooms. Much of their impetus fell away when Favager was called up for National Service in December 1948.

Though the tube journey between Barkingside and Golders Green was long and complicated, Revell and Barber became solid friends. Much of their time was spent playing records from Chris's prodigious collection, working out ideas on their instruments, enthusing over the possibilities of playing in a band together, trawling for treasure in the record bins at Dobell's and Colin Pomroy's, marvelling over Mezz Mezzrow's depiction of the jazz underbelly in *Really The Blues*, seeing new bands emerge and thinking they could do better, given half a chance. Going to see Humph's band at the 100 Club was like going to college. "I used to sit at Wally Fawkes' feet, watching his fingers, listening to his phrasing" says Revell. "I remember him leaning over towards me once and saying 'Alex, have a night off – please!' Chris and I were there all the time."

Getting hold of records was their other passion but this could be a dicey business. "Good ones were so rare that you were sometimes forced to take a chance," recalls Revell. "I was so excited when I bought a pirate pressing of *Hyena Stomp* backed by *Billy Goat Stomp*, highly desirable sides by Jelly Roll Morton, but the edge crumbled like a digestive biscuit because the shellac was so bad."

Barber was wandering about, sitting in with various bands, including one recently put together by Cy Laurie, a questing clarinet player from the East End, who had fruitlessly auditioned for both the Crane River Jazz Band and the Original Dixielanders. A year earlier, Laurie had never heard of Johnny Dodds but (thanks to a crammer course with Dixielanders leader Owen Bryce) was now his most fervent disciple, and would soon turn his club at 41 Great Windmill

Street into a temple to his memory. "Cy gave me the sack after two weeks because I wasn't loud enough," says Barber. "The bloke he got instead of me was a terrible player; I've forgotten his name, I'm proud to say." Chris also played a few gigs with a band led by record collector cum Vogue Records employee cum trumpeter Doug Whitton but that too proved an unfulfilling experience.

Meanwhile, Revell was still rehearsing at Gearies School with a shifting personnel. Not a lot happening, except that they were playing and learning and having fun. One night, riding the late tube train back home to Barkingside, he found himself sharing a carriage with a kid he recognised as another 100 Club regular. They got talking. It turned out this lad knew a few chords on the guitar, so Revell invited him over to Gants Hill for a blow. Alex Revell must shoulder the blame for introducing Lonnie Donegan to showbiz.

He was still Tony Donegan then, 17 years old, living with his mother in Forest Gate. Although he had taken a few lessons, his proficiency was limited: he knew enough to busk *St Louis Blues* and he could just about find his way through a few Frank Crumit songs. Revell gave him a list of chords to practise and, with the help of a local dance band guitarist, he quickly got to grips with the basic positions. He was enthusiastic enough not to get the bullet.

Chris Barber ventured over quite a few times but though his interplay with Alex Revell and Ben Cohen raised the tone and raised the spirits, he felt that the composition of the band was still rather too inexact to pursue wholeheartedly. Which, of course, it was. The only gig they played, at least the only one anybody can remember, was a school dance at Gearies that happened to coincide with a rehearsal evening. They were persuaded to take the stage and play the one number they felt most comfortable with, their ragged but passionate rendering of *Muskrat Ramble* – learned from the 1926 Okeh recording by Louis Armstrong & his Hot Five. No one could accuse them of lacking ambition.

In the interests of being heard above the front line and giving the band some rhythmic stability, it was suggested that Donegan invest in a banjo. Years later, the story was woven into his cabaret act. "Alex convinced me to buy a banjo," he would chuckle, as if recalling it for the first time in years. "This was not an easy task, but I found one in a second-hand shop in Walthamstow. The guy wanted four and a half quid for it. I had to make a quick decision – should I buy the banjo or an engagement ring. I thought, well, a banjo you've always got – so I bought it!"

On leave for a few days, prior to a posting to Hong Kong, Ferdy Favager showed Donegan a few chords on his new instrument and left him a piece of paper covered in diagrams. Not long afterwards, Donegan was called up too. The band lost impetus.

The Musicians' Union operated a mystifying policy of refusing permission for foreign musicians to play on British stages, even if their appearance would have generated work for their own members. However, through various subterfuges, the great clarinettist Sidney Bechet, who had played on some of the most influential records ever made (including sides with Clarence Williams and Louis Armstrong), was able to give British jazz fans a taste of the real thing when he appeared on a concert at the Winter Garden Theatre in Drury Lane (closed in 1960; site now occupied by the New London Theatre) on Sunday 13 November 1949. The quickly-sold-out show was billed as a concert by the Humphrey Lyttelton Band but Bechet was in the audience (sitting in the Royal Box, no less), having decided to visit London after gigs in Paris, and he was lured onto the stage to play. This was no surprise to members of the London Jazz Club, who had been alerted to Bechet's appearance by mail, or aficionados in clubs around the capital, who were tuned in to the grapevine. Fortunately, it was a late-night performance.

That evening, Barber and Revell (no band, looking for a break, high hopes) were guesting with Beryl Bryden's Washboard Band (completed by Dave Stevens on piano and Alan Wickham on trumpet) at Cooks Ferry Inn in Edmonton. They were supporting club residents, Freddy Randall & his Band ("I liked Freddy very much," says Barber, "though I wasn't that keen on his music"), and after opening the proceedings, they travelled down to see Bechet ... standing there in all his glory, glistening under the spotlights, clarinet playing note-sequences they had marvelled at on record. A big night on which to lower the safety curtain on a chilling and thrilling decade. An instructive one, too. Cocooned as they had been in post-war isolation, it made the English guys sit up and think.

"In the excitement and joy of actually seeing a jazz giant in the flesh," wrote historian Jim Godbolt, "the audience didn't seem to notice a nervous and stumbling Lyttelton band, some of whom were nowhere near the standard of the man they were accompanying, and the rhythm section, at times, floundered helplessly. The performance of a genuine original with a band of different race, generation and country, who had largely received jazz music through the agency of jazz records in their front rooms, highlighted the difference in stature. It demonstrated sharply the inadequacies of the British revivalists."

That same month, November 1949, Barber was offered a gig. At the start of the year, some of George Webb's old Dixielanders had decided to get back together as the Original Dixielanders. With a pedigree stretching back six years, they quickly secured a reputation through jazz club residencies and guest spots, jobs at corn exchanges and *palais-de-danse* halls, on riverboat shuffles. They won the Essex heat of the National Dance Band Championships at the Royal Forest Hotel in Chingford and came second in the final, held in the art décor splendour of Dorking Halls. When Harry Brown left the band, Barber – who had bought his first trombone from Brown little over a year earlier – felt privileged to replace him.

He was already a good friend of Dixielanders leader Owen Bryce, day one pioneer of British jazz, a fellow collector and fanatic, because he had spent many hours at his record counter. Known as the Hot Spot, it had opened in February 1949, in the basement of Bryce's radio shop at 23 Thomas Street in Woolwich. Owen's friend James Asman had moved down from Newark to manage the establishment and the initial stock was most of Bryce's extensive record collection – which ensured frequent visits from Barber. There he acquired such treasures as *Stevedore Stomp* and *Shout 'em Aunt Tillie* – late twenties gems from Duke Ellington.

Within days of Barber joining, Dixielanders clarinet player Charlie Connor got into a little spot of difficulty and withdrew, affording Barber the perfect opportunity to add his mate Alex to the existing crew: Reg Rigden and Owen Bryce on trumpets, Bob Barratt on bass and Roy White on drums. It was great experience, playing the Wood Green, Catford, Cooks Ferry Inn, Red Barn circuit, though the music proved to be less exhilarating than they had anticipated, and not entirely to their taste. "To amuse ourselves, Chris and I would see how often we could weave snatches of *Peanut Vendor* into whatever we were playing. Needless to say, the others got very uptight," is the way Revell remembers it, though Bryce attributed even more ingenuity to the duo. "They drove us spare, despite their excellent musicianship," he recalls. "During solos they would turn to each other, shooting out of the corners of their mouths such loving asides as 'Paramount 20292', and then proceed to quote a phrase from that very disc. It became a source of great amusement to them; we thought they were mad."

According to Revell, their letter of resignation and a letter confirming their sacking crossed in the post but Bryce says the band was on its last legs, on the point of collapse anyway. It had simply used up too much of its fuel in the early stages and fell to earth, burned out.

Having had a taste of interacting on stage, in front of eager and appreciative audiences, Barber and Revell knew they wanted to stick together. They also recognised that the only way they would be able to concentrate entirely on classic jazz, as recorded by their favourites, was to form a committed band of their own. In February 1950, they started doing just that. "We were King Oliver fanatics," says Barber. "We thought that Oliver's music was the ultimate expression of the traditional jazz thing. We wanted to do that and we tried as hard as we could."

No more of this out-in-the-sticks business; they would rehearse in central London, heart of the jazz territory they intended to infiltrate. Ideally, they wanted two trumpets – and to this end arranged to meet Ken Colyer and Sonny Morris at the Hare's Foot in Goodge Street. Strange, since both seemed happy enough fronting the Crane River Band, which although a fairly recent creation, was already drawing punters out to Cranford. Maybe they were just checking out the competition. The four of them played together, but nothing came of it. "It was immediately obvious that they wouldn't fit," says Revell. "We didn't know much about music but they knew even less. Sonny's idea of harmony was to play a third from Ken, regardless of what chord they were on – and Ken seemed to have no idea of where a chorus began and ended . . . he would come in on the middle of a chorus. Chris and I realised that they would never be able to do the Oliver band stuff."

They went back to Revell's pal Ben Cohen, who was keen to join, and found a second trumpet player in Keith Jary. They also found a space to rehearse, in a basement in Gerrard Street.

Finding a bass player proved difficult, a piano player less so. Roy Sturgess, an insurance clerk from Southend, knew and loved ragtime and Chicago blues but could make a fair fist of almost every number on their proposed set list. He accepted an invitation to join. A drummer (whose name has been mislaid in the haze of time) set up his kit, where it remained undisturbed in a corner for three weeks. They never saw him again. Sturgess suggested that his girlfriend's brother might at least provide a background beat until someone better turned up.

Enter Brian Lawes, 17-year-old apprentice dental technician from Southend. His drumming experience was limited, if not laughable. He had been at some party where a small swing group was playing on the lawn. When they broke for refreshment, he got behind the drums and started tapping away. "I'd never hit a drum before," he recalls, "which surprised the drummer, who said I obviously had some talent." This inspired him to make his own drum by sawing the neck off an old banjo and mounting the head on a cardboard box. Using wire brushes, he played along to the radio and all his favourite records. This was the extent of his experience when he climbed behind the abandoned kit in the Gerrard Street cellar. Much to his amazement, he was offered the job. Next day, he went out and bought a kit of his own on hire purchase.

Revell wrote to Favager in Hong Kong, telling him about Barber (who Ferdy had yet to meet) and promising him the banjo role on his discharge. Meanwhile, Lonnie Donegan, now barracked over the river in Woolwich, was able to make a few rehearsals and would even get to a few gigs before the Army sent him to Vienna.

The newly constituted band knew in their bones that it was going to blend, as soon as they got stuck into their first King Oliver number. Big smiles. After a few more rehearsals, Barber announced that he had entered them into the First National Jazz Band Contest, organised by the National Federation of Jazz Organisations. On 25 April 1950, Chris Barber's New Orleans Jazz Band would make their début at the 10,000-seater Empress Hall in Earls Court. Only six months earlier, Winston Churchill had stood on the same stage, addressing the annual Conservative Party Conference, correctly predicting that he was going to depose Clement Attlee and become Prime Minister again. (Even if it did take him another couple of years.)

Rivals in the Contest included the Yorkshire Jazz Band, the Merseysippi Jazz Band, Roy Vaughan's Chicagoans, the Crane River Jazz Band, Ken Grinyer's Wolverines and Mike Daniels' Jazzmen. All did their best to impress the illustrious panel of judges: Jack Jackson, Ernest Borneman, Geoff Love, Harry Gold, Sid Phillips, Max Jones and Lord Donegall. Barber and his boys held their own.

Looking out into that cavernous hall, traditional home of important boxing tournaments and ice-hockey matches, big-deal ballet and ballroom dancing, Lawes (the self-styled "baby of the band") confesses "I was completely awe-struck, just couldn't believe it was happening."

Happening it was. A natural-born bandleader, Barber was buoyant, dynamic, brimming with self-confidence and ideas. The best way to put yourself on the map is to publish your own map. Rather than tout for gigs, which were thin on the ground anyway, they set up their own weekly Sunday afternoon residency in the cellar of 10/11 Great Newport Street, round the corner from Leicester Square tube station. They called it Lincoln Gardens. Dream big, or it's not worth dreaming. Lincoln Gardens, at 459 East 31st Street in Chicago, had been home to Joe 'King' Oliver's Creole Jazz Band – featuring Louis Armstrong on second cornet. "This, it may be asserted, was the greatest jazz band ever to appear in public," concluded historians Rex Harris and Brian Rust in their book *Recorded Jazz: A Critical Guide*. The Chicago venue became legendary throughout the jazz world.

Rather less so, the Great Newport Street branch, which opened for business on 16 July 1950. Free membership; half a crown to get in. As a result of its central location, *Melody Maker* small-ads and an underground buzz, it was soon attracting 250 jazz buffs every session, enough to make the walls sweat. Barber took over Tuesday evenings too and as well as his resident band, Lincoln Gardens began to feature such guests as the Crane River Jazz Band and the Riverside Stompers. The Mick Mulligan Band and even Humph's acclaimed crew were not too proud to book themselves in.

On other nights of the week, under its regular name the London Studio Club, the venue presented various styles of music and dance – but would eventually become famous, oh sweet irony, as Ken Colyer's Club. In fact, the Colyer band had a Monday night residency during Barber's time there, also starting in July 1950. Years later, in March 1963, the barely known Rolling Stones (indirect descendants of the Barber Band) would start a six-month Sunday afternoon residency there, inspired by a later cool, black, Chicago-recorded catalogue.

In June 1950, just in time for the Lincoln Gardens launch, Ferdy Favager (with the impeccable timing the band would come to expect of him) was released from the Army – about five minutes before North Korean troops, tanks, ship and planes began to invade South Korea. British troops would be sent in as part of the UN retaliatory force a month later. Only weeks after Ferdy got out, National Service would be extended from 18 months to two years. Too bad, Donegan!

Favager's banjo spiced up the texture and sharpened the tone: "he had the best ear of anyone in the band," Revell believes. (At a loose end for a job, Favager went for an interview at the head office of Friends Provident Insurance in Leadenhall Street – purely on the recommendation of pianist Roy Sturgess, who worked there too – and stayed with the company all his working life.)

It was at Lincoln Gardens that a young guitarist called Alexis Korner started sitting in. For anyone who saw them, they were seminal gigs. "Alexis played rhythm guitar in the band numbers and blues guitar in the blues numbers," says Barber, who (so he thought) had been at St Paul's School at the same time as Korner, but was not aware of him, "possibly because Alexis was on a different wavelength and always would be." In fact, Korner, an incipient juvenile delinquent, had been expelled from St Paul's before Barber arrived.

"Of course, I had little idea of how good Alexis was or what his playing was like," says Barber, "because you can't make a lot of noise with a semi-acoustic guitar and no amplifier. Nevertheless, at Lincoln Gardens, we specialised in King Oliver, with an interlude of Robert Johnson. Years later, when I heard Eric Clapton doing *Cross Road Blues*, I felt very pleased – because when I got my hands on that record in 1947, it might well have been the only copy in England. Eric does it beautifully, of course, and he stimulated enormous interest in that area of the blues. Now you can walk into any decent record shop in any part of the country and buy the complete works of Robert Johnson."

Alexis dropped out but their new double-bass player stuck around. Brylo Ford was from Trinidad and Tobago and, in the manner of calypsonians, fond of stage names, he sometimes styled himself the Iron Duke. A regular with the Jig's Club band throughout the 1940s, he was currently in a West End nightclub trio led by pianist Errol Barrow. He did the Barber gigs for fun and a few bob, same as everyone got. It was some buzz for young white guys to be playing alongside a black bass player, especially one who had been born in 1890 and knew a thing or two about the world.

"We played old numbers from the twenties," Barber explains, "but we didn't play them in an old way – nor did we wear wing collars or have our hair slicked down. We always intended to have a contemporary sound and attitude."

In September 1950, they played at the hallowed 100 Club for the first time and three months later, journeyed to Manchester for their furthest provincial concert to date. Slowly but surely, jazz was catching on. Word of this had even reached the *Daily Telegraph*, even stuffier then than it is now. "I visited the London Jazz Club for their regular Saturday night session," revealed their priggish novelty columnist in December 1950. "I went in to disapprove but I came out chastened. This is the reverse of a glorious pastime, but if ever I saw a harmless one, healthily indulged, it was here. The proceedings are solemn, strenuous and as respectable as a Victorian social. But, oh, the noise!"

One thing was plainly evident: he could not understand it, could not work out its attraction. Them and us. One would become used to it. Neither the *Daily Telegraph*, nor any of its readers, would ever have a clue what was going on in the grass-roots underbelly, not for years anyway.

Britain went into 1951 with petrol rationing, meat rationing, sugar rationing, sweet rationing, cheese rationing, tea rationing and God knows what else rationing. Because of the high price and widespread shortage of leather, dog skin (supplied mainly from dog homes) was used for lining footwear and manufacturing gloves. While our economy showed little sign of shaking off post-war austerity, the Americans were testing atomic bombs in the Nevada desert.

By April 1951, Barber had enough confidence in the band to phone John L. Hooper, a bigwig at BBC Radio, and talk his way into an audition for their token show *Jazz Club*. The bigwig wrote to Chris, inviting him to "prepare a specimen 25-minute programme based on some definite theme or style in order that we may not only judge the versatility of the Jazz Group but also your approach to any special jazz idea."

They not only prepared, but won the gig, playing live on the first day of December. Thirty-five quid between eight of them – "including the personal appearance," stipulated the contract, "of Chris Barber as conductor."

Their set list is an indicator of how they wished to project themselves to the radio audience: not those who were listening because there was nothing else on, but those who were actually interested in jazz. *Camp Meeting Blues, Mandy Lee Blues* and *Room Rent Blues* were sourced from 1923 recordings by King Oliver's Creole Jazz Band, *Brown Skin Mama* from a 1928 recording by Jimmy Blythe's State Street Ramblers, *Mama's Gone, Goodbye* from a 1923 recording by Peter Bocage & his Creole Serenaders, *Misty Morning, The Blues With A Feeling* and *Sloppy Joe* from recordings made by Duke Ellington during 1928 and 1929, and *When Erastus Plays His Old Kazoo* from a 1927 recording by Johnny Dodds' Black Bottom Stompers.

This BBC session was the last to feature trumpeter Dickie Hawdon, who had replaced Keith Jary earlier in the year. Hawdon, a stalwart of the Leeds-based Yorkshire Jazz Band, had moved to London to start his own band, which he soon abandoned to join Barber. His tenure was short, however. In November 1951, when Ken Colyer left the Christie Brothers Stompers to go back to sea on his New Orleans quest, Hawdon left Barber's band to take his place. He generously nipped back to bolster his old cronies on *Jazz Club*. Not that they'd really become old cronies in the few months he was with them.

Interestingly, Barber wouldn't get back onto the radio until August 1954, when he and his entirely different band guested on the 20-minute late-night programme *British Jazz*. From then on, however, appearances would be regular.

In summer 1951, Barber had waved goodbye to his day job and enrolled at the Guildhall School of Music, then on the Victoria Embankment near Blackfriars Bridge. "My father realised I was more interested in music than higher mathematics and offered to pay my fees if I could get into music school. If I'd known then what I know now, I could have gone to any music school in England, with a trombone in my hand, and they would have welcomed me with open arms and a scholarship – because there were so few brass players around. As it was, I was installed in the school orchestra almost immediately because I was the only trombone player there."

He didn't seem to do a lot of study, as such: just played in the school orchestra during the day and with his own band in the evenings. "The theory lessons were all at 9am, which was not good for me. Since I was out every night, either playing with my band or listening to Humph or whatever, I never made it. I think I attended a theory class once in three years – which is why I don't have LGSM after my name."

The laissez-faire college life allowed infinitely more latitude in what was proving to be a challenging year for the band. "The Crane River guys were more popular than us and they were swinging more than us," says Alex Revell. "Both bands were in it purely because they loved the music and wanted to play it – but we were passionate about different areas. They were playing Bunk Johnson/George Lewis stuff, as was currently being played by the old boys still living in New Orleans. We were revivalists, playing music from an older period, recorded by King Oliver and other master musicians – which we tried to copy faithfully, even though we'd only been playing for a couple of years. It could be very complicated and involved, and we were concentrating on our playing, because we didn't really have the technique yet – so we weren't swinging like they were. The dancers responded more to the rhythm of the Cranes, who got stuck into it headlong, never mind the mistakes." This was, after all, a period of intense, crazy dancing, extrovert central, art students and hoorays, look how cool I am, baby. "We thought that George Lewis, Jim Robinson and the other current New Orleans guys were amateurs compared with Oliver, Armstrong, Dodds, Bechet and their crowd. Sweet old guys, but not up there," says Revell. "So the Cranes weren't very interesting to us musically, but there's no denying that they had that beat, that swing. We would bump into them at railway stations here and there, and backstage at concerts, and Ken and Sonny would just grunt at us. Wouldn't speak. Sonny turned into one of the nicest blokes you could ever meet but he was a surly monster in the early days. Ken was always taciturn, of course."

As their reputation grew, the Barber band would spend weekends on trains or on the road, travelling to play concerts in Birmingham, Manchester, Liverpool, Newcastle, Southampton, Leeds, anywhere with a suitable hall and a jazz-bent promoter. Sometimes, they hired a charabanc, which came with its own driver, a cockney who told stories to keep himself awake. "Did I ever tell you about when I was living with a Polish countess during the war?" Twelve-hour journeys on Britain's winding, through-town-centres, pre-motorway road network, staying in memorable (for all the wrong reasons) digs and eating in pioneer Chinese and Indian restaurants, the only places open after ten o'clock. Gigs which saw them coming off stage flushed with exhilaration, gigs their followers would always remember.

They also made their first tentative recordings. At a Jazz Band Ball, held at Hammersmith Palais in March 1951, they cut *Snake Rag*, inspired by King Oliver's 1923 original, and *Oh Didn't He Ramble*, originally a New Orleans funeral song mixing sorrow and celebration of a life well spent (or hopefully well mis-spent), but soon a jazz standard. "Lay him down easy, lay him down slow . . . don't drop him, boys, he's got a long way to go." Barely audible vocals from their leader. Together for a year, the line-up still comprised Barber, Revell, Cohen, Jary, Favager, Ford and Lawes, but Brian Baker had replaced Roy Sturgess on piano. Still a bit stiff and careful, perhaps, but getting more relaxed and instinctive as the weeks went by, none of them afraid to come forward and have a go, all playing with gusto, verve and enthusiasm. *Snake Rag* is a primitive blueprint of the sound and style that, years later, would become nationally famous as 'trad-jazz'.

Just before he started college, Barber and some of the others went to a holiday camp at Yarmouth on the Isle of Wight for a summer break. While they romped and cavorted in the sea, Barber displayed little enthusiasm for the beach life, preferring his thick trousers and jacket to swimming trunks.

Not only were their spirited sit-in contributions welcomed by the resident ballroom band, but they were also able to put down a couple of tracks on the camp's prized tape-recorder. Featuring Barber on double-bass, Revell on clarinet, Cohen on cornet, Lawes on washboard and Favager on banjo, *Everybody Loves My Baby* (a 1925 hit by Clarence Williams' Blue Five – whose floating personnel included Louis Armstrong, Sippie Wallace, Coleman Hawkins and Sidney Bechet, among others) and *Whoop It Up* (a 1929 recording by another of his combos, Clarence Williams' Washboard Band) sounded so vibrant that Esquire released them as a single – credited to Chris Barber's Washboard Wonders. The primitive recording equipment gives them a dusty His Master's Voice sound-horn quality but the lads are so obviously having a blast, knowing they have something to say, something to impart. It's interesting to compare the complexity, imagination, integration and excitement with early records by later upstarts and upsetters.

Back on the circuit, in October 1951, the full band (now with cornettist Dickie Hawdon in place of Keith Jary, and bass player Mickey Ashman in for Brylo Ford) recorded four stage favourites for the Tempo label, in an arcade basement studio off Piccadilly. They were eventually issued simultaneously on two singles the following spring: *Camp Meeting Blues/Stomp Off Let's Go* and *When Erastus Plays His Old Kazoo/Misty Morning*.

"The ensembles are well knit and have a good round sound to them," opined the *Melody Maker*'s respected jazz critic Sinclair Traill, praising their "cleanly executed and well-timed breaks" and finding it "surprising that more has not been heard of this band." Barber was surprised too. His expectations, he knew, were being hampered by their amateur status and sensibilities. "We were two years into it, but now we were just plodding along, doing it."

1952 would be the watershed year. And not only for Barber.

Five

A musical giant whose influence has gone largely unrecognised by latter-day record buyers if not by rock historians, Lonnie Johnson spent a lifetime in blues and jazz. His pedigree was immaculate. Born in New Orleans in February 1889, he learned to sing and play in the whorehouses and gambling joints of Storyville, developing a unique guitar style, seemingly uninfluenced by itinerant contemporaries from bordering states. He worked riverboats, juke joints and the nascent 'chitterling circuit' during the twenties and thirties, recording tracks whenever the opportunity arose. His urgent, mellifluous guitar runs were copied by Robert Johnson but he was also dextrous enough to play solos on sessions by Duke Ellington (for instance, *Hot And Bothered*) and Louis Armstrong (try his Hot Seven's *Hotter Than That*).

In 1942, Johnson's rude anthem *He's A Jellyroll Baker* infiltrated *Billboard* magazine's newly inaugurated Harlem Hit Parade, which for the first time measured the popularity of records made for the race market.

In 1948, at the age of 59, he scored the biggest hit of his career when he revived *Tomorrow Night*, a nine-year-old song originally recorded by Horace Heidt & his Orchestra. Anticipating the anxious mood of the Shirelles' *Will You Love Me Tomorrow*, Johnson's intimate, vulnerable vocal gave wings to what was essentially a sentimental Tin Pan Alley ballad. A filigree guitar added an attractive Latin edge to a country/blues/pop melange that already defied categorisation, and the record easily outsold any other black-market contenders released that year – including *Good Rocking Tonight* by King label-mate Wynonie Harris, *It's Too Soon To Know* by the Orioles, *We're Gonna Rock* by Wild Bill Moore, *Chicken Shack Boogie* by Amos Milburn, and several others now regarded as seminal influences on the development of rock 'n' roll.

As the forties dissolved into the fifties, the teenaged Elvis Presley sat around his Memphis home, marvelling at the music of Lonnie Johnson, a turntable favourite at local radio station WDIA. (In

September 1954, during his third session for Sam Phillips, Elvis would bare his heart and soul in a moonlight-pure version of *Tomorrow Night* – only to watch it gather dust in the Sun vault.) Meanwhile, in a parallel universe some 4,000 miles away, an equally infatuated Tony Donegan – denied access to more recent material – was hooked on the nuggets Johnson had recorded for the Okeh label during the late twenties and early thirties . . . such rare, hard-to-find sides as *Racketeer's Blues, She's Making Whoopee In Hell Tonight, Mean Old Bedbug Blues* and *I'm Nuts About That Gal.*

Donegan was entranced – by the voice, by the guitar, by the image of the young virile bluesman, by the visions conjured by the songs, by the whole idea of singing and playing to a rapt audience. At the end of 1951, in a climactic rush of audacity and admiration, he somehow convinced all and sundry to start addressing him as Lonnie rather than Tony. It was an inspired move – far more dazzling than he could ever have imagined. There were no other Lonnies in British show business, or in Britain full-stop. Within a few years, Donegan would have the immediate single-name recognition enjoyed only by a handful of stars . . . Elvis, Mantovani, Liberace, Ringo, Groucho, Bing, Madonna, Cher, Sting, Elton, there aren't many more. If you said the name Lonnie, everyone knew whom you were talking about.

Anthony Donegan had been born in Glasgow on 29 April 1931, but poverty forced a relocation to London two years later: "If you're a classical violinist, you don't get any work in Glasgow," he reckoned, "but it didn't seem to matter where we lived; my father was still a failed musician with a capital F." So the young Tony spent most of his early life in Milton Avenue, around the corner from East Ham underground station. From there they moved to Derby Road in Forest Gate and when the Luftwaffe threatened to flatten the area, the eight year old was evacuated to Altrincham in Cheshire, where he stayed with his mother's sister and her husband. After further shuttling between his dad's place in Glasgow and his mother's in Forest Gate, he returned to Altrincham in a last ditch attempt to absorb some education at St Ambrose College, a Catholic school which is still regarded by many as the best in the area. Tony would eventually become their most famous old boy, even though he jacked school at 14 and moved back to London to start his first job, as an office boy at Shaw Loeble & Co, a firm of city stockbrokers with offices at 148 Leadenhall Street.

A fellow office boy spent his evenings playing guitar and pulling birds in a dance band. At lunchtimes, he would bring out his guitar and put ideas in Donegan's head. "We used to sit on benches in the courtyard," he remembered. "He would show me chord diagrams and say 'you put your fingers like this and go chink chink chink,' and I'd say 'Oh yes, I see . . . marvellous'. Then I bought his guitar off him for 50 bob when he got a new one." It was the start of a trend. Boys with guitars.

His early inspiration came from the *Radio Rhythm Club*, a half-hour programme broadcast weekly by the BBC throughout the war. Harry Parry & his Sextet would play approximations of jazz numbers, interspersed with the odd record. Listening in became a ritual, jazz became a passion.

Meanwhile, he was exercising his fingers on the fretboard and learning the lyrics of songs recorded by Frank Crumit, a novelty singer-songwriter from Ohio. Though a contemporary of Lonnie Johnson (seven months younger), Crumit's white skin, chirpy personality and folksy homespun ditties had earned Broadway fame by the time he was 30 and, thanks to the gramophone, such catchy curiosities as *Abdul Abulbul Amir*, *A Gay Caballero*, *Little Brown Jug* and *My Grandfather's Clock* became favourites in Britain too. Donegan loved the wry humour of songs like *The Pig Got Up And Slowly Walked Away* and *There's No-One With Endurance Like The Man Who Sells Insurance*. In a record-your-own-voice booth at the Kursaal Funfair at Southend, he cut his teeth on a naïve version of *Frankie And Johnny*, learned from a Crumit 78, and right up until his death, he would be pleased to recite the lyric of *Song Of The Prune* to anyone who cared to listen.

In summer 1948, Donegan bumped into Johnny Chown, who he'd known from his days in the boy scouts, and when a mutual interest in jazz was established they started hanging out together. At Chown's instigation, they journeyed over to Cooks Ferry Inn in Edmonton one Sunday evening to see Freddy Randall's band. Donegan's brain bubbled: live jazz! And not only that, but live blues too, courtesy of larger-than-life Beryl Bryden, who sang *St Louis Blues*. "That evening was the turning point of my life," Donegan would later assert.

Soon he was a regular at the 100 Club too, marvelling at Humphrey Lyttelton's band, always close enough to guitarist Nevil Skrimshire to study his chords. "This place was heaven for me," he would confess when he played the 100 Club in 1984, "this was my church."

Not for long, however. In summer 1949, after sporadic rehearsals with Alex Revell's band at Gearies School in Gants Hill, Donegan was called up. Of course, unless you were a two-short-planker, National Service was never more than a catastrophic waste of two valuable years, possibly the most valuable. "That insane little world of blanco, bootpolish, being broke and bullied," as Adrian Mitchell described it. One just had to be phlegmatic and positive and sit it out, while being hectored by pea-brained tin-god sergeants. This is what Private Donegan 22173387 intended to do.

Though the pain was excruciating, appendicitis brought him welcome relief from spud-peeling and square-bashing and, after surgery, he was ambulanced to hospital barracks in Southampton. As soon as he could get around, he located the city's jazz club and was soon on stage with local hot-shots, Ken Grinyer's Wolverine Jazz Band.

"They were quite good," Donegan recalls, "except that the drummer was a lemon – a six-foot schoolboy . . . sewper! It was more than I could stand, so when they took a break, cocky little bastard that I was, I asked the guvnor if I could sit in. So there I was, playing drums for the first time in my life – but at least I could hit them in time, which put me streets ahead of this other geezer. As soon as the set was over, I had to do a Cinderella number and shoot off without saying goodbye – but I was still late back and got confined to barracks for two weeks."

"When I eventually saw the band again, they wanted me to play with them on a regular basis, which was out of the question, of course." He did manage a couple of gigs, at one of which a snapper from *Jazz Journal* turned up. "They did articles on local bands – and I got lucky. In my first photograph as a musician, I was standing there in my army uniform, holding a pair of drum sticks."

Three years later, Ken Grinyer's Wolverine Jazz Band would receive a modicum of acclaim on the London pub circuit before fading out of the picture. Donegan, meanwhile, was sent back to Aldershot to complete his basic training.

The way he tells it, he volunteered for the Medical Corps to forestall overseas posting. Whether or not this is true, he ended up on a course in venereal disease – "you didn't have to catch it, just cure it" – at the Royal Herbert, the first British hospital with long corridors and separately partitioned wards. Its location, on the edge of Eltham Common, meant he could get to the odd Soho gig. Whether or not, too late for public transport, he actually walked the 12 miles back to Eltham, as he has claimed, is open to conjecture but one can safely assume that he quickly established himself as the Flash Herbert of the Royal Herbert. After medic duty at the Trooping of the Colour in June 1950 (the last attended by the King, who was too ill the following year), he was whisked off to Vienna and, having shown no aptitude or interest in the field of medicine, was put to work in the stores at one of the bases.

He knew what to expect, having seen Orson Welles' new film *The Third Man* – foreboding skies, cobblestones, grey buildings, stairways descending into rubble, and the Prater Wheel silhouetted against the skyline. "A smashed, dreary city of undignified ruins," Graham Greene had called it, and Donegan saw no reason to disagree. Statues and history were not to his taste and nor was the music in the cafés and bars. Vienna rang with zithers. In the hands of Anton Karas, the instrument had provided a novel and attractive soundtrack to the movie, but its sharp reverberating tones scraped at the psyche when you couldn't escape them.

He had his guitar with him and he and a friend, George Harlaw, would strum and sing whatever songs they knew, just for their own amusement. Harlaw was more accomplished and knowledgeable, acquainting Donegan with blues flourishes and folk standards. Guys in the barracks would gather round to listen. It was career-man Harlaw who introduced the young novice to the music of Lonnie Johnson, teaching him *Fly Right Baby*, a song that would become one of his favourites forever more.

As one of Harry Lime's friends advised, "everybody ought to go careful in Vienna," which in the after-burn of war had been divided into four zones, controlled by the British, the French, the Americans and the Russians. Off duty, Donegan often crossed the border into the American sector: he wasn't a drinker but he liked their ice-cream. He also liked their music. During the last half of 1950, listening to the American Forces Network, as he did most nights, he heard *Mona Lisa* by Nat 'King' Cole, *Music Music Music* by Teresa Brewer, *The Cry Of The Wild Goose* by Frankie Laine, *If I Knew You Were Coming I'd Have Baked A Cake* by Georgia Gibbs, *Frosty The Fucking Snowman* (Lonnie's modification) by Gene Autry, *The Old Master Painter* (or *The Old Masturbator*, as he and his mates called it) by Richard Hayes and, crucially, *Goodnight Irene* by the Weavers.

In 1951 came *Cry* by Johnnie Ray, *Mocking Bird Hill* and *How High The Moon* by Les Paul & Mary Ford, *So Long It's Been Good To Know You* and *On Top Of Old Smoky* by the Weavers, *My Heart Cries For You* and *The Roving Kind* by Guy Mitchell.

He would hear these records and smile. Silly, most of them – though unbeknownst to him, he had hummed along to songs by his future gods Leadbelly and Woody Guthrie. Whenever he got near a radio, he tuned it to AFN. The Weavers were stirring but more to his liking were the latest rhythm & blues records. At no time would disc jockeys play the old blues records he wanted to hear – they were now regarded as dusty artefacts from a bleak and bygone era – but he enjoyed the contemporary black music just as much: *Teardrops From My Eyes* by Ruth Brown, *Please Send Me Someone To Love* by Percy Mayfield, *Blue Shadows* by Lowell Fulson, *Blue Light Boogie* by Louis Jordan and *Black Night* by Charles Brown, unimaginable exotica ringing through the little speaker every night.

Country & western music was equally arresting, particularly records like *I'll Sail My Ship Alone* by Moon Mullican, *I'm Movin' On* by Hank Snow, *Shot Gun Boogie* by Tennessee Ernie Ford and two favourites by Hank Williams, *Why Don't You Love Me Like You Used To Do* and *Cold Cold Heart*. Too much to assimilate but he always went to sleep smiling.

Then it was back home to England, where you could hear bugger all on the radio.

At a loose end on civvy street in summer 1951, Donegan got a job behind the counter at Gray's, an electrical firm in Tottenham Court Road, and started to investigate the traditional jazz haunts of London, looking for an opening. With Ferdy Favager secure on banjo, Chris Barber's band couldn't use him but – with his mate Johnny Chown along for encouragement – Donegan took his guitar to the Wood Green Jazz Club, the Fishmonger's Arms, where promoter Art Saunders let him take the interval. Still only a kid of 20, but cocky with it. In a plangent, high-lonesome tone, he sang *Frankie*

And Johnny, his old stand-by, the American music-hall standard whose origins lay in the red-light district of St Louis, where the evening sun went down to the despair of many a blues-wailer, local heroine Beryl Bryden included. Frankie Baker was an "ebony hued" teenage prostitute who dispatched her "drunk, violent and unfaithful" lover at 212 Targee Street in October 1899. It was a story song, illustrative of a genre in which Lonnie would soon find himself comfortably imprisoned. When he first learned the song, he used to sing it in the style of Frank Crumit, but now he was trying to make it sound a little more raunchy and dramatic, rather closer to the version by Leadbelly, who, Donegan admitted, "made Crumit sound like Donald Duck". Saunders gave him expenses, his bus fare, and invited him back any time he liked.

"I was interested in blues, folk, country – the kind of songs that later became known, totally erroneously in my view, as skiffle. At Wood Green, I would sing them with a mixture of ineptitude, amateurism and lack of knowledge – but plenty of enthusiasm and I think that is what brought the punters back from the bar. I mean, at the interval, when the band came off, there would always be a mad rush for the bar, it was empty-room time, but over the weeks, more and more would trickle back to see me."

Of course, learning new songs was difficult. "The kind of stuff I wanted was hard to come by – but then somebody told me that you could order records from the Library of Congress if you went to the American Embassy in Grosvenor Square. So I signed myself in and spent days going through their anthropology room, where I found all sorts of treasures, including a record that Muddy Waters had made when he was a farm worker in Mississippi. I borrowed it and never took it back; I stole it. I told them I'd lost it and paid a fine . . . quite happily, of course." Thereby depriving others of the opportunity to hear it. Nice one, Lonnie.

On his travels, Donegan learned that Bill Brunskill's Jazz Band could maybe use a banjo player. Within a few weeks, it was being billed as Tony Donegan's Jazz Band. What he lacked in experience and contacts, he certainly made up for in ambition and cheek.

They were basically a fun band, typical of many on the circuit. Some short time after the turn of the decade, a clarinet player called Don Simmons had got a bunch of youngsters around him to play jazz. No-one remembers how they came together. Gordon Blundy (trombone) and Arthur Fryatt (drums), both from Southgate, seem to think that they first got the bug at some youth club near Barnet, from which they graduated to regular rehearsals at the church hall in Nether Street, Hendon. There, they successfully integrated themselves into the Georgia Jazz Band, run by the aforesaid Simmons, and started playing parties and pubs.

Investigating players came and went, including young banjo strummer Dickie Bishop, taking his first tentative steps. For reasons of fashion and fashionability, some of their infrequent gigs were at tennis clubs, one or two of which demanded that they present themselves in evening dress. While the others foraged in second-hand shops to find suitable garb, Dickie turned up in a uniform he'd borrowed from his uncle, his livery as doorman at the Regent Palace Hotel. "He was standing there in this beautifully tailored frock coat, with brass buttons and gold braid on the shoulders," recalls Blundy. "He would've looked just like some old colonel from the American Civil War, had he not had the name of the Regent Palace Hotel sewn onto his breast."

By all accounts, this chap Simmons had to leave town quickly. No one seems to know the details, which may be just as well. The band lost its centre and broke up. Only a few weeks later, however, Bill Brunskill (trumpet) got in touch to say that he'd met a couple of bods who were eager to audition. Both had recently emerged, relatively unscathed, from National Service: Geoff Kemp (clarinet) and Tony Donegan (banjo). They got going again as Bill Brunskill's Jazz Band: featuring Bill on trumpet, Geoff on clarinet, Lonnie on banjo, Arthur Fryatt on drums, Gordon Blundy (later Bob Dawbarn) on trombone and Woofer Barker on bass – soon to be replaced by Jim Bray.

Our Tony took little time to get the drop on the situation. "All of a sudden, we were no longer Bill Brunskill's Jazz Band, we were Tony Donegan's Jazz Band," says Fryatt, still somewhat mystified by the adroit hijacking half a century later.

The experienced, 31-year-old Brunskill had apparently stepped aside for a 20-year-old upstart. This was a bizarre and novel situation, insiders conjectured, a jazz band led by the banjo player, the bloke who just sits at the back going plunk plunk plunk. He knew his chords, his proficiency was never in question, but how could this plunker lead from the back?

"There were lots of bands around, but they were all playing for fun," says Lonnie. "The guys were all clerks and wallpaper hangers and students and what have you, and none had any thought of making it professionally. In fact, to most of them, the very idea of making money from playing jazz was preposterous."

So, although he merely grinned and strummed enthusiastically in the background, leaving any solos to the more glamorous tootlers up front, Donegan was the bandleader. "Whatever band it was, the most ambitious person drove it – and playing music was all I wanted to do, so I took over as organiser. The others didn't seem to mind." So he thought.

Badgering club promoters, Donegan landed gigs at all the pubs and clubs on the burgeoning trad-jazz circuit: the Queen Victoria at Worcester Park, the White Lion in Edgware, Cooks Ferry Inn at Edmonton, the Delta Jazz Club in Gerrard Street, the Harrow Inn at Abbey Wood, and the Fishmonger's Arms at Wood Green, where his champion, the dependable Art Saunders was so delighted with their pulling power that he advertised the band as Donegan's Demons! Already, 'the sensational new discovery' (as Saunders portrayed him in adverts) was making himself the centre of attention by pulling out his guitar and singing a selection of folk and blues songs during the interval.

He seemed to know exactly what he was doing: like a novice stand-up comedian or a music hall turn trying to elbow his way onto the ladder, he was promoting every aspect of his talent and remained oblivious to any criticism. Several people interviewed for this book remember their mates saying "Oh God, he's going to sing, let's go to the pub". Some even suggested that this was the cry of his girlfriend. Donegan's voice was an acquired taste if you'd been used to Bessie Smith and Big Bill Broonzy, let alone Donald Peers and Dickie Valentine.

One can only wonder what dream gave Donegan such turbo-driven conviction, dedication and self-belief that he started to call himself Lonnie. A nocturnal visitation from the ghost of Charley Patton, maybe, or a vision of his hero Lonnie Johnson telling him to adopt his name immediately if he wanted to become a star. Whatever, the transition was swift.

As early as February 1952 – the month King George VI died and Elizabeth ascended to the throne – he was being billed as Lonnie

Donegan in the weekly column advertising club dates in the small-ad pages at the back of *Melody Maker*. The first step to becoming larger than life.

Incidentally, the *MM* was already getting twitched about recent developments in popular music. In discussing the rapid rise of American newcomer Johnnie Ray, whose rabid female fans were trying to tear off his clothes wherever he appeared, their expert journalist Laurie Henshaw underlined the paper's fear of the unknown, a phobia which would haunt its staff until the Beatles eventually dragged them hollering and screaming into the real world.

"Surely there must come a time to call a halt to the never-ending search for sales-fetching gimmicks," Henshaw complained. "Johnnie Ray, a 25-year-old Oregon-born vocalist, has jumped from the $90 to the $2,000 bracket by hitting on the excruciating formula of virtually bursting into tears while singing a song. According to a US report, his stentorian sobbing sometimes so unhinges him that he has to rush offstage to compose himself. That this uninhibited and tasteless showmanship registers with audiences is indicated by the fact that, within eight weeks of issue, Johnnie's tearful version of his composition *The Little White Cloud That Cried* shot past the million sales mark. Listening to this recording was for me as much of a torturous experience as that obviously suffered by Johnnie during the actual session. The coupling *Cry* follows the same painful pattern. If an artist has to descend to this level to capture the masses, then the outlook for popular music is indeed bleak."

You had better believe it, baby!

Strangely, both Jimmy Young and Vera Lynn covered *Cry*. What were they thinking of?

It was under the name of Lonnie Donegan that the intrepid bandleader played his most important show to date: as a solo, just him and a guitar.

Along with George Melly and Beryl Bryden, he was a featured singer on what posters described as 'the greatest jazz event ever staged in Great Britain', an 18-band extravaganza held at the Royal Albert Hall on 2 June 1952. In a forerunner of the great annual outdoor festivals, the parade of bands – including those of Sid Phillips, Freddy Randall, Mick Mulligan, Sandy Brown and Charlie

Galbraith – were each given a 10-minute showcase, in which to blow their brains loose. Front row seats were six shillings, the cheapest half a crown.

Armed with only his guitar, Lonnie walked out onto one of the largest and most famous stages in the world and gave it his all. "OK, I was terrible," he admits, "just an ignorant little strummer who didn't know any better. I shudder to think what my voice sounded like in a place that big – but the response was as if I'd just raised the *Titanic* single-handedly. It was enormous, gigantic! The audience adored me!"

All except one, it seems.

From his elevated perch, the *Melody Maker* scribe Ernest Borneman liked little of what he saw and heard. In a generally disdainful review – "Whatever the musicians and the jazz lovers may feel about these three-numbers-per-band concerts, the general public have borne out the promoter's conviction that this is what the audience wants, but I can certainly vouch that musically they are getting worse" – he singled out Lonnie for special mention. "Why, oh why?" he lamented. "A cowboy-styled blues vocal with guitar accompaniment, *Lonesome And Blue* had echoes of Jimmie Rodgers and the hillbilly parade, falsetto notes and all. Really dreadful." Not a single word about the pandemonium Lonnie had generated.

Donegan has never forgotten this, his first press analysis. "I have a bad heart now," he confirmed, rubbing his chest, "and that review was the beginning, his words were written into the valves of my heart. He was so unjust."

Lonnie had the last laugh.

Ernest Borneman would soon be consigned to the pop-weekly scrapyard, the inevitable fate of old-and-in-the-way journalists reporting on the trite and ephemeral world of contemporary music. His fall from grace was probably hastened by readers' reactions to his review, some of which the *Melody Maker* fearlessly printed on their letters page. The most incisive included the observation that "Borneman must have ears as large as a donkey and as high an intelligence".

Incidentally, in the early hours of the morning following the Albert Hall concert, the promoter Maurice Kinn was burgled as he slept. Thieves broke into his Stanmore home and, although they failed to locate the night's takings, they looted over £2,000 worth of silverware. To add insult to injury, they made their getaway in his car, which was later abandoned near St Pancras station. Lonnie denied any involvement.

At the end of June 1952, against all expectations, Donegan found himself on the stage of the Royal Festival Hall. Two monumental gigs in one month . . . and this one was supporting his idol, the man whose name he had so recently appropriated. The coincidence, the synchronicity was astounding. What are the chances of this happening, a million to one? Somebody up there liked him, he was forced to conclude.

Since the beginning of the year, the National Federation of Jazz Organisations had been negotiating to promote two Festival Hall concerts featuring foreign and British musicians sharing the same stage. The first, set for 28 June, was to be headlined by American ragtime pianist Ralph Sutton and Donegan's idol, Lonnie Johnson; the second, lined up for 1 July, was to star Dutch saxophonist Rob Pronk and Swedish saxophonist Arne Domnerus. Work permits had been obtained from the Ministry of Labour – but officials from the Musicians' Union were behaving in their usual obtuse and bellicose manner, trying to prevent the concerts from happening. Not only had they instructed their members that "the proposal to present these foreign musicians must be vigorously opposed", they had been arrogant and impudent enough to express "considerable doubt as to whether any educational or cultural benefit" would be derived from their visit.

Sides were taken and a ding-dong battle ensued between the NFJO and the MU. The good guys against the bad guys. According to Lonnie, "it was something of a test case. American musicians used to come over and tour Europe but weren't allowed to play in Britain, which was ridiculous. The union rule was 'yes, they can come in at any time, as long as a British musician plays USA in exchange, for the same money'. Well, who could we send over in exchange for Dizzy Gillespie and Oscar Peterson, who were currently appearing in Paris? It was an absurdity – and it worked against the union members, who desperately needed to learn from the Americans. We were being shackled by our own union, which was largely run by non-musicians".

One puzzled official actually asked a jazz-fanatic journalist: "Why are you fellows so keen to have American musicians visit this country?" His failure to understand the agitation beggared belief. "The mills of the MU grind slowly, but always produce the same rotten flour," retorted one disconsolate fan.

So, while Paris was buzzing, London got increasingly bleak and stagnant – and the NFJO, deciding that enough was enough, thrust two fingers up the MU's nose. They advertised the gigs, sold tickets legitimately and booked the best British bands as support acts. However, at the eleventh hour, the union pulled a 'no, brothers'/Fred Kite-style ultimatum and threatened to black any members who dared to share the stage with these damned foreigners.

Fearing career-nixing reprisals, Humphrey Lyttelton thought it prudent to withdraw his band from the bill. Forced to cast around "and scrape the barrel" for replacements not beholden to the Musicians' Union, the NFJO fell upon the Lonnie Donegan Jazz Band. Amateur and non-Union. Would they be interested in doing the gig? What was Lonnie going to say . . . 'I might think about it'? He almost bit the guy's ear off down the phone.

Among others telling the Union to stick it were George Webb's Dixielanders (still refusing to lie down and not get up again) and George Melly. Said Melly: "I am in favour of unions; I disapprove of blacklegs and scabs – but I disapprove of the Musicians' Union policy towards American musicians." Said Donegan, who would have been happy to support Lonnie Johnson in a barn on the Isle of Skye, even if he had to row the boat himself: "I consider the NFJO is the jazz musicians' union – and, since professional musicians should uphold MU rules, the NFJO member should stick to his organisation."

Thus did Lonnie Donegan open the show for his idol Lonnie Johnson . . . who sadly didn't live up to expectations. "It was bitterly disappointing," says Lonnie, who was nevertheless too awe-struck and breathless to engage him in conversation, "and it was the same with Louis Armstrong when he first came over. We all lived in a time warp. All we were interested in were those old, old records – and we expected these guys to sound like those old, old records . . . which, of course, they didn't. They had moved on to maintain their careers."

"Lonnie Johnson had developed this very smooth voice, very warm and exciting, but smooth. He was playing electric guitar and singing Hoagy Carmichael sort of songs – which was not surprising because he was no longer working in gin mills and turpentine camps, he was playing well-paid night-clubs. The rather nice white suit and bow-tie were a bit of a give-away! He was very good, but not what I had been looking forward to."

The audience liked him, little realising that Lonnie Johnson was a yesterday man, while his opening act, the subservient and servile Lonnie Donegan was soon to become one of the biggest stars in show business.

Six

In late summer 1952, after the excitement of the Royal Festival Hall, Lonnie Donegan's Jazz Band had to content themselves with a handful of pub gigs and the occasional riverboat cruise from Westminster Pier. Their appearance on one of the Saturday afternoon concerts at the Battersea Pleasure Gardens was, however, memorable for several reasons.

Amid such crowd-pulling attractions as a funfair, a boating lake, a tree walk and the much-photographed Guinness clock, a big dance pavilion, complete with canvas roof and solid floor, had been erected as part of the Festival of Britain celebrations the previous year. They felt pretty good to be playing to such a large, non-partisan audience. Among those clustered around the band, sparkling with admiration, was an East End girl called Maureen Tyler, who took a shine to the banjo player. She was destined to become the first Mrs Donegan.

The band's performance, or part of it, was captured – not on tape but on wire. Some fellow they knew brought along a wire recorder marketed commercially as the Sound Mirror and Lonnie was later able to transfer his two vocal efforts onto acetate. The first was *Ace In The Hole*, an old jazz number which Ken Colyer's idol Bunk Johnson had unearthed and recorded with the Yerba Buena Jazz Band in 1944; the other was *The Boll Weevil*, 'the theme song of the Southern sharecropper', learned from a Leadbelly record.

The cheeky, chirpy chappie came off stage smiling, as usual. He wasn't aware that this would be his last appearance with the band, had no suspicion of what was going on behind his back, that the knives were out.

There was at the time an unpopular and unsavoury practice, which required all those who had completed National Service to interrupt their lives yet again and report for three weeks in the Army Reserve. It was known as call-back. Lonnie was called back. When he returned to the rehearsal room, only 21 days later, he was horrified to learn that someone had sneaked in and taken his place. He had been dumped by his own band.

"During his absence, we got another banjo player," recalls drummer Arthur Fryatt, matter-of-factly, "and Lonnie was given the elbow."

Melody Maker reported the changes. Bill Cotton (a chap who liked a laugh and a drink, by all accounts; no relation to the plump band leader of the same name) was the new banjo player and they were now called Geoff Kemp's Jazz Band. Lonnie had resigned, so readers were told. At least it gave him more time to spend with his new bird.

On the last weekend of September, he took her to see Chris Barber's band at Wood Green and learned that changes were in the air for him too. His New Orleans Jazz Band was about to undergo a complete overhaul and rebuild.

In retrospect, it could be seen that the signs had been pointing this way for almost a year and a half, since February 1951, when they had unsuccessfully auditioned to become resident band at the 100 Club, in place of the departing Humph. They lost out to the Christie Brothers Band, which was a much greater disappointment than they cared to let on.

"We had good ideas, our hearts were in the right place and we were all trying really hard but we just weren't proficient enough to be residents at the 100 Club," admits Barber. "It wouldn't have worked, unless we'd improved very quickly."

When trumpeter Dickie Hawdon left for the Christies later in the year, the band couldn't replace him. After six months, they found Jerry French – but by this time, the loss of momentum and lack of progress was gnawing at Barber. His inability to find a permanent bass player was another major frustration. During 1952, a succession came and went, including Frank Houghton, Johnny Willment, John Shaw and Pete Shorthouse. Some would be taught the numbers in the train carriage, on the way to the gig. "It's a piece of cake – it's the *Sweet Georgia Brown* sequence in A flat, starts on F seventh."

Playing a mixture of club dates and concert halls around the country, the band was enlarging its following quite dramatically but Barber still felt increasingly uncomfortable with his situation. "If you only play once a week, you realise you've made all the same mistakes as last week and not corrected any of them. You never get any better."

Alex Revell, his long-time sidekick and sounding-board, found himself sidelined and superseded by a new confidante.

"I was still at the Guildhall School of Music, playing a Brahms symphony by day and King Oliver by night," recalls Barber, "but during the summer break, I used to go into Soho most days and meet up with Monty Sunshine."

Monty was also a student. After RAF duty, he had taken a course on graphic art at Camberwell and was now continuing at St Martins School of Art in Charing Cross Road. As often as they had a gig or a rehearsal, he was still playing clarinet with the Crane River Jazz Band, which, since Ken Colyer's exit had sadly dwindled in popularity and spirit. After their morning trawl through the record racks at Dobell's, he and Barber would head for the Rex Café in New Compton Street, the stone-floored cellar of which had already housed such enterprises as the Delta Jazz Club, the Metropolitan Bopera House and most recently Club du Faubourg.

"The Rex was owned by a Cypriot couple, lovely people who encouraged musicians to eat there and sometimes, if they were broke, would lend them the train fare to make a gig in Leeds, or wherever," recalls Barber, who had himself benefited from this uncommon generosity on occasion. "Throughout that whole summer of 1952, Monty and I would sit around all day talking about jazz, drinking tea and coffee, and eating the cheapest meal on the menu, which was poached egg on spaghetti."

"He and I represented the two camps in New Orleans jazz. Because of Ken Colyer's influence, the Crane River band stood for the revived archaic jazz; my band stood for the classic New Orleans jazz, but played in a contemporary way. So the George Lewis versus Johnny Dodds debate used to rage . . . but we could see each other's point of view and we both shared the same goal: we wanted to make our living by playing music."

This was brought home in September, when Barber took his girlfriend to Copenhagen. He had been invited to play his trombone with local heroes the Ramblers in a two-day festival organised by the Danish Hot Club and Jazz Society . . . and he went down a storm. "His addition to the band made it sound like a new one, a much better one," wrote journalist Hans Pedersen. Said the *Melody Maker*: "His reception was the kind that fans give to big American stars." Interestingly, the clarinet player was Danish tennis star and renaissance man Torben Ulrich, whose son Lars would become world famous as founder of the heavy-metal group Metallica.

Barber came back to England with his mind made up. "I concluded that the way to become a proficient musician was not only to play more, but to play as if your life depended on it – and the way to do that was to make your life depend on it. In an amateur band, it's immaterial whether the musicians can play well or not, it's just personal fun. It needed to be more than that . . . it needed to be a professional band."

He sounded out the guys – who all thought he was mad.

"None of us believed that it was possible to make a living from playing jazz," says Alex Revell. "We knew that even our hero King Oliver had ended up working as a janitor in a Georgia pool-room – plus we'd had the importance of a secure job drilled into us since we first went to school. It was all right for Chris, he had an allowance, but we were all working. On top of that, I was getting married the following year."

They had helped to promote and enhance the name and reputation of Chris Barber but none felt able to commit to his vision. His eyes blazed with conviction but they had other strings tugging at their lives.

First to leave was Ferdy Favager. As soon as he realised that Donegan was sniffing around, waiting in the wings, he bowed out graciously and gracefully. Next to go was Brian Baker, who correctly sensed that a piano didn't feature in the new game plan. Then Barber said goodbye to his best friend, Alex Revell, who opted for the certainty of a career in engineering, his cornet player Ben Cohen, who had good prospects at Bush Radio, and drummer Brian Lawes, who was finishing an apprenticeship before being dragged off for National Service. "We were in each other's pockets for years . . . and then all of a sudden we lost touch." It was a process, a group-scene scenario that would be repeated at least a million times over the years.

Lonnie Donegan joined in a flash. Right time, right place, right vibe, right face. Since leaving school, he had been an office boy, a laboratory assistant, a salesman at Meaker's the gents' outfitters, a squaddie, a counter hand in an electrical shop, a counter hand at Ryman's the Stationer, and he was currently working as a window dresser at Millet's Army Surplus Stores in Oxford Street. He had nothing to lose, no qualms whatsoever about packing up work and becoming a professional musician. Are you kidding?

Monty was in too, of course. That made three. Now, what about a bass player and drummer? Less than 10 years later, another Chris would encounter difficulties recruiting a similar bunch of dedicated gunslingers in *The Magnificent Seven*.

Knowing that he was fed up with his job as a researcher at Shell, Lonnie talked his old bassist Jim Bray into joining the enterprise and Monty convinced Barber that the Crane River Band's drummer Ron Bowden was capable of being moulded into shape. Barber knew he was a good drummer but he couldn't disguise his scepticism. Other than wanting nothing more than to turn pro and spend the rest of his life playing drums, Bowden didn't exactly fit the bill. "Ron wasn't quite what we wanted," says Lonnie. "He was a bit too much of a smoothie, really, and totally passionate about be-bop. On top of that, he was always taking drum lessons – which was considered most uncool on the trad-jazz scene: 'oh, you can't take lessons, man, you have to play instinctively!' But he was enthusiastic, so Chris took him on board."

When no trumpeters seemed up to it or up for it, Barber had an aberration and produced from his collection two 78s to validate his contention that they could do without. Both were by the Eclipse Alley Five (comprising New Orleans faces George Lewis, Jim Robinson, Baby Dodds, Lawrence Marrero and Alcide Pavageau): *My Bucket's Got A Hole In It* and *Ice Cream*. No piano, no trumpet, but still a workable combination.

"We knew it was possible to play authentically with a five piece line-up and got on with trying to do just that. Straight away, we sounded marvellous, light years ahead of what any of the other bands were doing. And it made us work harder: in that line-up, you couldn't hide bad phrasing behind somebody else, it was just too transparent."

Chris Barber (trombone), Monty Sunshine (clarinet), Lonnie Donegan (banjo), Jim Bray (bass) and Ron Bowden (drums). A super-group years before such a concept existed, it looked good on paper and sounded spectacular on stage. Initial rehearsals were held in the first floor functions room of The Prince Albert, an East End public house with a friendly and accommodating landlord – Maureen Tyler's father. "It's every layabout's dream, isn't it?" laughs Donegan, "to meet a nymphomaniac whose dad has a pub! What a stereotype I was – the original lad!" (Ha ha, very funny, Lonnie; he didn't even drink at the time and Maureen was undoubtedly demure and virginal.)

"Old man Tyler loved to hear us playing and would bring crates of Ben Truman up so that we could blow all night – and the more we played together, the better it felt," says Donegan. "There was no other jazz band like it . . . we felt we could own the world!"

However, although the no-trumpet idea was novel, it was ultimately impractical. The music they wanted to play demanded a trumpet. Lonnie's friend Johnny Chown auditioned "and was awful," according to Barber. "He played one rehearsal and we asked him not to come again." They racked their brains. Whenever his old band played at the White Hart in Southall, Barber had admired the fire and fluency of Pat Halcox, who played trumpet with club residents the Albemarle Jazz Band. After a bit of smooth talking, Pat accepted an offer to switch camps. (Just to complicate the *Rock Family Trees* picture, Sonny Morris left the Crane River Band to replace him.)

The augmented line-up sounded amazing. "None of us had any doubts," said Lonnie, "we were going right to the top!"

They still congregated at the Rex Café to discuss repertoire and strategy, or merely to chat and dream. Amongst the other coffee drinkers were Richard Attenborough and Sheila Sim, who at the end of November opened in *The Mousetrap*, a new Agatha Christie play at the Ambassadors Theatre, just down the road.

On Christmas Eve, the new band made its début at the Creole Club at 44 Gerrard Street, operated by Barber's future business partner Harold Pendleton, and blew the place apart. "It was atomic," recalled Lonnie, though the more measured Barber considered it merely "very fine." On New Year's Eve they went back to the same venue and knew it was going to happen for them. Barber had a Danish tour up his sleeve and suggested that this would be the turning point of all their lives, the time to quit day jobs and education and become professional jazz musicians. None of them could wait.

Their euphoria was short-lived. "Pat Halcox turned up ashen-faced and dropped a bombshell," recalls Barber. "His parents had made him promise that he wouldn't leave his job at Glaxo. They had supported him through all his studies and he felt that he would be letting them down if he packed in his job."

But then, out of the blue, a new master plan was forged. The gods were not only smiling, they were pissing their pants. The band had been following Ken Colyer's adventures in New Orleans and it was now apparent that he would soon be deported, back to England. "He was locked up in prison. What else were they going to do but send him home?" asks Barber. "He'd been courting trouble, sitting in with black bands in the clubs on Bourbon Street. It was against Louisiana's state laws for black and white musicians to share a stage – and he knew it. But there are some things in life that are irresistible, no matter what the cost." The band had meetings and voted to get in touch with Colyer through his brother Bill, who was then working at Collet's, a leftie bookshop at 52 Charing Cross Road. Within days, a letter came back – Ken would be delighted to join the band when and if he ever got back to London. It was manna from heaven. Colyer was a hero, a God to every tuned-in fan of traditional jazz.

"We agreed that Bill Colyer would be our manager and that the band would now be called Ken Colyer's Jazzmen," says Barber. So far so good.

In mid-March 1953, Chris Barber and Monty Sunshine went to Waterloo with Bill Colyer, who was photographed by the *Melody Maker* snapper as he greeted his brother Ken stepping off the boat train.

It was a great week for jazz but a terrible week for popular music. Oriole Records released the latest American hit, (*How Much Is*) *That Doggie In The Window* by Patti Page.

Seven

On April Fools' Day 1953, after intense but assured rehearsals at a pub on York Way, augmented by the chugs and whistles of the numerous steam trains going in and out of Kings Cross station, Ken Colyer's Jazzmen left for Denmark. Art Saunders hosted a farewell party for them at Wood Green, the night before. Colyer told the *Melody Maker* "We are going to try to popularise New Orleans music without distorting it, aborting it, or slapping any gimmicks on it." He added, "I am very glad to have Ron Bowden, who is the best British drummer I have played with." These were words that might possibly come back to haunt him.

Thanks to the network of club promoters who had befriended Chris Barber on his earlier visit, they were able to play clubs, balls, restaurants, concert halls and bandstands dotted around Denmark, happy to sleep wherever they could find space. One of Lonnie's last duties at Millet's was to liberate enough pairs of fur-lined gloves to keep them all warm as they travelled through the cold nights. Thick, closely-woven checked shirts too. "Towards the end, I wasn't so much working as thieving," admits Lonnie.

A local fan and collector called Karl Knudsen followed them around with a Grundig tape recorder, amassing enough material to fill a library. He also issued a single of *Ice Cream/Down By The Riverside*, which ultimately sold more than a quarter of a million copies in Denmark, Germany and Holland, and became the corner stone of his Storyville label.

Ken Colyer was in his element in Denmark, feted wherever he went, enjoying himself immensely. As, indeed, were the others. Like the Hamburg-honed Beatles almost a decade later, they came back from Copenhagen tight and proficient.

They made their official UK début on 25 April 1953, at the London Jazz Club, by now running in the basement of a Catholic church at 34 Bryanston Street, behind the Cumberland Hotel, a block back from Marble Arch. Over 500 enthusiasts crammed in – as they would every Saturday and Sunday evening. It became the Colyer band's staple gig until it was closed down in September. They also played residencies at the Hot Club of London (now held at the Shakespeare Hotel in Powis Street, Woolwich) and the 100 Club, and quickly filled up their calendar with club dates, concerts, Coronation celebrations and the odd Jazz Carnival at the Royal Festival Hall. Everything was going according to plan for the first professional jazz band in Britain.

They gelled socially as well as musically, though niggles were not long in surfacing. "No problems with Monty or Ron," says Barber, "nor with Jim Bray, who was a bit older than us and clever with it. Typical of people with a high IQ, he could be a bit impractical sometimes, but he was fine. Lonnie was a good rhythm player – a bit pushy at times, but then some banjo players are. He wasn't as pushy as some that I could name. Neither he nor I drank at all – whereas Ken was soon drinking heavily, for what reasons we couldn't be sure. He may have been harbouring dark thoughts but he never told us about them. We were all just trying to get it right – because we all admired him so much. He was a lovely player."

"As far as I could see, Ken's problem was that he squashed things up inside him and got angry, maybe because he realised he wasn't very articulate. He knew an awful lot about the music but was totally unable to communicate his knowledge to other people. So the band would be hanging on to his every word, hoping he was going to tell them what they were doing wrong – and all he would do was grumble or swear at them for doing it wrong."

"Ken was becoming a bit of a fly in the ointment," according to Lonnie. "He was getting pissed-up with more and more regularity, sometimes being difficult and obstreperous, which was a great shame because there was no need for it. He started to bicker about Ron Bowden's drum technique, especially when he once had the brass neck to use brushes instead of sticks . . . and he took a dislike to me." Something of an understatement, Lonnie!

It was in this atmosphere of suppressed tension that Ken Colyer's Jazzmen recorded their first album for Decca, a label more associated with Vera Lynn and Mantovani. "An LP of New Orleans jazz by a British band would be something of a departure," noted *Melody Maker*.

"Decca's A&R man was Hugh Mendl and he approached me at Bryanston Street one night," recalls Bill Colyer. "They wanted some jazz on their label – and, of course, we jumped at their offer. At that time, you didn't think about royalties; we did it for MU session rates." Ken was always miffed that ex-art student Monty Sunshine got paid more for designing the sleeve than the musicians got for playing on the record.

The album was in the can for six months, before Decca finally released it in February 1954 . . . *New Orleans To London*, a 10-incher, 'microgroove, full frequency-range recordings', eight tracks, yours for 20s 4d.

More than merely demonstrating how proficient and accomplished they were, the album set down the parameters, laid out the guidelines and presented a formula. Many American records were influencing the jazz movement, constrained though it was, but this was the first British record to have a significant effect. It wasn't exactly the Rosetta Stone, but most players and would-be players of traditional jazz, throughout the country, moved in its direction, whether they knew it or not.

Released as a single, *Isle Of Capri* – a jaunty re-working of a classy Tin Pan Alley standard written in the mid-1930s – sold unexpectedly well, thanks to the support of crotchety BBC disc jockey Jack Payne. As an ex-bandleader, it was just the kind of thing he would latch onto; he knew the tune and was amused by the novel treatment. But it was just a novelty, all the same, minority music that had inadvertently floated down a rivulet, into the edge of the soggy mainstream.

Max Jones, coolest of the *Melody Maker* scribes, praised the LP's "remarkably authentic sound" and declared it "a very creditable achievement for a British jazz group." The sleeve note spoke of "experienced players whose mutual understanding is a miraculous thing very rarely achieved in jazz."

In May, only weeks after the album's release, this mutual understanding was hanging in the wind, shredded by a welter of recriminations. Their manager, Bill Colyer, told Chris that Ken wanted to fire the rhythm section of Bowden, Bray and Donegan.

"He was quite specific," recalls Barber. "He said Jim Bray doesn't swing. Well, quite right, he doesn't and never did – but he plays good solid bass, good notes and you can swing around it. He said Ron Bowden was too modern. No, he wasn't. He certainly looked modern, with his snappy Italian clothes – more like a Ronnie Scott clubber than a 100 clubber – but he played well enough. And, of course, Lonnie had to go because Ken hated Lonnie's guts. Well, that's not difficult! Anyone who's ever dealt with him hates Lonnie's guts, but that's not a reason to fire him."

"Ken and Lonnie were oil and water: there was no way they could ever mix – but they played together all right. On banjo, Lonnie was maybe a bit too flouncy for him, trying to play like Johnny St Cyr, while Ken preferred a more straight-ahead Lawrence Marrero approach . . . but it was hardly a sackable offence. Of course, musical differences had little to do with it."

Lonnie was a seasoned smart alec and smart-arse, always had a quip and a grin, always had the girls fluttering around him. Being more serious about everything, as well as a tongue-tied kind of guy who couldn't think of a chat-up line or a retort until hours later, Ken couldn't handle Lonnie, grew to loathe him, the fucking cocky little bastard. Look at him, he thinks he knows it all – but I know more in my little finger. There was no way they could have remained in the same band together.

"Bill told me that, because we were catching on fast, Monty and I could stay in the band," recalls Barber. "Well, it was always a co-operative, so we had a chat for about five minutes and I was able to tell Bill that he and his brother had been voted out; the rest of us would find a new trumpeter and carry on. We got the band fund shared out and gave them notice. They were not too happy about this turn of events."

Correctly citing musical and personal differences, *Melody Maker* broke the news of the split. Ken Colyer was quoted extensively: "Last weekend, I gave the rhythm section notice and this has been the outcome." Quizzed further, he admitted "there have been differences of opinion that have nothing to do with music, but I don't wish to comment on them."

He was happy to comment on what he saw as failings in the music. "I have been well aware of the band's shortcomings from the New Orleans Jazz point of view. We have experimented with a variety of styles, playing everything from ragtime to Ellington, and I think that has been a mistake. I feel a certain amount of relief about what has happened."

It was true they strayed from the path of the gods – partly through the need to develop as musicians, partly through the need to satisfy the growing, not yet clued-in audience. "All of us were perfectly willing to submerge our own personal ambitions into the band and what the band did as a unit – there was no hint of anyone trying to push or upstage," explains Barber. "It was still the days of dance-halls, and when we played in the provinces, we were expected to play waltzes. The patrons demanded it. Well, neither Monty nor Ken could play a waltz without losing time, so I had to play the waltzes. Someone had to do it! We used to do the *Theme From Moulin Rouge, Always* and *True Love* – just trombone and rhythm section. Must have sounded pretty strange!"

"In fact," Barber continues, "when I look back and listen back to some of the recordings made of us during that period, I think the only one Ken should have fired was me! My playing was rotten! But I have to say that, during the year or so we were together, I learned from Ken Colyer everything I knew about timing."

Even though Ken was ready to stitch his banjo player up, having created what he called "a social hiatus" between them, Lonnie still remembered him tenderly. "He was the best, the best ever in Europe, even to this day. If you're talking about pure New Orleans jazz, I don't think he has ever been equalled."

Barber concurred: "For that sort of music, Ken would still be the best were he alive today. He had a perfect understanding of how to make a New Orleans band swing – while doing almost nothing. He was a marvellous musician who became a pain in the arse."

There was a belief in the Barber camp that Ken's brother Bill was at the root of much of the trouble. "When we first got together with Ken," says Chris, "we told him we didn't want Bill anywhere near us: we didn't trust him and didn't like him anyway. Somehow, he became our manager despite that – and because Ken couldn't express himself, Bill was always the one who told us what he wanted or what he was thinking. In the end, Bill was telling Ken."

If Bill Colyer ever got on with Barber, he's long forgotten the good times. "He's got an accountant's mind," opines Bill. "I don't hear jazz in his playing at all. I call it Mickey Mouse Clinic music. The Barbers and Donegans rewrite jazz history: to me they're still tiny-minded shit heads."

Ken made his final appearance with Barber and company at the Hot Club of London in Woolwich on 30 May 1954. Then he and Bill disappeared into the night, leaving the band not only richer in knowledge and experience but also with a gift, a trinket whose value was then negligible but would soon be incalculable . . . the word 'skiffle'.

From the day they started playing together, in late 1953, Chris and Lonnie had indulged their passion for folk and blues in all its combinations and had been offering choice selections during the interval at gigs. Chris on string bass; Lonnie on guitar and vocal. Though his timbre was not to everyone's taste, Lonnie could catch the prison farm wail, the drifter's cry, the gambler's glee. He was in his element, standing at stage front, strumming at his guitar and pouring it out with all the authenticity he could muster. "One of the recordings Karl Knudsen made on that first trip to Denmark was of Lonnie singing Leadbelly's *Leavin' Blues*," says Barber. "I played it for Sonny Terry and he was convinced that it actually was Leadbelly! And he had worked with Leadbelly a lot – so that's not bad!"

This between-sets interlude had been reinforced when Ken Colyer came on board – though no descriptive name was attached to it until Bill Colyer suggested 'skiffle'. As its popularity increased, posters began to advertise them as Ken Colyer's Jazzmen and Skiffle Group. Ken and Lonnie played guitars and sang in turn, sometimes together. Chris played bass and Bill played washboard – as he had in the Crane River breakdown group. A growing number of fans were obviously more interested in the skiffle than the jazz.

Some historians contend that the skiffle tag was inspired by a 1929 single, *Hometown Skiffle Parts 1 And 2*, a promotional sampler-come-medley 78 rpm disc by the Paramount All Stars, a bunch of outlaws whose ranks included Blind Lemon Jefferson, Blind Blake and Papa Charlie Jackson – heroes all to the UK skiffle vanguard. "Here's the record everybody's been waiting for," claimed press adverts, "six of the great Paramount artists on one record, each one playing or singing for you at their big get-together party."

In fact, the term was purloined – according to Bill Colyer, whom all acknowledge to have suggested it – from Dan Burley & his Skiffle Boys, a short-lived recording group who cut half a dozen tracks for Rudy Blesh's Circle label and a couple (including *Skiffle Blues*) for Leon Rene's Exclusive label in 1948. Burley was a piano-playing newspaper man; his sidekicks were veteran New Orleans bassist Pops Foster and the McGhee brothers, Stick and Brownie.

"For some reason, out of the blue, my mind flew to the Burley records and returned with the word 'skiffle' – and that's how it first got into circulation," says Bill Colyer. "I wonder what would have happened if I'd decided to call it 'spasm' music."

"The Burley group had got together to do exactly the same as we were doing, having a giggle," explains Donegan. "They were improvisers too: they played suitcases with wire drum sticks, used kazoos and jugs, anything else that came to hand – and they played whatever appealed to them."

Though the style was still considered too much of an acquired taste for release on vinyl, or whatever they made long-playing records from in 1954, jazz club habitués and concert-goers were well familiar with it. Audience favourites had already been identified, none more so than *Midnight Special* – learned from a recording by Leadbelly.

Nobody could have imagined that, in a few years, this song would be one of the most performed numbers in Britain, the first of the skiffle standards, practically a teenage anthem. Not only was the melody catchy and easily memorised, punctuated at regular intervals by a simple sing-along chorus, but it was a new kind of song – quite different from the infantile stuff being dummy-fed by BBC radio, those silly songs about the cost of doggies in windows and seeing mommy kissing Santa Claus.

When they first considered introducing *Midnight Special* into the interval set, Ken and Chris were able to discuss the song like professors of anthropology and folklore. It had been learned and modified by Huddie Ledbetter – known to one and all as Leadbelly – when he was serving time in the Central State Prison at Sugar Land, 20 miles south-west of Houston, Texas, and it was one of many tracks recorded by John Lomax when he toured the southern states collecting folk songs for the Library of Congress in the mid-1930s.

The story is cinematic, transporting the audience into the heart of a black and white movie about Negro convicts, chained together in hooped uniforms, working the cotton and sugarcane fields under the guns of ignorant redneck guards, bent and sweating in the sun, yearning for a woman's touch as darkness fell but resigned to prison bunks and prison bars until God or the parole board spared them. Each night, they caught a tantalising glimpse of freedom as the ceiling flickered with the headlight of the Southern Pacific train,

which headed across Texas from Houston to El Paso, crossing the
plantations and skirting Sugar Land – "the hell-hole on the Brazos",
as it was known to the inmates.

Leadbelly's original was ragged and rough; Ken, Chris and
Lonnie tidied it up and turned it into a documentary. Their
performance was always soulful but, more than that, it was
authentic. As some of the audience knew, Colyer had done time in a
southern prison, had hung out with the descendants of slaves, had
lived and worked with them until getting deported as an
undesirable. This man had ridden a streetcar named Desire. It was
real, it was intense and passionate, it was mind-food, it was social
history, it was Americana incarnate.

However, it is at this point that Ken Colyer disappears from our
story. His importance in the development of skiffle and rock 'n' roll
would never be appreciated by those who embraced the emerging
styles, but his influence ceased on the penultimate day of May 1954
when he and Barber parted company. He lit the fires, but his work
was done. He formed a new hand-picked band but was on a slow
train for oblivion and posthumous cult-hero deification. The skiffle
records he made were largely ignored, too ponderous and
pedestrian, lacking the verve and excitement of his disciples – who
trampled him underfoot in the musical stampede he had helped to
instigate.

Practically all Colyer managed to salvage from his year or so with
Chris Barber and the boys was his stage suit. He dyed it black and
wore it when he married telephonist Delphine Frecker at the Fulham
Register Office, six months later.

Eight

On 31 May 1954, the night after they played their last gig with Ken Colyer, the modified line-up débuted at the 100 Club as Chris Barber's Jazz Band. No mention of New Orleans in the name this time: too restricting. The new trumpeter was Pat Halcox. Under siege for a second time, his parents had relented and let him follow his dream to become a professional jazz musician. Despite the hand-wringing, it turned out that his new job was considerably more secure and remunerative, not to say more interesting and rewarding, than the one he held.

They worked, or more accurately played, for six nights a week. "We had given Ken 14 days' notice," recalls Barber, "during which time I went to all the club owners and promoters and said 'Listen, Ken's been fired: if you want the same band, it's us . . . not him!' So we got the gigs. Then I went to Decca and told their A&R director Hugh Mendl what had happened. He immediately looked through his schedules and booked us into the studio to make an LP later in the summer."

Recorded on 13 July 1954, *New Orleans Joys* was another 10-inch microgroove album, comprising eight tracks . . . two of which were skiffle!

Always a great believer in promoting the legend if it held more interest than the truth, Lonnie was fond of telling the story (a fantasy of his own devising) that the producer was not keen to record his vocal numbers, *Rock Island Line* and *John Henry*.

"He didn't even want to hear them," laughed Lonnie. "Chris had to argue really hard that, in order to make the album truly representative of the band, it would have to feature a couple of tracks by the skiffle group. So, having done the band tracks, the guy said 'Well, I'm going for a coffee . . . there's the microphone, the tape is running, the engineer will take care of it. If you want to do some of this singing, go ahead. I'll see you in half an hour'. And he left the studio."

A good story, but no more true than the one he told about how he had personally contributed to Ken Colyer's bail fund, to secure his release from prison in New Orleans, or the one about how he adopted the name Lonnie after the announcer at the Royal Festival Hall Lonnie Johnson concert confused their names, referring to Tony Johnson and Lonnie Donegan.

What is certain, however, is that no-one at Decca had any idea what a goldmine they were sitting on. The tapes were considered so low-priority that they lay in the library for six months.

Meanwhile, the band continued to play as many gigs as they could handle. Traditional jazz was still mainly underground, pub-orientated music but wherever they played, whether in clubs, concert halls and theatres, whether in London or the provinces, or on European forays, the venues were always packed and buzzing. Something was definitely starting to happen.

When *New Orleans Joys* was finally released, in January 1955, it confirmed just how inventive and integrated, how confident and comfortable the Barber band had become, flowing and lilting, suppressing ego for the ensemble sound, a bunch of guys with one goal – to play the kind of music they loved.

"It was never a question of money or golden rainbows," said Lonnie. "The fact that we were able to make a living from it was enough – it was the key to heaven."

The *NME* asked Humphrey Lyttelton to review the album for them. He homed in on Lonnie's tracks: "Isn't it time to call a halt to the sloppy use of the term skiffle before it changes its meaning altogether?" he asked. "Country folk songs and urban rent party music are not the same thing!" Oh, let's get pernickety, shall we Humph? As if anyone outside a small circle of pedants cared a jot anyway. Whatever 'skiffle' may have been was no longer of any importance: though nobody realised it yet, the term had already been redefined by Lonnie, on those two tracks – *Rock Island Line* and *John Henry*.

Like Elvis Presley, on the other side of the Atlantic, Lonnie Donegan was about to change not only the music industry, but also the world.

Over at Sun Records in Memphis, Sam Phillips was hoping to find a charismatic white boy who could sing like a Negro. This was the last thing on the mind of Hugh Mendl, the upper-crust talent spotter at Decca, even though just such a performer had been delivered to his doorstep.

Elvis cut *That's All Right* during his first Sun session on 5 July 1954. Eight days later, Lonnie cut *Rock Island Line*. Elvis was 19; Lonnie was 23. Elvis had grown up with a rich diversity of music on the radio, surrounded by rednecks, rustics and blacks, a stone's throw from the Mississippi River. Lonnie had grown up in East London, hearing only a smattering of black music on AFN and on records at the houses of friends. Elvis took *That's All Right,* a 1947 song by black blues-man Arthur 'Big Boy' Crudup, and not only personalised it but took it to another planet. Lonnie did the same on *Rock Island Line,* which he had learned from a 1942 recording by Leadbelly. The same propulsive acoustic rhythm guitar, same string bass driving it along, same souping-up of the original tempo, same sense of urgency and passion. Elvis had a warm, good-old-boy, sultry southern sexiness to his voice; Lonnie sang with a high lonesome nasal whine, a cross between East Virginny and East Ham. Both their styles had developed naturally, almost accidentally, born of admiration for earthy American roots music and uninfluenced by commercial considerations.

Like *Midnight Special, Rock Island Line* was a song that Leadbelly had learned from another prisoner; he was as much a collector as his saviour John Lomax. The story spread that Lomax had secured Leadbelly's release from Louisiana State Penitentiary in Angola, where the singer was a second-termer with little hope of parole. Lomax had written to the Governor, explained his importance, and made various promises – as a result of which, Leadbelly was released in August 1934, so the story ran. It later transpired that the singer was shown "no clemency", no special treatment. His discharge was "a routine matter under the good time law, which applies to all first and second offenders". However, should he ever find himself in trouble in Louisiana again, he was assured, he would be required to serve the five years remaining from his old term before starting his new sentence.

No chance of that. He was on the straight and narrow, doing his best to impress his sweetheart Martha Promise and his mentor John Lomax, who took him on as 'research assistant' as he continued his quest. Leadbelly would drive, hump the heavy recording equipment and – most valuably – help to bridge the contrasting worlds of black prisoner and white hunter. In October 1934, they arrived at Cummins Prison Farm, south east of Pine Bluff, Arkansas. During Bill Clinton's tenure as state governor, it was still being described as "dark and evil" and the chilling 1980 Robert Redford movie *Brubaker* was said to have been based on tales emerging from its blood-stained walls. The skeletons of prisoners, beaten to death and secretly buried, were apparently discovered in the surrounding fields, and, in 1940, horrific conditions led to the most dramatic prison break-out in twentieth-century American history. Thirty six got out, none evaded capture, four were hanged.

Leadbelly was a good man to have on your side in a place like this, thought Lomax, well aware that it housed the state's toughest cons. A group of these, led by a man named Kelly Pace, sang a song Leadbelly had never heard before, *Rock Island Line*, extolling a stretch of what would eventually become the Chicago Rock Island & Pacific railway system, which took a tortuous route from Chicago to the Pacific, crossing Arkansas on the way. Leadbelly promptly learned the song and would record it several times over the years.

In January 1955, the week *New Orleans Joys* was issued, the Barber band unveiled a new dimension to their set, a new addition to their line-up. Twenty-two year old Belfast art teacher and blues singer Ottilie Patterson had guested with them the previous August but had been unable to extricate herself from a contract until now. Unknown and making a nervous début on a National Jazz Federation concert at the Royal Festival Hall, "a demure little fairy-like figure in a fluffy white dress", she sang three numbers and stopped the show dead. Critics immediately declared her to be the finest female blues singer in Britain. She wouldn't be distracting the limelight from Lonnie, would she?

There were some interesting developments on the British music scene during the last half of 1955. On the trickle of American R&B records considered suitable for release in Britain floated such hot items as *Don't Be Angry* by Nappy Brown, *Ain't That A Shame* by Fats Domino, *Play It Fair* by LaVern Baker and *As Long As I'm Moving* by Ruth Brown. For over a year, rock 'n' roll had been gathering momentum, though no-one could have known it from reading *Melody Maker*. Such was the clamour for his strange and exotic brew that Bill Haley & his Comets had seven new singles issued during 1955. Boosted by its inclusion on the soundtrack of *Blackboard Jungle*, premièred here in October, *Rock Around The Clock* stayed at number one on the *Record Mirror* hit parade for the last seven weeks of the year.

Ted Heath's trombonist Don Lusher was the first of many jazz players to cash in on the latest fad when he released a Decca single called *Rock And Roll*. Terrible, of course. Most bands tried their best to ignore what was happening; for them, it was business as usual. A typical week in October would find the Ronnie Scott Orchestra at Chiswick Empire, Jack Parnell's Band Show at Hackney Empire, the Eric Delaney Band at Bradford Gaumont, Ronnie Aldrich & the Squadronaires at Colchester Regal, the Ken Mackintosh Band Show at Liverpool Empire, the Denny Boyce Orchestra at the Orchid Ballroom in Purley, Johnny Dankworth at Plymouth Odeon, the Ted Heath Orchestra at Romford Odeon, the Kirchin Band at Kilburn State, Tony Crombie at Bedford Corn Exchange. Many different styles but none directed at teenagers. If a big upheaval was in the air, it was imperceptible to most.

The black New York-based folk and blues singer Josh White returned for his umpteenth tour. He was very popular here, but opinion was divided about him: he did all kinds of interesting songs and his dues-paying credentials were impressive, but now he seemed more cabaret than prison farm; he was safe enough to be a regular guest on BBC radio and television too. Touring Britain at the same time, Big Bill Broonzy let it be known that Josh wasn't quite the real thing. "He is intelligent and smart and has everything that it takes to meet all kinds of people, the low class, the middle class and the high class," Bill wrote to an English newspaper that had dared to bracket their names together. "He can make people like the blues that don't even know what the blues is. He can feed it to them in a way so that they will have to like his music, and like him too. Not like Big Bill Broonzy: he is just a big black country man, not smart, just got an old Martin guitar and a bellyful of Mississippi blues. And he loves his whisky. All other fancy things, he don't care much about – just the common and ordinary things for Bill."

Officials from the Musicians' Union were pulling their usual head-up-the-arse hanky-panky. Chet Baker, trumpet sidekick of Charlie Parker and Gerry Mulligan, was in Britain with his Quartet, touring US Air Force bases – over which the MU had no jurisdiction. He offered to play a London concert, free of charge, no fee, all profits to charity, which was the best news of the decade to the visionary musicians and punters who regarded him as the God of Cool and Hip. Sorry, said the MU, but we can't allow it.

In the end, they agreed to let him sing but not to play his trumpet! Colossal, indefensible stupidity. At least a few people got to see him in the flesh.

Week by week, the Barber band could see the audience for traditional jazz expanding; their album was selling well and new venues were opening around the country. In November 1955, *NME* readers voted them into seventh place in the Small Band section of their annual poll. Those placed higher were all modernists, except for Humph at number four.

Until recently, Barber's skiffle interlude had comprised only Lonnie (guitar and vocal) and Chris (string bass and backing vocal), plus Ron Bowden (drums) occasionally, so they tended not to feature *Rock Island Line* – which required a washboard to provide that train rush intensity. "Ron Bowden couldn't have played the washboard if you'd given him a thousand pounds," according to Lonnie.

In September, however, there were changes. Jim Bray switched places with Humphrey Lyttelton's bassist Mickey Ashman, and a second guitarist/vocalist, Dickie Bishop, was added to the skiffle group. "Lonnie wanted a fuller sound," explains Barber, "so we added Dickie, who was a good singer and harmoniser. By the end of the year, the skiffle group was Lonnie, Dickie, Ron and me – and we moved away from country blues and more towards a Folkways folk-music jam-session atmosphere." Their repertoire now embraced soulful laments like *Bury My Body* and risqué romps like *Digging My Potatoes*, as well as old sing-along favourites like *Wabash Cannonball* and *Midnight Special*. Lonnie was basking.

Indeed, the whole band was bursting with exuberance and optimism – and now that Ottilie was touching audiences with her blues homage diversions, their musical range and authority was light years beyond the reach of any others on the circuit.

By this time, frenetic dancing was becoming de rigueur at many traditional jazz clubs as increasing numbers of novices and provincials were drawn in, swept up and galvanised by the music.

Arms waving, legs flailing, bodies swooping, these places were paradise for the extrovert fan. Some of the old guard, pipe-and-pint kind of guys who had listened respectfully and respectably for years, were not amused. Criticising the behaviour and attitudes of the younger set, the buffoonery of teenagers, would become a regular feature in the media for evermore . . . but we must salute James Asman, record shop proprietor and jazz aficionado, for being among the first. Writing in *Record Mirror,* he deplored "the utterly stupid antics of fans and fannies, who cavort and prance like inmates of a mental home during recitals of music far beyond their comprehension". Oh god, our exclusivity is in danger!

He was particularly concerned about "the current popularity of skiffle amongst the teenagers who throng the outskirts of British jazz appreciation". The following week, he was carping about "a problem of youth, which must be solved in order to keep the true name and spirit of jazz clean".

Oh dear, it was going to be a bleak winter for James Asman and his ilk.

Nine

"Decca was a funny old company," Chris Barber conceded, as he recalled his relationship with the label on which his hopes were pinned, his future depended. "They appeared to show no interest, no understanding, no thought." It was not an ideal situation.

When, in late 1954, Denis Preston, an entrepreneur, studio owner, producer and piss-artist, invited him over for a chat, Barber was all ears. The first man to arrange lease-tape deals in Britain, Preston had been behind two West Indian underground hits, *Victory Test Match (Cricket Lovely Cricket)* by Lord Beginner and *Don't Touch Me Tomato* by Marie Bryant – and he was on first-name terms with a variety of famous people from Aldous Huxley to Orson Welles. He knew jazz, had industry-wide contacts, understood the music business and put together a contract that would see Barber product leased to EMI's Columbia-Export label, to satisfy the demands of the European market, and to Pye Nixa for the UK market.

As soon as Decca's A&R Director Hugh Mendl got wind of these developments, he went to see his boss Edward Lewis, in the hopes of persuading him to offer Barber a deal he couldn't refuse and thereby keep him on the label. Lewis had no interest in jazz and saw little future for Barber. "Give the boy a radiogram," he said, as if this wide-handed gesture would impress the bandleader and ensure his loyalty. "I think he already has one," Mendl replied, knowing that Barber possessed one of the most extensive record collections in the country.

"That was the end of our affiliation with Decca," says Barber. "We meant nothing to them."

Denis Preston's style of production – 'supervising', as it was then known – was rather more laid back than they had been used to. "He did bugger all!" says Barber. "All he did was drink brandy and leave it to the engineers. He was a producer like a film producer: he couldn't work the studio, but he could see to it that a record got made. If we said 'we weren't too happy with that take, could we do another?' he'd say 'Don't worry, dear boy, you're fussing too much.

Just play what's going down well in the clubs – you'll be all right'. Eventually, he let us do things the way we wanted."

In November 1955, just in time to gather Christmas sales, Nixa released a new Barber band long-play album *Echoes Of Harlem* and Polygon (soon to be absorbed by Nixa) issued a Lonnie Donegan 45 rpm extended player *Backstairs Session*.

As its title suggested, *Echoes of Harlem* took a new direction – concentrating on New York rather than New Orleans. Its composition was bizarre: 11 tracks, all from the late 1920s, perfectly paced and sequenced. There was a familiar though modified number by W.C. Handy, sung by Ottilie, and another by Duke Ellington, but never recorded by him. Three more had been composed by Fats Waller and his collaborators, Andy Razaf and Harry Brooks. The other six were by white Tin Pan Alley writers Dorothy Fields and Jimmy McHugh, and all were from their Negro revue *Blackbirds Of 1928*. The duo had first teamed up to work on shows for the Cotton Club but this one, featuring "an all-star cast of 100 colored artists" including Bill 'Bojangles' Robinson and Adelaide Hall, was staged at the Liberty Theatre on West 42nd Street, in the heart of Broadway theatre-land.

It was a far cry from King Oliver and, particularly when they discovered the source of the material, this was a cause of astonishment and perplexity to some stuffed-shirt traditionalists. Nevertheless, it was still, very identifiably, a Chris Barber album; it seemed as if the band could stamp its singularity on anything they wished. Forget fashion or the current mainstream, they seemed to be saying, we are going off into more esoteric territory and we hope that our audience will be either a) cool enough to follow, or b) too ignorant to know that we are moving on, into uncharted areas, they will love us just the same. Whatever, the audience went with them, growing larger by the day.

Nobody knew it then but *Echoes Of Harlem* was the last Barber band album to feature Lonnie plunking his banjo. None of its tracks had been given over to the skiffle group because Denis Preston had been perspicacious enough to take them into IBC Studio in Portland Place to record their own extended player, *Backstairs Session*. Juxtaposing the relatively obscure *New Burying Ground* and *When The Sun Goes Down* with future skiffle anthems *Midnight Special* and *Worried Man Blues*, it was a commercial enough package but was ignored or overlooked by most reviewers and radio programmers, and consequently by most record buyers.

Fortunately, this was not the fate of a simultaneous release on Decca. Some bright spark at the label had suddenly cottoned on to the growing grass-roots interest in skiffle and two tracks from *New Orleans Joys*, recorded 16 months earlier, were paired as a single: *Rock Island Line/John Henry* – credited to the Lonnie Donegan Skiffle Group. The same could not be said of many records, but the world would have been a different place without *Rock Island Line* having come out and taken off when it did.

Decca were not exactly twisters but, in common with most of the industry's middlemen, they lacked a generosity of spirit where finances were concerned. Lonnie was paid £3.10.0d for recording *Rock Island Line*, the standard union rate for a session. No royalties; that was it. £3.10.0d and you were lucky to get it. The record sold over a million copies. Sorry, boys, no royalties. Decca boss Edward Lewis (later Sir Edward, but not for services rendered to Lonnie) was able to buy another yacht or two, while Lonnie was out there strumming for his crust. Of course, Lewis lost Lonnie almost immediately; serves the tightwad right, says the rock 'n' roll fraternity. Lonnie was exploited in the same way that his blues idols were – and he was still cursing Edward Lewis until the day that he died.

Also paid minimum session fees for their contributions to *Rock Island Line* were Chris Barber, whose string bass drove that train up the rails, and Beryl Bryden, whose swishing washboard laid down the track. She was a long-time friend of the band, since the days when Barber was chatting up the promoter at Cooks Ferry Inn for an unpaid guest spot. From Decca, they received next to nothing, no ex gratia payments, no gratitude even. They were just factory hands. Such were the rationale, ethics and modus operandi of the record industry in the mid-fifties. "Give the boy a radiogram." Maybe Mantovani got a better shake.

Its ascent to the charts and beyond was as serendipitous as its journey so far. Jack Payne, a graveyard-faced BBC radio disc jockey who despised all things teenage with corrosive disgust, was for unfathomable reasons attracted to *Rock Island Line*. No one was able to discover why. Then boxer turned broadcaster Eamonn Andrews (who was soon to score with his execrable version of *The Shifting*

Whispering Sands) played it on his *Pied Piper* show. Lonnie thinks it was because "someone had requested that strange novelty record, of the man playing a guitar, singing very fast, through his nose."

Such was the power and reach of BBC radio, the nation's one and only broadcaster, that two plays were enough to light the fire. The single started selling in every town and city from Swansea to Sunderland. The people at Decca were nonplussed but assigned all their presses to *Rock Island Line*.

During the first week of January 1956, the Barber band was getting ready to play in some freezing suburban pub, when a fan approached them with that day's *Record Mirror*, whose chart showed *Rock Island Line* as a new entry at number eight. They looked at it in disbelief. Hang on a minute, wasn't that something we knocked off at Decca a couple of summers ago? That record has made the best-sellers list?

Decca's timing was perfect. Lonnie caught a wave and rode it. Also entering the chart that week were other scenes from American history: *The Ballad Of Davy Crockett* by Bill Hayes, eulogising the hero of the Alamo, and *Sixteen Tons* by Tennessee Ernie Ford, about the hardships endured by miners in Kentucky, though few listeners appreciated its seriousness. These songs were rather different from the kind of music-biz confections that usually filled the chart, the latest examples being *Never Do A Tango With An Eskimo* by Alma Cogan, *Twenty Tiny Fingers* by the Stargazers and *Pickin' A Chicken* by Eve Boswell.

As *Rock Island Line* continued to bob around in the Top 10, week after week, the Tin Pan Alley establishment scratched their heads in wonder: it was illogical, beyond reason. The recording was so crude and primitive, in every respect. The guy couldn't sing and it wasn't a proper song: the verses had no perceptible connection with the chorus. It must be a flash in the pan, a one-off novelty item. Of course, the money it generated was interesting; always at the top of their agenda were the pounds, shillings and pence.

"I was the luckiest guy in the world," says Lonnie, "I knew that straight away. Imagine a songwriter walking into any of the publishing firms on Denmark Street and saying 'Look, I've written this song and I think it could be a hit. It's about a train driver in the States who fools the tax inspector, the revenue man, by telling him that his freight train contains only live animals, which are not subject to a levy. The dumb-cluck takes his word for it, too stupid to notice that there's no sign of animal life, and lets him through without paying. Exhilarated, the engineer laughs his socks off as he speeds off down the track'. What publisher is going to fall for that? The guy would be kicked down the stairs. 'Oh, by the way, the lyrics go "ABCWXYZee, the cat's on the cupboard but he don't see me" – so you can see that it has hit potential.' The publisher would have thought you needed to see a psychiatrist."

The Barber band soon noticed changes in their fan-base: unfamiliar faces at pub gigs, younger faces in the theatres. "All of a sudden, the phone at our agency started ringing, strange people wanting to book us, journalists wanting to know about us," says Lonnie. "We became the hottest band in the land, playing the concert hall circuit and selling out wherever we went. But we were attracting people who had no interest in jazz . . . they only wanted to hear *Rock Island Line* and were shouting for it throughout the set." This, of course, was a little disconcerting for the other guys in the band.

Since the early days, they had always attracted the college crowd. For the intelligent, slightly wayward and boisterous element, their music offered many levels of enjoyment and sustenance. Even Barber's spoken intros were interesting and educational! They weren't just hacking it out, like so many of the contemporary dance-bands . . . these guys were grooving! One only had to hear a few bars of Monty Sunshine's swooping and sweeping clarinet to know that. How many of their audience would have loved to be up there on stage, one of the band. For the vast majority of them, this was out of the question, of course; such instrumental skill was way beyond their reach or their dreams – as they confirmed when they spontaneously applauded each virtuoso solo.

But the skiffle interlude was a different matter, some of them were beginning to realise. Nothing too complex about that, surely. Since the Colyer days, when Lonnie and Ken strummed and warbled while Bill thimbled away on *Good Morning Blues, Casey Jones* and *The Cotton Song*, aspiring youngsters felt that such musical activity wasn't impossible.

Lonnie didn't take long to emerge as the focus of attention, a role model. He was something new. Even on the songs where he was only supposed to add texture and counterpoint to Ken's lead vocals, he was cutting a swath through the auditorium with his high-yaller holler. Ken's voice lacked force and vigour and his guitar playing was rudimentary.

Lonnie might have admired his trumpet playing but he never saw him as competition in the skiffle stakes. "At an increasing number of gigs, Ken went to the bar. He was never serious about playing the guitar, and was totally inadequate as a result. He found it very entertaining and amusing, and he liked singing Leadbelly songs, but doing it for a living was never on his mind. That's not how I felt . . . it was always on my mind. I was driven!"

As *Rock Island Line* became a radio favourite, Lonnie got more than a whiff of stardom and he wallowed in it. Pictures in the papers, articles about his offstage life. How perfect if he could develop this side of his career, out in the spotlight like Tennessee Ernie Ford or Slim Whitman. At the same time, he could be a modern version of the black pioneers he admired. Never mind that the Delta blues singers had been the least respected and most disreputable of all strands of post-Civil War black entertainers, guitar-wielding hobo tearaways singing the devil's music, most of them dedicated to pussy and drinking and gambling. Well, Lonnie didn't drink and he didn't gamble but he had no aversion to pussy.

"I don't know if he was looking after my interests or his, but I remember Chris saying 'This hit record is a bit of jam, but your bread and butter is the band.' I mulled that over, but a lot of people were bending my ear at the time," says Lonnie. For a few weeks, he remained cautious. "The Barber band is a co-operative," he told a music paper journalist, one of the first to show any interest in him. "We play seven gigs a week and we're quite well off financially. I don't want to be swept along on the tide of the latest gimmick and then get left high and dry when it wears off."

Decca wished they had a follow-up, too dim to realise that two unissued Donegan sides had been had been lying in the can since the *Rock Island Line* session. *Nobody's Child* was a melodramatic weeper that Lonnie continued to sing for the rest of his life; *Wabash Cannonball* was a Carter Family classic, a dramatic train song, destined to become another skiffle staple. It could have been a second money-spinner for Decca, had they had more grasp – but both tapes nestled in their vaults, undisturbed, for decades.

Instead, in desperation, they issued two live tracks as a single. Recorded at a Royal Festival Hall concert, back in October 1954, *Bury*

My Body and *Diggin' My Potatoes* were never going to attract airplay. The former was a slow gospel blues by the Norfolk Jubilee Quartet (from Barber's record collection, of course), mournful and soulful, with the chorus "I don't care where they bury my body; my soul is gonna live with God." Play that on the radio and the church would be complaining about religion being cheapened by its association with lowlife musicians. The latter was a Washboard Sam song about a faithless woman, who is caught sucking off another man. Jack Payne wouldn't be playing that one but fans loved it because here was Lonnie, strumming as rhythmically and forcefully as Elvis would, singing about sex with gusto and enthusiasm. (Incidentally, Lonnie beat Elvis to the UK charts by a good four months.)

Meanwhile, Lonnie had been recording material for Nixa, who now had him under a royalty-paying contract, arranged by Denis Preston, who was also getting a slice. Chris Barber, Ron Bowden and Dickie Bishop agreed to accompany him for one-off session fees, much to Barber's subsequent regret. "I always wish I hadn't done that, actually – out of principle – but Lonnie was still in the band at the time and we wanted to support him." *Jesse James, Ol' Riley, Railroad Bill* and *Stackalee* were released on the extended player *Skiffle Session*, while *Lost John* and *Stewball* were paired for his next single, the official follow-up to *Rock Island Line*. Barber had suggested *Lost John*, which he had on a 1928 Paramount 78 by the Chicago-based Papa Charlie Jackson; *Stewball* was another Leadbelly song – "about a racehorse," wrote the clever dick in *NME*, "but not worth more than a few bob each way." This was the paper so unhip, so unclued to underground undercurrents that the name of Lonnie Donegan never appeared in their pages until he had reached the chart.

By the time *Lost John* was issued, in mid-April 1956, events had moved on a pace. The Barber band was touring provincial town halls with a *Daily Express* sponsored Jazz Ball package called 'Rhythm With The Stars', sharing the bill with trumpeter Eddie Calvert and Ronnie Scott's latest ensemble. The compère was George Melly, who had been singing *Rock Island Line* for five years or more, certainly long before Lonnie, but in a jazzbo style that could never have attracted pop music fans. He was snooty, made sport of Lonnie – who rose above it: he knew who the audiences had come to see.

"It was during that tour that Lonnie came to us and said he wanted more money," recalls Barber. "I reminded him that we were a co-operative and shared the money equally. He said 'I'm big! I can bring a lot of money in'. I said 'well, you're big now, but in a few years it might be clarinet solos.' He wasn't impressed; I think he'd made his mind up by this time."

Backstage at Finsbury Park Empire, Lonnie had run into American impresario Manny Greenfield, who was managing the smooth American star Don Cornell. Manny gave him the old soft-shoe and Lonnie fell for it. "How would you like to go to America?" he asked.

"Who is going to pay the air fare?" countered the suspicious Lonnie.

"Oh, don't worry about that, I'll sort it out . . . just sign here."

Lonnie did just that: "I signed a management contract for American representation, not knowing what the hell it was. Then I went to Chris, who said it was OK, they would get Dickie Bishop to play banjo in the band for a couple of weeks, until I got back."

By this time, *Rock Island Line* had also entered *Billboard* magazine's chart, a pioneering coals-to-Newcastle hit, on its way to becoming a top tenner in America too. People were telling Donegan that he had the ability to become an international star.

He must have believed them: within a month, Lonnie had left the Barber Band and was making his first solo radio broadcast on Cyril Stapleton's *Show Band Show*. Two weeks later, on 14 May, he flew to the States to promote his record – a very big deal. Several papers carried a photograph of him, standing on the steps leading up to the plane, giving fans and detractors his best cream-licking smile.

America was a nine-week blur and he didn't even have a camera. First stop was Perry Como's television show in New York, for which he was paid $800 – "an amazing amount to get in one lump!" He played a sketch with film star Ronald Reagan, 24 years away from becoming President. "Ronald taught me how to smile," he laughed, no doubt recalling the two faces of that crocodile-smiling actor, "and Perry Como taught me how to relax." Due to the dictates of the donkeys who ran the Musicians' Union, Donegan was allowed to sing but not to play his guitar. "Take my guitar away, and I'm lost; I don't know what to do with my arms," he told them – to no avail. On the show, he was backed by bassist Eddie Safranski (from the Stan Kenton Band), guitarist Al Caiola (of subsequent *Bonanza* fame) and drummer Ray Bauduc (a veteran of several orchestras, including

Jimmy Dorsey's). "They were sensational musicians, and really wanted to help – but they read my songs as country & western. They weren't familiar with this strange music we called skiffle and just had to busk it, which was very difficult because I tend to speed up and get frantic."

He was then dispatched to do a two-week residency at the Brooklyn Town and Country Club, backed by Weavers guitarist Fred Hellerman, whose group had been driven into extinction by Senator McCarthy's communist witch hunt, some three and a half years earlier, but had recently re-formed. Lonnie went to a reunion gig at Carnegie Hall.

During his fortnight in Brooklyn, Lonnie learnt to gesticulate, joke and communicate with an audience. Offstage, he learnt all about the Weavers, who had recorded *Midnight Special* and *Rock Island Line* years earlier, and Woody Guthrie, who was just submitting himself to Greystoke Park, the New Jersey mental institution that would be his home for the next five years. Hellerman had also worked alongside Leadbelly, a good enough friend to have played and sung at his funeral. Now here he was, backing a young guy from England who had become famous singing a song off one of Lead's old records.

(Lonnie would fly back to London four days before the House of Representatives voted by 373 to 9 to cite Hellerman's fellow Weaver Pete Seeger, and seven others, including the playwright Arthur Miller, for contempt of Congress for refusing to answer their impertinent questions – a foolish decision which only boosted Seeger's status as folk hero, true patriot and spokesman for truth and justice.)

After Brooklyn, Lonnie went to Cleveland to appear on Bill Randle's local television show. It was the first of many whistle-stops, including radio station interviews in Washington DC, New York, Baltimore, Philadelphia, Buffalo, Boston, Atlanta, Memphis and New Orleans. On his travels around the south, he learned about the racism, about the Montgomery bus boycott led by Martin Luther King Jr, about the recent assault on Nat 'King' Cole by white supremacists in Birmingham.

He played strange gigs at Folly Beach Pier in South Carolina (where he was fed lobster and hated it) and the Copacabana Club in Pittsburgh, played rock 'n' roll package shows with such cool black performers as Chuck Berry (charting with *Roll Over Beethoven*), LaVern Baker (between hits), the Cleftones (charting with *Little Girl Of Mine*) and Clyde McPhatter (hitting with *Treasure Of Love*).

In Detroit, he was backed by Johnny Burnette's Rock 'n' Roll Trio – destined to become cult heroes in Britain – on a bill he shared with Frankie Lymon & the Teenagers and Pat Boone, among others. He saw Elvis Presley singing *Hound Dog* on television, saw all the folk and jazz shows he could manage. The best of these was at Birdland: the Count Basie Orchestra featuring Joe Williams, who had "a voice like a tame bull," thought Lonnie.

He got back to England on 22 July, to find *Lost John* still in the Top 10, having peaked at number two. 'Skiffle' had become a media buzzword.

Among the first to fathom its appeal and point out its potential was *Melody Maker* freelancer Bob Dawbarn, whose trombone technique Lonnie had roundly mocked when both were members of Bill Brunskill's Jazz Band. Now Dawbarn was able to get his own back in an article headlined 'The Scots-born Irish Hillbilly from London'.

"It is a fact," he wrote, "that public taste has veered away from the obviously clever artist, towards the singer who makes it all sound so simple that our Nellie, or Fred next door, could do it as well and might one day also be a star. Perhaps skiffle, with its watered-down blues flavour, simple rhythmic tunes and primitive guitar work, gives the same impression." However, Dawbarn was astute and generous enough, less than half-way through the year, to describe Donegan as "the phenomenon of 1956."

Most people in the music business still couldn't see it. For Lonnie to assume the role and patois of a black train driver in Louisiana, delivering a load of pig iron, was as preposterous as Sid James playing Davy Crockett. Yet these same Tin Pan Alley traders could accept, took for granted even, something as patently ridiculous as Jimmy Young recording cod-cowboy ballads *The Man From Laramie* and *The Wayward Wind*, and could only heap praise on a hideous record like *Don't Cry Little Donkey* by 16-year-old Pauline Shepherd.

"They saw me as a novelty item," said Lonnie, "with about as much future as the Singing Dogs. I was a one-off, a flash in the pan, here-today gone-tomorrow, a gimmick. No-one expected me to be around in six months' time."

But Lonnie's fan-base was already large and growing, top heavy with teenagers who regarded *Rock Island Line* as a project, a blueprint. They loved the way Lonnie introduced the story in measured tones, before jumping a gear and accelerating up the rails towards a full-tilt, full-lather crescendo. It was *Boys' Own Paper*, it was Saturday Morning Pictures at the flea-pit, it was Americana, it was history, it was romance, it was offbeat and rebellious, it was unpalatable and incomprehensible to old fogies, a generation gap widener. What's more it swung like crazy and tore through the room like a tornado. It was exciting, even though no sex or dancing was involved. We could do this! The washboard was the key. Plenty of them lying around. Let's have a go.

Contrarily, Lonnie had already dropped the washboard in favour of having a competent, versatile kick-arse drummer behind him.

Ron Bowden had played on *Lost John*, providing rhythm and texture for a record whose appeal lay primarily in its story line, the unlikely tale of an escaped convict who fashions a pair of shoes "with heels on the front and heels behind – you couldn't tell which way Lost John was gwine." Consequently, he manages to evade the cops, for a while at least. A simple strum and an appeal for listeners to join in on the singalong chorus encouraged sales, but Lonnie's masterstroke was to personalise the song: "if anybody asks you who sang this song, tell them Lonnie Donegan's been here and gone." He stamped his authority not only on *Lost John* but on skiffle songs in general. It wouldn't be long before people were calling him the King of Skiffle.

Lonnie had left the trad-jazz world to forge a career in show biz. More importantly, though he had no idea at the time, he had already set himself up as teacher and guru to a new generation of aspiring musicians.

Ten

When Lonnie Donegan returned from America on 22 July 1956, a grass-roots skiffle movement was already underway and beginning to flourish. Of several clubs in central London, the first and most popular was held every Thursday evening, in the first floor bar of the Roundhouse, a pub on the corner of Brewer and Wardour Streets in Soho. It had been operating since 1 September 1955 and now styled itself 'Europe's only Skiffle and Blues club'. In a few years, the likes of Sonny Terry & Brownie McGhee, Big Bill Broonzy and Muddy Waters would perform there, but now the main attraction was Bob Watson's Skiffle Group, fronted by the club's founder.

Watson was a teenager when two classmates introduced him to jazz. A blast of New Orleans magic was all it took. When he found out that a local approximation of this music could be heard live at the White Hart in Cranford, he cycled over from his parents' house in Hayes to investigate. Immediately, he was drawn in: through 1951 and 1952, he saw the Crane River Jazz Band as often as they played there.

"I was only 16 when I first went there, but I was fairly tall," he says, "so I could get in and drink without being thrown out of the place and, because the audience was comparatively small, I got to know everyone to a greater or lesser extent."

Inspired by Ken Colyer's skiffle interludes, Watson bought a guitar but could find no way of learning how to play it in the way he wanted.

"By 1953, I was helping to run the Albemarle Jazz Club in Southall and, that summer, when the recently formed Ken Colyer /Chris Barber band played there, I forced myself on Lonnie Donegan and asked him if he'd teach me the rudiments. Much to my astonishment and delight, he said he would!"

Every Saturday morning for three months, Watson would tube over to Lonnie's house in Highgate. "I wasn't a teacher, not a good one anyway," admitted Lonnie in a rare moment of modesty, "but I was able to point the way."

When Lonnie's gig schedule made further lessons impossible, Watson sought the help of Alexis Korner, a guitarist and record collector, admired for his encyclopaedic knowledge of American folk music, already regarded as an expert on country blues.

Born in 1928, to an Austrian father and Greek mother, Korner had been a problem child and a teenage tearaway. His delinquency first revealed a musical dimension when he fell under the spell of boogie-woogie. "On Saturday afternoons, my friends and I would go to Shepherds Bush market on our bikes and nick 78s from the stalls. You had to have a saddlebag which took 10-inch records, because a quick getaway was essential." When his father, a Strauss enthusiast, forbade him to use the family piano for Jimmy Yancey style workouts, Alexis switched to guitar – which he could play anywhere. "I started to play the guitar," he laughed, "because it annoyed my father more than anything else I could do. He loathed the guitar, hated it, said it wasn't even a serious instrument, that ladies played it and tied ribbons on it."

Alexis started out playing country songs like *The Little Red Caboose Behind The Train* and *Roll Along, Covered Wagon, Roll Along* but his horizon broadened when he went to a series of record recitals given by Ken Lindsay – communist, bookseller, jazz and blues evangelist. "This would have been around the end of the war, when I was maybe 16 or 17," Alexis remembers (though chronology was never his strongest point), "but the effect of hearing records by Robert Johnson and Scrapper Blackwell and Huddie Ledbetter was just colossal."

He left school at 18 – Finchden Manor, a private school for intelligent but incorrigible boys – and managed to survive two years of National Service with his dreams intact. By summer 1950, he was strumming and picking and singing alongside Chris Barber during the blues interludes at Lincoln Gardens, already a familiar Soho face. "I had been hanging out in Soho since about 1941," recalled Alexis, describing his slump from academe to delinquency. "I used to bunk off school, whichever one I was supposed to be attending at the time, and spend days in the amusement arcades, speaking in a fake French accent and pretending that I was a member of the Free French Navy. Ridiculous! I wasn't even old enough to be a cabin boy. But I always had a love affair with Soho, such a wonderful place. I sold all of my father's dirty books there, a great mistake. He had a marvellous collection – and I didn't know much about them, except that they were worth money. Of course, the Soho booksellers saw me coming."

"Later on, I realised that being accepted in Soho was like being part of a very hip, secret society – you felt fantastically privileged. It was like joining the best club in the world, to be involved with the jazz scene. Although it came to nothing, some of us were convinced that we were on the edge of breaking down the British three-class system, that we could create a fourth class made up of refugees from the other three, and then say 'Fuck the class system altogether'. Jazz was one of the ways of doing that, as far as we were concerned."

After the Barber experience at Lincoln Gardens, Alexis played briefly in Dickie Hawdon's Jazz Band and the Galleon Jazz Band, some of whom "were determinedly alcoholic, some very straight". In summer 1953, he often joined in on the Colyer-Barber-Donegan skiffle sessions at the Bryanston Street club – and when Colyer split off in the following spring, Alexis was first choice for his skiffle group, as second guitarist/vocalist.

It was during this period that Bob Watson got to know him. "Alexis and Bobbie (who were married in 1951) were always very encouraging and let me spend hours at their house in Notting Hill. He seemed to think that I could sing and taught me as much as he could, showing me guitar chords and runs, playing records to illustrate different styles. Sometimes, he would play a number of records, to give a feel for a period, or a geographical region – identifying the singers and players that had been associated with that area. Records were like gold-dust in those days and his collection was an invaluable source for someone like me, who wanted to play that sort of music and learn all about it. I was fascinated every time I went over there. I remember the first time he played Blind Lemon Jefferson, it was almost incomprehensible – but he pointed things out and I began to pick up on them, began to appreciate him."

Watson also got to know Dickie Bishop, who was then playing banjo with the Brent Valley Stompers at the Viaduct in Hanwell, and Cyril Davies, who played banjo with Steve Lane's Southern Stompers at the Fox & Goose in Hangar Lane, Ealing. Both had guitars and knew about folk blues, both were always keen to discuss it. So was Adrian Brand, who Watson had met at the Crane River Club. "He was the sort of guy who could do everything – music, metalwork, electronics, whatever he put his hand to," says Watson, "and we began playing together, initially as a duo but always thinking about forming a group."

When attempts to find a string bass player proved fruitless, Adrian acquired one and asked Jim Bray, from the Barber band, to give him lessons. "Within a few weeks, he was playing quite competently – and that gave us the impetus to start playing gigs at Steve Lane's club. Other guitarists dropped in and out, but the basic unit was the two of us."

It didn't take long to find out that Lane's banjo player was also a prodigious 12-string guitarist. "Cyril would sometimes join in at the Fox & Goose and we seemed to take off on those evenings – because he was Leadbelly incarnate! He had a great feeling for the music and he was a bit larger than life in the sense that he wasn't afraid to go for something that others would consider beyond their grasp. Others were too inhibited even to try certain songs but he would go for it, and generally get it."

Playing interval spots to Steve Lane's Southern Stompers at the Fox & Goose every week, Bob Watson's Skiffle Group spent the first half of 1955 playing club favourites and learning new songs, all copied from old 78s. By now brothers in the unfolding skiffle fraternity, Watson and Dickie Bishop were among those backing Lonnie Donegan on his first session for Denis Preston, released as the extended player *Backstairs Session*.

"The results were far removed from the recorded versions that had been our inspiration, but that was fair enough because we didn't come from the Mississippi delta or Texas or wherever, and we were white anyway."

In a giant step, Bob Watson, Adrian Brand and Cyril Davies decided to start a club dedicated to skiffle music. Until then, no venue offered a continuous evening of skiffle; it was still very much interval music at traditional jazz clubs. "We went searching for premises," Watson recalls, "and the Roundhouse seemed to be perfect. It was a large room, in a central location, and the landlord seemed amenable, fairly free and easy about what we were proposing. He was an Irish chap and I think he liked the idea of something folky . . . but I remember when we started, he came up to have a look, listened for about two minutes and said 'I'll be in the bar if you want me'. I don't think it was his cup of tea."

"Cyril was a level-headed guy, capable of dealing with any administration, collecting money, paying expenses, putting adverts in *Melody Maker*, all that kind of thing . . . but the entrance fee was minimal: two shillings, with free membership on opening night. The intention was not to make money; we just enjoyed playing and we were happy to have created a scene for people who liked the music. If we could give guests a bit of travelling money and a small appearance fee, that was fine."

Through the autumn of 1955, the Roundhouse catered to a core of a few mates but gradually the audience grew "until some nights, it was jam-packed, with people cascading down the stairs as well. The landlord would gently take us aside at the end of such evenings and give us a twitchy lecture about fire regulations."

"Cyril and I would start the evening off, then we'd have a guest, and we'd usually get people turning up out of the blue – because its reputation spread and it quickly became the place to go. All sorts of people were guests in those early days, from Ken Colyer to Lonnie Donegan – and Alexis Korner, of course. He and Cyril hit it off immediately."

"At a time when it was difficult to find a record by Leadbelly, let alone an article about him, Cyril was a walking compendium," Bob Watson continues. "He didn't just know about the guy: he lived him . . . knew his history, his prison terms, where he lived and when, who his friends were, when he wrote his songs, how he played various runs, where he got his guitars. If anyone so much as mentioned his name, Cyril would reel off one of his diatribes. It was only when he packed his guitar away at the end of the evening that he remembered he was, in fact, a panel beater from south Harrow."

"Some people found his personality daunting; he could get a bit prickly and bad-tempered and he certainly wouldn't suffer fools gladly. Happily, we never fell out . . . after all, he idolised a man who wasn't averse to committing the odd murder or two!"

Also roaring out Leadbelly songs was a visiting American, Jack Elliott, who had serendipitously blown into town with his wife June just after the Roundhouse club had been launched. (It was the week that June's friend James Dean had been killed.) No-one had heard of Jack, of course, but it soon became apparent that he was the real thing – even though it later transpired that he was actually Elliot Adnopoz, born in Brooklyn, the son of a Jewish doctor. He wore a stetson, the first pair of Levi's that most people had seen, authentic Texan cowboy boots with drag-along heels, he sang like a cattle-drover and spoke with a prairie twang, puffed and sucked at a harmonica held in a harness around his neck, played a flat-top Gretsch Synchromatic (said by the company to be 'very popular with cowboy and other singing stars') and seemed to know the Americana song-bag inside out.

During 1951, a 19 year old done with schooling, Jack had lived with and studied under his hero Woody Guthrie, adopting and refining his guitar style, copying his vocal intonation. "He sounds more like me than I do," Woody was forced to admit. A couple of years later, hanging out with the bohemians of Greenwich Village, he 'stole' Allen Ginsberg's girlfriend Helen Parker, who had introduced the poet to heterosexual pleasures before running off with the dashing folkie. Later, in California, a guest of the actor Will Geer, at his 'herb garden' in Topanga Canyon, he met actress June Shelley, who was working on the Hugo Haas movie *Edge Of Hell*. They married in San Francisco; Jack's new friend and sidekick Derroll Adams was best man.

Everybody at the Roundhouse, musicians and audience, fell in love with Jack immediately. His repertoire encompassed not only Woody Guthrie and Leadbelly, but ranged through the Carter Family, Blind Lemon Jefferson, the Reverend Gary Davis, Jimmie Rodgers, Uncle Dave Macon, Dock Boggs, Clarence Ashley, Charley Patton, Charlie Poole. "He was like a visiting lecturer," recalls Watson. "He didn't just introduce his songs, he used to weave in these fantastic stories, so you could never be sure about what was truth and what was fiction. His playing was very influential too: he would manage to combine chording with single string runs, which gave a lot of variety to what he did. I used to do a few numbers with him but always felt very diffident about it, because I suspected that what I was doing didn't measure up to what he was doing. He was a very skilful musician, even then."

More than any other song he played, Jack's strident version of Jesse Fuller's *San Francisco Bay Blues* was an inspiration to anyone who ever wanted to flat-pick a guitar.

Besides several Roundhouse appearances in late 1955 and early 1956, Elliott starred in a Christmas extravaganza at the Theatre Royal in Stratford, East London: *The Big Rock Candy Mountain*, written by folklorist Alan Lomax (who had just taken up residence in London) and directed by Joan Littlewood. Jack played the Chorus, addressing the audience and singing songs; June played principal boy. Kids in the area, seeing him as the living embodiment of the cowboys they had seen in films, followed him around the streets. Jack and June also zipped over to Paris three times during this period, busking to pay expenses, and would later head on for Spain and ultimately the rest of mainland Europe. By the time he got back to London, he could legitimately call himself Ramblin' Jack Elliott.

Roundhouse hosts Bob and Cyril were always happy to see Alexis Korner turn up – which was not every week, because, in another attempt to find a day job he could not only tolerate but enjoy, he'd recently started as a trainee studio manager at the BBC in Portland Place. "Although he wasn't the world's greatest guitarist or singer, he had a very defined style and could really put certain songs across very well," recalls Watson. "He would always concentrate on those which suited his cracked, croaky voice. On top of that, he would talk to anyone who engaged him in conversation, discuss aspects of the music, direct interested parties to specialist record shops. Much of the time, he just sat in a corner smoking his dreadful roll-ups, liquorice paper things. They looked and smelt terrible. The place used to get pretty foggy."

In those days, his smoke merely contributed to the bohemian atmosphere – and at the end of the evening, the audience would spill out into the darkness of Wardour Street, free from menace unless they felt intimidated by the offers of prostitutes, lurking in the doorways. Maybe Soho was as near as you could get to Storyville but – the odd stabbing aside – much of its reputation was based on mythology set up to make the place more attractive to provincials.

The Roundhouse had been going for seven months, when, in April 1956, two more skiffle clubs opened: the first in a Gerrard Street cellar, not 200 yards away, the other at the Princess Louise in Holborn. Their founders were both enthusiasts with eccentric leanings, patrician swashbucklers with a passion for adventures involving music and maidens. One was a painter, the other a Doctor of Philosophy.

Eleven

Richardson's Rehearsal Rooms, housed in dank cellars below 44 Gerrard Street, a Soho backwater that was about to be earmarked for colonisation by the first wave of Chinese settlers, had already been home to several transient jazz clubs and now, every Tuesday starting on 3 April 1956, inquisitive punters descended the precarious wooden staircase to experience the strangeness of London's second skiffle club.

The enterprise was the brainchild of John Hasted, leader of the 44 Skiffle and Folksong Group – the motliest bunch ever to grace a stage. Did any other group, in the entire history of popular music, include a communist professor and a burglar?

A more unlikely guitar enthusiast would be difficult to imagine. In real life, John Hasted researched and taught atomic physics at University College – but when he dived into a convenient phone box and put on one of his other Superman outfits, he turned into an upper-crust cross between Woody Guthrie and Carl Sandburg, and taught folk music to lefties, bohemians and nubile women.

Born in Woodbridge, Suffolk, in 1921, the son of an officer in the Durham Light Infantry, Hasted emerged from deepest *Who's Who* territory. After winning science and choral scholarships, he turned up at New College, Oxford, just as the war was breaking out. He studied by day, engaged in political discussion by night – joining the university Labour Club, and becoming increasingly interested in left-wing philosophies. He also got involved with the New College choir and, finding his musical fervour needing further stimulation, started to explore political balladry and revolutionary music.

A rapidly secured degree under his belt, he went off to help repel the Luftwaffe as a junior officer in 321 Battery, 205 Heavy Anti-Aircraft Regiment, Royal Artillery, defending the citizens of Glasgow from bombardment. Then, after volunteering an interest in the development of radar, he became a research boffin, dispatched to the Mediterranean to carry out wireless maintenance on Churchill tanks and work on Malta's coastal defence radar.

He returned to Oxford after the war, became a post-graduate physics student and helped to set up the Oxford University Communist Party, of which he became secretary. Then, in 1948, Dr John Hasted, as he was now, moved to University College, London.

"In Britain at that time," he points out, "university teaching was virtually the only path open to anyone who wished to dedicate his life to physical science research." His work focussed on atomic collisions – but while some boffins were fogies, submerged in obsessive study that excluded practically any contact with or interest in the world outside, others were seekers and explorers, equally passionate about life beyond the lab. Hasted was definitely in the latter category. The day wasn't long enough to squeeze in all his extramural interests, which were primarily politics, music, theatre and combinations thereof.

On arriving in London, he and his wife Elizabeth had taken a basement flat in Notting Hill Gate – as cosmopolitan and bohemian an area as existed in the whole of Britain. At sundown, the aroma of West Indian cooking mingled with the heady perfume of marijuana and the distant strains of calypso as he and fellow subversives took to the streets to further the communist cause. This was done principally by selling the party newspaper the *Daily Worker* door to door, or by daubing political slogans on any appropriate stretch of wall. In the latter field, Hasted was a graffiti pioneer – devising a 'whitewash pentel', where a hot water bottle full of paint fed a tube inserted into the hollow handle of a brush, speeding up what was a hazardous operation. If you got caught, you could find yourself doing three months in Wormwood Scrubs.

To the first rock 'n' roll generation, for whom most things American were admirable, praiseworthy and generally wonderful, the notion of communism was anathema – but it was an attractive proposition for many post-war, pre-Hungary teenagers and intellectuals.

1948 was the centenary of what Hasted calls "the most important pamphlet since Martin Luther," the *Communist Manifesto*. "It has always been a source of wonderment to me," he says, "that those penetrating thoughts were written in a library not a quarter of a mile from my own laboratory." It was also the year Hasted joined the Workers' Music Association Singers, who, under conductor Alan Bush, sang at rallies and meetings in Trafalgar Square, the Royal

Albert Hall, at Wembley, in Hyde Park, at any Labour Movement gathering to which they were asked. "We were out at gigs most evenings – despite rain, shine or pea-soup fog. In the great fogs, we could hardly see our shoes in the street, and had to hang on to each other by our raincoat belts."

When Stalin died in March 1953, a 100-strong WMA choir sang his praises with the same funeral song the Bolsheviks had sung when Lenin was laid to rest. "It is no use pretending that British communists disapproved of Stalin," admits Hasted. He's not kidding. Check these *Daily Worker* headlines:

'ETERNAL GLORY TO STALIN!'
'THE GREAT SERVANT OF MANKIND'
'THE SAVIOUR OF HUMANITY'

Only the one with the ambiguous twist turned out to have any prophetic resonance: 'STALIN'S NAME WILL LIVE ON IN MEN'S HEARTS'. Some of the most hagiographic tributes were written by Harry Pollitt, the General Secretary of the Communist Party of Great Britain. He must have had to do a big swallow when the real story got out.

"Rumours of Stalin's oppression, imprisonment and murder of good comrades began to reach us," says Hasted, "but we discounted them right up to the time that Khrushchev lifted the lid on the whole can of worms."

For five years, Hasted spread himself between the WMA choir and other musical projects, the most significant of which were a folk quartet called the Ramblers, which he started in 1950, and the 40-strong London Youth Choir, which he organised the following year.

Similar experimentation was taking place here and there in the traditional jazz haunts of London, but the Ramblers were the first guitar/banjo/vocal group to be rooted in the folk tradition. Whereas the jazzers were inspired by black Americans, Hasted and his cronies were motivated mainly by their white counterparts.

In the United States, a strong national folksong movement was already underway; the Weavers spent a quarter of 1950 at the top of the popular music hit parade with their recording of Leadbelly's *Goodnight Irene*. The lilt of the melody and sentimental lyric belied the group's original *raison d'être* – to perpetuate the spirit and idealism of their parent group, the Almanac Singers, and the left-wing trade union singers before them – and their astonishing popularity left them somewhat bewildered.

The possibilities of advertising and influencing the class struggle in song, by commenting on social and political issues, had first been investigated around 1915, by activists in the radical union Industrial Workers of the World, colloquially known as the Wobblies. The Swedish immigrant Joe Hill, whose scathing *Pie In The Sky* was a favourite Depression comforter and rallying cry, became the best known of several functional topical songwriters – and when he was framed for murder and executed by a Utah firing squad, it was soon plainly evident that the authorities would never be able to eradicate either his ideology or his memory. Woody Guthrie, among others, took up his sword and was able to inspire subsequent generations with a validity, intensity and honesty absent from the work of most professional singers and musicians.

During the thirties and forties, folk music and topical song continued to thrive as the focal point of union rallies, Farm Aid-style fund-raisers, rent parties, strike meetings – and as pure entertainment. Up there with other mid-century biggies like *Rudolph The Red Nosed Reindeer* by Gene Autry, *If I Knew You Were Coming I'd Have Baked A Cake* by Eileen Barton and *Music! Music! Music!* by Teresa Brewer, *Goodnight Irene* sold over two million copies and would have made Leadbelly a wealthy man had he not died at the end of the previous year.

1950 also saw the emergence of America's first regular folk music publication *Sing Out!*, the front cover of whose first issue carried the words and music of the Weavers' anthem *If I Had A Hammer* – the source of the magazine's title. "All you left out was the sickle," wrote one disgusted browser. The printer (it was 16 pages monthly) was paid by money raised at hootenannies, and early supporters included Woody Guthrie, Cisco Houston, Pete Seeger and the other Weavers, all of whom would "come down and sing for the cause" whenever they were in town.

That folk music was widely seen as the province of Kremlin pawns and subversives, all part of a fantastic Bolshevik plot, was underlined the following year when two of *Sing Out!*'s founders, Israel Young and Betty Sanders, were served subpoenas by McCarthy's demented witch-hunters.

Throughout this period, even though in pop and jazz terms Britain was virtually a colony of the United States, only the skimpiest information about the folk scene drifted across the Atlantic. Here, the folk tradition had been repressed and regulated almost to extinction.

"In the Weavers, and all the other groups I'd been involved with, we had consciously avoided the mistakes made in Britain," says Pete Seeger. "Over there, they had tended to arrange their folk music for the pianoforte, with all the protest, sex, colloquial expressions and bawdy humour removed. They told the schoolchildren 'don't change a note - this is our national heritage!' and taught them to sing very elegantly and nicely. We, in contrast, sang old songs, new songs, rough and ready songs, political songs, uplifting songs, protest songs, work songs, union songs, rambling songs, whatever songs we felt appropriate to the situation."

In many ways, it was as if Hasted had taken Pete Seeger as a role model. The son of a prominent ethnomusicologist, Seeger had dropped out of Harvard University to travel around playing his banjo and singing with other politically committed friends. After meeting in New York, in March 1940, at a rural migrant workers' benefit concert organised by subsequent *Waltons* star Will Geer, Seeger and Woody Guthrie hitch-hiked across America, singing for trade unions and political action groups.

On his return, he formed the Almanac Singers (named after the *Farmers' Almanac*, one of the most influential books in pre-industrial America) with Lee Hays and Millard Lampell and various auxiliary members including Woody, Gordon Friesen, Sis Cunningham, Josh White, Cisco Houston, Brownie McGhee and Sonny Terry. The group ethos was that the message, not the performers, was all-important. In other words, total disdain for the Tin Pan Alley system of hit songs and star performers.

In 1946, a friend who was serving in the Merchant Navy, Bob Hinds, dropped by to play John Hasted a 78 he'd picked up in New York: the Almanac Singers' recording of Woody Guthrie's *Talking Union* – cut in May 1941, when the line-up was Seeger, Hays, Lampell, Bess Lomax and Pete Hawes. This was the first of many instances in British rock history of a hip Merchant seaman turning on potentially influential musicians with obscure records he'd picked up in the States. Hasted was galvanised; he had never heard anything like it before. Getting a guitar and learning to duplicate that style of music was all he could think about – but that was easier said than done. You could buy classical guitars and Spanish guitars, three-quarter size ladies' guitars (festooned with ribbons, of course), even lutes, but there was no demand for country & western or folk guitars and stores didn't stock them.

Just about the nearest one could get to a folkie in England was the radio and variety artist inevitably billed as Elton Hayes and his Small Guitar. A kind of prototype cross between Jake Thackray and Val Doonican, he specialised in jaunty nonsense like *Riddle De Diddle De Day*. When, in 1951, the Walt Disney studio was looking for a troubadour type to play Allan-a-Dale in their made-in-England version of *Robin Hood* (with Richard Todd – public school accent, Harley Street teeth, gleaming hairstyle, baby's bottom shave – in the title role), Elton was the automatic choice. He just put on a pair of coloured tights and pranced about as normal.

It was a year or more before Hasted found a flat top, round hole guitar capable of taking steel strings – a fine old Martin as luck would have it – and several more months before he got the hang of the 'Carter Lick'. "There were no tutors available. There were plenty of people around who could teach you dance band guitar or classical guitar, but I could find nobody who knew anything about folk picking or chording."

"I'd met a girl called Jean Butler, who was a good singer and banjo player," says Hasted. "She was an American who claimed not only to have sung with the Almanacs on occasion, but had also sung at rallies where it was just her and Woody Guthrie. She told me where to write to Pete Seeger – and he sent me a set of duplicated instruction sheets, for both guitar and banjo, with chord diagrams, tablature and picking techniques. It was obviously a service he performed regularly. For me, it was invaluable."

A year or so later, in 1950, Hasted was in the habit of meeting Bert Lloyd for lunch once a week, to discuss folk music. In his more formal role as A.L. Lloyd, Bert was a world authority, having worked as a sheep-shearer in Australia, a whaler in Antarctica, and collected over 500 songs on his travels. His 1944 book *The Singing Englishman* was the first general book on the subject since Cecil Sharp's *English Folk Song: Some Conclusions* was published in the early part of the century.

"One day, I asked Bert if he would like to help me organise an Almanacs-style group. To my astonishment, his voice dropped about an octave and he said, very quietly . . . 'passionately'! Jean Butler came in and suggested we call ourselves the Ramblers, after Woody's song *As I Go Rambling Round* – and that was one of the first songs we learned." The trio became a quartet with the addition of Lloyd's guitar-playing friend Neste Revald, brother of John, a leading authority on impressionist painting.

"There was a considerable history of singing connected with the trade union movement, but it was all choral – so we were a little apprehensive about appearing with guitars and banjos . . . but we were accepted and were soon playing at rallies and branch meetings." The most memorable was a gathering of the Clerical and Administrative Workers' Union, where the main speaker was the Prime Minister, Clement Attlee. They went down better than he did.

The Ramblers only lasted a couple of years, on and off, but their revolutionary repertoire, comprising British and American material, often adapted and modified to include denunciations of the atom bomb, curmudgeonly bosses and feckless politicians, formed an important, though largely forgotten bridge into skiffle and the CND movement. Jean Butler's versions of obscure Guthrie numbers, including all 17 verses of *Tom Joad*, were the first public performances of those songs in Britain, and *Amazing Grace* – written (Hasted would inform the audience) by the Reverend John Newton, born-again skipper of a Liverpool slave ship – was a popular staple of their set 20 years before it reached the pop charts.

Amazing Grace was also taken up by Hasted's concurrent venture, the London Youth Choir.

At the start of 1951, when the Cold War was at its iciest, John Hasted saw an opportunity to have a peek behind the Iron Curtain, something that no conventional channels would allow him to do. In the six years since the war, the super powers had shifted position. Once merely suspicious, East and West were now petrified of each other and governments were racing to develop nuclear weaponry capable of obliterating the opposite hemisphere. Not all citizens felt that this was a sensible plan. A better idea, surely, was to co-exist peacefully and happily.

In an attempt to breach the political and cultural barriers that had gone up even before World War II had ended, and to let interested visitors see that communism wasn't as virulent as the PR machines would have them believe, a series of World Youth Festivals were organised during alternate summers. Prague had hosted the first in 1947, Budapest the second in 1949. The third was scheduled for East Berlin in August 1951.

Hasted combined several local choirs into the impressively large and accomplished London Youth Choir, working as their musical director and conductor, rehearsing songs of peace for the festival. Along with morris dancers, sword dancers, clog dancers, mime artists, pipers, amateur actors, jazz musicians and curious students, they enjoyed two weeks of singing, dancing, music, poetry, camp-fires, pageants, plays, ballet, sport, processions, picnics, rambles, international friendship and unplanned fun in East Berlin.

The American army was obstructive, the British tabloids were paranoid: 'Parents Beware: Communism Wants Your Children'. "It's hard to remember what a dirty word 'peace' was at the time," says Hasted.

The theme was continued at the next festival, at Bucharest in 1953. Inspired by Picasso's *Doves Of Peace* drawings, a song celebrating "a little white dove bringing hope to the world; a bird with a leaf in her beak" won them a prize.

"Bucharest was the first one I went to," remembers choir member Hylda Sims. "It was a huge affair, incredibly organised. Hundreds of us went from Britain, thousands from other countries all over the world, but it was hardly mentioned in the newspapers – we were living in the shadows of McCarthyism, covered by a blanket of silence."

As soon as they got home, the choir reverted to busking, smaller units singing a programme of three or four songs in Petticoat Lane and the other street markets every weekend, collecting hundreds of pounds, enough to finance the next trip abroad. "This went on for years," recalls Sheila Finn, who was recruited, along with "half the cast", when Hasted was musical director on the Unity Theatre's production of *Reedy River*. "We would rehearse in his office at University College, which had been sound-proofed with egg boxes, and then take our music to the streets. Sometimes, a few of us would cram into his Morris 1200 and go down to Brighton, where we would sing everything from *Wimoweh* to *Careless Love* to *The Man Who Invented Beer*."

Taking their cue from the American folk magazine *Sing Out!*, Hasted and choir member/journalist Eric Winter launched *Sing* in May 1954. The first song they published was Leon Fung's calypso *The Atom Bomb And The Hydrogen*, which started with the line "In 1954, my friend, we have so many things to mend". In later issues, they followed with *Against The Atom Bomb, For Peace And Lasting Friendship* and *Fare Thee Well Westminster*, three Ewan MacColl songs which left no doubt about their political stance.

Although the Campaign for Nuclear Disarmament was four years away from formation, the seeds were being sown. A month earlier, Hasted and Winter joined trade unionists, Salvation Army representatives, Quakers, Members of Parliament, doctors, religious leaders, pacifists, socialists, communists and all-comers at the Royal Albert Hall, where Anthony Greenwood MP launched a campaign to oppose British participation in the development and manufacture of nuclear weapons. That same week, the *Daily Worker* reported that US troops had covertly flown to Vietnam to assist French forces following attacks by insurgents from the north. At a news conference, President Eisenhower propounded his 'domino theory', suggesting that allowing one country to fall into communist hands would lead to the fall of all nearby countries.

"John Hasted was one of those co-ordinating people that could make things happen, but he was a funny mixture," according to Hylda Sims. "He was Oxbridge, a distinguished scientist, lived with his wife in a pleasant house, had this astonishingly upper middle-class life and accent – but then he had his other side, the choir and communism. He was always rather self-conscious about his accent, so he used to put on a special folksy voice for his dealings with the choir, which irritated us all to death. I was quite close to John. If you went off to Oxford with him, to mingle with his scientific friends, his real voice would re-emerge – and that was a much nicer self, actually. He seemed altogether more comfortable in that setting."

By the time of the fifth World Youth Festival, held in Warsaw in summer 1955, Hasted was leading both the choir and a skiffle group. "There was a big struggle in my life: whether to concentrate on the choir, to which I had been passionately devoted, or the new skiffle. I had this idea, as so many musicians do, that we should try and bring our music to the people. I suppose I was a do-gooder. I eventually became convinced that in order to get the message across, the music had to change – which is why I went for skiffle. Of course, I was right: it became a craze."

The result of much experimentation, his first stable skiffle group comprised John Hasted (guitar, banjo, vocal), Chaim Morris (bass), Paul Fineberg (clarinet), John Cole (harmonica) and Dennis Finn (washboard). The principal singers were Redd Sullivan, a 25-year-old Merchant Navy stoker, and two choir members, Judith Goldbloom and Shirley Collins, both 20 years old. "Redd was big and red-haired, the best blues shouter around," says Hasted. "During his times ashore, he had travelled with me many miles to sing at Labour Movement meetings, complaining with justification that we were treated too casually – but always turning up next time. Judith was a drama student and the granddaughter of a Chief Rabbi. Shirley's clear tones came through like a peal of bells over the Sussex Downs: no trace of concert-style voice production or rubato – that was what held the audience."

It was this line-up which hosted the 44 Skiffle Club in Gerrard Street every Tuesday evening from April until July 1956, when they took a summer break. Of the many guests and floor singers during that first season, Hasted was particularly impressed by Isla Cameron, who had moved up from the west country to join Joan Littlewood's Theatre Workshop, the West Indian singer Eddy Thomas, who would later set up Jamaica's National Dance Theatre Company, and Margaret Barry, a street singer from Cork, who used to cycle to market squares and country fairs with her banjo strung across her back. Then there was Jack Elliott, of course. "He was our most welcome visitor; not just a Brooklyn cowboy but a genuine travelling singer. He had a great influence on skiffle."

"I always had happy groups and happy choirs, a stimulating night life, and more laughter and tears than in the rest of my life," says Hasted. "Some of the choir regarded me as a bit of a renegade when I deserted them to concentrate on skiffle – but not all of them." One who applauded his move was Hylda Sims.

Twelve

On 16 April 1956, two weeks after John Hasted opened the doors at 44 Gerrard Street, Russell Quaye's City Ramblers launched central London's third skiffle club in the first floor functions room of the Princess Louise, an elegant Victorian pub a skip away from Holborn Kingsway tube station. 'Monday Night is Studio Skiffle Night!' announced the fliers. 'Come on and hear Work Songs, Ballads, Blues, Union Songs and Stomps.' Singing and strumming her guitar alongside Russell was his girlfriend, Hylda Sims – a graduate of the London Youth Choir.

"I was brought up in a communist family," says Hylda. "My father was a romantic, who saw the Labour Party as middle of the road, compromising and revisionist, only concerned with rationalising capitalism; they weren't interested in trying to promote a socialist society like the Communist Party was. They may have nationalised the mines and the railways, but they didn't alter the power structure as far as the worker was concerned; it made no difference to him whether he was working for a nationalised industry or a private company."

At the age of seven, Hylda was dispatched to Leiston in Suffolk, to Summerhill, a free, progressive 50-pupil school that provided the setting for her 2001 novel *Inspecting The Island*. It was founded and run by A.S. Neill, whose main idea, he wrote, was "to make the school fit the child, instead of making the child fit the school." There was no uniform, no coercion: Neill believed in "self-government for the pupils and staff, freedom to go to lessons or stay away, freedom to play for days or weeks or years if necessary, freedom from any indoctrination whether religious or moral or political, freedom from character moulding."

"In an ordinary school, obedience is a virtue," he wrote, "so much so that few in later life can challenge anything. I believe that education should produce children who are at once individuals and community persons. Obviously, a school that makes active children sit at desks studying mostly useless subjects is a bad school."

Unsurprisingly, the school boasted no truants. Rounded and ready, Hylda left at 15, to go to ballet school in Kilburn, living in a little room of her own, in someone's house. An intrepid move, perhaps, but maybe not for a Summerhillian.

"I looked around for a social milieu and joined the local Young Communist League, one of whose haunts was the British Polish Friendship Society, who had very posh premises at 81 Portland Place. There was always something going on there. It was all to do with slightly masked communist organisations that existed to promote the idea and image of East European democracies, so-called. Looking back, it was probably quite sinister underneath. We all had a good time there, anyway, and that's where I came into contact with, and soon joined, the London Youth Choir . . . they used to rehearse there every Monday. I went to Bucharest with them in 1953, and to Warsaw two years later – but by then I was also getting into the bohemian scene, singing folk songs in the coffee bars."

Her friend Ivor Cutler, unknown then, and known to Hylda only because he taught at Summerhill for a short time, bought her a guitar and showed her the first chords she ever knew. "I was 17 at the time. He was in love with me and wanted us to get married." They stayed good friends.

The first songs she learned were from records by Burl Ives – *Skip To My Lou* and *Gimme Crack Corn* – but then her repertoire expanded to include English and Scottish ballads. Talented and pretty, with long straight raven black hair, she pioneered the femme folknik style several years before it became fashionable. A rippling underground coffee-house reputation led to occasional gigs further afield, including one at the Heritage Society at Oxford, where she met Russell Quaye. He too, played the occasional gig – strumming a quattro and singing such cockney music-hall staples as *Your Baby Has Gone Down The Plug-Hole* – but he was better known as a painter. As 'the Jazz Painter', in fact. His most talked-about commissions were portraits of Pearl Bailey and Big Bill Broonzy, both of whom sat for him after glowing recommendations from *Melody Maker* writer Max Jones. The AIA Gallery in Lisle Street had exhibited his work.

When Hylda bumped into him again at the Oasis Swimming Pool in Holborn, they started going out together. Russell had stories in his eyes, wore smocks, sometimes funny hats, had long unruly hair, a cross between Cézanne and Augustus John. By this time, Hylda had left ballet school and was working with Bill Colyer and Ken Lindsay at Collet's bookshop and record cellar in Charing Cross Road. Before long, she went to live with Russell, moved into his flat at 50 Pearman Street, in the cobweb of roads behind Waterloo Station.

Almost twice her age, Quaye had been through the wringer and was in need of some nourishment. Born in Bromley on Boxing Day 1920, he had been raised in a total-immersion Baptist, speaking in tongues, evangelistic religion. "The way Russell told it," says Hylda, "his mother had been in love with the hellfire preacher who ran the place – not realising that he was also screwing most of the other females in his congregation. When she found out, she committed suicide. Russell was 15 . . . he lied about his age and joined the RAF."

As rear gunner in a Lancaster, he survived nightly scrapes and occasional crash landings. Later, travelling to Malta, his ship was torpedoed and sunk. "He was one of a dozen survivors clinging to a coal-chute that had become detached, floating around in the Med, in total shock, with weaker ones dropping off and disappearing every so often," says Hylda. "He was on the last hospital ship to leave Tobruk before the Germans took it. By then he was pretty tight; they sent him to the Sudan to chill out a bit. I think he was in quite a mess when the war ended."

He started picking up the pieces at Beckenham College of Art but his life was fairly chaotic for the next 10 years. He bought a long lease on 50 Pearman Street for a few hundred quid, its price indicative of its tatty condition. He let the upper part as a self-contained flat and moved into the ground floor: two rooms, a small kitchen, a loo and a back yard. To supplement his precarious income, he let the smaller room to a lodger – who was still there when Hylda arrived. "To my surprise, I knew him. It was Johnny Pilgrim, one of the jazz-mad bods that used to hang around in Collet's."

For some time, Russell had been experimenting with ideas for an acoustic group. Not exactly an art-school rocker, but certainly an art-school jazz and blueser, he roped Pilgrim in on washboard and their mutual friend Harry Jackson on clarinet. Russell played his four-string quattro, surmounted by a kazoo, which he blew between vocals. Whatever they played had a quirky similarity, which was reinforced when John Lapthorne, an architectural student, joined on tub-bass. Made from a cheese barrel and a broomstick, it was the first such DIY instrument on the scene; wherever they performed – coffee bars, mainly – people would cluster round and marvel at it in wonder. "We were all broke," says Pilgrim, "but money was unimportant, we just played wherever we could find an audience. Busking was illegal but we often played under the arches at Charing Cross – until the police came down and moved us on. We were just spirited, inept New Orleans revivalists who wanted to make music ourselves and, to our surprise, some of the coffee bar crowd accepted and liked us."

Pilgrim, Lapthorne and Jackson dropped out; Alan 'Little Bear' Sutton ("he was short, cuddly and wore a baggy koala-coloured pullover") came in on washboard, Tony Bucket on tub-bass, and Hylda Sims on guitar and vocals. They now had their own snazzy logo, City Ramblers, hand-painted on the bass and their musical style moved towards what one might call proto-Fairport Convention, mixing Americana with English folk music, a varied, naturally evolving strand of jug-bandy skiffle. By early 1956, the creeping decay of Pearman Street having become pretty intolerable, Russell and Hylda moved into a studio in South Kensington – and it was there that they hosted their first skiffle club. The landlord was not amused by the noise and nor were local residents, resulting in an immediate relocation to the Princess Louise.

A pub venue ruled out teenagers but the audience grew every Monday, any profit going towards a projected summer tour of Europe. The City Ramblers were resident group; pianist Dave Riddell provided appropriate interval music every week, as did Nancy Whiskey, a pert Glaswegian who had recently moved down to London. Guests included Cyril Davies, Redd Sullivan, the Ted Wood (brother of Rolling Stone Ronnie) Skiffle Group and Jack Elliott, who quickly became a bosom pal. They kept it going for 16 weeks, until 30 July, when they headed for Germany in an old ambulance they'd bought and done up – not the last bunch of crazies to exhaust themselves in the clubs of Hamburg. Jack and June Elliott went along for the ride.

Johnny Pilgrim stayed on in the Pearman Street flat, which soon turned into a crash pad of the sort favoured by San Franciscan hippies a decade later. "It was a cold-water slum," he says, "no bath, damp everywhere, condemned as unfit for human habitation – but none of that really mattered. We thought of ourselves as a bit bohemian and just wanted to live differently, lead a less stuffy existence than our parents' generation." A working-class kid from a council estate in Barnes, he had joined the army in order to learn the clarinet: if you signed on for seven years, you could go into the band, so he thought. That didn't happen and, nauseated by what he'd seen while stationed in Egypt ("the dirty work of the Empire"), he turned pacifist and, by way of a Conscientious Objectors Tribunal and three months in Wormwood Scrubs, managed to extricate himself.

Back in 1948, during one of the regular lunchtime jam sessions at Regent Street Polytechnic, Pilgrim had seen Beryl Bryden playing her washboard and was impressed enough to swipe his mother's and get to grips with it. He joined in on the sessions, as visitors were encouraged to do, and a reassuring Bryden asked him "How do you get that Washboard Sam rhythm?" Pilgrim laughed. "It was pure ignorance, of course . . . I'd never heard of Washboard Sam." He would soon know everything about him.

By the time he was shot of the army, he and his friend John Jack were regular customers at the 100 Club, New Orleans jazz their passion. "Somehow there had gathered in central London this group of people who had different rules, rules which they made up as they went along," says Pilgrim. "We were beatniks before the term was invented and ours was a world where sex and jazz and drinking and having a good time weren't wrong. It was a white, working-class intelligentsia in a sense, although we would never have described ourselves as such. We read books. Henry Miller was the author we would all have loved to emulate and Mezz Mezzrow's *Really The Blues* was the jazz autobiography that everybody had to read. It was filled with this wild hipster language, which Mezz wanted us to believe was habitually used by black American musicians – though we suspected he'd embellished it somewhat and even invented some of it to create more of a romantic impact."

"Like most uneducated people, we believed what we read in books," says Pilgrim, "so my friends and I naturally concluded that marijuana was harmless. At the time, Lyons Corner House was open all night and tended to be both a haven and meeting place for the underworld, so you never had any trouble scoring. You could buy hash or grass or, if you were feeling flash, three ready-rolled reefers – pure leaf, no stems, no seeds – for half a crown. Of course, we dropped the word 'reefer' as soon as the newspapers started bandying it about."

Pot was the preferred drug of the modern jazzer; comparatively few New Orleans aficionados indulged. "The scene was pretty clearly defined," says Pilgrim. "One of the big myths about the early fifties was that all dealers were West Indian, but I never in my life bought marijuana from a black man. They didn't come into my purlieu; they tended to keep to their own culture until the modern jazz scene began to open up a bit. They certainly never went to revivalist jazz clubs."

Pilgrim and his cronies used to sit in Golden Square, rolling marijuana into liquorice paper joints and getting stoned in the sunshine. Though he is unable to remember ever being hassled or threatened by the police, who were unable to identify either the drug or its heady aroma, he seems to have been lucky. Less fortunate were modern jazz musicians like Tubby Hayes and Jimmy Skidmore, both of whom were busted and vilified. "Pot was never a big deal," says Pilgrim, "it was just something we did now and then – whereas the blues and New Orleans jazz were our religion."

After starting out as a messenger at the Fleet Street office of the *Manchester Guardian*, he was hired as assistant to the art editor on the *Reynolds News*, a Sunday paper owned by the Co-op – and he was still working there when another 100 Club habitué, Wally Whyton, asked him if he was interested in joining a skiffle group he and his friends had formed, the Vipers. "We've got a residency at the 2Is, a coffee bar in Old Compton Street," Wally told him, "and the place is packed every night."

Thirteen

The 2Is Coffee Bar would later claim, with ample justification, to be the cradle of British rock 'n' roll but a skiffle movement was already incubating in other coffee bars – in parallel and sometimes in tandem with the trad-jazz and choir-based developments previously discussed.

The first espresso bar was The Coffee House, on the corner of Northumberland Avenue, just off Trafalgar Square. A few oddballs got in there, including John Rety, an anarchist poet and novelist, and Tony Potter, one of the first long-haired bearded boho-types in London, but it was fairly conservative and straight, catering primarily to office workers. It only became part of the scene on Sundays, when it was one of the few places open for business. People sat in there reading papers and doing crosswords, but anyone attempting minstrelsy was quickly shown the door.

Not so at the Gyre & Gimble, a coffee bar at 31 John Adam Street, just down from Charing Cross Station. Here strummers were actively welcomed and allowed to make all the noise they wished. Being out of the way, in a back-street basement, the G (as the cognoscenti knew it) was the perfect refuge for those who liked to sit around chatting and socialising but didn't particularly like the ambience of pubs.

"When I started going down there in 1954," recalls Derek Duffy, who'd been alerted to its suitability by fellow magician David McDonald, "the folkie thing was just starting to happen. There were a few bods down there strumming on guitars but it hadn't become a craze."

Already it was attracting those nurses, writers, students and seekers who leaned towards the bohemian, who felt not only comfortable down there but part of a twilight-zone in-crowd. Dark walls, low lighting, a stone floor, higgledy-piggledy tables and chairs, benches around the sides. To be ensconced there, looking pensive over a Penguin paperback, a cup of frothy espresso and a smouldering Gauloise was about as cool and existential as you could get, outside of Paris.

So delighted was the owner with his clientele that he printed handouts proclaiming the G to be 'London's rendezvous for its famous bohemians, artists, models and musicians.' Very pleased, he was. 'The proprietor invites you to meet some of these amazing people,' his flier concluded, after plugging the reasonably priced snacks and beverages. The regulars were tickled pink, of course.

"Inevitably, tourists started coming in to look at the weirdies," says Derek Duffy. "Some were obviously hoping to merge and gain acceptance, but a lot of them were just getting off by being in the midst of what they imagined was exotic company. Pretty soon, the newcomers would be looking at other newcomers, thinking they were observing some of these famous bohemians they'd been hearing about. It was all too amusing."

In fact, the only customer who could legitimately lay claim to being a famous bohemian was Ironfoot Jack, whose picture appeared on some of the handouts. He was in his 70s, wore a misshapen Homburg and a black cloak, carried a shoulder bag full of antique rings and leaflets (mainly his own philosophical tracts), had been in the workhouse, in prison, a tramp, a fortune teller, an artists' model, and the subject of a 350-page biography entitled *What Rough Beast?* He could hold forth on yoga, phrenology, the occult and numerology at a time when such words were barely known and had run both the quasi-religious Temple of the Moon and the gay Caravan Club before the war. One of his legs was shorter than the other, corrected by the robust boot and steel extension which prompted his nickname. John Hasted embraced him and gave him a stage for his lectures and proclamations at the 44 Club.

Equally intriguing to any curious Gyre & Gimble rubber-neckers were Alan, the lank-haired accordionist who would optimistically pass the hat, Ernest Page, a homosexual civil servant who did astrology readings, and a character known as Dexy Dan, a pioneer dealer who had once done a roaring trade in pills but now looked as though he swallowed more than he sold. He was often slumped in a heap.

Weekend bohemianism became a cult; nine-to-fivers would dress up in appropriately scruffy garb – jeans and sloppy sweaters, duffle coats and sandals – and sit around in this hip milieu until Monday morning came around again . . . but all sorts of interesting folk, some far weirder than the resident weirdos, began to drop in too, and they invariably infiltrated the inner circle, such as it was at the time. A few of them were even learned enough to know that the coffee bar's name had been appropriated from Lewis Carroll's *Through The Looking Glass*. Well, the owner was a bookseller, and he did have his favourites.

There was also an increasing trickle of suburban girls, nice girls who wanted to give themselves, to be part of the scene, to have their intellect and emotions stimulated simultaneously, to share the talk of art and literature, and to get shafted by romantic swashbucklers. "You could usually tell the ones that were going to get pregnant as soon as they walked down the stairs," says one rueful regular.

The G's pearl diver, the guy who did the washing up, would often disappear for months. Of course, one didn't ask questions; when people suddenly went off the scene, it was assumed they had fallen foul of the law and were doing time. But this fellow turned out to be a noted conductor, who liked to relax over a sink-full of dirty crockery when he wasn't touring Europe with well-known orchestras. If anyone was having trouble tuning his guitar, they called him over: he had perfect pitch.

"When the tabloid newspapers started doing stories on the coffee bars, a couple of years later, they gave the impression that they were full of unwashed yobbos, smelly people with no brains and no future," says Redd Sullivan, who became a G regular in 1955, "but that's not what I found."

Nor Duffy, who listed the occupations of all habitués he could remember: "One doctor, one dentist, one university professor, two prostitutes, one pimp, a waiter, a couple of merchant seamen, an RAF person, several musicians, some nurses, numerous art students (mainly from St Martins Art School in Charing Cross Road) and sometimes their models, a typist or two, a sprinkling of bums, several burglars, one or two club bouncers, and a few shady types who would turn their hands to anything profitable, whether it was legal or not. If there were any painters or poets or writers or sculptors, they didn't sit around talking to us – but, of course, when the G got full, you couldn't move, so who knows?"

The archetypal female would sport a black jumper (possibly roll-necked, possibly huge and shapeless), either tight jeans or a long flared skirt, loads of beads, not enough make-up to notice, a minimum of professional hair modification, and sandals. Blokes would wear whatever they had, which often reflected a fairly abysmal income. Perversely, Duffy always insisted on wearing a suit and tie.

The guitar train was started by Diz Disley. Something of a roisterer and reveller, he had been a mainstay of the Yorkshire Jazz Band before moving to London at the end of 1953. He joined Ken Colyer's first post-Barber band in September 1954 and then, six months later, moved on to Mick Mulligan's band. Though trad-jazz convention required him to concentrate on banjo, he was also an accomplished guitarist and could often be found doodling in the G. Several admirers benefited from his instruction, notably Canadian Johnny, a 20 year old who'd come over from Vancouver and used different names to confound whoever might be on his tail. That was the rumour anyway.

In fact, John Martin Booker was no more Canadian than anyone else in the place. He had been born in the Horns Tavern, an imposing landmark on Kennington Road, not far from the Oval, in 1934. When his parents separated, he was shunted off to a succession of boarding schools – at the last of which, Clayesmore's, at Iwerne Minster in Dorset, he was elevated to lead chorister. His sweet renditions of Schubert's *Serenade* and Handel's *Where'er You Walk* were recorded and placed in the school library.

When he left, at 17, he went to visit his father, by now living in Edmonton, Canada. They soon fell out but Booker stuck around, teaming up with a country singer. "He had an old DeSoto car with a loudspeaker on the top, the sort politicians used to have, and he would go to all the small towns in the area, hire a hall for Saturday night, and then drive around advertising it. We would fill the place wherever we went."

After a few months of that, he travelled on to Vancouver, where he grooved around and worked casual jobs until hitchhiking the 3,000-odd miles to New York and returning to England on the *Queen Mary* at the end of 1954. By this time, he was a fully paid-up existentialist.

He rented a room in Brixton, which he lost after failing to make headway either as a tallyman or a travelling salesman. By summer 1955, around the time of his twenty-first birthday, he was living in St James's Park – "second bench up from Admiralty Arch". The Gyre & Gimble provided a perfect refuge; he could sit there, long into the night, warming his hands on a cup of coffee, chatting to new friends who respected his beat credentials.

Disley taught him chords and Mr Garfinkle, owner of the G and the bookshop upstairs, offered him the job of coffee bar manager. The G became his home, the store room at the back his bedroom. "The hours were 10am until 2pm, or whenever the last customer left. In between fiddling around with the Gaggia machine and making sandwiches, I would strum the guitar and sing."

A keen student, Booker was soon good enough for Sam Wanamaker to offer him a role in *The Rainmaker*, which he was about to stage at the Royal Theatre in Brighton. (Wanamaker also dropped into the Roundhouse and offered Bob Watson the same part. Both turned it down.)

"Diz taught me Django Reinhardt numbers like *Sweet Sue* and *Oh, Lady Be Good*, so I could back him up. Other guitarists started turning up: Alan Leat, who we used to call the Vanishing Prairie, because he was totally bald, and this kid from the Merchant Navy, Tommy Hicks. John Hasted came down, Redd Sullivan, Martin Winsor, Lionel Bart, Mike Pratt, Marion Amiss, all sorts of people who felt comfortable in that atmosphere."

"Having mastered a few chords, Booker passed them on to me," recalls Derek Duffy. "I would always take my guitar down there so that if no-one else was around, I could back whoever wanted to sing – but usually there would be several of us strumming away. People took it in turns to sing, and the rest of us would join in on choruses. Some people called it skiffle."

Booker got too sorry for Dexy Dan: it was winter and he had nowhere to go, so he allowed him to stay overnight. He was on prescription, scoring 25 tablets at a time from the chemist in Piccadilly, and the speed vied with the pills he took in order to sleep. He passed out lying against a steam radiator and had to be hospitalised with burns, after which he faded out of the picture.

The Gyre & Gimble stayed open until the early hours, whereupon nocturnalists would move on to Mick's, the printers' café in Fleet Street, which stayed open all night.

This practice was common until the visionary Cliff Pritchard converted a filthy cellar beneath 9 Monmouth Street into an all-night coffee bar, the Nucleus. Within weeks, if not days, it was vying with the G as the coolest dive in London.

"It quickly became a favourite haunt for musicians," says Duffy, one of several mates who rolled up their sleeves and helped to clean the place and redecorate. "At that time, few people had cars and musicians would often miss the last bus or tube home. Their days became a ritual: get up around three, potter around until it was time to go to work, and play until midnight or even later. Since the last tube left the West End at ten past eleven, or thereabouts, they were stranded – so they would go down the Nuke, have a meal, a few cups of coffee, maybe get into a jam session or a card game, and then emerge around five in the morning, in time to catch the first public transport and get home to bed."

Martin Winsor remembers the fun and games when the Nuke first opened. "It was immediately obvious that there weren't enough cups and saucers – so everyone went off to places like Joe Lyons, had cups of tea, and nicked the crockery!"

The atmosphere in both the Nuke and the G was a mixture of party and film-noir social club: many of the customers spent more time there than they did at home. There were no rules, no restrictions, but regulars knew and observed the behavioural boundaries. They could relax and not have to worry. They also knew that they couldn't find an equivalent ease in the other coffee bars that were becoming popular, like Bunjies in Litchfield Street, which was too prissy and proper for most of them and soon had a sign up saying 'Folk Songs but No Skiffle', or Orlando's in Old Compton Street, where the Ghouls had already become a fixture, the first resident skiffle group on the espresso scene.

Of course, the denizens of these, and other 'community centres' like the Colony Club, Torino's, the York Minster and the Caves de France, all thought the world revolved around their chosen haunts and that they were the hippest and most exclusive set in town – and who is to say that they weren't?

If the G and Nuke set ever imbibed in Soho, it was usually in the French (the coffee bar, not the pub) at 6 Old Compton Street, where Ironfoot Jack often held court and Quentin Crisp went to stretch his legs after posing for students around the corner at St Martins. It was on street level and they could gaze out of the windows at the circus parade. "Most of these coffee bar types didn't have two pennies to rub together, but they were still incredibly sniffy and cliquey," says Mick Robson, an art student drawn to investigate all the haunts his college mates were talking about. "Unless you had an 'in', you were excluded from most of the intrigue and laughter. Sometimes it could be very frustrating: you knew that the gods were up there frolicking on Mount Olympus, but you didn't have a ticket to get there and join in. On a more basic level, I liked the French because they sold fresh croissants there – the first I'd ever seen – and the best coffee in the world, I swear. It was real French coffee, with salt in it . . . and the experience of tasting that for the first time was like hearing *Be Bop A Lula* after a steady diet of Dickie Valentine."

"The best thing about the French coffee bar was that it functioned as a mailing centre," says Angela Bathurst, another student. "You could have letters sent there, which they would pin on the wall, awaiting collection."

A few years later, when Colin Wilson wrote about the French and Ironfoot Jack in *Adrift In Soho*, it became the number one attraction for incipient bohemians. As for now, the subterranean set kept mainly to the Gyre & Gimble and the Nucleus.

Unless they preferred to hang out in Fitzrovia, in which case they would make for the Breadbasket at 65 Cleveland Street, a block up from where they would soon build the Post Office Tower. When not distracted elsewhere, Wally Whyton would go down there looking for girls, looking at girls, talking to girls, doing everything he could to impress girls. He lived only a few minutes walk away, in Netley Street.

Wally had been born on 23 September 1929, in Stanhope Street, which threaded through the area he came to regard as his 'village' – bounded by Euston Road to the south, Hampstead Road on the east, Albany Street on the west, and Camden Town to the north. As soon as Adolf's bombers started making holes everywhere, he was evacuated to Minehead in Somerset, and was 16 when he returned to his patch in 1946. "At school, art was my main interest; from the age of eleven I knew I wanted to be a commercial artist. The 1930s had been a great period for posters, and I saw myself carrying on in that tradition."

When he got home to what was left of London, he did what he could to colour the grainy monochrome ration-book austerity. "I was in and out of pubs from the day I came back – simply because there wasn't much else in the way of entertainment, just after the war. There was a youth club, which was pretty tame, and a pinball arcade in Euston Road, which was considered a highly unsuitable place for intelligent teenagers. Fortunately, it had a shutter door, so you could creep in and not be visible from the street as you wasted all your money playing pinball or working those crane things that always managed to miss whatever you were trying to scoop up."

"I spent a lot of time wandering around the West End. There was a wonderful clothes shop in Charing Cross Road called Cecil Gee's. It later became huge and moved to Shaftesbury Avenue, but in the late forties, it was very small, very modern and very cool. It sold all the current American fashions – and that's what you aspired to: everyone wanted to look like a Yank."

That feeling was widespread, and persisted throughout the forties, into the fifties and beyond. There were no hip British role models for teenagers . . . who wanted to be like Billy Cotton or Ted Ray or George Formby or Donald Peers or Ted Heath? Infinitely more attractive were American stars like Robert Mitchum, John Garfield, Frank Sinatra, Humphrey Bogart, Perry Como and, as the decade turned, Eddie Fisher and Johnnie Ray. It was as Evelyn Waugh said: "We are all Americans at puberty".

Whyton's first hero was bandleader Artie Shaw – "partly because he married beautiful film stars like Lana Turner and Ava Gardner, but also because he wore the snappiest clothes I'd ever seen: jackets without lapels, and shirts which had great long pointed collars dropping down about a foot. I used to listen to his records and wonder how on earth anyone could play the clarinet so beautifully and so brilliantly . . . but then I did a total turnabout and went from swing to Louis Armstrong. I suddenly wanted to listen to black music rather than white, and swapped all my big band 78s for Hot Seven records."

"For the gang I knocked about with, Saturdays mornings would be spent walking down Oxford Street, going into all the record shops, blagging as many 78s as they would let you take into a listening room, and checking them out – five or six of us, crammed in those little glass-walled rooms they had. Then we'd take them back to the counter, say 'thank you very much, but we don't want to buy any' and mooch up the street to the next one."

"When I'd first started buying 78s, during the war, the shellac or whatever they used was so thin that you sometimes only got five or six plays out of them before they either turned grey or disintegrated

altogether. Steel needles just ripped through the surface in no time –
so you had to use thorns. The only way you could get rid of them,
trade them in, was to put black boot polish on them, shine them up,
go over the grooves to remove any excess gunge, and then sell them
or swap them with unsuspecting market traders."

Leaving school as soon as he could, Wally was apprenticed in the
design studio of Dorlands, an advertising agency which represented
such prestigious clients as Hennessey Cognac, Dunhill and Bentley
Motors. "Among the things we did was that Decca logo with
vibrations hitting an ear, and the words Full Frequency Range
Recording. Strangely, they started using it again in the late eighties
and it was fashionable on T-shirts for a while. We also designed one
of the first long players to be issued in Britain, a ten-inch album by
Anne Shelton."

"For me, the most interesting part of that job was going over to the
American Embassy in Grosvenor Square. Essentially I was there to
borrow Sears & Roebuck mail-order catalogues from their library, so
we could pinch ideas for the ones we were putting together for
Freemans and Great Universal Stores – but I spent much more time
in their record library, which was a goldmine, an Aladdin's cave.
You could actually take records home, which is staggering when you
think of it . . . all these extraordinarily rare field recordings done for
the Library of Congress. So as well as all the American jazz that I
absolutely adored, I started listening to Woody Guthrie and
Leadbelly and all sorts of obscure folk and blues." The selection
would have been wider, of course, had Lonnie Donegan not been
nicking them.

The first musical instrument Whyton tried was a cornet, which
proved impossible to master. "I used to sit up playing along to King
Oliver records, making the most dreadful din – and after putting up
with it for a while, my dad finally lost his cool and went bananas. He
forbade me to play it again until I'd had some lessons – so I went to
the only place I could think of – the Salvation Army. They told me I'd
have to join up and march around in their uniform, but I was a
Catholic boy, so the cornet got shelved."

"I continued to amuse myself playing the piano in our local pub.
Sometimes, late at night when I'd had a few and wanted to get
people stomping around, I'd play a bit of boogie-woogie – and after
one of these sessions, the publican asked me if I wanted a banjo. 'Not

really,' I said. 'Well, a busker left it here against a debt,' he said, 'it's been hanging around for months now. You can have it for ten bob.' 'It's a deal,' I said."

"I had no idea even how to tune it, so I enrolled for lessons at Kentish Town Institute, where they had a BMG orchestra – banjos, mandolins and guitars – and as soon as I'd learned a few chords, I was hooked. It was pretty simple stuff – the guitarists played a sort of strummed background fabric and the banjos plunked while the mandolin players did fancy runs, but it got me to the point where I knew what I was doing: I could play the changes and was soon able to get by in several keys . . . G, D, C, A, E and F. That was in early 1955 – and I started going down to the Breadbasket around the same time"

"Of course, once I'd discovered that place, I couldn't keep away. It was so different from the pub scene . . . for a start, there were loads of girls there. You didn't go to pubs to meet girls, and I loathed dance halls: all the rules about formal dress, and straight guys with neat hair and tuxedos up on stage playing from sheet music, that wasn't my cup of tea at all – but the Breadbasket was great."

"It was a cellar, with murals of Spanish dancers and flamenco guitarists wearing sombreros, and the tables had those spiky-legged lamps made out of steel rods with little red knobs on the end. Tremendously chic and trendy! I think the girls were the main attraction, though . . . they wore flared print skirts and all seemed so fresh and vibrant and youthful. It was a different world down there."

It was small enough for everyone to be mates, especially those who played instruments – whether they were Sunday bohemian novices like Wally or professionals like Diz Disley. "We tended to roam from one coffee bar to another, a bunch of layabouts," says Diz, who later redecorated the Breadbasket with new murals. Also in the floating gang were three guitarists: Alan Starke, Brian Silver and Bob Sturgess; two bass players: Clive Godden and Johnny York; sometimes a Scottish fiddle player, Bob Clark.

People came and went, moved around. At the Breadbasket, Wally formed a regular trio with Brian Silver on guitar and Johnny York on tea chest bass – just messing around, having fun. When he was able to find a Saturday night relief manager, Johnny Booker came up from the Gyre & Gimble and the four of them became a weekend house band. "That went on for a while," says Wally, "with others sitting in from time to time – including Tommy Hicks, who came down with Booker one evening. That was the first time I ever met him."

As soon as Wally saw a guitar in a pawnshop window he bought it. "All the pawnshops used to have banjos like mine hanging in the window," he recalls, "tenor banjos with a wooden sound-box, made to play chords on . . . but you never saw a guitar. So I was thrilled when I saw this one." Diz Disley re-strung it for him, tuned it and showed him some chord shapes. Wally dumped the banjo and started spending more time at the Gyre & Gimble, where he could practise with Booker long into the night. By this time, he was also frequenting the 100 Club, hanging out with Johnny Pilgrim and John Jack, who always seemed to know where the parties were.

The Booker/Whyton guitar duo became a guitar trio in spring 1956 when they incorporated another G regular, Jean Van Den Bosch. "Like me, Booker was a proficient strummer," says Wally, "but Jean – whose name and goatee suggested a Dutch painter, even though he had an English public school background and sold nails for a living – played in open tuning." Complementing their full, ringing guitar sound was a skiffle-perfect vocal blend: Booker sang a convincing, raspy lead, Wally was a tenor and Van Den Bosch a bass.

Although, at this point, they were just having glorious fun and there was no question of going professional, Booker decided to adopt a stage name, Johnny Martyn. Wally already had a name for the group: the Vipers . . . the first drug allusion in British rock. Most people thought it referred to the snake, poisonous and menacing, but had they examined the glossary at the back of Mezz Mezzrow's *Really The Blues* – several well-thumbed copies of which were in constant circulation among the membership of the 100 Club – they would have known that viper was also hipster slang for a marijuana smoker.

Vipers turned up in the lyrics of many race-market reefer songs of the thirties and forties, most memorably in *If You're A Viper*, written in 1936 by 'the King of Swing Violin' Stuff Smith. Wally had in his growing record collection a version by Rosetta Howard & the Harlem Hamfats, and this had inspired the name.

> *I dreamed about a reefer five feet long,*
> *Mighty mezz but not too strong.*
> *You'll be high but not for long, if you're a viper.*

Paradoxically, none of the trio smoked marijuana.

Sometimes augmented by Johnny York on tea-chest bass and Clive Godden on guitar, the Vipers Skiffle Group played regularly at the Gyre & Gimble and the Breadbasket, and – like all the other strummers on the scene – busked under the arches behind Charing Cross Station, dispersing swiftly when the law appeared. Their first advertised gig was supporting the City Ramblers at the Princess Louise at the end of June but their pivotal moment came a fortnight later, on 14 July 1956.

At the instigation of Gaston Berlemont, the French landlord of the York Minster in Dean Street, a Soho Fair was held on Bastille Day every year – a festival of arts, crafts, food and drink.

"It was open house, everybody enjoying themselves on the streets, and we had gone along to enjoy the fun," says Wally. "Suddenly, two guys we knew from the G – John Hasted and Redd Sullivan – saw us and grabbed us. One of Hasted's friends had got hold of a lorry and was going to tag on to the end of the main parade. Before I knew it, we were on this flat-bed truck, trying to keep our balance as we sang out to the people on the street – up and down Frith Street and Greek Street, round Soho Square, all over. John Rety was sitting on the back, handing out his anarchist leaflets or maybe some of Hasted's pro-communist rants, and the rest of us were singing *Sail Away Ladies* at the top of our voices. We must have sung it for at least half an hour – all dwarfed by Redd, of course, who could almost level buildings with his voice. I had never heard the song before but it was very catchy." Hasted had found it on an old record by Uncle Dave Macon and his Fruit-Jar Drinkers.

When the parade came to a standstill, they found themselves outside a coffee bar in Old Compton Street, the 2Is – not on the hip circuit and therefore unknown to any of them. Nevertheless, the Vipers dismounted and entered the premises for refreshment. They ordered coffee, sat down and began playing their guitars. The proprietor didn't seem to mind. He kept looking across at them, but not with any hint of displeasure or negativity. He didn't even object when they passed the hat and extracted a few coppers from the tourists who'd happened by.

As they were preparing to leave, he intercepted them. "Excuse me, lads," he said, "but I really enjoyed that . . . I'd be happy for you to come in and sing any time you like."

"Sure," they said, thinking to extend their territory, "we'll see you one evening next week."

It was as if a seed, blown across the desert, had lodged in a spot fertile enough to take root and sprout into a giant beanstalk, the like of which no one had seen before. The entire British rock scene is built upon that one chance visit.

Fourteen

In July 1956, Lonnie Donegan returned from America feeling he was already a star. First thing he did was order a car befitting his new status: a blue two-and-a-half litre Daimler DB18 Sports Special drop-head coupé, described in company literature as 'more a gentleman's carriage than a sports car'. During his absence, *Lost John* had risen to number two on the hit parade, his extended player *Skiffle Session* to number 20, and his manager/agent Lyn Dutton had been casting around for new sidemen. Never again would Lonnie play a subservient role in the beer-and-fags backroom world of traditional jazz; at 25, he was about to be launched as a variety artiste, fronting his own band.

Dutton first approached Mickey Ashman, a reliable bassist and a good friend, who had served four years with Humphrey Lyttelton, followed by brief spells with Chris Barber and Eric Delaney. He was easily persuaded, as was Nick Nicholls, a cutting-edge drummer who had paid his dues with the Christie Brothers Stompers and Geoff Taylor's rhythm & blues-inclined sextet. But finding a suitable, skiffle-savvy guitarist was proving more difficult.

Serendipitously, Johnny Booker visited Dutton at his office in Great Chapel Street, and invited him to check out the Vipers with a view to representing them. He did, after all, represent Humph, Chris Barber, Terry Lightfoot, Sandy Brown, Ken Colyer, Alex Welsh and several more jazzers . . . maybe he could use a skiffle group. Dutton duly showed up for one of their regular Monday night Breadbasket gigs, told them they were too green and too limited to get anywhere, and left. Don't phone us, we'll phone you. "The strange thing," says Booker, "is that he stayed for the second set, stayed for the entire evening."

A week later, on 30 July, Lonnie turned up out of the blue (tipped off by Dutton, obviously), sat there drinking coffee and whooping encouragement. In what was his first UK appearance for months, he joined them on the Breadbasket stage, or the steps that passed for a stage, and turned the evening into a memorable one for all who attended. As they prepared to leave, Lonnie drew Booker aside and offered him the position of guitarist/harmony singer in his band. Booker talked to Wally Whyton, who was still working at Dorlands and had no intention of packing it in to play music full time. Knowing that, since relinquishing his job as manager of the Gyre & Gimble, Booker had no visible means of support, Wally advised him to take Lonnie's offer: "it could be a good money-spinner for you," he told him.

The following day, the new band met for their first rehearsal. Lonnie had picked out two songs for his next single: *Bring A Little Water Sylvie*, from a recording by Leadbelly, and *Dead Or Alive*, from a recording by Woody Guthrie. The band had them worked out in no time flat. Donegan was a happy man. The studio had been booked for Thursday; there should be no problems.

Johnny Booker did have a problem, however . . . he decided he didn't want to work with Lonnie, felt no sense of camaraderie. The clincher came when, having finished working on the two scheduled songs, Lonnie asked Booker to teach him "that new song you were singing at the Breadbasket – what was it called, *Don't You Rock Me Daddy-O?*" Booker taught it to him, the band ran through it a couple of times.

"I think I'll record that," Lonnie told him – adding that he was going to copyright it the next day. "Don't worry," he said, "I'll take care of you."

Booker was not amused. "Wally and I had been working on that song for a fortnight solid, and Donegan was openly telling me that he was going to nick it from us. I was furious."

He had every right to be. Taking the rough framework of *Sail Away Ladies*, which they had sung from John Hasted's truck at the Soho Fair, he and Wally had remodelled the melody and rhythm, and written entirely new lyrics. Their masterstroke had been to modify the arcane chorus "Don't you rock 'im die-dee-oh" into the teenage war cry *Don't You Rock Me, Daddy-O!* – a change which transformed a 1920s rural Tennessee string-band knees-up hoe-down number into a contemporary skiffle classic.

Since its use in the film *Blackboard Jungle*, the term 'daddy-o' had been gaining currency only with smart alec kids and in radio comedy sketches. In the States, where two versions of a pop song called *Daddy-O* had recently reached the Top 20, it was already common teen parlance, but the expression only really entered British popular culture with the Vipers' song.

Hasted happened to drop into the G one evening when they were working on it, and was delighted. "This is the folk process in action!" he told them, little realising that this was only the first step in a continuing process. At a time when a million or more teenagers were latching onto skiffle, the Vipers provided the anthem, the obligatory number. It was the coolest thing they ever did. And Lonnie was about to claim it as his own.

In a bid to pre-empt him, Booker immediately phoned Wally and together they went to see the only Tin Pan Alley connection they knew, Bill Varley. His music-biz pedigree was not extensive. After a stretch in the RAF, a year as a student nurse, and a miserable spell as a service mechanic for National Cash Registers, Varley got a job as an air steward, working for the British Overseas Airways Corporation, flying transatlantic routes in Boeing Stratocruisers and Lockheed Constellations. These were the days when the trip from Heathrow to New York took 14 hours, with fuel stops at either Shannon or Prestwick, then Keflavik in Iceland, and Gander in Newfoundland. In first class, where he worked, dinner was served on china plates with silver cutlery; for breakfast, eggs were cooked individually to the passengers' requirements. The best thing about it: there was plenty of time off after each flight – five days in New York, even longer at home.

At training school, Varley had met Roy Tuvey and they stayed friends. "When we weren't working, we used to hang around together, and one day we went up to Denmark Street to see a friend of his, Peter Charlesworth, who was a song plugger and publicist. He also had a sideline, cutting 78 rpm acetates from publishers' demo-tapes. He reckoned it was a pain in the arse to mess around with this, when he could be yakking away on the phone, but Roy and I were fascinated."

At Charlesworth's suggestion, they set up our own business, a disc-cutting service for publishers: he channelled work their way and they were soon off and running, working in an office on the top floor of 6 Denmark Street, sub-let from an accordion repair specialist. They called themselves Trio Recording Service and ran it in their spare time, between flights. By 1955, business was so brisk that they were able to quit their day jobs.

"On the way home, we would often drop into the Gyre & Gimble," Varley recalls. "I lived in Hammersmith, Roy lived in Fulham, and both our late-night buses left from Trafalgar Square, which was just down the road. We got chatting to a lot of the regulars, particularly those with guitars. They would be thrashing away, singing their hearts out and having a great time, but it was not the sort of thing that could ever be accepted by the music business, we thought."

When Booker and Whyton went to his office and told him their story, Varley took them to see Gerald Benson, who had a little music publishing company a few doors away. He had his fingers in other pies too, doing a bit of song plugging and flogging the odd piece of jewellery, but he knew publishing and promised to copyright *Don't You Rock Me Daddy-O* as quickly as possible, as a Benson Music Co title. This he did – and Donegan was denied. Mysteriously, when the sheet music appeared, some months later, words and music were attributed not to Whyton/Booker but to Whyton/Varley.

Lonnie's recording session was booked for 10am on Thursday 2 August 1956, at IBC Studio. Naturally, Booker didn't appear. He and Lonnie would never speak to each other again.

The accepted story, printed many times, is that Booker overslept and missed the session. In fact, he missed it on purpose, sat there drinking coffee in the G as the clock ticked and the hour passed. Lonnie never forgave him, of course. When he discovered that they had been booked on the same bill in Vancouver in 1973, he refused to go on if Booker was even in the same building, let alone on the same stage.

So there was Lonnie, pacing the floor, getting increasingly agitated as Nick Nicholls set up his kit and began improvising with Mickey Ashman. "Where the fuck is he?" shouted Lonnie. "Don't worry, dear boy," advised Denis Preston, sitting in the studio control room, his cheeks already feeling the benefit of brandy, "if he doesn't turn up, we'll find somebody else."

When it became apparent that Booker was a no-show, Preston got on the blower to Denny Wright, who got in a taxi and was there almost before the engineer had finished setting the levels.

"I couldn't believe it," said Lonnie. "Of all the guitarists that I had ever played with, just for fun, messing around and jamming the night away, my favourites were Denny Wright and Diz Disley.

Denny was God, Diz was St Peter, and I was just a lowly disciple. I would never have dared to invite Denny Wright to join my band; surely, he would never come near a band like mine. He might pass by the window and wave, but that was it."

Not only did Denny play on the session, he was euphoric about the prospect of joining Lonnie's skiffle group full time. He was already portly and balding: too long he had suffered in anonymous night-club and hotel bands, playing as skilfully as he could, but without any sense of satisfaction, of fulfilment, of recognition. He did recording sessions galore, everything from Johnny Parker's Washboard Band to Edmundo Ros. Thoroughly irksome, much of it. Recently, he'd been in Martin Moreno's Latin American Quartet, playing for pissed-up poseurs at the Casanova Club in Grosvenor Street. They had moved on to a residency at the Albany Club in Savile Row, but it was hardly the atmosphere he craved. No one gave a hoot about how or what he played; most of the audience wouldn't have known a waltz from a tango. Small wonder that he jumped at the chance of joining Lonnie's group, of standing on stage next to him, singing choruses and floating out a few decent solos.

Bring A Little Water Sylvie was the first record Lonnie cut without the sage Chris Barber being around to keep him on track. He had to rely on Denis Preston, who had more commercial objectives. It was as if Lonnie got into costume and went out to perform some amateur dramatics. Another Leadbelly song, but a strange choice. For the third time in a row, he tells us "this here's the story . . . " – but this particular story was sung from the perspective of a black cotton picker in the broiling heat of Texas or a sugar-cane worker sweating his guts out in Louisiana, feeling hot and "thoisty", in need of the water girl. For Leadbelly, it had been a real and constant craving. Mule-drawn wagons would bring water barrels to the field workers, with water carriers dotted around each plantation, to carry the water bucket, to provide drinks and mop brows. It was a hard life picking cotton all day, every day – as Lonnie would surely know, living as he did in Wanstead.

Nick Nichols and Mickey Ashman eased themselves in as Lonnie worked himself up into a lather. Denny Wright played an acoustic solo that was barely audible above the pandemonium. Denis Preston's engineer caught the moment. One of the most unlikely songs ever to become a Top 10 hit, it proved that neither Lonnie nor skiffle were just a flash in the pan. The first generation of copycat groups learned the song immediately, but none could come close to Lonnie's manic intensity.

Denny gave a hint, though only a hint, of his instrumental dexterity on *Dead Or Alive*, about an outlaw on the run. "Lonnie collaborated with American folk singer Woody Guthrie in writing *Dead Or Alive*," the *NME* explained, helpfully if not accurately. In fact, he nicked half the credit for a song written and copyrighted years earlier by Guthrie, who had recently been committed to the New Jersey state mental institution at Greystone Park. In the lyric, the sheriff (of East Ham, possibly) sends the protagonist a wanted poster with his picture on it. He has to evade capture if only to see his little "sweet thing" one more time – possibly that bint who used to hang around the Fishmongers Arms in Wood Green. On the face of it, the whole idea was preposterous, ludicrous beyond imagination – but the thing was this: Lonnie could suspend our disbelief, transport us into the heart of the song. Which was more than Billy Cotton ever could.

His records appealed mainly to boys, but girls wanted to watch him too. Lowbrows of all ages were intrigued, not only by his music but also by his comedy patter. He was a beaming showman, a natural for the national variety circuit, the main stream of live entertainment. Into it headlong he was pushed, showing no sign of fear or hesitancy. This is what he was born to do.

After a trial run at Blackpool Palace, he made his London début at the Stoll Theatre in Kingsway, playing his hits and some of the new songs he and the group had been recording for his first long player. Then, headlining over a motley music hall bill, he spent the autumn playing, as was the practice, a week solid at each of 14 theatres, an itinerary which found him appearing within reach of much of the country's population. After Nottingham, Edinburgh, Glasgow, Birmingham, Sheffield, Newcastle, Manchester, Leeds, Liverpool, Sunderland, Hanley and Bradford, his 35-minute set was word perfect, note perfect and grin perfect, and audiences, reticent at first, were soon clapping and stamping along. He played a week at the Prince of Wales Theatre in London, followed by a week at the Finsbury Park Empire, by which time it was almost Christmas and in all those homes with a hip teenage son and a gramophone capable of playing at 33⅓ rpm, *The Lonnie Donegan Showcase* was on the list for

Santa. Pye could hardly press copies fast enough to satisfy demand; it sold in sufficient quantity to enter the best-sellers list, the first album to do so.

"I haven't gone commercial," Lonnie explained to reporters, "it's just that my act has become commercial."

In the *NME* poll results, published in Christmas week 1956, Lonnie shocked his old mates in the jazz world by being voted number five in the Small Band section. Even more incredibly, he was voted number two in the Outstanding Musical Personality category. Only Dickie Valentine out-polled him. Outstanding Musical Personality? Lonnie had arrived; he knew it, his band knew it, his audience knew it, his disciples knew it. Tin Pan Alley hoped it was just a momentary aberration.

On Christmas Eve, he was seen in most of the six and a half million households fortunate enough to possess a television set, playing a track from his *Showcase* album on Jack Payne's BBC show *Off The Record*. Payne winced visibly, both before and after the performance. He disliked skiffle almost as much as he disliked the year's other new trend, rock 'n' roll – as celebrated by another of his guests that week, Tommy Steele . . . who was already making his second appearance on the show.

Fifteen

Tommy Steele had become an overnight star even faster than Lonnie Donegan. His old mates, who had always known him as Tommy Hicks, weren't just shocked, they were flabbergasted.

"For most of the Gyre & Gimble dwellers with guitars, singing and playing was a way of life," says Derek Duffy, "but for some it was going to be a career and if there was one characteristic that those people shared it was drive. Tommy wanted to be up on stage and to be famous – there was never any doubt about that, as far as I was concerned – but if he'd tried to tell us then that he was going to be a household name in less than a year, and would be shaking hands with the Queen in less than two, we would have told him to go and see a shrink."

The Vipers knew Tommy from the G and the Breadbasket, where he was often strumming and singing Hank Williams or Red Foley songs, or getting to grips with the early Elvis Presley releases. "Some weekends in spring and early summer 1956, he would come down to Brighton with us on the train and busk on the beach," recalls Johnny Booker. "He was very good in front of a crowd, could pull an audience and generate money. He would sing his rock 'n' roll songs, Redd Sullivan would stomp and holler, and Wally and I would sing all the noisy, familiar songs in our repertoire. Various friends from the G, up to a dozen or so, would come too – singing choruses, dancing around and collecting money – so it was a great day out at the seaside for us all. We would usually end up spending all the money on cider and having a slap-up Chinese meal before catching the last train back to Waterloo."

Less interested in folk music than the other Gyre & Gimble strummers, Tommy was often berated for his contemporary taste, not to mention his cocky, cockney flamboyance. Why should he care . . . he played the songs he loved and the girls would sit gazing at him.

"He had a very infectious, happy-go-lucky presence," says Booker, "the girls were always flocking round him."

"Not long after I first met Tommy, he rolled me into a gig, somewhere in the East End," recalls Wally Whyton. "A bookie had asked him to play at his mother's birthday party, in a front room of a terraced house, out in the back of beyond – and, presumably because I happened to be around, he co-opted me, along with his mate Mike Pratt, who played piano, and our mutual friend Johnny York on tea-chest bass. We were called the Cavemen and, as far as I know, he had a floating group of Cavemen, depending on who was available."

"So there we were, a bunch of misfits with little idea of each other's material, and a piano that sounded as if it hadn't been tuned since 1927. I was into American folk music and calypso at the time, Mike was keen on ragtime, Tommy was singing rock 'n' roll, and the tea chest bass had little bearing on what any of us were doing . . . we were totally disparate in every way."

"The first big mistake they made was to give us a bottle of whisky, which Mike immediately got stuck into, as the rest of us tried to bash out recognisable versions of *Blue Suede Shoes* and *Heartbreak Hotel*. It must have been the most tuneless, cacophonous racket, because it was the first time I'd tried to play anything like that – but I just strummed and sang a bit behind Tommy, who must have known the words of every rock 'n' roll song released at that time. He really was the first kid in London singing that stuff, and he got totally carried away, even though we were only getting three quid between the four of us."

"Meanwhile, Mike Pratt was getting totally out of it – and at some point, he went up to this bookie and said, 'Tell you what, tosh, I'll toss you for our three quid, double or quits.' Of course, he lost! He came back, all pissed and sheepish, explained what had happened and collapsed in a heap, leaving Tommy and me to carry on – chanting 'no money! no money!' to each other between the verses."

"So after we'd sung ourselves to a standstill, Tommy went over to the old lady whose party it was – she was about 82 and dripping with gold – and said 'We're not being paid.' She said 'What do you mean?' 'Our piano player got drunk, tossed double or quits, and lost,' explained Tommy, 'so we're not getting any money.' With that, she opened her handbag, pulled out three quid and gave it to him – at which point Tommy suggested that it might be time to leave. So we jumped into this Ford van we'd borrowed for the night and took off like a jet – with Johnny York driving and Mike sprawled out in the back. We knew that if the bookie found out, he would probably chop our legs off! East End bookmakers were not known for their largesse!"

The only other gig that line-up did was a Sunday lunchtime pub date, again somewhere in the East End. Wally went back to his Breadbasket mates, while Tommy shared his time between the G, the unpredictable company of Mike Pratt and his clique, and the Merchant Navy.

"When I was a kid, my mates and I always used to wonder what people got up to north of the Thames – but we were frightened to go out of Bermondsey," Tommy explained in a BBC interview. "Everyone used to talk about London Bridge and Waterloo Bridge, and everyone used to dream about going over, because we were under the impression that people like us weren't allowed in the West End. That was reinforced the first time we tried it: a copper stopped us half-way across Waterloo Bridge. I think there was some sort of scare about air guns at the time and he grabbed one of my mates to search him. The rest of us just ran for our lives!"

Thomas Hicks was born on 17 December 1936, in Mason Street, off the Old Kent Road, the eldest of four children. The family would have been larger had three more not died in infancy and considerably smaller had the German Air Force come any closer. As it was, they were bombed out of two different houses in Mason Street and were forced to move some three-quarters of a mile to Dockhead, off Jamaica Road.

"We had the bottom floor in a block of flats called Nickleby House, which was the best one to have because you could jump around as much as you liked without disturbing the neighbours below," recalled Tommy. Of course, the only trouble with that was the possibility of getting dodgy ones upstairs, keeping you awake at night."

There would be parties in the street, initially motivated by news that one of the residents was coming home from a prisoner-of-war camp, and fights in the street, usually started by kids but sometimes with parents drawn in. Despite this, the feeling of community, of belonging, was strong.

Before long, the Hicks family was on the move again, this time a stone's throw away to a terraced house not far from the railway bridge in Frean Street, number 52. Thomas Hicks Sr was in the racing business, selling lists of runners at race meetings; his wife, Elizabeth, did piece work.

"We were never poverty stricken – our parents were too hard working for that – and we were always dressed properly. No one could ever point a finger and say he's got the back of his trousers hanging out. Our hard times were watching our mother work. She was ill and should have been in hospital, but she wouldn't go. My father would say 'please go into hospital, love,' but she would say, 'No, I won't leave the kids.'"

When Tommy was considered old enough, he would be allowed to accompany his mum and dad to the Gregorian Arms in Jamaica Road on a Saturday night. "I sometimes used to take a record along and mime to it. That was the first time I performed in front of people."

He'd gone to sea at 15, working first as a pantry boy, then as a lift-boy. (His hip-to-the-trip manager John Kennedy later put it about that he'd been a 'bell-hop', knowing full well that the only bell-hop most teenagers in England had heard of was the one who worked at *Heartbreak Hotel*.) He subsequently worked his way up to assistant steward and was now a gymnastic instructor – though a few months later, when he was getting famous and the press hadn't yet decided whether to be nice or nasty to him, the *Sunday Pictorial* quoted the Secretary of the Shipping Federation, Mr H.W. Greaney, as saying: "His story is extraordinary; we have no record of him as a physical training instructor."

Now assigned to the Cunard liner *Mauretania*, he was on the Atlantic run, with two weeks off in New York and two weeks off at home between crossings. On occasion, some of the 1,150 passengers were treated to his Norman Wisdom impressions. A friend was quoted as saying: "He's very popular with the old dears" . . . but it wasn't old dears on Tommy's mind. "I had the greatest thing in the world going for me," he said. "I had a job that I loved, which was the navy, and I had a guitar on my back, which was very rare at that time. I had a load of songs and I could sit in the corner of a coffee bar, start singing, and gather an audience . . . and nine times out of ten, in that audience would be a chick, and she would be intrigued by this highly tanned 19 year old with cropped hair, who sang and played and drank coffee and talked about the world – which he'd seen! I was in clover."

He had been taught guitar on board, by a scouser, who showed him enough basic chords to get going. "I was singing on the ship for a good two years, which is why, when I came ashore in summer 1956, I had this whole backlog of songs – mostly country, but with a few rock 'n' roll numbers mixed in."

All of a sudden, his music was fashionable. He had done more and seen more than any subsequent rock 'n' roll wannabe ever would, but he was 19, naïve and vulnerable, sailing into uncharted waters. "When I'm asked about South London," he would say later, "the first thing I think of is honest, down-to-earth people." It was his way to be friendly, to accept people at face value, to expect that South London integrity. He was planning to go back to sea, once his leave was up, and was bemused when music-biz types began to hover. "I loved my life. The idea of people coming up and telling me they were going to make a star of me was quite ludicrous really, because no-one was going to give me more than I already had."

Dennis Grayman, a photographer working for the Moss Empires theatre chain, arranged two auditions: one with Solly Black of the Lew & Leslie Grade Agency, the other with Ruby Bard of Freddy Randall's agency. Both proclaimed his talent too raw. Tin Pan Alley was about to undergo its biggest upheaval ever – but nobody could see it coming, mainly because they didn't want to see it coming.

There were exceptions. Having been consulted by Johnny Booker and Wally Whyton of the Vipers, who had written a song that Lonnie Donegan wanted to record, the guys who ran Trio Recording Service – Bill Varley and Roy Tuvey – sensed that change was in the air. Perhaps some of the skifflers down at the Gyre & Gimble could find a wider audience, even if they were a motley crew.

"We were doing well with our recording business," says Varley, "but neither of us knew much about management. Roy was more business-like than me. I was better at taking care of the equipment; he was better at doing the chat. We worked well together."

Tuvey wanted to sign Tommy Hicks and, to assist him in this enterprise, brought in the more experienced Geoff Wright, an agent with offices in Charing Cross Road. They apparently came to some sort of arrangement with Tommy – who didn't look as if he was ready to go back to sea just yet.

September 1956 would be the pivotal month of his life. Tuvey and Wright arranged for Tommy to play a guest spot with the Vipers at the 2Is Coffee Bar on Old Compton Street, where they now had a residency. Knowing they were not au fait with the world of publicity, they invited John Kennedy along, to see if he thought their boy had any potential and, if he had, to ruminate on ways in which he could be promoted. Kennedy was blown away. Not only by Tommy's performance of *Heartbreak Hotel*, but by the possibilities he felt raining down on them both.

A New Zealander, Kennedy had been, and still was, a photographer. At the start of 1955, just back in London after several weeks in Los Angeles, he was running the *Record Mirror*'s photographic studio at 21 Gerrard Street. Whilst in Hollywood, he'd photographed Marilyn Monroe at the 20th Century Fox studio, as she was filming the final scenes of *The Seven Year Itch*. Not the last John Kennedy to take an interest in her. And such an apposite title too. Why and how he branched out into PR and publicity remains hazy, but that was clearly his calling.

Kennedy had already worked (hence the summons) with Geoff Wright, doing the publicity for a stage-play in which he had financial involvement, *The House Of Shame*. It had opened, to paltry audiences, in November 1955 at the Grand Theatre in Luton, a decaying vaudeville relic, which normally tried to make ends meet by staging nude revues with such titles as *Yes We Have No Pyjamas* and *Eve Without Leaves*. Kennedy suggested the play be renamed *Woman Of The Streets*, did his best to get some favourable press, but quickly learned that all the promotion in the world would never give flight to a turkey.

This time, it was different. Tommy would soar like a golden eagle, glide like a golden goose, of this he was convinced. Total certainty, never a shred of doubt. There at the 2Is, he was looking at a star.

Tommy remembered the evening as well as he did, even years later, when he was telling his story to the BBC. "I'll never forget his first words to me. I'd left one coffee bar and gone to another, which is what I'd do, and this fellow followed me. He had been a photographer for the *Daily Sketch*, I think, and he said 'I've been watching you and I wonder if you'd be interested in doing it professionally, in the theatre?' So I looked at this nut-case and said 'What are you talking about?' He said 'Well, I think I could make you a star very quickly.' I said 'What do you know about show business?' and he said 'Absolutely nothing! What do you know about singing?'

I said 'Nothing' . . . so he said 'Why don't we try it?' – which is what we did."

No mention of either Tuvey or Wright, who were still very much involved at this point, the first week of September 1956.

Realising that Tommy Hicks would not look particularly alluring in lights, he and Kennedy huddled over a more dynamic name. It was Tommy who suggested Steel, after his grandfather Thomas Stil Hicks, but an E was later added by mistake (courtesy of Decca) and that modification stuck. Tommy Steele. It would last a lifetime.

Only days after their first encounter, Kennedy pulled off a classic publicity wheeze, a stroke of genius which purred like clockwork from the moment he had the brainwave. Presciently, he explained to Tommy that "rock 'n' roll music had got a bad name from Teddy boy hooligans who wrecked cinemas and broke up cafés – but it was coming to Europe nonetheless. It would get bigger, and anyone who went along with it would himself grow big on the crest of a wave. But someone has got to lift it out of its Teddy boy rut, give it class and get society as well as the thousands of ordinary decent kids singing and dancing it." He knew that Tommy was the boy to do it.

On Sunday 16 September, readers of *The People* (whose circulation was then in excess of 4.5 million) woke up to see a photograph of Tommy, cavorting at full tilt across the front page. 'ROCK AND ROLL HAS GOT THE DEBS TOO!' proclaimed the headline. "Now the smart set are at it," ran the story, "and here's what the camera saw happening at the first rock 'n' roll society party in London. They started at eight in the evening and they kept it rockin' until dawn."

At a house in Wandsworth, "demure debs leapt from their chairs. 'Keep it goin', chicks!' yelled Tommy, and soon the joint was really jumping." Among the guests were Patricia Scott-Brown, Valerie Thornton-Smith and Gerald Bernard, "an industrialist's son, who changed his stiff collar for a check shirt".

As the sun came up, "Britain's top rock 'n' roll guitarist Tommy Steel sagged helplessly in his chair and gasped 'Gee, you cats have rocked me to a standstill.'"

In his biography, *Tommy Steele; The facts about a teenage idol and an inside picture of Show Business*, Kennedy reveals how he had suggested the story to the newspaper's editor, organised the party at a friend's house, and had a photographer ready to capture Tommy sending the guests into an orgasmic trance with his exciting music.

The 'debs' were "a dozen girls from shows or model agencies who agreed to give phony, aristocratic sounding names if they were quizzed by reporters."

The first and one of the greatest hypes in rock history. But it could never have succeeded had Tommy not had the capacity and ambition to follow it through.

Immediately, he was asked to do a residency at the upmarket Stork Club, and again his photograph appeared in newspapers. Biographical details began to emerge: he went to the Gravesend Sea School at 15, learned how to make a sea bed and set a table, found out what a dipping lug rig was and what it did, passed the Board of Trade lifeboat test. Worked on tramp steamers and the *Queen of Bermuda*. He had spent three months at Guy's Hospital after being taken ill on board, bought a guitar when he was well enough to resume work and took it on every voyage. Rumours of his talents were so strong, according to *The Stage*, a trade paper for the theatrical set, that when he docked in August, after what was to be his last voyage, "at the quayside, Geoff Wright was waiting to audition him and give him a five-year contract."

As his three-week Stork Club season got under way, another manager entered the picture, the fourth man, Larry Parnes. He was known to both Wright and Kennedy, having put money into the ill-fated play *Woman Of The Streets*, and both knew that he was itching to get into show business.

Just turned 27, Parnes was bored with the fashion trade, with working in ladies' dress shops, the family business. According to Parnes, in an interview with a somewhat sozzled Jack de Manio, Kennedy approached him and asked him what he thought about rock 'n' roll. "I told him I didn't know what rock 'n' roll was, which I didn't, and he told me that it was going to be very big. He said 'I've seen this boy who I think has got talent and I need a businessman behind me – would you come and see him?' So I went to this little coffee bar (it was, in fact, the Stork Club) to see him work and thought there was something tremendously exciting about him. He said 'Hello, guv, I understand that you're going to be my new manager'. It all happened very quickly."

Later that week, Brian Daley, another guitarist on the scene, bumped into Tommy on the street. "How's it going, Hicksy?" he asked. "Oh, great," Tommy replied, "I've got four managers now!"

He seemed very pleased, and so he should: he was about to cut his first record.

After one company had turned him down, Hugh Mendl at Decca agreed to audition him, not at the 2Is but at the company's West Hampstead studios. The orchestra leader Frank Chacksfield had apparently put in a good word for him. "Unfortunately, no-one had checked to see whether either of the studios was free," recalled Mendl, "so I ended up listening to him in an artists' rest room; just Tommy, a bass player and a drummer, no microphone. He sang *Rock With The Caveman* and, although I had little idea of whether his voice would record, I detected an absolutely fabulous magic. Everyone was being rude about rock 'n' roll but this was such a magical performance and he had such a dynamic personality that, after only a chorus or two, I stopped him and said 'Yes! This is absolutely perfect!' It was only a few days later that we had him into the studio and made the first record."

John Kennedy had a *Melody Maker* photographer on hand to catch the moment and they put Tommy on the front page.

Two songs were cut that day, *Rock With The Caveman* and *Rock Around The Town*. Both were originals, the latter written by Tommy, the former a Steele/Bart/Pratt collaboration, the first of many. On occasion, on his way home from the Gyre & Gimble, Tommy would drop into the Yellow Door, a stand-alone house surrounded by bombsites in Baylis Road, not far beyond Waterloo Station. No number, just a yellow door. A commune before its time, it was sub-divided into bed-sits and small apartments and a party was usually in progress. Among the residents were Maurice Agis, later an acclaimed sculptor but then a student at St Martins School of Art, Tony Bucket from the City Ramblers, and Mike Pratt, a typographer then working at Dorlands Advertising thanks to a recommendation from Wally Whyton. Visitors included Kenneth Haigh, about to star in *Look Back In Anger* at the Royal Court Theatre, jazz fans John Jack and Johnny Pilgrim, future playwright John Antrobus, film star Shirley Eaton, and Lionel Bart, a young communist and aspiring songwriter.

It was at one of these all-night parties that Steele, Bart and Pratt sat in a corner and put together *Rock With The Caveman* – the words of which alluded to the Piltdown Man, skull fragments and bones found in a Sussex quarry which were originally thought to have been the missing link between apes and humans but had recently been exposed as a hoax. "Tommy had a melody and a riff and a title," Lionel recalled, "Mike threw in some changes, and I did a bunch of lyrics. We used to perform it as a party piece at the Caves de France on Dean Street, a little club run by a French woman, Philippe, who used to let us run up credit . . . not that I was into booze then – that came later!"

Cut on Monday 24 September, the record had the rhythm and drive of rock 'n' roll, but the words, though different and amusing, were more suited to a revue. The backing was basic, provided by respected players from the bop and swing world, including Detroit-born bassist Major Holley and Johnny Dankworth's pianist Dave Lee, who was considered to be one of the most innovative players on the scene but here sounded like a first year student on Sparky's magic piano. Fats Domino he wasn't. Some rock 'n' roll purists (a pedant class had already formed, a handful of obsessed kids in every town) saw the record as a novelty, a failure to grasp the genre, but all involved were working in the dark. Later, Tommy would reveal that the Cavemen used to describe themselves as a "country and comedy" team and that their theme song *Rock With The Caveman* was really written as a spoof.

By the time it was released, Roy Tuvey and Geoff Wright were fading from view. Very soon, it was as if they had been airbrushed from the picture altogether, as comprehensively as the pubic hair on photographs in *Health & Efficiency*.

What exactly happened remained unclear until a High Court case in 1960, in which John Kennedy and Larry Parnes brought a libel action against the publishers of *Weekly Sporting Review and Show Business*, and one of its journalists, Fraser White, who had written what he alleged to be 'The Real Steele Story'. White suggested that he had been threatened with violence if he went ahead with his article, which, after discussing Tuvey and Wright's entrance and exit, concluded "It's not only artists who get carved up in showbiz."

On the first day of the case, held before Mr Justice Havers, the man who had sentenced Ruth Ellis to death five years earlier, the plaintiffs' barrister detailed a clandestine meeting between Wright and Parnes. "Mr Wright put up what the jury might think was a thoroughly discreditable proposition. It was that he and Mr Parnes should exploit Steele through a company and that he should sign

Steele and sell his services to the company for £20 a week. The company would derive the profits of exploiting Steele. Mr Wright said Mr Kennedy would receive 10 per cent of the £20 a week it was proposed to pay Steele."

"Mr Parnes was horrified," continued Mr Helenus Milmo (for that was the barrister's magnificent name), "because it meant not only swindling Steele but was a scandalous proposition as far as Mr Kennedy was concerned. Mr Wright did not even bother to attend Steele's opening night. He refused to put a penny towards buying him a shirt for this great and all-important occasion."

When Kennedy heard about Wright's plan, he suggested that he and Parnes should see Tommy's mother and her solicitor. This they did.

"At that stage," Mr Milmo continued, "Steele said he had signed something at Mr Wright's request but had not been told what it was. Mrs Hicks' solicitor wrote to Mr Tuvey and Mr Wright giving notice of Tommy Steele's intention to repudiate any agreements between them."

Giving evidence, Larry Parnes said he "did not like the smell of Mr Wright's proposition. It was an unfair deal for a young man just starting in the business."

Three song contracts were also discussed. "The first was between Tommy Steele, Wright and Tuvey as the composers and authors of a song called *Rock Around The Town* and a music publishing company," reported *The Times*. "As far as the plaintiffs were aware, Wright and Tuvey had never composed one note of music at any time and certainly had not written any part of *Rock Around The Town*. Under the contract, Wright and Tuvey got 66 per cent of the proceeds of the sale of the song and Steele got 33 per cent. The jury might think that they were nice, helpful, kind and generous managers when that was the sort of thing they were doing behind this boy's back. Tommy Steele never signed that contract and was never told about it."

Wright and Tuvey had also added their names to *Pretty Daisy*, a song written by Tommy Steele, Lionel Bart and Mike Pratt – so the jury was told – with the result that each stood to gain 20 per cent of the proceeds. Furthermore, as Bart explained, the name of Frank Chacksfield had curiously been added to the credits of *Rock With The Caveman* – "so that he could get his cut of one quarter". Bart had contributed a rare moment of levity to the proceedings when asked if he was indeed the author of *Things Aren't What They Used To Be*. "Actually," he replied, "it was called *Fings Ain't What They Used To Be*." And, of course, in true Cocklecarrot style, Mr Justice Havers had at one point demanded "I think we should be told where Tin Pan Alley is".

Six days into the hearing, the defendants offered a full apology and retraction in respect of both the libel and the particulars of justification.

On 26 September 1956, after discussions with Tommy, his mother and her solicitor, Parnes and Kennedy entered a management contract with Steele, which guaranteed him 60 per cent of his gross takings. From their 40 per cent, Parnes and Kennedy would bear all costs, including "10 per cent to a booking agent, the expenses of travelling, accommodation, advertising, publicity, entertainment and every possible thing needed to keep Tommy on the road to stardom." It was a good deal for Steele, one that many a subsequent star would have loved to sign.

October was the breakthrough month.

On the twelfth, *Rock With The Caveman* was released. The *NME* was not impressed: "Decca's British rock 'n' roll record by Tommy Steele lacks the essential authentic flavour. Best thing on the disc is Ronnie Scott's driving tenor sax playing."

Three days later, Tommy made his television debut on Jack Payne's BBC show *Off The Record*. Viewers were left wide-eyed after a vigorous performance that must have shaken not only the staid presenter but also the show's other guests, Kenneth McKellar and Joan Regan. "Hopefully, he's just another of these here today, gone tomorrow novelty acts," thought the music-biz, "he won't be around for long."

By the end of the month, *Rock With The Caveman* was in the Top 20 and Tommy was suddenly in demand. After his appearance on Jack Jackson's Sunday night ATV show, the *NME*'s Alley Cat could not contain his antediluvian views. "Does Tommy Steele expect to gain more popularity by appearing with untidy hair, as he did on Jack Jackson's show?" Oh yes! Something is happening but you don't know what it is, do you Mr Cat?

John Kennedy must have been cock-a-hoop. Everything was going to plan, the next step of which was a national tour. In his book, dedicated to "the agents who showed us the door", he tells of those who ridiculed him out of the office and in doing so passed up a chance to laugh all the way to the bank. Only Harold Fielding shared his enthusiasm, agreeing on £150 per week for a six-week variety tour. Tommy would top the bill – which he has continued to do from that day to this. Starting on 5 November, he would play six nights a week (Sundays off for good behaviour), two shows a night, at Sunderland Empire, Nottingham Empire, Sheffield Empire, Brighton Hippodrome, Finsbury Park Empire and Birmingham Hippodrome. Supporting him would be the young comedy duo Mike and Bernie Winters, Johnny Laycock (renowned for his ability to play four trumpets at once!), singer and comic Reg Thompson, pianist Thunderclap Jones ('classics, boogie-woogie and pops from the wild Welshman of the keyboards'), soprano singer Josephine Anne and the Marie de Vere Dancers.

The world was in worse chaos and turmoil than usual, as the front page of the *Sunderland Echo* confirmed: 'Airborne landings in Egypt going well' and 'Hungary is cut off from outside world as Russian troops seize control' were the headlines. Inside was Tommy's maiden live review. "A 19-year-old youth, giving his first ever variety stage performance, couples boyish shyness with simple vibrant ability. Tommy Steele is a rock 'n' roll specialist but there is nothing raucous or discordant in the lilting, hilly-billy type tunes he has to offer – most of them his own compositions. He is gifted with a catching exuberance; he can please the old as well as send the young." The reviewer was spot on.

The Stage was similarly pleased: "Oh, how the crowd enjoyed his closing rock 'n' roll numbers. Yes, Tommy certainly made his mark. It was due to the pleasing way in which he presented his act and not the noisy fashion that was expected by some people."

Harold Fielding extended his tour from six weeks to 10; three weeks ahead of Christmas, Tommy's photograph was already in the identity bracelets being offered for sale in newspapers and magazines; and he featured twice in *NME*'s year-end readers' poll – number eight in the Outstanding British Male Singer section and number 12 in the Outstanding British Musical Personality section.

As he celebrated his twentieth birthday, on 17 December 1956, Tommy was already an acclaimed all-round entertainer, on his way to becoming the self-taught Renaissance man of rock 'n' roll.

Sixteen

"A year of what I can only describe as hysterical transition," was how jazz saxophonist/journalist Benny Green summed up 1956 in his last *NME* column of the year. Every modern jazz and dance band musician he knew was asking the same question: "What is to become of us all?" Their style of playing was old and in the way, last year's model. It was over. Teenagers had arrived and it looked as if he and his ilk were heading for the poorhouse – unless they could embrace the new music, as his sidekick Ronnie Scott had on *Rock With The Caveman*. "What are our prospects?" Green asked. "Pretty bad. None of us is getting any younger and, apart from Tommy Steele and Lonnie Donegan, none of us is getting any richer."

Bill Haley was largely to blame for the sad state of affairs. The American rock 'n' roll invasion had actually started two years earlier, with this trailblazing corrupter of youth out in front, waving the flag. Then, however, he was seen merely as a novelty.

In the States, rock had been seeping into the mainstream since white teenagers first got wind of how much more exciting than the processed fare fed to them was the music being made for the Negro market. *Billboard* magazine first noted the trend in April 1954 and by the end of that year, such records as *Earth Angel* by the Penguins, *Sh-Boom* by the Chords and *Hearts Of Stone* by the Charms had even made the national pop best-sellers lists as a result of crossing over from the black rhythm & blues field. Unlike Britain, best seller charts in America were not published for the curiosity and interest of the consumer, but exclusively for the business – so that stores knew which records to order, so that area distributors could keep abreast of national demographics, so that record companies and publishers knew what was selling and where – and, to the delight of some and the consternation of others, rhythm & blues seemed to be catching on, expanding its audience.

It had been a natural process but, as the trend for black music (we'll call it black music, even though that term wasn't invented until years later) picked up, white sharpies and enthusiasts became increasingly interested, influenced and involved. The canal connecting black music with the white teenage audience was completed in August 1954, when disc jockey Alan Freed, a wild but shrewd rock 'n' roll proselytiser, moved from Cleveland to New York, hired by the bigwigs at the hugely popular radio station WINS for purely commercial reasons. They had detected which way the wind was blowing and acted accordingly. To have Freed playing this new-fangled music that the teenagers seemed to admire would increase their audience and therefore their income. Everybody would be happy. (Except those bible-belters and bible-thumpers who saw rock 'n' roll as sinful, corrupt and depraved, of course.)

In Britain, rock 'n' roll sneaked in unnoticed and unheeded. A couple of weeks before Christmas 1954, a record called *Shake Rattle And Roll* by Bill Haley & his Comets crept into the *NME* chart at number 13. Radio Luxembourg and American Forces Network listeners had obviously fallen for it. It had never been played on BBC radio and it had not been reviewed in the music press. A case of spontaneous combustion, no less.

Though they knew practically nothing about it, the editor and his crew at the *NME* accepted rock 'n' roll and reviewed the odd record – but the staff of *Melody Maker* found it so contemptible and vile, so beneath them that they couldn't even bring themselves to acknowledge its existence. They, like the hidebound bods at the BBC, saw rock 'n' roll as dog-waste on the pavement they had to walk every day.

Nevertheless, despite the ostriches in the media, rock 'n' roll started to catch on, through a groundswell of American records and songs tickling the tills of the British recording and publishing industry. This process resulted in an increasing number of US rock 'n' roll hits being released here (though rarely, if ever, getting played by the BBC and thus having little chance of selling or charting) alongside cover versions of those hits, made by British artists. The latter always had far more chance of airplay; the Musicians' Union restricted needle-time (as playing music from records was described) and the BBC invariably favoured domestic artists. They also broadcast many hours of live music and could obviously assist the careers of acts like the Stargazers or the Beverley Sisters rather more than those of the Moonglows or the Penguins.

Thus, we saw (but preferred not to hear) a sudden splurge of rock 'n' roll cover versions. If American purists thought the vanilla interpretations of the Crew Cuts and Pat Boone were dire and wretched, they should have heard some of the excruciating efforts foisted upon us. Of which, more soon.

The state of Britain's pre-rock 'n' roll pop scene can be gauged by glancing at the top five best selling records of 1954:

1 *Secret Love* by Doris Day – the big romantic ballad from her hit movie, *Calamity Jane*.

2 *Cara Mia* by David Whitfield – an opera-style ballad that could never be sung by anyone not wearing a tuxedo and a very serious expression.

3 *The Happy Wanderer* by The Oberkirchen Children's Choir – catchy sing-along, chorusy, escapist fluff from Germany, of all places.

4 *Little Things Mean A Lot* by Kitty Kallen – a mushy, gushy, mawkish ballad from the States, where it was the year's top seller.

5 *Oh Mein Papa* by Eddie Calvert – po-faced singers mewl sentimental gloop while Eddie blows away on his celebrated golden trumpet.

The sixth record, however, was *Such A Night* by Johnnie Ray – with a lyric so torrid that American radio stations had banned the original by black vocal group Clyde McPhatter & the Drifters. "Just the thought of her lips sets me afire" ran the lyric and one sensed what lips Clyde was singing about. Despite the imprecations of *MM* scribe Laurie Henshaw and others, the histrionic Ray, the bridge between Sinatra and Elvis, had become a phenomenon in Britain. Wherever he appeared, women of all ages were screaming and swooning, waiting outside the stage door, anxious to tear off his clothes and handle his private parts. Much good would it have done them.

In Edinburgh, uncontrollable fans broke into his hotel and knocked him unconscious, ripping his £80 suit to shreds. "If I'd known I was going to get a reception like this," said Ray, "I would have worn some old clothes." Clamouring girls clambered onto his car, while others had toes crushed by its wheels. A thirteen year old was hospitalised.

At the end of his record-breaking fortnight at the London Palladium, he sat on the edge of the roof at the back of the theatre and waved to fans, who had blocked Great Marlborough Street as police looked on helplessly.

There was no British equivalent; only gentle pandemonium greeted performances by Dickie Valentine, David Whitfield, Ronnie Hilton, Dennis Lotis and the other smoothies.

Already, worship of America and all things American was an established religion among the young and progressive, who had spent their childhood in a battered and bruised world of Woodbines, war widows, ration books, bus queues, bomb sites, outside toilets, Butlin's, smog, fish and chips in newspaper, utility furniture, downcast faces, them and us. To British teenagers raised on films and comics, and force-fed Empire-orientated history lessons, much of Europe was rubble; Asia was communist or wog; the Far East was geeky Japs and slimy Chinks; Australia was convicts and people who talked like Chips Rafferty; Africa was mud-huts and Boers; South America was straw-skirts and blowpipes and cattle; Canada was where boring English people emigrated.

In his essay *Boys' Weeklies*, on many an O level syllabus, George Orwell had laid it out: "As a rule it is assumed that foreigners of any one race are all alike and will conform more or less exactly to the following patterns:

Frenchman: wears beard, gesticulates wildly.

Spaniard, Mexican, etc: sinister, treacherous.

Arab, Afghan, etc: sinister, treacherous.

Chinese: sinister, treacherous, wears pigtail.

Italian: excitable, grinds barrel organ or carries stiletto.

Swede, Dane, etc: kind-hearted, stupid."

Although written in 1940, Orwell's stereotypes were still alive and well in the mid-fifties.

But the United States! The United States had the best music, cars, girls, clothes, gangsters, Negroes, cowboys, songwriters, singers, jazz musicians, films, film stars, records, trains, planes, jukeboxes, flag, weather, beaches, history, geographical features, place names, rivers, hairstyles, money, television programmes, sport, street names, food, skyscrapers, athletes, boxers, confectionary, sunshine, comics, the best of everything, so we believed.

Even stentorian balladeer David Whitfield, a stiff and starchy 28 year old from Hull, decided to buy a Buick when he had amassed sufficient money. Did he want a black Rover or a black Morris? No. He'd seen the adverts in American magazines. He knew that across the Atlantic, cars came in ultramarine and cream, coral and charcoal, complemented by acres of chrome! Designed by people with the imagination of abstract artists, they were beautiful sculptures just like so many of the records that were coming out over there.

When rock 'n' roll arrived here, it was regarded as an aberration, a five-minute wonder. There was no intimation of a hell bent youth movement rising up and riding on its back. It was just another fad – exactly like the mambo, which was happening simultaneously. For those twixt school and marriage, or any working-class couple with a bit of spare cash, 'going out' meant either the cinema, the theatre (usually a variety show) or dancing. Dance halls thrived in every town, with creaky orchestras and bands reading from music stands. A waltz, a foxtrot, a spot of Latin American for the show-offs, a few perennial songs rendered by the resident vocalists, a quick-step, and maybe a bit of novelty rock 'n' roll for those energetic enough. Its UK publisher, Campbell Connelly & Co, had sheet music and dance band orchestrations ready for *Shake Rattle And Roll* as soon as it showed any sign of becoming popular. It was all very orderly. If you've ever seen *Come Dancing*, you've got the picture. Just imagine a primitive version in grainy 505-line black and white.

So, nobody got worried or even anxious when rock 'n' roll arrived in Britain. No sense of threat; no fear of change. It was just a bit of fun. A newly discovered vegetable thrown into the stew.

Strictly, Bill Haley's wasn't the first rock 'n' roll record to chart here. The Crew Cuts' version of *Sh-Boom* made the Top 20 during the first week of October 1954 – but no-one identified that as rock 'n' roll. The expression wasn't known here then, and that record was regarded as just another vocal group novelty, a zestful, playful piece of nonsense on a par with Max Bygraves' *Gilly Gilly Ossenfeffer Katzenellen Bogen By The Sea*, which was popular around the same time. When Stan Freberg's *Sh-Boom* parody charted the following month, everyone knew for sure that the song was a joke. (Everyone except the handful who admired the Chords' original, released here on EMI's Columbia label.)

Bill Haley's *Shake Rattle And Roll* bounced around the Top 20 for 14 weeks – joined for just a fortnight (the first two weeks of the New

Year) by his previous single, *Rock Around The Clock*. Haley was obviously the originator of this new genre, so the public at large believed. Well, maybe not . . . but he was the leading exponent. He'd been experimenting with the hybrid for a while, moving away from western swing and cowboy music towards the teen scene. His 1952 recording of *Rock The Joint* featured a strong back beat, a slapped bass and a lyric which described not only a party, but a scene of venery and vandalism. Danny Cedrone played a guitar solo of such intuitive brilliance that Haley got him to duplicate it on *Rock Around The Clock*, a couple of years later. Though *Rock The Joint* was not a hit, Haley saw the way audiences reacted to it and modified accordingly, changing the name of his band from the Saddlemen to the Comets and concentrating on contemporary music rather than cowboy weepers. Subsequent recordings *Crazy Man Crazy* and *Fractured*, both peppered with teen jargon, confirmed his new direction but, for a while at least, he seemed to be going nowhere fast.

When it fell out of the UK Top 20 after only two weeks, his record company thought they'd lost *Rock Around The Clock*, that its sales potential was expended. Often a record sold steadily over a year or so, but usually, once a single had dropped from the chart, that was the last one heard of it. It was beyond Haley's wildest dreams that the record could ever be revived – let alone become the eternal anthem of rock 'n' roll.

Through 1955, the genre (few would have dared to call it a style) showed no perceptible sign of stabilising. No one could have foreseen the coming avalanche from the trickle of rolling stones.

Released at the end of January, Bill Haley's *Dim Dim The Lights/Happy Baby* had all the fingerprints of another winner, according to the *NME*'s perceptive reviewer Geoffrey Everitt (who was moonlighting from his real job as a disc jockey on Radio Luxembourg): "two more fine sides . . . how these boys rock!" Sometimes he goofed, but Everitt was one of the very first journalists to see rock 'n' roll as a positive force; the first to pin his colours to his sleeve and declare unashamed love for it. His enthusiastic review hit quite a few nails on the head.

"I marvel at the wonderful beat, which is something we never seem to get in this country. The recording engineers have decided not to hide the drummer in the background. As for the gentleman on the guitar, he really can play."

"This is more than just a new record release; it is the answer to those who think that groovy records do not sell. The atmosphere on this disc is amazing; when you listen to *Happy Baby*, sit back and think when you last heard something as good. *Dim Dim The Lights* is also in the rave class – and when Bill Haley sings 'the beat is jumping like a kangaroo', he just about sums up the whole record."

"Sorry to say it again, but this is a fantastic rhythm section and if you can only afford one record this week, I suggest you make certain it is this one. You won't regret it."

One infers that he liked it.

Unfortunately, it didn't sell – which led optimistic fogies to hope that the rock 'n' roll craze was dead and buried, please God . . . but less than three months later, Haley found his way back to the charts by covering both fad-bases with *Mambo Rock*.

Geoffrey Everitt went overboard again: "Bill Haley's brand of music is the most exciting that I've heard for many years and this record looks like being another big hit. What is it that puts this group way out in front?"

"Well, first and foremost, I think is the terrific atmosphere, coupled with the tremendous driving beat from the rhythm section. Bill's singing has that essence of brightness and enthusiasm that is so rarely heard. These sides just rock from start to finish and every instrumentalist is just playing his heart out."

For two weeks only, it became another quirky, colourful thread in an eclectic chart tapestry that also included the tinkly piano of Winifred Atwell (described by her agency as 'Trinidad's Dusky Queen of the Keys'); the country & western strains of Tennessee Ernie Ford, whose *Give Me Your Word* was at number one; the jaunty whimsicality of Alma Cogan's *I Can't Tell A Waltz From A Tango*; the wild and slithering cha-cha-cha of Cuban-born Perez Prado, whose *Cherry Blossom Pink And Apple Blossom White* had surfaced after being featured in the Jane Russell movie *Underwater*; and the religioso schmaltz of records like *Hold My Hand* by Don Cornell and *Count Your Blessings* by Bing Crosby.

Also on a chart roll were the Prince and Princess of British pop, Dickie Valentine and Ruby Murray. Ruby was an open, fresh-faced, innocent, soft-voiced colleen from Belfast, straddling her twentieth birthday with a run of seven consecutive Top 10 hits that would propel her into cockney rhyming slang.

Teen and twenties heart-throb Dickie Valentine, who in a couple of years would be about as fashionable as Gilbert Harding's haircut, was peaking commercially despite his recent marriage. *Finger Of Suspicion* had seen the year in at number one. On a streak that had also sprung the Stargazers (*Broken Wings* and *I See The Moon*) and Lita Roza (*How Much Is That Doggie In The Window*) to the top of the chart, his adept producer Dick Rowe would still go to his grave haunted by his failure to have detected any commercial potential in the Beatles, poor bugger.

As soon as white-market covers of rhythm & blues hits started selling in America, British acts were pressed into recording even less subtle or respectful versions. It was the practice of record company Artists & Repertoire managers to obtain advance pre-release copies of US hits and see which songs they could match to artists on their roster. Not for a minute did anyone stop to consider how ludicrous this practice was. Jimmy Young would cheerfully go into the studio and make a pig's ear of *Unchained Melody* without batting an eyelid. Even more strangely, enough people would actually go out and buy it to lift it to number one! Then he would go in and warble *The Man From Laramie* – and that too would reach number one! That is how it was done.

It was all fantasy, suspension of disbelief, so no one gave it a second thought – and, of course, equally ridiculous charades were being enacted on the other side of the Atlantic. Take, for instance, the case of Frankie Laine, a 42-year-old, be-wigged, tuxedoed, Jewish, Italianate, Chicagoan cabaret singer who came on like a fringed frontiersman from the last century. In pre-TV days, before we got a good look at him, hits like *Mule Train, The Cry Of The Wild Goose, High Noon, Blowing Wild, Hawk-Eye, Sixteen Tons* and *Cool Water* gave him the aspect of a big wide-open-spaces adventurer, taking adversity in his stride.

The only adversity he had to worry about in those days was a bit of snow on the pavement between the stage door and the limousine – but in his youth, he'd been pretty cool: in 1932, he'd entered a marathon dance competition in Atlantic City, and achieved a world record of 3,501 hours in 145 consecutive days! (Don't ask me to elaborate on this – it sounds preposterous, but that is the accepted legend.) He and Guy Mitchell were acceptable enough; their records above all others made them seem like credible, hip, male-teen heroes before more basic music struck.

The first British R&B/rock 'n' roll covers came in 1953, led by such unforgettable monstrosities as *Crazy Man Crazy* by Lita Roza and *Crying In The Chapel* by Robert Earl. The following year we were assailed by *Sh-Boom* by Four In A Chord and the Johnston Brothers; *Goodnight Sweetheart Goodnight* by the Beverley Sisters, Anne Shelton and the Stargazers; *ABC Boogie* by the Five Smith Brothers (who also recorded *We Want Muffin, Muffin The Mule* – so they were obviously bona fide, certified rock 'n' rollers); and *Honey Love* by Dennis Lotis.

During the first half of 1955, everyone was (as the most over-used cliché of the year proclaimed) climbing onto the bandwagon: new music but the same old singers. The beautiful Moonglows' ballad *Sincerely* – already put through the flour mill by the snow-white McGuire Sisters – was pulverised by Rose Brennan and the Joe Loss Orchestra, Muriel Smith and the Wally Stott Orchestra, Jill Day and the Ron Goodwin Orchestra, and – yes – the man with the golden crumpet himself, Eddie Calvert. *Tweedle Dee* was mauled by Frankie Vaughan, Suzi Miller, Billie Anthony, the Kirchin Band and Alma Cogan, among others. *Dance With Me Henry* and *Pledging My Love* were stripped of nuances by Suzi Miller and Rose Brennan, respectively. *Shake Rattle And Roll* was comprehensively mutilated by Jack Parnell & His Orchestra and *Rock Around The Clock* was turned into acceptable BBC Light Programme fodder by the Big Ben Accordion Band.

These versions were all excruciating enough – but the worst fate awaited *Hearts Of Stone*, an astonishingly original work by black Los Angeles vocal group the Jewels. The song was turned into gold by another black vocal group, Otis Williams & the Charms, and covered again by the gleaming, pearly white Fontane Sisters, who took it to the very top of the American best sellers. Here, it was dismembered by that eminent student of black urban culture, Billy Cotton, who put it on the chopping block and turned it into dog-food. Fans of R&B should not approach this record. Not unless they want to become ill.

In January 1955, you could go to Romford Odeon and see the Ken Mackintosh Orchestra, plus Ruby Murray, Bill Maynard and Dickie Dawson; you could go to Lewisham Gaumont and see the Joe Loss Band Show, with Max Wall and the Three Monarchs; you could go to the Victoria Hall in Hanley and see Geraldo and his All Star Orchestra, plus Leslie 'Jiver' Hutchinson, Ralph Dollimore's Tip Toppers and Harry Roche's Sentimentalists; you could go to the Regal in Edmonton and see the Jack Parnell Band Show, with Joan Regan, Reg Varney and Barry Took. You could see trad jazz, modern jazz, big band jazz too. Wherever you happened to be, you could find some music – but you couldn't find any rhythm & blues . . . not until April, when Ronnie Aldrich and the Squadronaires, a popular 17-piece dance band that had grown out of the wartime RAF Dance Orchestra, suddenly announced a change of musical policy.

In a move motivated by sheer lunacy as much as opportunism, 39-year-old Ronnie leapt, not onto, but under the wheels of the R&B bandwagon. Intoxicated by "the tremendous furore which is sweeping America", he re-launched the band as Ronnie Aldrich and the Squads, giving an indication of their new direction on the single *Ko Ko Mo/Rock Love* ('with vocal refrain by Andy Reavley', as it said on the label). In the *NME*, Geoffrey Everitt gave it his 'Oscar of the Week'. Out of pity, one suspected.

It was a short-lived diversion. Ronnie's public were obviously unprepared for such swingeing changes and before long the Squadronaires were back on track, spending their fourth consecutive summer as resident band at the Isle of Man's Palace Ballroom, pleasing holidaymakers with their regular something-for-everyone brassy dance band programme. Interestingly, one of the band's premier assets was 'the singing saxophone of Cliff Townshend', whose nine-year-old son Pete would also find inspiration in rhythm & blues. One of the other sax-playing Squadronaires was Red Price – whose day would come.

In April, when Bill Haley's *Mambo Rock* plummeted from the hit parade after only two weeks, the BBC managed to turn a Nelson eye to the few decent American rock 'n' roll records that were being released here – preferring instead such confections as *Where Will The Dimple Be?* by Rosemary Clooney ("On the baby's knuckle, on the baby's knee: where will the baby's dimple be?" as if we gave a toss) and the Crew Cuts' hack-job *Earth Angel*, which reached the Top Five. The Penguins' original, of course, was nowhere to be seen or heard . . . but at least it was released here, which is more than could be said for records by the Drifters.

Then – by accident, surely – Al Hibbler's great brimming-over version of *Unchained Melody* got a flying start against Jimmy Young's Gloucestershire rendering and actually rose to number two, number one on some charts. But that doesn't really count as rock 'n' roll.

There was very little evidence of the new music all summer, particularly if you listened exclusively to the BBC. You had to have your ear pretty close to the ground to hear such new American releases as *Don't Be Angry* by Nappy Brown, *As Long As I'm Moving* by Ruth Brown, *Don't Roll Those Bloodshot Eyes At Me* by Wynonie Harris – or even Bill Haley's latest, *Razzle Dazzle*.

Paradoxically, you could see just about every American movie that was ever made, no matter how crappy, and every English one too. Cinemas were abundant in every town. The British movie business was booming: every week there seemed to be a new film starring either John Mills, Norman Wisdom, Diana Dors or Kenneth More. Laurence Harvey was our hippest young actor; Dirk Bogarde our most accomplished. Peter Sellers, a member of the *Goon Show* cast since 1949, got a leading role in *The Ladykillers*; Joan Collins went to Hollywood to become a star, playing Beth Throgmorton in *The Virgin Queen*.

Even if they were in colour, most British films were black and white. But so were many of the best American movies. Others came in Cinemascope or VistaVision, with magnetic stereophonic sound. Marlon Brando was the coolest star; Tony Curtis the "most promising". Lads whose parents allowed them to, copied his tousle-fronted hairstyle. Paul Newman made his screen début in *The Silver Chalice*, starring Virginia Mayo; Clint Eastwood made his in one of the Donald O'Connor Talking Mule series, *Francis In The Navy*; a brunette Jayne Mansfield played a saucy cigarette girl in *Pete Kelly's Blues*.

Already 1955 had brought a deluge of movies: westerns, musicals, dramas, comedies, adventure films, war films, historical films, biblical films, every kind of film. Winners included *Monsieur Hulot's Holiday, There's No Business Like Show Business, Seven Brides For Seven Brothers, The Colditz Story, Above Us The Waves, Bad Day At Black Rock, The Night My Number Came Up, Daddy Long Legs, A Star Is Born, The Man From Laramie, A Kid For Two Farthings, 20,000 Leagues Under The Sea, The Dambusters,* and *East Of Eden,* which introduced new star James Dean. "He isn't loveable, but he gets under the skin of the part in a way that will shake you," said *Picturegoer*. Within two months, he would be dead.

Dean's next film, *Rebel Without A Cause*, was already in the can; he was finishing up his contribution to *Giant*; and he was now lined up to play Rocky Graziano in *Somebody Up There Likes Me*. Paul Newman got the part: someone up there must have noticed him.

Before he died, critics were rude about James Dean. Respected journalist Donovan Pedelty had introduced him four months earlier with the headline warning 'You Can't Ignore the New Scowl Boy'. Pictures of him embracing his *East Of Eden* co-star Julie Harris revealed that he had the best haircut yet. He looked like a supercool version of Guy Madison.

Pedelty said he wore blue jeans, a white T-shirt, and rode a motor-cycle. "I was an actor before I became an actor," Dean told him. "A neurotic person has a necessity to express himself – and my neuroticism manifested itself in the dramatic." The original mixed-up kid, by the sound of it, but articulate with it. "I'm a serious minded and intense little devil, terribly gauche and so tense I don't see how people stay in the same room with me." Unlike the rest of the civilised world, Pedelty was not impressed. "I personally would rather pay money than see James Dean on screen again," he said. A bit of a hasty judgement, one felt.

But the impact of *East Of Eden* was nothing compared with that of *Blackboard Jungle*, which came along in October. Based on Evan Hunter's novel of juvenile delinquency in a tough urban American high school, it might have slipped in and out of the schedules as routinely as Glenn Ford's other films, had it not been for the music which played over the opening and closing credits: *Rock Around The Clock* by Bill Haley & his Comets – louder than anyone had ever heard rock 'n' roll before. Cinemas vibrated, audiences whooped. In America, where no age restriction was applied, teenagers from Frank Zappa to the Everly Brothers were terminally affected, but in Britain the censor denied access to anyone under 18.

Most critics attending the preview gave it a rough ride. The *Picturegoer* reviewer was more generous; she gave it four stars. "It's back to school for this classroom shocker. But hold on to your satchel. This isn't kid stuff. For its frightening realism it gets an X certificate; for its startling impact it gets full marks as one of the most gripping black-and-white action films of the year."

She also praised the music, describing it as "the blaring, rocking jazz of big city youth."

School films were usually light-hearted romps with Will Hay or Max Bygraves types playing the teacher, or melodramas where the pupils were played by precocious brats from the drama schools. From a rock 'n' roll point of view, *Blackboard Jungle* was a seminal work, the curtain raiser to a new and exciting era.

To locate the exact point where 'civilised society', as cherished by Sir Anthony Eden and his pals, started disintegrating and going off the rails, look no further. The rock 'n' roll revolution begins right here.

A scrolled preface was inserted to give the film sociological import, asserting that it was not intended as an exploitation movie, but a serious examination of a growing problem. Oh yes? The UK censor was not mollified.

"We, in the United States, are fortunate to have a school system that is a tribute to our communities and to our faith in American youth," ran the disclaimer. "Today we are concerned with juvenile delinquency; its causes and its effects. We are especially concerned when this delinquency boils over into our schools."

"The scenes and incidents depicted here are fictional. However, we believe that public awareness is a first step toward a remedy for any problem. It is in this spirit and with this faith that *Blackboard Jungle* was produced."

War veteran turned teacher Glenn Ford turns up for his first day at North Manual High to find kids jiving to Bill Haley's music. Boys with greased-up pompadours and attitude problems.

When he announces his name, Richard Dadier (pronounced Daddy-A), the thuggish Belazi (played by Dan Terranova) re-christens him Daddy-O, introducing the first of several new US teen locutions to British audiences.

The moral, decent, dedicated Dadier, who wants "to shape young minds, sculpt lives", is confronted by a cauldron of Spics, Niggers, Micks (their words), Italians, Jews and other bad-neighbourhood riff-raff. Nearly all insolent, truculent, ill-bred oafs, they intimidate him, take the piss out of him, beat the shit out of him, and try to foul up his marriage.

One of his colleagues, the jazz buff Edwards, foolishly brings in his priceless collection of 78s, built up over 15 years, to let the students share his exhilaration. Egged on by the others, prime troublemaker Artie West smashes them. Edwards quits teaching; all his dreams are shattered, along with his prized copy of *The Jazz Me Blues* by Bix Beiderbecke.

Dadier refuses to submit. In the term leading up to the Christmas concert, he begins to win some respect – particularly from Miller, played by Sidney Poitier. Miller wears white T-shirts, jeans and an oversized sports jacket, works in a garage after school, smokes, calls Dadier "chief", and uses expressions like "square". He also plays piano, leads a gospel harmony group, and gives us an inkling of how black teenagers feel. Dadier gives him hope.

Meanwhile, we are intrigued by the clothes – jackets with logos on the back, for instance – and the hairstyles: flat-tops or Tony Curtis affairs, with duck-tails. All our school photographs looked as if we were waiting to go into the army; theirs looked like police mug-shots.

The kids are eventually converted into true Americans through stimulating, imaginative teaching – all except the recidivists West and Belazi. A confrontation is inevitable. West pulls out his flick-knife: "Step right up and taste a little of this, Daddy-O". Dadier advances. "He's floating on Sneaky Pete," warns Miller. One of the students grabs the flagpole from the corner of the classroom and charges West, who is disarmed. Dadier clutches the Stars And Stripes as audiences are reassured that justice and right always triumph in the land of the free. All very symbolic.

And all very fascinating too – especially for graduates of the British school system . . . blazers, ties, grey flannels, short back and sides, discipline, uniformity, conformity. Could this film really be an accurate depiction of what was happening in America?

Blackboard Jungle not only introduced a plethora of ideas and expressions to adopt and imitate, it also romanticised teenage rebellion and rock 'n' roll. The ripples propelled Bill Haley's *Rock Around The Clock* back onto the charts. Dead and buried months ago, it was resurrected and guaranteed immortality. By the end of November, it was number one on the UK hit parade, the best selling record in the country!

The bad news was that rock 'n' roll was now inextricably associated with anti-social behaviour, flick knives, leather jackets, preposterous hairstyles, swearing, disrespectful louts, moronic tearaways and blood curdling hoodlums. Not only was it noisy, it just wasn't nice.

And, of course – there was that word again. Jungle. Where primitive people and wild animals live.

Seventeen

As far as the British music-biz was concerned, 1955 had been the year not of rock 'n' roll, but of mambo. Few of them sold in any quantity, but the record shops were ankle deep in mambo singles – for instance *Papa Loves Mambo, Everybody Loves Mambo, Early Dawn Mambo, Mambo At Midnight, Cool Mambo, Short Hair Mambo, Long Hair Mambo, They Were Doing The Mambo, Can't Do It Mambo, She Wants To Mambo, Let's Mambo, I Don't Want To Mambo, Happy Mambo, Jungle Mambo, Five Bottles Mambo, Hot Potato Mambo, Hill Billy Mambo, Tennessee Mambo, Mississippi Mambo, The Ooh And Ah Mambo, Mambo Italiano, Mambo Americano, Mambo Society, Mambo Rock, Manhattan Mambo, Mardi Gras Mambo, Marilyn Monroe Mambo, Lazy Mambo, Middle Age Mambo, It's Mambo Time, Minor Mambo, Saturday Night Mambo, Seven Kisses Mambo, I Wanna Dance To A Mambo Combo, Olé Mambo, New Kind Of Mambo, Irish Mambo, Nursery Mambo, Good Mambo Tonight, Arthur's Mambo, Bo Mambo, Baby Doll Mambo, Mambo Baby, Mambo Blues* and about a million more, all released in 1955. A February BBC Light Programme favourite was *Mambo Is In The Air*. They weren't kidding.

There was also the usual spate of quasi-religious twaddle, in records like *The Bible Tells Me So, Cast Your Bread Upon The Waters* and *A Teenage Prayer*; an unpleasant dose of pretentious philosophical conjecturing, in records like *There Must Be A Reason* and *I Wonder*; and a liberal sprinkling of songs with foreign titles, to administer a dash of spurious sophistication to the proles – *Cara Mia, Por Favor, Tino Tino, Domani, Arrivederci Darling, Croce Di Oro, C'est La Vie*. Mosta-le Crappe, I fear.

To begin with, it looked as though 1956 would be the year of Americana. There were about 257 versions of *The Ballad Of Davy Crockett*, for a start. The film was released here as the year began and, just as they had in the States, the pioneering pop-culture merchandisers made a mint out of pre-teen boys as they began mining a rich, inexhaustible vein that would ensure fat profits from the Beatles during the sixties, and on through the rest of the century and beyond with wombles, turtles, dinosaurs and God knows what else.

Davy Crockett hats everywhere, from expensive replicas in real fur to cheap and nasty market-stall copies made from suede-effect fake leather-cloth, dyed brown, with a dismal tatty tail reminiscent of a dead cat. In gardens and streets around the nation, kids felt noble and glorious as they died defending the Alamo.

Among the barefaced band-wagoners trying to make a few bob out of the theme-song were Billy Cotton and Max Bygraves (an unlikely pair of buckskinned buccaneers), but the only versions to make any real impact were those by Tennessee Ernie Ford, who gained a handy dollop of accidental authenticity by having been born in the same eastern end of Tennessee as Crockett, and Bill Hayes, who had scored the definitive American hit – five weeks at number one. (Hayes' subsequent screen-star cash-in attempt, the lamentable *Message From James Dean*, flopped disastrously.)

The most bizarre *Davy Crockett* cover was by Ronnie Ronalde, a variety/radio/TV turn whose speciality was whistling. He took his art very seriously, sticking his fingers in his mouth and waggling his hands around his lips to give his performance a professional and artistic sheen. Backed by an orchestra, he warbled his way through it, his version enhanced by a unique touch. According to his PR hype, Ronnie "had borrowed, from the Disney Organisation, a recording of a Tennessee thrush, a bird heard in the film" – and had listened to it over and over "until he had the impersonation note-perfect." An interesting way to spend one's days, we thought.

Even more popular than *Davy Crockett* was another Tennessee Ernie hit, *Sixteen Tons*, which knocked *Rock Around The Clock* off the top of the UK chart in the middle of January and stayed there for a month. Whereas the Crockett song was full of patriotic guff about "the land of the free", *Sixteen Tons* detailed the plight of Kentucky coal miners, for whom Eisenhower's America contained no heroes or saviours. Written by Merle Travis, whose own father "owed his soul to the company store", the song was nine years old but none the less current for that. Needless to say, its message of despair and resignation bounced off most of those who bought it – and most of those who sung it, come to that, like Michael Holliday, for instance, whose promotional pics showed him manhandling a shovelful of nutty slack.

Mitch Miller's modified, singalong version of the Civil War marching song *Yellow Rose Of Texas* was still lurking in the chart and was soon joined by *The Shifting Whispering Sands* – a dramatic recitation, supposedly by a grizzled old gold prospector wandering through "the bones of cattle and burros, picked clean by buzzards and bleached by the desert sun." American readings at least had the tumbling tumbleweed feel of a black and white cowboy film – but here the best-selling version was by boxing commentator and *This Is Your Life* host Eamonn Andrews. What kind of person would want to sit around at home listening to Eamonn Andrews going on about "the coyotes and horned toads of the thorny chaparral", one wondered? It was a strange and unpredictable time.

Tailored perfectly, though entirely accidentally, to the style and mood of this Americana boom was Lonnie Donegan's *Rock Island Line*. Right time, right place, what a lucky laddie he was.

Perhaps as a patriotic antidote to all this yankee-doodle business, the theme-song from ITV's red-hot children's series *Robin Hood* was rushed out in several versions – with Gary Miller's outselling the original by Dick James, who had not only been singing it over the credits every week but had also hedged his bets by covering *Davy Crockett* on the B-side. Miller then mugged him again with his version of *Garden Of Eden*. It must have been the last straw.

"Blow this," thought Dick, who had paid his dues prancing about in front of orchestras led by Henry Hall, Billy Ternent, Geraldo and Cyril Stapleton, "those music publishers cop all the money without having to do any work. I think I'll become one myself" – which he did forthwith, going into partnership with the firm of Sheridan & Bron. Due to taking care of these interests, the man who would a decade later swan around town in the most vulgarly decorated Rolls Royce ever seen, restricted future variety appearances to the London area. At the Gaumont cinema in Edgware Road, he gave bows and arrows to those children giving the best performance of *Robin Hood*. His nine-year-old son Stephen judged the candidates.

For the whole of January 1956, Bill Haley had two singles bobbing around the Top 10 – *Rock Around The Clock* and *Rock A-Beatin' Boogie* – but his toehold was nothing compared with what was happening in the States. "Rock 'n' roll is the order of the day now," reported publicist Ken Pitt (the London-based PR for Eric Delaney, Billy Eckstine and Liberace, among others), freshly returned from a quick business trip. "Originally an emanation of the Negro temperament, there are now several white groups doing well in the idiom. Of these, I was most impressed by Freddie Bell & his Bell Boys at the Sands Hotel in Las Vegas." Unbelievable! Rock 'n' roll was already acceptable cabaret fare; it was already being assimilated into ad-mass popular culture. What was going on?

Pitt continued: "The strength of the craze can be judged from the fact that Alan Freed grossed $154,000 when he presented a rock 'n' roll show at a Brooklyn theatre, while Johnnie Ray, headlining at the same venue a week later, drew only $65,000."

Still no sign of any home-grown rock 'n' rollers – even on the new BBC-TV talent show, *Camera One*. Their first 'discovery' was 'a young electrician from the provinces, Ronnie Carroll.' He turned out to be a 21-year-old Belfast boy from the same street as Ruby Murray. Small world, isn't it? He sang only one number on the show, but within minutes of his appearance he had been contacted by "two major recording companies and two famous bandleaders."

Said Michael Winner, trying a spot of journalism before infiltrating the film business: "Television is still not quite on the ball in screening the very latest in popular music." But a few people were already thinking about it.

Meanwhile, the string of frightful covers continued – with *Only You* by Malcolm Vaughan, *The Great Pretender* by Anne Shelton, and *I Hear You Knocking* by Jill Day among the most embarrassing. Few critics waved the flag for anything original, though Geoffrey Everitt remained alert: in the 20 January issue of *NME*, over reviews of *Donkey Tango* by Cyril Stapleton, *Piano Tuner Boogie* by Winifred Atwell and *Young And Foolish* by Ronnie Hilton, he gave top billing to *My Boy Flat Top* by Boyd Bennett & the Rockets. "Here are some Rockets who really rock!" he said. A Haley-style outfit from the southern States, Boyd and his band had seen Frankie Vaughan cover their first US hit, *Seventeen* – and blow me if he didn't cover *My Boy Flat Top* too! And he had a hit with it. Sadly lacking in original ideas, these English chaps. We had seen Vaughan on television, looking like something out of Moss Bros window: no way was he going to be messing around with a 17-year-old hep-cat doll with peroxide hair! He must have been a-c-t-i-n-g. He was highly regarded as a cane-and-boater, 'gimme the moonlight' adult entertainer, so why was he pretending to be part of rock 'n' roll?

The big news of the month took up only a few lines on the back page of the *NME*: "Bill Haley & his Comets are to be featured in a forthcoming musical for Columbia Pictures – appropriately titled *Rock Around The Clock*". Producer Sam Katzman had been in New York looking for other rock 'n' roll acts and was going to start filming as soon as he got back to Hollywood.

Not only will we be able to hear rock 'n' roll, we will now be able to see how it is played! We'll find out what the singers and musicians look like, and what they wear! The only intimation of how it was actually performed had been in *Record Mirror*, back in June. In an overview of the 'craze', Len Gutteridge described the antics of black singer Nappy Brown in a show at Newark, New Jersey. "He bellowed his off-colour lyrics over the loud honking of the tenor sax back of him. After throwing enough contortions to make Johnnie Ray look like a robot, Brown finished up writhing on the floor. By then, half the audience was writhing with him." Before getting entirely carried away, Gutteridge added a health warning: "Such goings-on are heavily panned by anti-rock 'n' roll music critics and disc jockeys, who claim it hurts both morals and music." It sounded amazing! Did all performers behave like that? Or were there variations? It looked as if we were going to have to wait for the movie to find out.

The bad news of the month was the BBC's renewal of Billy Cotton's contract, guaranteeing him a radio show until 1959. Worse than a prison sentence! Whenever one heard that blood-curdling, brain-petrifying cry of "Wakey Wake-e-e-e-ey", one could be sure of half an hour of musical torture.

It didn't seem to affect their rivals, but between the middle of February and the end of March 1956, a localised print union dispute kept the *Melody Maker* off the news stands for seven weeks – thus forcing them to miss out on any contribution to the pandemonium surrounding Elvis Presley's first UK release, *Heartbreak Hotel*. Though it had yet to appear in the US Top 10, as printed in the *NME* that week, it had arrived from America on a flying bedstead of fanfare and hype. How much was bullshit and how much the truth, there was no way of knowing.

This piece was typical: "Here are the facts. He's 21, dark, looks like a junior Rock Hudson. He shakes, rattles and rolls a lot in his act. Called a dry-eyed Johnnie Ray, with twice the locomotion when he sings, he likes life to be colourful. Dresses in pink and black, or clover. Owns two Cadillacs; one canary yellow, the other pink. He sells himself hard with publicity and insists on two giant cut-out figures of himself being displayed wherever he appears. He's nick-named the Cat – because he's slinky and sneers slightly when he smiles." Is that how cats smile?

Every publication had its own version. This was the *Daily Mirror*'s: "Take a dash of Johnnie Ray, add a sprinkling of Billy Daniels, and what have you got? Elvis Presley, whom American teenagers are calling The King of Western Bop. He is 21, single, and scorns western kit for snazzy, jazzy outfits. Will British fans fall for him? I think it's likely."

His impact on the public consciousness was instantaneous, as if he'd been beamed into their lives by the process later perfected on *Star Trek* – and immediately it was a case of "do you like Elvis or not?" It was as if everyone felt compelled to make an instinctive and intuitive on-the-spot assessment and decision. Like "do you believe in flying saucers?" or "do you believe in ghosts?" It was a yes or no answer; no equivocating. You had to choose which side you were on. For Elvis, or against him.

In a move they are mortally embarrassed about to this day, the *NME* came out on the side that reckoned he was rubbish. With his last shreds of credibility dissolving even as he typed, their singles reviewer Geoffrey Everitt nailed himself into a lead-lined coffin by boasting that he had not been positively affected by *Heartbreak Hotel*. So often in the past, his comments had been incisive and accurate – but this was tantamount to admitting that he was too old and uncool to be reviewing records made for a new generation.

"If you like gimmick voices, Elvis will slay you," he wrote, "but if you appreciate good singing, I don't suppose you'll manage to hear this disc all through." Never mind, Geoffrey . . . with a bit of luck, Presley and his record will be forgotten by the end of the year.

"Of the two sides, *I Was The One* is the better, but this half-brother of Johnnie Ray fails to make any impression on me," he continued. "If this is singing, then I give up, and furthermore, if this is the stuff that the American record fans are demanding, I'm glad I'm on this side of the Atlantic."

It seemed to be the generation gap he was standing beside, not the Atlantic, especially when he moved on to the next single in the week's pile. "For a breath of fresh air, we turn to Billy Cotton and his Band. Let me at once say that our Billy still knows what the majority of us like to listen to. His version of *Lizzie Borden* is entertaining, musical and well performed."

We felt hurt and betrayed, as if our leading ally had deserted us. Poor Geoffrey somehow seemed to have lost his perspective – and there must have been mutterings to this effect in the smoky rooms of the *NME*, because his days as their reviewer were numbered.

Released here in the middle of March, *Heartbreak Hotel* was, to many people, the most astonishing record ever made in history up to that point – and this buffoon couldn't see that? It was the most emotional and atmospheric performance that most teenagers had ever heard; the bleakest, most hand-wringing, heart-wrenching desolation – and all because his bird has dumped him? He's only 21, surely he'll find another. God, it's not the end of the world – but he sings as though it certainly is. In an incredible "if I die tomorrow at least the world will always remember this" performance, he sounds as if he's singing from inside the actual hotel room, so sparsely furnished as to absorb no echo, with the microphone placed in the open doorway.

It was a sequence from some unmade movie, shot in the same subdued twilight Technicolor as the swimming pool scene in *Rebel Without A Cause* – released here simultaneously – except that this was Lonely Street, where a pulsing No Vacancies sign in the window of this run-down, beaten-up Skid Row hotel provided scant illumination. Only when the camera zoomed into the open window could we see Elvis.

It was a stark, shadowy scene from a cheaply printed American pulp magazine like *Dime Detective*, a cross between Cornell Woolrich and Raymond Chandler, with everyone holding back from the verge of suicide, leading wretched lives that had only been saved from extinction by the fact that every single person in the place, guests and employees, was in the same boat.

This extraordinary drama was hung with glowing, volcanic, dripping rock 'n' roll, overlaid with delicate sprinklings and abstract stripes of otherworldly guitar and piano weirdness, making it irresistibly attractive, like a book you can't put down or the prospect of a casual shag with a girl who looks like Kim Novak. For many, it was the first record they ever bought and played ten times in a row non-stop. Then went and got their friends round and played it another ten times.

If the most ridiculous name ever conceived was Dick Hyman (whose female counterpart was probably called Pussy Foreskin) – currently in the US chart with *Theme From A Threepenny Opera* – then the greatest was Elvis Presley. Elvis Presley!

Who had ever heard of a name like that before? Elvis! Mention the word, one word, and everyone in the world knew whom you were talking about. Instantly. Like Hitler or Brando . . . only they were surnames. This was the name given to him by his mum and dad. Teenagers everywhere were sitting there listening to *Heartbreak Hotel*, thinking "how on earth could they have ever come up with a name like Elvis?"

It wasn't just the name; everything about him was unique and mysterious, more thrilling than anything teenagers had ever heard or seen or read about before.

In and around Memphis, during 1954 and 1955, it later transpired, savvy white kids were playing music in the same way that a handful of hip kids were starting to play skiffle here . . . but the Yanks (and we called all Americans Yanks, irrespective of whether they came from north, south, east or west) were playing like people they'd heard on the radio or seen around. A bit of blues, a bit of country, a bit of gospel, a bit of hit parade pop – in absorbing all these influences, they were unwittingly evolving a style all their own. Toss into a mincing machine all these different kinds of music concocted to entertain the poor blacks and the poor whites, add the pepper of youthful enthusiasm and naiveté, crank the handle for a while, and out of the other end comes rock 'n' roll. Elvis Presley, Scotty Moore, Bill Black, Carl Perkins, Johnny and Dorsey Burnette, Paul Burlison, they were all playing bits and pieces they'd picked up, messed around with, and personalised.

Then Elvis, through a handful of regional breakers on the local independent label Sun, promoted by saturation touring through the south, started attracting notice nationally. Observations like "He may be unknown north of the Mason Dixon line, but down here the girls are ripping his clothes off everywhere he goes" alerted RCA Records, who outbid their rivals by forking out a fortune to sign him.

With that kind of money at stake, they had to pull out all the stops to promote him – which they did, on national television. Within weeks, *Heartbreak Hotel* was the biggest record in America and the name of Elvis The Pelvis was on everyone's lips.

We didn't see him on television; we only saw pictures – but we soon knew he was wilder, younger, more graceful, more sexual, more lithe, more grease, more beautiful, more tender, more respectful, more vulnerable, more sensitive, more soulful, more exquisite, more animal, more naturally elegant, more sussed and more us than anything else that was ever likely to visit our planet. The God of rock 'n' roll, Elvis was going to change the world. Frozen in that emerging moment, he makes Jim Morrison look like a sack of fertiliser, Michael Jackson a bag of spanners.

Helpless through the strike, the people at *Melody Maker* must have been doubly depressed by all the media kerfuffle about Elvis. They were probably thinking "People will associate his ghastly noise with jazz – you know what the proles are like: they call any music they don't understand 'jazz'. They'll think we should be writing about it. Let's hope the bastard falls flat on his face and all the ballyhoo dies down quickly."

But Elvis wasn't just being touted as this year's model; he was this generation's model, ready to go after decades of research and development. He had been swept over the Atlantic on a wave of spontaneous quim-wetting and hero-worship unseen since the hey-days of Valentino and Sinatra. He wasn't about to go away – not with so many girls anxious to know about his every move, dreaming about being his fantasy lover; not with so many boys wishing they were him, wanting to experience everything he experienced; not with every newspaper dying to find a new angle so they could tell the story again and print more pictures.

Every newspaper except the *Melody Maker*, that is. When they came back into circulation in the first week of April, they did manage to print a letter from some reader complaining that Tampa Red was a Lonnie Donegan imitator, but – as they had with Bill Haley – they studiously avoided any comment on Elvis.

The people at *Melody Maker* managed to keep a safety valve on their boiling anxieties for a month, but in their 5 May edition, the bubbling cauldron exploded spectacularly when columnist Steve Race, a 35-year-old dance-band pianist, arranger and composer, could stand it no more. Now Steve Race sounded like a good egg – he had recently railed against racial intolerance, for instance – but something inside him snapped when Elvis started setting fire to the edges of his world.

"We know the plain, unvarnished fact, which is that the term 'Rock and Roll' derives from a slang allusion to the sex act," he wrote. "Many of the most treasured names and terms in jazz (not to mention the word 'jazz' itself) stem from the same origin; a fact which makes all the more difficult the business of defending jazz in a world less obsessed with sexual imagery."

Admirable so far. None of the prudishness and moral indignation which was already spreading in some of the national tabloids. But then the lid blows off spectacularly.

"Viewed as a social phenomenon, the current craze for Rock and Roll material is one of the most terrifying things ever to have happened to popular music. And, of course, as in all modern forms of entertainment, we blithely follow the lead of the American industry. When father turns, we all turn."

The notion that rock 'n' roll might possibly develop as a musical form, as had his beloved jazz, either doesn't strike him or else is too ludicrous to contemplate. And it could all have been prevented had not those greedy fools who run the music business here opened up the sluice-gate and allowed that torrent of repulsive filth from America to pollute our comfortable little scene. Our only hope is that the media sees sense and puts up barriers to forestall its spread.

"I hope the gimlet-eyed men of commerce who are at present trying to bring about a Rock and Roll boom in this country are aware of what they're doing. I also hope that the BBC Song Committee will be more vigilant than ever when vetting the cheap, nasty lyrics on which the Rock and Roll movement thrives."

Cheap, nasty lyrics? Maybe someone in the office – the waggish Max Jones, more than likely – had played him secretly imported copies of *Big Ten Inch Record* by Bullmoose Jackson or *Big Long Slidin' Thing* by Dinah Washington, because we hadn't heard any cheap, nasty lyrics. We had heard plenty of pathetic, infantile ones, of course, but they were on *MM*-approved records like *Hot Diggety* by Perry Como and *Pickin' A Chicken* by Eve Boswell.

"Musically speaking, of course, the whole thing is laughable," Race continued. "All the composer has to do is to remember the 12-bar blues, dot it out with the usual melody line, and put his copyright stamp on the bottom. The lyric writer needs one line, repeated ad nauseam, and a little store of suggestive couplets at the traditional place."

It sounded like saloon bar or taxi-driver talk, yet Race was well known to be an intelligent, musically educated man. Good job that early Elvis fans like Paul Simon and Paul McCartney, both of whom would later be praised by Race, weren't put off rock 'n' roll by his remarks.

"The Rock and Roll technique, instrumentally and vocally, is the antithesis of all that jazz has been striving for over the years – in other words, good taste and musical integrity."

One imagined the disconsolate *Melody Maker* staff, heads in hands, resigned to defeat at the hands of these uncouth marauders, even as Race tried to rally the ranks for a desperate rearguard action.

"The promotion and acceptance of the Rock and Roll cult is a monstrous threat, both to the moral acceptance and the artistic emancipation of jazz. Let us oppose it to the end."

We rock 'n' roll addicts had a couple of questions. As he typed his column, did Mr Race have the demented look of a Hollywood B-movie professor, warning the world about an invasion by giant ants or creatures from outer space? Or was the ghost of James Dean standing over him, wearing a King Canute costume and smiling?

Why was the *Melody Maker* so antagonistic towards rock 'n' roll? Why didn't they just accept it as a new strain of popular music and hire a couple of youngsters to write about it, like the *NME* did? By making such a fuss, they merely exposed and emphasised their fusty outlook. They liked to think of themselves as sages – and indeed were promoted as such in advertisements – but they were petrified because this was crude, primitive, unschooled music that they neither liked nor understood, but which was attracting punters outside their sphere of influence.

The simple truth was that most rock 'n' roll fans couldn't have cared less what anyone on *Melody Maker* thought. They didn't need *Melody Maker*. They saw it as an archaic bastion of the square world, a champion of old people's music. How dare the *MM* even poke their nose in and make judgements on our music? They should stick to their own world – jazz and prole fodder.

Well, the *Melody Maker* tried to ignore it, tried to decry it, tried to belittle it, but rock 'n' roll spread through their domain like cancer. Eventually, they had to accept it and change – but not for years yet.

A month or so after Race's splenetic diatribe, another *MM* columnist decided it was time to get hot under the collar in print – the self-righteous oldie, Jack Payne. His article, a seminal document in the 'Them and Us' divide, was headlined 'SHOULD WE SURRENDER TO THE TEENAGERS?' and one could just imagine the acid coursing through his cranium as he typed that question. On one side of the page was Payne's lugubrious cut-out face – looking across at a picture of Elvis, just ticking over for the camera, like a Porsche at the traffic lights anxious to tear away.

Payne began by explaining how the BBC's disc-jockeys (of which he was one) had the ultimate power in the music business. "Generally speaking, the public buys only that which it has heard and likes. A record is played on the air and is heard by thousands of people. If it 'clicks', then the cash registers in music shops are going to set up a merry jingle – and that jingle is Tin Pan Alley's favourite music."

He talked about the integrity of the corporation's disc jockeys and their imperviousness to bribes and favours, their steadfast refusal to be flattered or persuaded into playing a record. "The disc jockey, as a window dresser, serves only one master – the public, which gazes in at the goods." And if the goods they want to look at, with a view to purchase, happen to be those manufactured by Elvis Presley? Well, now we find out what has provoked this stream of paynefully trite philosophy.

"He is, they tell me, the latest teenage craze in America. Personally, I don't like his work and nor will, I feel, the vast majority of our listening public." If Jack Payne wasn't already considered a turd by most teenagers, this sentence finished him off. Here was a man held up to be some kind of expert in his field, and he obviously didn't have a clue what he was talking about. It also alerted rock 'n' roll fans to the notion (invariably borne out) that any act on his abysmal TV show *Off The Record*, that he prefaced with the disclaimer "I don't like this particular style of music", was bound to be the best thing on the programme.

In his article, Payne went on to outline his idea of hell: radio which reflected public taste, "with whole programmes completely devoted to new records and absolutely bulging with best selling singers. The programmes, and those who ran them, would be the servants of the industry rather than of the public."

"Teenagers are the most vociferous of fans," he continued. "With the enthusiasm of youth, they really get down to the job of writing to the BBC requesting their favourites. And believe me, they are anything but sympathetic toward the tastes of other sections of the community. Anyone who doubts that should take a look into my own postbag."

We didn't doubt it for a minute – we had contributed to it – but here was Jack Payne openly admitting that the BBC was turning its back on a considerable body of disenchanted teenagers trying vainly to find anything remotely interesting on the radio.

Instead of looking for a positive solution, or at least a compromise, know-it-all Jack suggested that disc jockeys follow his policy. "One doesn't play to the gallery in the theatre. One doesn't, with any sort of wisdom, surrender to those who shout the loudest. The question of how far one should pander to teenage tastes is, I submit, a very knotty one. Adolescence is, we are told, a difficult time of life; a phase, some sociologists say, of emotional unbalance." Holy cow! Jack Payne isn't even aware that he went through a period of adolescence himself! He's forgotten it! He must be even older than we thought.

"Are we going to let youth become the sole judge of what constitutes good or bad entertainment? Are we to move towards a world in which the teenagers, dancing hysterically to the tune of the latest Pied Piper, will inflict mob rule in music?"

No, Jack. It's very simple. We'll have our music and you can keep yours. All we want are a couple of hours a week . . . the BBC is supposed to be public service radio, after all. There's room for everybody, without any stepping on each other's toes.

But no. Jack wants everything his way. "I still believe that good entertainment – *with something for everybody* [his italics] – should be allied to good taste" . . . which, presumably, means his taste.

After Elvis, *something for everybody* would never be a feasible concept. Any fool could see that.

Heartbreak Hotel rose to number two on the Hit Parade. Quite a few people enjoyed his music, obviously.

In July, Jim Davidson, who as BBC Radio's Head of Light Music was not only Jack Payne's boss but also the supreme arbiter of public pop music consumption, went on record to reassure listeners who were perplexed by the sudden popularity of Elvis Presley and Bill

Haley. "Those freaks are the bottom of the gimmick noise barrel," he said. No shilly-shallying; the fellow obviously loathed rock 'n' roll.

"We have heard too many songs by too many singers without talent," he continued. Funny . . . that was our conclusion too – after listening to the Light Programme all weekend.

And how did the BBC intend to engage with combat rock 'n' roll? Simply by ignoring it. Mr Davidson had the perfect solution: "We're getting back to, say, the 1938 era, when singers had to have a basic entertainment value and a show business personality. We've proved, through the success of the BBC Band Show, that this is what the public wants."

God spare us!

What to do? Best sit tight. Stick *Heartbreak Hotel* on the turntable and hope Alan Freed's prediction, written on the back of an EP by Sam 'The Man' Taylor, comes true: "The strong solid beat will rush like a gigantic tidal wave of happiness and, as in the past, the shrill outraged cries of critics will be lost beneath the excitement of a new generation seeking to let off steam the happy way – to the new Big Beat in popular music."

Eighteen

To a great extent, Presley's meteoric arrival dimmed Haley's comet. As soon as Elvis was unveiled in all his glory, in large photographs in every admass publication and on a couple more UK singles (*Blue Suede Shoes/Tutti Frutti* in May 1956 and *I Want You, I Need You, I Love You/My Baby Left Me* in July), it became clear that the corpulent, suddenly somewhat elderly Haley had been the messenger rather than the Messiah, the herald who came along and blew the horn to get our attention so that we'd be facing the street when the King came along. But he was still making an incalculable contribution to the small corner of the rock 'n' roll tapestry that we in Britain could see.

In *NME*, Geoffrey Everitt gave *See You Later Alligator* the lead review, even though the record obviously hadn't excited the same emotional reactions as Haley's previous releases. As it slithered up the chart to number seven, the staff of the splendidly named music publisher, Box and Cox, celebrated its success by clustering round a stuffed crocodile for a press photo. "Money for old rope," they seemed to be saying.

With *See You Later Alligator*, *Rock Around The Clock* and *Rock A-Beatin' Boogie*, Haley kept rock 'n' roll alive in the UK chart until Elvis burst in, a few days before yet another effervescent Haley offering, *The Saints' Rock 'n' Roll/R.O.C.K.*

Lack of BBC airplay, lack of awareness and lack of interest suppressed the sales of various other authentic releases, including *No Money Down* by Chuck Berry, *Bo Weevil* by Fats Domino, *Seven Days* by Clyde McPhatter and the original version of *See You Later Alligator* by Bobby Charles, but – wondrously – Fats Domino scraped into the Top 30 with *I'm In Love Again*. It was a genuine black rhythm and blues classic, delivered exuberantly in an all but indecipherable New Orleans patois guaranteed to mystify and disturb the Jack Paynes of the world. Brilliant!

We would soon read that the engaging, chubby, bubbly, friendly, bouncing Fats was 28 years old and had seven children. Those who cared thought that Fats was the genuine article, a crafter of esoteric records, an *éminence grise* to be respected.

Pat Boone, whose shameless appropriation of *Ain't That A Shame* had the previous year obliterated the Domino original, was back in the UK Top 10 with *I'll Be Home* – a ballad originally recorded by black Chicago vocal group the Flamingos. Boone reached number one in the middle of June and stayed there for five weeks.

The record was intriguing to British rock 'n' roll fans if only for the line "at the corner drug-store each Saturday we would meet." He would meet her at the chemists? Why? Did she have a Saturday job on the counter, selling medicine and hot water bottles? Or was a drug-store something different? It must be. But what? "Once more our love will be free" . . . what the hell does he mean by that?

In the Flamingos' original, the song (in the form of a letter) is sung by a soldier posted away from home – but any such context is vague in Pat's version, which substitutes "My mind's made up" for "My time's 'bout up". Nevertheless, Pat retains as the punch line, "so long – until I'll be home to start serving you." (To start "servicing you" would have been even more interesting.)

The record's extraordinary sales figure (it became the year's biggest seller) was in no small way due to its suitability for the popular Sunday lunchtime radio programme, *Forces Favourites*. Because it was a request show, one sometimes heard a good record on it, a comparative rarity for BBC listeners. "This one goes out to Flight Sergeant Fred Wilks, in BFPO 27 at Munchen Gladbach, with lots of love from his wife Hilda and their three-year-old son, Robert. They say they're counting the days until they see you again in December."

Any new record with an optimistic message and a military connection was bound to get played for weeks on end. So it was with *I'll Be Home* – and again, two months later with Anne Shelton's lilting chart-topper, *Lay Down Your Arms*.

The B-side of Boone's hit, *Tutti Frutti*, was – one could see from the *NME*'s *Billboard* chart reprint – a big American hit for Little Richard, but neither his records, nor those by the Platters, were available in Britain. Accordingly, during the first six months of 1956, we saw such mouth-watering titles as *Long Tall Sally*, *The Great Pretender* and *The Magic Touch* enter the US list, but all we heard were factitious covers.

We did get to hear *Lipstick And Candy And Rubbersoled Shoes* by Julius LaRosa. A promising title, but a useless record. If you're going to sing about shoes, make sure you know what you're talking about.

To the average teenager, most politicians were remote figures in ivory towers. Unlike today, they didn't appear on television every night, pampering their egos and oiling their way round questions about their duplicity and incompetence. They just sat up there in London ruling the country – because they knew what was best for everybody.

Only occasionally did they acknowledge the existence of pop music, and then usually in the most deprecating terms. The most laughable instance was in June 1956, when the bean-brained Labour MP Lt-Col Marcus Lipton (whose hobbies, according to *Who's Who*, were "giving advice and scything") questioned the Home Secretary about two allegedly indecent records: *Don't Touch Me Nylon* by Marie Bryant & Jackie Brown's Calypso Kings and, unimaginably, *John And Marsha* by Stan Freberg – the most harmless morsel of innocent nonsense this side of *Round The Horne*, and a radio Family Favourite for the previous six years!

"Have you taken the trouble to listen to the two records of which I sent you details?" asked the demented, 55-year-old Lipton. "No paper in the country would dare to print the words used on one of them. Is it in the public interest that these wretched things should continue to be on sale?"

Since the lyrics of *John And Marsha* are just that – "John . . . Marsha . . . John . . . Marsha . . . " repeated a couple of dozen times each, over the course of two-and-a-half minutes – it would seem that the deranged tea-bag was referring to *Don't Touch Me Nylon*, an obscure slice of Caribbean humour, in which Marie admonishes an over-ardent lover, who is "very swell" but whose hands are "roaming all over the place".

> *I have to say "Don't touch my nylons, Johnny;*
> *You've really got to stop this carry-on."*

Suggestive, it might have been – but indecent? It was more like a morality tale. A warning to young girls . . . don't let those naughty lads get their hands inside your knickers. They should have played it in schools. (And to some future Members of Parliament, come to that.) To the surprise of nobody, the Home Secretary gave Lipton short shrift: "I have not had a chance to hear either of these songs and feel it is unlikely that I will. In any case, it is not my responsibility to prosecute; it is a matter for the police."

Lipton's extraordinary outburst had been pre-empted – and prompted, presumably – by similar condemnations in that paragon of good taste and virtue, the *Sunday People*, which claimed that complaints about *Don't Touch Me Nylon* had reached the Public Morality Council (one can only imagine what sort of stiff-arsed pontificators sat on that) and that such organisations as the Moral Welfare Council of the Church of England were expressing fears about the damage such indecent records might be doing to young people. We were living in loony land!

Strangely, there are no recorded instances of teenagers being driven into frothing sexual frenzy by *Don't Touch Me Nylon*. Most people who read about Lipton's quest wondered why he was wasting Parliament's time on such trifling matters; many thought he'd gone stark raving barking bonkers. But one person was deeply affected by the ballyhoo . . . Stan Freberg! He was appalled to hear his record described as indecent. "Any unclean meaning must be entirely in the person's mind," he said, when *Melody Maker* asked for his response. "Quite definitely, nothing dirty was intended."

"The recorded lyric of *John And Marsha* was actually the middle section of a skit on American soap operas," he went on – and since few of their readers had any idea what a 'soap opera' was, the *MM* helpfully explained that "the nearest British equivalent is possibly *Mrs Dale's Diary*". "I have done it at church socials for many years," continued the injured Freberg. "Only two weeks ago, I was invited to perform it at a Youth for Christ meeting." No thunderbolts had struck him down – so stick that in your pipe and smoke it, Marcus!

Ironically, Lipton had cried wolf a little too early. The real wolf – a slavering, ferocious, unmanageable beast – came padding down the high street a few weeks later. If only he had waited, he would certainly have had something to get twitched about. *Rock Around The Clock*, a cheap Hollywood exploitation movie rushed out to capitalise on the current American rock 'n' roll fad, really did stick a dagger into Britain's staid way of life, opening up a festering wound – later described as a 'generation gap' – which grew wider and deeper by the day. Its star, the amiable, avuncular, roly-poly Bill Haley (now over 30 years old) was obviously the devil in disguise.

When the film was previewed, no one in the media had the
slightest inkling that such a maladroit farrago would, or could, have
such a devastating impact on youth culture and deliver such a
divisive jolt to society. You either dug rock 'n' roll or you were
square and past it, daddy-o!

The film opened at the London Pavilion on 20 July. "With odd
contortions and odder noises, *Rock Around The Clock* extols the
virtues of rock and roll," said *The Times* reviewer. "American youth
finding fulfilment in what seems to be a mingling of primitive dance
and ritual." No condescension there, then. "This is not a film which
can profitably be discussed in the terms of normal criticism," he
continued, writing it off as rubbish. He was right, of course.
Compared with some of the year's other films – *Around The World In
Eighty Days, The Ten Commandments, Moby Dick, The Searchers, High
Society, The King And I, Bus Stop, Carousel* and *Lust For Life*, for
instance – it was rubbish, in the same way that records like *Razzle
Dazzle* and *See You Later Alligator* were rubbish if they were judged
against Gershwin or Mozart. What he was actually saying, albeit
tacitly, was "This film wasn't made for snooty, middle-aged,
middle-class egg-heads . . . it was made for working-class teenagers."

As expected, *Melody Maker*'s review was terse and curt. Quaintly
describing rock 'n' roll as 'cod jazz', they discussed the spread and
effect of the music as though it were a newly discovered incurable
virus. "What it threatens to do to musical standards, the film doesn't
discuss," they observed.

The *NME* sent Charles Govey to see it. "This isn't a film for the
square," he wrote, "or for the person with any degree of musical
taste." Supercilious upstart!

Other reviewers saw it for what it was: candyfloss entertainment.
No better nor worse than any of a hundred movies cranked out every
year. Giving it one star, *Picture Show*, the film buff's favourite,
described it as a "lively, up to the minute musical with a slight story
– of a manager in love with a singer, trying to get a band better
bookings, while an agent, in love with him, jealously puts obstacles
in the way – interwoven between rock 'n' roll numbers. Well
presented, it is a film which should not be missed by jive
enthusiasts."

The quirky *Weekly Sporting Review* said "rock 'n' roll rhythm is
sweeping adolescent Americans off their feet, and this movie-taste of

their latest enthusiasm will, I fully expect, spread the dynamic disease round those noisy haunts of self-expression known as jazz clubs." Very unlikely! Trad-jazz fans loathed rock 'n' roll with a passion – though probably not as passionately as rock 'n' roll fans loathed trad-jazz.

In many respects, *Rock Around The Clock* was a ludicrous, exploitative, hastily cobbled together load of tat. No one connected with the film denied that – but no one who saw it cared. What mattered was the music, its performance, and the insight – however limited and distorted – into the milieu surrounding it. How American teenagers dressed, spoke and behaved. How they danced. Why some adults enjoyed the music, but others loathed it. It was just an escapist film for young people, but at the same time was infinitely more interesting and educational than, say, *Land Of The Pharaohs* or *My Teenage Daughter*, which were also on general release.

The film's producer, Sam Katzman, obviously knew as little about rock 'n' roll as anyone else in the film industry – he could never have imagined the shekel gush from his measly investment – but he was still prudent enough to have signed Alan Freed, Bill Haley & his Comets, and the Platters.

Miming to all-time definitive versions of *Only You* and *The Great Pretender* – two of the most memorable songs that would ever be written – the Platters shimmered. Tony Williams, we knew for sure, had the most exquisite voice in rock 'n' roll and if Zola Taylor wasn't the first black girl to win white hearts, she was the latest. She was so lovely. (Significantly, they and various backing musicians were the only black people in the movie.)

In introducing the acts, Alan Freed was everything that Jack Payne wasn't. He was unquestionably the world's greatest authority on rock 'n' roll – so we truly believed. He fought the law. Always had a fag on, too.

There were strange sequences. The gawky Freddie Bell & the Bellboys, singing asinine numbers like *(We're Gonna) Teach You To Rock* and *Giddy Up A Ding Dong*, looked like faked-up bandwagon jumpers. They didn't have the authentic ring of Elvis Presley – but what the hell? At least they were more spirited and intense than anything in Britain at the time, and they did have a bass that was shaped like an oversized, long-necked guitar with only four strings. No one had ever seen anything like that before.

Bill Haley's music, in abundance, was as exciting as it had been on record (it couldn't have been otherwise, since he and his band were miming), but his appearance was an eye opener. He was patently portly, and not just avuncular but adult. The celebrated kiss curl, which was mentioned in every single article one read about him, couldn't disguise the overall impression of a suburban insurance salesman on a golfing holiday. He looked as though he might well be wheezing after jumping around like that for a few minutes. Nevertheless, contrary to popular belief, his popularity would wane not because of what he looked like but because his producer lost the knack of picking sure-fire hit songs for him to record.

When the Platters sang, they struck whatever made the strings of the heart go zing, but not so with Haley. He was just antics and excitement. It's all very well for the saxophonist to remove his jacket without missing a note, and for the bass player to roll about on the floor like a circus seal, but there was one thing missing. There was none of the unconstrained sex that was so obviously exuding from every pore of Elvis.

It later transpired that in his heyday, Haley had a goat-like sexual appetite to rival that of Lloyd George, but he couldn't express any sexuality on stage or on record, no matter how much he wrenched his guitar about. Excitement is what he was about – and so he was quite justified in stressing the "good clean fun" aspects of rock 'n' roll whenever he was interviewed.

Parts of the film were so silly as to make *The Grove Family* look like Pinter and the 'stars' were B-movie hopefuls who were never again seen by most cinemagoers. Johnny Johnston played a Liberace type who fancied himself as a ladies man and Alix Talton was an overbearing female agent who looked like Marc Anthony. For both, it was the peak of their Hollywood careers – unless you were impressed by Talton in *The Deadly Mantis*.

The story line was risible, but for any rock 'n' roll fan, it was a must-see, must-hear movie. Through the columns of enormous cinema speakers, it was the loudest and clearest that anyone had ever heard rock 'n' roll played. The only drawback was that it wasn't in colour.

It is not an exaggeration to say that the film changed lives. Of how many movies can that be said? Most people who saw it left the cinema uplifted and exhilarated. "Forget Billy Graham . . . give me

Bill Haley." Some felt inspired. Hundreds of kids wanted to start bands. Thousands wanted rock 'n' roll to be the soundtrack of their lives. Some were affected more than others.

On 3 September, magistrates were told of disturbances after noisy, jiving fans had been ejected from Gaumont cinemas in Dagenham and Leyton. Ruffians were rounded up and fined for insulting behaviour and jeering at the police.

Outside the Gaumont in Stratford, East London, teenagers were shouting, whistling and jumping over flower beds – and in Church Street, Twickenham, three youths were arrested for "singing and shouting rock and roll songs."

While John Davis, the managing director of the Rank Organisation, who distributed the film, studied reports on the audience reaction, one of his publicity department played down the furore by reminding concerned stuffed-shirts that the incidents had only occurred in London: "It has caused no trouble in its provincial showings," he said. Wishful thinking, mate! He had spoken too soon.

Rank acted swiftly but prudently. They weren't about to withdraw a potential money-spinner if they could fudge the issue. They tried to appease religious factions by banning Sunday screenings. Said an official at the Trocadero, Elephant & Castle: "We have been instructed to show the film *Gun Fury* on Sunday, instead of *Rock Around The Clock*." That's all right, then – just a film about people shooting and beating the shit out of each other.

Around the country, Watch Committees, local censors, went further. In the second and third weeks of September, the film was banned from cinemas in Blackpool, Flint, Taunton, Ipswich, all of Gloucestershire, Stockport, Blackburn, Preston, Birmingham, South Shields, Brighton, Gateshead, Belfast, Bristol, Carlisle, Bradford and various other "civilised communities". In towns where it was shown, such newspaper headlines as 'THE ROCK AND ROLL MENACE', 'YOUTH ON THE RAMPAGE' and 'ROCK 'N' MAYHEM' put the fear of God up law-abiding citizens.

After cinema seats had been slashed with cut-throat razors, electric light bulbs and lighted cigarettes had been hurled from balconies into the stalls, fights had broken out between rival Teddy boy gangs, fire hoses had been squirted over sections of the audience, fireworks had been let off, post-film singing and jiving had halted traffic, milk bottles had been thrown at innocent bystanders,

parked cars had been danced on and damaged, constables had been
assaulted and injured, pavements had been blocked, and youths had
turned cinemas into dance halls – even dancing onstage in front of
the screen – there were arrests in Croydon, Manchester, Welling,
Woolwich, Burnley, Lewisham, Liverpool, Carshalton, and God
knows where else. In most cases, police reinforcements were needed
to disperse gangs of jiving, charged-up teenagers. In all, some 60
miscreants – though one would have thought it was 60,000 from the
way the newspapers reacted – were hauled before the beak to be
admonished and fined.

"The film has turned them into packs of wild animals," said a
senior policeman in Bootle; "It really is organised hooliganism," said
a stipendiary magistrate in Leicester; "This so-called music is an
insult to civilised society," fumed a vicar in Colchester. The Bishop of
Woolwich, no less, wrote to the *Times* to express his disgust: "The
hypnotic rhythm and wild gestures have a maddening effect on a
rhythm-loving age group and the result of its impact is the relaxing
of all self-control." Oh, ban that evil addictive music! One would
have thought the Plague had returned.

On 15 September, in an editorial headed 'STIMULUS BEHIND
ROCK 'N' ROLL DISTURBANCES', *The Times* attempted to dissect
the problem. "Bill Haley, the principal band leader in the film and
the chief exponent of rock 'n' roll, is reported as saying that its beat
'stems from old Negro church music'. He and his band keep to the
simple formula of an obvious beat, prominent guitar, and repetitive
tune." Surprise was expressed at the film's ability to inspire any form
of turbulence: "There was more exciting dancing in *Hellzapoppin* and
hotter music in a score of other films." It was like sheet metal
workers attempting to penetrate Egyptian hieroglyphics.

You either felt rock 'n' roll or you didn't. It was as simple as that.
If you did, you were hooked; if you didn't, then you never would.
You might like the odd record now and then, but rock 'n' roll would
never course through your heart and soul. It was not unlike *Invasion
Of The Body Snatchers*, a movie in which extra-terrestrial forces
occupied the bodies of the chosen ones and took over their lives.

The so-called riots, the disturbances were just red herrings. They
were all over in five minutes. That was just a narrow band of teenage
sheep reaping centuries of pent-up frustration, celebrating liberation.
Rock Around The Clock had unlocked the door. Once the media had

described in detail the kind of behaviour which had greeted the movie in one or two London cinemas, it became de rigueur in the provinces. It was like putting on a football scarf and chanting after your team had won. Their exhilaration and exuberance was merely the cork being pulled from the bottle, which had been heartily shaken and was ready to explode. After the pressure had been released, life got back to normal. For some of them.

Basically, the whole episode was press driven. Newspapers sensationalised a few isolated incidents and a handful of unimaginative buffoons went on imitation binges. It set a pattern which has kept smug tabloid editors happy ever since.

As usual, most Fleet Street hacks failed to convey the full picture. The film had gone on release in August and had enjoyed trouble-free showings in over 300 cinemas before a few half-bright Teds went on a spree. Glasgow and Sheffield – neither known for teen rectitude – suffered no disturbances, for instance.

Most teenagers who saw and liked the film did so because it made them feel part of a new movement, one from which previous generations were excluded, or because they loved the music ... it was their music. Music which parents and teachers couldn't relate to or identify with; music they were unable to understand; music they disliked. And when an establishment spokesman, like the wrinkled Jack Payne, mocked and criticised, it was a reflection on him, not the music: he was obviously past it. It's rock 'n' roll, mister, and it's here to stay!

To their credit, Oldham watch committee refused to ban it. "There is nothing wrong with the film," they said. "Although we have not seen it, we know all about it." Berkshire County Council, on the other hand, banned it from every cinema in the county. (One could be forgiven for thinking that decision might have been the origin of the derogatory term 'berk'.) This led to coachloads of fans from the Reading area descending on High Wycombe, where police became territorial and heavy-handed, causing more aggravation than they would have needed to suppress.

The public at large, the unthinking majority who believed what they read in the papers, were left with the impression that rock 'n' roll had sinister overtones, that it was an entirely negative trend leading inevitably to hooliganism. It was probably the first time that teenagers actually had a clearer perspective than politicians, churchmen and other upholders of traditional Christian values (which, of course, allowed for a bit of discreet adultery, a little worship at the temple of Mammon, a spot of hypocrisy when it was needed, the making of promises which couldn't be kept, etc, etc).

"If they showed *Rock Around The Clock* in dance halls, without seats," said one of the teenage tearaways, "then we could really enjoy it" – implying that a degree of audience participation was mandatory at a rock 'n' roll performance. The south London magistrate, Miss Sybil Campbell, was unimpressed: "It's about time you realised you are grown up and stopped behaving like a silly little boy," she said. Yes, lad, get a uniform on and go to Suez.

That it was unsophisticated, working-class music didn't escape the notice of Sir Malcolm Sargent, chief conductor of the BBC Symphony Orchestra, who had already amused his privileged audience by referring to skiffle as "piffle". Ho! ho! ho!, so very comical, Malcolm. At the height of the *Rock Around The Clock* furore, he told promenaders at the Last Night Of The Proms that "in London, more than a quarter of a million young people find Beethoven as exciting as roll and rock". There was a sycophantic roar of laughter. "Oh dear," said Sir Malc, "I gather I got the name wrong. I am delighted."

The following day, he felt moved to expound on the music's deficiencies. "It is nothing more than an exhibition of primitive tom-tom thumping," he said. "The amazing thing about rock and roll is that youngsters who go into such ecstasies sincerely believe that there is something new and wonderful about the music. There is nothing new or wonderful about it: rock and roll has been played in the jungle for centuries."

Sir Malcolm was just off to South Africa for five weeks, to conduct a series of concerts commemorating the 75th birthday of the city of Johannesburg – the city which the previous year had been cleansed of its black population, all of whom had been forcibly moved to purpose-built coloured settlements 11 miles away. The largest city in a country which had just withdrawn from UNESCO rather than modify its racial policy of apartheid. Nice one, Malcolm. Don't stray too near the jungles – your senses might be assailed by some of that nasty primitive tom-tom thumping.

Sargent's view was mirrored by most of the establishment, as can be gathered from a priceless remnant in the BBC Radio archives. On

Does The Team Think?, an *Any Questions*-style diversion featuring prominent opinion-spouters of the day, the panel was asked: "Does the team approve of the action by the watch committees of certain cities in banning the film *Rock Around The Clock*, to the disappointment of many young enthusiasts?"

First to speak was the eminently sensible Labour MP, Emanuel Shinwell, then 72 years old. "I thoroughly disapprove of their action," he said. "I think we've got to try and understand the fundamental nature of the problem. This is a social problem; it's a problem of youth – and we who are somewhat older have got to take full cognisance of what is happening among the youth of the nation. You know, it seems to me that the whole world is rocking and rolling; certainly this government that Bob (Sir Robert Boothby) supports has been rocking and rolling, and sometimes I think that he's rocking and rolling! You get all these Teddy boys, these people who want to jive and dance their heads off, and play all kinds of tricks – well, there's something happening to the youth of the nation: they're trying to free themselves, they're trying to escape. They want more liberty, more freedom. They resent the routine, being in a rut, getting up in the morning, being clocked in, being liberated only when the employer decides they can be liberated . . . the same routine, morning, noon and night. They're getting a little bit tired of it, tired of being in a rut. Therefore, I don't worry about Teddy boys and Teddy girls, whether they come from the slums of London or the universities, when they do a bit of jiving. If they want to dance their heads off in the street or elsewhere, then why not let them have a bit of fun?"

Next up to the microphone was Sir Robert Boothby, the sozzled, self-righteous, adulterous (he had been having an affair with the Prime Minister's wife for many years), huffing-puffing bore. Ex-Eton and Oxford; 56 going on 113. "The question says 'enthusiasts' – well! Enthusiasts for what? For jiving! Jiving! What a thing to do! Can you see me jiving? I've never had the faintest temptation; it's not my idea of fun at all. I think one of the purposes of us old fogies is to stop young people from being silly – and they're being very silly. There are better things to do in life, and much more fun to be had, than jiving – and if they cause a lot of trouble in cinemas, and upset people, well, I'd rather they went off to Cairo and started Teddy boying around there. I think the sooner this ridiculous film is banned altogether, the better. It's causing a lot of trouble to a lot of people, and giving no pleasure except to a few irresponsible lunatics."

Shinwell interjects: "We were nearly all silly when we were young, weren't we?"

Boothby: "Not I."

Shinwell: "Well, you started rather late in life. I'm bound to say that if you did a bit of jiving you'd get some of your weight off."

The token woman panellist, Mary Stocks – 65 years old; an economist, lecturer and author – the blueprint for many a Monty Python sketch: "I think the watch committees are quite right to ban a film if it causes disturbances of this kind, and gives trouble to the police, and encourages young people to behave in this silly way. I am quite convinced that the young people of today, on the whole, have more leisure and more money and more variety of entertainment than they've ever had before – and they have unexpended animal spirits. Now, if those boys had been born rich, they would have been at public schools and their brains would have been kept on the stretch, and when they weren't thinking, they would be made to take violent exercise, and they would go to bed not exhausted, but comfortably tired. Now, I don't think these young people do. I think they work very short hours, at comparatively light jobs – and they've got a lot of animal spirits. The less educated they are; the sillier they are. What can you expect of a generation brought up on such literature as *Reveille* and the *Weekend Mail*?"

Shinwell: "So university students at Oxford and Cambridge do nothing but go to bed? What about their rag weeks? What about some of the stupid, insane things they do – what is the difference? The fact is, the world is in turmoil. Don't we all sometimes feel we'd like to have a break and kick up a bit of a row? It would do a lot of you good if you did!"

Finally, that exemplary Liberal Jeremy Thorpe – also ex-Eton and Oxford; relatively youthful at 27; a barrister, journalist and broadcaster, yet to be elected to Parliament: "I am a lover of music; therefore I am prejudiced and don't like jazz. Jazz to me comes from the jungle, and this is jungle music taken to its logical conclusion. This is musical Mau-Mau. What worries me is that a fourth-rate film with fifth-rate music can pierce the thin shell of civilisation and turn people into wild dervishes. If that's what's going to happen and police genuinely think there is a threat of breach of the peace, then I think the film should be banned. If we are convinced that police-men's hats will be knocked off, and people will be dancing in the street, dustbins will be turned over, lamp posts will be smashed, milk bottles will be strewn around, and two thousand hooligans will be marching down the street – well, faced with that, I think it is not unreasonable to ban it."

A few decades later, we watch *Rock Around The Clock* when it comes round on television and wonder what all the fuss was about. A more quaint, innocuous slice of hokum would be impossible to imagine. But in September 1956, respected sages and pillars of the community saw the film, and rock 'n' roll music, as a threat to civilised society – an evil, pernicious, coded exhortation, a clarion call to anarchy.

Despite *Melody Maker*'s haughty censure, it didn't put off many of their readers from seeing *Rock Around The Clock*. Some of the more open-minded modern jazz players were among those most affected. Though the music they were playing in the cool clubs of Soho was probably the most avant-garde in London, they must have identified with the old-fashioned band at the start of the film: they couldn't attract an audience of any size, their future looked bleak.

Then the action moved to some hick town where Bill Haley and his crew had the joint jumping; his gigs were packed solid with happy-go-lucky dancers. "Mmmmm," thought a few of these old jazzaroonies, "we could rustle up a bunch of boys and make a racket as bad as that. Maybe we could smoke a few bales of hay while the sun shines."

Nineteen

"One afternoon, I was sitting with a bunch of friends at the Harmony Inn in Archer Street, and we decided to go and see *Rock Around The Clock*," recalls Tony Crombie, "to check out what all the fuss was about and maybe to have a laugh. But I came out of there knowing what I had to do. I started putting together a rock 'n' roll band that same evening." He called it Tony Crombie & the Rockets. This was in the last half of July 1956. Within a month, he had signed a recording contract with EMI's Columbia label and had convinced the Bernard Delfont Agency to put him out on a bill-topping variety tour.

Crombie was widely recognised as one of the best modern jazz drummers in Britain, "twice as good as anyone else," according to Benny Green. He had recently been leading his own big band – 10 or 11 pieces, plus Annie Ross on vocals – but business had been dwindling and in January 1956, he and Ronnie Scott, who was in the same boat, broke up their bands and put together a "super-orchestra" of the best players. People like Les Condon (trumpet), Pete King, Benny Green and Derek Humble (saxophones), Lennie Bush (bass) and Stan Tracey (piano). Their first gig was the Gaiety Ballroom in Grimsby, and it went downhill from there. Some gigs were good, some were average, but the general lack of appreciation for their music was too dispiriting. It led to a lot of bad language in the band coach. They played their last date in April. In the weeks that followed, a lot of tea was consumed at the Harmony Inn. "You would often see Crombie standing astride the junction of Archer Street and Windmill Street, looking like one of Al Capone's lieutenants," said Benny Green.

Ronnie Scott and Tony Crombie had known each other since the war, when they were still teenagers, playing at such dives as the Fullado, the Bouillabaisse and the Jamboree, drinking dens come pick-up joints frequented by black American servicemen and Soho prostitutes. In summer 1947, they scraped up the money to fly to New York, where they saw Duke Ellington and Lionel Hampton at the Apollo Theatre in Harlem – the only two white faces in the place. Eighteen months later, together with other be-bop fanatics, they started Club 11, the first modern jazz club in Britain, at Mac's Rehearsal Rooms, opposite the Windmill Theatre, a hop away from Archer Street. During the early fifties, they played wherever they could, trying to keep body, soul and wallet together. Bands came and went, some more successful than others. Summer 1956 found them at something of a loose end. During its opening week, in late July, they walked round the corner to the London Pavilion, where Shaftesbury Avenue meets Piccadilly Circus, and saw the writing on the wall. *Rock Around The Clock*. "That film closed the door on a lot of jobs," reckoned Benny Green, "but, strangely, in ways that few of us predicted, it opened the door to a lot more."

Tony Crombie & the Rockets made their début at the Theatre Royal, Portsmouth, on 10 September, the first British rock 'n' roll band on the national touring circuit – two months ahead of Tommy Steele & the Steelmen. Facing criticism from some of his cynical old mates (including Tubby Hayes, who could not bring himself to accept an invitation to join the Rockets), Crombie was quite candid, admitting that it was a financial rather than an artistic endeavour. "I've tried playing swing and straight dance numbers – but to empty halls," he told a local newspaper reporter, adding that he was now in his sixteenth year as a professional musician. "I've been a martyr long enough – now I want to eat! That's the great thing about rock 'n' roll . . . we get an audience! It's a question of economics: I am merely giving the public what it wants."

His sidemen were all disenfranchised jazzers. Sax player Rex Morris had played in bands led by Tito Burns, Ken Mackintosh, Johnny Dankworth, Vic Lewis and several others but had most recently been with the Courtley Seymour Band. When he left for the Rockets, he took along their pianist, Red Mitchell – who would now be required to stand while playing. Rex would be required to roll on his back while playing and, if he could manage it, to remove his jacket at the same time. Heading into strange territory. Singer Clyde Ray and bass player Ashley Kozak (who would one day manage Donovan) came from the Kirchins, a respected father and son outfit that won the Small Band section of the 1956 *NME* readers' poll. They must have wanted a bit more fun. Surrounded by top-credential modern jazz musicians from respected bands, guitarist Jimmy Currie

had to put his hands up and admit some unexpected interludes in his
career: the Vic Ash Five, Mick Mulligan's (very traditional) Jazz
Band, the Stan Bernard Trio, and a six-week tour of Scandinavia
backing Canadian vaudevillians Fran Dowie and Candy Kane.

They trooped off to see *Rock Around The Clock* again, en masse.
Picking up on the style, the feeling, the tricks, the rhythms, finding
out what made the music tick, what made it tickle the fancy of a
generation. Out on the road, in cool plum jackets and grey slacks,
they played several numbers from the movie – *(We're Gonna) Teach
You To Rock, Razzle Dazzle, Rock Around The Clock* and *R.O.C.K.* –
interspersed with a couple of Elvis songs and a few ideas of their
own.

"Why is it that good players consider it beneath them to entertain
as well as play?" asked Crombie. "I look along the front lines of some
bands and it reminds me of a roll call at a political execution." His
new band would entertain full speed ahead. They were all fans of
Wynonie Harris and Louis Jordan and other R&B swingers and
would essentially be playing jazz under the guise of rock 'n' roll,
letting their hair down and blowing wild.

Early on in the tour, one provincial newspaper reported "shrieks,
whoops, squeals and moans of rapture." Everybody, the band
included, was having a great time. Crombie's agent, Bernard Delfont
was beside himself: "Seasoned troupers on their bill are saying they
haven't seen anything like it, in an English act, for 20 years!"

"The sound they produce would seem to come from 10 men
rather than five, the tenor-and-guitar riffs producing a remarkably
full effect," said the *NME*, when they reached the Finsbury Park
Empire. Extremely pleased to be able to thrash away and have full
houses watching his every move, Crombie told the *NME* guy that
there had been "occasions when a few spirited kids lunged into an
informal jitterbug routine along the gangways – just as if they were
watching THAT film."

"The ironies of the music business seem never ending," mused
Benny Green. "For 10 years, Crombie has played the best jazz drums
in the country and gone almost unnoticed. He then slightly pollutes
his style for the benefit of the variety audiences and finds himself
suddenly acknowledged as all sorts of things."

The *Evening Standard* reckoned Crombie resembled "an elongated
George Raft", the *People* described him as "the East End wild cat who

likes his music tough". Live onstage, his band was fun, a good novelty spectacle for bumpkins, but too music hall to sustain the personality-orientated teenage audience. They would do until the real thing came along. Their records weren't that great either, having the atmosphere of old jazzers play-acting if not slumming. On ballads, Clyde Ray often sounded as though he were making demos for Johnnie Ray, while their rock 'n' roll records sounded old fashioned the moment they were issued, not powerful enough, lacking that primitive, pronounced backbeat. Crombie couldn't help letting you know how good he was and producer Norrie Paramor couldn't disguise how little he understood the style. A sexual element was missing too: almost exclusively, their records concerned dancing rather than having a balance of romance and shagging to excite other than purely physical reaction. Their original lyrics veered towards parody . . . for instance, "We're licking a stick of rock beside the seaside." A little on the Billy Cotton side, one felt. If it had been "She's licking my stick of rock" it might have been different. A version of Freddie Bell's *Teach You To Rock* nudged into the Top 30 for a couple of weeks but never looked like becoming a hit.

They were up against terrifying competition during that last half of 1956. Every week or so, another great (no other word) American record arrived like a rocket ship from Venus. Other than by the zealots, not that many of them were appreciated.

Back track to summer 1956. In one of his columns – by far the most erudite and interesting journalism in the *NME* (or any of the pop papers, come to that) – Benny Green mocked a recent publication called *Teach Yourself Songwriting*. "Throughout history, nobody has yet figured out a way of imparting the creative process to others by instruction," he reminded the opportunistic author. "In short, you can't learn to write a beautiful melody, or an enduring poem, or paint a masterpiece. If you could, those who could afford the most exclusive instruction would become the best creative artists."

Tin Pan Alley songwriting, however, was not always the product of genius. By now, sharp publishers – and artists who wanted to appear hip and youthful – were beginning to realise that any song with the word 'rock' in the title was going to attract attention. As usual, this idea first got underway in the States – with records like *Rock And Roll Waltz* by Kay Starr, *Rock Around Mother Goose* by Barry

Gordon and *Rock And Roll Wedding* by Sunny Gale – but it soon caught on in England, where we suffered such frivolities as *Rockin' And Rollin'* by the Stargazers, *Rock Candy Baby* by Frankie Vaughan, *Rock A Boogie Baby* by Diana Decker, and *Rock Around The Island* by Don Lang. Fakes trying to get exhibited in the same gallery as the real stuff.

Don Lang – real name, Gordon Langhorn – had been playing trombone with Ken Mackintosh's Dance Band since 1950. He also sang in their in-house vocal group, the Mackpies. He drove a Morris 12 but fancied owning a racing car. Nice geezer, but hardly a rock 'n' roll animal. He looked more like a woodwork teacher or a bloke who might open a cycle shop.

However, anxious to boost home-grown talent and genuinely convinced of his potential, the guys at *NME* predicted that "by this time next year", Lang would establish himself as "our top rhythm singer." The *Weekly Sporting Review* joined in and called him "Britain's own rock 'n' roll boy". Yup, he's going to knock old Elvis right off that perch. But don't hold your breath.

The 'rock' obsession quickly radiated through the whole of British show business. As early as May 1956, the wily birds who ran the Moss Empires circuit had added a touch of derring-do (so they thought) to a straightforward variety show by calling it *Rock This Town*. Starring Alma Cogan, Winifred Atwell and Peter Sellers, it packed the Palladium for weeks. By November, there would be half a dozen revues doing the rounds with the word 'rock' in the title.

The King Brothers, a square *Workers' Playtime*-inclined variety act, were suddenly being described as 'Britain's Rock 'n' Roll Kids'. Hardly. Then 17-year-old Pauline Shepherd was billed as 'Britain's Rock 'n' Roll Princess'. Some disagreed. A rock 'n' roll princess would not record a song like *Don't Cry Little Donkey* nor would she allow herself to be photographed in a studio listening approvingly to the playback of Edmund Hockridge's latest waxing – Edmund Hockridge being straighter than the A5.

A cringeworthy version of *Rock A Bye Baby* by Johnny Brandon was described by his record company as 'a hard hitting rock 'n' roll record'. His press picture, posed to make him look like a personable Presley, actually made him look like a deluded and gullible Johnny Come Lately who would soon be a Johnny Gone Quickly.

One knew it was getting beyond a joke when *Melody Maker*, in their 14 July issue, acknowledged a 'Club, Disc Boom As Rock And Roll Craze Spreads'. Bandleaders were reporting a clamour for rock 'n' roll numbers at dance halls. Said Denny Boyce, resident at the Orchid Ballroom in Purley: "I think the clientele would be happy if I played rock 'n' roll all night." Rock 'n' roll clubs were starting up "throughout the country," we were told, and sales of rock 'n' roll records were "soaring".

It must have hurt like hell, but *Melody Maker* was forced to admit it: "Although music critics and the press continue to blast off at rock and roll, the craze is gaining ground." "Because the fans know something we don't," they should have added.

Had someone at *MM* actually taken his head out of the sand to see what was going on out there? It certainly seemed so, because the week before, they had printed – shock! horror! gasp! – a photograph of Gene Vincent & the Blue Caps. Strangely, the *NME* also printed a similar photo that week. The people who ran the Press Office at Capitol Records must have been exceedingly pleased with themselves – and with good reason. He was a completely unknown entity, but Gene had just released his first single, *Be Bop A Lula*.

Heartbreak Hotel, See You Later Alligator and *Blue Suede Shoes* had been eerie and arcane enough, but this was a flying saucer of a record that defied imagination. Even through the fading signal of Radio Luxembourg, the guitar cut through like a switchblade. The musicians made the resident group on *Workers' Playtime* sound like someone laying the table. It must have been made by people who picked up their instruments like Jackson Pollock picked up a paint pot. Gene sounded as if he were in a trance, just this side of sexual hysteria. His energy, his drive, his passion for life simply didn't exist in our grey world. At one point, someone in the studio screamed with uncontrollable excitement. What was this? Someone called Sheriff Tex Davis was credited as a writer! A girl called *Be Bop A Lula*? A name even more bizarre than Elvis. She wears RED BLUE JEANS! She has flying feet. Who could this woman be to inspire such an incredible space-floating monument? Where did she live? What did she do? Did she have a face and body like Natalie Wood in *Rebel Without A Cause*, but a brain like Artie West in *Blackboard Jungle*? She walks around the store. What does that mean? Why would that aspect of her daily routine be interesting enough to incorporate into a song? Was it all in code? This was esoterica beyond interpretation. One hearing on Lux, and you knew that the most important thing in life was to own a copy of that record. Get it home and play it to death. The B-side too.

Be Bop A Lula/Woman Love by Gene Vincent & the Blue Caps. Capitol CL 14599. Two and a half minutes a side. Five minutes that would last forever.

Only an incipient psychopath could have made such a fantastic record, one which no adult could possibly listen to without scoffing. Bill Haley, Elvis Presley, Carl Perkins, and now Gene Vincent . . . all these extraordinary American singers making remarkable records! How do they do it? Where does it come from?

However they did it, they were making them especially for teenagers – to play when their parents weren't around. They were making them to sound celestial on jukeboxes in coffee bars and cafés and amusement arcades. They were making them to sound ethereal and unearthly as they cut through the squealing from the dodgems, blasting out of competing loudspeakers at funfairs.

To the poor deprived citizens who didn't have the right antennae attached to their taste buds, they were just noise.

They were just noise to the *NME*'s new singles reviewer. That man of passion, Geoffrey Everitt, who blew hot and cold like a faulty hairdryer, had left to give his undivided attention to Radio Luxembourg, where he was now Programme Director. And who did the *NME* get to replace him? The obvious man for the job, of course . . . Alex MacIntosh, the Chief News Announcer on BBC Television. A bit like getting Sir Anthony Eden to write about football.

The guy was as square and dense as an Oxo cube, if his review of Gene Vincent's single was anything to go by. "Young Vincent's party pieces are a couple of ditties titled *Be Bop A Lula* and *Woman Love*," he wrote. "The first is a straightforward junior idiot chant. The second is the idiot some years older – still drooling but apparently having come to realise that candy bars and funny clothes are no great substitute for the opposite (if I may use the expression) sex. The Old Lady of Portland Place (the BBC) has boggled at *Woman Love* and very properly so; you won't hear it on the airwaves. Whichever way you slice it, it's still vocal pornography. Strictly from the booby hatch. Much more of this and my advice is to pack a grip and make a quick run for the hills."

The more they ranted and railed, the better we liked it. Few people older than about 20 liked rock 'n' roll. It's a wonder we ever got to hear it. Somehow, *Be Bop A Lula* got to number 16. Gene's equally astonishing follow-ups, *Race With The Devil* and *Blue Jean Bop*, also charted. It had started.

The only possible reason that these and similar records were even released here was that they might make money. The city gents who controlled the record companies wouldn't become acclimatised to rock 'n' roll for decades, but they always appreciated that there might be a profit to be made by following current trends. That was their job – making money, not encouraging creativity or art. They also knew that before they were likely to sell, records had to be heard, to which end they employed specialist pluggers to bend the ears of BBC producers and disc jockeys. Only now and then, did they manage to get a rock 'n' roll record on the playlist . . . but one big hit could wipe out the deficit caused by a dozen or more non-hits. Basically, few music bizoids had any idea what they were doing, whether a record was intrinsically good or bad, whether it was likely to sell or not. Their methodology was enshrined in the maxim 'Throw enough shit at the wall and some of it is bound to stick.' It was a philosophy that would serve the industry well for many, many years.

One record that did stick was an amazingly primitive, vital and revolutionary rock 'n' roll creation called *Why Do Fools Fall In Love*, by 13-year-old Frankie Lymon and his vocal backing group the Teenagers. Immediately, it found its way into the hearts and minds of 'the British record buying public' – now obviously changing and expanding furiously – and, in the middle of July, reached number one. A record made for America's rhythm & blues market, by a bunch of black kids who happened to like singing together in their New York schoolyard, was outselling all the David Whitfields and Ronnie Hiltons and Doris Days and Teresa Brewers. It was number one for three weeks.

The business saw little merit in Lymon's record. In his widely syndicated review column, the utterly hopeless, sub-Dean Martin, grinning Light Programme crooner Benny Lee, wrote "Sometimes I wonder if this dizzy roundabout they call the record business isn't the craziest set-up under the sun. When five schoolboys, who can't read a note of music, sling together what they imagine is a song and the resulting record sells 100,000 copies in 10 days, I don't just wonder, I know!"

"The Teenagers are five coloured kids, all under 17, whose vocalising has earned them a record contract with the small Gee label in America and first disc sales are already topping half a million. The leader of the group, pocket sized Frankie Lymon wrote the lyric for *Why Do Fools Fall In Love* when he was 13. The group literally made up the music as they went along."

"After hearing the result, my opinion is the kids would be better sticking to their school books. To my ears, their singing, if you can call it that, is distasteful and completely unmusical. When I think of the number of talented people who write songs, and never a note is published, I feel disgusted." Poor old washed-up geezer, we thought. Young fresh-faced virgins swooned when they listened to Frankie Lymon and BBC mediocrity Benny Lee would never be able to understand why.

Clearly, the world as we knew it was changing. For the better, we felt sure. For some, however, accepting rock 'n' roll was as difficult as accepting Richard Hamilton's pop-art creations, currently on display at the Whitechapel Art Gallery. If you were raised on Rembrandt and Gainsborough, or even Van Gogh and Lautrec, they just didn't make sense. It wasn't real art.

"Not until the Stargazers performed their version of *Why Do Fools Fall In Love* on Cyril Stapleton's show," some nitwit on the *NME* observed, "was it noticeable, by comparison, that the Teenagers scored a hit through lack of real competition from a top vocal group." You have to feel sorry for a chap who could write something like that. The only good thing about the Stargazers was their name. In October, they made a jingle for Murraymints, the too-good-to-hurry mints, which was more their métier.

Only on Radio Luxembourg could one hear *One Night* by Smiley Lewis or *The Fool* by Sanford Clark, but *Blueberry Hill* by Fats Domino found reluctant, restricted BBC airplay once it rose to number six. Said the *NME*'s Alley Cat: "It seems a great pity that a delightful song like *Blueberry Hill* must be massacred by a weapon like the voice of Fats Domino."

Meanwhile, the Elvis Presley controversy was gathering momentum, with journalists queuing up to expose him as the devil's agent. One such was Tom Hutchinson of *Picturegoer*, who headed his piece

'THIS MAN IS DANGEROUS' and wrote like the prophet of doom. It would have been easy to dismiss some of the nonsense coming out of Fleet Street as a calculated attempt to create sensationalism and thus sell newspapers – but sometimes one felt that these articles were being concocted by people who actually believed what they were writing.

"I have never met Elvis Presley but already I dislike him intensely," Tom began. "The news that he is coming to England early next year (as if!) fills me with advance revulsion. If the Musicians' Union could prevent his working here, it would suit me fine. For I feel that I *do* know Presley via the vicious effect he has on his American fans. I know that this man is *dangerous* and I don't want to see British youngsters hacking out his name on their arms with clasp-knives, or see sex treated as an appalling commercial freak show."

"This is what is happening in America. *Picturegoer*'s men on the spot – Leonard Coulter in New York and Guy Austin in Hollywood – have sent me the facts about Presley. Coulter tells of a Kansas City concert at which an army of girl teenagers swarmed onstage and began ripping Presley's trousers off."

"Austin says that records such as *Heartbreak Hotel* and *That's All Right, Mama* are selling by the million. At concerts, 'his powerful voice rises above the din like a mating call in the jungle'. Audience fever is spurred on by Presley's suggestive leers and postures. Johnnie Ray was never like this, I am told. Neither were Sinatra or Crosby. They did not, and do not, rely on a tom-cat's caterwauling to achieve their vocal effects. And their fans are not unhealthily stimulated to morbid hysteria."

"This 21-year-old Tennessee boy is hailed as the new Marlon Brando. I hope his 'streetcar' will not reach England. Perhaps this crazy cult will have gone off the rails before then."

Needless to say, such ravings only consolidated Presley's position. Devil or angel? Either way, you were already under his spell. Most people believed what they read in the papers.

In September 1956, *Hound Dog* was a hair-raising hit single; weeks later, *Blue Moon* was a hit EP. His first movie *Love Me Tender* opened a week before Christmas.

"Can Elvis survive this film?" asked *Picturegoer*. Most people seemed to think he would be around for a while yet. So too, we hoped, would Little Richard, whose first UK release *Rip It Up/Ready Teddy* was released in November. Back then, the editor of one national newspaper thought it perfectly acceptable to describe him as "an animated golliwog".

At the end of the year, Tony Crombie gave his Rockets some time off and flew to New York to see some jazz and presumably to try and rehabilitate himself. It had been the weirdest six months of his life – the strangest moment coming when he appeared on *Sunday Night At The London Palladium* with fellow guests Alma Cogan and Harry Secombe dressed up in rock 'n' roll outfits.

In his slipstream had already come a surge of other rock 'n' roll bands, some containing old modern jazz cronies. Two of his former big band vocalists now led groups of their own: Art Baxter & his Rockin' Sinners and Bobby Breen & his Rock 'n' Roll Rockers. The latter made little headway, while Art and the boys (crimson and black uniforms, abundant exuberance, a live set based entirely on Haley numbers) cut a handful of foolish sounding records and just about managed to make it into 1957. Behind them were Dave Shand & his Rockin' Rhythm, Don Sollash & his Rockin' Horses and the Geoff Taylor Band.

A devoutly non-jazz strand of bands was also emerging, enough of them to stage a Rock 'n' Roll Jamboree at Wimbledon Palais. Rory Blackwell's Rock 'n' Rollers, the House Rockers, Leon Bell's Bellcats and Oscar's Hot Icebergs. They had chosen the wrong venue.

The real revolution was happening at the 2Is Coffee Bar in Soho.

Twenty

Since stumbling into the 2Is Coffee Bar on 14 July 1956, the day of the Soho Fair, the Vipers Skiffle Group had been playing there regularly. "We started going in two or three nights a week, then four or five nights, then six, and finally every night!" says Wally Whyton. "Within weeks, literally, the place went from being practically empty to being crammed solid every night."

By this time, the original guitar/vocal trio of Wally Whyton, Johnny Booker (aka Johnny Martyn) and Jean Van Den Bosch had been augmented by washboard player Johnny Pilgrim, a friend from the 100 Club, and double bass plucker Tony Tolhurst, who Wally had known for years and managed to entice into the fold.

Before the Vipers arrived, business at the 2Is had been erratic to say the least. In April, when Paul Lincoln and Ray Hunter had borrowed money to purchase the lease from Freddie and Sammy Irani (the two Is after whom it was named), they felt that the prime location – 59 Old Compton Street, on the south side between Wardour Street and Dean Street – would ensure abundant passing trade . . . but the whole street was jam-packed from end to end with coffee bars and cafés and, after three months, they were becoming concerned.

Both partners had been, and continued to be, all-in wrestlers, first in Australia and later in England. When he arrived at Tilbury in 1951, with a suitcase and an envelope of newspaper cuttings proclaiming him holder of the New South Wales title, Lincoln had 20 pounds in his pocket. Wearing a mask, he wrestled under the name of Dr Death, the first of several to adopt the name, and, wearing a smile, he promoted wrestling matches around the country. He stood only 5 feet 8 inches, while 'Rebel' Ray Hunter was gigantic, and would become British Empire and Commonwealth Heavyweight champion three times.

"In all the time I was singing at the 2Is, I only saw one act of violence," recalls Wally. "Some guy came in and managed to get some blood on Ray's shirt – he had obviously just been involved in some skirmish on the street. Now Ray was always terribly fastidious about his clothing and he was aghast! He just whacked this guy, knocked him straight out of the door and halfway across Old Compton Street."

To begin with, the Vipers' sessions were informal. "I still had my day job, so I would wander up from work, meet the others in the Swiss Tavern, just along the road from the 2Is, and then we would play all evening," says Wally. "No pressure at all. We played every song we knew and tried to work in one or two new ones every night, rehearsing as we went along, working out harmonies, reading the lyrics from bits of paper strewn around our feet. Once it started getting crowded, that became impossible, of course."

As soon as it got around that Tommy Steele had been discovered at the 2Is, "singing for buns and coffee", according to the papers, teenagers started arriving from every corner of the suburbs. Paul Lincoln began charging sixpence entrance fee, and when queues started forming, he split the evening into two houses. The Vipers would play from 7.30 until 9, then nip up to the Swiss Tavern for a swift pint before returning for a second set, from 9.30 until 11. During the interval, Lincoln would have cleared out the first bunch of punters and admitted another load.

Ironically, Tommy had only ever played there twice, and then only briefly, but the story of his discovery turned the 2Is into a goldmine. Lincoln was a happy man, although he would later admit that he had been "completely indifferent to Tommy Steele – he didn't impress me one way or the other."

During the day, the 2Is functioned as any other coffee bar, specialising in cappuccinos, goulash, toasted cheese, sesame seed rolls and Coca-Cola, while at night, the somewhat claustrophobic, drab and dusty basement throbbed and echoed to the sound of skiffle.

Lionel Bart, who made a point of investigating any new haunt, suggested that the place could do with a bit of tarting up – and he, Maurice Agis and Mike Pratt agreed to paint the walls "for a few bob, a crate of beer and free entrance for life". They painted what Wally describes as "a sort of abstract cubist thing in bright colours" on the back wall and then, along the side walls, Bart added the *pièce de résistance*, a series of Cleopatra-style eyes. "I must have used the wrong kind of paint," says Lionel, "because it took ages to dry and kept coming off on punters' clothes." The eyes on the wall led some people to think it was the Two Eyes Coffee Bar.

Denmark Street opportunity-seekers Bill Varley and Roy Tuvey were in the Vipers picture long enough to arrange (through music publisher Stan Bradbury) for George Martin to come down and see them, but various members of the group were reluctant to involve themselves with managers and they decided to make their own way. They did, however, sign a contract with George Martin and had their first Parlophone single *Ain't You Glad/Pick A Bale Of Cotton* issued in November. It was well plugged on Radio Luxembourg but didn't catch on.

By now, Tommy Steele was in the charts and on television, and the 2Is myth was carved in stone. The coffee bar's popularity was such that on 9 November, Paul Lincoln was able to open a second venue, the New 2Is Club, which ran every weekend in that multi-scene cellar at 44 Gerrard Street – where John Hasted's Skiffle Group still had their Tuesday-night club running. The Vipers opened it on Friday night and on Sunday, Kirk Denning's Dynamos became the first of many rock 'n' rollers to enjoy the 2Is' patronage.

The Vipers started winding down their reliance on the 2Is in early December, when they landed a weekly 100 Club gig, supporting Terry Lightfoot's Jazzmen.

Thinking they were beyond cool, they bought matching black shirts for the season. "We wore whatever we felt like wearing in the coffee bars but felt a responsibility to dress up a bit for the jazz people," says Wally. "After all, we were about to play at the 100 Club, where a few weeks ago we had stood as awe-struck punters. I had been over to Paris a couple of times and black shirts had become fashionable there, so we thought we'd look pretty natty if we got some. But then some of the jazzers, who resented us playing there anyway, gave us a hard time, said we looked like a bunch of fascists. We dropped them pretty quickly and started dressing more flamboyantly. Well, what the fuck, we thought . . . we're in it now, we might as well go for it."

By the end of 1956, skiffle was the music-biz buzz word. Every agent in Tin Pan Alley suddenly felt he needed a skiffle group. It was the big thing, and it was getting bigger every day; a craze that needed exploiting. If you didn't have a skiffle group on your books, you were nowhere. Audiences were demanding skiffle. If you didn't give them skiffle, you were not going to make as much money as you could have made. This would mean nights of regret, sleepless nights. Bernard Delfont, of course, was on the case.

Unfortunately, Wally wasn't. "During that period, I was acting as the group's manager – and I got a call from Delfont, who asked me to go and see him, which I did. He asked me how much we wanted for two weeks at the Prince of Wales Theatre and I, in my ignorance, asked for the same money as we had been getting at the 2Is." Mr Delfont didn't express any surprise but merely pencilled in the dates, the first two weeks in February, and said that a contract would be in the post.

Thus they were hurled into variety. Music Hall. What remained of vaudeville.

To their embarrassment, they were billed as headliners – over a mind-boggling list of performers, some of whom had been at it for years. Experienced hoofers and comedians Jimmy Wheeler and Dickie Henderson, for instance, and singer Gary Miller, who had scored a couple of hits and was currently in the chart again, with his version of *Garden of Eden*. Not to mention sex goddess Yana and another skiffle group, led by Bob Cort. Additionally, there were such old hands as Brian Andro ('dancing on a wire'), the Marthys (balancing and juggling), Bob Hammond's Feathered Performers and Fernando's Dogs. Most were vaudeville veterans, though the compère was a relatively new face, Des O'Connor, who "fared well with rather creaky material," according to one reviewer.

The Vipers were particularly intrigued by the much-vaunted television siren Yana, who wore sheath dresses that accentuated her shape and purred her way through such silly songs as *Climb Up The Wall*. Some critics had not fallen for her sexual allure: "The noise she makes when she takes a breath is as loud as the noise she makes when singing. It sounds like a large female concertina being unsqueezed between each musical phrase," said one.

The Vipers had been to John Stephen's shop in Beak Street, to buy strawberry pink corduroy shirts, and then to Vince's Man's Shop in Fouberts Place to buy faded blue jeans in sanforized shrunk denim. "We were upstarts, but we thought we were the bee's knees," says Wally. "Everybody seemed to enjoy the shows, even though we had three microphones, one for each singer, but none at all for the bass or the washboard. God knows what the sound must have been like."

The Prince of Wales, a fine old theatre in Coventry Street, had a seating capacity of 1,140 and a performing area that measured 43 feet by 22 feet, far greater than the whole 2Is basement. There was a revolving stage, and every night, twice a night for a fortnight, the Vipers came round singing and grinning. The first night, they pissed their pants with fear but after that, they pissed their pants with laughter. It didn't matter in the slightest, because the happy-go-lucky audience laughed with them. The critic from *The Stage* was somewhat concerned about "their lack of stage craft" but nobody else seemed to notice. Except for the critic Kenneth Tynan, who was singularly unimpressed. "Two skiffle groups loudly expose the monotony of their atavistic cult," he wrote. "Here is phony primitivism run mad."

On the two Tuesdays, between shows, the Vipers beetled up Wardour Street and managed to squeeze in their 100 Club spots. But these were soon a thing of the past.

At the Prince of Wales, they had been bearded by Stanley Dale, an agent who ran a company called Associated London Scripts from an office in Shepherds Bush. They fell for his patter and before long he was representing them. Meanwhile, their second single *Don't You Rock Me Daddy-O* had reached the Top 10 and an equally potent follow-up *Hey Liley, Liley Lo* was set to go. Somehow, they managed to get onto Jack Payne's television show.

"He didn't like us at all," says Whyton. "He was surly at the rehearsal and worse when the show went out. He introduced us by saying 'These people have been put on the programme against my wishes, but here they are, the Vipers Skiffle Group' – straight out, no messing!"

The group's first out-of-towner was a one-night stand in Cheltenham on 23 February 1957. They were topping the bill over a trad-jazz band led by drummer Lennie Hastings – who wore a wig, which he used to like flipping around. "If you were trying to chat up a bird, he would manage to get behind her and start lifting up his wig with a drumstick, so you were distracted from your mission," recalls Whyton.

They made the trip in a lorry belonging to Oatsman's, a furniture shop in Tottenham Court Road. Wally's brother knew the driver, who was happy about making a surreptitious weekend variation. Into the back climbed the Vipers, with all their gear, and Lennie's mob with all their gear. Sitting on the floor, in pitch black, having to feel around for the crates of beer and worrying in case someone should drop the bottle opener.

"That was the first time I ever remember an audience screaming," says Wally. "That was the start of our brief career as teen idols. Lennie went on and did the first half and all through his set, the audience was shouting out for the Vipers. He was really pissed off. Then we went on and there was this wall of screaming. It was sold out and the whole house was clamouring for us – and there we were, congregated round the solitary microphone that the theatre had provided, trying to put on a show. It was an amazing thing."

"Going home, we were locked up in the back of this lorry again, everyone smoking and singing and drinking and being stupid. Lennie's band were drinking because they suspected it was all over for them; we were drinking because we were the new kids on the block. When Charlie took his lorry into work on the Monday morning, he was fired. There was piss and dog-ends and beer everywhere and he was sacked on the spot."

The Vipers played a string of one nighters, as far north as Edinburgh and Glasgow, as far south as Ryde on the Isle of Wight. "We looked like ghosts up onstage until a comedian called Dickie Dawson gave us some lessons on how to apply stage make-up," recalls Booker. Dawson was a flash Harry from Hampshire, a young comic who would marry Diana Dors before moving to America and getting the part of Private Newkirk on the comedy series *Hogan's Heroes*. During his music-hall career, he specialised in impressions of Robert Mitchum, Humphrey Bogart, Groucho Marx, Edward G. Robinson, Billy Eckstine, Jerry Lewis and Rod Steiger. "Dickie was this fast-talking hipster type, very sharp, wore Italian suits," says Wally. "He had a coffee percolator in his dressing-room when most of us were lucky to find a coat hanger. He may have been ninth on the bill but somehow always managed to get the star dressing room with the settee. He sold me a couple of suits but also told us how to rub this Tan 29 pancake stuff on our faces, so that we looked like South Americans. Then he made us put all this eye-liner on and paint our eyebrows. We had no idea what we were doing: some nights we looked like chipmunks, others we looked like wooden dummies."

By the spring of 1957, it seemed as if every schoolboy in Britain was in a skiffle group – and the Vipers were seen as the prime role model. Lonnie Donegan may have been the main source of material but he had an electric lead guitarist and a jazzy drummer; the Vipers, with their boisterous vocals, synchronised strumming and the all-important washboard (the key to the do-it-yourself boom), laid down the style that all provincials sought to emulate.

Realising this, Stanley Dale suddenly flashed on the perfect money spinner. He would organise a nationwide skiffle contest, hosted by the Vipers, with heats in every part of Britain and the most deserving contestants progressing to a grand final, where the ultimate winner would be showered with riches.

Thus did the Vipers embark on an interminable, enervating slog around the country. Reading, Hull, London, Derby, Nottingham, Sheffield, Leeds, on and on it went, a week at each venue, two shows a night, a local final on Saturday nights, and a national final at some unspecified time in the future.

"Stanley Dale knew that as well as drawing our fans, he would draw fans and friends of local groups," says Johnny Booker, "and because their popularity was judged on applause, they obviously got as many people as possible to the gig, hoping they could win and eventually become famous."

"It was all a big con," agrees Wally. "Stanley Dale was only interested in getting the maximum number of punters into the theatre; musical ability had nothing to do with it. He used to put three or four local groups on each night – and whoever had the biggest following would be sure to play again on the Saturday night."

"For us, it was all too depressing. Practically every group would have a go at *Don't You Rock Me Daddy-O* – and then, at the end, we would have to sing it too. The schedule was very disciplined and discipline was not what we were about. The reason we'd started singing was because we were bohemian free-spirit types, and here we were pinned down to a 17-minute showbiz act, twice a night for what seemed like a million years."

They got tired of hearing the same old jokes too, night after night. Two of Dale's comedians were permanent fixtures on the tour – Jimmy Edmundson and Stan Van 'the Zany Man', who had wild frizzy hair and played frantic violin for light relief – and his namesake Jim Dale (no relation) was the compère. He also told jokes and sang a few numbers with the pit band, who provided incidental music throughout. Jim was from up near Kettering, a kid who had only ever wanted to be in show business and had started out as a juggler and comedian. His life would change dramatically after his George Martin-produced single *Be My Girl* reached number two, at the end of the year.

Also on the touring show were a conjurer, tumblers, a knife throwing act, Susan & Valerie Pardoe ('Two misses with the hits'), Betty Fox's Eight Dancing Teenagers (kicking and whirling in unison, in the style of the Television Toppers), and Campbell & Rogerson, a traditional music hall duo who had been treading the boards since before the war. "They were amazing," says Wally. "One of them would come out in a baggy shirt, dancing around, and you suddenly became aware that his arms were getting longer – they kept extending until he had this massive wingspan of about 18 feet. And then you realised that his face was a mask on the back of his head – and that he had his back to the audience. Then the other guy would come on, dancing furiously with a partner, which turned out to be a dummy whose feet were attached to his feet. They had a whole truckload of props, which they loaded into the theatre each Sunday."

Naturally, liaisons were formed between some of the Vipers and some of the girls on the bill, and good times were plentiful, but these were precarious times for the old troupers. *The Stage*, their professional newspaper, applauded skiffle, grateful that it was helping to support the Music Hall tradition: "Variety needs some new blood and this is a healthy way of getting it."

Sadly, the truth was rather more gloomy. By the autumn of 1957, television was already in the homes of 20 million people – most of whom no longer saw any point in going out to see a live show. They would rather stay in, sit around the fire and attach themselves to the 'glass teat' (as Harlan Ellison called it), watching *Hancock's Half Hour*, *Opportunity Knocks*, *Amos 'n' Andy*, *The Dave King Show*, *Take Your Pick*, *The Adventures Of Robin Hood*, *Alfred Marks Time*, *Emergency Ward 10*, *The Phil Silvers Show*, *Treasure Island*, *Dixon Of Dock Green*, *The Benny Hill Show*, *What's My Line?* and any number of other programmes.

Only young people were propping up the variety circuit – and they knew what they liked (rumbustious music) and what they didn't like (equilibrists and dog acts). "Fortunately, they liked us," says Johnny Booker. "The boys would cluster round asking questions about guitars and chords and lyrics, and the girls would treat us like people from another planet. There were times when I'd look down at the girls in the audience, screaming up at us, and I'd just wonder what the hell was going on, why people would pay money to watch us bashing out a few songs. Sometimes, we would try to leave and there would be women crammed solid from the stage door to the car. There were times when my clothes were all but ripped off me, other times when girls had broken into the car. They would scratch messages into the paintwork with their nail files. It was mayhem."

The tour and the skiffle contest rumbled on beyond Christmas and on into 1958, still with no end in sight. Said John Jack, who was now working as the Vipers' road manager, general factotum and hustler-bustler: "It was like a long, increasingly dull shag that never reached a climax."

Twenty-one

The order was changing, the old guard were toppling. 1957 would be a transitional year for the music business – alarming for some, exhilarating for others. One thing was clear: like it or loathe it, teenage music was here to stay. The orchestra leader Geraldo was among those who wished it were otherwise. "Skiffle is sheer unadulterated piffle which cannot be classed as music," he opined. Silly old fossil, we thought.

There had been a symbolic moment in November 1956, when that cherished notion 'the show must go on' had been dashed in the dirt – by the Queen, no less. So distraught was she about what was happening in Hungary and Egypt that she took the unprecedented step of vetoing the Royal Command Performance. Scheduled, amusingly, for Guy Fawkes night, it was cancelled five hours before the curtain was due to go up. She was advised against attending by the frock-coated *éminences grises*, who told Her Majesty that it would be unseemly to be seen laughing at court jesters like Harry Secombe or Max Bygraves. That was the official explanation – though she had perhaps discovered that the nauseating Liberace was on the bill and simply couldn't face having to sit through his act. She would happily sit through Tommy Steele's, a year later.

By the end of 1956, as the Prime Minister Sir Anthony Eden was being helped out of the back door of Downing Street and shipped off to Jamaica to prevent the populace from seeing what a bumbling nutcase he'd become, attitudes towards the hydrogen bomb had divided the sane from the loony – although each side, the ban-the-bombers and the supporters, thought they were the rational party. On the record scene, improbably, the H-bomb divided the generations.

The icons of the new and old, Tommy Steele and Dickie Valentine, would, throughout the coming year, tussle for audience control and loyalty. Maybe Dickie's fans were getting married and couldn't afford to buy so many records. Maybe it was this year's fashion replacing last year's – everyone wanted the new design.

Dickie might have had a premonition that it was game-over in December 1956, when his latest Decca release *Christmas Island* peaked at number 8 and, as it turned out, became his last ever Top 10 hit. At least he went out with a bang – a bigger bang, in many respects, than even American rhythm & blues star Johnny Ace had, when he blew half his head off playing Russian roulette two Christmases before.

Valentine was Camden Town's answer to Dean Martin, except that he didn't drink as much. He was a dance orchestra smoothie, whose lilting voice floated sensuously on a featherbed of muted trumpets and soft strings, caressing the erogenous parts of many yearning women. His forte was expressing not his own sentiments, but those of Tin Pan Alley tunesmiths who knocked out songs as easily as their television equivalents wrote soap opera episodes.

In 1955, he had put five singles into the Top 10: *Finger Of Suspicion, Mr Sandman, A Blossom Fell, I Wonder* – whose greeting card-style lyrics typified the 'infantile songs for undiscerning adults' syndrome on which so many music publishers depended: "I wonder who paints the sky so blue; who paints the snowflakes white; who wakes the sun up every day, and lights the stars at night" – and the biggest, *Christmas Alphabet*. Although it kept Bill Haley's *Rock Around The Clock* off the top of the charts for three weeks, it was a truly abysmal record: C is for candy, H is for happiness, R is for reindeer, I is for icing on the cake, S is for stocking, T is for toys, M is for mistletoe, A is for angels, S is for sickly saccharin shit – er, oh no, sorry – Santa Claus.

The original version of *Mr Sandman*, by jaunty Wisconsin quartet the Chordettes, was dreamy and romantic, an imaginative prayer for the speedy deliverance of a dreamboat lover: "give him a lonely heart like Pagliacci, and lots of wavy hair like Liberace". (Though not his libido, presumably.) Dickie obviously had to change the lyric . . . would he concoct something equally ingenious – for instance "give her a mouth like a vacuum cleaner, and lovely breasts just like Sabrina"? Not a bit of it. He merely left out the verse – but even so, his lacklustre, zing-free version still outsold the sprightly Chordettes.

His currency was on the wane as soon as rock 'n' roll hit. When the cowboys rode into town, he had to put his hands up. What else could he do? He didn't have the wherewithal to fight, and joining them was out of the question. *Christmas Island* was where he met his

Waterloo. "How would you like to spend Christmas on Christmas Island?" he warbled – at the very time that the British government was preparing to obliterate the tropical paradise by using it as a testing ground for a nuclear bomb many times more powerful than that which destroyed Hiroshima. They went ahead with the explosion on 15 May 1957. For years afterwards, geiger counters went berserk when passed over the crayfish and lobsters living in the clear blue waters on a waist-deep shelf stretching 300 yards around the island.

As a result of this, *Christmas Island* remains the only interesting record Dickie Valentine ever made. It marked the point where working-class youngsters in their droves started rejecting adult values and behavioural patterns and began immersing themselves in an exclusive new culture of their own making.

Until now, they had had no Alan Freed figure to cater for them, to guide them, to let them in on his passion. Jack Jackson was the first British disc jockey playing rock 'n' roll records on a regular basis – but he wasn't a crazed evangelist like Freed. He was being paid by Decca to play them. In Britain, we were extremely fortunate to have a legal payola system, which ensured that we were able to hear practically every great record as it was released. The record companies bought half-hour chunks of air-time on Radio Luxembourg and plugged all their latest records, as many as they could cram in. The disc-jockeys would talk over the introduction, let us hear the first half and then fade out over the instrumental break. Rock 'n' roll fans knew the times of all crucial programmes and listened religiously. Thank God for Radio Luxembourg, a lifeline without which the development of rock music in Britain would have been all but stifled.

The BBC was loath to play any noisy record unless it had accidentally become a hit, in which case it got an occasional spin. Even though Jack Jackson had a BBC show as well as his Luxembourg slots, he wasn't saying to his producer "Look, we've got to play this stuff – it is totally amazing!" in the way that Freed had. Jackson didn't like noisy teenage music.

Most BBC disc-jockeys, it seemed, were merely announcers; graduates of either drama school or mediocre dance bands. Pete Murray (who was also paid to play great records on Luxembourg but seldom played one on the Light Programme) made no bones about his stumbling entry to the business. "To put it bluntly," he admitted, "I was lumbered. I had the notion that I was an actor – Royal Academy of Dramatic Art and all that. I try to forget it now, but I was actually a Rank starlet. Diana Dors and I got the push at the same time. Then my agent had a brainwave: 'How would you like to work abroad on a radio station?' he asked. I saw myself giving dramatic eye-witness accounts of floods and riots . . . but then he fractured the picture by telling me he meant Luxembourg. That's how I became a disc jockey." Not a lot of messianic zeal there, then.

For the most part, Light Programme presenters were told what to play by highbrow producers who'd left university with degrees in whatever and ambitions to climb the BBC ladder. Not a single one of them had succumbed to rock 'n' roll – and even if they had, they wouldn't have dared to play it. Anyone seen actively endorsing that kind of thing was likely to be castigated by the starchy bosses on the fifth floor, given a black mark on his Personnel Dept file – forever stigmatised as "that man who played the Smiley Lewis disc on *Housewives' Choice*".

For a few months only, we were able to hear the real thing, thanks to former *NME* singles reviewer Geoffrey Everitt, now Programme Director at Radio Luxembourg and obviously back on track. In retrospect, it seems almost dreamlike. For two hours every Saturday night, from 8 until 10, sandwiched between *Irish Requests* and *Scottish Requests*, Luxembourg broadcast a youth-orientated programme called *Jamboree*. The host was Gus Goodwin, a keen teen who ran the British branch of the Bill Haley fan club, and the show was divided into sections – the best of which was a 30-minute segment specially recorded by Alan Freed and air-mailed from New York.

For the rock 'n' roll cognoscenti, this became the most important half-hour of the week. He played Chuck Berry, he played Fats Domino, he played Nappy Brown, he played records from the American chart, he played records by people we'd never heard of. He played records by Little Richard when they were still unobtainable here. He was always exuberant, sometimes shouting and whooping over the introduction or fade of records, as though he was jumping around in his chair as they played. He read out requests . . . this one is for Deborah in "St Albans, Herts . . . I guess that's short for Hertshire." Alan Freed was beaming out of our radios, playing our music. How one prayed for optimum atmospheric conditions so the wavering signal didn't fade. How we cursed when it did.

In February 1957, British teenagers got a champion of their own, the unlikeliest of rock 'n' roll maniacs, a man as eccentric as Freed but as upper-crust as the Home Secretary. He was to do everything in his power to expose young people to the music he loved. Born in Greenford, Middlesex, on 7 August 1931, Jack Good had been President of both the Oxford University Debating Society and Balliol Dramatic Club during the early fifties. Since coming down, he had acted in 94 performances of *The Queen And The Rebels* at the Haymarket Theatre and, in a double act with Trevor Peacock, had worked as a stand-up comic at the Windmill Theatre, between nude tableaux vivants and whirling dance routines.

"I was very depressed with the state of British theatre: it had become degenerate, too fancy," he quickly concluded. "I preferred the old Globe Theatre style, where the audience would get up, join in the fight, shout, enjoy themselves . . . and that is exactly what happened when I went to see *Rock Around The Clock*. Bill Haley shouted out 'On your marks. Get set. Now ready. Go! Everybody razzle dazzle!' and with one accord, the audience leapt to its feet and started bopping about in a way I had never in my life seen before! I was looking at the screen and then the audience, back and forth, as though I were at Wimbledon. I was totally bowled over by the simple display of animal force and energy – and I loved it."

"I had never been interested in pop music, which always seemed sickly, the worst sort of commerciality. Rock 'n' roll didn't suffer from that. Granted, some of the lyrics were inane, but that didn't matter. It was like abstract art, a very simple abstract art with a definite beat. It was vigorous and unpretentious and I was just completely sold on it."

Without too much optimism, he applied for a job as trainee television producer at the BBC – and managed to convince them of the need for a teenage show with rock 'n' roll overtones. Thus was launched a Saturday evening series aimed at young people of all ages; in essence, a weekly 55-minute variety show on which a milling, dancing audience was integral.

The *6.5 Special* was a big deal for the paternalistic BBC. Up until now, their schedules had closed down for an hour at six o'clock – so that mothers could get the children to bed before adult programming began at seven. Now, every Saturday, starting on 16 February 1957, this hour would be devoted to teenagers – and the signature tune, "over the points, over the points", would burn deep into the nation's consciousness.

Jack Good's co-producer was former film starlet Josephine Douglas, who'd sat in the ops room in the 1952 Battle of Britain movie *Angels One Five*, looking glamorous but forlorn as Hurricane pilot John Gregson radioed in (with stiff upper lip) to say the Fokkers had done for him. Josephine also presented the programme, along with disc jockey Pete Murray and, later, Freddie Mills, who had briefly been the world light-heavyweight boxing champion but had luckily retained enough marbles to switch careers.

Tommy Steele starred on the first show and the next five, leading viewers to think that the *6.5 Special* had been created especially for him. Not so, although it could hardly have been created without him. Lonnie Donegan was a frequent guest and the Vipers appeared on a memorable show that also featured Big Bill Broonzy. Sadly, such highlights were rare. For the most part, it was a weekly dose of *Workers' Playtime*-style pabulum, with the likes of Michael Holliday, the King Brothers and Dennis Lotis jumbled up with trad-jazz bands, unimaginative vocal groups, weedy comedy sketches, discussions on make-up and cookery, and ersatz rock 'n' roll. Don Lang & his Frantic Five were hardly Bill Haley & his Comets.

"Genuine rock 'n' roll was thin on the ground," admits Jack Good, "and that was always our problem. It was universally despised by anyone who could play any sort of scale or arpeggio on any instrument at all. The jazz people thought it was a joke, a sick joke that would be over in a couple of months, just a passing phase, and it was impossible to reproduce the music except by bringing in antagonistic talent. Sometimes it wasn't too bad, because these guys were competent, but they just thought it was funny. It was a struggle. Few of them could think of rock 'n' roll as creative music."

The *6.5 Special* was a start, but proved to be little more than a training camp for Good, who would find his feet and his focus over at ITV the following year.

Twenty-two

In summer 1956, when Russell Quaye's City Ramblers had converted an old ambulance and taken off for Europe with an entourage of bohemian adventurers including Ramblin' Jack and June Elliott, their skiffle club at the Princess Louise public house in High Holborn had been taken over by Nancy Whiskey. She kept it going until she found herself in the charts.

Nancy had been born in Glasgow on 4 March 1935, in a two-room flat on the top floor of a tenement slum in Bridgeton. "I was one of six children, all crammed in there, and I have few happy memories of my childhood," she said. "A lot of drinking went on in our block, with parties every weekend, most of them ending in a fight. I grew up taking clothes to the pawnshop on Monday morning and getting them back on Saturday morning – before taking them back again on Monday. That's what I remember . . . poverty, booze, lice, mice, bed-bugs and thick hellish fogs caused by a million coal fires and factory chimneys."

The family stayed there until the place was in danger of collapsing and the council moved them out of town, to Pennilee. At school, Anne Wilson (as she was then) was taught to be a good Catholic but learnt more from her uncle's collection of country and folk records. On his guitar, she worked out how to play Jimmie Rodgers and Burl Ives numbers, as well as Scottish songs. One she felt particularly close to, because Calton and Bridgeton were neighbouring areas in the east end of Glasgow, was *The Calton Weaver*, with its singalong chorus "Whisky whisky, Nancy Whisky". It became her signature tune, a few years down the line, when she needed a professional name – even though, unaware of the distinction, she spelt Whiskey the Irish way.

As soon as she could, she left home and got a bed-sitter in the city centre. By day she hand-painted pottery for Govancraft; by night she attended classes at Glasgow School of Art, where Josh McCrae and Jimmie MacGregor would sit around playing folk songs whenever the opportunity arose. Her life changed dramatically when she met

Bob Kelly, a railway worker who played boogie-woogie and blues piano in the pubs of Glasgow, where (because of his hairstyle) he was known as Crew Kelly. "It was Students' Day and I was out with my can, collecting money," she recalls. "I was wearing my brother's RAF cap and jacket, but no trousers. I was the RAF officer who forgot to wear his trousers. I had super legs!" Bob must have noticed. He bought her coffee and then took her to the Arts Ball that evening. They fell in love – which created a few problems as he was due to marry someone else a few months hence. The wedding went ahead as planned but lasted less than a year. On 5 November 1955, with two quid between them, Bob and Nancy found themselves on the coach to London, watching fireworks from the window as soon as it grew dark. With them was Bob's friend Broken John McKerrow, who had a job lined up as clarinet player with Mike Daniels' Jazz Band. So he thought. When they arrived at the rehearsal room, as agreed, he found that the gig had been given to someone else.

By a stroke of fortune, the three of them found a small flat near Hampstead Heath. The men got casual jobs; Nancy worked as a waitress. No thought of singing in public entered her head until one Thursday night Bob and Broken John returned from a swift reconnaissance trip to Soho, where they had stumbled upon the Roundhouse – and had booked an audition for her the following week. Nervous as a sparrow, she borrowed a guitar and did a floor spot, her first public performance. Jack Elliott was sitting there: told her she "sang pretty". Club organisers Bob Watson and Cyril Davies went further: they booked her for a weekly spot and loaned her £6 to buy a little Spanish guitar.

One gig led to another . . . 44 Gerrard Street, the Breadbasket (where she got a couple of quid plus supper!), the Baker Street Jive Club and the Princess Louise – which she took over from the beginning of August 1956, changing the name from Studio Skiffle to the Nancy Whiskey Club, and moving it from Monday night to the more hospitable Sunday. Her repertoire was mainly Scottish, songs like *The Blantyre Explosion* and *The Braes Of Yarrow*, but she booked a wide range of guest artists, including such traditionalists as Ewan MacColl and Bert Lloyd, skiffle groups like the Satyrs (led by John Hasted group refugee Judith Goldbloom) and the Vipers, blues specialists Alexis Korner and Cyril Davies, who now seemed to be an indivisible duo, and Nicky Thatcher, an American 12-string guitarist who had taken up residence at the Yellow Door. Nancy also started a Monday night residency at Cy Laurie's Jazz Club – and Bob Kelly joined Ken Colyer, playing piano in his band and during the interval at Studio 51, where Ken now held sway five nights a week.

At the beginning of 1957, after a glorious Hogmanay party at Cy Laurie's Club, Nancy surrendered her independence. She joined Chas McDevitt's Skiffle Group.

Chas was another Glaswegian, born in Rutherglen on 4 December 1934, but his family moved south and he was educated in Farnborough, Hampshire. At 16, he was in isolation hospital for a year with pleurisy and suspected tuberculosis and learned to play the banjo, which must have been an interesting experience for the other people on the ward. After he got out, he took a job in the transport division of Unilevers, in Blackfriars, and was set to climb the corporate ladder. But destined not to. Evenings were spent playing banjo with a Camberley trad jazz band, the High Curly Stompers – until, in 1955, he graduated to the Crane River Jazz Band, at least a band going out under that name, although no original members remained. Chas fronted their skiffle and blues interlude and then an independent breakaway group, the St Louis Trio . . . which gradually built into the Chas McDevitt Skiffle Group over the last half of 1956.

His washboard player, Marc Sharratt, a busy photographer about town, happened to bump into two guys who were trying to get involved in management . . . Bill Varley and Roy Tuvey. They had just lost the Vipers and McDevitt's group was perfectly placed to step into the breach. They made some test recordings in the Denmark Street office of Trio Recording Services – part of which had now been converted into a demo studio, sound-proofed with egg boxes stuck onto the walls and ceiling with wood glue. Varley was impressed enough to move forward; Tuvey was less enthusiastic and dropped out.

"Roy and I lost contact soon after," says Varley, who now put his faith in McDevitt's boys. "I became their manager, roadie (none of them could drive), negotiated with agents, bought a mini-bus, co-ordinated their bookings, arranged their digs, did their press and publicity as well as I could, everything – all for 10 per cent! By then, because of the publishers and record companies who used Trio, the network of people I knew was quite wide – and I thought I would

have no trouble getting a deal. So I went round to various labels . . .
and they all turned us down."

It was Varley who sensed the potential of adding Whiskey to the
mix. "Chas and the group had entered a talent contest, organised by
Pye and Radio Luxembourg, and had won it three weeks running.
During the final, a Scottish girl came on, a petite young folksinger,
and I was intrigued by her performance. Then it struck me: a lady
skiffler! She was Scottish, so was Chas . . . what a combination!"

Both were dubious. "It was the first time I'd seen her, but they
knew each other from the club circuit, had even shared the odd bill
together," continues Varley. "Neither seemed too impressed by the
other – but I was convinced that Nancy would give the group that
distinctive extra element, that commercial boost. She was giving me
all this 'och, I dinnae think so' and Chas was worse, giving me one of
those moodies: 'If you have no confidence in us, you'd better stop
managing us'. So I explained that we were going nowhere, that we
needed to do something different if we were going to get away. In
the end, I convinced them to meet up in our little studio and see how
they sounded together."

Chas had already been singing *Freight Train* at half the tempo –
but Nancy spiced it up and speeded it up, made it chirpy and catchy,
even though it concerned an outlaw who had killed his friend: "got
no future, got no hope, got nothing but the rope."

Convinced it was a hit, Varley trawled the record companies once
more but could interest no-one other than Jack Baverstock at Oriole,
an independent label with little or no reputation, even though it had
been in existence since 1932. *Freight Train* would assist the company
to its best year ever.

Although she saw herself as a folk singer and had no faith in
skiffle's ability to sustain or survive, Nancy reluctantly agreed to join
the group for six months. "McDevitt phoned me up and talked me
into it," she says, "telling me that they wouldn't get anywhere unless
I joined." The relationship would end in bitterness, if not tears.

In January 1957, the Chas McDevitt Skiffle Group featuring Nancy
Whiskey made their grand début in the week-long Skiffle Show at
the Metropolitan Theatre in Edgware Road, topping a variety bill
which included Joe 'Mr Piano' Henderson, comedian Larry Grayson,
comedienne Joyce Golding, the Brawns (jugglers), the Marcias
(balancing duo), the Three Quavers (a vocal and instrumental trio)

and compère Digby Wolfe. "An agent called Joe Collins (father of Joan and Jackie) and former orchestra leader Bert Ambrose decided to cash in on skiffle," recalls Chas. "They saw how Lonnie had taken off and wanted to get in on the action – but they lost a lot of money."

Since they had never worked a big venue before, Ambrose took them into a Soho rehearsal studio and coached them on stage craft – but the reviews were not too kind. "This was skiffle in the raw," said one, "with coffee bar type clothes and a style of guitar playing as monotonous as a string of sausages. The group has enthusiasm, lots of it, but little else."

The group fared better on their own turf, playing for younger audiences more attuned to skiffle. They played regularly at the 2Is and resumed Nancy's residency at the Princess Louise. In March, they were filmed performing *Freight Train* for *The Tommy Steele Story*. Later that month, at Romford Odeon, they starred in the first teenage package show, 'Meet For Cats' – promoted by 2Is owner Paul Lincoln and featuring his new discovery Terry Dene.

In April, after six weeks up a siding, *Freight Train* suddenly chugged into the chart, eventually reaching number five. The archetypal skiffle record, it flitted on a compelling washboard-driven strum-along rhythm, its lyric a compendium of the genre's favourite themes: Americana, trains, travel, romance, open spaces, convicts, love beyond grasp, the certainty of death. Carrying coals to Newcastle, it also began to make headway in the States – on the Chic label, a tiny independent operating from Thomasville (population 15,000) in Georgia. Mainly because of a fast-selling cover by Rusty Draper on the powerful Mercury label, McDevitt stalled at number 40. Nancy and Varley flew out to address a music operators' convention in Chicago and a press conference in New York.

As business moved up a few gears, the McDevitt group split into two. Unwilling to give up their day jobs, three guys left to carry on as a part-time group, the Old Timers. Chas, Nancy and Marc Sharratt recruited two seasoned modern-jazz pros, electric guitarist Bill Bramwell and bassist Lennie Harrison, plus the youthful Tony Kohn, formerly with the Ghouls and the Cotton Pickers. They toured the country, playing theatres, cinemas and civic halls, supporting Slim Whitman and Frankie Lymon & the Teenagers. In June, they headlined a ten group 'Rock Across The Channel' day trip, from Gravesend to Calais, before flying to New York for 'a two-week concert and cabaret tour' which somehow didn't materialise. Their only gig was the *Ed Sullivan Show*, where they shared the billing with another act enjoying their first hit, the Everly Brothers. Most of the time, they kicked their heels at the Sheraton Hotel, with Chic label owner Chick Thompson.

Nancy was threatening to leave, saying her six months were up, and Chick Thompson was not happy about it. He threatened Chas with all manner of unpleasantness if he could not prevent her departure. Chas didn't like to tell him that the band had no kind of written contract with Nancy.

When they got back to London, their second hit *Greenback Dollar* (again with Nancy taking lead vocal) had already been and gone – and so, it appeared, had Nancy. It was soon front page news in *Melody Maker*: 'Freight Train Pair Uncouple'. "I'm sick and tired of skiffle," she told reporters, "I never wanted to sing it in the first place." Grudgingly, she agreed to stay on for a five-week tour, during which time a replacement could hopefully be found. Chas auditioned girls at every city they played; none was acceptable. At the eleventh hour, he was contacted by a Belfast girl, Babs McEvoy, who had been taught to play guitar by Val Doonican. She proved eminently suitable: the only modification deemed necessary was a name-change to Shirley Douglas. The group continued to tour but would never find the charts again.

Meanwhile, a copyright dispute had blown up over the author-ship of *Freight Train* – which was published here by the Pan Musik Company and credited to Paul James and Fred Williams ... who turned out to be none other than Chas McDevitt and his manager Bill Varley.

The song had been introduced to Britain by Peggy Seeger, who by coincidence had been a fellow passenger of Jack and June Elliott on the *Maasdam*, sailing from New York to Europe in September 1955. They knew her because she was Pete Seeger's half-sister – and because she played the banjo and sang. The Seeger family employed a domestic at their home in Washington DC, a black woman called Elizabeth Cotten, who as well as ironing and cooking, played the guitar and taught Peggy various songs – including *Freight Train*, which she had written in the early part of the century. (Libba, as Peggy called her, had been born in Chapel Hill, North Carolina in 1893.)

Peggy sang the song many times in the skiffle clubs and coffee bars of London during 1956. According to Denny Carter, one of the guitarists in the McDevitt group, they copped it at the Princess Louise one evening. "I've got a very good ear for melody: once a song has been sung, I know it. So I concentrated on the tune, Chas noted the chord shapes and sequence, and the girlfriend scribbled all the words down."

"We tried to find the publisher of *Freight Train*, but we couldn't find any trace – so we copyrighted it ourselves, using our middle names," says Bill Varley. When Elizabeth Cotten's representative threatened to sue, Pan Musik apparently countered with the suggestion that the song would have been worth nothing without the McDevitt record. According to *Sing Out!* magazine, Cotten had insufficient funds to bring the case to court and it seems that "the English company quietly made a settlement with her", adding her name to those of 'James' and 'Williams'. "She agreed that we should be co-owners," says Varley.

Also on that first visit, Peggy Seeger had been responsible for another hit, albeit a dormant one. In March 1956, three months shy of her twenty-first birthday, she met Ewan MacColl, 20 years her senior, at the rehearsal for a television show on which they were both appearing. He lost his heart to her, although he was currently married to the dancer and choreographer Jean Newlove, with whom he had sired a son, Hamish. He was still married in January 1959 when his folk-singing friend Alex Campbell ("a sweet crazy man, a harum-scarum lovely guy," according to Seeger) very graciously depped for him in a wedding ceremony to keep Peggy in the country as a British subject. Peggy was soon to bear McColl's child Neil (born that March), while Jean Newlove was about to fall pregnant again, with his daughter Kirsty (born in October). How he managed to juggle his life was a mystery to most of his friends – but Ewan and Peggy lived together for 31 years, until his death in 1989. The song Ewan wrote for her, *First Time Ever I Saw Your Face*, eventually escaped into the wider world and into the hearts of millions, billions even, inadvertently turning the humble communist into a multi-millionaire.

By leaving the Chas McDevitt Skiffle Group to go solo, Nancy Whiskey was making life more difficult for herself. Whereas she had enjoyed an easy ride, coming onto the stage only for three numbers, she would now have to organise and rehearse a new group, deal with wages and bookings and places to stay, sing a whole set – and to further complicate matters, she was pregnant. She tried to conceal the fact for as long as possible. No mention of it in the 25 July 1957 issue of the *Daily Sketch*, in which she talked about her split from Chas and her secret boyfriend Bob Kelly, whom she intended to marry "when I've got enough money".

On 4 August, the *Sunday Mail*, 'Scotland's National Sunday Newspaper', revealed another dimension to the romance. Bad news on the doorstep. "Bob Kelly is already married," they reported. "In March 1955, he was married to Mary Burns of Gallowgate, Glasgow. Their marriage was unhappy and six months later Bob went to live in London. Mary still works in a factory."

While filming her contribution to *The Golden Disc*, Nancy stood behind a large music stand to conceal her bump; a journalist described her as plumpish. She did a month of variety, topping the bill over Michael Holliday and the John Barry Seven, in a show called the Big Beat but it all got a bit too much in early November. Said her agent, Sonny Zahl: "The Christmas period is not a good one for variety. That is why Nancy is ending her stage appearances this week and not resuming until about February."

Twenty-three

Skiffle, skiffle, skiffle. It was everywhere, throughout 1957. This was not to everybody's taste. The staff of *Melody Maker* were not enthusiastic on several counts. The decline in musical standards made them wince and the idea of unschooled youngsters outselling and out-drawing long-time professionals made them furious. The reduction of popular music to three chords gave them apoplexy and the fact that events were getting beyond their control gave them nightmares. Yet they still felt obliged to cover the developments. They devoted two pages of their 9 March issue to a discourse headed 'Skiffle On Trial – Music Or Menace?'

Bob Dawbarn, unsung trombonist-cum-*MM* scribe, felt eminently qualified to expound on its deficiencies. "Skiffle is piffle," he wrote. "It is also the dreariest rubbish to be inflicted on the British public since the last rash of Al Jolson imitators. My chief reason for disliking it is that I love jazz and therefore hate its parasitical offshoots. It is a bastardised commercialised form of the real thing, watered down to suit the sickly, orange juice tastes of musical illiterates. Incompetent musicians are drawing good money for a kind of musical fraud."

His words fell on stony ground. Skiffle groups formed in every school, in every youth club, in every town and city across Britain – and new 'stars' were hailed every month. The pecking order was in constant flux. As Tommy Steele, the Vipers and Nancy Whiskey proved, the age of overnight stardom was upon us. You could be playing in a tiddly basement coffee bar one day and on television the next.

Bob Cort, a 27-year-old from Loughborough, was a case in point. Balding and bearded, he had been working as a visualiser in a West End advertising agency and was all but unknown until January 1957, when, with the assistance of Ken Sykora (a jazz twiddling guitarist with BBC connections) and Nevil Skrimshire (Humphrey Lyttelton's guitarist and banjo player, at whose feet Lonnie had studied), he landed third billing on the National Jazz Federation's Skiffle Concert at the Royal Festival Hall. Sykora was the compère.

Cort then managed to get himself onto the bill (in amongst the ladder-climbing cockatoos and the jugglers and the dancing poodles) for the Vipers' fortnight at the Prince of Wales Theatre in February. By this time, his lacklustre version of *Don't You Rock Me Daddy-O*, the first of several singles for Decca, was getting airplay but few sales – relegated to the shadows by the Vipers' original, which scraped into the Top 10, and Lonnie Donegan's vigorous re-working, which reached number four.

That Bob Cort was a nondescript performer seemed to matter little in the world of skiffle, where (as Dawbarn had correctly pointed out) originality was not a requirement, where one group sounded scarcely different from the next. Still hanging on to his day job, he cut an insipid version of *Freight Train* with 'Liz Winters' (in fact young Australian actress Lorrae Desmond, who had recently made her television début in a series with Terry Thomas) and on Easter Monday appeared in London's First (sic) Big Skiffle Session at the Royal Festival Hall, alongside Chas McDevitt and Nancy Whiskey, the Avon Cities Skiffle Group (from Bristol) and two more expectant pecking-order upsetters, Johnny Duncan and Dickie Bishop – both Chris Barber acolytes.

Dickie Bishop had joined Barber from the Brent Valley Stompers and the Albemarle Jazz Band, ostensibly to strengthen the skiffle group, and had briefly taken over from Lonnie when he went solo. At the end of 1956, he left Barber to join Lonnie's band but within weeks had formed his own group, Dickie Bishop & his Sidekicks – one of whom was Bob Watson, founder (with Cyril Davies) of the Roundhouse Skiffle Club. Another Sidekick was Don Wilson, who had one of the first, possibly the first electric bass on the scene, as early as February 1957. "After breaking the neck of my stand-up bass, I visited Lew Davis's music shop in Charing Cross Road," recalls Wilson, "and I emerged with a Framus bass and a 12-watt amplifier, which was considered to be quite adequate for the task. It was one of only three in Britain and was a talking point wherever we went – even though some of the purist skifflers thought it was heresy."

Though they made only limited commercial headway, they toured steadily and recorded the underground skiffle classic *No Other Baby* – written by Bishop and Watson, and years later revived by Paul McCartney on his album *Run Devil Run*. When Watson was called up, his replacement Pete Korrison and Dickie electrified their guitars –

creating, along with electric bassist Wilson and drummer Stan Bellwood, a prototypical Beatles-style beat group. Says Wilson: "We finished up with so much gear that Dickie and I would go to gigs by train, while Stan and Pete went by road, in a big estate car loaded with equipment."

Johnny Duncan proved little more than a stopgap in the Barber band, though a welcome one at the time. "In May 1956, about a week after Lonnie Donegan left us, Johnny walked into the 100 Club, looking quite similar to Lonnie and wearing identical clothes," recalls Chris. He was soon fronting Barber's interval skiffle group. "He was a likeable guy, a fine guitarist and mandolin player, but his thin, high-pitched voice was taking us away from country blues towards bluegrass."

This could have been predicted from day one. Duncan was from bluegrass country, having been born and raised in a coal-mining community near Oliver Springs, Tennessee, on 7 Sept 1932. He grew up listening to gospel, country and bluegrass on radio stations beaming out of Oak Ridge and Knoxville, and he sang around the area as soon as his hands were big enough to hold a guitar. Unwilling to follow his father into the mines, he joined the US Air Force for a journey which took him from Lubbock Army Airfield in Texas to the USAF base at Molesworth in Cambridgeshire. He met and married (on Independence Day 1953) a local girl, Betty Gardner from St Neots, who yearned to see the wide open spaces of America but wasn't too impressed by Wichita, Kansas, where her husband, freshly demobbed, had taken a job. At Christmas 1955, they returned to Cambridgeshire, where Johnny worked on his father-in-law's market stall. His exploratory trip to London, and his visit to the 100 Club, proved to be a perfect right time, right place moment.

He stayed with Barber until February 1957, when they parted by mutual consent. "It was too constricting with Johnny; it worked for a while, but it wasn't right. On top of that, we were just about to go on tour with Big Bill Broonzy and Brother John Sellers – and we knew that Big Bill could spot even mild inhospitability at 500 yards. We also knew that Johnny's wife was not always circumspect in her use of language. He wanted more room to expand his act, anyway." Perversely, although he had cultivated the style, which had now reached a commercial peak, Barber abandoned skiffle forthwith. He was always looking for new ideas rather than recycling old ones.

Guided by the ubiquitous Denis Preston, Duncan launched his solo career with a bet-hedging single featuring country blues on one side and C&W on the other. However, skiffle fans were impressed neither by Leadbelly's murder ballad *Ella Speed*, set in the hardcore drinking dens of Dallas, nor by the sad story of a storefront wooden Indian *Kaw Liga*, which four years earlier had been a posthumous hit for Hank Williams, topping the US country charts for three months solid. The story was put around that Duncan had once been a member of Bill Monroe's Blue Grass Boys – but his only connection with that outfit came when he unashamedly appropriated their name, calling his own group Johnny Duncan & his Blue Grass Boys.

Preston changed tack for his second single, suggesting that Duncan update a calypso originally recorded in 1950 by the Duke of Iron, a Trinidadian who had become popular in the folk clubs of New York. Duncan hated the song but acquiesced under pressure. Luckily for him. The infuriatingly catchy *Last Train To San Fernando* became his signature tune, his passport to success – albeit short-lived. After it reached number two on the best-seller list, Duncan was all over television and radio, even landing a series on the BBC's Light Programme playing records which suited the title *Tennessee Song Bag*. Suddenly, he was the acknowledged expert on country & western music – and his affected stage costumes and repertoire verged in that direction, although a heavy reliance on Hank Williams, Eddy Arnold and Jimmie Rodgers material was leavened with an assortment of bluegrass, blues, folk tunes, gospel songs and originals.

His chart career was over in less than a year, once *Blue Blue Heartaches* and *Footprints In The Snow* (an old Bill Monroe hit) had made brief showings in the lower reaches, but he maintained his reputation as a live act – thanks mainly to his band. No skiffle group they. Managers Denis Preston and Lyn Dutton, who had overseen Lonnie's launch, used the same tactics and found experienced sidemen. Bassist Jack Fallon had accompanied Josh White, had played with avant-garde jazz groups, and had led one of the first country bands to play the American air base circuit. Drummer Lennie Hastings was a legend (not only for musical reasons) on the traditional jazz scene, having played with Freddy Randall and Alex Welsh before forming his own band. When he shared the bill with the Vipers in the last week of February 1957, on their first out-of-town gig, he saw how much audiences enjoyed the new music and how little they cared for his. Within days, he was a Blue Grass Boy. Guitarist Brian Daley had been playing in Bobby Breen's Rock 'n' Roll Rockers alongside such temporarily disaffected and disenchanted jazzers as pianist Harry South and sax-player Harry Robbins. They had been the first rock 'n' roll band to play Belfast, a gig so successful that they needed a police escort, despite whose best efforts Bobby was raised high and carried through the air by over-excited fans.

Johnny Duncan & the Blue Grass Boys made their début at Leeds City Hall on 3 March 1957 – but by the end of the month, Daley had gone, having decided that studio work was preferable to touring. He was later in Jack Good's session crew, played the intro on 1967's *The Day I Met Marie* by Cliff Richard and – most importantly (from a wallet perspective, certainly), he wrote the words and music for *Postman Pat*.

Replacing him in the Blue Grass Boys was Denny Wright, who had been in Lonnie Donegan's band for eight months and probably could stand it no longer. Or possibly he preferred Duncan's eclectic range and his emphasis on music rather than personality. The new band was the most integrated on the skiffle scene, enjoying the music, stretching out, rocking country style – far too accomplished for teenage amateurs to copy. None of them could have attempted the stuttering guitar solo on *Last Train To San Fernando*, or Johnny's mandolin on *Get Along Home Cindy*, or his singing on *Footprints In The Snow* – not without looking and sounding foolish.

In September 1957, at the peak of the skiffle 'boom', as it came to be called (quite correctly), the *NME* published a four-page Skiffle Supplement – discussing all the front-runners like a racing tip-sheet. Out in front was Lonnie, of course, followed by Johnny Duncan, the Vipers, and Chas McDevitt with Nancy Whiskey. Attempting to come up on the outside, though appearing to pose little threat, were Dickie Bishop and Bob Cort; flexing their muscles in the paddock were Jimmy Jackson, Sonny Stewart and the 2.19 Group; still weighing in were Les Hobeaux.

Jackson was destined to be an also-ran. A 21-year-old Glaswegian, he had signed up with the Royal Air Force for 12 years and was currently a corporal, stationed near Bedford. Much ballyhoo was attached to his first Columbia release *California Zephyr*, which was described as 'rock 'n' skiffle' and predictably fell between two stools.

After extricating himself from the RAF, he toured with the 'Stars of Six-Five Special' package, alongside Kenny Baker's Jazz Band, Don Lang, Rosemary Squires, Jackie Dennis, Mike and Bernie Winters and various others who few concert-goers particularly wished to see or hear. A lamentable version of Eddie Cochran's US hit *Sitting In The Balcony* sealed Jackson's fate.

Sonny Stewart and his over-optimistically named Skiffle Kings cut a single for Philips, *Black Jack/The Northern Line*, but neither they nor the 2.19 Skiffle Group – who allegedly won 'an international skiffle contest at Bury St Edmunds' (which received minimal publicity) – would make it into the books that list hit records, or into rock and pop encyclopaedias, or even into the memories of other than latter-day skiffle obsessives.

By April 1957, a year after he'd left Chris Barber's Jazz Band, Lonnie Donegan was already so far ahead of the field that no-one would ever catch him, making a smooth transition from King of Skiffle to show-biz superstar. Said the *NME*: "There is no question that Lonnie is here to stay as a top-line variety attraction for as long as he has the strength to knock himself out twice nightly!" *Don't You Rock Me Daddy-O* had made the Top five and *Cumberland Gap* took only two weeks to reach number one.

The lyric was incomprehensible to most of the people who bought it, and – he freely admitted – incomprehensible to Lonnie too. Cumberland Gap had been made a National Historical Park two years earlier, a 20,000 acre tract covering the point where Tennessee, Kentucky and Virginia meet – only 50 miles from Johnny Duncan's home town. It was a narrow, steep-sided natural pass through the Appalachian Mountains used by bison, Indian tribes and white trappers, and later by pioneer settlers moving west and the Union Army invading the south. It had been 'discovered' in April 1750 by Thomas Walker, who named it after the Duke of Cumberland, butcher of the Scots at Culloden four years earlier – and, as Lonnie correctly points out, it was only 15 miles from the Kentucky town of Middlesboro. It was the only verse that made sense; the rest were non-sequiturs – for instance "I've got a girl, six feet tall, sleeps in the kitchen with her feet in the hall and Two old ladies sitting in the sand, each one wishing that the other was a man." In the midst of the mayhem, Lonnie, earnest yet lathered, urges Denny Wright to play a strenuous guitar solo and then yawps throughout. Across the country, thousands of skiffle groups added the song to their repertoire.

When Denny left for the Blue Grass Boys, after a final appearance on the *6.5 Special* on 23 March, Lonnie made Jimmy Currie his right hand man. Currie, a fellow Scot (from Edinburgh), had played jazz with Mick Mulligan's band and rock 'n' roll with Tony Crombie's Rockets, and though technically not in his predecessor's league, he stayed with Lonnie for a year and a half.

The schedule was relentless. Weeks of variety, interspersed with television appearances, followed by 21 days in the States, supporting the Harlem Globetrotters – a showbiz basketball team! They travelled by plane: Madison Square Garden, Chicago, Cleveland, Buffalo, Raleigh, Hershey, Detroit, St Louis, Louisville, Kansas City, Seattle, Eugene, San Francisco, Los Angeles, Denver, Omaha, Evansville, Milwaukee, and Cincinnati – all on consecutive nights. Sanctioned by the Musicians' Union, the visit was an exchange with Bill Haley & his Comets, who were greeted with pandemonium when they arrived in Britain but dropped from the charts like a stone when they left.

Back home, Donegan and his group returned to the variety circuit for four months solid, touring provincial theatres before ending up with two weeks at the London Palladium (supported by the Platters). There, Denis Preston set up microphones and recorded an entire show – from which two tracks were selected as their next single: *Gamblin' Man* and *Putting On The Style*.

The former, another in the series he 'wrote with' (filched from) Woody Guthrie, was the most rocking record made in Britain to date. "It's the simplicity of it, the attack of it, the energy behind it," says Lonnie modestly, "there's not a lot of music in it really. It's a bit like jazz: you state the melody and theme, insert a solo, then allow it to build to a climax." QED. He had initially stumbled on the formula, but now he had mastered it. Take an old song and speed it up to make it more exciting. Get carried away, get raucous. It was a manoeuvre later adopted by the Rolling Stones and the Yardbirds, the Sex Pistols and the Clash. Absorb the song, chew it thoroughly and then feed it to your audience in a form they can relate to. It's a generational thing: personal, instructive, educational, inspiring even. Lonnie was the first to see it and his band was proficient enough to keep up. Rehearsed enough too: they had, after all, been playing together every night for months. Kids would sing *Gamblin' Man* in the playgrounds and youth clubs in the same way that doo-wop groups sang on the street corners of urban America.

Putting On The Style was adapted from a 1926 Victor recording by Vernon Dalhart, a country & western pioneer who had recorded the genre's first million seller *The Prisoner's Song* two years earlier. (A Texan born Marion Slaughter, Dalhart had taken his professional name from two places on the local map, as Conway Twitty would do many years later.) It was Lonnie's most novel release, signalling his natural impulse to move away from skiffle and become more of an all-round entertainer. He modified the lyric to include today's youth, but only whimsically. Lonnie would hardly bite the hand that fed him, even as he fed them.

He and his group were soon wearing tuxedos and bow ties. He no longer had a Millet's check shirt in his wardrobe, not one. In the last week of June, he started a month at the 1,300-seater London Hippodrome, with Alma Cogan and Des O'Connor in attendance. Des told jokes and sang *99 Ways* (currently in the charts by Tab Hunter, though true rock 'n' roll fans preferred the original by Charlie Gracie, on the b-side of *Butterfly*), *Sioux City Sue* (that he learned from a 1946 Bing Crosby record), *Rock Around The Clock* (blatant crowd pleaser) and *Shine On Harvest Moon* (that had even reached the clubs of Northampton, where he started climbing the ladder). He looked no younger than he did at 70.

Lonnie was soon back on the road, playing ABC cinemas and Moss Empires until December, when he began a month at Chiswick Empire, playing Wishee Washee in this year's Christmas pantomime *Aladdin*. Would you catch Chuck Berry or Jerry Lee Lewis fooling about in a pantomime? Lonnie had gone over to the other side – and who can blame him? He would go on forever.

By this time, he'd had two more hit records: *My Dixie Darling* and *Jack O' Diamonds*. It was Lonnie's big year.

On 14 October 1957, the Royal Albert Hall presented another Skiffle Jamboree – this one starring Johnny Duncan & his Blue Grass Boys (headliners now), Cy Laurie (no skiffler he), Bob Cort (inevitably), the Cotton Pickers and the Eden Streeters.

The last two, along with *NME*'s pick-to-click Les Hobeaux, had been resident groups at the 2I's Coffee Bar and frequent guests at the Skiffle Cellar.

Twenty-four

The Skiffle Cellar was the brainchild of Russell Quaye, who towards the end of 1956 arrived home from his 'continental tour' to find skiffle taking off, its audience expanding uncontrollably. Back in spring, when he and his group the City Ramblers were running their skiffle club at the Princess Louise they saw more or less the same core of aficionados every week. When they left for Germany at the end of July, they said goodbye to everyone in the place – all were familiar faces, all had become their friends.

Proto hippies, taking an adventure bus to wherever, they had bought and modified an old Chevrolet ambulance. "It was forever going wrong," says singer and guitarist Hylda Sims, "with bits falling off, other bits malfunctioning. We had no idea how far we would be going or even where we would be going."

Only a handful of gigs had been lined up, at jazz clubs in Hamburg, Wuppertal and Frankfurt. "We got them purely by chance," says Hylda. "We were busking under the arches in Villiers Street one afternoon and a guy came up and told us he was a German impresario, involved with a string of clubs. He offered us work, so off we went – playing from 9pm to 4am, with only the odd break, to audiences of heavy drinking sailors, American servicemen, happy-go-lucky jivers, a good cross section of night-life characters. Years later, the beat groups would discover what a rigorous schedule it could be. Hell of a stint, but we got through it . . . and then we thought we should drive on to Denmark and tour around up there."

By this time, the ambulance was losing not only hubcaps and bumpers but passengers too. There had been ten to begin with, crammed in pretty tight. The Ramblers numbered five: Russell Quaye (quattro, kazoo and vocal), Hylda Sims (guitar and vocal), Tony Bucket (tub bass), Alan Sutton (washboard) and Chris Bateson (jug and trumpet). Pete Maynard was driving, and his girlfriend Shirley Bland was along for the ride. So too was Sutton's sister Blossom, who was in a relationship with Bucket. Rambling Jack and June Elliott wanted to explore more of Europe and knew they could find no better travelling companions – so they joined for the first leg and were last seen erecting a little tent on the outskirts of Frankfurt. They would travel on to Switzerland, Paris, Spain and Tangier before making it back to London.

"After a while, we were all at each other's throats," says Hylda, who was pregnant at the time, as indeed was June Elliott. Bucket went home after a red-mist disagreement with Quaye, and Sutton had to go back to school in September. So Pete Maynard, who had been on the door at the Princess Louise, and fancied going on the trip for the fun of it, took over the bass and Shirley started playing washboard. "We did a mixture of gigging and busking, and made much more from busking. The impresario we hooked up in with Denmark was even more of a nutcase than the German guy had been. He didn't pay us, so we were stuck in Arhus, daggers drawn. Eventually, it got into the papers and the Danish jazz union gave us enough money to get moving again."

They stopped over in Brussels, busking by day and playing a swish nightclub, the Tour de Babel by night. The police arrested and jailed them for playing in the street, refusing to believe they had a posh cabaret gig to play.

No sooner were they back in London than the Bernard Delfont Agency came on the phone offering them a slot on a touring variety show, '(S)Cool For Cats', which opened at Brighton Hippodrome on 4 February 1957. Also on the bill were petite singer Suzi Miller, comedian Dickie Dawson and Little Abner, a black American described on posters as 'Harlem's King of Rock 'n' Roll'. Wearing gaudy jackets trimmed with feathers and beads, he shimmied on stage, leaning backwards like a limbo dancer, and bawled out *Hound Dog* and *Blueberry Hill* to acquire six weeks of localised fame.

By this time, the City Ramblers line-up had expanded to six. Jimmie MacGregor had come down from Glasgow at Nancy Whiskey's suggestion and was going to join Chas McDevitt's group – until he was distracted. "Jimmie was staying at our place in Hampstead," says Nancy, "and he came to some rehearsals, even had his photograph taken as a member of the McDevitt group, but then at the eleventh hour he met Shirley Bland, who was playing washboard in the Ramblers. She had been a ballet dancer – with the Royal Ballet, I think – but then she outgrew her tutu. She used to walk around the streets barefoot, this statuesque woman, stepping delicately with her head in the air. One night, Jimmie said 'do you mind if I bring Shirley back?' and that was it . . . he joined the Ramblers!"

On Saturday 13 April 1957, Russell Quaye launched the Skiffle Cellar at 49 Greek Street in Soho. 'Music every night of the week, from 7.30 until 11pm', it said on the handbills. Resident group was the City Ramblers, of course; the Vipers and the Chas McDevitt/ Nancy Whiskey Group made sure the opening night was a memorable and newsworthy affair. Over the weeks, the Duncans, Corts and Bishops all played there but the venue's real importance was as a central London showcase for young hopefuls – who arrived in droves.

As the skiffle craze snowballed, newspapers began to offer advice. "A British-made washboard of heavy gauge metal is best. Remove the wood from the back, pad with newspaper, rags or papier mâché, and replace the wood. Buy some thimbles – a heavy gauge is kinder to the fingers. Lay the board flat on the knees, holding it with the left hand and making an easy, relaxed stroke across the ridges with the thimbled right hand, accenting the first and third beats of each bar. Do not play too loudly – too much noise from the washboard can ruin the group." Of course, any dextrous player used both hands – and the best of the professionals, Johnny Pilgrim and Marc Sharratt, became role models for a generation of percussionists.

The NME suggested that when buying a guitar, the novice should look for cracks in the bodywork, warping of the finger-board and wear in the machine heads. "The instrument must also be checked to see if it is in tune."

The girls' magazine Mirabelle, recently launched to exploit the teenage market, invited Mr Teazie Weazie, celebrated hairstylist to the gullible rich, to create a look for the ultra-hip skiffle girl. "For evening, crown your Skiffle Bob with a gilt Alice band," he counselled. This would complement your skiffle skirt ("look for one with a deep, nipped-in waistband, and lots of dancing room") and your trim, brushed-rayon skiffle waistcoat ("in a host of colours, including peacock, red and lime"). The fashion industry, such as it was, saw an opportunity and began to home in on the youth market.

There was even a spread in Woman advising housewives how to plan their own outdoor skiffle party. "It's the gayest newest way to have fun with your crowd!" readers were assured.

Experts were called in to explain the origins of the music. "Skiffle is New Orleans' oldest, most primitive jazz form," David Hammond told *Picturegoer* readers. "In the Negro poor quarter, these songs became popular at parties where people got together to have fun and pass the plate around to raise the rent. They called their music skiffle." The story of Lonnie and *Rock Island Line* was told and re-told a hundred times.

By summer 1957, in every town, in every school there were dozens of skiffle groups, all playing much the same repertoire, drawn from a list that included *Rock Island Line, It Takes A Worried Man To Sing A Worried Song, Bring A Little Water Sylvie, Don't You Rock Me Daddy-O, Cumberland Gap, Freight Train, Gamblin' Man, Putting On The Style, The Midnight Special, Lost John, Pick A Bale Of Cotton, The Wabash Cannonball, Mama Don't Allow* and *Stewball*. Few of the singers and strummers knew anything about Woody Guthrie or Leadbelly or the Weavers; they merely copied records by Lonnie Donegan and the Vipers, which were sufficient to fill their heads with dreams. Below the top layers, skiffle became a very English style of music, with the original flavour and emotion washed out of the songs, the nuances ironed flat, black or rural American patois unconsciously translated into cockney or the BBC English taught at school. It was youngsters with new jeans, matching shirts and institution haircuts, having a bash and feeling part of a strange movement that was sweeping across the country like an epidemic. The only thing many had going for them was enthusiasm.

Any rainbow-chasing group living within striking distance of London made a bee-line for the Skiffle Cellar, which, having no alcohol licence, was open to teenagers. "In the first few weeks, we had two hundred skiffle groups here for auditions, and we let them all have a go," said Russell Quaye. In increasing numbers they came, toting guitars and dragging tea-chests, hoping for a floor spot. "We made one night a week over entirely to new groups, some of whom were dire," says Hylda Sims. "You heard the same songs over and over again until you thought you were going to go mad."

For many groups – the Quakers, the Spiders, the Sunrisers, the Streamliners, the Sapphires, the Wayfarers, the Black Shadows, the Skeletons, the Moonshiners, the Adders, the Southdowners, the Hornets, the Saints, the Sinners, the Nomads and scores more – a few numbers at the Skiffle Cellar represented the peak of their musical career, but others contained the odd member who caught the bug and had the suss and talent and luck to progress. In early May came the Worried Men, from Acton, fronted by lippy, cocksure Terry Nelhams, who would turn into Adam Faith, and towards the end of the year came the Spacemen, mates from Wanstead Aero-modelling Club in East London, whose zippy jack-the-lad guitarist Joe Brown would always be Joe Brown. The Smoky City Skiffle Group, from Kentish Town way, included John Foreman, who became known in folk clubs as 'the Broadsheet King' and whose son Chris (as yet unborn) would play guitar in Madness.

Wanting and needing more variety, the City Ramblers cut their residency to three nights a week. Other groups became regulars: firstly the Cotton Pickers (fronted by songwriter Mike Pratt), followed by the Eden Street Skiffle Group (led by future *Sunday Times* journalist and travel writer Brian Jackman), the Pete Curtis 4, the Boll Weevils, the Old Timers (former McDevitt men who had opted not to turn pro), and the New Hawleans.

A prostitute, Angie, had a room a floor or two above the club and used to stand in the doorway listening to the music when not otherwise occupied. She got to know some of the visiting musicians. Denny Wright was rather fond of her.

The City Ramblers appeared on the *6.5 Special* every so often and on BBC Light Programme's *Skiffle Club*, which began weekly transmission on 1 June. Looking like a cross between the Carter Family and the New Christy Minstrels, they toured with package shows, played at peace movement gatherings, got their fair share of publicity but never broke through with a hit record. "On successive days, we got telegrams from two record companies, Columbia and Tempo, both of which wanted to sign us," says Hylda Sims. "One was a big commercial label, the other was a prestigious, cult jazz label . . . so, of course, Russell went with Tempo. Had we gone with Norrie Paramor, who was very keen to get us, the whole story might have been very different."

In August 1957, they went to the sixth International Youth Festival, held this year in Moscow. The Soviet authorities went to vast expense to impress the various delegations from all over the world but it did little to increase communist influence; they were either preaching to the converted or entertaining the curious. It worked both ways: curious natives were being entertained too –

there are even photographs of Khrushchev listening to skiffle music with a bemused look on his face. Viewed as honoured guests, the Ramblers went to a party in the Kremlin and were guided around the sights, at a time when few Britons could even dream of seeing Moscow. John Hasted was there too, of course, as he had been at the previous five festivals. He had just split from his own skiffle group. For the second time.

In July 1956, when Hasted closed his 44 Skiffle Club in Gerrard Street for the summer recess, most of his group had flown off for other adventures. They were the kind of questers for whom the world was now ripe for further exploration. When he re-opened the club on 16 October, he already had a new line-up, with only singer Redd Sullivan remaining from the old one. The rest had been recruited from the coffee bars. Guitarist David Tick, who even this early in his career adopted the stage name Zom (for his zombie visage), was a 17 year old from Stepney, in the East End. He spent his days schlepping bolts of cloth in a warehouse on Commercial Road and his evenings in the Gyre & Gimble – which is where Hasted also found 18-year-old Marion Amiss, a short-hand typist at a brokers' firm in the City. For reasons beyond her control, she had been drawn to folk and blues music and the bohemian life. "She had a tremendous voice, with a great range, a marvellous singer," recalls Hasted. Frank Ogrodovitch, who owned and could play a real string bass, was an accountancy student of mysterious provenance.

Completing the six-piece group was washboard player Martin Winsor, who was already sewn into the upholstery of Soho and the subterranean coffee bars just beyond its fringes. He was 25, a burglar, pimp, gambler and *bon vivant* – the kind of maverick raconteur that the patrician Hasted liked to have around him now and then, as a change from the predictable chatter of his scientific colleagues. Winsor lived in a room above Chez Auguste, a restaurant on Old Compton Street, his window to the world.

"I felt at home in Soho about two minutes after I arrived," he says. "It was lovely in those days, a hub for everything: literature, painting, skulduggery, drinking, discussion, music. You had the best of all worlds within walking distance – French bread and cheeses, Italian pasta, German sausage, wonderful coffee, street markets, bookshops, theatres, pubs and the most interesting people in London."

What he got up to was nobody's business. "I came to know most of the criminal fraternity, so there were quite often little bits of business thrown my way – like I'd be given £25, a fair sum of money in those days, to go on a bus or a tube to deliver a verbal message to an accomplice. Nobody liked to write anything down or say too much on the phone. It would usually be something like 'be at such-and-such a place at such-and-such a time' – and I knew better than to ask any questions. I knew Jackie Comer and people like that enough to talk to, but you always had to be careful how you spoke to them; they expected respect in the same way that politicians did. I never had any trouble . . . I was a face, known and trusted, I suppose."

For Winsor, a night on the tiles meant a spot of burglary, "but never domestic stuff", and there were various other nebulous activities, anything to finance his interest in gambling. (Naturally, there was a reluctance on his part to disclose too many details.) Much of his time was spent in his favourite coffee bars, the Gyre & Gimble and the Nucleus – both of which had now achieved a degree of notoriety in the press.

Some journalists saw mud, some saw stars. Among the former was one Grub Street hack, who wrote of "people who have not had a wash for so long that your first instinct is to hold your breath. The waitress is barefoot and pregnant." The customers, he continued, "eat only when someone buys them a meal, or when they can scrounge rotten cabbages at Covent Garden. They herd together in cheap digs and pair off to live on a Woolworth's wedding ring."

It was not a description which rang true with any coffee bar denizens encountered by the author. As they recall, their refuges incubated and fostered the swinging sixties, tolerance, spirituality, social and sexual equality, inter-racial and gay relationships, beat culture, ban-the-bomb communality, an interest in poetry and jazz and folk music, not to mention decent coffee. People wrote, read books and newspapers, played chess, played guitars, sang, ruminated, discussed, argued – or, if they were Diz Disley, drew on the walls. A jazz-bent guitarist, often forced to take skiffle gigs for the money (on stage, he would work out how much he was getting per chord), Diz also contributed cartoons to *Melody Maker*. On the walls of both the Nuke and the Breadbasket, he painted American jazz greats and Boticelli-style angels – in return for mountains of spaghetti bolognaise . . . 'spag bollock-naked', as it was known.

Fighting was unknown in the Nucleus as was the presence of any pugnacious yob element. "They would wander in, but soon wander out again, feeling and looking as if they'd strayed into alien territory," says Derek Duffy, who tended to see the Nuke as his social club. "There was a place across the road that they frequented, the Casa Savoia, a sort of greasy and unsavoury scene for unsophisticated people. Lots of fights. We used to call it the Karsy."

Not long after Cyril Pritchard opened the Nucleus, there had been a fracas with a protection-racket gang that tried to put the bite on him. A big guy, he had put two of them in hospital. More trouble was expected but none came, possibly because various underworld faces became regular customers. Martin Winsor, for one.

"Martin was a scallywag but such a nice chap, very kind and gentle," says Derek Duffy. "His personality filled the room, anytime he wanted it to – whether or not he was performing. A devil with the women too: he had the sort of charisma that encouraged them to follow him."

It was in the Nucleus that Winsor first ran into Redd Sullivan. "He was a merchant seaman and he'd obviously just got back from a trip," Winsor recalls. "He came clattering down the stairs, a mass of ginger hair and a big red beard, a duffel bag on his shoulder, sat down at a table and was immediately the centre of attention. 'Where have you been this time, Redd?' someone asked, 'tell us all about it' – and he went into this long dramatic spiel about native girls in Brazil. Then someone asked him to sing – so he stood up and let fly! I could barely believe it: everyone else who sang in the Nucleus used to sit down and strum a guitar – but this bloke was standing there, unaccompanied, roaring his head off . . . "On a Monday, I was arrested; On a Tuesday, I found myself in jail". I think we became inseparable friends from that moment on."

Naturally, Redd introduced Winsor to John Hasted – and by the time Hasted got his skiffle group going again, the former burglar was proficient on both the washboard and the lager-phone, a percussion instrument made from beer-bottle caps nailed onto a broomstick and banged on the floor. Hasted also recognised that he had a terrific bass voice and a talent for parody.

The 44 Skiffle Club ran in the Gerrard Street basement every Tuesday night from October 1956 until the following June. "Folk song has been dead in English cities for many years," Hasted told

The Observer. "We want to re-build a living urban folk music. It will take a long time." Guest performers at the club included Alexis Korner and Cyril Davies, John Cole, Rory MacEwen, Ramblin' Jack Elliott, Judith Goldbloom and Brian Silver, Ironfoot Jack, Beryl Bryden, Dave Stevens and whoever else wanted a spot. The group also played in coffee bars, in prisons and at demonstrations – including a Suez protest in Trafalgar Square where over-zealous police smashed Hasted's beautiful Martin guitar. In April 1957, when Nancy Whiskey suddenly became famous, Hasted's group took over her club at the Princess Louise – but by then, their days were numbered.

Three, sometimes four nights a week, they rehearsed, worked up new songs in Hasted's office at University College. Their repertoire was vast, greater than any other group on the scene. On club nights, they would regularly sing over 30 songs. Skiffle was taking over their lives. For most of them, this was fine – but Hasted felt the need to pull back. "My scientific work was going downhill," he says. "My colleagues were insisting that physics should come first. It was too serious an antagonism: I couldn't live with it. In the end, I went back to the lab and refocused my life there. For me, too, there had always been a struggle between skiffle and the pure ethnic folk song. In the beginning, it had been necessary for me to compromise, or we wouldn't have got anywhere at all, but now I felt quite disheartened by what was happening around us, the cheapening of fine songs and music into a mass produced commercial product."

A further complication was Hasted's forthcoming marriage to Lynn, a 'mystery' from Liverpool, who he had first met at her engagement party to someone else. She made him tear up his skiffle scrapbooks and notebooks. He was a very active chap . . . God knows what they contained.

As Hasted correctly predicted in one of his *Sing* columns: "When skiffle dies down, it will split in two directions: rock 'n' roll and folk music. When that happens, we shall have a legacy of serious singer/ guitarists to develop."

His 44 Skiffle Group continued without him, hoping to pursue a more commercial line, but soon lost impetus and folded. Singers Redd Sullivan and Marion Amiss would re-surface in the Thames-side Four, with Pete Maynard from the City Ramblers and a lanky guitarist called Long John Baldry – and after he left to go solo, they incorporated a 20 year old that Marion had seen at the Witches Cauldron in Belsize Park. Said Redd: "She told me about this kid with a nylon string guitar, very cadaverous and pale, looked like he never had anything to eat. She said he can play and sing – so Martin Carthy joined us." Later, for many years, Redd and Martin Winsor ran the folk evenings at the Troubadour in Earls Court.

Although the 44 Club closed in summer 1957, London's first skiffle club was still thriving at the Roundhouse in Wardour Street. In March, to distance itself from the fadsters, it had undergone a name-change – to the Blues & Barrelhouse Club. Bob Watson had left to become one of Dickie Bishop's Sidekicks, but Cyril Davies was still there, as large as life, educating the audience as well as entertaining them. He and Alexis Korner worked the club separately, and as a duo – one that would last until late 1962.

Recordings from the period confirm Cyril's worship of Leadbelly, both in his unabashed vocals and in his 12-string guitar. Since they'd started, Leadbelly's songs had become popular, sung by teenagers all over Britain. It was barely credible; the music had been so esoteric and unfamiliar back then. Cyril and Alexis quickly acquired reputations as professors, sages – not only able to play country blues better than anyone else on the scene, but knowing its history inside out. Still, of course, they had no idea of quitting their day jobs (Cyril was still a panel beater, Alexis a BBC studio manager), to turn pro. Blues was their hobby, and they loved sharing their passion with fellow enthusiasts, who never knew who might drop in for a blow. Big Bill Broonzy, for instance, probably the greatest living bluesman at that time.

Broonzy was over to play a tour – and Jack Good, already displaying all the flair he became famous for, booked him onto the 6.5 Special. Big Bill Broonzy on prime time Saturday evening television! Of course, he was presented as something of a curiosity – but any blues fan could tune in to see him playing and singing and chatting briefly about his background.

At rehearsals, during the day of the show, Broonzy took the Vipers (who were also appearing that week) into his dressing-room and invited them to sip whiskey with him. "He locked the door and we all got boozed to hell," says Johnny Booker. "They were hammering for us to go out into the studio for a soundcheck but we were having a brilliant time, playing our guitars and singing together." Broonzy taught Booker the chords to his version of *Summertime*.

A week or so later, Booker and Wally Whyton happened to be in the A&A Club, an all-night hang-out for Soho nocturnalists (at 6 Flitcroft Street, off Denmark Street), when Broonzy came in and greeted them like old friends. They watched him eat a whole chicken and a trayful of baked potatoes. "Then," says Booker, "he sat there with his legs spread out in front of him, a bottle of whiskey in his hand, a girl on each knee, and a huge smile on his face. It was a great night for all of us!"

Naturally, the Roundhouse clientele were thrilled to bits, felt privileged beyond imagination, when Big Bill (who knew Alexis from previous visits) ambled in and played a set. They knew his records, some had read his biography *Big Bill's Blues*, all would remember this evening for the rest of their lives – as would Cyril and Alexis, who even played with him.

Ramblin' Jack Elliott had recently returned from Tangier and he re-established himself as a regular Roundhouse performer. In February 1957, he sent for his pal Derroll Adams, a deep-voiced banjo player he had sung with briefly, back in California. Derroll dressed like a riverboat gambler, with a black frock coat, a bow tie with long tails and a wide-brimmed hat. Looked like he maybe kept a derringer in his waistcoat pocket. They often dropped into the Roundhouse or into Hasted's 44 Club en route to a nightly cabaret gig that kept them going for months, at the Blue Angel in Berkeley Square. They also recorded tracks for Topic, which made up the seminal 10-inch albums *Jack Takes The Floor* and *Rambling Boys*.

At the suggestion of Tony Bucket, erstwhile tub-bass thumper for the City Ramblers, Jack, his wife June, and Derroll had moved into the Yellow Door in Baylis Road. Bucket collected a pound a week rent from each resident, although no-one ever discovered if he had been authorised so to do. Other transient tenants included Nick Thatcher, a Dylan fore-runner from Boston, who wore a peaked cap and army fatigues, smoked pot and played all the folk clubs. For as long as he was around (after six months he went back to the States and promptly disappeared), Thatcher was an object of adoration – along with Wally Whyton and Johnny Booker – to Iris Orton, an existential poet, who swept around Soho in a black cloak. Her first poems appeared in *The Dreamer And The Sheaves*, which had been published by Oxford University Press, but further anthologies, *With Music In Mind* and *A Man Singing* – inspired by and dedicated to these musicians – appeared only in limited editions. She and Christopher Logue would share jazz and poetry evenings at the Nucleus.

On Sunday lunchtimes, Jack and Derroll would go up to the pub on the corner, the Spanish Patriot in Lower Marsh, and sing for beer and food. Jack would sometimes still be wearing pyjamas, with his big racoon coat over them. According to June Elliott, when the Yellow Door was demolished for a road-widening scheme that summer, the residents held "the party of all time, roasted an ox in the back yard and destroyed the place afterwards." The Elliotts, and Derroll, moved on to Paris, St Tropez and Italy, where they bought Vespa scooters and toured in a package show with the Platters.

"Whenever I went to the Yellow Door, I always felt as if I were stepping into the pages of one of those classic Henry Miller books, like *Sexus* or *Plexus*," says Vipers washboard artist Johnny Pilgrim. "Mike Pratt was the moving spirit in that place. If he wasn't holding court in the kitchen, he was in bed with some voluptuous big-breasted bird. I remember going round there one day and he was licking marmalade off this woman's tits. I thought that was very impressive. Of course, by the time they pulled the Yellow Door down, he was starting to make some money. He had got into songwriting as a result of Nick Thatcher's influence and was now working with Lionel Bart, providing material for Tommy Steele."

Twenty-five

In Britain, the sale of gramophone records reached a new peak in 1957, partly due to the expansion of the teenage market, but cinema attendance fell by 20 per cent, to its lowest level for years. This was attributed to the extended reach of commercial television rather than any failing on the part of the film industry, which provided an unusually varied bill of fare.

During the year, critics went wild, or at least fell for (in order of appearance) *Friendly Persuasion, Ill Met By Moonlight, Oklahoma, The Rainmaker, Kismet, Giant, Baby Doll, Brothers In Law, Anastasia, Doctor At Large, The Teahouse of the August Moon, The Sweet Smell of Success, The Spirit of St Louis, Love In The Afternoon, Gunfight At The OK Corral, Saint Joan, An Affair To Remember, Silk Stockings* and *War And Peace*.

In the film magazines, there was undue emphasis on the brief careers of the late James Dean and the man supplanting him as a screen adonis, Elvis Presley, but neither saw anything like the acreage devoted to Jayne Mansfield. Unless one believes the editors wanted an excuse to publish photographs of a scantily clad woman with an unusually large chest, this was unfathomable – because although Jayne quickly became the rock 'n' roll generation's first and favourite pin-up (well ahead of Diana Dors, Joan Collins, and other contenders), she had no career to speak of. She had been a dancer in *Hell On Frisco Bay* and a cigarette girl in *Pete Kelly's Blues*, but then, at 23, she won the part of the gangster's moll in *The Girl Can't Help It* (released here in March 1957), which turned out to be the greatest rock 'n' roll film of the year, of any year.

One sensed it at the time. For many, it was the moment that the drab, monochrome post-war world suddenly bloomed in full spectrum colour. Some scenes would glow in the memory for the next 50 years. You can't get any better than Gene Vincent and Eddie Cochran in their most intense hungry-for-it prime, dressed splendidly, performing vitally their epic recordings *Be Bop A Lula* and *Twenty Flight Rock*. Or Julie London, floating erotically at the peak of her singing and acting careers on *Cry Me A River*. Or Fats

Domino, rolling around on his piano stool, singing *Blue Monday*. Or Little Richard standing there vamping the keys in his baggy suit, looking heavenward as he bawled out *She's Got It* and *Ready Teddy*. Enormous and loud in CinemaScope, blazing DeLuxe colour and high fidelity sound.

As a bonus, it actually had a story line, a sharp and witty script and fine acting – plus, one couldn't help but notice, the gigantic breasts of Jayne Mansfield, jacked out like Oldsmobile tail-lights underneath a wardrobe of tight fitting sweaters and the kind of motorcycle-fairing dresses which encourage the dumplings to boil over. "If you've got a figure like mine, 40-18-35, you're bound to be stared at," she admitted. No-one in grey and grainy Britain could imagine encountering a girl with such a remarkable physique, such lips, such hair – she was as exotic, unique, other-worldly as Gene Vincent or Little Richard.

Over the year, musically inclined teenagers were served by a spate of exploitation movies, the first of which was Elvis Presley's début *Love Me Tender*, which went on general release in January. A dreary, post-Civil War, black-and-white, B-picture western, it would have been quickly forgotten had Elvis not been involved – mainly as an 'actor', although room was made for a few songs. Most critics were snooty and condescending; not so his female fans, who were dismayed only when he was shot dead towards the end.

More interesting were the movies (like *The Girl Can't Help It*) where rock 'n' roll stars recreated elements of their stage show. Trivial and inconsequential though most of them were, these films were illustrated lectures on how the different strands of American rock 'n' roll music were performed. In Britain, they were studied, to learn how it was done. *Shake Rattle And Rock* (February) was accused by journalists who knew no better of having a slender story. Who cared, as long as it featured some great music? Which it did – Fats Domino singing *I'm In Love Again*, *Honey Chile* and *Ain't That A Shame*; Big Joe Turner (about whom little was known, except by Johnny Pilgrim, Alexis Korner and a few other collectors) singing *Lipstick Powder And Paint*.

Don't Knock The Rock (March) was a crass sequel to *Rock Around The Clock*, shot in two weeks on a budget of $600 thousand – but it had Alan Freed (personifying the disc jockey we never had), Bill Haley & his Comets (about to hit the downhill chute after their interesting but not too exciting UK tour), and Little Richard miming to his hits *Tutti Frutti, Long Tall Sally* and *Rip It Up*. We had read about him – "the little Negro with the big haircut" was *NME's* tantalising description – and we had heard his astonishing, hair-raising voice, but it was spring before anyone in Britain had ever seen Little Richard in action. He became an immediate hero forever.

Rock Rock Rock (April) had no pretensions; a pitiful story, abysmally acted, held together by a showcase of acts promoting their latest records. Alan Freed acted nobly – even though he was probably getting a cut from all of them. British fans admired and respected him for having a job as important as the Secretary-General of the United Nations, and they lusted after pretty 13-year-old Tuesday Weld. The film was worth going to see for performances by LaVern Baker, the Johnny Burnette Rock 'n' Roll Trio, the Flamingos, Frankie Lymon & the Teenagers, the Moonglows and especially Chuck Berry, ducking and bobbing and looking into the camera to see if anybody out there was on his wavelength. If they were, they could come along.

Loving You (August) showed hillbilly truck driver Elvis Presley in shining Technicolor and VistaVision magnificence, "the sexiest screen sinner since Valentino," according to reviewer Margaret Hinxman. For the first time, aspiring Brits could see him gyrate and sneer and put women into a coma. They would practise curling their lip and trying to comb their hair like his. The girls liked *Teddy Bear*; the boys preferred *Let's Have A Party*.

Of passing interest were *Rock Pretty Baby* (March) and *Untamed Youth* (September). The former was high school rubbish, starring the slightly talented Sal Mineo, Rod McKuen (trying to find himself at this point), Kim Fowley's father Douglas and Fay Wray, who some 20 years earlier had struggled in *King Kong's* gigantic fingers. The latter turned "a searing spotlight on teenage cons in a House of Correction . . . kids gone wrong, and the Farm's disgraceful penal abuse." It starred "the girl built like a platinum powerhouse" Mamie Van Doren (not in Jayne's league) but more importantly gave a cameo role to Eddie Cochran – already a big star to the rock 'n' roll cognoscenti, who admired and probably owned his first two London American singles.

Calypso Heat Wave (October) and *Bop Girl* (November) were silly attempts to cash in on the American calypso fad that had already fizzled out by the time they were released. The first featured the Tarriers singing *Banana Boat Song* and an early screen appearance by Maya Angelou, then a calypso singer.

There was the usual parade of duff British films, none more chronic than *Rock You Sinners*, released in August. If *The Girl Can't Help It* offered a glimpse of the world we wanted to inhabit, *Rock You Sinners* showed the world we were stuck with. The true wretchedness of the early 1957 British rock 'n' roll landscape can be gauged from this quickie hotchpotch featuring Tony Crombie & his Rockets, Art Baxter & the Rockin' Sinners, and Don Sollash & the Rockin' Horses – all acts from the Jeffrey Kruger stable and all lacking any originality or rock 'n' roll heart. It ran for only 59 minutes and was roundly panned, most thoroughly by *Picturegoer*. "If rock 'n' roll is really dying, as everybody says it is, this film should stand as a tombstone. For by its monumental ineptitude, it finally closes the lid on whatever was fresh and exciting in the harsh, twitching beat."

Little did they know that, far from feeling death pangs, the home-grown rock 'n' roll scene had barely got started, and that these parasite bands were as fake as plastic flowers. "The acting is so wooden you could light a fire with it," *Picturegoer* continued, "and the story is so wet it would douse it." Little more was heard of the stars, Philip Gilbert and Adrienne Scott (who turned out to be the producer's daughter), and the film belly-flopped more ignominiously than any other that year.

Rather better (though some felt only marginally so) was *The Tommy Steele Story* (June), described by *Picturegoer* as "a modest little biopic which presents the well-known incidents of his life with a simplicity well within the scope of his limited acting ability." Elsewhere it was variously described as "a bean-feast for the teenagers" and "delightful entertainment". Quaint would probably have been nearer the mark. What nobody realised at the time was that Tommy, very shrewd and very sussed beneath that grinning façade, was merely serving his apprenticeship, getting hands-on experience in as many fields as possible. Here he was, intrepidly diving into a new medium, shouldering a full-blown Beaconsfield Studios production less than six months after his discovery.

He had started the year with a rising hit, his version of Guy Mitchell's chart-topping *Singing The Blues*, a country & western song which changed personality with each new recording. Tommy gave it a Bermondsey twist that took it to number one again. More television, more concerts, everything going to plan; soon there would be no-one in Britain unfamiliar with his name.

He had already filmed a coffee bar scene for *Kill Me Tomorrow*, a nondescript thriller starring Pat O'Brien and Lois Maxwell, and now, with unprecedented brass, managers Larry Parnes and John Kennedy approached Anglo-Amalgamated Pictures with the idea of making Steele the star of his own movie. It was an outrageous suggestion but one which the company grasped with both hands. The film was put into production immediately, shooting to begin on 18 February. Norman Hudis, who had written screenplays for *The Crooked Sky* and *West Of Suez*, and would later write the first six of the *Carry On* series, was hired to cobble a script together as quickly as possible. Tommy's friends, Mike Pratt and Lionel Bart were rolled in to work on a dozen new songs – a task they completed in little more than a week.

Bart had been born Lionel Begleiter in Petticoat Lane on 1 August 1930. He was nine when war broke out and almost 15 when it ended. As a schoolboy athlete, he ran for London and teachers also praised his flair for English, drama and painting. "They reckoned I should try for a scholarship at St Martins School of Art, and I got in," says Bart. "Because there was a grant involved, and because I was the baby of the family, my dad let me go. He was a ladies' tailor, and all my brothers and sisters worked with him, in his workshop in the backyard."

Bart spent his National Service as a clerk in the RAF, based at Innsworth, near Gloucester, where he painted murals on the NAAFI walls. On release, he and a fellow inmate, John Gorman, borrowed 50 pounds each from relatives and started a silkscreen printing business in the basement of a sweet shop in Elderfield Road, Hackney – but his main interests lay elsewhere. "I was a Young Communist and used to go to various meetings organised by them, and I started going to jazz clubs too. Some of my mates from art school had become musicians and I took to hanging out with them, in the coffee bars and drinking dens of Soho, which was quite a bouncing place, I quickly discovered."

He also got involved with the fiercely left-wing Unity Theatre, run by Alfie Bass and housed in a reconstructed church hall at

1 Goldington Street, up beyond St Pancras station. "It was just a little dump," he says, "but it was quite a heavy thing, theatrically – changed a lot of lives." He first went there in spring 1952, to help paint the scenery for a sexual equality play (in 1952!) *The Wages of Eve*, "just to be part of a team, with no ideas in my head about writing."

A year later, in the run-up to the Coronation, they staged *Turn It Up*, a political satire whose main target was the Conservative government. "I was painting scenery again, but during the rehearsals I wrote a couple of lyrics which I thought might be appropriate – and as soon as Alfie heard them, he got me doing a bit of songwriting, a bit of acting and a bit of sketch-writing. I did a duet with the actor Julian Glover, and I think that Warren Mitchell and Johnny Speight were involved in that one too." In their review of the show, which ran for several weeks, the *Daily Worker* singled out Bart for special praise.

In December, as well as writing much of the Unity's Christmas pantomime, *Cinderella* – transmogrified into the daughter of an impoverished John Bull figure, dominated by his ghastly American wife – Bart played the part of an ugly sister. The lead role was taken by London Youth Choir member Hylda Sims.

Between the two shows, in summer 1953, Lionel went with the Unity Theatre troupe to the International Youth Festival in Bucharest – there meeting the Choir and its musical director, John Hasted. He also went to the 1955 Festival in Warsaw. "We were treated like Lords," he says, "and we felt we were part of something. Masses of people from all over the world, mixing together in a very positive, friendly way. It was very moving. We were going to change the world!"

It was at the Yellow Door that Lionel first ran into Mike Pratt, who lived there, and Tommy Steele, Tommy Hicks as he was then. "We used to go there after the coffee bars closed and party through the night," he recalls. "It was a good place to be, so different from the usual basic humdrum. We had been through the war and everything was pretty grim, what with rationing and so on – and scenes like the Yellow Door seemed liberating and glamorous."

Bart's biggest buzz, one which no doubt endeared him to Tommy, was writing a song for Billy Cotton: *Oh For A Cup Of Tea (Instead Of A Cappuccino)*. "That was the first song of mine to get on the radio –

and it was about Soho! The second was *Rock With The Caveman,* after which the ball was rolling."

"Next thing we knew, Anglo-Aggravated wanted us to write a load of songs for Tommy's film. Tommy's film! Things were moving so fast that we barely had time to blink! Anyway, we sat with Norman Hudis, who was doing the screenplay, and I talked him into letting us do songs in a variety of styles, not just rock 'n' roll, to reflect the episodes of his life – some cockney stuff, some calypso for when he was on the boats, some humour, some romantic numbers, maybe. 'Yes, I like it,' Hudis said, 'a handful of songs to hold the story together' . . . and we had our first title."

Lionel Bart and Mike Pratt were not exactly sure of the film's market or its projected audience, but they knew Tommy's personality well enough, knew what kind of stuff he enjoyed singing when he was relaxing with his mates, knew what he was capable of, and knew they could stretch him – and maybe stretch his audience too, while they were at it. Only later would Bart master the art of writing for a show; now he was working on instinct. Not only was *The Tommy Steele Story* an exemplary training camp for all concerned, but some of the songs, and the performances, remain memorable. Tommy was already flying beyond rock 'n' roll, although that would remain his anchor for some years yet.

"Mike and I worked well together during that period," says Bart. "He might write a melody for the first verse, then I might think of one for the bridge or the chorus. He sat at his piano and I sat beside him, both of us scribbling down notes, singing bits of song at each other. It was Mike who came up with the melody for *A Handful Of Songs,* which is probably the best thing we did for that film."

The Tommy Steele Story surprised the critics, not least Margaret Hinxman, who wrote: "Even his dearest fans couldn't call him a polished actor. But whatever he isn't, this lean, hungry-looking dynamo is a thoroughly likeable screen personality. Surprised? I'm amazed!" Before the end of the year, every female from five to 95 would love Tommy.

But only one would catch him.

Back in early February, in his slick blue jacket and blue suede shoes, Tommy played a week at Chiswick Empire, topping a variety bill that included singer Josephine Anne, comedian Reg Thompson, one man band Johnny Laycock, puppeteers Paul and Peta Page, the grandly named Ballet Montmartre dancing team, and nutty boys Mike & Bernie Winters. He was relaxing in his dressing room, taking it easy between shows when Lionel Bart came in with a girl he'd met, a 20-year-old dancer from the Windmill Theatre, Ann Donoughue. Within minutes, she and Tommy were chatting and laughing.

His manager John Kennedy didn't like girls hanging around his star, wanted to preserve the notion that Tommy was within reach of every single one of his adoring female fans. On that fragile thread his success depended, thought Kennedy – whose heart suddenly started beating twice as fast when he realised what was happening before his very eyes. "I was a fool not to have recognised the symptoms at once," he wrote in his book. "This was love at first sight." He refused to speak to Ann – until it became impossible not to. During the filming of *The Tommy Steele Story*, she was at the studio every day, obliging Kennedy to invent the story that she was there in an administrative capacity.

Photographs of Ann began appearing a few weeks later. "She's Tommy's secretary while he's filming," ran one caption, "and he bans pictures of them together. 'They said I needed a secretary,' said Steele, 'but I don't usually like people to fetch and carry for me.' Her name is Ann Donoughue." If any journalists saw through the fiction, they didn't let on.

In March, Tommy was the first British rock 'n' roller to release a live album *Stage Show* (mostly covers, not memorable) and two months later the first to release a film soundtrack album *The Tommy Steele Story* (all originals, with a stage musical atmosphere). In between, he appeared at the Royal Albert Hall, on the BBC Light Programme's *Festival Of Dance Music*, and was later the castaway on *Desert Island Discs* – an honour for someone so youthful. The staid and formal interviewer Roy Plomley was clearly confounded by some of Tommy's selections, which included *Rudy's Rock* by Bill Haley & his Comets, *What A Mouth* by the Two Bills From Bermondsey and his own revue-style rocker *Cannibal Pot*.

Throughout the summer, he and the four-piece Steelmen continued to tour the country. "Originally, we were contracted for six weeks, but somehow that got extended to two years," says string bass player Alan Weighall, who along with saxophone player Alan Stuart had been recruited from Teddy Foster's Orchestra. Drummer Leo Pollini had worked as an engineer in the Harold Fielding

Agency's recording studio but neither he nor Denis Price, who played piano standing up (as was the current requirement), had a famous-band pedigree. "We didn't make much money but we enjoyed ourselves," Weighall continues. "John Kennedy would instruct us to jump around and look as though we were having a ball. We were serious musicians before that!"

For their appearances on the 6.5 *Special* and various other television shows, the Steelmen were augmented by guitarist Roy Plummer – but he was seen as an expensive luxury, to be used only when the BBC stumped up, possibly because the hysterical screeching of Tommy's audiences overwhelmed the sound coming off the stage. This "indescribable din" perplexed, all but unhinged the crusty *Daily Telegraph* reporter sent to cover a concert (sold out, as they all were) at the Dominion Theatre in Tottenham Court Road. Unable to understand the furore around him, he tried to be amusing, describing the singer as "no more than a crazy mixed-up minstrel with ants in his pants." Very droll. "In the modern idiom, this was an evening out for the cats," he continued. "Personally, I'll take the more soothing, more civilised caterwaulings of the four-legged kind."

Steele and his band did four weeks with visiting American group Freddie Bell & the Bellboys, whose only hit *Giddy Up A Ding Dong* had been in Tommy's set since day one, followed by a summer season at Blackpool, and then several more weeks at provincial theatres, spread around from Bristol to Aberdeen. Meanwhile, his parents moved out of Bermondsey, where their house had been condemned and scheduled for demolition, and into a four-bedroomed residence in Catford, purchased by their son. Said Tommy: "I know that I've shot up to the top very quickly – too quickly, some people say. Now I'm learning all I can about show business because I want to stay at the top for my mum and dad's sake, if nothing else."

In October 1957, exactly a year after his first record had been released, Tommy was voted number one in the British Musical Personality section of the *NME* readers' annual poll (how that must have hurt and upset a few people), and number two in the British Male Singer section, below Dickie Valentine, who was now clinging on by his fingernails. That same month, he started work on his second film *The Duke Wore Jeans* – on a financial package which made him "the highest paid film star in Britain", according to his managers, who, feeling he was now worth more than the flat fee of £2,500 he received for *The Tommy Steele Story*, had negotiated an astronomical £20,000 plus 10 per cent of the box office take. This at a time when the Prime Minister, the Rt Hon Harold Macmillan, was governing the country on an annual salary of £1,000.

Having more pressing matters on his mind, Macmillan tried his best to ignore rock 'n' roll – as did everyone of his class – but the Queen was forced to take a passing interest. They must have been tuned in to the *6.5 Special* in the royal household. Her children, Charles (days away from his ninth birthday) and Anne (then seven), both liked Tommy Steele and had been to see his film. She told him so when she shook his hand at the Royal Film Performance in early November. "Her Majesty was the most charming woman I have ever met," Tommy was reported as saying.

A fortnight later, Tommy was singing for Her Majesty. Along with such showbiz notables as Judy Garland, Count Basie, Gracie Fields, Harry Secombe and Max Bygraves, he had been chosen to appear in the Royal Variety Performance at the London Palladium. Against a backdrop representing a coffee bar, he sang three numbers: *Rock With The Caveman*, *Hound Dog* and *Singing The Blues*. According to John Kennedy's biography, the Queen, Princess Margaret and the Queen Mother all clapped along.

Steele ended the year in pantomime, in *Goldilocks And The Three Bears* at the Royal Court Theatre in Liverpool. He jumped at the chance to work on a stage with people other than his Steelmen, to be moved around by a director, to be part of a production, to spend a month studying at another training school.

Interviewed earlier in the year, he had revealed an ambition to become an 'entertainer', as he called it. "I don't need rock 'n' roll crutches," he said. He had never wanted to be Elvis Presley or Bill Haley or Hank Williams or anyone other than Tommy Steele.

Down in the coffee bars, a lot of boys were wishing and hoping that they could be 'the next Tommy Steele'.

Twenty-six

If Tommy Steele had been discovered at the 2Is Coffee Bar, then that was obviously the place to go. To see or be seen. Or just to hang out. Some teenagers began to treat it like an exclusive youth club, one serving the whole city rather than just the local community, and naturally, having all been drawn by the same need, kids from different parts of London became mates. Among the first to arrive, in November 1956, were two 17 year olds, Brian Gregg from Brixton and Terry Williams from Waterloo. Williams would soon be the first of several contenders to find himself launched as "the new Tommy Steele".

Gregg and Williams were friends already, had been for almost a year, ever since starting work together on the same day in the stockroom at HMV in Oxford Street. The former's introduction to rock 'n' roll had been at the Warwick, a youth club over the river in Victoria, frequented by the local Teddy boy faction. "People would bring in records by Ruby Murray and Dickie Valentine," says Gregg, "but this one particular guy brought in all the early Bill Haley records, like *Crazy Man Crazy, Dim Dim The Lights* and *Razzle Dazzle,* plus really weird stuff like *Don't Roll Your Bloodshot Eyes At Me* by Wynonie Harris and *Don't Be Angry* by Nappy Brown – records so good that you felt you had to go out and buy them. When skiffle got going, I went to some of the coffee bars, like the Gyre & Gimble and the Nucleus, but I never felt comfortable in them. The people down there were a bit older – they didn't like rock 'n' roll or riff-raff types like me."

A more congenial atmosphere could be found at the 2Is in Old Compton Street and the Cat's Whisker in Kingly Street, coffee bars with rock 'n' roll jukeboxes and no objection to the lavish use of Brylcreem. Resident at the Whisker was the Leon Bell Hi-Fi Four, one of the first rock 'n' roll groups on the scene. How hi-fi they were is questionable. A hairdresser by day, the short and curly Bell had attracted attention for singing skiffle songs with a cigarette drooping from his lip, but he had acquired a minuscule amplifier and was now keen to move onward and upward. By November 1956, sensing how duff their name was, the group had become Leon Bell & his Bellcats and as such were featured regularly on the weekly rock 'n' roll nights at Studio 51 and Wimbledon Palais.

It was during one of Bell's sets at the Cat's Whisker that Terry Williams first got up and let rip. "We were down there one night," says Gregg, "and I must have been in a mischievous mood. Most of the people thought Leon Bell was pretty good, but not me! After he'd sung *Green Door* for the third time, I grabbed hold of his trouser leg – he used to sit on the counter to sing, because the place was so small – and asked 'Can my mate sing with your group?' He said 'Is he any good?' 'He's better than you are!' I told him."

People were looking on expectantly, so Leon could hardly say no. "Terry sang *Blue Suede Shoes* and tore the roof off the place," says Gregg. "I knew he would. He used to sing in the stockroom when there wasn't anyone else around, and I knew he could blow Leon Bell out of the back door."

His confidence boosted, Williams took his guitar to the 2Is and strummed out a few songs. Margaret Rooke, a girlfriend of Gregg's and a fan of Rory Blackwell's band (and a few years later the wife of Gene Vincent), tipped off Rory and on 24 January 1957, the novice was fronting Rory's Rock 'n' Rollers at the Razzle Dazzle Club (as Studio 51 was known on Thursday night rock 'n' roll sessions), billed as 'the new singing sensation Terry Williams'.

Twelve days later, Blackwell and his band (minus Terry) were given the honour of playing on the *Daily Mirror*-sponsored train which took fans to Southampton to meet Bill Haley & his Comets off the *Queen Elizabeth* at Southampton and bring them up to Waterloo, ready to start their first UK tour. Newspapers described mob scenes outside the station as 'the Second Battle of Waterloo'.

By this time, Williams was already on his way out of the band. Most of their gigs were in boisterous pubs like the Castle at Tooting and the White Hart in Willesden, and having alcohol in close proximity was a temptation he was sometimes unable to resist. Coffee bars were a better bet – and it was to these that he returned after being fired by Blackwell, allegedly for becoming over-refreshed and fighting.

Almost immediately, 2Is owner Paul Lincoln started making enquiries about how he could assist Terry to the kind of overnight stardom Tommy Steele was now enjoying, less than six months after meeting John Kennedy in his very own establishment. Lincoln saw how it had been done and sought to get in on the act, putting in a few calls, putting out a few feelers. The clique of kids who hung out there were full of ideas, about what sort of group he should have, what clothes he should wear, what songs he should sing. "He won't get anywhere with a name like Terry Williams," warned Michael Hayes. "Why not call him Terry Dean?" Everyone knew that Hayes idolised James Dean. After further discussion, the acquiescent Terry Williams became Terry Dene. Star in waiting.

"I don't know what it was about him," Lincoln told a reporter, "but he seemed to have just that little something that attracted attention." A month was spent auditioning musicians, rehearsing an act, buying clothes – "one long spending spree," according to his novice manager.

During this time, the original set of 2Is coffee bar cowboys – Brian Gregg, Terry Dene, Michael Hayes and Alex Wharton – earned a bit of cash by working as extras on St Joan, which was being filmed by Otto Preminger at Shepperton Studios. "We only lasted a couple of days," says Hayes. "You had to be there at seven in the morning, for make-up and to get into costume. All I remember is falling asleep all over the place because I was so tired. Everything took hours, all of us milling about while the cameras were moved around. It was the burning scene . . . I get killed in it."

Dene's launch progressed as smoothly as Lincoln had hoped it would. Step one: Hymie Zahl, a partner in the respected Foster's Agency, agrees to represent him. Step two: Lincoln and Zahl mount a showcase début on a well-publicised rock 'n' roll package show 'Meet for Cats' at Romford Odeon on 31 March 1957. (Also on the bill are Bobby Breen's Rockers, the Chas McDevitt/Nancy Whiskey Skiffle Group and Rory Blackwell's group, now called the Blackjacks.) Step three: Terry makes the first of several 6.5 Special television appearances on 27 April. Step four: Decca issues his first single A White Sport Coat (a US hit by Marty Robbins, currently at number five on the Billboard chart) on 31 May. Step five: the record breaks into the Top 20 a week later. Step Six: he headlines a national variety tour – twice a night, six nights a week at each venue. Step seven: a second single Start Movin' (a US hit by actor Sal Mineo) reaches number 15 on 19 July. Step eight: he is signed for a starring role in *The Golden Disc*, to be filmed at Walton Studios during late August and early September. Step nine: he appears at the Royal Albert Hall on 8 September. Step ten: he buys a house in Camberwell for his parents in November.

The ten step method. It ran like clockwork. At the start of 1957, Dene was unknown, too awkward and shy to talk to girls, sleeping on a camp bed in his parents' cramped flat. By Christmas, he was one of the biggest stars in the rapidly expanding teenage market, a white sport coat and a pink carnation his trademark. Of course, his appeal was mainly to girls; the rock 'n' roll cognoscenti wouldn't have touched his records with a barge-pole – mainly because they were so pitifully inept. At a time when astonishing American records were being released every week, Dene suffered from poor choice of material, tepid arrangements and wimpy, gutless productions. It was all too dispiriting.

"Terry was a much better singer than most people realise," says Brian Gregg. "He's judged on his records, most of which were rubbish because the record company dictated every move. I remember him saying 'Listen to this crap they want me to sing!' In fact, he was a good, forceful rock 'n' roll singer. They should have let him make at least one powerful record that people would remember as more than just a novelty." Hopefully the fan worship and the money provided ample compensation.

Everyone was learning. Including Gregg, who had joined Les Hobeaux in January. It was an unplanned move. He was walking through the HMV record store, on his way back to the stockroom where he worked, when these guys asked him if he knew where the Blues section was. They got chatting and when he discovered they were in a skiffle group, he arranged for them to audition at the 2Is – where he already had the ear of the boss. When they did so, Gregg played along on the tea-chest bass that was kept in the corner – and they asked him to join. They took over as the main attraction when the Vipers went off to do their fortnight at the Prince of Wales Theatre.

Les Hobeaux were distinguished not only for the existentialist ring of their name but also for having two singers out front, one of them black – the direct descendent of an African chief, if you believed the publicity. Behind them were Gregg, soon playing a real double-bass though with only one string, and three guitarists, including Les Bennetts, who would later become a mainstay of Lonnie Donegan's group.

Alternating with the Worried Men, Les Hobeaux provided entertainment at the 2Is until summer 1957 – when they decided to go for it. "We all dumped everything to turn pro," says Gregg. "Most of the others were students at Regent Street Poly; I was still at HMV, who actually wrote to my mum asking her to try and talk me out of leaving – because they had 'big plans' for me within the company, so they reckoned. They hadn't tried to talk Terry Dene out of it when he left; they were glad to get rid of him. He used to take the piss out of our manager."

In late August, Les Hobeaux were given a cameo in Dene's movie *The Golden Disc*, performing *Dynamo* – with nattily quiffed Rory Blackwell guesting on drums – and at the beginning of September, they played their first out-of-towner at the Commodore Ballroom in Ryde on the Isle of Wight. By chance, EMI producer Norman Newell had travelled down to see a new lad who was just starting out, local boy Craig Douglas. He passed on Craig but was waiting in the wings to offer Les Hobeaux a contract as they came off the stage. It was as easy as that.

For the rest of the year, they toured as a package, supporting Terry Dene and the Southlanders, a West Indian vocal quartet whose *6.5 Special* appearances had broadened their audience. The compère was Zom, erstwhile 12-string guitarist in John Hasted's 44 Skiffle Group, who had developed his repertoire to include talking blues numbers and badinage.

By this time, Dene was working with a new backing group. The first line-up, professionals assembled by Hymie Zahl, had hardly fitted the bill. Guitarist Eric Kershaw was a refugee from the swing era, who could play rings around practically every other guitarist in the country. In 1946, he had published *Eric Kershaw's Dance Band Guitar Chords*, a tutor that nourished every aspiring player of the era, but he was already in his forties and had neither feel nor respect for the mishmash music he was expected to play behind Dene. On bass and drums were Pete Elderfield and Dave 'Benny' Goodman, modern jazzers trying to earn a bit of bread and do the best they could. They had played together in avant-garde bands led by Tubby Hayes and Don Rendell, gods in their subterranean world, and now they were volunteering for this rock 'n' roll freak circus of screaming teenage girls and a bloke "stuttering and twitching, wiggling his legs and hips in rhythmical ecstasy," as one paper described it.

After a few weeks, the two guys who didn't look or feel or sound rock 'n' roll enough left. If they were fired, it probably came as sweet relief. Pete Elderfield stayed and was joined by Terry Kennedy's Rock 'n' Rollers, who now became the Dene-Aces. They were younger and snappier and played rock 'n' roll like the passionate, grooving kids they were.

Mates from Peckham, Terry Kennedy and Clem Cattini had felt rock 'n' roll taking over their minds as they sat in awe-stricken wonder watching *Rock Around The Clock*. "It was 28 August 1956, my seventeenth birthday," recalls Cattini. "We came out of the cinema and Terry said 'Right, we'll form a group. I'll be the singer and guitar player'. So I said 'What'll I do?' He said 'You can play drums'. My whole career was based on that one moment of madness."

With two friends, Mick McDonagh and Ron Prentiss getting to grips with guitar and bass, they rehearsed every evening, trying to sound more rock 'n' roll than skiffle. Girlfriends complaining that all they cared about was that music. For their début, they hired the hall at the Adam & Eve pub in Peckham one Sunday lunchtime. By December, they were playing regular gigs at the Cat's Whisker and the 2Is Club at 44 Gerrard Street, where more noise could be made than at the coffee bar. Originally billed as the Rock City Ramblers, they upgraded to the more descriptive Terry Kennedy's Rock 'n' Rollers. Fired up and ready to go.

They had a taste of variety when they went out on a package with spindly comedian Max Wall, whose act had been modified to include a rock 'n' roll skit in which he wore a Bill Haley-style plaid jacket, but they felt more comfortable as a featured act on Terry Dene's first tour. They became his backing group in August, on cue to make an appearance in *The Golden Disc*.

Les Hobeaux had two singles released on HMV during late 1957. Both sides of the first – *Toll The Bell Easy/Oh Mary Don't You Weep* – were old Negro spirituals but here they sounded more Sunday school than southern Baptist. Allusions to Jesus and Moses meant neither side was played on BBC Radio. The next, *Mama Don't Allow* and *Hey Hey Daddy Blues*, featured session men brought in by musical director Geoff Love to make their sound neater and more attractive to his own audience, the square audience. He saw them more as a cabaret group; they were happier being part of the teenage maelstrom.

While their mates spent the summer evenings jumping around on stages, Alex Wharton and Michael Hayes were working at the 2Is for a quid a night: Alex upstairs selling coffee, Mickie in the basement selling Coke.

"Mickie and I went to the same school, Chandos Secondary, between Kenton and Kingsbury," says Wharton, "and we started going up to the West End together. He was two years older than me and seemed so worldly . . . he introduced me to the porn shops and coffee bars of Soho."

Hayes turned 19 on 20 June 1957, by which time he was known to the 2Is crew as 'Mickie the Most'. "It was his favourite catchphrase," says Brian Gregg. "Every new record he heard was 'the most', every new film he saw was 'the most', every new girl he met was 'the most'. He was always posing around, miming guitar to the records on the jukebox, combing his hair, coming out with hip sayings like 'I've got a pocketful of green; I'm gonna split this scene'. He certainly enjoyed life."

"Look at him! The Mostest-with-the-Leastest!" observed Margaret Rooke, who was now going out with Terry Dene.

Mickie Most, as he would one day become known to just about everybody in Britain, was a fan of James Dean. Even though he was underage, he got in to see the X certificate *Rebel Without A Cause* and realised that he wanted his own life to be like a movie. "This was in early 1956, before anyone over here had even heard of Elvis Presley," says Most. "James Dean was the role model – and he certainly was for me. In my mind, I was already living in Hollywood, while most of the people I knew were living in Cricklewood, if you know what I mean. Dreaming away, you believed you were capable of anything. Of course, you weren't really, but you didn't know that. While you had that innocence or that ignorance, which is what it really was, you had a chance in life. So *Rebel Without A Cause* and then a year later *The Girl Can't Help It* had a big influence on me. I saw myself in both of those films."

"After I left school, I found myself employed as an apprentice welder and sheet metal worker, which was the last thing I wanted to do," Most continues. "I never used to go. I left home in the morning, as if I was going to work, but then I would go up to Soho and hang around the coffee bars. The 2Is especially had a warm and friendly atmosphere; it was a very easy niche to slide into."

He and Wharton became adept at riding trains without a ticket. "We used to jump off at Kenton Park, where it slowed down for the curve," Wharton remembers. "One night, Mickie jumped off first and yelled this blood-curdling scream . . . he'd straddled a stay-wire supporting an electrical pole, almost castrated himself."

Some Saturday afternoons, they also used to go across to the Riverside Studios in Hammersmith and mingle with the audience at the 6.5 *Special*, hogging the camera whenever they could. Life was one long party.

Not wanting to be left out of the 2Is house-fun, Wharton and Hayes began singing the odd song with Les Hobeaux and the Worried Men, not as a duo but individually. Both had toyed with guitar. "It didn't take too much talent to learn three chords," reckoned Most, "a bit tough on the fingers, but if you practised enough you got round it." They paired up as the Most Brothers when Paul Lincoln and Hymie Zahl wanted an opening act for Les Hobeaux' provincial début, a Sunday gig at the Ryde Commodore on the Isle of Wight on 1 September 1957.

Lincoln told reporters that he had chosen their name "not because they were the most talented but because they were the most troublesome", always nagging him to make them stars – as if he had the magic wand, the Midas touch. He also put it about that Tommy Steele had been very supportive, instructing them on stagecraft.

"All Tommy did was show us a few chords," says Wharton, "but then again, we never learned to play more than a few chords, so maybe you could say he did teach us all we knew!"

"We were kind of like the English Everly Brothers, without the harmony or the musical ability," admits Most. "What we were really doing was saying 'isn't this great?' It was so great to be playing and singing in front of people."

After a second concert, the Trocadero at the Elephant & Castle, supporting their pal Terry Dene (billed as 'the local star'), they were offered a recording contract with Decca. Such was the clamour for teenage acts. They took it. "I used to carry my recording contract in my inside pocket, everywhere I went, so that I could show it around," says Most. "I mean, how many people made records in 1957? Not many. I thought I was one cool kiddie!"

"We got loads of publicity," says Wharton, "because we were young, blond, photogenic and could be linked into the glamorous 2Is story. We felt we couldn't fail."

Lacking fire, flair or substance, their first single, *Whistle Bait*, released just before Christmas 1957 was a dismal affair, despite – or maybe because of – the presence of such jazz luminaries as Tony Crombie, Lennie Bush and Bert Weedon. A bunch of farcical backing singers and wolf whistlers gave it a Billy Cotton Show atmosphere, demonstrating once again that English producers (in this case Dick Rowe) had little insight into the adolescent mind and little idea how to record teenage music. The song was a mediocre rockabilly number, written and recently recorded by Texan singer Don Johnston; the Mosts were given copies of his single and told to learn it. Few record buyers considered it an essential purchase but the duo remained optimistic about the future.

Following on from Terry Dene, Les Hobeaux and the Most Brothers, Paul Lincoln's fourth act of 1957 was the oddity launched as Wee Willie Harris. That he was never regarded as anything but a fringe novelty, a figure of fun by most people worked in his favour, enabling him to turn this eccentric guise into a lifelong career. "Is he a clown in the circus tradition, a latterday Little Tich, a budding Harpo Marx?" asked one puzzled reviewer, "or is he taking the everlasting mickey out of rock 'n' rollers and skifflers, making his own wry comment on the raving, raucous out-of-perspective idols of the modern teenage world?"

He'd been born in Bermondsey, that cradle of rock 'n' roll, on 25 March 1933. As Charlie Harris, he had sung in pubs and social clubs. As 'Fingers' Harris, he had played the piano at jazz clubs, often played into the night, down at the Nucleus. As Steve Murray, he started singing rock 'n' roll at the 2Is Club with different backing groups, sometimes Terry Kennedy's Rock 'n' Rollers, sometimes jazz-mates like drummer Bill Eyden and bassist Ashley Kozak. Most of the kids singing down there were teenagers; he was already feeling old at 24 – and was desperately hoping for a way out of his boring dead-end job at Peak Frean's biscuit factory.

On 1 June 1957, still calling himself Steve Murray, he was a featured performer on '2Is Rock Across The Channel', a ferry trip from Gravesend to Calais and back. Lincoln liked him, thought he was a good bloke, but felt he was lacking the "little something" he had detected in Terry Dene, the little something that made a singer gaze-worthy and memorable. "You need a gimmick, something that will get you noticed," Lincoln told him.

The singer returned the next day with his hair tousled up and teased – and dyed a bright shade of pink. A plot was hatched that day; he would be launched as Wee Willie Harris. Plenty of Max Wall-style tongue in cheek. He would wear an oversized polka-dot bow-tie and a garish red Teddy boy drape with his name emblazoned on the back, like a wrestler. A new act was devised. Journalists could not wait to write about him and his 'sputnik red' hair. Said one: "He plays piano standing, kneeling, occasionally with his chin and gyrates like an exploding Catherine wheel, emitting growls, squeals and what sounds like severe hiccuping."

According to one newspaper, happy to regurgitate the hype, Wee Willie's hair was "insured for £12,000 against falling out – by the same firm that covers Sabrina's bust against shrinking".

He confounded viewers when the 6.5 *Special* was broadcast live from the 2Is Coffee Bar on 16 November 1957 and was featured leaning against the servery, gently mocking Gilbert Harding and calling him "daddy-o". What was Gilbert Harding doing there? One may well ask. The standard of 6.5 *Special* was never high, but there was nothing else to watch. Jack Good was still there but a new co-producer had arrived, Dennis Main-Wilson . . . "who admits he is an off-duty Mozart fan". It didn't augur well.

The 2Is 6.5 *Special* cemented the coffee bar's reputation. They even had an interview with Paul Lincoln, whose voice, according to journalist Fraser White, "rang with a sacred softness that made him sound like the Billy Graham of the teenage movement". The show also featured Terry Dene, Larry Page, the Chas McDevitt Skiffle Group with Shirley Douglas, Mike and Bernie Winters, Lucille Mapp, Don Lang & his Frantic Five, Jim Dale, the King Brothers, Joe Henderson and current 2Is residents the Worried Men. The cellar was barely big enough for the cameras to fit in; singers, musicians and comperes were flying up and down the stairs like firemen. Half of Old Compton Street was blocked off by outside broadcast vans; police diverted the traffic. Anyone would have thought something important was going on.

In the last week of the year, Decca (which seemed to be signing up anything that moved) released the first single by Wee Willie Harris,

Rockin' At The 2Is, a celebration of the womb, a work of his own
creation. It was a silly trifle of a song, with a quasi-Fats Domino intro
and a catchy chorus. The arrangement was laid-back and thrust-free,
with heavy reliance on trombone, which may sound cool and
innovative now but then sounded like one's worst BBC Band Show
nightmare. It was regarded as a curio. Willie was well chuffed, many
years later, when he bumped into Ian Dury somewhere and Dury
sang the entire song to him, word perfect.

Twenty-seven

On 1 June 1957, perhaps a little early in the year for this kind of thing, Paul Lincoln promoted a rock 'n' roll ferry crossing on the *Royal Daffodil* – a bit of a tub, despite its noble name. It was a 16-hour round-trip, including five hours in Calais. The first rock 'n' roll hooligans in France. Those who made it had a good time – as did Lincoln, though he lost a lot of money, so it was reported. The venture was billed as '2Is Rock Across The Channel'. Get that brand name up there.

The bill was as solid as it could have been: Terry Dene & the Dene-agers (precursors of the Dene-Aces), Rory Blackwell & the Blackjacks, Steve Murray (not yet Wee Willie Harris), Leon Bell & the Bellcats, the City Ramblers Skiffle Group and several more. Historically, the trip was memorable for two reasons. Dene was due to perform in Calais, where even local dignitaries had booked seats, but he was as pissed as a newt by the time the boat docked, and the show was nixed. However, a new 'star' emerged: 16-year-old Colin Hicks, who was backed by the Bellcats. He was blond and James Deanish, and looked a bit like Tommy Steele, which wasn't surprising because they were brothers. Most articles about him were headlined 'Big Brother Is Watching You'. As if he didn't know.

Colin's praises were first sung by *Weekly Sporting Review*'s Fraser White. Ironically, both the journalist and the newspaper were brought down by the action brought by Tommy's manager Larry Parnes, a few years later. White was a fervent champion of the 2Is, where the regulars were always pleased to see him whenever he dropped by.

Published weekly, the oddly named *Weekly Sporting Review – Show Business* was an unlikely mixture of boxing, horse racing, film news and music-biz chat. The front page usually had a picture of some blood-splattered boxer wincing as he got another fat glove in his face and inside they often printed photographs of the country's leading fight promoter Jack Solomons sucking on a fat cigar. (The parallels between boxers and pop stars became more interesting as the years went by.) The same old photographs, especially those of Lonnie Donegan and Diana Dors, were printed several times over the weeks, leading one to believe that resources were limited. The editor also found excuses to publish pictures of pin-ups, girls in negligées or towels, which just covered their nipples, or sitting up in baths, with improbable mountains of suds camouflaging any rude bits. Among regular contributors were Kenneth Wolstenholme, Jimmy Wheeler, Alex Forbes, Richard Hearne, David Hughes and Fraser White – whose column was called 'Window on Tin Pan Alley'. He kept his eye on the youth market particularly and he was convinced that Colin Hicks was going to be as big a star as his brother.

"He hugs his guitar as a frightened child hugs his teddy bear," White gushed, "and his eyes at times have the look of a haunted gazelle. As he gains confidence, his blond mane shakes and then, without warning he jumps into a shuddering war dance."

Within a fortnight, Hicks had been auditioned by Johnny Franz at Philips, who apparently saw little potential. At Nixa, Alan Freeman had no such reservations and signed him forthwith. It soon emerged that Colin was being managed by Larry Parnes, who, having got Tommy up and running was now seeking to increase his power, influence and territory. Why not keep it in the family?

Colin's first single, *Wild Eyes And Tender Lips* (good title, shame about the song), was released in November 1957, to coincide with a seven week package tour – sharing the bill with the usual acrobats and jugglers, plus the Most Brothers and another Parnes protégé Marty Wilde.

Some papers reported that Hicks faced a non-stop hail of rotten fruit when he opened in London, at Finsbury Park Empire on 9 December, but Fraser White maintained that "only two apples and one tomato hit the stage and the gang of Teddy boy trouble-makers who were responsible were immediately ejected by the management." It was something of a shaky start; 1958 would be the make or break year for Colin Hicks.

Even at this early stage, the future looked rosier for Marty Wilde. He was long and lean, endowed with a husky presence and a sexual pout. Lionel Bart knew a good looking laddie when he saw one – even if this one was "a bit gauche and had enormous feet, very large shoes" – and it was Lionel who brought him to the attention of Larry Parnes.

Wilde had been born Reginald Smith in Greenwich on 15 April 1939. "I was a real dumb ox at school," he says. "My great loves were art and music, but technically I wasn't any good at either. I lived in my own world, looking out of the window and daydreaming most of the time . . . always getting told off for whistling or tapping out rhythms on my desk."

Other pupils at Charlton Secondary School for Boys in Sherington Road made fun of him when he revealed his ambition. "When I was 15, I wrote on the back of a photograph that I would be a major star within a few years. People were laughing at me, saying I'd never make it, but it was all I wanted to do."

He had a skiffle group going by November 1956, Reg Smith & the Hound Dogs. Strumming a black Grimshaw guitar with white trim, "a gorgeous looking guitar", he belted out a selection of Lonnie and Elvis numbers at youth clubs and hospital dances. Their early set, acoustic but loud, included *Rock Island Line, Bring A Little Water Sylvie, Down By The Riverside* and *Mystery Train* – sourced from the just-out first Presley long player, his favourite at the time, his favourite forever. "That album changed everything for me, a massive influence. The power and ingenuity and soul of tracks like *Lawdy Miss Clawdy* and *Trying To Get To You* just took my head off. How could anyone create pieces of music like that? I must have played that record a thousand times."

Saturday mornings he would go to the record shop in Trafalgar Road, Greenwich, operated by Mr Everest, a man in his forties who was passionate about rhythm & blues and had a Merchant Navy contact who always brought back the latest releases from the States. "I went there to buy *Hound Dog* by Elvis," says Reg, "and he asked me if I wanted to hear the original by Big Mama Thornton. I ended up buying them both." That year, he also bought import copies of *Manish Boy* and *Forty Days And Forty Nights* by Muddy Waters and *Smokestack Lightning* by Howlin' Wolf – so when he arrived in Soho, he was the hippest kid on the block. (In July 1959, when asked by a newspaper to pick his 10 favourite records, he included *Smokestack Lightning* – four years before the London blues groups started playing it.)

"There was a girl fan used to follow the Hound Dogs about, wrote for a film magazine, and she told whoever she could about me – including a music publisher called Joe Brannelly, who got me some reasonable-looking clothes and a couple of gigs in the West End. No contract or anything, he just wanted to help."

Brannelly, a former dance band guitarist, also got him an audition with Decca, having gatecrashed a recording session for the Ted Heath Orchestra, who were good friends. Drummer Ronnie Verrell and bassist Johnny Hawksworth broke ranks to back Reg on an impromptu jam but producer Dick Rowe was not impressed.

Under his new professional name of Reg Patterson, inspired by boxer Floyd Patterson who had recently succeeded the undefeated Rocky Marciano as heavyweight champion of the world, the singer played a week at the Condor, a gloss-veneer club at the lower end of Wardour Street. Out on the town, making the rounds, Lionel Bart happened to see him and reported in terms so gushing that Larry Parnes turned up the next night with a contract in his pocket.

How much John Kennedy had to do with what happened next is open to question, but Parnes would always take full credit for catapulting Reg Patterson to stardom. For the most part, Parnes had merely sat and watched, marvelled and learned as Kennedy masterminded Tommy Steele's magical ascent – but he was a player now, had contacts and spieling prowess, already had the ear of Tin Pan Alley's Jewish hierarchy. His first task was to re-christen Reg Smith, to bestow upon him a name that would serve him well until he could retire a happy man. Thus began the Parnes name-game, where he contemplated his latest charge, assessed the areas of attraction, and provided a new surname to suggest the sexual characteristic with which female fans could most relate. How light he made of it in interviews; how deep each frisson must have invaded his psyche. Eager and Gentle would come later, as would Fury; the first was Wilde. Nowhere is there evidence to support those advancing the theory that the theatrical Parnes might have been thinking of Oscar Wilde when he proposed the name.

Reg was dropped for Marty, which had a hunky ring and was the title of a recent movie Parnes had enjoyed, a gritty romance starring Ernest Borgnine. Reg was unfamiliar with the film and protested but Parnes assured him that from this day forward, no-one would ever know him as anything other than Marty Wilde. So it would be.

To confirm that his brand of rock 'n' roll was not a menace or a threat to society and had no hoodlum connotations, spin-doctor Parnes put out the story that Wilde was a Sunday school teacher. It was nearly right: "In fact, I was going out with a Sunday school teacher," he says, "but I did go to church every Sunday."

Parnes also invented a more romantic backdrop, spinning the yarn that Marty had formerly worked in a timber yard, heaving those big heavy planks about with his muscular arms. He had a series of photographs taken to substantiate this – even though Marty had never been near a timber yard. His had been a collar and tie job, working as a messenger boy at a firm of commodity brokers in Rood Lane, off Eastcheap.

Tommy having given credibility to *6.5 Special* and vice versa, Parnes was on congenial terms with the show's producers Jack Good and Josephine Douglas – both novices like himself. He asked them to audition Marty, who passed despite Good's hesitation.

"He was tall and gangling," says Good, "and carried a guitar which he could hardly play. He shuffled uncomfortably from one foot to the other and when he sang, it was only Presley numbers." It was Good's wife Margit who persuaded him that the boy had talent.

Marty made his *6.5 Special* début on 7 September 1957 and was signed to a recording contract within the week. Johnny Franz at Philips had just the song for him – he would cover *Honeycomb*, an American hit by Jimmie Rodgers which was heading for number one on the *Billboard* chart but had no chance of getting BBC airplay, because it mentioned "the Lord".

The BBC was very correct about this sort of thing. Before any record could be aired, it had to satisfy the standards of the Dance Music Policy Committee. In April 1956, it was revealed that the DMPC had passed 957 numbers, plus another 26 with restrictions enforcing referral before broadcasting. A total of 19 numbers had been banned altogether: five after consideration by the Head of Religious Broadcasting, six on the Controller's recommendation, and eight by the Committee, without reference to anyone.

The most contentious had been *Sixteen Tons*; versions which said "Brother don't you call me" were passed, but those saying "St Peter don't you call me" got the red pencil NTBB verdict . . . 'Not to be broadcast'. Everyone in the biz mocked the DMPC and artists adversely affected by their decisions cursed them roundly. One or two went further, including American singer Don Cornell, who thought he could bring down the BBC temple by appealing to the Archbishop of Canterbury. He complained that his record of *Hold*

My Hand had been banned because it contained the phrase "the Kingdom of Heaven", whereas other versions which had been modified to "the wonder of Heaven" had been passed for broadcasting. His recordings of *I'm Blessed* and *I Still Have A Prayer* had also been booted out and now he was being given the cold shoulder over *The Bible Tells Me So.*

"The heads of various American churches have written to me stating that they are wholeheartedly in favour of recordings like *The Bible Tells Me So,*" Cornell wrote to the Archbishop. "They maintain that if young people, who will not go to church, hear recordings like this when they are in restaurants and milk bars, it is a good thing. I have taken the liberty of attaching the words of *The Bible Tells Me So,* and enclosing copies of the records which have been banned by the BBC. I would look upon it as an honour if you are able to give me your own opinion on the words of the songs – which have been sung and recorded in all sincerity."

His Grace replied to Cornell, but gave him short shrift. "Let me say that I do not in any way doubt your sincerity. I do not for a moment suppose that the BBC is banning your records on any religious ground, but on general grounds of taste. In this respect, we differ in many ways from the United States, and there is a general unwillingness to have religious subjects loud-speakered into restaurants and milk bars."

"I have not played the records over, but I must say that the words of this song would, in my own judgement, be found somewhat discordant when heard out of a religious context – and even in a religious context, they would hardly accord with taste in this country."

So put that in your pipe and smoke it, you unsophisticated vulgarian. One wonders if Don showed the letter to Roy Rogers' wife, Dale Evans, who had written *The Bible Tells Me So.*

Prior to this episode, Cornell had blotted his copybook by promising to sing *Hold My Hand* with a revised, innocuous lyric when he appeared on *In Town Tonight* – but had gone back on his word. The BBC was affronted. Cornell could expect little sympathy.

If he thought he could wreak some vengeance on the Brits by covering *Rock Island Line* for the American market and cutting out Lonnie Donegan's version, he was out of luck. Lonnie got to number eight on *Billboard*; Don stalled at number 59 . . . and he never saw the

Top 40 again. He probably went to his grave wondering if the Archbishop had something to do with it.

Recent BBC bans covered *Mack The Knife* – unless it was played as part of an entire performance of *The Threepenny Opera*, whence it came – and the theme from *The Man With The Golden Arm*, a highly acclaimed Frank Sinatra/Otto Preminger movie about the horrors of heroin addiction. That the latter was an innovative piece of music, without any lyric, had no bearing; the title alone was enough to give the Dance Music Policy Committee the heebie-jeebies: it must not be mentioned on the air. Showbiz pillars Eddie Calvert and Ted Heath, who had both recorded versions of the number, were beside themselves with fury but the BBC would not relent. Until the original recording, by Billy May & his Orchestra, was re-issued as *Main Title*. Same record; different title. That was all right. Consequently, May's version was programmed by BBC producers and became a hit. Eddie Calvert and Ted Heath were even more outraged.

"In considering the lyrics of songs submitted, the Committee is guided by stated BBC policy governing Light Entertainment generally in matters of taste, advertising, political references, vulgarity and so on," explained an official memo dated 15 March 1956. And, of course, any popular song with a melody derived from classical music was automatically banned. The sentence was always final; no appeal was ever entertained.

Soon, the BBC panel would reject *Chicken* by the Cheers (glorifying irresponsible behaviour), *No Money Down* and *Maybellene* by Chuck Berry (mentions of Cadillacs and Fords), *Ice Cream* by Chris Barber (mentions Coca Cola), *Hard Case* by Alan Lomax (unsuitable ideas expressed in lyric), *House Of The Rising Sun* by the Chas McDevitt Skiffle Group, (unsuitable subject matter), *Croce Di Oro* by Patti Page ("a rather nauseating mixture of sentiment and superstition"), *This Silver Madonna* by Kirk Stevens (poor taste), *Glow Worm* by the Mills Brothers (mention of "Mazda brightness"), *On Bended Knee* by Bobby Charles (suggestion of prayer), *To Love Again* by the Four Aces (based on Chopin's E-flat *Nocturne*), *Answer Me* by Frankie Laine (seeking guidance from above) and *A Corset Can Do A Lot For A Lady* (subject matter too vulgar for public discussion) from the soundtrack of a Ginger Rogers movie *The First Travelling Salesgirl*. They also banned Perry Como's rendition of the title song from *Somebody Up There Likes Me* (religious objections), the boxing film turned over to the young and hungry Paul Newman following the death of James Dean.

This level of censorship had been initiated by Lord Reith, first Director General of the BBC, who actually believed to his heart and soul that the Corporation had been "entrusted to him by God". Here was a man who knew what the public wanted but felt superior and confident enough to give them what he thought they ought to like. The BBC's Royal Charter, after all, was one of the most serious documents ever drawn up – and was there not an inscription in the foyer of Broadcasting House which trusted that 'the people inclining their ear to whatsoever things are lovely and honest, and of good report, may tread the path of virtue and wisdom'?

All very noble and worthy, but where does Billy Cotton and his Band Show fit into that ethic?

For the Dance Music Policy Committee, religion was the thorniest subject of all. Dubious cases had to be referred to the highest authority, the Head of Religious Broadcasting (at this time Reverend R. McKay), who would give them a spin and make his prudent judgement. Some got the thumbs up – *Garden of Eden, Have You Ever Bought A Bible?* and *He's Got The Whole World In His Hands,* for instance – while others, such as *From Your Lips To The Ears Of God, Crying In The Chapel, The Fourth R (Religion), Toll The Bell Easy, Without Him* and *If God Can Forgive You So Can I* were ruled inadmissible.

The Committee's brief, as far as religious records were concerned, was this:

1) Each song to be considered on merit.

2) Where religious content is slight or incidental, no ban is necessary.

3) Where the religious aspect is an integral part of the lyric, one should discriminate between:

a) words which are at least consistent with Christian teaching and which are considered inoffensive if sung straightforwardly, and

b) words which are inconsistent with Christian teaching, which are near blasphemies in the sense of 'taking the name of God in vain', which encourage a totally false idea – for example, of prayer – or which are manifestly commercial exploitations of near-religious feeling.

Singers queued up to complain when their records were banned. The hapless (not to mention hopeless) Robert Earl, who cut what he thought was an adequate Light Programme cover of *Crying In The Chapel*, was mortified. He countered with piety: "Local theatre chaplains have gone out of their way to tell me how much they appreciate these songs, and the message they convey in a simple, palatable form." His simpering cut no ice with the Dance Music Policy Committee, nor did the protestations of Malcolm Vaughan, a junior Harry Secombe style balladeer from Merthyr, whose *St Therese Of The Roses* was on their proscribed list.

Having fallen foul of them in the past, the people at Philips were now hip to the BBC's rules – and sought to give Marty Wilde an advantage in his recording of *Honeycomb*. On his fast rising American hit, Jimmie Rodgers sang

> *It's a darned good life and it's kind of funny*
>
> *How the Lord made the bee and the bee made honey*

which for Marty's début disc was altered ("harmonised" as the BBC called it) to

> *It's a darned good life and it's kind of funny*
>
> *How the bee was made and the bee made honey.*

Much better, as far as the Corporation was concerned. The offending reference to "the Lord" had been removed. Even though his version was comparatively poor (his producer made it a light and peppy novelty, zestless and hook-free, with a laughable guitar solo), Marty was rewarded with all the airplay on the song and was allowed to sing it on the *6.5 Special* and Jack Payne's *Off The Record* . . . but it wouldn't fly. Ironically, thanks to Radio Luxembourg, the Jimmie Rodgers original sold more copies and even reached the UK chart, albeit fleetingly.

Lionel Bart seemed to take an uncommon interest in Wilde's early career. Not only did he 'discover' him at the Condor Club, but he also helped him cobble together a B-side for his first single, *Wild Cat* – a song to reflect his new name, to help project Larry's fantasy image of this hunky teenager on the prowl for playful girls, but only in their dreams. He's a wilde cat and he's attracted to wild kittens. Thousands will scream at him every night, but that doesn't mean that he isn't available to you. You can look at his pictures on your bedroom wall before you fall asleep. It wasn't happening yet, but it would. Bart and Parnes were quite right about that. Marty sang *Wild Cat* well enough, but had to contend with jazz-tootling session men and a banana fingered guitarist.

Bart's work was not yet done. He now went looking for a backing group – and found one playing in a talent contest at the Mayfair in Tooting, a seven-piece outfit called the Merry Men.

"We had been doing gigs all over south London, usually at venues where Rory Blackwell had done all the groundwork," says guitarist Ken Orpen, who had just turned 17. "Some of the audiences were pretty rowdy and menacing, with rival gangs of Teddy boys fighting each other. You'd see these insane characters brandishing knives and razors, sometimes bike-chains and even axes. It could get quite terrifying, knowing that out there people were getting chopped, cut, bottled and beaten. We always played through it, knowing that the stage was the safest place to be."

"Lionel told us that this new singer Marty Wilde needed a professional group to go on the road; *Honeycomb* had just come out and a full tour had already been booked. Were we interested?" The others didn't want to know but three of them – Ken Orpen (rhythm guitar), Jack Potter (drums) and Bert Lankester (double-bass) – became the core of Marty's first group of Wild Cats. Stan Waterman, an older guy, a jazzer who'd been in the cod rock 'n' roll band Art Baxter & the Sinners, was recruited to play lead guitar and they rehearsed at Dinely Studios in Blandford Street, Marylebone ('39 studios from two shillings an hour'), before they were whisked to Sunderland Empire to start the slog to stardom.

"Larry Parnes was always fussing about," says Orpen. "He insisted that our first week was at Sunderland Empire because that was where Tommy Steele had started – he seemed very superstitious about that. He bought Marty a new electric guitar and a little amplifier from Selmer's but there was no way that anybody could have heard him play: it was just a wall of screaming girls, wherever we went."

The Wild Cats also backed the Most Brothers on that tour; Colin Hicks had his own group, the Cabin Boys – including guitarist Tony Eagleton, who would write the B-side of Marty's next single *Afraid Of Love*, and drummer Jimmy Nicol, who would suddenly become famous seven years later when he played Denmark, Holland, Hong Kong, Australia and New Zealand as a substitute Beatle.

During the seven weeks leading up to Christmas 1957, Marty Wilde, Colin Hicks and the others took their show to Sunderland, Newcastle, Nottingham, Sheffield, Birmingham, Finsbury Park and

Chiswick. Most of them had never been away from home before and now found themselves sleeping in strange places. "It got easier later, but it was always digs on that first tour," recalls Marty. "I remember the shock of having to get into a cold, damp bed. I slept in rooms where there was as much ice on the inside of the window as there was on the outside. Absolutely freezing – like Siberia. At one place, I opened a cupboard to hang up my jacket and there was a guy asleep in there. At another, I had a room right opposite a big, chiming town hall clock – I had the shock of my life when it suddenly struck midnight."

"We couldn't find any digs in Birmingham," says Ken Orpen, "so we had to stay in this navvies' doss-house, with holes in the ceiling, straw in the mattresses and pubic hairs on the sheets. At the other end of the scale, we stayed in a very posh hotel when 6.5 *Special* did a live broadcast from Whitley Bay. That was because the BBC were paying and not Larry."

"I didn't get on with my father but as soon as I hit the road, I realised how much my home and my parents meant to me – and we were very close from that day forward," says Marty. "I was able to spend Christmas 1957 at home but after that I was only able to make flying visits – Larry had me out there working my socks off."

Twenty-eight

Larry Parnes and Paul Lincoln had a monopoly on rock 'n' roll management until others saw the rewards. Overnight, it seemed, the 2Is Coffee Bar became a showcase, if not a cattle market for young hopefuls – all of whom would be assessed by impresarios, lotharios, agents and record company men. "I make a regular visit to Soho," Parlophone boss George Martin told the *Daily Mirror*. "Six months ago, I wouldn't have dreamed of going there but now it has become a breeding ground for talent."

"I remember Adam Faith coming up to me and asking my advice," recalls Wally Whyton of the Vipers, who were venerated by the younger skifflers. "He was genuinely concerned, on the point of giving up, because he had been singing and playing in the 2Is for three months – and no-one had tried to sign him up! He wasn't joking; he thought it was a natural progression and he couldn't understand what he was doing wrong." He needn't have worried.

Adam had been born Terence Nelhams at 4 Churchfield Road East, just round the corner from Acton Central station, on 23 June 1940. His dad was a lorry driver; his mother a cleaner. School held little importance or interest and became an increasing irritation. All he wanted to do was to strut around looking snappy, and to facilitate this ambition he did a paper-round each morning and as many jobs as could be fitted into evenings and weekends without disturbing the essence of his social life – which revolved around the cinema, the youth club and the recreation ground. "I paid for all my own clothes from the age of 12 onwards," he boasted in the first of several autobiographies, the most recent of which begins with the line "My grandmother was a prostitute".

At 15, he left school to work for a local silk-screen printer but then moved on to get a taste of central London, working as a messenger boy for Rank Screen Services in Hill Street, Mayfair.

When the music and the conversation at the weekly YWCA youth club dances veered towards skiffle, he and his mates formed their own group – which, in a matter of weeks, underwent radical personnel and ideological changes. "One evening, Terry and his friend Hurgy turned up at my door and asked if I was interested in teaming up with them," recalls Freddy Lloyd, who lived in East Acton and led rival skiffle group, the Sinners. "At that time, he really looked like James Dean, no question about it . . . hair brushed up in an exact copy, white T-shirt and blue jeans, leaning up against the wall looking exceedingly cool – as only Terry the poseur could! He was certainly very image conscious, even then."

"I think he was probably more interested in my car than my musical ability. Hardly anybody had wheels in those days and I had a 1932 London taxi, large enough to accommodate a tea-chest bass. I'd painted it bright yellow, and covered it with graffiti, so it was pretty well known in the locality."

By May 1957, when they started playing in Soho, they had settled on the name the Worried Men – after the most popular number in the skiffle catalogue – and Terry Nelhams was calling himself Terry Denver. He was now working as a messenger boy at TV Advertising Ltd in Wardour Street and could scout the area for gigs, the first of which he obtained at Russell Quaye's Skiffle Cellar at 49 Greek Street, the Mars Club at 77 Berwick Street and the 2Is Coffee Bar at 59 Old Compton Street. Terry and Freddy sang lead vocals and played guitars; Terry's cousin Dennis Nelhams played another acoustic guitar; Chas Beaumont played electric guitar, an old cello-bodied Epiphone with a DeArmond pick-up; Pete Darby played bass; Terry's schoolmate and best friend Roger Van Engel (aka Hurgy) played the washboard. They wore matching silver grey slacks and dark blue shirts.

From the outset, the Worried Men had their sights set on the 2Is and, through the summer, they increased their tenure there until Les Hobeaux's expanding tour schedule allowed them to take over as main resident group. Paul Lincoln 'guided', them, according to Hurgy, but there was no formal contract. Much to Terry's chagrin, it was their guitarist who became the centre of attention. "Chas Beaumont was a revelation, the first guitarist in the 2Is to play single string runs and solos with any real fluidity," says Wally Whyton. "Several times we asked him to join the Vipers but he didn't want to turn professional."

Terry did: it was his dream. "He was always convinced he would become a star," says Freddy Lloyd, "always big time!"

They bashed away, sometimes backing such guest singers as Wee Willie Harris and Mickie Most. "Get off the stage Mickie and get back to selling coke," Paul Lincoln would cry.

November 1957 was the watershed month. "I remember Jack Good coming down to the 2Is to see us," says Freddy Lloyd. "He wore an American baseball jacket and looked down through his glasses, with his head raked back. I think he was hard pushed to find enough interesting talent to fill his programmes. We were the next act along, and he came to see if we were any good."

He booked them. In terms of vérité, Good realised, it was important to feature the coffee bar's current residents on the 6.5 Special to be broadcast live from the 2Is on 16 November. He may also have sensed a future for young Terry and wanted to see how he would look on camera. He was pretty telegenic, so it seems, and television was already the surest and quickest way to break anyone with star aspirations if not star quality.

Meanwhile, Decca had agreed to record a few tracks. This Little Light Of Mine and 900 Miles From My Home appeared on the dreadful hotchpotch of an album, Rockin' At The 2Is – the first example of exploitation in the rock marketplace. To feature Wee Willie Harris and the Worried Men was legitimate . . . but the Graham Stewart Seven (a dull trad jazz band), the Blue Jeans (of unknown provenance, though a few people vaguely remember them) and Beryl Wayne (of whom nothing had hitherto been heard)? To the 2Is regulars, it did the coffee bar a disservice by its mere presence in the record racks.

Terry's distinctive vocal and a burst of Beaumont's guitar can also be heard on Fraulein, their cover of an American hit by country & western singer Bobby Helms, which appeared on another commercially-expedient Decca 10-inch album Stars Of The Six-Five Special.

In the midst of all this wild activity, the Worried Men plunged into deep metamorphosis, setting a precedent for many a similar scenario. Terry Denver left to go solo, Freddy Lloyd left to replace Jean Van Den Bosch in the Vipers and, in the weeks to follow, the others left too, all except guitarist Chas Beaumont. Within six months, the group was barely recognisable, having been infiltrated by two members of Rick Richards' Skiffle Group – bass player Tex Makins and Rick himself. Others came and went over the months that followed and the 'Worried Men' brand name was driven until it was no longer useful.

It seems that, on Jack Good's advice, Terry was signed by an agent called Teddy Summerfield, who had no difficulty in securing him a recording contract with HMV. "I'll build you up as Britain's singing James Dean," Jack told him, "you know, the black leather jacket lark." The singer also understood Good to expect a sense of menace, the projection of 'moody rebellion' – the very aspect of youth culture that all other impresarios and star-guiders had sought to avoid. Terry couldn't quite carry it off.

Never a reliable witness on the details of his early career, Terry claims to have 'cooked up' the new name of Adam Faith all by himself – he plucked it from a book of names, published for the benefit of prospective parents who had no ideas of their own. Adam was from the boys list; Faith from the girls. Subsequent research suggests that it was confected by Jack Good, in whose Goldhawk Road flat the singer's launch was plotted. He took the names of two friends from Oxford, now living nearby: future lawyer Adam Fremantle and wine connoisseur journalist Nicholas Faith.

Adam's new name had legs but the same could not be said for his début single, the mournful and wretched *Brother Heartache And Sister Tears*. When he sang it on the *6.5 Special* he looked and sounded close to death.

Equally abysmal was Larry Page's first release, *Start Movin'*. He was Columbia-EMI's big entry into the new teenage market and had come all the way from their packing department. "I failed my 11-plus, failed everything, left Townfield Secondary School without any qualifications, as early as I could," says Page, who had been born in Wales but raised in Hayes, conveniently located for EMI's factory. "I used to cycle to work at six o'clock every morning and spend the day packing records."

His singing career started inauspiciously at the Blue Anchor in Printing House Lane, where he would take drink and then take the stage, often so pissed that he could remember none of his performance the next day. He was urged to enter the Carroll Levis Discoveries Show when it visited the Shepherds Bush Empire, and a *TV Times*-promoted 'Find the Singer' talent contest at the Hammersmith Palais, favourable reactions spurring him to audition for EMI. "I applied for a recording test, which I did at Abbey Road with Russ Conway, then unknown, accompanying me on piano . . . and Norman Newell signed me up. I do think pressure was put on him; when they got wind that I actually worked in the factory, it speeded things along a bit."

Naturally, he was treated as a junior employee rather than a star-in-waiting by Newell, a man known to some in the business as 'the Queen of Denmark Street'. "He dictated everything," says Page. "I had no say whatsoever, not that I cared because getting a record deal was like winning the football pools. They gave me a copy of *Start Movin'* by Sal Mineo, told me to go away and learn it – which I did, every vocal inflection, every swish of the rhythm – but when I arrived in the studio, the arrangement was nothing like the record. They felt they had to put their own personality on the song. The band struck up and I was given two chances to run through it, then they went for it. The musicians didn't even think about it – they just played what was in front of them. You spend endless hours getting word perfect and nuance perfect, then you get in the studio and find they're like a marching band. Then there were the Rita Williams Singers, about eight of them. She was maybe 45. I wasn't allowed to object to anything or even make suggestions. I had to do as I was told. Even the key was picked for me."

Page continued to work at Hayes until *Start Movin'* backed with *Cool Shake*, his version of an American hit by cool Pittsburgh vocal group the Del-Vikings, was released in July 1957. "It seemed to be nothing but ballads at EMI; I spent all day packing records by Ronnie Hilton and Malcolm Vaughan . . . but one of my last jobs was packing my own record."

The audience for rock music was growing faster than it could be supplied. With barely a decent review for his record, let alone any airplay, Larry Page was able to go out on a variety tour, topping the bill. The first UK rocker with no instrument, just a microphone and a handful of songs: *Blue Suede Shoes, Rip It Up, Butterfly, Cool Shake* and *Start Movin'*. He made his début at Reading Palace, where business was so brisk that the gods were opened up for the first time since whenever. The previous week's attraction had been a nudie revue starring Peaches Page (no relation). Hardly anybody had come out to see that.

In September, during a week headlining (over the City Ramblers, Dickie Bishop & his Sidekicks, and Zom) at the huge Metropolitan

Theatre in Edgware Road, Page was summoned to Abbey Road to cut his second single, a version of a song by unknown Texan group, the Crickets. *That'll Be The Day* was currently at number three on *Billboard* and rising, a certain number one, but Norman Newell was convinced that the record was too 'un-British' to make it here. Larry was assigned to cover it; Geoff Love and his Orchestra would work on a more anglicised arrangement, to harmonise the number for the UK market.

No one extols Page for being the first person to cover a Buddy Holly song, far from it. The version that went out under his name is among the most excruciating records ever made and was quickly buried and forgotten, justly so. In their advertising, EMI described it as 'the most sensational record of the year'. If this was merely hype, the people who devised the slogan were criminals; if EMI believed it, they obviously knew nothing about anything.

"The label saw no future in rock 'n' roll," says Larry. "They had to make all the great American records sound like *Workers' Playtime*. They didn't have a clue. Consequently, I made the Mickey Mouse version of *That'll Be The Day*." Indeed he did, backed by a ricky-tick brass band, a meaningless tenor sax solo and an uncomprehending bunch of women, wailing away like freshly recruited canteen-ladies having a bit of fun. Norman Newell and his pals turned *That'll Be The Day* into a novelty item, as inconsequential as a market-stall trinket. They didn't realise that this was serious stuff, this was art. What they were making was artificial, devoid of the fluidity, the rippling liquid incandescence of the original.

The Crickets' remarkable creation was previewed, its first UK airing, as 'Record of the Week' on the *6.5 Special*. On the following Monday, it was discussed during school milk breaks and lunchtimes all over the country, everywhere a rock 'n' roll clique flourished, a sense of wonder coursing through excited, arcane conversation. Everybody was going to buy it and everybody did: it was number one by the beginning of November and Buddy Holly's picture and story were all over the music press. He had our attention.

The Crickets were still number one when Larry mimed to his version, live from the 2Is on the *6.5 Special*, with (according to one review) "a cup of coffee balanced in each hand, a roll stuck in his pocket and a constant smile on his face". Even though he lost the race, the first print run of the sheet music for *That'll Be The Day* had

Larry's smiling face on the front and made no mention of the Crickets. Thanks to Jack Bentley, show business columnist on the *Sunday Pictorial*, he now had a tag-line, like a vaudeville star: from that day forward, he would always be known as Larry Page the Teenage Rage. He revelled in this description, of course.

The records were duff but the gigs were going well. In July, prior to going out on tour, he had gone to the 2Is in search of suitable backing musicians. Coincidentally, a young guitar player called Ian McLean had started doing guest spots down there, after finishing a three-month stint with the Teddy Foster Orchestra, his first professional job. He was now on the lookout for something more exciting. Paul Lincoln told him about Larry and directed him to a rehearsal hall, where he was introduced to the other members of the Page Boys, as Larry had decided to call them: drummer Ray Taylor and bass player Jet Harris.

"Larry Page could sing all right for someone who couldn't sing," says McLean. "He had managed to acquire a sort of pseudo confidence from somewhere. I think his record company saw him as England's answer to Pat Boone."

This is not how Jet Harris saw him. "He was the most awful singer I've ever worked with," he told Shadows biographer Mike Read. Despite this, Harris was still happy to give up his job at the Dairy Supply Company in Park Royal, where he was an apprentice sheet metal worker, making milk churns. He and Ray Taylor lived on opposite sides of Brenthurst Road in Willesden and had been in experimental groups since their years at Dudden Hill Secondary. Modern jazz was their preferred taste but it was quite impossible for lowly amateurs to get a blow in the Soho clubs so they gravitated towards the 2Is, where they were welcomed. Jet was a few days past his eighteenth birthday when he quit work to become a Page Boy.

Melody Maker shared Jet's apprehension. "Mr Page sounded flat to me," concluded their reviewer, "and I caught about one word in 10."

By the end of the year, McLean and Harris had left the Teenage Rage to join Tony Crombie's latest set of Rockets. There was a long package tour in prospect, one featuring Wee Willie Harris, Colin Hicks & the Cabin Boys, Les Hobeaux and the Most Brothers. It promised to be a lot of fun.

Larry was far from perturbed. He just dyed his hair bright blue and formed a new group, the Front Page Men.

Although neither Larry Page nor Adam Faith got within hailing distance of the charts during 1957, a couple of other precocious youngsters saw their careers peak in a shower of sparks.

Former Butlin's Holiday Camp redcoat Russ Hamilton, a quiet lad from Beacon Lane in Everton, recorded two of his own chalet compositions for the profoundly uncool Oriole label and scored one of the most popular hits of the summer, with the wimpy ballad *We Will Make Love*. Ron Hulme, for that was his real name, protests innocence and pure thoughts only, but lustful interpretations prevailed. It was the first British record to celebrate sexual congress for its own sake, for its purity, for its possibilities, for its potential to change the course of people's lives – in this case, towards the aisle. The music business was amazed to see an unknown Merseysider reach number two with his very first single . . . even more amazed when some American disc jockey flipped the record and started a surge which took the B-side *Rainbow* into the US Top five – seven years ahead of the full-scale Liverpudlian assault.

That Hamilton had written both sides of a million seller was an extraordinary achievement, but the record did not further the cause or course of rock music and neither did Laurie London's freak hit *He's Got The Whole World In His Hands*. He was only 13 years old when, in September 1957, he climbed up onto the BBC stand at the Radio Show in Earls Court and broke into song, so impressively that he was invited back. Word reached Norman Newell, who signed him to Columbia – releasing his début on the heels of Larry Page's *That'll Be The Day*. While the latter crashed on take-off, London's record flew to number 12 in Britain and all the way to number one in the States.

Envisaged by some as an East End Jewish version of Frankie Lymon, Laurie left school to develop a singing career but though he was often on television and released several follow-up singles, he would never return to the charts. Chances became even slimmer when his voice broke. He had his day in the spotlight, however, and every skiffle group in the land sang his song. Strangely, inexplicably even, the BBC played *He's Got The Whole World In His Hands* frequently, even though it was an old Negro spiritual rendered happy-clappy and singalong, the travails of the Almighty trivialised by Geoff Love's musical setting. Did the Head of Religious Broadcasting not object?

Jim Dale emerged from the anonymity of jesting compère on the Vipers' never-ending national Skiffle Contest tour when his Parlophone single *Be My Girl* rose to number two during the last weeks of the year. His toothy grin and wacky disposition were made for the screen, which is where he now concentrated his attention. Eventually his contribution to British cinema would bring an MBE (in the Queen's Birthday Honours list, 2003) but for now, at 22, he learnt to smile at the cameras on the *6.5 Special*, where he would soon become anchor-man. He was better looking than Freddie Mills, that's for sure.

The *6.5 Special* worked wonders for some but not for Terry Wayne, from Plumstead in south London, whose trajectory proved too low, leaving him to become a footnote in rock history. He was just a kid but he knew what he liked, which was rockabilly – especially that area occupied by Carl Perkins – and this awareness put him in the vanguard of a UK rockabilly movement that has never gone away. For reasons difficult to fathom – a tribute, perhaps, or some sort of transmutation – he recorded both sides of Carl's most recent single *Your True Love/Matchbox* (issued here five months earlier) as his own début, which was released on his sixteenth birthday in September 1957.

Of course, from the moment it hit the Radio Luxembourg airwaves, Carl's recording of *Your True Love* was regarded as not only fabulous but definitive by the rock cognoscenti, as was his version of *Matchbox*, featuring Jerry Lee Lewis on piano. With his languorous southern face, Perkins was then as mysterious as a voodoo man, the 25-year-old son of a sharecropper, whatever that was, who wrote momentous songs and played impossibly intricate guitar runs and solos. This was only his second UK release, following his Top 10 hit *Blue Suede Shoes/Honey Don't*, 11 months earlier. What had gone on in the interim, one wondered? *Your True Love* was the A-side but had no chance of airplay because of the line *God made the world and he made it round*. To avoid this nonsense, Wayne made *Matchbox* the plug side of his record.

How could he compete? Obviously, he couldn't. His record is one of the silliest of the era. A bunch of footling session musicians bungling around without any inkling of their task or their inadequacy. A producer who thought he could have a stab at this new teenage music. The Perkins original was about atmosphere, feeling, undercurrents, experience, it was an impossible mission. On top of that, it wasn't a hit song. Nevertheless, Wayne was on radio and television, got his picture in a few papers and went out on tour.

1957 was a vintage year for rock 'n' roll (and related) records – but all were American. *I Walk The Line* by Johnny Cash, *Mystery Train* by Elvis Presley, *Long Tall Sally/Tutti Frutti* by Little Richard, *Blue Monday* by Fats Domino, *Baby Let's Play House* by Elvis Presley, *I'm Not A Juvenile Delinquent* by Frankie Lymon & the Teenagers, *Love Is Strange* by Mickey & Sylvia, *The Girl Can't Help It /She's Got It* by Little Richard, *Little By Little* by Nappy Brown, *Twenty-Flight Rock* by Eddie Cochran, *Come Go With Me* by the Del-Vikings, *Butterfly* by Charlie Gracie, *Too Much* by Elvis Presley, *I'm Walkin'* by Fats Domino, *Bi-Bickey-Bi Bo-Bo-Go* by Gene Vincent & the Bluecaps, *Little Darlin'* by the Diamonds, *Party Doll* by Buddy Knox, *Gone* by Ferlin Husky, *Roll Over Beethoven* by Chuck Berry, *Sittin' In The Balcony* by Eddie Cochran, *Bye Bye Love* by the Everly Brothers, *All Shook Up* by Elvis Presley, *School Day* by Chuck Berry, *Lucille/Send Me Some Loving* by Little Richard, *Fabulous* by Charlie Gracie, *Valley Of Tears* by Fats Domino, *Searchin'* by the Coasters, *Whole Lotta Shakin' Goin' On/It'll Be Me* by Jerry Lee Lewis, *Whispering Bells* by the Del-Vikings, *Lotta Lovin'* by Gene Vincent & the Blue Caps, *Stardust* by Billy Ward & the Dominoes, *White Silver Sands* by Don Rondo, *Wandering Eyes* by Charlie Gracie, *Jenny Jenny* by Little Richard, *Short Fat Fannie* by Larry Williams, *Paralysed* by Elvis Presley, *That'll Be The Day* by the Crickets, *Mr Lee* by the Bobbettes, *Party* by Elvis Presley, *Susie Q* by Dale Hawkins, *Wake Up Little Susie* by the Everly Brothers, *Be Bop Baby* by Ricky Nelson, *Happy Happy Birthday Baby* by the Tune Weavers, *Silhouettes* by the Rays, *You Send Me* by Sam Cooke, *Keep A Knockin'* by Little Richard, *Peggy Sue* by Buddy Holly, *I'm Available* by Margie Rayburn, *Reet Petite* by Jackie Wilson, *Raunchy* by Bill Justis, *Lawdy Miss Clawdy/Trying To Get To You* by Elvis Presley, *Could This Be Magic?* by the Dubs, *Glad All Over* by Carl Perkins, *Little Bitty Pretty One* by Thurston Harris & the Sharps, *Great Balls Of Fire* by Jerry Lee Lewis, *Oh Boy* by the Crickets and *Rock And Roll Music* by Chuck Berry were, in order of appearance, some of the best, all imbued with magical elements. Surprisingly, many of them reached the UK charts.

Pinching American hits and giving them a Light Programme treatment continued to be the basis of the British record business.

None of those involved seemed to question the ethics, the morality, the total lack of imagination, the inferior quality of the copy. To true rock 'n' roll fans, however, it was the same as a painter, with no ideas of his own, making manifestly bad Picasso replicas and putting them up for sale as though they were worthy pieces of art. British session men and producers were in the Third Division (South) compared with the people who made these records. Even with an eternity of tuition, no pianist on the Musicians' Union register could even get close to the intro of *Whole Lotta Shakin' Goin' On*. No guitarist on their books could begin to figure out the sound and feel of *Baby Let's Play House* or *School Day*. No producer could dream of catching the eerie intensity of *Searchin'* or *You Send Me*. No Denmark Street songsmith could conjure from the air a song as compelling as *Great Balls Of Fire*. Our stuff all came out sounding the same, tailored towards BBC sensibilities – and this was no coincidence, of course, because although their influence was being noticeably eroded by Radio Luxembourg, the BBC ruled the roost.

As rock 'n' roll gathered momentum, BBC brows knitted into permanent expressions of consternation, not only in the room where the Dance Music Policy Committee auditioned the latest offerings, but all the way up to the top. The Director General sent his lieutenants a memo headed 'Popular Songs And Music By British Composers'. In it, he outlined his objective: "the creation of a market and a taste for songs and music which are British not only in the sense of being written by British composers, but British in sound and idiom and capable of performance in a British way".

He went on to say "a large amount of the best foreign material is rightly included in our programmes, but we should make more determined efforts to create substitute vehicles for material of British type. If we embark wholeheartedly on such a policy, and make it known throughout the profession that we are doing so, the response may be better than we now believe likely. Broadcasting is a great power in this field and we must use that power to the full."

The Controller of Sound Entertainment passed on the memo with some additions of his own: "We should look at existing programmes with an eye to the ultimate possibility of removing the American element and replacing it with something un-American, if we can find it, which will do the same job." Anticipating the deluge of protest from those record labels and music publishers who relied on

American material, not to mention the fans who clamoured for it, he concluded: "Nobody is more aware than I that we shall be swimming against a powerful tide. I only hope we can prove to be web-footed!"

Cobweb-brained, more like.

When complaints were received about the pitiful amount of airtime allocated to teenage music, they were met with paternalism and the reiteration of maxims laid down by the first Director General of the BBC, Lord Reith. "To set out to give the public what it wants is a dangerous and fallacious policy, involving almost always an underestimate of public intelligence and a continual lowering of standards," he contended. "It is not autocracy, but wisdom, that suggests a policy of broadcasting on the basis of giving people what they should like and will come to like."

This appeared to mean plenty of Cyril Stapleton and Billy Cotton; no Little Richard or Chuck Berry.

It all went back, it could reasonably be assumed, to 1933 when Eric Gill created a monumental sculpture of Prospero and Ariel over the heavy brass and glass entrance to Broadcasting House. When a Member of Parliament noticed the length of Ariel's penis, declaring it "objectionable to public morals and decency", the board of governors immediately caved in like quislings and instructed Gill to get the ladders back up there and shorten it. The puritanical, Victorian tone of the institution was circumscribed (or something like that): moderation in all things. In the realm of popular music, even during the days of its most turbulent revolution, the BBC succeeded in broadcasting mediocrity of the highest order. It would take them another 10 years to pick up on what was happening out there and reflect it in their programming.

Again, it must be stated: Thank God for Radio Luxembourg.

Twenty-nine

Variety was on its last legs. A symbolic moment came in August 1957, when top-flight singing star Dorothy Squires kicked up a fuss and flounced out of a show due to start at the London Hippodrome. She had refused to accept second billing to a rock 'n' roll singer, especially one of whom she had never heard. Then a swishy 42 year old, Squires was a showbiz legend, a girl from the Welsh valleys who had made her name as featured vocalist with Charlie Kunz and his Band and was currently married to barely known screen actor Roger Moore, a dozen years her junior. When it was explained to her that she was no longer selling seats, that the audiences wanted to see Charlie Gracie, and that he would be billed over her in much larger letters, she walked.

Gracie was a modest but exuberant singer from Philadelphia, whose two singles *Butterfly* and *Fabulous* had endeared him to the teenage audience, especially aspiring guitarists, who admired the way he played his beautiful and exotic sunburst Guild, festooned as it was with knobs and pick-ups and switches. For two weeks (the start of a national tour, the first of many), he headlined over a motley cast of variety acts that merely tested the patience of his audience.

As soon as his engagement finished, the Hippodrome – as old as the century, a splendidly ornate theatre on the corner of Cranbourne Street and Charing Cross Road – was closed down and re-modelled as a bourgeois nightclub, the Talk of the Town.

This left the Metropolitan Theatre at 267 Edgware Road the only traditional music-hall venue in central London – and it was here in January 1958 that Wee Willie Harris began his first headlining tour. It was an appropriate choice: he was, after all, the bridge between the old and the new, the last music hall creation, a vaudevillian caricature singing and playing rock 'n' roll. "He sang six numbers, or was it the same number six times?" wondered the *NME*'s reviewer. "He travels noticeably downhill after the impact of his big gimmick, his flamboyant and startling entrance." Willie's old jazz pal Tony Crombie had put together a new line-up of the Rockets, who would back him through thick and thin for many years. "Crombie was a very relaxed person, just enjoyed playing and never took it too seriously," says guitarist Ian McLean. Just as well.

The Wee Willie Harris/Tony Crombie partnership outlived the Metropolitan, which was soon demolished – but not before many of the new-music pioneers had enjoyed the privilege and pleasure of working there, from Lonnie Donegan to Larry Page, Chas McDevitt to the Vipers. It was run by a man in his seventies, Albert Vasco, a trouper who had first played London during Queen Victoria's reign, when he and his mother were a trapeze act, Alexandra and Bertie. His father had been known as Vasco the Mad Musician, whose frantic act involved playing 25 different musical instruments.

When skiffle attracted younger audiences, Albert modified the Metropolitan's 500-seater gallery – where "the hard boards will be replaced by soft seats," he assured the press – as well as sprucing up the stalls and the backstage area. "He redecorated the dressing-rooms and put in these Formica units," says Wally Whyton of the Vipers, "but the rats had eaten their way back in within two weeks. Most of the wash basins had soon come away from the wall too, because the chorus girls used to rush offstage and piss in them rather than use the loo. That was the hallmark of most variety theatre dressing rooms and it was certainly true of the Met. Even when we got the star dressing-room, the sink was off the wall, held up by the plumbing."

The Met was also distinguished by an ineradicable aroma, which pervaded the auditorium. "There was a wonderful SPO café next door, selling sausages, potatoes and onions," says Wally. "You could get them on a plate or in a box – the first takeaway food I ever saw. The smell from that place would carry for miles and punters would take boxes into the theatre and stink the place out."

"As we toured around the country, we could almost touch the despair in the music halls. When we became popular, our skiffle shows at least drew an audience but television had just about killed off any interest in variety. In the old days, comedians could have the same patter for decades and people went to see them because they wanted the familiarity of their act – but now they preferred to stay at home and watch the box. So theatre managers saw their income dwindling, yet they still had to pay the ushers and all the guys in the pit orchestra, all the backstage staff and the cleaners, and the heating bills, which must have been enormous because they were cavernous places."

Ironically, skiffle was next to feel the draught. Its demise had first been predicted in spring 1957, when a conspiracy of pundits foresaw a replacement craze – calypso. This on the basis of three versions of *The Banana Boat Song* reaching the UK charts: one by New York folk group the Tarriers, another by New York-born actor Harry Belafonte and a home-grown effort by Cardiff girl Shirley Bassey. No calypsonian she! A craze? It was preposterous. Rock 'n' roll fans laughed for five minutes, knowing it was nothing more than a novelty blip. Which is all it turned out to be.

Since then, 'Skiffle is Dying' headlines had been appearing in the music press on a regular basis and eventually they came true. "It just died overnight," says Wally Whyton. "By about March 1958, it was virtually all over – and so were the dreams of all these poor local groups that had been hoping for a crack at the big time in our National Skiffle Contest. We were supposed to have the grand finals at the Metropolitan in April, but if there ever was a winner, nobody cared by then! I don't remember a winner ever being chosen!"

Having worked themselves to a standstill, the Vipers came off the road for a breather. Tony Tolhurst and Freddy Lloyd promptly quit, leaving the other three to ponder the future. Other groups were doing the same, modifying their style to prolong their active lives. Russell Quaye's City Ramblers attempted, with little joy, to introduce 'spasm music' (more of a name-change than a progression in their music) but they had secure employment, not least in their own Skiffle Cellar, which was now abbreviated to the Cellar. Chas McDevitt, whose group was still attracting plenty of work, hedged his bets by taking over a shop on the corner of Noel Street and Berwick Street and opening his own coffee bar, the Freight Train. A prime Soho location. He had a big new shiny Gaggia espresso machine, the latest releases on his jukebox and he stayed open all night – tending the counter himself when he wasn't off strumming somewhere.

After all of six months as a professional, Bob Cort returned to his advertising agency day job. Dickie Bishop got married, disbanded the Sidekicks and reverted to traditional jazz, playing banjo with Kenny Ball's band. Buoyed (though only slightly) by a cameo in *The Golden Disc* and safe on a five-month package tour with Wee Willie

Harris, Les Hobeaux kept going until summer but then packed it in. Johnny Duncan plunged deeper into country & western music, expanding his territory to Ireland and Europe and releasing an album *Johnny Duncan Salutes Hank Williams*. Lonnie Donegan was out on his own, of course, an established showbiz star, flying high above all competition, always on radio and television, headlining here there and everywhere, back in the Top 10 with another song he 'co-wrote' with Woody Guthrie, *Grand Coolie* (sic) *Dam*. He was now directly contracted to Pye Nixa, whose directors gave independent producer Denis Preston a colossal £10,000 pay-off. As if to confirm his multi-talented versatility, Lonnie was also selected for the Showbiz Soccer XI's first fixture, scoring a goal in their 5-1 defeat of the *Daily Sketch*.

Meanwhile, Donegan's disciples were still streaming towards Soho, hoping to be discovered . . . but now they were coming from further afield. In November 1957, the Saints Skiffle Group (a hopeless name; there were several in every town) hitched a ride in the back of a lorry, rain-soaked and windblown, all the way from Norwich, just to audition at the Skiffle Cellar. When they were assessed as having insufficient originality and informed that they wouldn't be getting further bookings at this stage, they split up there and then. Andy (drums), Taff (tea chest) and Moon (guitar) went back to Norwich. Tony Sheridan (guitar/vocal) and Kenny Packwood (guitar) decided to stick around in London.

Although the population of Britain (according to the 1955 *Hulton Readership Survey*) was three per cent upper class, 25 per cent middle class and 72 per cent working class, the entire population of the 2Is Coffee Bar was working class. Storemen, packers, sheet metal apprentices, cabin boys, messenger boys, and the like. Sheridan was a different animal entirely. His full name was a clue: Anthony Esmond Sheridan McGinnity. He had been born at 38 Glenmore Gardens on 21 May 1940 and the family stayed in the middle of Norwich until the early fifties when they moved to the outlying village of Thorpe St Andrew. His distinctly middle-class father, Alphonsus, was an official in the Ministry of Labour and National Service.

At City of Norwich School, Sheridan played violin in the orchestra, sang in the choir and the madrigal society, and took part in Gilbert and Sullivan operettas – lavish productions with costumes hired from London. At 16, after passing several O levels, including Art at Grade 1 and English at Grade 2, he moved on to art school. Under the spell of Lonnie, who they saw giving a typically maniacal performance at Norwich Theatre Royal in February 1957, he and four schoolfriends formed the Saints. "After 10 years of playing classical violin and singing sacred songs in choirs, I was anxious to get into the sexual side of music," says Sheridan.

Earliest gigs were lunchtimes in the pub next door to the art school and evenings at the Red Lion in Thorpe St Andrew. Their peak was winning £15 in a skiffle contest at the Industries Working Mens' Club.

With guitars and suitcases, Sheridan and Packwood found a room above a pub in Seven Sisters Road and began infiltrating the 2Is scene. "Roy Young was screaming out Little Richard songs the first time I went down there," recalls Sheridan, "and the Worried Men were still resident. Their guitarist, Chas Beaumont, used to back up any new singer that wanted a shot – and since it was obvious that I needed an electric guitar if I was going to get anywhere, I bought a Grazioso."

In February 1958, his pal Kenny Packwood was offered the job of replacing Stan Waterman in Marty Wilde's Wild Cats. "Waterman was a disgruntled jazzer," according to rhythm guitarist Ken Orpen, "and a bit of a drinker. He was about 6 foot 4 inches tall, 18 stone, and he was about twice the age of the rest of us. He didn't like the music and he could get a bit difficult. One day, we were going somewhere in the group van and he got into an argument with our driver, Keith Rippingdale. Keith wanted his window open and Stan wanted it shut. He sat there shouting and fuming and then suddenly whacked Keith on the back of his head, almost pole-axed him."

The incident never left Marty's memory either. "The force of his punch smashed Keith's head against the wheel and we went careering across the road into – as luck would have it – a pub car park, where Keith was able to pull up. Then there was this terrible fist fight and Stan was fired the next day. He was such a crazy guy. Sometimes he could be hysterically funny, lying on his back and waving his legs in the air at the end of the show, but other times he could be so withdrawn and moody that you didn't like to speak to him." They made do with a Musicians' Union temp until they found Packwood.

"Although our paths crossed now and then, I never played with Kenny again," says Sheridan. "He became a Wild Cat and I became a 2Is regular, singing most nights, backed up by whoever was playing there." This was usually the Worried Men, the house-group already on their way to becoming a Bluesbreakers-style training school for fledgling musicians, but sometimes by two guys from Les Hobeaux: Red Reece (drums) and Rex Dabinett (bass).

"Les Bennetts from Les Hobeaux seemed to be at the centre of everything happening in Soho at that time and was a great inspiration to me, both as a guitarist and a person," says Sheridan. "I was only 17, obviously very impressionable, and I was swept up by the 2Is crowd, especially what I saw as the bohemian element. There were a lot of parties and some very attractive girls. Zom gave me my first hit on a joint – incredibly strong. I just laughed for two days."

Sheridan's first steady gig was playing lead guitar with the Vagabonds, led by another recent arrival, Roy Taylor – who was trying to get used to his new identity, Vince Eager.

Taylor was a Grantham lad, conceived as war was declared and born on 4 June 1940. He sang in the church choir, acted in school pantomimes and learnt to play chords on a banjo gifted by his parents – all good training for his skiffle group, formed with other members of the local YMCA youth club. Roy 'Vince' Taylor played guitar and sang, as did Roy Clark; Brian 'Licorice' Locking played a tea-chest bass, constructed by Taylor (who worked as an apprentice joiner), and John Holt played washboard.

In September 1956, rampant Lonnie-fan Taylor bought tickets for all 12 of Donegan's concerts at the Nottingham Empire (the start of his first ever variety tour), and a year later, at the same venue, the Vagabonds won the local heats of the Vipers/Jim Dale National Skiffle Contest, which boosted their confidence considerably, even though no reward (other than getting to shake Wally Whyton's hand) was forthcoming. There were, however, cash prizes to be won in another competition they had entered.

In conjunction with Mecca ballrooms, the trifling admass magazine *Weekend* launched the absurdly titled World Skiffle Championships. On page three of their 19 June 1957 issue were a few paragraphs headed 'Great Chance for Skiffle Cats!' Any group fancying a crack at the big-time could strum their stuff at one of the many Mecca ballrooms scattered across Britain. Local heats would be advertised in the magazine.

There were dozens of similar scams on the go but this one had a guaranteed pot of gold at the end. The final would be televised live from Streatham Locarno, in front of millions, on the popular BBC show *Come Dancing*. Top prize was £250 cash and all the fame that would surely follow.

For weeks, contestants from across the country selected their best songs and their snappiest clothes and performed with all the enthusiasm and energy they could muster. Six made it through to the final: the Creoles from Glasgow, the Excelsiors from Carrickfergus, the Lumberjacks from Stamford Hill, the Moonshiners from Barnsley, the Vagabonds from Grantham and the Trentside Five from Nottingham.

On Monday 11 November, BBC Television die-hards would have sat through *This Is Your Life* with Eamonn Andrews, *Hancock's Half Hour*, *Panorama*, *Picture Parade* with the man puzzlingly described as "television's most eligible bachelor" Peter Haigh, and the *News*. At 10.15, after Bob Miller & his Orchestra finished their opening number, also-ran Canadian actor turned compère Paul Carpenter announced the main feature of tonight's *Come Dancing*, the grand final of the WORLD skiffle championship, telling viewers that they would have the first opportunity to see the stars of tomorrow. Backstage, the groups were shaking with anticipation; back home, parents and relatives and friends were clustered in front of little veneered television sets doing the same.

Roy Taylor was hefty and handsome, possessed of a confidence and charisma ideally suited to television, and the Vagabonds played well enough to feel that the prize was theirs. "We thought we had walked it," says Taylor. "The only threat to us were the Trentside Five, who had a great guitarist, but we had beaten them before, in Nottingham, and were sure we had out-performed them. They read out the winners in reverse order – and the Trentside Five came third. 'We've got it! Piece of piss!' we thought . . . but we hadn't reckoned on the composition of the judging panel. That was my first taste of the Jewish fraternity in our beloved profession."

Oscar Rabin, Ben Warris and Anne Shelton awarded the prize to the Lumberjacks, from a Jewish youth club in north London. They collected a silver cup and a cheque for £250 but it was the last anybody ever heard of them. As runners-up, the Vagabonds were given £150, enough to placate them temporarily.

"The following night, we found our way to the 2Is, where there was a long queue – so I went up to the guy on the door and told him we wanted to play. He wasn't interested: 'Get in the queue with the rest of them.' So I said 'But we came second in the World Skiffle Championship on television last night' – at which point his attitude changed completely. He let us through right away and before long, we were on stage at the 2Is! We played for an hour in the most sweltering airless heat, almost pressure-cooked ourselves to death."

Back home in Grantham, they savoured their adventure. They scrutinised the next issue of *Weekend*, looking for any mention of their near triumph. Not a word. They had to content themselves with learning a few phrases from the magazine's 'Jive Talk Guide for Cool Cats'.

Blow your top	become wild
Cat	a great guy
Crazy	marvellous
Dig	listen to
Fly right	behave correctly
Groovy	wonderful
Gutbucket	earthy music
Hep	enlightened
Kick	pleasurable feeling
Killer diller	terrific
Sends me	gives me pleasure
Square	unenlightened
Corny	out of fashion
Cut a rug	dance
Gone	inspired
Latch on	join in
Solid	good
Zooty	stylish, in the fashion

"I say, you guys, I feel killer diller; I think I'll go and cut a rug," said Roy. "That sounds like a solid idea," said Licorice, "do you mind if I latch on? There's a crazy cat blowing his top at the Guildhall, and I'm sure his hep gutbucket will send me!"

Paul Lincoln had offered the Vagabonds a residency at the 2Is. "He said he would give us £20 a week, so we talked it over and decided to go back to London in the New Year," says Taylor, who travelled down with a slightly modified line-up. Mick Fretwell had come in on drums, replacing their former washboardist, who had gone back to school. "When we got there, we found it was £20 between the four of us, a pound a night each – almost impossible to live on." Nevertheless, they decided to give it a whirl, playing skiffle-rock versions of Elvis Presley and Gene Vincent songs.

"We found these cheap digs at a hostel in Paddington," recalls Licorice Locking, "but that was a horrendous place – I came out in boils, all over! We had so little money that we all sold our watches, and we used to walk miles rather than spend money on bus fares. The highlight of the day was having a modest meal at the café in Denmark Street."

In April 1958, Paul Lincoln phoned up Decca producer Dick Rowe, who already had three of his acts on the label: Terry Dene, the Most Brothers and Wee Willie Harris. "You should come down," he said, "I think I've got a sure-fire winner." Rowe was not keen on the Vagabonds but saw potential in their singer – which naturally caused hackles to rise among the three musketeers. Was it not an 'all for one and one for all' situation?

Caught in a whirlwind of subterfuge and intrigue, Taylor found himself in the studio – and, only days later, journalist Bill Halden revealed that "Paul Lincoln is staking his all on a new star, a 17 year old from Grantham named Roy Taylor, who has already made his first record for Decca".

Before it could be released, events took an unexpected turn. Larry Parnes suddenly emerged from the shadows and offered the Vagabonds a Sunday night gig at the Gaumont in Coventry, opening for Marty Wilde. Excited by the prospect of playing on a decent sized stage for the first time in months, and in such illustrious company, they took it.

"In the coach, on the way back to London, Larry buttonholed me and said he wanted to manage me," says Taylor, who had no formal contract with Lincoln. "I'd heard about his tendencies but I also knew that he was the most famous rock 'n' roll manager in Britain, so I told him I was interested. I went back to his place and there was the usual pillow fight, holding him at bay – all the guys would have to go through it. Next day, he told me I needed a more dynamic name than Roy Taylor. I suggested Vince, because Gene Vincent was my idol, and Larry came up with Eager because he thought that described my attitude. I've been Vince Eager ever since."

Vince was an earnest, honest, trusting kid from the Lincolnshire boondocks, who believed that his new handler knew what he was doing. He was, after all, Mr Parnes, the famous rock 'n' roll manager who had launched Tommy and Marty so successfully – a man acclaimed not only for his street credibility, his ability to spot and nurture talent, but also for his standing in Tin Pan Alley, where he had quickly gained the respect of the showbiz and music-biz establishment for his capacity to charm and schmooze as skilfully as any among them. Larry had been welcomed to the club. Two years earlier he was selling dresses but already he was beginning to believe in his omnipotence. Vince Eager and the Vagabonds would soon be bill toppers and show stoppers, he assured them.

Locking, Clark and Fretwell were put on wages, sufficient for them to escape the wretched doss-house and move into a flat on Cromwell Road but, anxious for more stability, Clark returned to Grantham to resume his engineering apprenticeship. Already something of a 2Is hero, Tony Sheridan came in on lead guitar and took up residence with the other two. Meanwhile, Vince moved into Larry's apartment in Gloucester Road. "He had guys back every night; I stayed out of the way. We didn't see eye to eye, didn't get on that well together. I knew he was an old queen and I didn't like him trying it on. For his part, he didn't like me having birds around. 'You can't have girlfriends: you'll lose your fans,' he used to tell me. The more he said it, the more girlfriends I had."

Set for release in May 1958, Eager's first single for Decca paired non sequiturs: *Yea Yea*, a cover of an ephemeral US hit by the Kendall Sisters, and a run-before-you-can-walk version of *Tread Softly Stranger*, the title song from an instantly forgettable new film starring George Baker and Diana Dors. (The only interesting moment comes when Baker, in a bookmaker's, peruses a list of runners and suggests 'Moonraker looks like a good bet' – *Moonraker* being the title of his concurrent movie, which certainly had more commercial impetus.) However, after test pressings – which bore the name Vince Eager rather than Roy Taylor – Parnes decided he didn't like it, disputed Decca's right to issue it, and the record was squashed.

Eager's career was effectively put on hold for the whole of the summer. In order to smooth him out, make him more palatable to the universal audience, Larry had him playing a residency at Churchill's, a club for the swanky set in Bond Street, where he was seen as an amusing novelty interlude. It was plainly the wrong audience; his constituency was the teen set, especially the girls. "The groupies down the 2Is used to faint when Vince Eager got on stage and wiggled about," says Tony Sheridan, "and it was genuine too! It nonplussed everyone. I clearly remember girls collapsing and passing out. He was a bit of an Elvis imitator, but he was good at it."

The five tracks Vince cut for Decca were eventually released on an extended player, but few noticed. This was partly due to the producer's insufficiency, partly due to lack of promotion, partly due to the silly nature of the musical settings. One cannot expect scoffers from the Ted Heath Orchestra to play teenage music with any degree of authenticity or feeling, so they played the way they knew how. The most horrifying track was *Lend Me Your Comb*, their ridiculous attempt to better the atmospheric, down-home Carl Perkins original by turning it into fodder for the Light Programme low-brow/accept-anything audience. It not only missed its target but was also disrespectful. To rock 'n' roll fanatics, Carl was a kingpin, up there with Gene and Elvis, and although *Lend Me Your Comb* was by no means one of his finest moments, Vince was ill-advised to tamper with his material – and that was to be a constant problem throughout his career: he was poorly served by his manipulators. Especially Parnes, who flew by the seat of his pants and those parts of his body contained therein. His spontaneous ideas and ejaculations were those of a butterfly.

Ambition and megalomania prevailing over rationality, Parnes decided to launch his own record label Elempi – after his initials L.M.P. Vince, now free from his Decca contract, would be the guinea pig, in on the ground floor of something quite stupendous, Larry hoped. "There hasn't been a label as exciting as this for a long time," he told reporters, as he unveiled his A&R director Ron Grainer. It was a perceptive choice although Grainer had yet to find his niche or his groove.

"We recorded some awful cover stuff," says Vince, "so bad that my memory has lost trace of the details. None of it was released and the whole project went sour, didn't happen."

By this time, Eager was using temporary backing musicians on his Churchill's Club residency, the others having fallen out either with him or with Parnes. "What put me off Parnes was the fact that he was a raving queer," says Tony Sheridan. "He tried it on with me and I was scared out of my wits." There was also a bit of friction with Vince. "On more than one occasion we got into fisticuffs. Personality differences you could call it." Seventeen-year-old country cats up in London trying to make their mark and get somewhere.

Among Vince's new sidemen were bassist Tex Makins and drummer Tony Meehan, who were now playing with the Worried Men at the 2Is every night but then rushing to Churchill's to back Vince, who didn't go on until after midnight. By September, he was sufficiently 'groomed', Larry's favourite process, for exposure to the wider world. He had his first provincial tour mapped out, he had been booked for his 6.5 *Special* début, George Martin had signed him to Parlophone and the future was looking rosy and bright.

The same could not be said for Colin Hicks. Larry's faith in him had cooled, a development which some observers saw as tantamount to the kiss of death, at least a serious impediment to further progress. After his first provincial tour, through November and December 1957, the gig-sheet seemed to lose all momentum.

Whether as a test of endurance or some kind of sinister experiment, Parnes sent Hicks and his group to play two one-night stands on the top edge of Scotland, over a thousand miles away. By train, change at Inverness. This in April, season of mist, wind, lashing rain, late snow, cold and damp. At the Town Hall in Thurso and the Boys' Brigade Hall in Wick, towns on the same line of latitude as Juneau, Alaska, they faced and attempted to entertain the restless natives. It was not easy. Maybe no other work offers were forthcoming. At least their next trip would take them to sunnier climes.

Colin's group, the latest line-up of the Cabin Boys, was quite formidable for the time, containing Jimmy Nicol on drums, Johnny Stanley on sax, Ronnie Mills on piano, Tony Eagleton on guitar, and Brian Gregg on bass guitar – a shiny cello Hofner purchased in September 1957, one of the earliest on the beat scene. Gregg had quit Les Hobeaux to play rock 'n' roll and found every opportunity to cut loose when Hicks was booked on a package tour of Italy, sharing an oddly conceived bill with the Platters and Ramblin' Jack Elliott. Intrepid teenagers on a bizarre working holiday, able to snoop around Milan, Venice, Bari, Brindisi, Naples, Rome, Genoa, every

major town up and down the length of Italy – an impossible dream
for most people.

The Platters were polished and sophisticated, celebrating their
third US number one, *Twilight Time,* and yet they were no match for
this wild bunch. "We used to go down amazingly, stole the show
every night," says Gregg. "We were the first rock 'n' rollers to get
over there and the Italians had never seen anything like it. So, of
course, we gave them the full Bill Haley bit, tearing about, lying on
our backs, leaping around, shouting and whooping, encouraging
them to clap and stamp and sing and dance. We would be practically
dead at the end of the set but the audiences just stood and cheered,
wouldn't let us off. At home, we often met either apathy or hostility,
but it was utter pandemonium over there. Weeks of it, non-stop."

In early June, Hicks left Italy a massive star and returned to
London to find that Parnes was no longer prepared to represent him.
Another single *La Dee Dah* had failed and promoters were reluctant
to book him because – not wanting to be accused of riding on his
coat-tails – he allowed no references to his brother, either in publicity
or on posters. After a year of uphill struggle, Parnes wasn't prepared
to extend his contract, nor was he disposed to accept any more
truculence. "Colin used to give Larry lip, he took the piss, and if
there was one thing Larry demanded, it was respect," says Gregg,
"but I'm sure it was a purely commercial decision. Colin just wasn't
happening in England and despite him being Tommy's brother, he
had to go."

Instead, to complement his current trio of Steele, Wilde and Eager,
Parnes signed "a beautiful Anglo-Indian girl" called Shari – so the
compliant press reported. However, short of her turning up at the
première of *Ice Cold In Alex* with John Kennedy, there was never any
sign of her.

Significantly, Kennedy, the visionary who facilitated Larry's
spectacular rise, was about to break away from the management
partnership in all areas except those concerning Tommy Steele, to
whose career he once more devoted all his energies. Larry loved
gambling and flamboyance, had aspirations and a lifestyle not
entirely to Kennedy's taste – and after two years of inspiration and
sweat, Kennedy's future was now laid out exactly as he wanted it,
both challenging and secure.

Thirty

In March 1958, Tommy Steele played dates in South Africa, the first rock 'n' roll star to do so. "I suppose that is half the secret of Tommy's £14,000 a month or whatever it is – you want to mother him," concluded the *Cape Times*. "The other half is real cool smooth rhythm music to flip to. And that smile!" The tour caused friction when Tommy insisted on playing to black audiences as well as white. Years later, he would recall the rows of stone-faced white men, who commandeered the front stalls at one concert and sat in silence, protesting against what they thought he represented. "I didn't have that great a time over there to be honest," he confided, but at least he drew attention to apartheid.

Everywhere he went, from South Africa to Southend, from Copenhagen to Kettering, he was mobbed by hordes of screaming teenagers – and after a year or so, the novelty was beginning to wear a little thin. Several times, he had escaped injury by the skin of his teeth but on May Day, during a week of concerts at Caird Hall in Dundee, he was not so lucky. So great was the clamour for tickets that the promoter had also sold the choir seats at the back of the stage and, at the climax of his act, a spontaneous stampede pinned him to the floor.

"Like a spark on dry tinder, a sudden gust of hysteria swept over the audience and girls hurled themselves at him from every direction," wrote John Kennedy. Steele's guitar was smashed, one of his arms was all but wrenched from its socket, clumps of hair were torn out and his clothes were ripped. Hospitalised and traumatised, out of action for six weeks, all the while hounded by promoters and agents who suspected he might be bilking, he had ample time to consider his future.

One thing was never in doubt: he was going to marry Ann Donoughue. Their engagement was announced at a midnight press conference on 11 June 1958. He resumed touring a few days later, an ill-conceived itinerary taking him from Llandudno up to Aberdeen, back down to Margate and then across to Bournemouth. He and the

Steelmen, initially hired for six weeks, would part company in November, after working together for two years.

Meanwhile, Steele had starred in his own television show *Saturday Spectacular* and had turned disc jockey for a series of eight BBC radio shows. Internal correspondence reveals how the BBC was now forced to acknowledge his importance, how much he had already influenced the course of popular music. "In the past there have been policy points in connection with rock 'n' roll, with which Tommy Steele is so closely associated," wrote the Light Programme's Head of Planning, "but we know he has a pleasant microphone personality and he has already broadcast a most attractive *Desert Island Discs* programme." Panic had set in because Radio Luxembourg's *Top Twenty* show was drawing more listeners than the BBC's *Pick Of The Pops*. The plan was to switch *Pick Of The Pops* to Saturday and, in an attempt to fire a broadside at Luxembourg, "we should broadcast a programme of gramophone records presented by Tommy Steele." So desperate were they to secure his services, that they allowed Larry Parnes to extract a fee of 100 guineas ("Tommy won't do it for less") per 35-minute show – more than twice the weekly wage of Radio One disc jockeys, 10 years later. "I strongly make the point that this exceptional fee must not be the beginning of a train of embarrassing problems," wrote the Head of Planning – but another high-ranking executive had no qualms: "I heard about half of Tommy Steele last night. Just the ticket, I'm sure: really natural and most refreshingly un-BBC. I see by this morning's papers that he is to star in pantomime: a reason to sew up a second series right now?"

The reply was curt. "I suspect that Pete Murray will do at least as well for less than half the money."

Steele's disc jockey days were over but his film career was flourishing. Going on general release in March, his second movie, *The Duke Wore Jeans*, was an English musical, a hokey low-budget cross between *Oklahoma* and *The Prisoner Of Zenda*, with Tommy playing a cockney who happens to resemble the upper-crust Hon Tony Whitecliffe. He agrees to take his place on a trip to the oil-rich monarchy of Ritalla, to impersonate him in a complicated plot involving valuable bulls and the king's daughter. Tommy's fans hear eight new Bart/Pratt/Steele songs and sigh over his first screen kiss, with Redcar lass June Laverick. "The director didn't say cut," said

June, "and we held the kiss for ages, until we got the giggles." Critics agreed that Tommy had a natural screen presence. For him, it was a stepping stone towards *Half A Sixpence*; for Bart, it was training for *Fings Ain't What They Used To Be* and *Oliver*.

During the year, four Steele singles reached the hit parade: *Nairobi, Happy Guitar* (from his movie), *The Only Man On The Island* and the Ritchie Valens cover, *Come On Let's Go* – backed with an early Joe Meek composition *Put A Ring On Her Finger*.

During all this excitement, his fiancée took the stage name Ann Donati and joined Millicent Martin, Victor Spinetti, Barry Cryer, Susan Hampshire, Trevor Griffiths and Carol Ann Ford in the cast of a new West End musical *Expresso Bongo*, written by Wolf Mankowitz, about a coffee bar cowboy catapulted to fame by an imaginative manager. No parallels there, then. Starring Paul Schofield as the manager and James Kenney as the young protégé, it opened to widespread acclaim at the Saville Theatre on 23 April 1958.

Ten days earlier, *The 6.5 Special*, a full-length cinema spin-off from the television series, reached screens across the country. Far from exhausted after writing the convoluted screenplays for *The Tommy Steele Story* and *The Duke Wore Jeans* (for which he received a total of £400), Norman Hudis now turned his attention to devising a plot involving a train and abundant music. Easy.

Believing her vocally adept friend Ann (Diane Todd) to be a potential overnight star, Judy (Avril Leslie) persuades her to go to London. They board the 6.5 departure, only to find it packed with regulars from the show, all of whom are taking the opportunity to rehearse . . . and, much to their surprise, compères Pete Murray, Jo Douglas and Freddie Mills are also on the train, returning from a search for amateur talent in the Midlands. Ann gives them a song in the dining car and is naturally booked for a spot in the following Saturday's show.

During 85 minutes of bunkum, viewers were subjected to such curious performances as *The Train Kept A-Rolling* by Jim Dale, *Hand Me Down My Walkin' Cane* by the King Brothers, *Gypsy In My Soul* by the Kentones and *Midgets* by Desmond Lane the Penny Whistle Man. In contrast to the antiquated Dickie Valentine and Joan Regan was the show's latest discovery, Jackie Dennis, a 15-year-old Scot who invariably appeared in either the kilt or tartan trews. He had recently been launched by Decca and was high in the chart with *La Dee Dah*, a song that only emphasised his novelty value. Calling him 'the loneliest boy in show business', columnist Tom Hutchinson was sceptical about his chances. "I'm not saying that Jackie Dennis could not be a star," he wrote, "but the build-up could crush a talent that is slender at the moment. It is too sudden and too soon. If he is not careful, he's going to be a kind of freak because of his youth, a human gimmick." At least wee Jackie enjoyed a few months in the spotlight.

Despite the presence of Johnny Dankworth and Cleo Laine ("what are we doing here?") and the John Barry Seven, the *6.5 Special* movie was memorable only for the appearance of Lonnie Donegan and his group, all bow-ties and tuxedos, who were able to relieve the torture with *Jack O' Diamonds* and *Grand Coolie Dam*.

The television show, fairly pathetic to start with, was now on the slippery slope to oblivion. Mike and Bernie Winters were the resident unfunny comedians, Jim Dale had taken over from Pete Murray as compère, and such new faces as Little Johnny, the Mudlarks and Barry Barnett were of mild passing prole interest only. It would soon be wiped off the face of the earth by *Oh Boy!*, the new ITV show devised and produced by Jack Good, who had left the BBC 'by mutual consent' in February 1958.

Against all odds, the *6.5 Special* did help to create an American chart single. The Three Tons Of Joy, a trio of colossal black women who were then affiliated to the Johnny Otis Show, scored a freak UK hit with *Ma He's Making Eyes At Me*, and in the wake of this were featured on the show. On returning to Los Angeles, they and their manager reported back to Otis, telling him about this most peculiar phenomenon they had witnessed, the hand jive – which had reached a peak of popularity at the time of their visit. There was even an instruction book for those too moronic to copy the simple movements. Otis promptly wrote and recorded *Willie And The Hand Jive*, which became the most successful of all his multifarious recordings. On the principle of credit where credit is due, it should be noted that the hand jive had originated at Wimbledon Palais at least a year earlier, and the group who first encouraged and popularised it were the unsung Leon Bell & his Bell Cats.

Among the worst films of 1958, *The 6.5 Special* was greeted with rather less enthusiasm than *The Pride And The Passion*, *Paths Of Glory*, *Witness For The Prosecution*, *The Bridge On The River Kwai*, *Disc Jockey*

Jamboree, The Big Beat, Peyton Place, A Farewell To Arms, Violent Playground, The Ten Commandments, South Pacific, Dunkirk, Touch Of Evil, The Long Hot Summer, Sing Boy Sing, The Vikings, Dracula, Vertigo, A Night To Remember, King Creole, Raintree County, The Fly, Cat On A Hot Tin Roof, The Left Handed Gun, Carry On Sergeant and *The Old Man And The Sea.*

However, woeful though it was, *The 6.5 Special* looked like *Ben Hur* alongside *The Golden Disc.* A terminal embarrassment to all concerned, this fiasco was a rose-coloured interpretation of Terry Dene's rise to stardom and purported to represent coffee bar culture. It was produced by Butchers (an apposite name), a studio at Walton-on-Thames which appeared to make do with sets donated by local amateur dramatic societies. The storyline was asinine, the screenplay was piffle and the acting was wooden – yet the business accepted it without censure.

As a time capsule, it holds a squirmy fascination. Singing *Johnny-O*, the matronly Nancy Whiskey is unable to disguise her pregnancy, despite trying to hide it behind a music stand; gaunt and ghostly, with fag in mouth, Phil Seamen (drumming with the Don Rendell Six) can barely conceal his self-loathing for having accepted his cameo role; Les Hobeaux and Sonny Stewart's Skiffle Kings mime to their latest releases, and Terry Kennedy's group back Terry Dene on *Candy Floss*, one of several unspeakably bad songs he is required to sing. The poor lad looks thoroughly uncomfortable throughout, although the *NME* reviewer was moved to praise his "convincing acting".

Released in April 1958, the film was intended to expand Dene's audience but already the pressure was getting to him. Since leaving school, he had been a bicycle messenger, a timber-yard labourer, a plumber's mate, odd job boy in a clock factory, a crate maker, a record packer and, for the past 12 months, a pop star, touring up and down the country with barely a day off. Faced with such a schedule, who wouldn't have needed a drink now and then, just to soothe fraying nerves?

The trouble began on 26 January, when Dene was fined 40 shillings for being drunk and disorderly, after having been caught smashing shop windows and wandering the West End in a state of undress – providing a field day for the tabloids and all rock 'n' roll deprecators. He would later shrug it off as a bit of fun: "I was walking down the street in my underpants – and it was blown out of all proportion. These days, it would be looked on as some kind of joke, you'd be some kind of streaker. But because I'd done that, and thrown a no-waiting sign through a window, it caused a sensation."

He could make light of it later but it was serious at the time, a potential career-buster. Not only was it a disappointment to his girlie fans and ammunition for those in the media and establishment who loathed rock 'n' roll, but it was also a defining moment for his manager, who was stuck with a large bill for the costs. Obviously time for a damage-limitation plan.

At the end of the week following the hearing, *Melody Maker* had a hastily organised picture of Dene on their front page, sipping milk through a straw as he signed a pledge promising not to touch alcohol again. The first rock star (at the front of a long line) to get wasted and ridiculous, out of his tree and gone, the first to offer lavish apologies for his unpardonable behaviour. "It will certainly be a long time before I have another drink," the contrite singer was reported as saying, "I was very foolish and I couldn't feel more ashamed. In future, it is soft drinks for me."

Less than a month later, during a package tour with Chas McDevitt and Edna Savage, he was up before magistrates in Gloucester, facing charges of causing wilful malicious damage and being drunk and disorderly. "Terry Dene's got a pretty bad name now," reported Fraser White, who had travelled up to cover the case. "You may think he deserves it or you may not, but whatever you think, if you'd been in that court you would never forget the sight of that lonely, frightened youth in the box."

Dene had spent the night in police custody, following his arrest on suspicion of smashing glass in a phone box, damaging two plate glass windows and two motorcycles, and damaging another shop window. This had happened in the early hours, following an altercation at Gloucester Regal and a visit to the Infirmary to treat his fists, which had apparently been injured when he struck a wall.

Sitting at the back of the court, watching the proceedings through dark glasses – to cover the black eye that Dene had apparently given her – was Edna Savage, who put up £50 bail to free him. However, with Colin Hicks and Marty Wilde roped in as replacements, the tour continued without him. After paying his fine, £155 plus £122 for damages, Dene returned to London.

"Terry is seeing a psychiatrist this week," explained manager Paul Lincoln. "He will then have to receive treatment and will not resume work until both he and the doctors are satisfied he is better." Their pronouncements would not satisfy Lincoln, however. His composure and faith had been rattled beyond endurance and, regardless of his 30 per cent stake in the singer's future, he quit. "Don't get me wrong," he told one inquisitive journalist, "it really wasn't because of Terry's trouble. It was just that we didn't see eye to eye . . . and I figured it wasn't worth it."

Fortunately, Dene's agent Hymie Zahl was not prepared to let him slip out of his life. Gay, though in no way predatory (he was in an inviolable long-term relationship with his partner Glen), Zahl had fallen for the singer's cherubic charm and was determined to hold his career together to the best of his ability. "Hymie was a lovely little man," says Brian Gregg, "and straight as an arrow, too; no one ever had any problems with money from him. His agency, Fosters, had a massive list of clients, mainly variety acts and the penguin-suit brigade, but he couldn't do enough for Terry. Of course, we used to have fun with him. We used to call him Mr Magoo, because he wore these jam-jar bottom glasses and was always bumping into door-posts. He was obviously very fond of Terry."

He wasn't the only one. At the Queen's Theatre in Blackpool, on 30 December 1957, the first day of a long headlining tour, he had met support act Edna Savage. A romance developed – but it was ill-starred from the start. She was more than two and a half years older, and two and a half light years more worldly-wise. A telephonist in Warrington by day, she had been singing with the Eric Pepperall group at a club in Ashton-In-Makefield when a *Melody Maker* journalist put in a good word for her. Soon, she was performing with the BBC's Northern Variety Orchestra and on her nineteenth birthday recorded her first single for Parlophone. She was something of a star by the time she met Dene, popular on radio, television and the stage, her picture on magazine covers, her story told and re-told in the press – the perky singer who escaped from her switchboard and was now living life to the hilt, touring all over the country and in between times having a high old time in her posh Marble Arch flat.

As the tour progressed, a week in each town, penned up in theatres and hotels at Blackpool, Taunton, Oldham, Dublin, Manchester and Peterborough, an intense affair developed. Too hot to handle, impossible to sustain or contain; the siren and the callow, besotted teenager. It turned turbulent and exploded across front pages during their week in Gloucester. "Young singer went berserk," reported *The Times* after his window-smashing rampage. As he was carted off to the cells, Dene told police that Edna had rejected him. He was in love with her, couldn't stand the thought of her in another's arms, couldn't bear even to hear the names of other men she knew.

Dene was off the road and in the doldrums for almost three months, trying to shake his twin addictions, the bottle and Edna. There were no fireworks for the première of *The Golden Disc*, at the Rialto Cinema in Piccadilly, and his band – forced to take any employment on offer – went on tour backing Decca's latest discovery Bill Kent. But eventually those investigating his mind and body declared him fit and able to resume his schedule and optimists saw Dene's life getting back on track in May, when his latest single *Stairway Of Love* made the Top 20. "He's going to be a good boy now," David Jacobs assured the audience as he made a tentative comeback, but many were not convinced, especially when details of his summer tour were announced. Who should be sharing the bill but Edna Savage, femme fatale, the author of all his woe – now in a happy relationship with either Ronnie Carroll or Andrew Ray, depending which newspaper you read. Would Dene dedicate his hit to her . . . close your eyes, hold me tight and we'll climb the stairway of love tonight? How long before another incident?

All were confounded. On 25 June 1958, Terry and Edna announced their engagement and on 8 July they were married at Marylebone Register Office. Wee Willie Harris was best man, Larry Page a witness – their contrasting coiffures glinting in the sunlight, red and blue. Off the happy couple flew, for a honeymoon in Torremolinos, and then it was back to work – at the Glasgow Empire, most paralysing of all variety venues, its patrons capable of reducing hardened troupers to jelly. Coping with them was a cakewalk; it was his own demons Terry Dene had to worry about.

Thirty-one

The 2Is Coffee Bar was changing. Paul Lincoln was often out on the road with his acts and had appointed a new manager, Tom Littlewood – an acquaintance from the wrestling world, who quickly began to throw his weight around. In the old days, Roy Heath, the gentle 22-stone doorman/deputy manager had adopted a laissez-faire attitude.

"We were like family in the 2Is: we could go behind the counter and help ourselves," says Brian Gregg, one of the earliest regulars. "We sometimes used to sleep down there too, several of us – a den of iniquity it was at times – but that all got messed up when Tom Littlewood arrived. He was strict – plus he used to demand 10 per cent commission from anybody who played down there . . . so he'd give you a quid but then take back two shillings. It was daylight robbery but, of course, but none of us dared to complain."

"The presence of the wrestling fraternity is usually overlooked when anybody recalls the 2Is, but there was quite a contingent," according to Tony Sheridan. "You had these characters like Henry Henroyd and 2Is Norman, who were involved in wrestling promotions, and a lot of hard people used to strut around down there, intimidating characters in Italian suits and pointed shoes. I don't think they had a lot of interest in the music."

Young hopefuls were still coming down in droves. It was as if Paul Lincoln had put a horn on the roof, broadcasting messages that couldn't be denied. Few would infiltrate the established order but they never stopped trying. "It was pointless playing anywhere except the 2Is," says Wally Whyton of the all-but-defunct Vipers. "Even if you were playing at the coffee bar next door, you were nowhere. You might as well be playing in Wales."

Well aware of this, Bruce Welch and Brian Rankin moved down from Newcastle in April 1958, hoping to find acceptance within the 2Is inner circle. They came with good references: Chas McDevitt had been telling everyone about "these Geordie kids, the Railroaders", and the Vipers had been encouraging when the National Skiffle

Contest heats had been held at their local Empire, two months earlier.

For Johnny Booker, the abiding memory of the Vipers' visit to Newcastle had been the beer. "Newcastle Brown had a disturbing effect on us, not having drunk it before, but we didn't realise until we'd knocked back several pints," says Booker. "A couple of us got diarrhoea on stage, really bad. The smell was terrible, the agony of having to carry on singing was indescribable. To make it worse, the theatre manager came out during our set to beg the people in the balcony to stop stamping because it was shaking. When we eventually got offstage we just removed our waffle blue pants and threw them away. That was the first and last time I touched Newcastle Brown."

Born within days of each other, in late 1941, Rankin and Welch had first met in the shadow of Newcastle Brewery, next door at Rutherford Grammar School, where by 1956 they were playing and singing in rival skiffle groups. Hank Rankin, as intimates called him, played banjo in the Crescent City Skiffle Group, who followed the Ken Colyer tradition of placing conviction and respect above commercial considerations. Their versions of *Go Down Old Hannah*, *Streamline Train* and *Stack-O-Lee* helped them to first place in a skiffle contest at South Shields Pier Pavilion in May 1957 but they disbanded only weeks later, when school broke up for summer.

By this time, Rankin had abandoned the banjo for a borrowed guitar, a much more versatile instrument on which he could learn not only chords, but intros and solos and fills. "The guitar seemed to be the way to go," he says, "it had so much potential, so much variation, so much more possibility of expression." His natural aptitude couldn't escape the notice of Bruce Welch, who invited him to join his group, the Railroaders. "I only knew him vaguely at school, even though we were in the same year, but I recognised him as a fellow traveller," says Hank. Pretty soon they were best friends, stomping it out at working men's clubs in Newcastle and the mining villages of Northumberland.

"That's when we started playing rock 'n' roll," Hank continues. "I had been more inclined towards jazz and blues, listening to records by people I could never hope to emulate – like Big Bill Broonzy and Django Reinhardt and Barney Kessell – but Bruce had been fanatical about rock 'n' roll from the moment he heard it and he gave me a crash course on its esoteric delights, playing me stuff by Gene Vincent, Elvis Presley, Chuck Berry, brand new records by the Crickets and the Everly Brothers. I plunged into it headlong, trying to copy the way the guitarist was playing behind the singer, how he integrated with the rest of the band, trying to work out the essence of American guitar playing, which was so different and exciting. Of course, you have to remember that we were only 15 at the time."

On his sixteenth birthday, 28 October 1957, Hank's parents bought him a guitar of his own, a Hofner Congress – an acoustic archtop with cello-style f-holes and a simple trapeze tailpiece. "It was their budget model, priced at around 16 guineas, but it was a joy to behold, a joy to hold. Then, I found that I could turn it into an electric guitar simply by screwing a little square metal pick-up onto the end of the neck and that opened up a whole new world of possibility for me."

Bruce decided not to go back to school after Christmas and his pal would drop out a few weeks later. "I was totally wrapped up in the guitar by then," Hank explains, "it's all I wanted to do. We were supposed to be taking our O levels in the summer but we left long before that – which is probably just as well because it saved us the embarrassment of failing. We certainly weren't doing any work; we were out every night playing wherever we could get an audience and a couple of quid. Then, afterwards, we would go to this open-all-night railway workers canteen behind Newcastle Central Station. The tea was only tuppence and you could get hot-pot, probably been there all day, but delicious, all subsidised for the workers. Other local skiffle groups and jazz bands would congregate there too and we'd swap stories. It was hardly the Café Royal but at that time of night it had a wonderful charm and atmosphere."

The Railroaders made a couple of trips to London, the last to lose out in a national skiffle contest (number 257 in a continuing series) at the Granada in Edmonton on 6 April 1958. They broke up that night – but while the others went home to Newcastle, Hank and Bruce got the address of some theatrical digs within easy travelling distance of Soho. "We moved into a bedsitter in Holly Park, round the corner from Crouch Hill underground station, where a kind-hearted soul called Mrs Bowman kept us alive for quite a few months. She was from the north-east and I think she felt rather sorry for us, a couple of kids lost in London – so she allowed the rent to pile up, all that stuff. Without her generosity, we would have been history, no doubt about that."

They made an immediate impression at the 2Is and were soon fronting a four-piece band with drummer George Plummer and whichever bass player was around, sometimes Licorice Locking or Jet Harris. "It was just a little cellar but it had such a presence, an aura that actually made your heart beat faster. Bruce and I were always interested in singing in harmony – and as fast as the Everly Brothers' records came out, we had been learning them and practising them, and the B-sides too. Then, not long after we'd moved down, we got their first album and learned the whole of that. Bruce could sing quite high and we worked hard to get that American country sound and feel, rather than adopting a British approach to it."

Hank had just begun calling himself Hank Marvin, his new surname inspired by Marvin Rainwater, a Cherokee Indian (so his record label claimed) who felt no embarrassment wearing a fringed buckskin shirt and a headband with a feather sticking up at the back. His boastful country-pop novelty *Whole Lotta Woman* was about to replace Perry Como's *Magic Moments* at number one. "Hank Marvin? Are you sure?" asked Bruce. It was a whimsical choice that would last forever.

In the middle of May 1958, Wee Willie Harris, Tony Crombie and the Rockets, Les Hobeaux and the Most Brothers returned from the north after four months on the road.

"It was a prototype package tour, all of us travelling on a 30-seater coach, complete with a road manager to look after us," recalls Alex Wharton, Mickie's partner in the Most Brothers. "We got home and strutted into the 2Is, all flash and arrogant, posing furiously after having been everywhere from Liverpool to Edinburgh on a national tour. We really thought we were stars but we got a rude awakening because there on the stage were Hank and Bruce, who had just blown into town, we learned. They were amazing, everything that we weren't. They had perfected the Everly Brothers harmony, had it off to a tee – and they played their guitars to complement each other, rather than strumming in unison the way we did. We played the wrong chords and we couldn't sing harmony at all. When I saw Hank and Bruce, I felt like giving up there and then. The game's up, I thought."

"Hank always played better than anyone else – he had all the Buddy Holly licks off before anyone else could play them," says Mickie Most. "He and Bruce were both good: they sang well together and were definitely going to make it. There were the ones who were destined to become stars and the ones who just used the 2Is as a social club. I always admired Hank and Bruce . . . young, living from hand to mouth, holed up in a room somewhere, they didn't have mum to go home too. It wasn't easy for them – but they were going to make it and nothing was going to stop them."

Eager to make new friends, Hank and Bruce had fallen in with drummer/songwriter Pete Chester, son of the famous and wealthy comedian, Charlie. In conjunction with singer and harmonica player Gerry Furst and piano player Neil Johnson, they made a record as the Five Chesternuts – financed by Leslie Conn, then the UK representative for the New York based Carlton label. He got them a one-off deal with Columbia, who scheduled *Teenage Love/Jean Dorothy* for August release. "It was never going to be anything permanent even though it was a roaring little band," says Hank. "Neil Johnson wore a cravat and had a very cultured speaking voice but he was a maniac on piano, foot up on the keyboard and all that stuff, and Gerry was a good harmonica player, but they both had careers mapped out." Hank and Bruce were looking for something to get their teeth into, but the Chesternuts only managed a couple of gigs before dispersing.

The Vipers, though road-weary and weather-beaten, seemed to hold more promise. Anxious to capitalise on the name and get back on track, Wally Whyton and Johnny Booker revamped the group, offering jobs to Hank Marvin and Jet Harris. Both accepted. Hank had nothing to lose, experience to gain; Jet had just finished a tour with Tony Crombie's Rockets and fancied a change. With Johnny Pilgrim now on drums rather than washboard, they guested on BBC radio's *Skiffle Club* on 29 June and then drove to Birmingham for a week at the Hippodrome.

"By then we were travelling in my 1951 Nash Statesman, which had overdrive and a long torpedo back," says Booker, "big enough to take the instruments and everyone in the band except Wally, who liked to travel separately in his TR3. Maybe he didn't like my driving. Cars were my passion: I had five of them, including the Nash, a Lanchester and, my favourite, an Allard with a supercharged flathead V8 engine – all parked around Eccleston Square, where I shared a flat with my sister."

"We still had to play our hits but we were trying to move towards rhythm & blues, which wasn't that easy. Pilgrim found that you needed more than a couple of weeks to learn drums and I don't think Hank was comfortable playing with guys who were so much older; I think he missed his mates at the 2Is."

"The week in Birmingham was a total disaster, the beginning of the end for me," says Whyton. "We tried to go electric and immediately blew up the little amps we'd got. As soon as Jet got started, the speaker cone in his just gave up and died. As well as that, we were trying to play raunchier numbers like *What Am I Living For* and *Johnny B. Goode* but the audiences only wanted to hear familiar skiffle songs – so we fell between two stools, died a death. It was not a good time: we had an album out, *Coffee Bar Session*, which nobody was buying and we had recently released our worst-ever single *Make Ready For Love*. It was becoming painfully obvious that our days were numbered."

On Saturday night, after the last show, they loaded up the Nash and drove straight back to London in gloomy silence. As he was dropped off, Hank – knowing that there were no pressing commitments on the Vipers' calendar – announced that he was leaving.

"Who could blame him?" asks Pilgrim. "The group had become a shambles and I felt that I was largely to blame. I was paralysed with fear behind that drum kit but Wally insisted that the washboard was a thing of the past . . . and it turned out that I was a thing of the past too. I wasn't so much fired as not asked to go to the next gig."

Determined to mount a last desperate rearguard action, the Vipers (now reduced to Wally Whyton, Johnny Booker and Jet Harris) resumed battle with two new recruits from the 2Is: drummer Tony Meehan and guitarist Zom.

Meanwhile, Hank Marvin did a quick two-step back to the Five Chesternuts, just in time to appear with them on the 12 July edition of *6.5 Special*, plugging their single. "I had a loyalty towards Bruce," he says. "We could have stayed in Newcastle and tried to get something going up there but we'd taken a punt and moved to London – and Bruce had been the prime mover, the motivator who persuaded me to go with him – and even though we were barely making enough to exist at the 2Is, we were both optimistic that something was going to happen and we were going to stick together, no matter what."

It was summer, it was warm, things were happening around them, they felt part of the scene. Days were spent at the bedsit, playing records on their Dansette, or in the 2Is cellar practising and sharing ideas with anyone else who happened to be down there – usually Tony Sheridan, Licorice Locking, George Plummer and various members of the Worried Men, who were still the main resident band. Adam Faith and Freddie Lloyd were long gone from the line-up, which seemed to be in constant flux. Adam's cousin Dennis Nelhams, who had taken over lead vocals, had insufficient power to hold the audience and Paul Lincoln replaced him with Rick Richards, who débuted with the group in April 1958, the week Hank and Bruce arrived.

Already 24 years old, Richards had been born within the sound of Bow bells but had moved out to Edgware and on to Watford as a child. After national service, he bought a Hofner Senator guitar and travelled the trad-jazz route, playing and singing with the local Colne Valley Stompers before forming his own skiffle group – which won a weekly residency at the Skiffle Cellar but folded when guitarist Johnny d'Avensac was called up. After a few guest spots with the Worried Men, Richards became a permanent fixture, turning them into a tight musical unit.

Chas Beaumont was a respected guitarist and would stay the course but when bassist Pete Darby attempted to graduate from tea-chest to the real thing, it quickly became apparent that he was no Charles Mingus. "He just seemed to be moving his fretting hand haphazardly, pulling the strings in any position, never in tune," says Richards, "so I brought in Tex Makins from my old group. He was always practising, trying to become a better player. Then we had problems when Adam's old school friend Hurgy switched from washboard to drums. He was a very good washboard player but he had a bit of trouble getting to grips with a pair of sticks – and he got the bullet while he was on holiday, I'm sorry to admit. It seems pretty ruthless, looking back, but we wanted to sound good. His downfall was the arrival (on Sunday 22 June 1958) of Tony Meehan, who was only a young kid but swung like the clappers. None of us could believe how good he was, how he managed to establish such an instant rapport with the rest of us. It was finally a great little rocking band."

For a year, Rick Richards was the regular resident singer at the 2Is – but whenever he took a night off, Tony Sheridan jumped at the chance to take centre stage.

"Tony Sheridan was lurking around the 2Is from the day we got there, sometimes singing and sometimes playing guitar behind other guys," says Hank Marvin. "He wasn't all that good at the time but he was a quick learner, very anxious to improve. I showed him a few bits and pieces I had picked up and we spent hours talking about records. The guitarists that interested me most of all, the ones I was always trying to copy, were those with a southern-states country background, like the guys who played behind Gene Vincent and Ricky Nelson."

Their names were known only to serious rock 'n' roll addicts at the time. Cliff Gallup, who had fired the imaginations of so many with his incandescent guitar solos on such Vincent classics as *Be Bop A Lula*, *Blue Jean Bop* and *Race With The Devil*, had returned to his day job as a plumber with the Norfolk, Virginia schools maintenance department and a new guy, Johnny Meeks, had played on recent favourites like *Lotta Lovin'*, *Dance To The Bop* and *Baby Blue*. For Hank, the big new discovery was James Burton, an 18 year old from Shreveport, Louisiana, whose stunning brilliance thrust every Ricky Nelson release into the must-buy category.

"Those of us who had been strummers in skiffle groups and now wanted to concentrate on playing guitar rather than singing were mesmerised by those players," says Hank. "We spent hours trying to work out their country picking techniques, how sometimes they would use a thumb-pick and their fingers rather than a plectrum – but even when we got the right sequence of notes, we were let down by the sound. We had cheap guitars, tiny amplifiers and big heavy strings – whereas James Burton used strings so light that he could bend them and produce cascades of notes that left us shaking our heads in disbelief. How on earth could he play like that? Same with Cliff Gallup and Scotty Moore, who not only had a natural fluidity but also benefited from that tape echo, which gave their playing such atmosphere. We had neither the knowledge nor the equipment to get anything but a very basic, dry sound . . . but we were trying as hard as we could."

Marvin's first visit to a recording studio had pointed up his limitations, everybody's limitations. Employing skiffle chords in a teen-beat format, Peter Chester's *Teenage Love* was garage rock, pure and simple. Hank managed a few rudimentary bits and pieces behind the verses but the record was lost in the shuffle. It could have been seen as a setback but he and Bruce saw it as their first tentative step. Skint they might have been, but they were in love with the life they had chosen, in love with girls that came to the 2Is to glow in the light of the jukebox upstairs or to gaze up at them as they played in the cellar, in love with the dreams that had brought them there. Boats had been burnt, bridges even, and nobody was about to give up and go home. Doors would open.

An honest and guile-free record, *Teenage Love* was interesting as far as English releases went, but was off the map in posterity terms. All the best records were coming from America and 1958 was another bumper year for teenagers whose lives had been transformed by rock 'n' roll. Readers of a non-zealous disposition may well be advised to skip this disconcertingly solid chunk of titles and names, but among the many great (exceptional in one or several respects) records released here during the year were, in rough order of appearance, *Bony Moronie/You Bug Me Baby* by Larry Williams, *The Bright Light* by Jim Lowe, *Stood Up/Waitin' In School* by Ricky Nelson, *I'm Left, You're Right, She's Gone* by Elvis Presley, *At The Hop* by Danny & the Juniors, *Jailhouse Rock/Treat Me Nice* by Elvis Presley, *Buzz Buzz Buzz* by the Hollywood Flames, *Teardrops* by Lee Andrews & the Hearts, *Good Golly Miss Molly/Hey Hey Hey Hey* by Little Richard, *Maybe* by the Chantels, *Maybe Baby/ Tell Me How* by the Crickets, *Get A Job* by the Silhouettes, *Oh Julie* by the Crescendos, *Listen To Me/I'm Gonna Love You Too* by Buddy Holly, *Don't* by Elvis Presley, *Walkin' Home From School* by Gene Vincent, *La Dee Dah* by Billie and Lillie, *Short Shorts* by the Royal Teens, *Bad Motorcycle* by the Storey Sisters, *Tequila* by the Champs, *Sweet Little Sixteen/Reelin' And Rockin'* by Chuck Berry, *To Be Loved* by Jackie Wilson, *Ballad Of A Teenage Queen/Big River* by Johnny Cash, *Who's Sorry Now?* by Connie Francis, *Click Clack* by Dicky Doo & the Don'ts, *Breathless* by Jerry Lee Lewis, *Believe What You Say/My Bucket's Got A Hole In It* by Ricky Nelson, *Betty And Dupree* by Chuck Willis, *Dizzy Miss Lizzy/Slow Down* by Larry Williams, *Rock 'n' Roll Is Here To Stay* by Danny & the Juniors, *Lend Me Your Comb* by Carl Perkins, *Skinny*

Minnie by Bill Haley & his Comets, *Oh Lonesome Me/I Can't Stop Loving You* by Don Gibson, *Wear My Ring Around Your Neck* by Elvis Presley, *All I Have To Do Is Dream/Claudette* by the Everly Brothers, *Baby Blue* by Gene Vincent, *Rumble* by Link Wray, *Big Man* by the Four Preps, *Don't You Just Know It* by Huey 'Piano' Smith & the Clowns, *Book Of Love* by the Monotones, *My True Love/ Leroy* by Jack Scott, *Sick And Tired* by Fats Domino, *Johnny B. Goode* by Chuck Berry, *What Am I Living For* by Chuck Willis, *Do You Want To Dance* by Bobby Freeman, *Rave On/Take Your Time* by Buddy Holly, *I Wonder Why* by Dion & the Belmonts, *Ooh My Soul/True Fine Mama* by Little Richard, *Endless Sleep* by Jody Reynolds, *Jennie Lee* by Jan and Arnie, *Guess Things Happen That Way/Come In Stranger* by Johnny Cash, *Think It Over* by the Crickets, *Hard Headed Woman* by Elvis Presley, *Yakety Yak* by the Coasters, *Splish Splash* by Bobby Darin, *No Chemise Please* by Gerry Granahan, *Stupid Cupid* by Connie Francis, *Rebel Rouser* by Duane Eddy, *Rocky Road Blues/Yes I Love You Baby* by Gene Vincent, *Poor Little Fool* by Ricky Nelson, *Born Too Late* by the Poni-Tails, *Little Star* by the Elegants, *Western Movies* by the Olympics, *Susie Darlin'/Living's Loving You* by Robin Luke, *Beautiful Delilah* by Chuck Berry, *Sail Along Silvery Moon* by Billy Vaughan & his Orchestra, *Over The Mountain, Across The Sea* by Johnnie & Joe, *One Summer Night* by the Danleers, *Bird Dog* by the Everly Brothers, *For Your Precious Love* by Jerry Butler & the Impressions, *Just A Dream* by Jimmy Clanton, *Break Up* by Jerry Lee Lewis, *Summertime Blues* by Eddie Cochran, *Tears On My Pillow* by Little Anthony & the Imperials, *You Cheated* by the Shields, *The Ways Of A Woman In Love* by Johnny Cash, *Nothin' Shakin'* by Eddie Fontaine, *Carol* by Chuck Berry, *It's Only Make Believe* by Conway Twitty, *Betty Lou Got A New Pair Of Shoes* by Bobby Freeman, *Ramrod* by Duane Eddy, *It's So Easy* by the Crickets, *C'mon Let's Go* by Ritchie Valens, *Git It* by Gene Vincent, *Rockin' Robin* by Bobby Day, *La-Do-Dada* by Dale Hawkins, *Someday* by Ricky Nelson, *To Know Him Is To Love Him* by the Teddy Bears, *Queen Of The Hop* by Bobby Darin, *Lonesome Town* by Ricky Nelson, *Poor Boy* by the Royaltones, *Gotta Travel On* by Billy Grammer, *A Lover's Question* by Clyde McPhatter, *Real Wild Child* by Ivan, *This Little Girl's Gone Rockin'* by Ruth Brown, *Lonely Teardrops* by Jackie Wilson, *Heartbeat/Well, All Right* by Buddy Holly, *Whole Lotta Lovin'* by Fats Domino, *Cannonball* by Duane Eddy, *Baby Face* by Little Richard, *Chicka-Chicka-Honey* by Robin Luke, and that's just a handful. If your soul and psyche had been invaded, you listened to the appropriate Radio Luxembourg shows, Grundig at the ready.

For many skifflers, the turning-point record had been Buddy Holly's first solo single *Peggy Sue*, which had been a Top 10 hit at the beginning of the year. Not only were the lyrics, the melody, the chord sequence and the vocal delivery the essence of simplicity but the potent guitar solo was within the grasp of any budding player. During 1958, Holly became a significant influence – not only through his records but as a live performer. In March, he and the Crickets (drummer Jerry Allison and bassist Joe Mauldin) began a 25-date tour at the Elephant & Castle Trocadero, heading a bill which included the archaic Tanner Sisters, balladeer Gary Miller, the Ronnie Keene Orchestra and compère Des O'Connor. Never before had anyone seen a Fender Stratocaster up close or heard such powerful amplification.

"Without doubt, the Crickets are the loudest, noisiest trio I've ever heard in my life," wrote *NME* reviewer Keith Goodwin, a new, young journalist who actually felt the music. "They completely overpowered the 13-piece Ronnie Keene Orchestra in relation to the volume of sound produced. Everyone loved the group's spirited lusty rock 'n' roll style and they went for Buddy's easy-going natural stage personality in an equally big way."

Among those trying to get his mind and fingers around the guitar work on all Holly's records was Tony Sheridan, who, having been at art college for a year appreciated how it was done: you started out trying to understand and copy the artists you admired and, if you had any natural talent, you began to develop a style of your own. He worked at it, day and night at the 2Is, only getting paid when Rick Richards had a night off. The most remunerative work he'd had was his short but educational interlude backing Vince Eager at twin nightclubs, Winston's in Clifford Street and Churchill's round the corner in Bond Street. There, lad that he was, he was able to hob-nob with upper crust punters (preferably the females) and play percussion with the resident band after Vince had done his set. Later, he would hang out in the Freight Train coffee bar, discussing the world with Chas McDevitt and the nightbirds of Soho.

Then, in August, another Vince turned up. Sheridan heard about Vince Taylor before he saw him, this tall sun-tanned American who was asking around, wanting to know who the best young rock 'n' roll musicians were. Along with his rich manager and a Hollywood guitarist, he was intending to form a band and take Britain by storm. He was going to be a star and he already had all the mythology in place – some even now impossible to unravel.

His manager, Joe Singer – also his brother-in-law – was claimed by some to have been Joseph Barbera, the former MGM animation artist famous for having produced over 200 *Tom & Jerry* cartoons. Since Barbera was 47, had recently formed Hanna Barbera Productions and was currently involved with the launch of *Huckleberry Hound*, this was never a credible story. It seems more likely that Joe Singer was Barbera's son or some more distant relative. Possibly no relative at all. One contemporary report described him as 'a news announcer'. Taylor was said to have been a former pupil at Hollywood High School, to hold a pilot's licence and to be something of a star in the clubs of California.

Some of it may have been true; he carried off any deception with consummate panache. Only years later did it emerge that Taylor had been born in Isleworth, Middlesex on 14 July 1939 and that his real name was Maurice Brian Holden. His family had emigrated to New Jersey after the war and by whatever convoluted route, he had ended up in Hollywood. He had just turned 19 when he investigated the 2Is cellar, coming down like a wolf on the fold, a fully-fledged rock 'n' roll animal the like of which had never been seen in the flesh, within touching distance.

The plan was audacious but sound. For a charismatic media-friendly American act, England would surely provide a sure-fire launch-pad. A few years later, the ploy worked perfectly for P.J. Proby, the Walker Brothers and Jimi Hendrix, but Taylor had a small problem: he was tone deaf.

"Joe Singer said that Vince was going to be the biggest thing since Elvis," recalls Tony Sheridan. "The only trouble was, he couldn't sing. He was a bad singer, had no voice . . . but he was a great showman, knew how to get an audience going."

Rick Richards agrees. "He was the greatest mover I'd ever seen and he had the kind of looks that sent the girls into a trance. As a package he would have been fantastic – if only he'd had a voice!"

Such considerations were considered relatively unimportant, it would seem, and Taylor recruited the cream of the coffee bar kids to become his backing group, the Playboys: Tony Sheridan on guitar,

Tony Meehan on drums and Licorice Locking on bass. They sallied forth, making little headway. Meehan quickly left, to be replaced by the latest 2Is live-wire Brian Bennett – at 18, already a veteran of Erroll Hollis and the Velvets, the Worried Men, the Red Peppers and Vince Eager's Vagabonds. Next to leave was Taylor's American pal Bob Frieberg, who felt that London's climate compared unfavourably with the 365 days a year sunshine he could experience back home. "He was hardly the best guitarist in the world," says Sheridan, "his best shot was *Rumble*". Into the band came Tony Harvey, 2Is innocent, most recently the driving wheel in one of many skiffle groups called the Spiders.

Strangely, gigs were few but Taylor soon scored a short-term contract with Parlophone. The subordinate status of the band was confirmed on the label of his début single, released in November 1958, which was credited to Vince Taylor 'with Rhythm Accompaniment'. *Right Behind You Baby* was a Charlie Rich song, recorded and released by Ray Smith on the Sun label earlier in the year and the Playboys did their best to duplicate it – doing the same on the B-side *I Like Love*, another Sun original, this one by struggling rockabilly singer Roy Orbison. Even if Taylor sounds gauche and overwrought – out of tune, time, tone and timbre – the guitar solos have panache and fluency. The single was an early favourite of rock history connoisseur Jimmy Page, who would later affirm that, in his opinion, "the only English guitarist who was any good during that time was Tony Sheridan". Page's session buddy Big Jim Sullivan, then a 2Is inmate keeping tabs on Sheridan, agrees: "He was the best rock 'n' roll guitarist around, no doubt about it."

Television producer Jack Good believed this too – and would give Sheridan the opportunity to shine on his new show *Oh Boy!* But then, to the surprise of all who knew him, Sheridan blew it.

Thirty-two

Seen by vicars and Sunday school teachers as good clean fun, a positive and creative influence on the nation's youth, skiffle had been approved and embraced by the church. Indeed, the first book on the subject *Skiffle: The Story Of Folk Song With A Jazz Beat*, published towards the end of 1958 (just in time to miss the wave and miss the boat), was written by Brian Bird, who – when he wasn't out jiving or raving it up with his band, the Box River Jazzmen – served God as the Vicar of Edwardstone and Groton, two small parishes in Suffolk. This did not impress Ken Colyer, the originator of the genre, who had little time for the clergy: "The Bible is the most boring book I ever tried to read," he wrote in his autobiography, "except for the psalms and the bit about a time to live and a time to die." Nor could he stand the Salvation Army, which had, in many towns, introduced skiffle into its evangelistic activities. "A bunch of damned God-botherers!" he ranted. "Half these people don't know a thing about true Christianity; they seek refuge in religion because they are moral weaklings."

It needed Jerry Lee Lewis to come in and shake them up a bit. He had studied at the South-western Bible Institute at Waxahachie, Texas, intending to become a preacher, like his cousin Jimmy Swaggart, but had ditched college to play the devil's music and, as his biographer Nick Tosches suggested, was prey to "the fate befalling those who served Satan with their God-given gifts". In May 1958, he arrived in London to start a 35-date tour, hot on the heels of his third Top 10 hit *Breathless* – another manic celebration of lust and lechery to match *Whole Lotta Shakin' Goin' On* and the number one *Great Balls Of Fire*. "Like most rock 'n' roll fans in Britain, Bruce and I couldn't wait to see him," says Hank Marvin, now scuffling in London but going without food to buy his ticket for Jerry Lee's show at Kilburn State Theatre on Sunday 25 May. "It was a great thrill, just to see him walk out on stage and start running his hands up and down the keyboard, but in some ways, he was a bit of a disappointment. He was very arrogant and we couldn't work out if it was part of his natural personality or an act, all the hair-combing and snarling. It got up a lot of people's noses, him being so cocky."

Cocky he most certainly was, and cock-happy too, apparently. Jerry Lee might have been a lion on stage but he was a lamb ready for slaughter when tabloid journalists realised what a story they had. Quite open about his past, the unsophisticated 22-year-old Louisiana country boy admitted: "I was a bigamist when I was 16". He also revealed that Myra, the young girl at his side – described by one newspaper as "a tiny, snub-nosed honey blonde, who wore no make-up and no wedding ring" – was his third wife. On Monday 26 May, the morning after his Kilburn concert, the *Daily Mirror*'s front-page headline screamed: 'Police Check Up On Child Bride'. The *Daily Sketch* was even more dramatic: 'Police To Act In Case Of Mrs Rock, Aged 13'.

It all came out. Lewis had married Dorothy Barton at 16 but soon impregnated Jane Mitcham, whose brothers enforced a shotgun, albeit bigamous, wedding. He was still married to Mitcham when, on 12 December 1957, he secretly married 13-year-old Myra, the daughter of his bass-player, Jay Brown – who was the son of his Aunt Jane. His divorce came through four months later, on the eve of his British tour. Goodness gracious, great balls of fire! Jerry Lee, a man who claimed to have been born "feet first with a hard-on", was even now sharing a room and a bed at the Westbury Hotel in Conduit Street with his 13-year-old cousin. Shake it, baby, shake! Was this revolting specimen a suitable role model for British teenagers, wondered self-righteous journalists? Reluctantly, after only three dates, agents Lew and Leslie Grade were pressured into cancelling Jerry Lee's contract and he was sent packing. "If the tour had been allowed to continue, it might have done irreparable damage to British show business and pop music in general," claimed Leslie Grade. "It seems such a great shame that Lewis had to make public his private life; we are now forced to suffer in many ways for his actions." It broke his heart to see all those shekels going down the drain.

The tour continued with Chas McDevitt's Skiffle Group and Terry Wayne substituting for the disgraced Jerry Lee. Rather like Marlon Brando dropping out of a picture and being replaced by Donald Sinden and Michael Medwin. On his return to the States, Lewis was forced to humble himself and beg forgiveness from the industry, the disc jockeys and journalists and tour promoters. "There were some legal misunderstandings in this matter that inadvertently made me look as though I invented the word indecency," he explained in a full-page apology, ghost-written by Sun Records boss Sam Phillips and published in both *Cash Box* and *Billboard*. "I hope that if I am washed up as an entertainer it won't be because of this bad publicity, because I can cry and wish all that I want to, but I can't control the press or the sensationalism that these people will go to in order to get a scandal started to sell papers."

Never again would he find the US Top 20 and he would spend 10 years in the wilderness before clawing his way back via country music and Nashville. All for the love of a girl, as he ruefully accepted.

Their paths had yet to cross those of Hank and Bruce, but also at the Kilburn State gig were a clutch of fans so committed that they talked their way backstage and even managed to get their photograph taken with their idol. Capturing a seminal moment in British rock 'n' roll history, it shows Johnny Foster, Harry Webb, Terry Smart and Ian Samwell flanking Jerry Lee like a close-up from the Last Supper – which is what it turned out to be. But even as the singer was being publicly crucified, his disciples were preparing to go out and spread the word, celebrating real country music that just drives along, in all its inspirational glory.

Harry Webb had been born in Lucknow, India, on 14 October 1940, and had started his education in Howrah, on the opposite bank of the Hugli River from Calcutta, during what were literally the last days of the Raj. Thinking they would be able to weather the transition to home rule, following Britain's capitulation in August 1947, the Webbs stayed put for another year – but when the situation turned ugly with religious and anti-colonial riots, they traversed the country by train, some 1,400 miles to Bombay, where they caught a P&O liner for Tilbury.

Neither Harry, nor his two sisters, nor even his parents had seen England before – his father had been born in Rangoon, Burma; his mother in Lahore, India – but they made their way to Carshalton in Surrey, where all five shared one room in his granny's house. For a family who had known no other life than respect, privilege, comparative wealth, servants and sunshine, it was an upheaval impossible to imagine, difficult to endure.

Harry's dark complexion (a legacy from his half-Spanish great-grandmother, according to assiduous biographer Steve Turner) and his Indian-inflected diction were strange to classmates accustomed to suburban conformity. The crueller ones mocked him, called him 'nigger' – and this taunt followed him when the family moved to his aunt's house in Waltham Cross, and finally to their own council house in Cheshunt, in April 1951. Only when he revealed a talent for sport was he treated civilly. He failed his 11-plus but at Cheshunt Secondary Modern, he excelled at football, rugby and athletics, track and field. At Holy Trinity Youth Club, he rehearsed with a two-boy, three-girl vocal harmony group, the Quintones, although by this time he was under the spell of rock 'n' roll and could only summon maximum intensity for his solo spot, *Heartbreak Hotel*.

In March 1957, after bunking off school to secure his ticket, he saw Bill Haley & his Comets at the Regal, Edmonton – a concert that filled his head with dreams. Four months later, he left school with one O level, enough for a position in the credit control department of Atlas Lighting, a division of Thorn Electrical at Enfield. If he worked hard for the next 49 years, he could leave with a gold watch and a decent pension.

Although he preferred rock 'n' roll, he joined the Dick Teague Skiffle Group and rolled with the flow, learning the standard lyrics and enjoying the confidence-boosting admiration of youth club audiences – but ideological differences, usually those concerning presentation and repertoire, always simmered and in January 1958, Harry and drummer Terry Smart broke away to form a Presley-orientated group, the Drifters.

"I hated skiffle and the leader of the group was always trying to show me how to sing," Webb told journalist John Ennis. "I left and the drummer left with me – but he had to wait until I learned the guitar. My father had an old one and promised to buy me a new one if I learned to play it. It took me three weeks to learn six chords, enough to play in the keys of G and C."

Long-time friend Norman Mitham was co-opted as second guitarist and, as a trio, they disguised musical shortcomings with unrestrained energy and enthusiasm. Whenever he sang, Harry Webb was gripped by the conviction that this was what he was meant to do – a notion confirmed by whatever supernatural forces were guiding him. He had suffered enough during his first 17 years;

from now on, he would enjoy a charmed life. 1958 would unfold like a fairy tale.

The Drifters made their début in March, during a social evening at Forty Hill Badminton Club, just north of Enfield. "I said to the club secretary 'Would you like us to do a show for you?' He said 'No, not really' – but we did. We whipped up 20 minutes of frenzy, people were clapping like mad, amateurs getting away with murder." Among the numbers they performed that night were *Be Bop A Lula*, *Ready Teddy* and *Long Tall Sally*. Later that month, they performed at the Five Horseshoes, a pub in Hoddesdon, a few miles up the road from Cheshunt. Lounging at the bar was sewage worker and rock 'n' roll fanatic Johnny Foster, who, in a spontaneous gesture inspired by Webb's magnetism, offered to become their manager. His experience in the field was non-existent although he had been to the 2Is Coffee Bar a couple of times and knew Tom Littlewood enough to stop for a chat. An audition was arranged, followed by a handful of unpaid gigs. At the first, they persuaded Rick Richards, another 2Is hopeful, to augment their line-up in a talent contest at the Trocadero, Elephant & Castle, on Wednesday 9 April. They came nowhere and four days later, Richards became leader of the coffee bar's resident group, the Worried Men.

It was during the Drifters' second 2Is appearance that Ian Samwell came up and introduced himself. Did they want a lead guitarist, he asked?

Born in Lambeth on 19 January 1938, Samwell was a bit older, a former public school boy now finishing his national service in the RAF. Only two months to go; out in June. The whole episode had been a waste of time, of course. "They asked me what my interests were, and I told them I was keen on electronics," says Samwell, "but they stuck me in an office and made me a typist."

Most of the time, he was shunted around – from RAF Cardington in Bedfordshire, on to some base on the Wirral, then down to Herefordshire, all over the place. Some weekends he accompanied a barracks-mate to Ashford in Kent, to play in the Ash Valley Skiffle Group – but he was soon looking to play more adventurous music, which is what led him to the 2Is. "My mother was suffering from asthma, was in and out of hospital, so I was given a compassionate posting to Hendon Aerodrome, which meant I could go up to St Albans on the train and out to London Colney, where she was living.

I was assigned to a squadron leader at Hendon, typing out reports, and the only interesting interludes were occasional route-training flights to Jersey, which was a duty-free zone. I could come back with a load of cheap liquor. Far more stimulating, however, was the fact that I could jump on the tube and explore Soho, whenever I managed to skive off for the evening. Sometimes I would take my guitar, other times a set of bongos, which I used to bash in a variety of cafés. I had no idea what I was doing but it all seemed wonderfully bohemian."

Samwell had been to the 2Is before but on that evening in April, he was galvanised by the Drifters. "There was this kid, shirt collar up, legs flailing, belting out all my favourite songs, almost in a trance. I think they were a bit apprehensive about me. Standing there in my corduroy trousers, check shirt and duffle coat, I must have looked a bit naïve and country but as soon as we started talking about Elvis and Chuck and Jerry Lee and Gene, they realised that I was on the same wavelength." He joined the group, managing to escape from Hendon for the odd rehearsal, even made another gig at the 2Is. There they were told by Tom Littlewood that a man called Harry Greatorex had been in, looking to book a band for his dance hall in Derbyshire. Tom had recommended the Drifters.

It was Greatorex who prompted the expansion of their name – convincing them, with little difficulty, that a name like Bill Haley & his Comets or Gene Vincent & the Blue Caps would have more panache, would add dazzle to posters and publicity. They retired (some say to Heaven & Hell, the coffee bar next to the 2Is, others to the Swiss Tavern, a few doors further up Old Compton Street) to confect an identity that Harry Webb could inhabit comfortably. Out of the blue came 'Cliff', which seemed to jigsaw well with 'Richards'. It was Samwell who suggested dropping the S, partly in deference to their hero Little Richard, partly to add distinction and memorability. "We've just borrowed your name," Samwell told Rick Richards, when they returned to the 2Is. A few months down the line, Cliff signed a publicity photograph for him: "To my pal Ricky, Sorry I pinched your name, Cliff".

On Saturday 3 May, they travelled up to Ripley by train and bus to play their first out-of-town gig – and Greatorex was absolutely spot-on: the guys were highly impressed to see their name displayed outside the Regal Ballroom: Cliff Richard & the Drifters. They were less impressed to discover that they would have to spend the night, locked in, trying to sleep on wooden benches or the floor. Welcome to the world of rock 'n' roll.

It was a world Norman Mitham would barely glimpse. On the grounds that his guitar was superfluous, he was aced out – the first of the Drifters to get the bullet.

The morning after the Jerry Lee Lewis concert, on a rare day off (for the Queen's official birthday), Samwell went to see an agent whose name and address he had plucked from *The Stage*.

George Ganjou had an office at 26 Albemarle Street, just off Piccadilly, and described his organisation as "Booking agents for high-class acts and artistes, home and abroad". Though Samwell could have had no inkling, it was something of an overstatement. Ganjou in fact had very little in the way of durable or even promising acts. When Samwell bounced through his door it was as if the golden goose had waddled in, the one all agents and managers dream about.

"He was a very distinguished looking Jewish gentleman, eastern European, elegant, refined, a sweet man," says Samwell, who sat and drank tea as he explained to the bemused agent that he and his friends had a rock 'n' roll group. "I'm not sure that he had a clue what I was talking about but I obviously aroused his curiosity."

Until the previous year, Ganjou, born to a Russian father and Polish mother, had been performing himself, in the Ganjou Brothers and Juanita, one of the most successful acts on the international variety circuit. Their speciality was adagio, a mixture of dance and acrobatics in which the girl (Joy Marlowe, a classically trained ballet dancer who was married to Serge Ganjou) was twirled, spun, thrown around and caught by the three brothers. They called their lavishly costumed and choreographed act Romance in Porcelain. When the bottom fell out of variety, and they were reduced to playing Luton's Alma Theatre with Mrs Shufflewick, the Two Redheads and Puposy's Marionettes, they quit. Serge (who, in 1998, would leave over £1.25 million in his will) opened a Polish restaurant in South Kensington; George, addicted to the smell of the greasepaint, started a theatrical agency.

George Ganjou agreed to see the group at Shepherds Bush Gaumont, a gig organised by Johnny Foster. "When he saw what was happening, the kids going nuts over Cliff, running down the aisles, causing pandemonium, he took us on," says Samwell. "The screaming had started and he knew something was going on; Cliff was so good, even then."

On Ganjou's advice, they recorded two sample tracks in the demo studio above the HMV shop in Oxford Street. *Lawdy Miss Clawdy* was inspired by Elvis Presley's impassioned early 1956 revival, so intense that it eclipsed Lloyd Price's original. While the Drifters could manage only a rudimentary approximation, Cliff already had the oxygen in his voice, the baton in his hand. *Breathless*, a song they had so recently seen Jerry Lee Lewis perform, bonded them as brothers as much as any other. Ganjou listened to their crude skiffle-rock, played as if their future depended on it – which it did – and asked if they would rather be on Decca or Columbia. They told him Columbia.

"Looking back, it seems amazing that everything fell into place so smoothly," says Samwell, "but we accepted it as the way things were done. What you did was form a group, do some gigs, make a demo, go and see a man with a big cigar, he got you a recording contract, you went on television and signed autographs, and all the girls loved you. That's exactly the way it happened; we hardly gave it a second thought."

True to his word, Ganjou arranged a meeting with Columbia's recording manager, Norrie Paramor, who agreed to give them a whirl. As was the customary practice, he gave them a copy of an American record to learn – in this case *Schoolboy Crush* by Bobby Helms. The song was Tin Pan Alley dreck, the B-side of Helms's latest release *Borrowed Dreams*, which itself only managed to stagger up to number 60 on *Billboard*'s Hot 100. Paramor was in his mid-forties, a former dance band pianist who had made his name creating hits for such middle-of-the-road acts as Eddie Calvert, Ruby Murray and Michael Holliday. His latest success was the Mudlarks, a Light Programme trio from Vauxhall Motors in Luton, who were currently in the chart with a vapid version of the Monotones' clever US hit *Book Of Love*. As straight as a rifle barrel, Paramor obviously possessed no rock 'n' roll antennae.

On 24 July, he got Cliff, Samwell and Smart into EMI's number 2 studio at Abbey Road and went to work. With the usual canteen ladies cooing and whistling in the background, and a couple of session bods attempting to give it a *Music While You Work* veneer, *Schoolboy Crush* was silliness incarnate, but Paramor was eminently satisfied. Having put all the eggs into the A-side basket, he allowed the lads to record their own song on the B-side. It was called *Move It* and they got it in two takes.

While their single was being readied for release, the group, along with Johnny Foster, went to Clacton for a two-week stretch at Butlin's Holiday Camp – organised by Ganjou. It would get them into shape, allow them to rehearse as they played, let them get used to being bona fide professional musicians. Cliff quit his life-time position at Ferguson's on 7 August and they left for Clacton the next day. Terry Smart had given up his job as a butcher's boy and Ian Samwell was free of the RAF. "My family always believed that I would go off to university," says Samwell, "but I didn't want to – and I didn't have to, because we had a residency at Butlin's and a record coming out. We were going to make it; there was never any doubt in our minds about that. We knew we were really good at what we did, in the sense of being the real thing as opposed to the fake stuff. Obviously, nobody here could hold a candle to Chuck Berry or Gene Vincent or Little Richard, but we were closer to the real thing than anyone else around."

Unsure how to present a rock 'n' roll trio, the entertainment manager at Butlin's put them in the bar, then the ballroom and finally in a theatre as part of the variety show. "It was Butlin's Concentration Camp," jokes Samwell, "and we never went beyond the fences the whole time we were there. All we did was just sit around in the sunshine playing guitars all day. Johnny and I had one chalet, because we smoked; Cliff and Terry had the other, because they didn't. We used to put on our white stage outfits, with a B for Butlin's embroidered on the front, and go out and do the show thinking that this was probably the way Elvis had started"

Cliff's first live recording, made by redcoat Stanley Edwards on a Grundig TK5, on a wooden chair, on a wooden floor, in a sparsely populated ballroom, captured the 17-year-old kid who wanted to be famous. He could sing every song that Elvis had ever recorded, and did, from *Heartbreak Hotel* to *Hard Headed Woman*, *Milk Cow Blues* to *Money Honey*. All the Jerry Lee, much of the Gene and Little Richard, some Chuck Berry, and the Eddie Cochran classic *Twenty-Flight Rock*. Sang their own song too, at every opportunity: *Move It*.

The publishers of *Schoolboy Crush*, Aberbach Music, sent out their plugger Franklyn Boyd with test pressings of the single, to see if he could persuade radio and television producers to feature Cliff on their programmes. There were no enthusiastic takers, just as there had been no positive feedback from journalists and reviewers. No one thought much of his record, so it seemed. It looked as if Cliff was destined to become just another mouse on the EMI treadmill to nowhere, like Adam Faith and Larry Page, both of whom had fallen through the rungs, so it seemed.

Strangely, Norrie Paramor had seen no merit in *Move It*, nor had anyone at the record company. To them, it was nothing more than a filler B-side.

Thank God for Jack Good. Everything changed on that day in August 1958 when Franklyn Boyd went to see Good and pleaded with him to listen to *Schoolboy Crush*. Cliff's career hinges on that moment. Without Good, he may never have dreamed of a fabulous mansion in Barbados, let alone a knighthood.

Boyd was only working as a plugger until his own singing career took off, although there was little sign of this happening in the near future, or the far future, come to that. A recent peak had been duff versions of *Bye Bye Love* and *Teddy Bear*, available only if you sent a postal order for 1/6d and three milk chocolate wrappers to Nestlé's head office.

He played *Schoolboy Crush* for Jack Good, who must have rolled his eyes heavenward and dismissed Cliff as nothing more than another pretty wimp being jerked around by the string-pullers of Tin Pan Alley. Spare us all! Nondescript beyond nondescription. What possessed him to turn the record over and listen to the B-side has never been adequately explained, not even by him, but Good was out of his chair and jumping around in amazement before it was 30 seconds in.

Good looked at Boyd. Boyd looked at Good. What was going on here? "Where can I see this fellow?" Good asked, perspiring freely, as Boyd remembered. Jack Good heard in Cliff what Sam Philips had heard in Elvis. He was the first.

Boyd reported back. "Why?" wondered Paramor. The record was flipped. *Move It* became the A-side. Even the rock 'n' roll cognoscenti, those purists who refused anything non-American on principle, had to admit that this was a fantastic record. In schools across the country it was discussed with a reverence reserved for the greats. It was a milestone, a breakthrough, a turning point. The road had suddenly forked off; English acts were capable of producing great stuff too.

Ian Samwell had written *Move It* on the bus between London Colney, where he lived with his mother in Peters Avenue, and Cheshunt, where Cliff lived with his family at 12 Hargreaves Close. Fate having thrown them into the same quadrant of suburbia, they were able to meet regularly during the summer, to rehearse in Cliff's front room, to play records, to talk about records, to go into the town centre and buy records. "I remember rushing in, terribly excited, telling him that I had written a song," says Samwell. "It was just a few lines and just a few notes, nothing really, but it was my first attempt."

The lyric, born of fury and written with brimming-over passion, had been prompted by Steve Race's most recent diatribe in *Melody Maker*. The grumpy old fossil who had two years earlier urged readers to "oppose rock 'n' roll to the end", describing it as "a monstrous threat, the most terrifying thing ever to have happened to popular music", was now crowing over its demise.

"So rock 'n' roll is dead, is it?" he wrote, although how he had come to arrive at this conclusion is unclear. "My funeral oration consists of just two words: good riddance. Perhaps now we shall see some sense of proportion returning to the pop music business." Or perhaps not. How ironic that his causticity should have inspired the greatest record to have been made in Britain, up to that point.

"So thank you, Steve Race, and God bless you," says Samwell. "I owe it all to you. Please know that to me, at least, you are the true father of British rock 'n' roll."

In the studio, Ian Samwell's surging rhythm guitar and Terry Smart's drumming drove the song, setting the tempo and feel. Session guitarist Ernie Shear, working under Samwell's direction and happy to experiment, played the intro, the fills and the solo; Frank Clarke, another dance-band veteran, gave it a solid bass line. Meaning every word, Cliff sang it with an assurance and authority that belied his youth and inexperience. Up in the control room, recently recruited recording engineer Malcolm Addy added echo, boosted the sound and set the levels to create a hotter, more atmospheric mix than anything that had ever come out of Abbey Road before. In less than half an hour, the six of them had painted the first masterpiece of British rock.

Without telling him the name of the artist, Jack Good played *Move It* for Marty Wilde. "Yes, it's marvellous," said Marty, "but, of course, you could never get a sound like that on this side of the Atlantic."

"He's from Hertfordshire," Good told him. "His name's Cliff Richard and I've just booked him for *Oh Boy!*"

Thirty-three

Marty Wilde had killed himself for over six months, on the road almost continuously, standing up there with his guitar, going for it every night, twice a night. He did what Larry Parnes told him, even when Larry told him to sing *Who's Sorry Now* wearing a straw hat and whirling a cane about like some variety pillock. He was not amused by some of Larry's ideas. Making him sing current hits like *Witch Doctor*, for instance. It seemed as if he'd seen every dreary town in the country, as if he'd sung *Treat Me Nice* and *Mean Woman Blues* a million times. Meanwhile, three singles – *Honeycomb, Love Bug Crawl* and *Oh Oh, I'm Falling In Love Again* – had barely registered any sales and he was beginning to wonder what else he could do to make something happen.

June 1958 was the turning point month. His recording manager Johnny Franz actually identified an American hit that matched his moody aura.

When Marty recorded it, the original version of *Endless Sleep*, by its composer Jody Reynolds, was heading for the US Top 10. The lyric concerned his girlfriend's threatened suicide by drowning, following an argument he feels guilty about, so guilty that he rushes to save her from the angry sea, intending no doubt to hold her close forever more – an interesting and unusual conceit-laden film-noir scenario, rather more provocative than traditional pop fare. For Marty's version, the studio musicians, hired session mercenaries, were asked to duplicate the American record note for note, as closely as possible. This they did – even though they had no emotional interest in the task. Guitarists Ernie Shear and Bert Weedon treated it as just another job; drummer Phil Seamen scowled throughout. Although Jody Reynolds must take full credit for the concept and realisation, from the musical arrangement to each and every vocal inflection, Marty was able to improve on the original. Some newspapers called the record sick and perverted, *NME*'s reviewer considered it "morbid and unpleasant", but fans loved it. "I'm not really mixed up," said Marty at the time, "I've just got my problems like anybody else." Very soon *Endless Sleep* was at number four on the charts and Marty was an overnight star.

This was no surprise to Jack Good, who, since leaving the BBC in February, had been mulling over ideas for another television series, and had come to the conclusion that Marty Wilde was the ideal man to carry it. For the ITV network, he made two pilot shows in June, transmitted only in the Midlands. He called the new programme *Oh Boy!*, after the Crickets hit, and he had his team in place.

Good's idea was to recreate the pace and excitement of Alan Freed's stage shows, to have a versatile orchestra of experienced but brash and ready-to-rock musicians, drawn from jazz and dance bands, and a parade of singers, one after the other, minimum chat between them. Tony Hall and Jimmy Henney were suave, hip and laconic compères; Marty was the main man, over a supporting cast which included the John Barry Seven, Lord Rockingham's XI, Neville Taylor & his Cutters, the Dallas Boys, the Vernon Girls and his latest discovery, Cliff Richard & the Drifters. A relentless half-hour, it made the *6.5 Special* look like *Woman's Hour* – which was a pity for the BBC. Starting on 13 September, *Oh Boy!* was broadcast nationwide every Saturday night, in direct competition with its rival. By the end of the year, three times as many viewers were tuning in to the new show.

Larry Parnes had Marty working to maximum capacity, touring right up until the television series started. Reviewing his show at the Finsbury Park Empire, during the first week of September, the *NME* described his backing group, the first set of Wild Cats, as "a solemn lot" – which was hardly surprising because Parnes had just told them that their services would no longer be required after Saturday. Out on the street. Most backing musicians were serfs as far as he was concerned. Guitarist Kenny Packwood got lucky and was given a job in Lord Rockingham's XI, some of whom would become familiar faces over the weeks. Wearing shades and a devious expression, Red Price became the country's leading tenor sax honker and Cherry Wainer, a South African who sat at an upholstered Hammond wearing low-neck gowns and a radiant smile, introduced the flowing organ sound to British pop.

The *Oh Boy!* cast were required to rehearse for four days each week at the Four Provinces of Ireland Club at 13 Canonbury Lane in Islington, to work on songs and arrangements, camera angles, lighting effects, staging and continuity, everyone getting vibed up, accelerating towards the Saturday night show, transmitted live from the Empire Theatre in Hackney. No other television or radio programme, newspaper or magazine, exerted a greater influence on teenage taste – but although the personable Marty Wilde quickly won his way into the hearts of viewers (those with sets capable of receiving ITV), his chart progress was severely hampered by his record company's lame choice of material. Even as he was cutting it, he knew his fifth single *Misery's Child* was hopeless: "It's a bad record," he admitted. "If it gets into the hit parade, it doesn't deserve to." It didn't. Knowing its all-pervading gloom would compromise the upbeat momentum of the show, Jack Good refused to let him sing it on *Oh Boy!* – a decision that incensed the self-important Larry Parnes.

The hapless Wilde found himself a pawn in his manager's ego-flexing power plays. "Has a craving for publicity influenced Larry Parnes to make unwise decisions on Marty Wilde's behalf recently?" asked the *NME*'s Alley Cat. In late October, after six *Oh Boy!* shows, Parnes pulled him from the series, claiming at a press conference that Good was "trying to develop a virtually unknown artiste (Cliff Richard) at the expense of Marty." As another doom-laden single *No One Knows* bit the dust, Wilde was shuffled off into the wilderness. Instead of building on his considerable television success, he was forced to play a string of one-nighters in such backwaters as Worksop, Wombwell, Scunthorpe and Pontefract. A teenage idol, a national star, he was back spending his nights in a succession of theatrical digs – Mrs Wilson's at 1 Cromwell Street, Burnley and Mrs Cronin's at 30 Salisbury Road, Cardiff. At least they had indoor lavatories.

There was worse to come at the end of the year. While his rivals were thriving on *Oh Boy!*, Wilde was dispatched to Stockton-on-Tees, to spend a whole month – including Christmas and the New Year – marooned in pantomime at the Hippodrome, playing Will Scarlet in *Babes In The Wood*. "I want to end my contract with Larry Parnes," he told the newspapers. No chance: it still had three years to run. Marty had to swallow. "This will be my first and last pantomime," he swore. "I'm not awfully keen on the idea but I realise the experience will be good." It was certainly interesting. Chas McDevitt's Skiffle Group were also in the show: Chas played Richard the Lionheart,

Shirley Douglas was Maid Marian, drummer Red Reece was Little John and pianist Roy Powell was Friar Tuck. Shirley would declare "Look, here comes Will Scarlet!" – at which point Marty would appear, clad in red tights, and sing *I'm Dreaming Of A White Christmas*. Unlike the others, he took no part in the plot, merely returning at the end to sing *It's Only Make Believe, Someday, I Can't Give You Anything But Love, King Creole* and *Maybe Baby*, backed up by McDevitt and his group.

Larry Parnes had his other acts in pantomime too. Tommy Steele was at the London Coliseum starring in *Cinderella*, a show so successful that its run was extended until April 1959. Vince Eager was playing Simple Simon in *Mother Goose* at the Garrick Theatre in Southport. At least he had a couple of mates with him: Tex Makins from the Worried Men, who had backed him at Churchill's Club during the summer and had just traded in his string bass for a bass guitar, and Joe Moretti, a 20-year-old Glaswegian freshly arrived in London. He'd barely had time to unpack his suitcase before he was on his way to Southport, where they used the pit-band drummer to round out their sound.

Eager was making headway, slowly but surely. He was having a high old time: it was better than being an apprentice chippie in Grantham. During the autumn of 1958, he had toured with Marty Wilde and the John Barry Seven, had appeared on both the *6.5 Special* and *Oh Boy!* (though only once, thanks to the Good-Parnes feud), and had been signed by Parlophone. His first single for them was *No More*, copied from a recent Atlantic release by the ridiculously named Two Chaps. Drivel. Among the most cretinous records of the era. Poor Vince was doing the best he could but was surrounded by record company people with little or no idea.

Meanwhile, Cliff Richard's career was picking up speed like a runaway train. Columbia had released his début single *Schoolboy Crush/Move It* on 29 August 1958 – along with such contenders as *Luxembourg Waltz* by the Big Ben Banjo Band, *My Lucky Love* by Johnny Duncan & the Blue Grass Boys, *Belonging To Someone* by Dennis Lotis and *Land Of My Fathers* by the Band of the Welsh Guards. Ten days later, Cliff showed up for his first *Oh Boy!* rehearsal and followed Jack Good's instructions to shave off his sideboards and drop the guitar. Elvis comparisons were bound to be hurled, but the fewer the better, Jack told him. "Has it ever struck you what awkward lumpy silly things hands can be?" asked Cliff in his first autobiography. Jack Good taught him to relax and move his arms naturally. On the first show, his first television appearance, Cliff sang *Move It*, which slowly climbed the chart to number two.

Immediately recognised as a natural born star, he was offered a slot on the latest package tour. Having seen him on television and bought his record, the promoters correctly figured, teenagers would flock to see him at their local concert hall – boosting ticket sales, which had so far been sluggish. And who could wonder? The bill juxtaposed Eddie Calvert, the profoundly square golden trumpet virtuoso, and the anonymous Kalin Twins, an American duo whose candyfloss single *When* had been catchy and innocuous enough to attract maximum BBC airplay and rise to number one on the chart. It would remain their career peak: sadly, they came to epitomise the term (yet to be coined) 'one hit wonder'. Also on the tour were the sharp-looking peroxide-blond Most Brothers, whose third single *Dottie* had already missed the boat.

The Drifters suddenly felt inadequate. Unwilling to commit, their latest recruit, guitarist Ken Pavey, had already dropped out and they were back to two: Terry Smart and Ian Samwell. Thinking that he might be able to lure Tony Sheridan into the fold, Johnny Foster made a beeline for his usual hang-out, the 2Is coffee bar. "He'll be in later," Tom Littlewood told him – even though he should have known that Sheridan was on the road with Vince Taylor, a fully paid-up member of his Playboys. While he waited, Foster got into conversation with Rick Richards, who told him about Hank Marvin. On Friday 19 September, on a day off from the 2Is, Richards had played at the Bridge House in Canning Town, taking along a group comprising Tony Meehan (still nominally in the Vipers, although their gig sheet was barren), Bruce Welch and Hank Marvin, whose dexterity had astonished him. He gave Hank's number to Foster, who was surprised to find that he was already booked for the tour – as a member of the Most Brothers' backing group.

Hank agreed to double up and play for Cliff too, but only if his mate Bruce could be part of the band. This suited all parties. Ian Samwell would switch to bass guitar; Hank would play lead guitar; Bruce would play rhythm guitar; Terry would play drums, as usual; Cliff could ditch his instrument and concentrate on singing, as he had on *Oh Boy!* On Sunday 5 October, the revised Drifters line-up took the stage of the Victoria Hall in Hanley – the first of 12 one-nighters, spread around the country. "Were we intimidated? Not at all!" says Samwell. "That's what we did . . . we had seen the films!" It was the start of a long journey – but only for some of them.

Already, kids were coming backstage, wanting to meet Cliff in the same way that he had wanted to meet Jerry Lee Lewis, less than five months earlier. Admiration, respect and, for some of them, sexual frisson. He was going places and everybody let him know it, not only the media, the business whisperers and the fans but also his mates and the boys on the bus, the tour charabanc.

Playing in the Most Brothers' band, alongside Hank, were drummer Pete Chester, whose Chesternuts had already folded, and bass player Jet Harris, who had recently left the disintegrating Vipers. Ideas were discussed, plots were hatched. "I suddenly got the impression that I was going to be edged out," says Samwell. "Cliff needed better guys in his band – and Jet was a much better, more experienced bass player than I was. He looked very cool too. So that was it for me. I was out. I'd sold my guitar to buy a bass; now I had to sell my bass to eat. I stuck around for a while, though, writing songs."

Novice manager Johnny Foster was on the way out too, out of his depth as Cliff's workload increased. Under pressure from both Norrie Paramor and Cliff's father, he downgraded to road manager and allowed Franklyn Boyd to take over the reins. During the last two months of 1958, Cliff's schedule was particularly merciless: press and radio interviews, photo-shoots, Sunday concerts, three full weeks of variety, more *Oh Boy!* shows (bringing his total for the year to 12), sundry other television shows, rehearsals, recording sessions, travelling huge distances, getting completely debilitated. Some days his voice was so blown that he could barely speak. Christmas off. Twenty-four hours, at least. In amongst it all, he was also making frequent early-morning journeys to Stevenage and Borehamwood, locations for his first film *Serious Charge*.

In what was called 'a dramatic role', a part Tommy Steele was said to have turned down, Cliff played Curly, a nervous pouting teenager caught up in a plot involving God, death, pregnancy and homosexuality. An X certificate excluded his fans, who probably wouldn't have understood or liked it anyway – but they still demanded the release of an extended player of the songs he recorded for the soundtrack. Not that good, not in their current state, anyway – but one of them, in a different guise, would soon become a classic.

"I put Cliff Richard up for the part in that film," says the author of those songs, Lionel Bart. "They wanted a Presley clone and some songs for him to sing, and they asked me to suggest somebody. I had seen Cliff on *Oh Boy!* and I'd heard his record, so I put him forward." He had not seen Cliff in the flesh, but he had seen his agent George Ganjou, in his adagio act. "Cliff did a screen test and got it. I went up to Cheshunt with the songs I'd written for him – *Living Doll, Mad About You* and *No Turning Back*. I remember taking this girl with me, a girl I was friendly with called June Wilkinson, who had enormous tits. Only 16 or 17. She had just had a photo-spread in the latest issue of *Playboy*." Well, Lionel always did have a wide circle of friends and an even wider imagination.

Cliff's fan-base was mushrooming daily, growing more vocal. Screaming fans mobbed him wherever he went. "I've had Johnnie Ray here, but it was never like this," said the manager of the Walthamstow Granada. "I've never seen anything like it . . . they just went wild."

As one would expect, a lot of adults didn't like it, thought he might herald a further decline in standards. Even though he had won the 'Most Promising Newcomer' category of the *NME*'s annual readers' poll, their Alley Cat castigated him for "the most crude exhibitionism ever seen on British television. His violent hip-swinging was revolting, hardly the kind of performance any parent could wish their children to see. If we are expecting to believe that Cliff was acting naturally, then consideration for medical treatment may be advisable. While firmly believing he can become a top star and enjoy a lengthy career, it will only be accomplished by dispensing with short-sighted, vulgar tactics." Watch that generation gap, you old creep.

"Nothing I did was shameful," protested the innocent singer. "I behave in a decent, proper manner." Clearly upset by the criticism, he addressed it at length in his autobiography. "The very word 'sexy' bothers me," he wrote. "It's used as if it were something not quite nice and in this way, it becomes smutty. Do the negroes in the jungle dancing to their drumbeat automatically think they are being 'sexy'? Of course they don't. The music gets into their blood and each movement they make is forced out because it expresses the music.

That's how it is with me, and that's how it is to all of us who love beat music."

By the end of the year, Cliff's father had stepped in. His Indian management sensibilities surfacing after a decade dormant, he felt unable to trust some of the natives to do a bang-up job. Only recently demoted, Johnny Foster left the organisation and was replaced by a more experienced road manager, Len Saxon – and, although he had only been his son's manager for a few weeks, Franklyn Boyd was summarily fired. That he had not even had time to organise a written contract facilitated this. Mr Webb now appointed – on the recommendation of *Oh Boy!* organist Cherry Wainer, so it seems – a new business manager, Tito Burns, who had an office at 39 Wardour Street and a list of clients with a limited shelf life: the Dargie Quintet, Dinah Dee's All Girl Orchestra, the Three Deuces, Bob Hammond's Cockatoos, the Three Kingpins, Isabelle Lucas and Zack Matalon, among them. Like Norrie Paramor, Tito disdained rock 'n' roll but knew he had to get his hands on some of it. For Cliff and his father, the appointment was a prudent move. Burns looked and acted the part: humorous, hard-working, protective, respected, well connected, big smile and big cigars, pencil-thin moustache, bespoke suits and an impressive phone manner. That he knew how to secure the most advantageous deal for his acts would later be confirmed in the Bob Dylan movie *Don't Look Back*. Tito had managed to land his first big fish, which must have pleased him no end. After all, as one of the antiquated resident bandleaders on *6.5 Special*, he had only recently given up playing the accordion to supplement his crust.

One of his first duties was to preside over the sacking of Cliff's best mate, Terry Smart. "He always had a hankering to join the Merchant Navy," explained Cliff in his autobiography.

"I think Terry knew his limitations," says Hank Marvin. "If he did a fill, he sometimes turned the beat around and it was difficult to keep in time. We had to put Cliff in the picture, had to say something – because he thought it was his fault, that he was coming in too late or too early. I felt sorry for Cliff, having to tell him, but in fact Terry was relieved because he was having trouble sleeping; he knew he wasn't playing well enough, that Cliff was in a different league now." Into the group came Tony Meehan, 2Is mate of Hank and Bruce; prodigy drummer. Just in time: he had been thinking of joining the Army.

Should Smart be seen as a Pete Best figure? Possibly not. He had been on wages. Even though *Move It* was released under the name of Cliff Richard & the Drifters, the naïve Smart and Samwell had been paid £7 session fees. The EMI contract was with Cliff alone. According to Samwell, neither he nor Terry ever received a penny in royalties.

January 1959. Cliff now had an entirely new set of Drifters and an entirely new management team. He had dumped his day job in August. After five months in the business, he was ready to go. It would still be an arduous climb.

Thirty-four

"Kids would rather listen to a jukebox than the Prime Minister," suggested Marty Wilde in one of his runaway interviews, admitting "Well, I would, really." Who could blame him? Harold Macmillan and the chaps in his government weren't exactly tuned in to teenagers. In fact, they didn't appear to have much in common with great swathes of the population. Rab Butler, the Chancellor of the Exchequer, had let the cat out of the bag when he said in a speech: "We must not drop back into easy evenings with port wine and over-ripe pheasant" – little realising that this lifestyle was unimaginable to most people. "He's dropped his silver spoon on the polished floor," mocked the *Daily Mirror*'s Cassandra.

Westminster was a different planet. The Conservatives had been in power since Winston Churchill brought them back to start a 13-year run in October 1951. Leading us through the cold, grey fog of post-war readjustment in their bowlers and Homburgs, they seemed to be honest and decent, the kind of people teenagers were taught to look up to and respect, and it was assumed that they knew what was best for the country. That was their job. But they had been testing atomic bombs since October 1952 and opposition to this policy was now beginning to spread. At the first meeting of the Campaign for Nuclear Disarmament, in February 1958, Bertrand Russell described how the whole human race was threatened by the continued development of nuclear weapons.

Unlikely though it may seem, Tommy Steele's manager John Kennedy was the first to express this anxiety in a teenage context. In the last chapter of his Steele biography, written only days after Russell's speech, Kennedy introduced a philosophical thread. "On the horizon there is a grisly spectre, a pall of mushroom-shaped smoke climbing into the sky. The threat of nuclear destruction. This is what every teenager, consciously or otherwise, is rebelling against."

If this were true, there was little evidence of it in April 1958, when only 4,000 hardy souls braved bitter cold, incessant rain and the first

Easter snow for a century, to take part in the first CND march, from
Trafalgar Square to the Atomic Weapons Research Establishment at
Aldermaston (subsequent marches took the opposite direction),
where the bombs were manufactured in *Quatermass*-style secrecy.
The CND symbol was seen for the first time, painted on banners and
printed on leaflets, and John Brunner's song *The H-bomb's Thunder*
was quickly adopted as the national anthem of the peace movement.
John Hasted and Eric Winter collaborated on the chorus, which
climaxed with the lines "Make your minds up, now or never: Ban the
bomb forever more!"

Ken Colyer's Jazz Band played at various points along the route,
as did the City Ramblers Skiffle Group – ignoring the muddle-
headed God-botherers who tried to prevent them from making
music on Good Friday. Also singing and handing out song sheets
were Ian Campbell and John Foreman, whose sons would eventually
become influential rock stars in UB40 and Madness.

No sign of any rock 'n' rollers at this stage, but plenty of CND
conscripts from the bohemian coffee bars. A new tag was about to be
applied to them: they would soon be derided as beatniks. The word
was coined by *San Francisco Chronicle* columnist Herb Caen in April
1958 and it would quickly cross the Atlantic to become a media
cliché. It sat well with some of the inmates of the Gyre & Gimble.
Jack Kerouac's *On The Road* was being passed around and people
were soon calling him a beatnik, so they felt they were in good
company. There were new faces in the G, but the core of the clientele
had changed little since the departure of Tommy Steele and Johnny
Booker.

John Hasted still went down there. "I'm sure some of them used
to say 'here comes that stupid academic cunt again' but they were
fine people." Respected not only for having organised so much
musical activity over the years (his latest role was musical director
for CND), Hasted was now accorded even greater admiration for
actually having met Woody Guthrie. "I was surprised they even let
me into the country, with my political background," he says, "but I
went over to New York for some scientific lectures. While I was there
I went to MacDougal Street in Greenwich Village to meet a girl who
had been in the London Youth Choir and was now married to a Yank
– and I got into conversation with a guitar player who was there,
Jerry Silverman. When he learned that I knew people like Rambling

Jack Elliott and Alan Lomax, he told me he was going to see Woody the next day and asked if I'd like to come along. So we went to Greystone Park in New Jersey, along with Millard Lampell, and there was Woody, his face very thin. He was just sitting there, couldn't walk. But he could communicate, he could speak and understand what was going on." Hasted didn't tell him that Lonnie was claiming co-authorship on several of his songs.

Two of Hasted's former skifflers, Redd Sullivan and Martin Winsor, were now singing as the Thameside Two – sometimes the Thameside Three if Alex Campbell was around. They had been busking under the bridge at Waterloo, outside the National Film Theatre for weeks on end and, after stopping to watch and listen many times, the owner of the nearby Thameside Restaurant had given them a residency, entertaining the diners. They kept the name, conferred by the restaurateur. The group would soon expand to include another former Hasted skiffler, Marion Amiss (by now Marion Gray), and this beanpole of a kid called John Baldry, who had made the Gyre & Gimble his second home.

That Easter of the first CND, Baldry was an intrepid 17 year old. He lived with his parents at Edgware, worked as a trainee designer in a commercial art studio, but was only really interested in music. Primarily blues music. He had started coming into Soho on Thursday nights, to go to the Blues & Barrelhouse Club at the Roundhouse, which Alexis Korner and Cyril Davies still kept up religiously. As Alexis said, "what other religion is there?" Baldry had just started playing guitar himself and was gaining confidence playing floor spots – and when he discovered that the Gyre & Gimble was open every night and that he could sing and play there at will, he was lost to the bohemian tradition.

"Much to Baldry's discomfort, his father came down to check the place out," says the subterranean Derek Duffy, "to find out where his errant son was spending his evenings. Of course, he saw a lot of guys with beards, which was the mark of the scoundrel as far as the establishment was concerned – and, being a policeman, he wasn't too happy. A bit later, when Baldry was talking about dropping his day job to concentrate on a career in music, both his parents came down and tried to get us to talk him out of it. Of course, we weren't prepared to do that because it was all he ever wanted to do. I can still picture him now, sitting there with his long legs stretched out in front of him (fully grown, he would achieve 6 feet 7 inches), one foot tapping on the floor, working furiously at a version of Big Bill Broonzy's *Hey Hey Baby Hey*: 'I love you baby, but I sure ain't gonna be your dog'."

"I consider myself to be lucky beyond description to have been able to see Broonzy at the 100 Club, singing and playing not more than a few feet away from me," said Baldry, recalling his first foray into central London. "He was such an idol to me. I was lucky enough to get my hands on a couple of singles he had cut for the French Vogue label when he first came to Europe, and another on the Melodisc label – the best records he ever made, in my opinion – and they were the ones I played all the time, and tried to copy. There was just something about their earthiness and directness that transported me. I had borrowed a 12-string guitar from a friend of mine in Edgware and couldn't wait to buy one myself – but that was easier said than done. Fortunately, at the Gyre & Gimble, I met a friend of Marion Gray's called Tony Zemaitis, who agreed to make one for me. He was a very skilled cabinet maker and wanted to get into building guitars – and I had the very first one he ever made."

1958 was shaping up to be a great year for blues aficionados, thanks in no small way to Chris Barber. When Johnny Duncan and Dickie Bishop had left his band to start their solo adventures in early 1957, Barber, who had done so much to popularise the style, dispensed with skiffle and concentrated entirely on jazz and blues. Already there were purist critics who knocked his band for being too calculating, too efficient – "there is nothing clever, nothing even original in their method of playing jazz," opined the respected egghead Sinclair Traill – but Barber and his team never stopped stretching and their professionalism was a result of telepathy rather than design. They had by now defined 'traditional jazz', as their fans and the media described it, and their rousing, well programmed shows made them phenomenally successful wherever they went. The more perceptive of Barber's following had always admired the educational aspects of his music and he now took this further, using the band's popularity to provide a platform for some of the American pioneers. This not only broadened his audience's knowledge and enjoyment but his own too, of course.

Guest star on 20 of the Barber band's late 1957 concerts was the great gospel singer Sister Rosetta Tharpe. All but unknown in

Britain, she was 42 years old, a spiritual soul stirrer, a formidable guitarist and an expressive, sometimes exuberant, sometimes bluesy singer. Barber was familiar with her recordings from the late thirties, through the forties, loved her singing with Lucky Millinder's Orchestra, loved her singing with Marie Knight, loved her singing solo to the accompaniment of her raunchy guitar. He could talk to her about her days in a gospel string band in the churches of rural Arkansas, about playing the Cotton Club with Louis Armstrong and Cab Calloway, about touring with the Dixie Hummingbirds. Ottilie Patterson could sing with her, and did. Under Sister Rosetta's influence, she would soon record *Lonesome Road* and *Strange Things Happen Every Day* with the Barber band.

International acclaim meant a lot to a woman who had been born in a back-of-beyond cotton plantation shack in 1915, the year that the Ku Klux Klan received its official charter from the Superior Court in Fulton County, Georgia.

(Interestingly, Long John Baldry, who saw Tharpe and was mesmerised, revived a song she had recorded with Marie Knight, *Up Above My Head*, as his first solo single – a 1964 duet with Rod Stewart.)

Chris Barber's next coup, or rather his next beneficent under-taking, was to bring in the legendary blues duo, Sonny Terry and Brownie McGhee, whose records were treasure to collectors. Writing in the specialist magazine *Jazz Journal*, Tony Standish spoke for all blues fans when he thanked Barber profusely for arranging the tour, which hopped around England during April and May 1958, before moving on to Germany. "It is really quite fantastic," he wrote, his mind comprehensively blown, "that jazz enthusiasts in Britain are able to see these giants of jazz. It is also a flattering indication of the European's appreciation of jazz that Sonny and Brownie, two uncompromising, honest-to-goodness blues singers, are able to undertake a nationwide tour and be assured of packed, enthusiastic and generally well-informed houses. This sort of recognition must be unexpected and gratifying to men such as these, whose contributions to their own country's culture are largely overlooked at home."

As a member of Dan Burley's Skiffle Group, after whom Bill Colyer had named the British style, Brownie could legitimately lay claim to having been an influence on the skiffle movement as well as helping to promote an interest in the blues. From Knoxville,

Tennessee, he had started out in the 1920s, playing on travelling minstrel shows and sleeping in graveyards to prevent being robbed, making light of mobility difficulties caused by childhood polio. His long-time partner Sonny Terry, from Durham, North Carolina, blind after childhood accidents, had started out singing on the streets. Most recently, steady work in the long-running Broadway production of *Cat On A Hot Tin Roof*, singing *John Henry* every night for three years, had brought an element of security to their precarious lives.

"Sonny and Brownie were great," says Chris Barber. "We used to call it 'the halt leading the blind'. Wonderful people. It was such a privilege to be able to put them on at the Royal Festival Hall."

"The good crowd were silent as Sonny's foot stomped and his cupped hands fanned incredible music from the tiny harmonica," wrote Tony Standish. "Brownie's head was back and the familiar words came singing out, new and fresh and real at last – and underneath it all was the type of guitar you'd been listening to for years on beat-up, hard-to-get records. The music was monumental and the stage presentation flawless. For nearly an hour, they held a huge audience and, at the end, had them screaming for more."

Strangely, no such pandemonium greeted Barber's next tour guest, who made his UK debut at Newcastle City Hall on 18 October. Muddy Waters was an acquired taste, regarded with some suspicion by both the jazz community, who felt his music was too raw, and the rock 'n' roll fraternity, who considered it too restrained. Only rabid rhythm & blues fans, of whom there were precious few around, appreciated his artistry, his subtlety.

Since making the pioneering Library of Congress records, so admired by Lonnie that he had stolen them from the American Embassy, McKinley Morganfield (as Muddy was then known) had travelled north from Mississippi to Chicago, where his superb electric group became a cornerstone in the transformation of Delta blues into R&B and, shortly thereafter, Chicago rock 'n' roll. Few of his records had been released in Britain – just three singles, of which *Rollin' Stone* had (significantly, it would turn out) been the first, and two extended players. In his review of the most recent of these, *Jazz Journal's* Graham Boatman warned the uninitiated that "on many records, Waters is difficult to take, for if his voice and rough delivery are not too strong to stomach, his curious twanging guitar can prove a deterrent." Correctly singling out *Manish Boy* as the most striking track – "an odd autobiography, full of yells from the band, over a stuttering riff" – he summed up the record as "strong, passionate music, very carnivorous".

When the tour (only a handful of cities: Newcastle, Leeds, Bournemouth, Bristol, Glasgow and London) reached St Pancras Town Hall on 20 October, the entire audience of the Blues & Barrelhouse Club were there to acclaim Muddy – for the second time. Unannounced, he and Otis Spann, the pianist who was travelling with him, had visited the Wardour Street club on a carefully arranged night off, savouring the prospect of finding an appreciative audience.

"At most venues on that tour," recalls Barber, "we had fans coming up to us complaining about the electric guitar, saying why are you letting that bloody awful guitar player share the stage with you – and we'd say, we think he's pretty good, why don't you shut up and listen? And some of them did, I'm pleased to say."

"I don't think many trad-jazz fans were ready for Muddy Waters," says Alexis Korner, "and it is to Chris Barber's great credit that he sponsored his tour." A long-time champion, Korner had written the sleeve notes for his first EP, *Muddy Waters With Little Walter*, and had been singing his praises to anyone who would listen. "For Cyril and me, it was one of the greatest pleasures of our lives to be able to present him at the Roundhouse. The place only held 90 at the best of times but I doubt if he had ever played in such an atmosphere of deep respect. He went back and told everyone at home about the Roundhouse and it sometimes seemed as if the club was better known in Chicago than it was in London."

In the audience that night was John Baldry. "I'm not sure if I was aware of it at the time but, looking back, I can see that it was one of those transitional evenings. Only a few weeks before, Cyril Davies had told us that Big Bill Broonzy had died – and everyone was very cut up about that, some crying openly. He and Alexis had got to know him very well, of course, but to some extent we all felt we knew him. He was certainly the first black American blues singer I ever saw and he had a profound effect on the way I wanted to go – but if Broonzy's death was the end of one chapter, the arrival of Muddy Waters was the start of the next. I remember he played *Got My Mojo Working* and that song would become very important to me over the years. The Rolling Stones took their name from one of his records; I named my band, the Hoochie Coochie Men, after another."

Max Jones proclaimed Muddy's St Pancras Town Hall concert to have been "remarkable, the nearest we'll get to a Chicago South Side blues performance in London." For once, *Melody Maker* could be positive about the latest musical undercurrent. "He sang and played with a fierce intensity and Otis Spann played rolling blues piano such as we have never heard before in this country." The moody harmonica, a prominent feature of many of his current records, was missing but Barber band members Graham Burbidge and Dick Smith, on drums and bass, did their best to emulate the slinky beat of his own cool rhythm section. It was good enough for Max Jones. "It was tough, unpolite, strongly rhythmic music, often very loud but with some light and shade in each number," he concluded, "pure blues in a vital, uninhibited style."

In the States, Muddy Waters would wait in vain for a hit single – but his new English friend Chris Barber was on the *Billboard* Hot 100 within weeks. Released as a result of public demand, *Petite Fleur* had been recorded over two years earlier as an album-track showcase for Monty Sunshine's clarinet. His idol Sidney Bechet had written the tune, an uncommonly pretty and attractive piece, and this was Monty's tribute to him. Accompanying him were Ron Bowden on drums, Dick Smith on bass and Dickie Bishop on guitar – three band members who had moved on since then. Neither Chris Barber nor his trumpeter Pat Halcox were anywhere to be seen, or heard – and nor was nominal producer Denis Preston. It was left to fastidious apprentice recording engineer Joe Meek to balance the instruments and catch the moment.

The record was at number 22 on 9 February 1959, the day the Barber Band left on SS America for their first US tour: two months, culminating in New York. While they were there, *Petite Fleur* went gold – the first ever British jazz record to sell a million copies, the first to reach the US Top Five. For good measure, it even scraped into the R&B chart.

In a Musicians' Union exchange deal involving George Lewis' New Orleans Jazz Band, they had been specifically forbidden to appear on television – but their US label, Laurie (currently hot with Dion & the Belmonts) obviously had good connections. "Somehow, we were pushed onto the *Ed Sullivan Show*, where we managed two minutes of *Diga Diga Doo* and half a minute of *Petite Fleur*," says Barber. "Then we were presented with our gold record. I can't say I warmed to Sullivan. He was a nasty man, most unpleasant. All he needed were the steel marbles and he was Humphrey Bogart in *The Caine Mutiny*. He was as evil as Captain Queeg." They also played live jazz on Dick Clark's *American Bandstand*, odd-footing teenage dancers more familiar with the rhythms of the Walk and the Stroll, the Shake and the Shag.

Back home in Britain, where *Petite Fleur* had reached number three, they were treated not only to an extravagant welcome home party thrown by Pye Records at the Savoy Hotel but also to lavish coverage in the press. Week by week, more fans were drawn to the Barber Band and their music as a trad-jazz boom began to gather momentum. May saw the première of *Look Back In Anger*, the movie version of John Osborne's turning-point stage play, in which they had a cameo. Richard Burton, looking every inch the angry young man, played trumpet with them, miming to the soundtrack recorded by Pat Halcox.

On 12 November 1959, Chris crowned a spectacular decade by marrying Ottilie Patterson . . . and then, before the year was out, he and the band were back on the road, touring with their latest guest-star blues man, Memphis Slim.

Thirty-five

Many accept 3 February 1959 as the day the music died. Nothing could be further from the truth: there were deluges of interesting records, many of them memorable or influential, coming over from America every month during 1959 and, once again (ignoring the counsel of sensible editors), I have no qualms about listing the best of these, in rough order of arrival, as one solid slab, a dense jungle of titles for fanatics to explore. The less intrepid may choose to fly over it. *One Night/I Got Stung* by Elvis Presley, *Letter To An Angel* by Jimmy Clanton, *High School Confidential* by Jerry Lee Lewis, *Problems* by the Everly Brothers, *Say Mama* by Gene Vincent, *Shame On You Miss Johnson* by Bobby Freeman, *Peek A Boo* by the Cadillacs, *I Cried A Tear* by LaVern Baker, *C'mon Everybody* by Eddie Cochran, *I'm A Man* by Fabian, *Sixteen Candles* by the Crests, *Stagger Lee* by Lloyd Price, *Lucky Ladybug* by Billie & Lillie, *The All American Boy* by Bill Parsons, *Donna/La Bamba* by Ritchie Valens, *I've Had It* by the Bell Notes, *Goodbye Baby* by Jack Scott, *It Doesn't Matter Anymore* by Buddy Holly, *Plain Jane* by Bobby Darin, *Never Be Anyone Else But You/It's Late* by Ricky Nelson, *Charlie Brown* by the Coasters, *The Lonely One* by Duane Eddy, *Telling Lies* by Fats Domino, *Since I Don't Have You* by the Skyliners, *By The Light Of The Silvery Moon* by Little Richard, *Who Cares* by Don Gibson, *Pink Shoe Laces* by Dodie Stevens, *Oh Why* by the Teddy Bears, *Lovin' Up A Storm* by Jerry Lee Lewis, *Where Were You On Our Wedding Day* by Lloyd Price, *Love's Made A Fool Of You* by the Crickets, *I Go Ape* by Neil Sedaka, *A Fool Such As I* by Elvis Presley, *Come Softly To Me* by the Fleetwoods, *Turn Me Loose* by Fabian, *She Said Yeah/Bad Boy* by Larry Williams, *Tragedy* by Thomas Wayne, *Luther Played The Boogie* by Johnny Cash, *This Should Go On Forever* by Rod Bernard, *Sea Cruise* by Frankie Ford, *The Happy Organ* by Dave 'Baby' Cortez, *Three Stars* by Ruby Wright, *That's Why* by Jackie Wilson, *Almost Grown/Little Queenie* by Chuck Berry, *Poor Jenny/Take A Message To Mary* by the Everly Brothers, *I'm Ready* by Fats Domino, *Dream Lover* by Bobby Darin, *So Fine* by the Fiestas, *Tiger* by Fabian, *A Teenager In Love* by Dion & the Belmonts, *I Think*

I'm Gonna Kill Myself by Buddy Knox, *Kansas City* by Wilbert Harrison, *Kookie Kookie* by Edd Byrnes, *Personality* by Lloyd Price, *You're So Fine* by the Falcons, *Peter Gunn* by Duane Eddy, *The Battle Of New Orleans* by Johnny Horton, *Guitar Boogie Shuffle* by the Virtues, *Teenage Heaven* by Eddie Cochran, *Along Came Jones* by the Coasters, *That's My Little Suzie* by Ritchie Valens, *Midnight Shift* by Buddy Holly, *Here Comes Summer* by Jerry Keller, *There Goes My Baby* by the Drifters, *Just Keep It Up* by Dee Clark, *What'd I Say* by Ray Charles, *Lavender Blue* by Sammy Turner, *Back In The USA/Memphis Tennessee* by Chuck Berry, *Forty Days* by Ronnie Hawkins, *Lipstick On Your Collar* by Connie Francis, *Bongo Rock* by Preston Epps, *The Class* by Chubby Checker, *Lonely Boy* by Paul Anka, *Only Sixteen* by Sam Cooke, *Tallahassee Lassie* by Freddy Cannon, *A Big Hunk O' Love* by Elvis Presley, *Hushabye* by the Mystics, *There Is Something On Your Mind* by Big Jay McNeely, *I'll Be Satisfied* by Jackie Wilson, *It Was I* by Skip & Flip, *The Way I Walk* by Jack Scott, *This I Swear* by the Skyliners, *Just A Little Too Much* by Ricky Nelson, *Peggy Sue Got Married* by Buddy Holly, *The Night Is So Lonely* by Gene Vincent, *Forty Miles of Bad Road* by Duane Eddy, *Linda Lu* by Ray Sharpe, *Til I Kissed You* by the Everly Brothers, *Sea Of Love* by Phil Phillips, *I'm Gonna Get Married* by Lloyd Price, *Crackin' Up* by Bo Diddley, *Mona Lisa* by Carl Mann, *Baby Talk* by Jan & Dean, *Poison Ivy* by the Coasters, *Mack The Knife* by Bobby Darin, *Let's Talk About Us* by Jerry Lee Lewis, *I Want To Walk You Home* by Fats Domino, *Somethin' Else* by Eddie Cochran, *Mary Lou* by Ronnie Hawkins, *Red River Rock* by Johnny & the Hurricanes, *Love Potion Number Nine* by the Clovers, *Don't Tell Me Your Troubles* by Don Gibson, *Hey Little Girl* by Dee Clark, *Sleep Walk* by Santo & Johnny, *Leave My Kitten Alone* by Little Willie John, *The Angels Listened In* by the Crests, *Come On And Get Me* by Fabian, *Run Boy Run* by Sanford Clark, *Just Ask Your Heart* by Frankie Avalon, *Mr Blue* by the Fleetwoods, *Teen Beat* by Sandy Nelson, *The Shape I'm In* by Johnny Restivo, *Shout* by the Isley Brothers, *Always* by Sammy Turner, *There Comes A Time* by Jack Scott, *Say Man* by Bo Diddley, *Tennessee Waltz* by Jerry Fuller, *When You Ask About Love* by the Crickets, *In The Mood* by Ernie Fields, *Woo Hoo* by the Rock-a-Teens, *Oh Carol* by Neil Sedaka, *A Lover's Prayer* by Dion & the Belmonts, *Dance With Me* by the Drifters, *Little Queenie* by Jerry Lee Lewis, *Rockin' In The Jungle* by the Eternals, *Be My Guest* by Fats Domino, *Pretend* by Carl Mann, *Some Kind-a Earthquake* by

Duane Eddy, *Wild Cat* by Gene Vincent, *Reveille Rock* by Johnny & the Hurricanes, *I'm Movin' On* by Ray Charles and *You Got What It Takes* by Marv Johnson. In the States, many of these singles had been released in stereo – a luxury we would not enjoy for years.

As usual, Radio Luxembourg was the obsessive rock 'n' roll addict's lifeline, the only chance to hear most of them, unless you spent every Saturday in the listening booth of your friendly local record shop.

Although they rarely commented on pop music, even *The Times* was moved to report the deaths of Buddy Holly, Ritchie Valens and the Big Bopper, albeit in two short paragraphs. The story was relegated to the back page of the *Melody Maker*, which plastered the front with coverage of Count Basie's arrival in London – where he spent all of 24 hours, en route to Switzerland. Fair enough. The *NME* carried the torch and would continue to do so.

To this day, it seems, every Holly fan remembers the circumstances in which he or she heard the news – whether on the radio, in the newspaper, a phone call from a friend (for those fortunate enough to have phones), on the school bus or in the playground. Terry Dene, however, probably remembers February 1959 for rather different reasons. For several months, his career had been falling out of the sky in slow motion and it was about to land on broken glass.

During the last half of 1958, since his marriage to Edna Savage in July, Dene had managed to hold it together, had been able to play most of his contracted gigs – but two more feeble singles, *Can I Walk You Home* and *Pretty Little Pearly*, had failed to impress either his following or his friends. "Terry had been one of our little team," says Mickie Most. "Him and Brian Gregg, Alex Wharton and me, we went everywhere together, just hanging out, playing and singing – and Terry had a lovely voice. He was a better singer than the rest of us put together but he was never recorded correctly. Our singles were bad enough but his were dreadful. We used to cringe when they got played on the 2Is jukebox."

"Terry's records were rubbish," confirms Brian Gregg. "When he started, he was definitely the best rock 'n' roll singer around, without a shadow of doubt. You ask anyone: no-one could touch him. He had power, conviction, always sang in tune, looked great, had all the girls screaming at him – but Decca picked all the wrong songs and every time another duff record came out, his confidence took a knock. On top of that, he had National Service looming over him."

"I've had enough messing about," Dene explained to the press in November. "I want to get in the Army and get it over with. Other lads have to serve two years – why shouldn't I? I'm watching every post for my call-up papers." They arrived shortly before Christmas, forcing him to cancel his one solid booking: he and Edna were lined up to appear in panto at Sheffield Empire, playing twin leads in *Babes In The Wood* for two months. Laurie London, hitless for a year but still popular on television, was called in to replace him.

Thinking perhaps to attract the same sort of favourable publicity as Elvis had, 10 months earlier, smiling even as his greased-up pompadour was clippered off, the Army had arranged for Pathe News to be at the gates when, on 22 January 1959, Dene reported for duty at Winchester Barracks. Because his father had served with them, he had elected to join the Royal Green Jackets, a regiment with a reputation for hard, iron-rod discipline, running at the double until they dropped.

"I imagine it will be much less worry being a soldier than it is a singer," ventured the newly conscripted Private Terence Williams, somewhat optimistically. "Obviously it's going to be a change, but I don't really mind. It's like going back to my old job: I'll have the same amount of money." The following day, opportunistic Decca issued a new Dene record, *Bimbombey*. They needn't have bothered: it was even sillier than the others.

By the first week of February, it was obvious that a mistake had been made. Dene was not soldier material – as his psychiatrist had concluded months before. Just being confined within the walls of the barracks with a bunch of braying meat-heads was bad enough but it was a letter from Edna Savage, apparently, that finished him off. According to Brian Gregg, "she wrote to him and said 'if you think I'm waiting around for you for two years, you've got another think coming . . . in fact, I'm with another man at the moment.' Of course, Terry flipped, had a nervous breakdown."

Sensing that he may require more than an insensitive loud-mouthed sergeant-major to pull him back into shape, officers transferred him to the army hospital at Netley and on to a civilian hospital specialising in mental health, St Ebba's in Epsom. There he was pronounced "unfit for further military service" and by the end of March, he was back home at the flat with Edna, planning his show business comeback.

As the press lampooned him, Dene was subjected to a spate of hate mail, not only vicious insults but envelopes containing white feathers. The self-righteous Gerald Nabarro MP went so far as to raise the case in Parliament, suggesting that Dene had swung the lead to escape National Service. Friends rallied round, including those he asked to be his new Dene-Aces: Brian Gregg on bass, Clem Cattini on drums and Tony Eagleton on guitar, all of whom, to their great relief, had managed to avoid Army service on medical grounds. They went into action together for the first time at the Majestic Theatre in Chaddesden on 26 April 1959, supporting fading pin-up Dickie Valentine, who was out promoting his latest single, a useless version of Frankie Avalon's cloying *Venus*. Valentine was unsettled by the audience, most of whom had come either to scream or to jeer at Dene, and he was even less impressed when he left the stage door and saw the state of his car, a chrome and ivory Cadillac, his pride and joy. Thinking it was Dene's car, macho pin-head detractors had gouged the paintwork with pennies and covered it with unflattering lipstick graffiti.

"Everywhere we played, Terry had to face ignorant wankers, shouting at him, booing, telling him what a weed and a coward he was," says Brian Gregg. "If the gig was within lorry distance of a barracks or a Territorial Army headquarters, we would get these army thugs threatening to do him over. At one place, the promoter heard the talk, saw what was going to happen, phoned the base and got a bunch of military policemen to line the stage. It was very heavy, every gig a drama; no fun at all."

According to his loyal manager, Hymie Zahl, Dene's recording contract had been renewed for a further year – but only two singles emerged. Neither sold; Decca got cold feet. So did concert promoters and, tortured beyond endurance, so did Hymie. He had put up with the singer getting legless, smashing windows, being arrested, having breakdowns, blowing gigs, getting booed, getting married even ... but his patience snapped in June, during a season of well-paid concerts at the Tivoli Gardens in Stockholm.

"We played the fairground in the afternoon and the theatre in the evening," Gregg remembers, "but Terry was simultaneously missing Edna and becoming fond of this very strong Swedish lager. One evening, he didn't turn up for the show – but we expected him to arrive at the last minute, so we went out and played the intro riff, over and over. It turned out he had taken a cab to the airport because he wanted to see Edna. I had to impersonate him, sing all his songs. As soon as Hymie found out, he ditched him . . . it was the final straw."

Gregg and Cattini accepted Larry Parnes' invitation to become the core of the Beat Boys, backing his singers on package tours – and at their instigation, Parnes welcomed Terry Dene into his stable of stars. This arrangement didn't make it to Christmas, however, and nor did his marriage. As if to rub salt into the wound, Decca paired *Thank You Pretty Baby* with *A Boy Without A Girl* as his last single. It had been less than three years since he first smelt and tasted stardom on the *6.5 Special*, his triumphant entry into show-biz, but his days in the spotlight were over. Some newspapers were keen to cast him as rock 'n' roll's first casualty but fortunately his wounds weren't fatal. After attempts to resuscitate his career proved futile, he withdrew for a period of recuperation – said to have been facilitated by the Kray Brothers, with whom he had been acquainted since doing a week of cabaret at their favourite hang-out, the Astor Club. It seems their influence was less pervasive than that of Christ, to whom Dene committed himself soon afterwards.

February 1959 was also a pivotal month for several more of the original coffee bar cowboys. For some it was the moment their dreams fell into place, a time for celebration, for others the end of the line. In the latter category, the Vipers were in no doubt that the music had died for them.

The previous autumn, by which time skiffle had become about as unfashionable as a Woolworth's Davy Crockett hat, they sought to toughen their stance by recording a rival version of a current US rock 'n' roll hit, *Summertime Blues*. Of course, nobody – let alone the Vipers – could have improved on the impeccable original, an instant classic, cleverly constructed and brilliantly performed by Eddie Cochran . . . and this became abundantly clear when their abysmal effort bombed.

Since the interminable National Skiffle Contest had withered to a halt, their gig sheet had been all but barren. "The bottom dropped out of everything," says Vipers co-founder Johnny Booker, "leaving

Wally Whyton and me scuffling to survive." Their latest recruits, Jet Harris and Tony Meehan, both of whom played on *Summertime Blues*, soon skipped: Jet to back the Most Brothers on the Kalin Twins/Cliff Richard tour and Tony to rejoin his mates, the Worried Men, at the 2Is. Nineteen years old, and already worldly wise as a result of touring with the sardonic Tony Crombie, Jet could give as good as he got – but Tony Meehan was only 15, fresh out of school and shy, on the road for the first time. With a couple of jaded old bohemians. Of course, Whyton and Booker joshed him mercilessly, holding him down and painting his fingernails purple, making him wear bright red lipstick on stage, telling him he might have to sleep with the gay promoter to ensure they were paid. They also had him running around the Derby moors, trying to catch a sheep – having told him that on Sundays they always caught and roasted either a pig or a sheep for lunch, on their way to the gig.

"Jet didn't stay long; Tony came and went even more quickly," says Wally Whyton. "It wasn't the level of glamour he'd envisaged – and by that time, it wasn't the level of glamour I'd envisaged either. In fact, I'd just about had enough of it by then. Even at our peak, when we were packing them in, two full houses a night, six nights a week, it was beginning to get to me. We would arrive in town on the Sunday, go to the theatre stage door and get the list of places to stay for the week. The guy would give his recommendations, having been slipped a few bob, no doubt, and we would go round, see some old dear, check the room and take it. Invariably, there would be the stench of cat's piss and you got used to seeing dinner served up on tea plates. You weren't expected to hang around the place all day, so after breakfast you would wander out and try to fill up the day, before the first house in the evening. You'd wander around Woolworth's, check out the market, sit in cafes, go to the pictures, do anything to waste a bit more time, marooned in the same dump for a week . . . a very depressing lifestyle."

Like a couple of gunfighters, ragged and old at 24, Whyton and Booker fought one last rearguard action together, taking on a 12-string guitarist to fill out their sound. Zom had been a Soho face since his days in John Hasted's Skiffle Group and had most recently been the singing compère on 2Is package tours.

"At the end, we were shoplifting and stealing fruit from market stalls, just to survive," says Whyton. "Our fees had slumped and we were really struggling, sometimes sleeping in horrible lorry-drivers' places, smelly old flop houses where you could bed down for five bob a night, lying on sheets stained with bodily fluids. That's when we decided to knock it on the head. It was a pretty inglorious end for the Vipers."

The decision to disband was accelerated by a visit from the Inland Revenue. "They came to my flat in Eccleston Square, looking for Johnny Martyn – which was my stage name, the one under which I signed contracts," says Johnny Booker. "We were usually paid in cash, often quite handsomely – and I'd spent the money on cars and good times. None left over to pay tax, unfortunately. I told them that Martyn was out on tour and they went away, leaving behind a huge income tax bill. I knew I had to get out fast – which is exactly what I did. I sold my cars, went and got a passport and left the country . . . and Zom came with me."

One morning in February 1959, they left from a dock next to London Bridge, on a Spanish banana boat, under ballast, going back to Las Palmas. "It was a pretty choppy voyage and Zom spent most it being sick, but the accommodation was good and we ate at the Captain's pleasure, which meant interesting Spanish food, but often heavy on green slimy olive oil. Zom usually took one look at it and barfed up again."

They busked, played clubs, got to the Spanish mainland, played more gigs, worked as clowns in a circus, had all their possessions stolen and were repatriated by the English consulate at the end of summer – by which time, Wally Whyton had found a sinecure, working for Associated Rediffusion Television as host of the children's programme *Small Time*. All he had to do was sit at a desk, sing the odd nursery rhyme and chat to a trio of glove puppets: Joe Crow, Simon Scarecrow and, the most popular, Pussy Cat Willum, who received more fan mail than Wally ever had. Realising it was money for old rope, he consolidated his position by providing the voice for a new puppet, Ollie Beak.

Booker moved to Vancouver and became a Canadian citizen; Zom toured with Colin Hicks & the Cabin Boys and played briefly with the Thameside Four, before taking to the needle; after his Pussy Cat Willum episode, Whyton went out either as a solo folkie or in partnership with Redd Sullivan, helping to establish the early 1960s folk club circuit.

February 1959 should have been the month that everything clicked for Colin Hicks. The previous summer, far from reeling in ignominy as the first 'star' to be ejected from Larry Parnes' celebrated 'stable', he had fallen on his feet, attracting the patronage of Frederick T. Clifford, a wealthy insurance broker who was soon pouring money into his protégé's war chest. "I had met this guy at the Freight Train coffee bar," says Brian Gregg, who was currently playing bass for Hicks. "He was a Dr Barnardo's boy who had made good and he used to enjoy the coffee bar scene. I told him that Parnes had dumped us and confiscated a load of our gear – and immediately you could see the wheels turning in his head. Before you knew it, he was buying us new equipment, taking us to Morris Berman's in Irving Street and ordering up these fantastic stage clothes: green metallic-looking jackets that glowed under the lights, silk shirts, suede shoes . . . we looked incredible! And we sounded incredible too!" Clifford spent £2,000 on instruments, amplifiers, microphones and a mixer – "to give a resounding quality to the whole thing."

They rehearsed in the first floor room of the Roundhouse, home of the Blues and Barrelhouse Club, until the manager blew a fuse. "It's the worst row I've ever heard," he told one reporter. "I've stood it for two days but now they'll have to clear out."

Though every record company had shown him the door, Clifford prepared to re-launch Hicks with a series of newspaper interviews, all of which, predictably, wondered whether he would ever escape from the shadow of big brother, Tommy Steele. "I don't mind waiting," said Hicks, a teetotal chain-smoker, "I'm only 17; he's 21. I'll give him a run for his money." Asked why he used his real name, he countered "Hicks may not have been good enough for Tommy, but it's good enough for me."

Not for the punters, however. They stayed away in droves. "No-one was interested," says Gregg. "We were playing these big ballrooms up north – places like Whitehaven and Barrow and Crewe – but we would be lucky to get an audience of a dozen. It was obvious that it wasn't going to happen and I quit. He was a cocky little git at times, thought he knew it all. Wouldn't take any advice from anyone in the band, wouldn't even consult us." The band folded.

One door closed, another opened. Colin Hicks was selected to star in the touring version of *Expresso Bongo*, one of the year's hit West End musicals. His co-stars would be pantomime veteran Hy Hazell and south London ingénue Jill Gascoigne. Starting in February 1959, the show would run for consecutive weeks at the Chiswick Empire, Streatham Hill Theatre, Golders Green Hippodrome and Brighton Hippodrome, before slowly moving north for a further eight weeks. It lost momentum almost immediately, however, and Hy Hazell was soon rehearsing the part of Mrs Squeezum in the Mermaid Theatre's opening production *Lock Up Your Daughters*.

Unable to make any headway at home, Colin Hicks chose to concentrate on Italy, where – as a result of his tour and a cameo in the Italian financed and directed documentary movie *Europa di Notte* – he was regarded as some kind of rock god. In September, he went to the 2Is Coffee Bar, checked out the latest arrivals and recruited a new set of Cabin Boys: guitarist Zom (freshly returned from his Canary Islands adventure), bass player Boots Slade and pianist Mike O'Neill. Jimmy Nicol, the drummer from his last group, provided a thread of continuity. For several weeks, they hit the high spots of Italy – though meeting and hanging out with Chet Baker was the brightest memory for Mike O'Neill. Back in Britain, he and Boots Slade would form Nero & the Gladiators, claiming to be pioneers of 'the Italian Sound'. Colin Hicks would quickly fade into the small-print footnotes of rock history.

The 2Is was still London's most powerful teen magnet but since opening in April 1956 had seen a complete turnover in clientele. The last of the original wild bunch, the Most Brothers had made little impact on the Kalin Twins/Cliff Richard package tour and had not been invited back to Decca's studios since their third single *Dottie* had followed the other two into oblivion. After a few Sunday concerts, as a filler act on package shows, they split up. Both had plans for a change of scenery.

Mickie Most had fallen in love and would not be denied. "I met a girl from South Africa, a girl called Chris," he recalls. "She had just finished school, at a convent school in Natal, and her parents were taking her on a trip around Europe. When she got to London, she demanded to be taken to the 2Is Coffee Bar, which she had read about at school – so, even though he was reluctant to take her into Soho, her father used to drop her off at eight o'clock and pick her up again at 10, just so she could sit around in a coffee bar for a few evenings. I invited her out to the pictures and we went to see the funnies in Leicester Square and we saw more of each other – but then she was whisked off to other parts of Europe. That was in September, just before the Kalin Twins tour. We met up again in November, when she was back in London, about to fly home and it was obvious that her parents were glad to see the back of this peroxide blond West End wallah. 'If you want to see her again, you'll have to come to South Africa,' her father said, laughing. He knew it couldn't happen: South Africa was like the moon! It used to take three days on a plane in those days."

On 31 December 1958, Mickie was knocking on their front door in Johannesburg. Her parents must have been impressed by his resolve, allowing him to marry their daughter that February. "And that's pretty much how it's been ever since."

They returned to London in late summer 1962 and Most resumed his stage career as a makeweight on the Everly Brothers, Little Richard, Bo Diddley, Rolling Stones package tour, rolling on his back, singing *Sea Cruise*, looking archaic. Nobody suspected that he would be a millionaire before the end of the decade.

Alex Wharton, aka Murray, auditioned for and won a part in the latest production at the Theatre Royal in Stratford, East London. In fact, he won three parts – playing Frank, a builder and a Teddy boy in the Frank Norman/Lionel Bart musical *Fings Ain't Wot They Used To Be*, which opened on 17 February 1959. He rolled his mates Tony Eagleton and Jimmy Nicol, between jobs with Colin Hicks, into the pit band. In October, Murray moved to the West End to understudy Alfred Lynch in Brendan Behan's *The Hostage*, again directed by Joan Littlewood – and it was there that he was spotted by Frank Lee, head of A&R at Decca.

"He took a fancy to me and signed me up," says Alex. Three singles did nothing but, rather than let him go, Lee made him a producer. His first session was with Ken Dodd, singing *Love Is Like A Violin*. "I told him to save his voice on the run-through, 'just sort of whisper the vocal' – and, because it was so intimate, it was the run-through that got released. I had a Top 10 record, first time out." Later, as an independent producer, Murray took the Moody Blues into a four-track garage studio behind the Marquee and produced their milestone hit, *Go Now*.

Thirty-six

For Marty Wilde, February 1959 was the day the music came to life. He had started the year miserably, wasting his time in red tights, mincing around as Will Scarlet, twice nightly at Stockton Hippodrome in a cobbled-together pantomime, *Babes In The Wood*. Fortunately, by the time he returned to London, towards the end of January, his manager Larry Parnes had met up with Jack Good and eaten rare humble pie, contriving to expunge any bad feeling he might have created between them. As a result, Marty was reinstated as the central star of *Oh Boy!* – which suited Good admirably. During the autumn, his show's viewing figures had soared, thanks largely to Marty, who had proved immensely popular with the television audience. Preferring to watch him on *Oh Boy!*, they had been deserting the *6.5 Special* in such numbers that the BBC soon admitted defeat and, after a run of almost two years, consigned their tired old warhorse to the knacker's yard. The final edition was broadcast on 27 December 1958 . . . but there was bad news too: they already had a replacement programme lined up . . . *Dig This*.

One watched with an open mind, quite prepared to dig it as instructed, but with a weekly dose of acts like the Polka Dots and Bob Miller & his Millermen, it was little more than *Workers' Playtime* transferred from radio to television. That it was profoundly hopeless was obvious to all, including the BBC's Youth Programming Dept, who pulled the plug on *Dig This* on 28 March, after a run of only 13 weeks.

Meanwhile, over at ITV, *Oh Boy!* continued to cruise on high ratings under the intuitive direction of Jack Good, who not only catapulted the careers of Marty Wilde and Cliff Richard, but also made Saturday tea-time stars of his residents: Lord Rockingham's XI, the Vernons Girls, Cuddly Dudley, Cherry Wainer, Red Price, Neville Taylor & his Cutters and the Dallas Boys. To these he added a stream of new faces . . . Vince Taylor & the Playboys, Roy Young, Billy Fury, Dickie Pride, Tony Sheridan, Vince Eager, even visiting Americans Brenda Lee and Conway Twitty. For anyone craving public recognition, there was no better exposure. Of course, it always helped if you had a new record to plug.

The most successful year of Marty Wilde's career began four days after the Buddy Holly/Ritchie Valens/Big Bopper plane crash, on 7 February 1959, when he returned to headline *Oh Boy!* Recorded a day earlier, his overwrought version of *Donna* (20 minutes of rehearsal with session men and backing singers, cut live, in the can to the producer's satisfaction on take six) would rise steadily to number three, all but obliterating Valens' mawkish original.

Later that month, Wilde was at London Airport, filming location scenes for his début movie *Jet Storm*. It wasn't exactly what he had in mind. In one of his ever-candid (often too candid for Parnes) press interviews, he had confided: "I want to act and not just look good. I want to play opposite people like Sinatra, Brando and Montgomery Clift. I want to be in films like *From Here To Eternity*. I'd like to go to Hollywood, because I think someone like me can waste a whole lifetime waiting for a chance in British films." No sign of Brando or Clift, but Marty did get to play alongside Stanley Baker, Sybil Thorndyke, Hermione Baddeley and other stalwarts of the British film industry, most of them cooped up in an airliner which a deranged Richard Attenborough was threatening to blow up with an exploding suitcase. Cardboard sets and a plastic model plane whose strings were plainly visible on screen. No Academy Award winner, but good fun for Marty, who played a rock singer on the way to the States for his honeymoon with 'curvaceous' Jackie Lane. She was not familiar with any of his records and he, like most people, was unaware of her performances in *The Gamma People* or *The Truth About Women*. It was not a marriage made in heaven, obviously, but back on terra firma, he had begun a relationship with one of the Vernons Girls, Joyce Baker. He wasn't even 20 years old but already he had met the love of his life. Still in the butterflies and daydream stage, the romance added a frisson to his next single, *A Teenager In Love*.

By the time he came to record it, he had assembled a most capable backing group, on a par, he felt, with Cliff's Drifters. They had initially come together for the benefit of fellow Parnes act, Vince Eager – who was also recovering from a protracted pantomime, in his case *Mother Goose* at Southport. Charged with finding suitable musicians, Eager's bass-player and best mate Tex Makins went to the 2Is and hired the latest drum prodigy, 18-year-old Bobby Woodman, a Coventry kid who had first come to London as a band boy, humping gear for Eric Delaney. He had recently been playing with Davy Keir's Elizabethan Jazzmen at the House of Sam Widges, sleeping in the damp cellar and existing on free meals and coffee, but when Tony Meehan went off to join Cliff Richard, Woodman was invited to replace him in the 2Is house band – backing not only long-time resident Rick Richards and returnee Freddy Lloyd but also such hopeful newcomers as Clay Nicholls, Dave Sutch and Paul Raven. A steady paying gig with Vince Eager tempted him away and also lured two of Rory Wilde's (no relation to Marty) sidemen, guitarist Tony Belcher and pianist Alan LeClair. Makins led the new band.

The first thing they did was bleach their hair blond, all four of them, an act of rebellion guaranteed to attract derision from every quarter of the straight world. It was nothing more than ostentatious flag-waving, a well-aimed V-sign from kids who had just learned that all males born after 1 October 1939 were to be spared national service. Call-up was going to be phased out! Glory hallelujah and great balls of fire, this was momentous news to the rock 'n' roll generation. They could now behave just as they wished, forever: there would be no attempt to collar them at 18, lock them up for two years and re-programme them into fully-fledged adults.

As they prepared to make their début, backing Vince for a week of shows at Streatham Locarno, Tex Makins – a seasoned panto performer after four weeks in *Mother Goose* – introduced the others to stage make-up. "What's that shit you're putting on your face?" scoffed Scottish saxophonist Billy McVay, one of several musicians from the resident dance band to poke fun at the cocky Young Turks who were stealing their spotlight.

Bass and drums solid, piano and rhythm guitar buffering Eager as he got back into rocking mode, they were exciting to watch and to hear, but – it was immediately clear – they were missing the most important element, a lead guitarist. At the end of the week, Eager, Tex Makins and Bobby Woodman went to the 2Is looking for one – on a night when this lanky, curly-haired kid happened to be down there, rattling out solos for the Soho Group. Originally the Soho Skiffle Group, they had (along with all surviving contemporaries), ditched their washboard in favour of drums and modified into a rock 'n' roll group. Jim Sullivan, a kid from Hounslow, had been with them for exactly a year, initially going electric by fitting a pick-up to his acoustic arch-top Framus Black Rose but then moving on to a Roger, a German guitar with a hand-carved top. He'd only turned 18 the previous month, but already he was fluent, a blend of Perkins, Moore, Burton, Holly and Gallup.

"We asked him if he wanted to join the group and go on Larry Parnes' payroll," Woodman remembers, "and, whoosh, he was in like a shot." They took him to "some hooker's place around the corner" and gave him the peroxide bottle-blond treatment over her kitchen sink. Then it was off to Colchester Regal and the road that goes on forever.

Within days, they were called to Larry Parnes' office and reassigned. Keen to get Marty Wilde back on the treadmill, Parnes had booked him on a long schedule of one-nighters, to fill the days when he was neither appearing on nor rehearsing for *Oh Boy!* – and rather than go through the arduous process of forming a new group for him, he merely appropriated Vince Eager's. Subject to Marty's approval, of course. They auditioned for him while he was rehearsing for that week's *Oh Boy!* No problems; they walked it.

Even though Marty's single of *Donna* was climbing the best sellers lists, their first tour was a low-key affair, visiting mainly provincial cinemas on the Star circuit – Worksop Regal, Newark Palace and Pontefract Crescent, for instance, where films were cancelled for the evening. Out came the teenagers, full of the joys of spring, to see the star of *Oh Boy!* in the flesh, to wallow in the radiance of his fame. And look at those musicians! Five boys with platinum blond hair and deeply tanned (pancake 30) faces. Never seen anything like that before, not round here. Mayhem every night.

Already possessed of an energetic technique, Bobby Woodman kept finding his drums moving forward on the shiny stages as the set progressed. "The spurs on the bass drum wouldn't hold it secure," he explains, "so I went out and bought a bag of long nails and this axe thing, with a hammer on one side and a chopper blade on the other. I used to nail the kit down to the stage, good and proper." Some cinema managers, Larry Parnes learned, were not too happy about this peroxide wild man wandering about with an axe, destroying their stages. Not too happy, either, was support act Russ Conway, a pianist not only nimble on the keyboard but also light on his feet. "He was just coming off his big number one hit *Side Saddle* and he insisted on having me accompany him," says Woodman. "He used to sit there with his great big smile, winking across at me as he played. Almost every night, he tried it on. 'Oh, Bobby, would you like to come up to my hotel room? I've got a bottle of whisky.' 'No chance, mate!' I used to say, 'What do you think I am?' " For one thing, Woodman didn't drink in those days (although he may have made up for it later) and for another, he was rather more interested in girls. Two years earlier, he had been fired from his first roadie job by band leader Sid Phillips, when "instead of bringing him his tea and sandwiches at the interval, I was pulling the birds like crazy!" – and this hobby was now being amply nourished by a constant stream of young fans, some hoping to escape their drab lives, if only for a few minutes. At Maidstone, there was an indignant confrontation with a magistrate, who was enquiring about the age of one of these girls.

Aberrant behaviour may have contributed to some overnight changes. Within a month of forming, the Wild Cats divided: Tex Makins, Bobby Woodman and Alan LeClair left to become the core of Billy Fury's backing group – and into Marty's band came drummer Brian Bennett and bass player Licorice Locking. Recently, they had been playing both in Vince Taylor's Playboys and the Tony Sheridan Trio; Marty knew them from their appearances on *Oh Boy!* and Jim Sullivan had become friends with them at the 2Is, where they always congregated and often jammed on their nights off.

"That was a fabulous band," says Marty, "without doubt the best rock 'n' roll group in Britain at the time. I remember the jolt of excitement I used to get every time they started up behind me. Wherever we played, all the girls would be gazing at me, while the boys would have their eyes riveted on Jim's fingers. Sometimes his hand would dart around on the fretboard so fast that you couldn't even see it." Wilde was so happy with Sullivan that he presented him with his prize guitar, a 1955 Gibson Les Paul Gold Top that he had bought from Sister Rosetta Tharpe when she was touring Britain with Chris Barber's band in late 1957. It was an inspired purchase and a generous gift. Due to trade restrictions, American guitars were all but impossible to acquire – and this was surely the coolest, the most exquisite instrument in the whole of Britain.

In one of his celebrated press outbursts, Marty laid into session men. "In the past," he ranted, "my record backings have been corny and square – and the kids can spot them a mile off." It was unheard of; never before had a singer dared to criticise his A&R manager. Feathers were ruffled. "I'm afraid Marty doesn't know a crotchet from a hatchet," sneered elitist jazzer Phil Seamen, who could have become the Earl Palmer of England had he not preferred to become a jaded old junkie.

Even if he didn't know a crotchet from a hatchet, Marty knew what a great rock 'n' roll record should sound like – which was more than his producer Johnny Franz did. This was confirmed when Franz caved in and let the Wild Cats back their boss on his début album *Wilde About Marty*.

"He poked his nose in all the time," says Sullivan, who on stage generated a whirlwind of reverberation and cone-stretching. "I was only comfortable with the controls of my guitar adjusted to give me exactly the sound I wanted – but Johnny Franz insisted on removing any presence or echo, and he wasn't happy until he had got the flattest, driest sound possible. Consequently, that album was something of a disappointment to us – because it lacked all the excitement of the rehearsals."

Franz brought in Wally Stott and Ivor Raymonde to pour their straight arrangements over several tracks but despite all his attempts to impose traditional values, the album stands as a milestone in British rock music. Atmosphere may be missing but the performances are fine. Free at last in the studio, singing songs he had picked himself, Marty is feeling good, singing heart and soul, meaning every word, so delighted to be floating on this cooking band. At this point in time, as a singer, he could cut all competition to ribbons – as could his group: the 2Is generation gone electric, serious young rock 'n' rollers doing it for themselves, playing their hearts out, learning the game. Excellent though it is, one wonders how much better *So Glad You're Mine* – a Big Boy Crudup song from 1946, later redefined by Elvis and now anglicised by Marty – would have sounded, had it been recorded in Memphis or Clovis or Nashville, with a producer who better knew how to cut rock 'n' roll.

Released on 18 September 1959, *Wilde About Marty* sold well, not just to the screamers but to boys who normally only bought American records. Wilde had become their representative, out on the front line. If Lonnie Donegan and the Vipers had dug the trenches, then Marty's début album and the first clutch of Cliff singles were the foundations on which the British rock music pantheon is built.

Throughout 1959, Parnes continued to work Wilde to the point of exhaustion but he had no cares. Born six months before the cut-off point, he had been called to attend a medical, to assess his suitability for National Service – but his big flat feet saved the day. He laughed for 24 hours straight and then grinned every time he sang the Bill Parsons call-up song *All American Boy*, which he did on all his shows – including the Northern Royal Variety Performance at the Palace Theatre in Manchester. That rock 'n' roll had infiltrated the music business establishment was confirmed by the fare they served up for the Queen Mother and Princess Margaret: Marty Wilde, Cliff Richard and the *Oh Boy!* cast. Marty wore his gold lamé jacket – and not just as a tribute to Liberace, who was also on the show. He had both silver and gold lamé jackets, which he wore every time he took the stage – except on Sundays, when entertainment was controlled by the Lord's Day Observance Society. They still had a grip: no dancing or theatrical costumes allowed. Marty wore sober attire, his Sunday school teacher look, but the fans went bonkers all the same.

Every afternoon for a month, he played matinees at Blackpool Palace, in a package show with Billy Fury, Dickie Pride, Tony Sheridan, Mike Preston, Sally Kelly, Cuddly Dudley, Cherry Wainer and Red Price. While most of the acts stayed at Squires Gate Holiday Camp, Marty stayed with Joyce Baker, at her parents' house in Liverpool. The intensity of the relationship was giving Larry Parnes nightmares.

Marty's credibility among rock 'n' roll purists was strengthened when a music paper asked him to list his favourite 10 records. *Dream Lover* by Bobby Darin, *Tallahassee Lassie* by Freddy Cannon, *Lipstick On Your Collar* by Connie Francis, *You've Got Love* by the Crickets, *Blue Moon Of Kentucky* and *A Fool Such As I* by Elvis Presley, *Cry Me A River* by Julie London, *3.30 Blues* by Duane Eddy and *Smokestack Lightning* by Howlin' Wolf. An astonishingly cool selection! Pity he blew it by also including *Gigi* by Liberace.

To widespread puzzlement and dismay, Jack Good killed off *Oh Boy!* at the end of May 1959, after a final show featuring the stars it had created – Marty and Cliff. Good took the summer off and on 12 September, returned to Saturday evening television with his new series *Boy Meets Girls*, starring Marty and the Vernons Girls. Less furious and more boy-next-door, it saw Wilde suppressing his sexuality – reflecting what Good saw, accurately, as a general softening of rock 'n' roll, a move to make it palatable to a wider audience. Naturally, the trend had started in the States, with a vanilla revolution (revulsion, according to many) spreading radially from Philadelphia. "Good has scored another bull's eye," concluded the *NME*'s scribe, "demonstrating his brilliance by converting Marty Wilde into a well-groomed versatile performer." A new single was released to coincide with the series – a version of the fast-rising American hit, *Sea Of Love*, an exotic and mysterious epic by Louisiana group Phil Phillips & the Twilights.

Johnny Franz had reached a compromise with Marty: his own musicians could play on the record, but a lavish arrangement would be overlaid, replacing the primitivism of the original with a polished theatrical sheen. A harp, an ethereal choir, whatever the song needed to move it from the Gulf of Mexico to the North Sea.

"We started at 10 in the morning, at the Philips studio, but nothing went right," says Jim Sullivan. "There was a lot of sitting around waiting for microphones to be repositioned and there were continual problems with the sound balance – so, after about 78 takes, we all trooped over to Lansdowne Studios and started again. The engineer there had it down in no time. That was Joe Meek." Although he had been responsible for the sound quality of such hits as *Bad Penny Blues* by Humphrey Lyttelton, *Petite Fleur* by Chris Barber, *Puttin' On The Style* by Lonnie Donegan and *Last Train To San Fernando* by Johnny Duncan, Meek was still very much an anonymous backroom boy, working for the prickly Denis Preston but dreaming of owning his own studio, maybe his own record label. He would get his chance in November, when Preston fired him.

On *Boy Meets Girls*, Marty came on like an older brother who was saving up to get married – which he was. He and Joyce were going to tie the knot at the Greenwich church where his parents had been married, where he had been christened Reginald Smith. They had started dating in February, became engaged in May, went public in October and now the date had been set: 2 December 1959. Of course, fearing a mass desertion by distraught girls and a consequent reduction in the cash flow, Larry Parnes had done all he could to talk him out of it.

"Larry and I had a few heated meetings," says Marty, "to discuss what it would mean to my career. I'd been a 'teen idol' for a couple of years and I was getting pressure from newer guys like Cliff and Billy Fury. But I just wanted to be me – and I'd always done what I wanted to do, so I got married. Larry wanted me to live with Joyce, just move in together, but I didn't want to do that. In those days, you just didn't. He predicted a decline in fan-mania and I said 'Well, I accept all that – just let me get on with my life' . . . which I did. And it was the best thing I ever did."

A new single, *Bad Boy*, a soft-rock Joyce-inspired love song written by Marty and cut with his Wild Cats on the first take, followed *Sea Of Love* into the Top 10 and even reached number 45 on *Billboard*'s Hot 100. In the annual *NME* poll, readers voted him number 18 in the World's Outstanding Male Singer category – above Mario Lanza, Johnnie Ray, Nat 'King' Cole and his latest hero Bobby Darin. And soon, two weeks into the New Year, Fleetway Publications would launch a new teen-girls' romance weekly called *Marty*, named after him . . . the pin-up dreamboat heart-throb.

And here he was married.

Thirty-seven

Until 1861, a chap could be hanged if he were caught engaging in a spot of sodomy. Such behaviour was still regulated by the Buggery Act of 1533, adopted during the reign of that pillar of rectitude Henry VIII, and, ever since its publication 78 years later, the notion that homosexuality was an 'abomination', punishable by death, was reinforced and held to be an incontrovertible truth by those who believed everything they read in the King James authorised version of the Bible, written to satisfy conditions set down by a monarch who believed in the divine right of kings, a man succinctly described as the wisest fool in Christendom. (In the world of rock music, one learnt never to trust an 'authorised' book.)

In 1885, responding principally to the sexual exploitation of adolescent girls, Parliament passed the Criminal Law Amendment Act, which raised the age of consent from 13 to 16, strengthened existing legislation against prostitution, and confirmed the criminality of all homosexual activity. Any man found guilty of 'gross indecency' with another male, either in private or in public, could expect a prison sentence of two years hard labour – as Oscar Wilde would soon find out.

During the 1950s, particularly, the forces of law and order were zealous in their pursuit and persecution of homosexuals, locking up more than a thousand in 1955 alone. Many others were sent for psychiatric treatment. The newspapers loved it, of course, especially when there was any sort of celebrity involved. It was headline news in October 1953, when a newspaper reporter happened to be in court to hear John Gielgud pleading guilty to lewd behaviour in a public lavatory. He was 49 years old, had been knighted only four months earlier and had given a false name to the police in an attempt to conceal his identity. Humiliated but fortunate to escape prison, he was fined ten pounds and instructed to seek help from his doctor.

Tory MP Ian Harvey, Under-secretary of State at the Foreign Office, was caught in the bushes (by a policeman who heard rustling noises) at St James's Park, allegedly committing an act of gross indecency with a Coldstream Guardsman. The charge was dropped but he was fined five pounds for breaching park regulations. This, however, was nothing compared with the shame of being blacklisted by his club and having to hand over his job to a more reliable fellow, the resolutely heterosexual John Profumo.

It was after old Etonian Lord Montagu of Beaulieu, founder of the motor car museum, was banged up for participating in illegal activities at his beach hut that the Home Secretary appointed John Wolfenden to head a committee to examine the current law and suggest possible changes. Their report, published in September 1957, concluded that "homosexual behaviour between consenting adults in private should no longer be a criminal offence" but it would be another 10 years before their recommendations were implemented.

The bohemian set was used to homosexuals, accepted them without question. Quentin Crisp, a beautiful talker, would often hold forth at the French coffee bar in Old Compton Street, taking breaks from modelling naked at St Martins Art School round the corner, and dancers from the West End shows would often be sitting around at the Gyre & Gimble. "They had to tread carefully," says Derek Duffy. "The police were always on their trail and the plain-clothes guys were often difficult to spot. One gay meeting place they used to hang around at was a gents' toilet in Soho Square, a sort of black-painted steel structure. It was known as the Iron Lung because there was often the sound of heavy breathing coming out of the windows."

Over at the 2Is, the rock 'n' roll crowd were less tolerant. Having been conditioned by contemporary moral values and newspaper stories deploring 'the homosexual menace', they spoke mockingly of homos, queers and – since the conviction of Lord Montagu – monts. It was Eddie Cochran who introduced a new description.

"I was up at the Astor Club one night with Terry Dene, who was trying to drown his sorrows, as usual," remembers Brian Gregg, who had just landed a gig as one of Johnny Kidd's Pirates. "The Krays, who were acquaintances of Terry's, were there too – buying us loads of drinks – and Larry Parnes came in with Gene Vincent and Eddie Cochran, who had only been in the country for about a week. We all got chatting – and when Larry left the table for something, Eddie asked me 'is he a fag . . . you know, queer?' Of course, I nodded – at which point, he turned to Gene and said 'I told you, man, the guy's a fucking faggot!' "

Parnes certainly was homosexual and, though usually charming, at times exhibited a darker side. How he avoided legal or music-biz censure is a mystery – although his interest in adolescents was by no means unique.

In May 1960, during his famous auditions at the Wyvern Social Club in Liverpool, Parnes examined a parade of hopeful groups, lined up for him by local impresario Alan Williams. Some of his acts had been offered tours of Scotland and it would be cheaper and more convenient to hire some of these youngsters as backing groups, rather than shipping up London guys. A couple of them might do, he thought – but the best thing he saw that day was a cherubic, chubby-cheeked teenager, playing enthusiastically in one of the bands. Hinting at the possibility of a recording contract, he arranged for Williams to bring the lad to London for a second, solo audition.

They travelled down by train and, that evening, after a sight-seeing tour of London in Larry's flashy car, Williams was dropped off at a hotel, while the wide-eyed lad went home with his host. "First thing he asked was 'did I want a bath?' Well, OK, why not? He showed me to the bathroom, which had two deep-buttoned upholstered armchairs and mirrors all over the walls . . . and then, when I was in the bath, he came in and sat in one of the armchairs, looking at me as he told me how he saw my future."

Later, in the expansive and expensive living-room, Larry plied him with whisky and Coca-Cola before guiding him to a bedroom containing only a double bed. "I was used to sleeping with my brother – we didn't have a lot of room at home – so I innocently asked 'which side shall I sleep on?' I was totally unfamiliar with homosexuals, what they did or how they behaved. I certainly hadn't ever met any before. Anyway, he climbed into bed and started trying to touch me. I spent the next hour resisting his advances and eventually he gave up."

Larry took him out the next day, bought him a suit from Cecil Gee's and sent him home with Williams.

Laurence Maurice Parnes had been born on 3 September 1929 at the family home, 98 Christchurch Avenue, a gentle walk from Brondesbury Park tube station. His father Nathan made a very respectable living as a ladies costumier and his mother Stella hoped her son would succeed him in the business when the time came. This he did, starting at 16, "picking up pins with a magnet", although he always harboured a wider ambition – to break into show business somehow. This was achieved through John Kennedy.

It was in September 1956, three weeks after his twenty-seventh birthday, that Parnes embarked on his new adventure, managing a singer who specialised in rock 'n' roll, a musical form about which he knew nothing. Tommy Steele became an overnight star and Parnes, a fast learner, became a star manager. As will have been noted, he added Colin Hicks and Marty Wilde to his roster in summer 1957, followed by Vince Eager in April 1958 – by which time he was being fêted as the sharpest, shrewdest operator in his field, a reputation he was always keen to foster.

"If you don't take a gamble in this business, you never get anywhere," he told showbiz journalist Tom Hutchinson. "There is a lot of star material in this country if you take the trouble to find it – and I'm going to find it!"

And, as if by magic, he did. His next discovery was a one-in-a-million find, a gold strike, in Birkenhead, of all places. He saw this kid and he just knew.

The latest Parnes package show had just hit the road, the extravagantly named 'Extravaganza', headlined by Marty Wilde and dovetailed into his *Oh Boy!* schedule. Also on the bill were Vince Eager & the Vagabonds, the Sophisticats, Sonny Roy 'the funny boy', Pat Laurence, Rae Young and the John Barry Seven – who, as well as having their own spot, backed Marty, who had recently jettisoned his first set of Wild Cats. After starting out at the Savoy in Burnt Oak, they moved on to the Essoldo at Clacton, the Troxy at Portsmouth, the Essoldo at Loughborough and, on 1 October 1958, they reached the Essoldo at Birkenhead. There waiting, hoping that Larry Parnes would see him as arranged, was 18-year-old local lad Ronnie Wycherley.

Wycherley had been born at Smithdown (later Sefton General) Hospital in Liverpool on 17 April 1940 and had grown up in a terraced no-garden outside-loo house in Haliburton Street in the Dingle. It was not the prettiest suburb of the city, boasting the biggest refuse tip on Merseyside – not only household rubbish but also the spoil from the Mersey Tunnel and bomb debris from the devastating Luftwaffe blitzes of 1941 and 1942 – and the oil jetties of the Herculaneum Docks, serving the spreading cluster of storage tanks.

Like another pupil at St Silas's Infants School, Richard Starkey (three months his junior), Wycherley was a sickly child, contracting the rheumatic fever that would always haunt him. After failing the 11-plus, he moved on to four years of torture and boredom at Wellington Road Secondary School, a short walk from his home.

"I hated school: it was like being in jail," he told writer Royston Ellis, describing his last day there. "There were about five minutes to go before the final bell. I couldn't stand it. I put my feet up on the desk and lit a cigarette. The teacher told me to put it out but I just laughed. 'Go on, teach, make me,' I said. With only a minute to go before the end of school, he caned me. He thrashed me six times on my hand. With each stroke, I laughed louder, until the bell rang as he brought down the cane for the sixth time. Then I was free! I went wild, running out of school shouting 'I'm free, I'm free, I'm free!' "

Blackboard Jungle in the Dingle. It was a tough life but you were programmed to lurch through it, even if the misty, monochrome neighbourhood seemed to be crumbling around you. Dingle Station, the southern terminus of the Liverpool Overhead Railway, was closed in 1956 and so was the Beresford Cinema, where he longed to be like the cowboys riding across the screen at Saturday morning pictures. The only thriving businesses seemed to be pubs – four of which were less than five minutes from his front door: the Masonic, the Pineapple, the Dingle Arms and the Pheasant. He would pass them on his way to the Florence Institute, on the corner of Wellington Road and Mill Street, to meet his mates. A boys' club where some played table tennis and others played guitars, the Florrie had been purpose-built in 1889 by a wealthy Liverpudlian trader, to give local lads a refuge where they could let off steam and make some noise. Skiffle addicts, fired up by Lonnie Donegan's records, strummed in groups that would eventually bloom into Gerry & the Pacemakers and the Fourmost, while Ronald Wycherley worked away at C, F and G and made futile attempts to win approval at talent contests.

He also started jotting down ideas for songs, developing some – including one inspired by a work colleague, Margo King – into finished pieces. He liked them, his mates liked them . . . why not send them to England's most famous rock 'n' roll impresario, Larry Parnes, and see if he liked them too? This he did, in summer 1958, but Parnes was now being pestered to death by wannabes and ignored it. Wycherley's mother then sent a letter boosting her son and Parnes agreed to meet him backstage at Birkenhead.

One can imagine his delight on seeing the lad, who had been cultivating an Eddie Cochran hairstyle and stance since seeing him in *The Girl Can't Help It*. He watched as Wycherley unsheathed his guitar from the bolster which served as a carrying case and sang a couple of his compositions. In their raw state, in this impromptu setting, Parnes could have detected little potential in these simple songs – but he saw all he needed in the teenager's shimmering natural beauty, his simmering sexuality, his spine-tingling voice and his naïveté, so ripe for moulding.

Without showing his hand, Parnes allowed Wycherley to stick around and see the show from the wings – and at an appropriate moment, tapped him on the shoulder. "Have you got guts?" he asked. "Sure I have," Wycherley replied.

Parnes would recall the occasion a few years later. "I then said firmly to this fair-haired boy 'Go on to the stage and start singing!' There was a brief instant in which he looked blankly at me. Maybe he didn't understand, maybe he thought I was kidding. So I pushed him out on stage. He got the message then! He ran to the microphone and started to perform. Well, he was sensational, a real gas! He only did a couple of numbers but that was enough to get the fans rooting wildly for him. Then and there I was convinced this boy would become a star."

His adrenalin bubbling, Parnes promptly invited Wycherley to join the tour. "It was a matter of going home and saying to my father that I'd been asked to join a rock 'n' roll show, was it OK with him?" he told radio presenter Stuart Colman. "He was pleased to get rid of me – I'd been making a lot of noise around the house!" The next morning, with a few clothes crammed into a cardboard suitcase, he was on the bus, leaving Liverpool on the East Lancs Road, heading for the Essoldo at Stretford and the start of a new life.

When they reached London, Wycherley moved in with Vince Eager, sharing the Gloucester Road flat which Larry had recently vacated in favour of more opulent accommodation in Great Cumberland Place.

Unwilling to blow it (though it might have crossed his mind a few times), Parnes exercised great care planning his new singer's launch. He learned that, since leaving school at fifteen, Wycherley had

worked his way through various casual jobs, including several
months as a Mersey tugboat deckhand, an occupation which
immediately took on a romantic *On The Waterfront* glow in Larry's
mind. He tutored his shy and awkward protégé in how to answer the
sort of questions he would be asked by the press, how to show
respect to authority figures in the business. He bought him smart,
trendy clothes to replace the drainpipes and Millet's shirts he
favoured and took him to his own West End hairdresser. A new
word slipped into the pop lexicon: 'grooming'.

Most importantly, Parnes needed to confect a more dynamic and
memorable identity than Ronnie Wycherley.

It so happened that a film director called Cy Endfield had got in
touch regarding Marty Wilde. He had seen him on *Oh Boy!* and
thought he would be ideal for the movie he was currently putting
together, *Jet Storm*. Although Parnes had never heard of Endfield, he
agreed to meet him and, in preparation for this, went to see his
current film *Sea Fury*, which had just gone on release. Dreadful tosh,
set on the coast of Spain, it starred Stanley Baker as the leading
crewman on a tugboat. Tugboat? *Sea Fury*?

He told Wycherley that, from this day forth, he would be known
as Billy Fury – a suggestion which received little enthusiasm. The
singer wanted to be known as Stean Wade, a stage name he had
thought up months earlier and had cherished ever since. After some
discussion, Parnes agreed to toss for it . . . and lost. But when the first
publicity material was prepared, it was under the name of Billy Fury.

In an interview with broadcaster Spencer Leigh, Parnes recalled
that the 'nice, ordinary, friendly name' Billy had been inspired by
Billy Cotton – fat, square, bald, anathema to any self-respecting rock
'n' roller – but this could well have been another example of Larry's
myth-making. We should also take with salt Larry's claim to have
signed no formal contract for five months. "I didn't sign Billy right
away," he revealed. "I knew it might take several years to build him
into a top name and therefore strong loyalty on both sides would be
needed. I preferred to go ahead without a contract until March 1959."
Hardly likely. By this time, he was on television and in the charts. "I
think Larry's gone senile," joked Hal Carter, his adjutant and road
manager. "His memories certainly don't match mine."

One thing was certain, however: the name he bestowed on Ronnie
Wycherley was a stroke of genius.

Billy Fury took no time at all to grow into it. His first professional appearance was a gift. John Moxey, who directed episodes of Associated-Rediffusion's 'Television Playhouse', phoned Parnes to say he was looking for a louche and lascivious guitar-strumming lad to slouch around in the coffee bar and beat-basement scenes of his next production. "I have just the boy," said the Parnes. Written by Ted Willis, *Strictly For The Sparrows* revolved around bohemians Tago and Al, played by Kenneth Cope and Philip Locke – but although Fury strummed and sang, his contribution went uncredited. Unless you, like Billy's family, were tuned in to Channel 9 at 9pm on Friday 31 October 1958, you would have missed it; the play was broadcast live and no tele-recording was made.

Obviously hoping to start a bidding war, Parnes next arranged an audition for two record companies. Philips turned him down but Decca's A&R manager Frank Lee saw in Fury the same qualities Parnes had seen and knew he must take him under his wing. The former General Manager of Radio Luxembourg, Lee had joined Decca in 1951 and had improved the company's fortunes immediately, producing million sellers in Vera Lynn's *Auf Wiederseh'n Sweetheart* and Winifred Atwell's *Black and White Rag*. He had even devised Atwell's tinny 'other' piano – so his meddling with the impressionable Fury, who knew what he wanted but would never have dared to speak up, could have been disastrous. Fortunately, Lee was sufficiently taken with Fury to give him his head, to accede to Larry's demand that he be allowed to record his own compositions, in a musical setting which did them justice, with a producer he could respect. This arrangement, unprecedented in the British recording industry, resulted in Fury's best work, initially with musical director Harry Robinson, leader of Lord Rockingham's XI – who, when Billy first met them in the studio, were cock-a-hoop, having just been told that their raucous novelty *Hoots Mon* had gone to number one.

He had seen them on television, of course. The brainchild of Jack Good, they were the backbone of *Oh Boy!*: an 11 piece band unashamed and versatile enough to play muddy rhythm & blues, startling rock 'n' roll, smoochy ballads, the whole spectrum, anything that might be required. Robinson was MD and MC, rapping out nursery-rhyme couplets in a broad Scottish brogue. He arranged much of the music for the series but looked quite mad, grinning hideously and waving his arms about. Most of his players were refugees from big bands and jazz groups, who had passed through the stage of wringing their hands about the paucity of work and were now quite prepared to embrace the spirit of the age and go for it, turn it into fun. The front line boasted four sax players: Rex Morris, Cyril Reubens, Red Price and, hiding behind shades, Benny Green – wry crony of Ronnie Scott and former *NME* columnist. Cherry Wainer played glamorous, swirling organ, Ron Black played bass, Don Storer played drums and Reg Weller percussion. Ian Fraser was pianist; former Wild Cat Kenny Packwood played rhythm guitar and Eric Ford played lead. When the band went on tour, Ford's spot in the programme would be a version of Duane Eddy's *Cannonball* but he could play in any style, having worked in dance bands, jazz groups and the pioneering rock 'n' roll bands of Rory Blackwell and Leon Bell. Until Jack Good hired him for the pilot show of *Oh Boy!*, he held down a day job, running the guitar department of Selmer's music shop, opposite Foyle's in Charing Cross Road, and had sold or demonstrated instruments to everyone on the London scene, from Terry Dene to Bert Weedon.

It was Ford's guitar figure which underpinned Fury's first single, *Maybe Tomorrow*. "I copped the idea for that from a record called *Looking Back* by Nat 'King' Cole," he admits, "just a simple repeated arpeggio which seemed to carry the song along – and the singing saxophone was inspired by the one on *Born Too Late* by the Poni-Tails, which was a big hit at the time." Put these ideas and influences into a blender, add Benny Green's understated baritone grunts, unobtrusive drum and bass interplay, and the Vernons Girls' neurotic wailing and you have the perfect carriage for Fury's soulful vocal. Wide and deep, it had the sound and texture, the authenticity and atmosphere of a record issued by some cool American independent label.

A B-side, *Gonna Type A Letter*, another of Fury's compositions was also attempted that day, 26 November, but time ran out and Harry Robinson took the song home to polish. Whereas only a few musicians had been required for the sparse arrangement of *Maybe Tomorrow*, Robinson brought in more of his band when they reconvened in the studio on the last day of the year. The result was a characteristically brash and boisterous *Oh Boy!*-style performance, punctuated by a percussive typewriter. The drummer sounded as if he had just come from a Fats Domino session, guitars and saxes ran together and the record clattered along like a train.

Slow, fast, ballads or rock 'n' roll, Fury had an instinctive touch. Far from feeling intimidated by his first studio experiences, the 18-year-old novice had created a landmark single. During the last week of January 1959, he mimed to *Maybe Tomorrow* on two ITV pop shows – *Cool For Cats*, which Kent Walton had been presenting for two years and which was rarely cool for real cats, and the *Jack Jackson Show* – but it wasn't until the middle of February, when he smouldered for the cameras of *Oh Boy!*, that he reached his core audience. A fortnight later, he was in the Top 20, and two weeks after that, he was heading north to start his first one-night-stand variety tour . . . billed down among the trick cyclists and jugglers.

Parnes wanted Fury to learn stagecraft, work up his act in such obscure locations as Worksop Regal, Wombwell Plaza, Matlock Ritz and Mexborough Empire – and since it was essentially a rehearsal, he economised by taking along only one accompanying musician, Colin Green. "We set off together in Larry's shiny Vauxhall Cresta, pink and grey with white-wall tyres – Billy in the passenger seat and me in the back with my guitar, on our way to a list of towns I'd never heard of."

Thirty-eight

On 11 January 1959, taking a quick Sunday break from his stultifying pantomime season at Stockton, Marty Wilde appeared on the *NME* Poll Winners' Concert at the Royal Albert Hall. He chose to sing *Rockin' Robin, Fire Of Love* and *I Can't Give You Anything But Love* – backed by the tuxedoed Ken Mackintosh Orchestra and his own guitarist Colin Green, brought in by Larry Parnes to provide a youthful, rock 'n' roll element. It would be his only gig with Wilde, but Green became a mainstay of the Parnes operation.

A 15-year-old guitar fanatic, he made school more palatable by playing truant whenever he had amassed enough dinner money for the train fare from Woking up to town, where he spent his days at the Freight Train coffee bar, playing along to every record that came on the jukebox. By some right place, right time coincidence, he was seen and heard by Mark Forster, who had recently been hired by Parnes to take care of correspondence, accounts and administrative duties. Next thing he knew, he was in Larry's office, suite 52 in Oxford Circus House, being offered a job – a weekly wage, whether he was working or not.

"My mother was very anxious about me missing school and even more anxious about me quitting to become a musician," says Green, "and she came with me to see Larry, full of apprehension. Luckily, Tommy Steele happened to be there – 'Go on, luv, give the lad a chance!' he said – and that was it. I only had an acoustic, so I had to borrow an electric guitar and an amp for my début . . . backing Marty at the Royal Albert Hall! The kids at school couldn't believe it."

He was assigned to Billy Fury and they spent many days at his flat, working out songs and keys, before setting off on the road, two wide-eyed rock 'n' roll kids under the care of their suave, confident protector. It was a strange initiation. A touring variety show catering for all tastes. Comedians, acrobats, straight singers, country skifflers and rock 'n' rollers, all crammed into makeshift dressing rooms. Topping the bill were Johnny Duncan & his Blue Grass Boys, hitless for over a year but still a popular draw. Further down was ferocious rock 'n' roller Vince Taylor & his Playboys and sandwiched in between was Jill Day, wondering what was happening to her career. Billed as "the sapphire blonde with the diamond personality", she had made films and records, starred in West End theatre, even had her own BBC Television series only two years earlier – and here she was in the boondocks, a fish out of water in a world that was changing too quickly.

Providing incidental music for the jugglers and backing the singers on the show, including Jill Day and Billy Fury, were the Wise Guys, a trio led by former Lonnie Donegan guitarist Jimmie Currie. He switched to drums for Fury's short set, allowing Colin Green to jump around and act out his fantasies. Every night, Parnes would suggest ways in which Fury could refine his act, loosen up and let his instinct guide him.

"We were terribly resented by the music-hall guys, the die-hard pros who had been in the business for years and suddenly saw these rock 'n' roll kids taking over," says Green. "The comics, in particular, could be pretty scathing when they introduced you."

The tour was instructive not only to Fury but his manager too. As if he needed any confirmation, Parnes could see that music hall – a tradition he adored as he was growing up – was in its death throes. This was partly due to skiffle and rock 'n' roll, but more to the epidemic spread of television, which for most people was now an easier, far more comfortable way of being entertained. Judging by the audiences at these concerts, Parnes knew for sure that it was only teenagers and unmarrieds who were still interested in going out and having a good time. Their parents were now glued to the screen, the first generation to complain that there was nothing worth watching on the telly that night, but watching it all the same.

What was needed was a fast-paced touring show, wall-to-wall rock 'n' roll, no fillers, singers and backing musicians who looked and felt and sounded like 1959. Teenagers wanted a teenage show – a package of their favourites – and Parnes knew just the man to give it to them.

On the road for the first time, Fury and Green became mates with the other rock 'n' roll act on the tour, Vince Taylor & his Playboys, seeing them as older brothers, hearing stories about the old 2Is days, the various groups they'd been in. Always good company. They were waiting for their break, a hit record or media acclaim, and

Taylor – who thought he was going to show the Brits how it was
done – was both bewildered and dismayed by his lack of progress.
His first single had died a death before Christmas and now, after
only two appearances on *Oh Boy!* it seemed as if Jack Good was no
longer interested in him. Maybe it was because he insisted on
wearing black leather. It was not quite time for that yet. Then Taylor
had fallen out with Tony Sheridan, whose guitar solos, most of the
2Is crowd agreed, were the best bits of Vince's record. To add insult
to injury, Jack Good had hired Tony Sheridan and two of Taylor's
Playboys to be *Oh Boy*'s resident trio. Brian Bennett and Licorice
Locking had a foot in each camp: on television with Sheridan and on
the road with Vince.

The other two Playboys, recently recruited, were pianist Lou
Brian, formerly with Colin Hicks & the Cabin Boys, and Glaswegian
guitarist Joe Moretti (known as Scottie to avoid confusion with the
other Joe, manager Joe Singer), who had just spent a month in *Mother
Goose*, backing Vince Eager. They appeared on the new single, issued
during the first week of April: *Brand New Cadillac*, an unrestrained
rumbling blues with an erratic vocal from Taylor but sizzling guitar
work from Moretti, his first time in the studio. It sank like a stone but
was destined to become a decade-crossing cult record, a treasured
relic revived by the Downliners Sect and the Clash, among others.

No sooner had the tour finished than Bennett and Locking
defected to Marty Wilde's Wildcats – replacing the platinum blond
trio of Bobby Woodman, Tex Makins and Alan LeClair. . . who joined
Colin Green to become Billy Fury's backing group. (And people ask
me why I invented rock family trees.)

That summer, feeling he needed a sax player, Parnes expanded
Fury's group to a quintet, adding Billy McVay, the former Streatham
Locarno guy who had teased Woodman and company for dyeing
their hair and wearing stage make-up. Colin Green succumbed to the
bleach – but McVay held out, fearful of what his rugged Scottish pals
might say, but then he went half way with an effeminate blond
streak.

By this time, a second Billy Fury single had been issued to little
effect. Despite another shimmering Harry Robinson arrangement, his
plaintive plea to former Liverpool love *Margo*, written on the tugboat
between tides, was in and out of the chart in a week. But although
his records weren't hitting the spot – two more singles, *Angel Face*

and *My Christmas Prayer*, would fail during the year – his live performances were filling halls wherever he went. His confidence boosted by five appearances on *Oh Boy!*, a long tour with Marty Wilde and Wee Willie Harris, and a bunch of solo gigs, he had rolled with the flow, gone where the music took him, got even looser than Parnes had suggested, into an area which the *NME* found rather distasteful. "Whatever Cliff Richard once did in his act to provoke the outcry that it was 'too sexy' has nothing on some of the things Billy Fury does," reported their incredulous reviewer. "Indeed, some of his antics during a 'love scene' with the microphone were downright disgusting."

During the last half of July, the first half of August, every afternoon for a month, Fury was a star attraction in the Marty Wilde Show at the Palace Theatre in Blackpool. For years, the town had been the nation's favourite holiday destination and every house was packed, mostly with squealing teenagers. "It was an *Oh Boy!*-style show, featuring Tony Sheridan, Cherry Wainer, Red Price and Cuddly Dudley, as well as a few of Larry's recent signings," says Bobby Woodman, "but it was Billy who got the crowd going. Onstage, he turned into this sensuous sex machine – but offstage, he was a shy, quiet guy. Generous and thoughtful too. He knew we were only getting paid 12 quid a week, out of which we had to pay our own expenses, and he used to take us out and buy us clothes. A very sincere, beautiful guy."

Woodman and Makins were in paradise: plenty of time off and a constant, ever-changing supply of fun-seeking girls, out to make the most of their week's holiday by the sea. "Just before the end of the season, we met these two Scottish girls," says Woodman, "and they invited us to go back home with them, to stay in the house they shared. We had some days off, so off we went . . . but we stayed up there a bit too long and missed some rehearsals. When we got back, Parnes fired us."

Now at a peak of megalomania, Parnes was about to launch his most ambitious project, the dream scheme that would confirm his superiority, so he believed, over the slow thinking yesterday men who still imagined that they ran the music business. A package show, nothing but rock 'n' roll, all his own singers and musicians, no other agents would get a look in. It was a one-man show, his show. Only three years in the business and he was cock of the walk.

During the year, Parnes had been collecting singers the way that some people collected Dinky toys. That he had no 'ears' – music business jargon for the ability to recognise musical talent – was no impediment since he made most of his signings on a hunch, on the way they looked, on the way they made him feel, and his intuitive understanding of what appealed to impressionable teenagers. All his signings were young and virile, all exuded the innocence of lambs.

He had already contracted Johnny Gentle, Dickie Pride and Duffy Power by March, when BBC Television's *Panorama* investigated the phenomenon that was Parnes. The impresario was delighted – even the staid old BBC had heard about him – although their upper-crust reporter, Chris Chataway, was clearly mystified by the young men's career choices and by Larry's epic self-belief. "He owns a batch of golden boys, all in the lucrative business of putting teenage growing pains to music," he told viewers and then tried to wrong-foot Larry by confronting him with the truth: "What perplexes a lot of people is that no training seems to be needed for success in this sphere." What a suggestion! "My boys are not untrained," Parnes protested, clucking like a mother hen.

The reporter turned to the boys: "Do you feel manipulated?" "Nah, not really: it all amounts to having faith in your manipulator." "Do people tell you that your manager is taking you for a ride, making a lot of money out of you?" "Very often." "When your audiences go hysterical and shout and scream, what do you think of that?" "We love it." As Chataway sat there, at a loss to understand why anyone should want to inhabit such a world, the class divisions fell open for all to see. Chataway, an Olympic athlete with a plum in his mouth and an honours degree from Magdalen College, Oxford, soon to become a Conservative member of Parliament; Parnes, a Jewish trader, nouveau riche; and a bunch of ill-educated working-class lads. The interviewer homed in on Johnny Gentle. "What do you do for amusement?" he asked. "I date girls." "Anything else?" "Not really, no."

Under his real name, John Askew, and his first stage name Ricky Damone, Gentle had started singing in the dance halls and working men's clubs of Liverpool. In summer 1958, he sang *Poor Little Fool* in a talent competition at Butlin's Holiday Camp in Pwllheli and one of the judges, Clinton Ford, told him he ought to go to London. "I wrote to Larry Parnes, sent him a photograph and a bit of history, and he wrote back, inviting me to come in for a chat," says Gentle. "I went to see him but I didn't take my guitar – so he put on *Endless Sleep* by Marty Wilde, which fortunately I knew, and asked me to sing along with it. That was my audition! Then he said, 'I'm going to send you to Johnny Franz at Philips, for a recording test' – which I passed – and next thing I knew, Larry was giving me a contract to sign." Gentle, who had been born on 8 December 1936 (the Parnes publicity machine would drop not one but three years off his age), was now over 21 and able to sign a binding contract.

"It just proved how powerful he was," says Gentle. "His whole life was creating pop stars and if he thought someone had talent, he could literally take them off the street, get them a recording test and give them the opportunity to shine. If they didn't pass, he would discard them . . . he did it many times. Luckily, I passed."

In his case, 'grooming' consisted of leaving the lad to his own devices, to choose his own clothes and work out his own stage act, but Parnes had to provide a new name, of course, convincing him that although it lacked the dynamism of Wilde or Fury, Gentle gave him that alluring *je ne sais quoi*. Then there was the question of money. Instead of working out a percentage deal, it would save a lot of trouble if his new acts went on wages. If they did well, he was in pocket; if they failed to progress, he was in essence subsidising them – so they should be grateful. And they were. "I would say he paid us about 20 per cent of what we earned," reckons Gentle, "but we were happy to go with him because it was an opportunity to make the big time. We weren't at all streetwise, we signed whatever was put in front of us." Parnes had learned a few lessons since the early days: his new, one-sided contracts tied up the singers for four years but there was an annual option which allowed him to get out and dump them if he saw fit. "We should maybe have had a lawyer look over them," says a rueful Gentle, "but we were so full of ourselves, so excited to be going on tour and making records, that we didn't even think about things like that."

Next to sign was Dickie Pride, a tousle-haired Teddy boy from Croydon, who became entangled in Larry's web after Russ Conway 'discovered' him singing at the Union Tavern in the Old Kent Road. So the authorised story goes. Dickie wasn't around to face the first generation of probing rock historians: he died in 1969, forgotten at 27. His death went unreported in any music paper even though, 10 years earlier, when he was a regular face on *Oh Boy!*, he was all over the press. Some teenage girls' magazines even featured him as their centrefold hunk.

According to Larry's shtick, which may very well have been true, Pride had been a student at the Royal College of Church Music and had sung in the choir at Canterbury Cathedral. He had bumbled his way through several jobs, including stone mason's assistant, paint sprayer, electric plater and lorry driver's mate. Nothing to lose. After assessment at the Oxford Circus office, he was easily persuaded to lose his given name, Richard Kneller, in favour of Dickie Pride, an identity which suited his leer. Norrie Paramor signed him to EMI's Columbia label in the first week of February 1959 and he made his *Oh Boy!* début later that month. Jack Good had already introduced him in *Disc*, the latest addition to the flourishing music-weeklies market. "He is a truly amazing wag," he wrote. "His legs look like bent matchsticks inside his drainpipe jeans, making his shoes look like size 14. He has a strange gnome-like face, reminiscent of a cartoon of Gene Vincent. His hair is thick and wavy and stands up like crimped steel wool." How could he fail?

Not long before Christmas, Parnes had gone to Shepherds Bush Gaumont, to see if Scottish singer Clay Nichols was as good as people said, but he was unimpressed. However, he couldn't take his eyes off one of the boys in the dance competition. His name was Ray Howard, he was 17, lived in Fulham and worked in a laundry . . . and, as fortune would have it, he also did a bit of singing on the side.

As Howard's fifteenth birthday, 9 September 1956, coincided with the end of the summer holidays, he hadn't bothered returning to school but embarked instead on a series of casual jobs – satisfying only because they financed his flourishing social life. By 1958, this revolved around singing at various youth clubs and pubs, including the Greyhound in Fulham Palace Road, still very much a family pub, and hanging out with older, flashier boys from the area. All had a sense of style; some were gay. "They seemed to be very well-connected and they sort of adopted me," says Duffy. "We would go off to parties in the West End and to Dorothy's club in Knightsbridge, where you would see celebrities like Lionel Bart and Ben Lyon, as well as underworld figures like Albert Dimes. It was exotic beyond belief, to be driven through Berkeley Square at night in a hand-painted lavender-coloured Armstrong Siddeley – and yet, next morning, I was back at the laundry, scrubbing collars and cuffs and getting dermatitis."

The manager of Shepherds Bush Gaumont ran not only the usual Saturday morning pictures for schoolkids – cartoons and cowboy films, *Flash Gordon* serials – but also presented live music and, on occasion, dance competitions. "One Saturday, the girl I was with dragged me up onto the stage and we won first prize," says Duffy. Parnes liked the way he moved. It was arranged with the cinema that Duffy would appear again the following week, this time singing. He was backed by his group, the New Vagabonds, and the pianist from the Greyhound. "I sang all the usual stuff – *Mean Woman Blues* and *Let's Have A Party* – and the kids began screaming, as they did automatically for anyone who appeared on the stage. Larry told me he was very interested. Although I was never gay myself, I had several gay friends and I clocked him straight off – but this was Larry Parnes! The biggest name in rock music, the man who could turn people into overnight stars!"

Parnes arranged for a recording test with Jack Baverstock at Fontana, who agreed the lad had potential, and, once his parents had signed the contract – a generous £20 a week for the first year (and a fiver more than Pride or Gentle were getting) – Howard was able to dump the day job. And change his name . . . to Duffy Power. Power? As in strength, energy, control, dominance? Ray, who was already known as Duffy to all his mates, thinks the inspiration for his new surname was Tyrone Power, the Hollywood swashbuckler whose face would appear on the *Sgt Pepper's* sleeve. He had recently dropped dead during a strenuous fight scene with George Sanders, on the set of *Solomon And Sheba*, and his obituaries were everywhere.

Parnes may have fantasised about his boys, and he clearly revelled and radiated in their company, but he did observe the proprieties. At least, most of the time. "He was gay but he wasn't open about it, you'd never know," says Johnny Gentle. "He never laid a hand on me, nor any of the other lads as far as I'm aware; our relationship was strictly business." He would never have dared to touch Tommy Steele, and Marty Wilde would have knocked his block off, but Duffy Power was a trusting kid of 17. "In the weeks between him 'discovering' me and actually signing me, I knew I had to play it clever and not upset him," says Power, "but I always made sure I kept him at arm's length. One weekend, he drove me down to this party in Brighton, thrown by Sally Ann Howes, who was currently very big on Broadway and was back to see her friends – and the guests, people like Gilbert Harding and Hughie Green, all looked at me with a knowing twinkle in their eyes, as if they suspected that something might be going on."

"The closest it ever got to that happening was when Larry told me that I would have to stay at his flat overnight because we had an early start the next day, had to be at London Airport for a promotional trip to Luxembourg. 'You're sleeping in there,' he said, directing me into his bedroom – and of, course, he got in bed beside me. I had to put up with his hand on my leg – and that's when I made it clear that he was never going to have sex with me. I mean, if he had been a woman, I might have given it a go, but there was no way I was going to let some greasy 30-year-old stick his cock up my arse. He had devoted quite a lot of time to me, taking me out to restaurants, taking me to his barber's to get my hair cut to his satisfaction, buying me sharp clothes, coming round to the house and socialising with my parents even, but I think that's when he started to go off me."

The impresario now had seven singers under contract – Tommy Steele (detached and well away from the teen circus by now), Marty Wilde, Vince Eager, Billy Fury, Johnny Gentle, Dickie Pride and Duffy Power – and he added two more during the summer. Taking pity on Terry Dene, on the skids with no manager and no work but promising once again to be a good boy from now on, he hired him for one trial tour – along with, surely some mistake, Sally Kelly, a token girl, who wore skin-tight trousers and was billed as 'Miss Rock 'n' Roll'. Something of an overstatement, one felt.

It was *Melody Maker* journalist Bob Dawbarn who, in August 1959, coined the two phrases with which Parnes would become inextricably linked for evermore. In a two-page spread headlined 'The man behind Britain's Big Beat', he described Larry as 'the pop Svengali' and his clients as 'a stable of stars'. The trainer and his colts. "They go through a very extensive grooming," he told Dawbarn. "I have their hair cut – that is very important – and sometimes they may have bad skin which has to be attended to. Then I get them suitable clothes. I like them to live in a good home, get three good meals a day, get to bed early and have plenty of fresh air." He stressed the importance of image and manners, the promotional value of press, radio and television, and the transitory nature of the pop-music industry. "The idea is that these boys have a run of three years with the teenagers and then, if they have the talent, I will groom them for other spheres of show business."

Digging deeper into what this might entail, another newspaper was told: "Don't get me wrong. I'm no Professor Higgins. My business is to distil not dispel a singer's naturalness. That's why I care not a hang about speech, so long as the boy can be clearly understood."

His 'Big Beat Show' was already on the road, locked into a non-stop rolling schedule of piers, theatres, Odeons and Gaumonts, his young bucks inducing hysteria wherever they went. Marty Wilde had exclusive use of his own band, the Wild Cats; backing the others was a handpicked supergroup: Clem Cattini on drums, Brian Gregg on bass, Billy McVay on sax, Brian Goodey on rhythm guitar and Kenny Packwood on lead guitar.

"One after the other, they would jump out on stage," recalls Gregg, "all looking the same, silhouetted in the spotlight, in their sparkly jackets. 'Which one's this?' Clem would shout. 'I think it's Dickie,' I would shout back. Most of the time, it was just an endless blur of Elvis Presley and Little Richard songs."

The 'stars' of his stable soon discovered that signing with Parnes was only the first step. The key to longevity, survival even, was a hit record. If you had a good song and a hip producer, and your record took off, you were laughing – but you were going nowhere if you left the studio knowing that you had just made another travesty.

"I never sang any of my records on tour, I hated them all," says Johnny Gentle. "Even though I was allowed to write a lot of them myself – thanks to Larry's power – I just didn't like the way they turned out. They were five years behind the times at Philips but I wasn't allowed to suggest how they could be improved. I tried once and the guy told me I was out of order, that as a newcomer to the business I shouldn't be spouting my opinions. The session men weren't saying 'let's make this a great record', they were more interested in looking at their watches, seeing if they were going to get any overtime. They couldn't adapt to the current trends; my records had no feeling to them, no soul." Novelty items, every last one, ballads set in weak *Workers' Playtime*-style arrangements, indefensible on any artistic level.

Nevertheless, Gentle could hold an audience and the girls were always milling around, wanting his autograph, giving him presents. "One fan knitted me a sweater, gave it to me at the stage door and pleaded with me to wear it that night – which I did. Jack Good happened to be standing in the wings when I came off and he said: 'Who knitted that pullover for you, Johnny, was it your grandmother?' I never wore it again after that."

"If one of my records had been a hit, my story might have been rather different," says Gentle. As it was, Parnes would drop him after two years, but not before he had done the tour which assured him a precious place in rock history, the seven dates he played in Scotland in May 1960, when he was backed by fellow Liverpudlians the Silver Beetles.

Duffy Power looked great, sang passionately and in tune, and had a sense of how a record should sound and feel but, as a 17-year-old greenhorn, was expected to trust his elders when it came to working in the studio. It didn't look too promising: the other acts on Jack Baverstock's roster at Fontana included Al Saxon, Barry Cryer, Rikki Price (anybody uncool enough to spell Ricky this way never stood a chance), Jimmy Blair, the Chacquito Orchestra and other oddities. Hip teenage fare was not his forte – as was soon clear. Why construct cover versions of *That's My Little Suzie*, *Dream Lover* and *Whole Lotta Shakin' Goin' On* when the originals were definitive? Riddled with banana-fingered guitar solos and Mickey Mouse arrangements, Power's Fontana catalogue was a farrago of ill-chosen material, poorly played.

Dickie Pride somehow managed to scrape into the Top 30 for one week with his lamentable cover of *Primrose Lane*, the tinkly theme-song from an American television soap series, but that was to be the start and end of his chart career. His records were uniformly silly, inept pastiches, clueless productions which missed every target – and his early stage exhibitions were quite ludicrous. Promoted as 'the Sheik of Shake', he would vibrate like a pneumatic drill as he sang. The impressionable admass might have found this amusing but the rock cognoscenti could never take him seriously: he made dud records and came on like a slippery barrow boy. He lost any residual audience when *Pride Without Prejudice*, a pretentious album of cabaret standards, left him with no direction home. "Regrettable though it may be, there are undoubtedly some people who will not give this record a second glance," said the prophetic sleeve note. After learning that Pride had been dabbling with drugs, Parnes reluctantly tore up his contract.

His place in history has never been fully acknowledged. According to almost all his cohorts, Pride had the most potential, was the best singer in the stable, a smooth balladeer, a convincing rocker, the most visionary in his outlook, could even have become a formidable stand-up comedian but, sadly, all subsequent projects foundered. His last band, the unsung and underrated Sidewinders (including Tex Makins on bass), backed Stevie Wonder on his first solo tour of Britain in January 1966, by which time he was seriously messed up.

"We all had problems after Larry let us go," says Johnny Gentle. "Prospective managers and agents would say 'If Parnes couldn't do it, what chance have I?' Brick walls appeared when we tried to take a new path, doors slammed in our faces. It was pretty tough at times."

"Larry thought he was infallible, thought he had the Madras touch [sic]," says Hal Carter, his number one road manager. "He used to tell people that he had a God-given gift for spotting talent – but he had as many failures as successes . . . and he was very good at brushing his failures under the carpet, simply forgetting about them." But it wasn't Parnes who let these youngsters down; it was their record producers. Their counterparts in America, many of whom could not sing as well, were making records which struck deep into the heart while theirs left only a blurred shape in the memory.

Thirty-nine

Brian Gregg and Clem Cattini, dapper prefects surrounded by noisy schoolboys, were intrigued by the new kid on the bus, brought in as a last-minute replacement for their indisposed guitarist Kenny Packwood. It was the morning of 23 August 1959 and the Big Beat Show was on its way to Southend. "Clem and I had been around the block a few times by then," says Gregg, "and we were a little fed up with Larry Parnes sending out boys he fancied, only to find that they were hopeless . . . and we thought this new kid must be the latest one of these. He didn't look like a guitar player – he had short hair all sticking out, as if he'd had an electric shock. So we went back to where he was sitting and started taking the piss. 'Was that suit made to measure?' 'Yeah.' 'Well, who was it made for? – obviously not you.' He wasn't rising to the bait. 'What name has he given you, Terry Terrific?' He just laughed. It turned out that Larry was paying him ten bob to do the gig."

The ever-solicitous Parnes was already there when the bus arrived at the Odeon, faffing around as the singers and musicians prepared for their soundcheck. "He told us all to be on our best behaviour, as professional and impressive as possible, because the soundcheck was doubling as an audition," Gregg continues. "Jack Good was sitting in the empty auditorium, ready to cast his eye over the talent. Everybody knew that he had a new television series starting soon, *Boy Meets Girls*, because Marty Wilde had already been lined up as the star – but he was obviously looking for more acts to book. So all the singers were primping like prima donnas, hoping that Jack was going to jump out of his seat when they came on – but the only one he called down was this new kid off the bus, who turned out to be a really nifty guitarist. He didn't seem at all interested in anyone else."

Larry had stumbled across another star.

"What's your name?" Jack asked the new kid.

"Joe Brown."

"And is Larry your manager?" asked Jack.

"Yes, that's right, Jack," Parnes interjected.

"He wasn't at all," says Joe, "but he was in there like a shot. If Jack hadn't been interested in me, I doubt if I would ever have seen him again."

Brown was eighteen and a half, an East Ender from Plaistow. He had been born on 13 May 1941 at Swarby, a small village in the Lincolnshire Fens but, as a child, had moved south with his family, to take up residence in his uncle's pub, the Sultan in Grange Road. Although he passed the 11-plus without difficulty, a mutual teacher/pupil understanding was reached at Plaistow Grammar and he completed his formal education at Pretoria Road Secondary – leaving to work as a tea-boy for a local electrical firm and a packer in a Covent Garden printing company before getting a job on the railways, working his way up from cleaner to fireman. Meanwhile, a parallel existence had been fired-up by Lonnie. After strumming in the Ace of Clubs Rhythm Group, he graduated to the Spacemen Skiffle Group, built around bassist Pete Oakman and rhythm guitarist Tony Oakham. They rehearsed in the storeroom behind the Oakham family's newsagents shop in Leyton and played wherever they could – usually in the East End but occasionally in Soho.

On 20 June 1959, Joe started his first professional engagement, at Butlin's Holiday Camp in Filey, Yorkshire, as lead guitarist in Clay Nicholls' group, who had a summer residency. "It was the worst band I'd ever been in," says Joe. "I'm not kidding, they were rotten, so bad that the camp commandant was going to chuck us out. Like a fool, I told the others that we needed some sort of outrageous gimmick – and suggested that one of us should shave his head. At the chemist's shop on the camp, they had one of these newfangled electric razors on display, so it should be easy. Well, of course, I drew the short straw, and I had to go down to the chemist's and get my head shaved so I looked like Yul Brynner. Then the others painted a red, white and blue target on my head, like an RAF roundel – and that increased our popularity a bit. People were curious to see this bald maniac with a target on his head. Of course, it buggered up my sex life."

By the beginning of August, Brown felt he had endured enough and Tony Harvey, from the 2Is, went up to Filey to replace him. With his hair growing back like a beard, Joe returned to his mates in the Spacemen, who played the 2Is a couple of times that month, attracting the attention of Tom Littlewood – and it was Tom who

tipped off Parnes when he called seeking a guitarist. Within days of
the Jack Good audition, Larry had the boy under contract: £15 a week
for the first year and an astonishing £30 a week for the second. Plus
expenses! He also promised faithfully to keep up the hire purchase
payments on Joe's motorbike – but didn't.

"We had a great relationship, Larry and I. Most of the others
treated him with reverence but I took the mickey out of him
something rotten – which he couldn't understand, because he had
absolutely no sense of humour. He couldn't work me out at all; it
was a battle of wits from start to finish, beginning with my refusal to
have one of his silly names. 'You can't walk around with a name like
Joe Brown,' he told me, 'you've got to have a name that rolls off the
tongue.' 'What, like dribble?' I said, 'all right, I'll call myself Daryl
Dribble.' I just wasn't having any of it."

No image-building, no grooming, no name change, no nonsense,
no Parnes hanky-panky . . . Joe was a natural star. And fortunately
for everyone, he had been delivered into the hands of Jack Good.

On *Boy Meets Girls*, every Saturday evening starting on 12
September, he worked his magic on the girls and his music on the
boys – a guitar hero before Hank and a chirpy, cocky little cockney
funster to boot. He played behind them all, on grinning terms with
Johnny Cash and Gene Vincent, larking around with Marty and the
Vernons Girls, having a great time. Initially, he was just one of the
resident group, the Firing Squad – Eric Ford and Brian Daley also on
guitars, Alan Weighall on bass and Andy White on drums
(augmented at times by Red Price, Cherry Wainer and Don Storer) –
but he was such a galvanising screen presence that Good brought
him to the fore. "I only ever wanted to be a guitarist but Jack said
'we've got to give this boy a song to sing every week' – and the first
one he gave me was *Seven Little Girls Sitting In The Back Seat*, which I
had to sing sitting at the wheel of this plywood, mock-up motor car,
with seven of the Vernons Girls in the back. I felt such a fool – but
even in that short time, I'd already learned that you never argued
with Jack Good. If he said 'do it', you did it. He might have said it
with a smile on his face, but he meant it!"

As well as producing *Boy Meets Girls* for ABC Television, Good
was producing records for Decca as an independent A&R manager –
but his first studio date, with Italian group Little Tony & his
Brothers, resulted in the undistinguished single *I Can't Help It*. It

wasn't as easy as it seemed, this production game; everybody had to learn the ropes. Since three versions of their composition *A Teenager In Love* had reached the Top 30 that summer, Good arranged to fly in the New York songwriting team of Mort Shuman and Doc Pomus (only just getting into their stride) to appear on a special *Boy Meets Girls* devoted to their work, to savour the scene he was helping to create and to provide a song or two for his acts – but *People Gotta Talk*, the song they 'wrote' for Joe Brown (in fact a recent non-hit for US rocker Ersel Hickey) proved to be an inauspicious début.

The next Good-Brown collaboration, *Darktown Strutters Ball* saw some action and Joe was on his way, but their best work together would be on Billy Fury's remarkable album *The Sound Of Fury*.

It was Jack Good who suggested that Brown's backing group be called the Bruvvers (Joe always called him 'bruv' – as in 'brother', trade union parlance) and Larry Parnes who financed it. "I had my disagreements with Parnes and I've said a few nasty things about him over the years but he had a lot of good points. He was all right. One thing I will always thank him for was letting me have my own group – so I could roll in my mates Pete and Tony Oakman from the Spacemen and one of the best drummers in the country, Bobby Graham. He just about worked me to death, of course – I did the first two years without a single night off – and he was very sparing with the money but then nobody earns much during their apprenticeship, and I have to say that it was a bloody good apprenticeship."

Feeling he could do no wrong, Parnes backed another hunch.

Like Johnny Gentle, Georgie Fame got his break at Butlin's in Pwllheli. He was still called Clive Powell then, working in a Leigh cotton factory by day and playing the pubs with local group the Dominoes at night.

"Egged on by my mates, I entered a talent competition at the camp, doing my Jerry Lee Lewis-Fats Domino thing, and I got through to the final – beating, incidentally, the Texans, a Liverpool group with Ringo Starr on drums. As soon as I came off the stage, Rory Blackwell, whose band had the summer residency, offered me a job and I took it! I went home, persuaded my parents to let me do it, worked out two weeks' notice at the factory and then went back to Pwllheli to finish the season, before moving down to London with them. This was the end of August 1959 and I was two months past my sixteenth birthday."

Powell moved in with Blackwell, who had two rooms above the Strava Ballroom in Islington, where his Blackjacks played a couple of gigs to single-figure audiences and promptly split up. Bobby Woodman and Tex Makins, who had just been elbowed from Billy Fury's band, turned up hoping to get something going with Rory but nothing came of it and they left . . . though not before persuading Powell to let them bleach his hair.

Blond hair and a winning smile – like a young Tommy Steele – but no work, no money, no future. Feeling bad for having brought the young innocent into this Dickensian nightmare, Blackwell got him a job playing piano at the Essex Arms, by Silvertown Bridge in Canning Town. "I used to take a couple of trolley buses over there, play all the tunes I knew, sing a few that I knew the words of, and then pass the box around – maybe make a couple of quid a night, which was just about enough to keep me going." One evening, Blackwell pulled a most unlikely fairy godmother act when he came into the pub with an acquaintance, Lionel Bart. "Clive came back to my place," says Bart, "and stood there playing Jerry Lee numbers on this little upright piano I had – a great big smile on his face. I always called him Bertie Beamer, for years and years, because of his wide non-stop smile. Of course, I really lumbered him, because I sent him to see Larry Parnes. I used to send them all to Larry."

It was agreed that Powell should present himself at the stage door of the Lewisham Gaumont the following Sunday, 20 September, and ask for Mr Parnes, who would detach himself from the stars of his 'Big Beat Show' and interview him. Parnes must have arranged for a piano to be on the stage because the teenager was sent out, Billy Fury-like, in mid-concert, for a trial by fire. From that moment on, he was part of the show, part of the stable. Sign here for four years of servitude – but more perks, more fun and ultimately more future than the cotton factory could ever have offered.

"You're no longer Clive Powell," Parnes told him, "from now on, you are Lance Fortune" – forgetting that he had already bestowed that name on another would-be star. Birkenhead schoolboy Chris Morris had travelled down to the 2Is, auditioned for Larry and impressed him enough for a contract to be proffered – along with a new stage name. After due consideration, Morris took the name but not the management deal. He signed instead with the George Cooper Organisation, which gleefully announced his acquisition in the press.

Already beside himself with rage, Parnes would boil over when *Be Mine* by Lance Fortune hit the singles chart a few weeks later.

Another name was hastily confected for Clive Powell. If thoughts of Billy Cotton had sparked Billy Fury's rechristening, as Parnes claimed, the inspiration for Powell's new name was even more bizarre. He told the blond piano pumper that something about him triggered comparisons with Wee Georgie Wood – a 64-year-old music hall and pantomime star best known for having grown no taller than four feet nine inches! "You're going to be Georgie Fame," Parnes told him. "Fame? Fortune? What's the difference?" Powell was not amused but grew to accept it.

With pianists at a premium, he not only had his own singing spot on Larry's various package shows but also played himself to a standstill backing all the other acts on the bill. By 1961, however, he was working exclusively as a member of Billy Fury & the Blue Flames – along with Colin Green on guitar, Tex Makins on bass and Red Reece on drums – but, at the end of that year, the band was fired for having developed a soulful, jazzy groove.

"During a soundcheck at the Paris Olympia, our road manager Hal Carter came running down the aisle, waving his arms for us to stop . . . 'it's not rocking! It's not rocking!' he shouted – and that's when we parted company with Parnes." That was the end of Billy Fury & the Blue Flames, the beginning of Georgie Fame & the Blue Flames.

"I have to say that the two years I spent in the Parnes stable was the best learning experience I could have had," says Georgie. "When I joined, I could only play in a couple of keys, in a very limited style, and I was busking it much of the time – but working with so many different singers, and with musicians who were as keen to progress as I was, gave me a very solid footing in the business."

Still they came, the young hopefuls, and still Parnes was unable to resist them – but Julian Lee, his final signing in 1959, would be remembered only for the ridiculous name Parnes expected him to bear, the most feeble he ever invented: Julian X. A former merchant seaman from Camberley in Surrey, he would disappear from the front line as quickly as he had arrived – as would two more discoveries the following year, Peter Wynne and Nelson Keene.

Blind to any possible failure, Larry could look back on 1959 as the year he turned his little allotment into an empire. He had started with an investment of a few hundred quid and now sat in a two thousand square-foot prime-rent suite of offices overlooking Oxford Street, watching the money roll in. In three years, the inquisitive novice had become the expert, the most energetic force in Tin Pan Alley, with a dozen singers and some 15 musicians depending on him. Not to mention administrative staff.

The careers of his first two stars, Tommy Steele and Marty Wilde, were now panning out exactly as he had envisaged. Marty was the biggest star on Saturday night television, his records were popular, his shows were sold out, his fan-base was growing. No problems there, except maybe a little anxiety about the new wife and her possible effect on business. And Tommy, too, was lined up to get married. "Why do these people do it?" he must have wondered.

Of course, Parnes didn't have to worry about Tommy; he had long since withdrawn from the creative side of his career, allowing John Kennedy to assume full control. For Steele, the year had started as the previous one finished, in pantomime – which he saw not as a chore but as an opportunity to embrace the theatre, to learn stagecraft beyond jumping around with a guitar. And he could do so in one of London's most beautiful theatres, the Coliseum in St Martin's Lane, built in 1904 and designed to be the largest and most extravagant 'People's Palace of Entertainment and Art'. God, less than five years ago, he would have been too awed and scared even to set foot in the place. Starting on 18 December 1958, he played Buttons in *Cinderella*, a lavish upmarket pantomime with music by Richard Rodgers and lyrics by Oscar Hammerstein. Jimmy Edwards played the King, Kenneth Williams played Portia and Yana was Cinderella. A runaway hit, the show closed on 11 April, after 168 performances.

Then it was off to Spain to shoot location sequences for *Tommy The Toreador*, his third film – a big budget, colour production, expensive enough to show that the studios were now taking him seriously. If only the scriptwriters were. Tommy Tompkins is a carefree sailor, singing and strumming wherever his ship docks. When he arrives in Spain, he is mistaken for a famous bullfighter. A tricky situation for Tommy, maybe, but challenging neither to the audience, nor to Sid James and Bernard Cribbins, playing Cadena and Paco. Kenneth Williams completists cherish the film for his performance as the Vice Consul. Parnes boasted that Steele was paid

£50,000 for the film – twice the fee that John Mills could command. "If he's not careful, Tommy is going to price himself out of films," warned jilted director Gerald Thomas. "It only needs Steele's star to wane at the box-office," suggested *Picturegoer*, "and he may find himself out in the financial cold." It did not seem likely.

The rebellious rock 'n' roller was finished with being mauled to death at concerts and would soon bid farewell to the singles chart, moving away from the ephemeral world in which success was measured by record sales. In 1959, *Tallahassee Lassie*, a brash cover of Freddy Cannon's American hit, sold moderately well to his core audience – but *Little White Bull*, written with Lionel Bart and Mike Pratt for the movie, was a pop-culture crossover, appealing to every age group from toddlers to grannies. It jumped class barriers too: everyone loved Tommy, from ragged kids to the Queen.

One of the few editions of the radio programme *Does The Team Think?* that the BBC chose to retain in their archives concerns his influence on end-of-the-decade society. The question was asked: "Would members of the panel prefer their children to have as their hero Field Marshall Montgomery, Peter May (the patrician captain of the England cricket team) or Tommy Steele?"

Panellist MacDonald Hastings revealed that, in his house, the question had already been answered. "Until he was about 12, Montgomery was emphatically my son's hero; he used to act the part of Monty with his little sister as Rommel. We've now passed out of that phase and our current hero is, in fact, Tommy Steele. My ears are bemused, day after day, with a song which goes 'little white bull, little white bull.' " So, even Max Hastings was once a Tommy Steele fan, maybe still is.

Parnes was a little perplexed about the accusations being levelled at Billy Fury, that his act was pornographic, but he stood by his star and faced down all criticism. This peaked during a six-week tour of Ireland in late 1959, when he was prevented from going onstage at the Theatre Royal in Dublin.

Billy had always protested his innocence: he delivered his songs as an actor would his lines, with maximum intensity, for maximum impact. He wasn't a cardboard singer who just stood there; he had to get inside the song in order for the audience to derive the full benefit of his performance. If that entailed writhing on the stage in orgasmic delight, so be it. "Basically, I'm a very shy person and I think it was a way of not being shy," he told BBC Radio's Keith Skues. "I hated talking to anyone because I was even too shy to speak – but once I was singing, I was fine. I think with being so retiring, it gave me a way of letting off steam, to lay it on a bit heavily."

On *Oh Boy!* Jack Good had given him a free hand with stage movements and facial expressions, knowing that close-ups would hold the viewers no matter where the camera was pointed – but Fury's television appearances were merely appetizers. Onstage, he could allow himself to get carried away.

"With hunched shoulders and agonised expression, he undoes the zip of his yellow jacket. Down, down it comes, while the screams increase in volume," reported *Picturegoer.*

"His act was certainly explicit," says Jim Sullivan. "Billy had obviously seen the early Elvis films and had learnt from the way he moved – but he took it one step further, doing all the gyrations and curling his lip. Then he would be down on the floor with the microphone stand, rubbing his body against it – and, of course, the more he did it, the more the girls screamed and the more he liked it!"

"He did go down on the microphone and he did roll around on the floor doing things to the microphone stand," says Brian Gregg, who led his backing band on the tour of Ireland, "but by then, that's what he was expected to do and everyone knew he was going to do it. No-one objected during the first part of the tour, which was in the north, but then we drove down to Dublin for a week of gigs and that's where the trouble started. It was all 'you're not in England now: you're in a Catholic country and you can't do that sort of thing'. On the first night, they brought the curtain down on us – and, of course, the audience went nuts." They had been going nuts throughout the tour, especially at the ballrooms. In some places, as soon as Billy had finished his act, most of the audience had rushed around to the stage door to try and get a closer look at him, maybe even get to touch him – leaving the headliner, Bridie Gallagher, to come on to the sound of her own feet. She was not happy.

Nor was the manager of the Theatre Royal, who ordered Fury to censor his act. No chance. Billy phoned Parnes, who flew over. My boy is going to do the same act he has done all year. Not in my theatre, said the manager, instructing ushers to prevent Billy and his band from taking the stage. He was sent home in shame, Jerry Lee style. "It was all over the papers," says Gregg, "and Billy was told that he and his like would never be welcomed back to Ireland. Larry was dead pleased, of course – he'd got loads of publicity and he'd already been paid for the whole tour – but fair play to him for backing his boy."

Friends could see that Billy was well in control of his destiny. He knew exactly what he was doing and where he was going, and Parnes and Jack Good shrewdly gave him all the latitude he needed. Good, who had now been appointed his record producer, encouraged him to work on his songwriting, which had started on Woolworth's notepads as he sat on the tugboat, waiting for the tide to turn, lost in a reverie, grasping for lines that rhymed.

He let him use all his own songs on his 10-inch début album *The Sound Of Fury*, recorded from start to finish on 10 March 1960 – marking the new decade with the best album of the era. Billy wrote and sang with a rock 'n' roll authenticity and authority that none of his contemporaries managed to acquire and his producer provided a setting to match . . . the echo, the slapped bass, a pianist who felt the songs, a guitarist born to the genre. *Turn My Back On You* was pure Gene Vincent & the Blue Caps; *Alright Goodbye* had *Chirping Crickets* overtones; *That's Love* and the seven other tracks had a sound based on Sun or early RCA Elvis. The Four Jays – a London vocal group and not his pals from the Florence Institute in Liverpool, as some believe – provided a creditable Jordanaires-style backing.

Fury's rise had been textbook smooth, leaving Vince Eager in the doldrums – but his career began picking up speed when he was selected as one of the resident singers on BBC television's new teen-music series. Starting on Saturday 4 April 1959 – going out at 6.30 to avoid competition with ITV's *Oh Boy!* – *Drumbeat* provided weekly prime-time exposure for Eager, leading to more press and more clamour at concerts, where he could be seen in the flesh, in living colour rather than grainy black and white.

However, Parlophone dropped him after the failure of three singles on which he had been all but smothered by the Rita Williams Singers, the Geoff Love Orchestra and other studio antiques. It was all too depressing, being expected to throw his heart and soul into such middle-of-the-road mediocrities as *When's Your Birthday Baby?* and *No Other Arms, No Other Lips*. He did his best but there was no way Eager could forge an identity, any kind of individuality, when his producers seemed to be treating him as just another kid on the hit-and-miss fingers-crossed conveyor belt. Did Bobby Darin or Conway Twitty have to put up with this nonsense? He was glad to escape – and Dick Rowe, who had supervised his earliest recordings for Decca and was now running the Top Rank label, was glad to step in and sign him. But if Eager thought his chart breakthrough was imminent, he was in for a disappointment.

Rowe adopted exactly the same ploy as his predecessors, scanning the *Billboard* Hot 100 for a likely American hit to cover and selecting Floyd Robinson's *Makin' Love* – a song in which the protagonist habitually bunks off school to spend the day shafting his girlfriend, yet sings about it decorously enough for Top 40 radio. And, indeed, for BBC radio. Robinson's original was a UK hit too, obliterating Eager's over-jaunty *Music While You Work* version. That he was now being seen as a hunky Fabian-cum-Frankie Avalon equivalent was confirmed when Rowe followed up with *Why*, an Avalon ballad, on its way to the top of the American chart. It seemed as if Eager might be onto a winner – but the plan was foiled when Anthony Newley also recorded the song and annihilated all competition. The B-side was an ill-advised and futile attempt to improve on the immaculate Marty Robbins epic *El Paso*, another American number one. Whereas the original benefited from the contributions of Nashville's most creative minds, Eager had to work with studio musicians who allowed any tension and drama to drain away, even as he looked on helplessly.

At least he was in command onstage. After much cajoling, Larry had agreed to allow him his own exclusive hand-picked backing group, the Quiet Three, named after the B-side of Duane Eddy's current hit. Colin Green played guitar, Jimmy Nicol (back from touring Italy with Colin Hicks) was on drums and Tex Makins had been permitted to return on bass. "We were anything but quiet," says Green, "a very loud band for a trio. Vince wanted to create an act – which he did: we worked up quite a powerhouse show. Lots of contrast, light and dark; plenty of pace and movement. He was a big lad, a good-looking boy, and he had good ideas about stage presence. It wasn't a natural thing, but he could look at it and see what was needed, get some choreography into it. We spent a lot of time rehearsing, so it looked spontaneous – but it wasn't . . . it was very carefully worked out. We used to go down a storm wherever we played." All he needed was a hit record, as his manager constantly reminded him. Meanwhile, Parnes tried to generate some publicity by putting it around that, as a result of the sequin-covered velvet jackets Vince wore on stage, promoters had taken to calling him 'the Liberace of British Showbiz'. It was not a description he savoured.

"Larry used to run so hot and cold," says Eager. "He had flavours of the week: It'd be me one week, Marty the next, Billy the next, he seemed to have no overall strategy, just flitted like a butterfly – very petulant and very petty."

And always ready with a new scheme. Larry's final coup of 1959 was to set up a tour which would give every British rock 'n' roll fan access to a legend.

With record company assistance, Jack Good had been able to present American guests on *Boy Meets Girls*: Johnny Cash, who came over to promote his Philips single *I Got Stripes/Five Feet High And Rising*, and the Browns, a brother-and-two-sisters country & western trio who had found a mainstream million seller in their dramatic revival of *The Three Bells*. But he wanted a biggie. Elvis was in the army, Buddy Holly was dead, Jerry Lee Lewis was *persona non grata*, Little Richard had renounced rock 'n' roll to praise the Lord, the Everly Brothers were unavailable, Bill Haley was history, Carl Perkins was going through a fallow patch, and Chuck Berry was too busy touring in the States. (Unluckily for him. It was on 1 December 1959 that he met the Apache Indian girl who landed him in prison.) Who else was there? What about Gene Vincent?

The idea gathered momentum; a deal was struck. Gene would appear on *Boy Meets Girls*, go over to France and Germany for dates and then return for a full UK tour, promoted by Parnes. Every singer and musician in his stable was paralysed with excitement. Gene Vincent! Idol of every big beat fanatic in the land, the pioneer who had set impossible standards from day one. *Be Bop A Lula, Race With The Devil, Blue Jean Bop*. Three monumental singles, one after the other, works of art received with deep respect and reverence.

He made his début at the Granada in Tooting, South London, on Sunday 6 December, special guest on a Marty Wilde package show which also featured Vince Eager, Billy Fury, Johnny Gentle, Duffy Power, Dickie Pride, Terry Dene, Sally Kelly, Julian X, the Wild Cats, the Beat Boys, the Quiet Three, the Viscounts and Joe Brown & his

Bruvvers, who had the daunting task of stepping into the Blue Caps' shoes to back him. Everyone on the show had been instructed to bring a guitar to the theatre, so Gene could have his own guard of honour and walk to the microphone through an archway of guitars. "Wearing a red and black sweater and jet black trousers, Gene closed the first half with a performance that put him way above the rest of the artists in stagecraft and showmanship," reported the *NME*.

"We were crowded in the wings when Gene came on, because he was a hero to all of us," says Johnny Gentle. "This was going to be one of the great moments of our lives, to be sharing a stage with Gene Vincent – and it was. The place just erupted as soon as his name was announced."

"Quite unexpectedly, he swung his iron-braced leg right over the mike, spun round a complete 360 degrees, and tore into *Be Bop A Lula*," wrote Jack Good. "The effect was electrifying. The nervous, silent, bewildered Virginian was suddenly transformed into a crouching wildcat. A Jekyll and Hyde story come true." It was a prophetic observation. In the months that followed, Vincent revealed a psychotic side which gallons of whisky could not subdue. One by one, his new friends lost their admiration for him.

In stark contrast, his touring partner, Eddie Cochran, whom Parnes brought in on 10 January 1960, was a sweetheart. Not only a gentleman with a warm personality and a great sense of humour but also a masterful guitarist, who was happy to sit around teaching licks and tricks to his travelling companions – including Jim Sullivan, Joe Brown, Colin Green and Tony Sheridan, all of whom benefited from his instruction, all of whom took his advice and replaced their third string with a thinner gauge second string, allowing them to bend the notes. He pointed Georgie Fame in the direction of Ray Charles and soul music and explained to the others how the engineer at Gold Star Studio in Hollywood had given his marvellous records such vibrancy. He talked about California, invited them all to come and visit. It was as if Larry had hired a professor to lecture to his troupe. Everybody loved him, everybody wept when he died.

"Larry Parnes brought the whole British scene to life," said Marty Wilde. "He was an ideal manager – and a star in his own right." It was true. While giving dozens of youngsters a launch pad, an opportunity to fly if they could, Parnes had transformed himself into a mythical figure of his own design – astute, wealthy, successful, caring, important – whatever he told journalists was dutifully written down and reported. In his heyday, he swanned around like an actor whose ego would never allow him to be offstage – but it was time to move on. By 1961, he was operating from his penthouse flat at 24 Great Cumberland Place and had trimmed his stable to four: Tommy Steele, Marty Wilde, Billy Fury and Joe Brown.

Returning to his first love, the theatre, he took a lease on the Cambridge, producing shows – including the smash hit *Chicago*, which ran for 590 performances – until February 1981, when he retired following a brain haemorrhage and meningitis. He then devoted his time to the loves of his life, his two Alsatian dogs, Prince and Duke.

Forty

When BBC Television announced details of their new pop music programme *Juke Box Jury*, on which a panel of celebrities would pass judgement on a selection of the latest singles, voting each a 'hit' or a 'miss', Jack Good could not resist a dig at his former employers. "Will this mean that while one channel is creating hit records, the other will be discussing them?"

The panel for the first *Juke Box Jury*, transmitted on 1 June 1959, comprised disc jockey Pete Murray, sparkle-eyed singer Alma Cogan, stoical balladeer Gary Miller and future *Magpie* presenter Susan Stranks – billed as 'a typical teenager' (though hardly typical in my purlieu). As the records played, they tapped pencils, looked thoughtful and nodded heads while a live audience awaited their verdicts. If the votes tied, chairman David Jacobs would cast the decider, banging his palm on a hotel-reception bell for a 'hit' or, to the delight of the easily-amused audience, squeezing the bulb of a vintage-car klaxon for a 'miss'. Over the next few weeks, the unlikeliest experts, ranging from comedians to actresses, pontificated on music they knew little about. *There Goes My Baby* by the Drifters was written off as "just a noise"; *What'd I Say* by Ray Charles was roundly mocked. As rock historian Dave Laing would write: "The stupidity of most of the guests made for compulsive viewing".

Unsure of its potential, schedulers had given *Juke Box Jury* a Monday evening slot but the simple, undemanding format proved instantly successful and, starting on 5 September 1959, it replaced *Drumbeat* to become a Saturday evening fixture for the next eight years. Only one change was made, in early 1960, when the original signature tune *Juke Box Fury* by Ozzie Warlock & the Wizards was replaced by the specially commissioned *Hit And Miss* by the John Barry Seven.

Barry played the trumpet, an instrument which had little connection with rock 'n' roll and teenage music, yet he had cleverly concentrated on that field, working at the cutting edge of contemporary music rather than sinking into dance-band oblivion.

After leaving school at 15, he had started work as a projectionist at his father's cinema, the Rialto in York, where he fell under the spell of the great movie composers. Dimitri Tiomkin, Max Steiner, Alfred Newman, Alex North, Franz Waxman. Their names flickered briefly on screen; their music held the films together in an intricate web few viewers appreciated. Barry studied the way their scores integrated with the action, the way their orchestrations rose and fell, giving mood and atmosphere to every scene, and he found their interpretations, the whole process of adding music to film, endlessly fascinating.

During National Service, he took an informal correspondence course in arranging (his tutor was Stan Kenton's composer and arranger, Bill Russo, who would correct and annotate his manuscripts) and, on leaving, set about forming his own seven-piece band. Three of the guys had been in the Army with him; the others were from local Yorkshire bands. After much experimentation, they made their professional début at his father's cinema on 7 April 1957, supporting the touring American singer Mitchell Torok, who was savouring the afterglow of his novelty hit *When Mexico Gave Up The Rumba (To Do The Rock 'n' Roll)*.

A competent and versatile unit, the John Barry Seven soon had offers rolling in: a four-week summer matinee season at Blackpool Palace with Tommy Steele, regular appearances on the *6.5 Special*, a nationwide tour with Paul Anka, a recording contract with Parlophone, 10 *Oh Boy!* shows, a package tour version of the *6.5 Special*, the 'Extravaganza' tour with Marty Wilde and Vince Eager, and a residency on the latest BBC show *Drumbeat*. Although, by this time, April 1959, they had been going only two years, no one except Barry remained from the original line-up. The most recent change saw pianist Les Reed coming in for rhythm guitarist and vocalist Keith Kelly, who went searching for solo recognition (and would score minor hits), but the turning point had come a few months earlier, with the recruitment of a young guitar virtuoso whose name was worthy of Larry Parnes.

Vic Flick had entered show business in 1957, playing a summer season with Les Clark & the Music Maniacs at Butlin's Holiday Camp in Skegness. "He was barely out of school when he joined us," says Roy Powell, the band's pianist. "His mum came with him on his first day, entrusting him to our care and instructing us to look after his moral welfare. But he was a good looking boy and he was soon spending a lot of time with Jackie Trent, who sang with the Alan Kane Big Band in one of the other ballrooms." By the end of the year, Flick was playing alongside Diz Disley in Bob Cort's Skiffle Group, down the bill on the Paul Anka/John Barry Seven package show. Barry took his name and number – and eventually, in November 1958, the phone call came. "After a hectic rehearsal, having to memorise not only the band's 20-minute set but also Marty Wilde's, I took the stage at the Metropolitan Theatre in Edgware Road," says Vic, who would, less than three years later, play the most famous notes the band ever recorded, *The James Bond Theme*.

Meanwhile, Barry was winning commissions to arrange music for other acts, starting with a young trio on Decca, the unrelated (to him) Barry Sisters. Together, they cut two singles, *Tall Paul* and *Jo Jo The Dog-faced Boy*, which had been consecutive American hits for Annette Funicello. Neither excited retail interest – and nor did any of the three singles he made with Larry Page, the alleged Teenage Rage, whose future as a singer already seemed to be in jeopardy.

Page had been dropped by Columbia after the failure of a third single, the nondescript *This Is My Life*, and had changed managers in a vain bid to maintain his currency. He also signed a one-off deal with Saga, a label with even less credibility than Oriole, unknown to most people, possibly because it was a shoestring enterprise, operating from a small office in the corner of a toy warehouse in Holloway Road. (The owner, William Barrington-Coupe, would soon launch the Triumph label, in partnership with Joe Meek.) Saga issued three singles simultaneously – all 'directed' by John Barry and credited to Larry Page & the 'Saga Satellites', a thin disguise for the Seven, who were under contract to EMI. Dire, each and every one. "I think we all did the session just to earn a bit of pocket money," says Page. Barry wrote two of the six songs, *Little Old Fashioned Love* and *Throw All Your Loving My Way*. One can understand why he has rarely made reference to them in interviews.

> *I need your loving, I need it so bad*
> *The kind of loving that I've never had*
> *Without it, baby, I'll feel so sad*
> *So just come close and make me feel glad*

Sheer poetry – but still not enough to resuscitate Larry Page's career. He got the picture and withdrew to Wales to manage a pub. At least he had enjoyed a few years of fun. "I learned how to play a stage and work an audience," he says. "I knew what it was like to receive great applause and I knew what it was like to die on my arse. I'd done all that. I think I sold my life story to the papers when I was 21, and most of that was about 'these I have bedded'. It was a unique situation: kids from working-class families were being hailed as stars – and society women would chase after you too, hoping to bed you. Of course, I fought hard to resist them!" After running ballrooms in Newport, Swansea and the Midlands, Page returned to London to make his fortune in publishing and management, nurturing the early careers of the Kinks and the Troggs.

In April 1959, Adam Faith was in the same position as Larry Page – washed-up and forgotten – but, in his case, John Barry was able to work some magic, facilitating the unlikeliest comeback of the year.

Following the failure of his first single *Got A Heartsick Feeling/ Brother Heartache And Sister Tears* and the completion of a *6.5 Special* package tour on which he made little impact, Faith was cut adrift. Nobody wanted to know. Rather than return to the 2Is with his tail between his legs, he dug out his Cinema and Television Technicians union card and found employment at Borehamwood, back in the film world where he obviously belonged, back in comfortable anonymity as Terry Nelhams. A vacancy at Elstree Studios soon found him working as an assistant dubbing editor, adding the sounds of quivering arrows and slamming doors to episodes of *William Tell*, an ITV series starring Conrad Phillips, and the prospect of a promotion to the cutting-room was on the cards. "All the time, I had this nagging feeling that I wasn't cut out to be a backroom boy," he says. "Fame is a heady drug, especially when you've had a whiff of it – and I became an expert at taking days off work."

He was given the chance to make another single for HMV, but his laughable version of Jerry Lee Lewis's rabid *High School Confidential* bombed, as any cool kiddie knew it would. "Norman Newell, my producer, had about as much knowledge and, I suspect, interest in rock 'n' roll as my mum," he would complain in one of his books.

Then, out of the blue, his old mentor Jack Good phoned with an idea: he should get together with Freddy Lloyd, his erstwhile partner in the Worried Men, and learn a song called *Go Tell Aunt Rhody (The Old Grey Goose Is Dead)*, which Lonnie Donegan had out on the B-side of his latest hit. "I hadn't seen Terry for months on end," says Lloyd, "but he suddenly appeared at my door with this record, saying that we were lined up to sing it on *Oh Boy!* It was thoroughly awful – and to make matters worse, we had to do these synchronised dance steps. Heaven only knows what Jack Good was thinking about."

Their wretched performance, as Terry and Freddy, would lead to no further bookings, of this they were convinced – but John Barry happened to see it and, having noted his number when they were on the *6.5 Special* tour together, was on the phone to Faith the next day. The John Barry Seven were to be the backbone of the new BBC series *Drumbeat*, he explained, and, although Vince Eager and Roy Young had already been hired, they were still looking for another resident singer. Taking a further day off work, Faith rushed to audition – and was hired for the first three weeks. When this was extended to 22 weeks, he packed in the day job.

Cramming all he could into a fast-paced half-hour, *Drumbeat's* producer Stewart Morris tried to cover all bases with a something-for-everyone format. Sylvia Sands, the Barry Sisters, the Kingpins, the Raindrops and Bob Miller & his Millermen catered for *Music While You Work* aficionados; Adam Faith and Vince Eager covered the Presley, Vincent, Holly, Nelson, Cochran songbooks; the John Barry Seven, as well as backing the singers, played novelty instrumentals; Roy Young, a quiffed-up rocker from Oxford, stood vamping at the piano in a baggy suit, bawling out Little Richard and Larry Williams numbers. Enthusiastic reviews followed the first edition, broadcast on 4 April 1959, but by the end of August the formula had worn thin and the programme was axed. Faith and Eager were both rewarded with Top Rank record deals, while Young was signed by Fontana, where he was required to cover consecutive Dee Clark hits, *Just Keep It Up* and *Hey Little Girl*, as his first two singles.

Drumbeat's compère, Trevor Peacock, who had started as Jack Good's stand-up comedy partner at the Windmill before helping him to script the *6.5 Special* and *Oh Boy!*, went back to his pal to write links for *Boy Meets Girls*. He would make a tidy sum when Herman's Hermits sold a few million copies of his song *Mrs Brown You've Got A Lovely Daughter* and would eventually become a household favourite playing Jim Trott in the television comedy series *The Vicar of Dibley*.

At Top Rank, Faith and Barry, who had been appointed MD on the session, were given an obscure year-old rockabilly single by Bill

Craddock and told to re-jig it. Dick Rowe had a hunch that it could be a chart breaker. But although Adam and the Seven hammered away with all the verve they could muster, *Ah Poor Little Baby* was never going to sell out the initial contingency pressing – and he was, as had been agreed, dropped from the label. A blow to his ego, but one Faith was now confident enough to shrug off.

Before he had been able to sign anything he might regret, Barry had guided him to the tenacious Eve Taylor, his own manager – and she had assured Adam that things would fall into place. He even had an agency to represent him, Starcast, run by Eve's husband Maurice Press. Keep it all in the family. "I very soon came to rue the day I'd signed a contract giving her a five-year franchise on my life," he would later write – but for now, he was in clover.

The past few months had witnessed fascinating developments in American popular music, with previous boundaries dissolving in the face of Top 40 radio, which now played whatever was popular, across the board, whether it be rock 'n' roll, rhythm & blues, pure pop, or even the odd country & western record. Taking advantage of this, the more ambitious producers and arrangers were making records which could ease their acts into new territory – and, of these, the ones which interested John Barry most were those with prominent string arrangements. In making *There Goes My Baby* with the Drifters, a vocal group who had never sold beyond the black market, Mike Stoller had set their elemental doo-wop in a sea of swirling strings inspired by Rimsky-Korsakov and Borodin. On *To Be Loved*, Berry Gordy floated Jackie Wilson's operatic voice on the lush orchestration of a very white orchestra, lifting him out of the R&B backfield. Strings too were an attractive feature of *Lavender Blue* by Sammy Turner (another Leiber and Stoller production) and *Since I Don't Have You* by Pittsburgh vocal group the Skyliners – but the record that set his pulse racing was by Buddy Holly.

Unable to live comfortably in redneck Texas with a Puerto Rican wife, and losing confidence in his manager, Holly had moved to an apartment in Greenwich Village and was looking forward to a new phase in his career. At the art deco Pythian Temple – the New York studio where Bill Haley & his Comets had recorded *Rock Around The Clock* only four and a half years earlier – Coral Records staff producer Dick Jacobs persuaded Holly to lay down his guitar and put aside his own song-bag to record Paul Anka's composition *It Doesn't Matter*

Anymore, with not only a top-flight rhythm section but eight violins, two violas and two cellos.

Its influence would permeate much of John Barry's turn-of-the-decade work, including his arrangement (Parlophone would only spring for four violins) for *What Do You Want*, the song which would secure Adam Faith's future. Simple and catchy, festooned with radio-friendly gimmicks, hooks and catchphrases, the record caught fire immediately and Faith saw in the New Year at number one. He always knew it would happen.

After also embellishing Lance Fortune's *Be Mine* and his own group's *Juke Box Jury* theme, pizzicato violins became something of a John Barry trademark until James Bond came along. By then, he had already stowed his trumpet in favour of composing music for films; his scores for *Born Free*, *The Lion In Winter*, *Out Of Africa* and *Dances With Wolves* would bring Oscars.

With his non-greasy combed-forward gamin hairstyle, owing more to Leslie Caron than James Dean, and his smart casual clothes, Adam Faith became a role-model for clean-cut youth – until he revealed that he had enjoyed pre-marital sex and saw nothing wrong with the practice. A shocking admission for the time.

Even as the hits kept coming, he began to branch out, into films, television, theatre, record production, management, journalism and finance, becoming extremely wealthy in the process. A self-improver who kept a dictionary on his desk, he eventually came unstuck when he tried to launch his own television channel – and he had not long been declared bankrupt when, in March 2003, aged 62, he died the perfect rock 'n' roll death, of a heart attack, in the Stoke-on-Trent hotel room he was sharing with a lover 40 years his junior.

Although *What Do You Want* fitted Faith like a hand-tailored suit, he was not the first singer to attempt it. The song had been written by Johnny Worth, whose three-boys one-girl vocal group the Raindrops were regulars on *Drumbeat*, and had been mapped out on the piano by his friend Les Reed – who not only played in the John Barry Seven but also rented the basement of the 17-roomed Edwardian house in Southfields that Worth had inherited from his father. "I tried to interest a few publishers in Denmark Street but, of course, they were the last people to know a decent song when they heard one, so I got rejections galore," says Worth. "Then, one night, on one of our jaunts, Les and I saw this group playing at

Wandsworth Town Hall – Freddie Heath & the Rock 'n' Roll Combo – and the singer seemed to be the sort of chap who could tackle my song. They got as far as rehearsing it and even made a demo of it – but they went at it hammer and tongs, a hundred miles an hour with thumping drums, and none of us were happy with the result."

Several months later, when Adam Faith looked like being signed by Parlophone, Worth got into a huddle with Les Reed and John Barry, and a hit record began to take shape. "Because, as a singer, I had recorded for both Oriole and EMI, I became the centre of a contractual dispute between them," says Worth, "and I knew that if anyone saw my name on the top of a song-sheet, it would be thrown into the wastepaper bin – so I had to devise a new one quickly. My phone number was Vandyke 7987 and my best friend was Les Reed – so I became Les Vandyke." Under that name, he would write a further number one, *Poor Me*, for Adam and another, *Well I Ask You*, for Eden Kane.

Freddie Heath was only just beginning to create a buzz in Wandsworth, but he was already a well known figure in Willesden, where had had grown up. There, everyone had a Fred Heath story: he used to work as a bookie's runner, taking illegal bets; he had been rejected from National Service as impossible to discipline; he had worked as a painter at a warehouse in the locality and had appalled staff by urinating from his high scaffold onto the concrete floor. Heath and his group, the Five Nutters, had been unable to find work locally after fairground workers caused trouble during one of their weekly gigs at the White Horse in Church Road and he had taken to busking as a way to maintain his presence and make a few bob.

He was already 23 (another who lied furiously about his year of birth) and worried that his time was past when he ran into Guy Tynegate-Smith, a frightfully posh former public school fellow who now called himself Guy Robinson. Royalty were among the pupils at his mother's exclusive dance studio at 15 Baker Street, where, in his first showbiz dabbling, he had run a series of skiffle and jazz evenings. He now promoted pop nights at Wandsworth Town Hall and thought that Heath could add some verve to his resident group, for whom he had high hopes. Mike West and Tom Brown, who shared vocals, went along with their manager's suggestion and almost immediately saw their roles diminishing. Soon, the posters outside announced Freddie Heath & his Band, sometimes Freddie

Heath & his Rock 'n' Roll Combo – and it was Heath who HMV's
A&R manager Wally Ridley and his deputy Peter Sullivan saw as the
star of the show.

Written by Heath (with enough input from his manager to justify
the jokey credit 'Heath Robinson'), *Please Don't Touch* soared on Alan
Caddy's fluid guitar and Fruit Gordon's rumbling bass. Heath's
navvy vocal and Sullivan's savvy production would ensure not only
a few weeks in the charts during the summer of 1959 but recognition
as one of the year's more innovative singles. When it was in the can,
Sullivan and Robinson emerged from the control room to tell the
band that they were now called Johnny Kidd & the Pirates. It was the
first time any of them had even heard the name.

By Christmas, Robinson had been down to the 2Is and hired Clem
Cattini and Brian Gregg, who had fallen out with Larry Parnes over
money, and – after the other Pirates had been forced to walk the
plank – they joined Alan Caddy as the gritty new power trio behind
Kidd. They rolled in their mate Joe Moretti to give them a hand on
the first record they cut together, another Heath original, *Shakin' All
Over*, and were soon at number one, basking in the certainty that
they had made a timeless hall-of-fame classic.

It was on television appearances promoting this record that Kidd
began wearing a piratical eye-patch to complement his fluky change
of name. "He was boss-eyed," says Brian Gregg. "He had a cast in his
eye that got worse as the day wore on. When he was really tired, he
looked like Clarence the Cross-Eyed Lion – and so he started
wearing the patch to hide it when the cameras closed in. The word
was put around that a guitar string had snapped and caught him in
the eye, but that was bollocks."

A formidable live band, Johnny Kidd & the Pirates would help us
through the lean years.

After 14 months, singing six nights most weeks, Rick Richards, who
had succeeded Adam Faith as leader of the Worried Men, finally
relinquished his residency at the 2Is Coffee Bar in May 1959. John
Barry's former singer and guitarist, the bespectacled Keith Kelly took
over. "He bears a striking facial resemblance to the late Buddy
Holly," suggested his publicist, and journalists readily agreed.
Richards moved on to the Top Ten Club, which Vince Taylor had
recently opened in the cellar below the House of Sam Widges, a

coffee bar on the corner of Berwick and D'Arblay Streets. His timing could not have been worse. It was the week that Taylor's world fell apart.

His manager, Joe Singer, suddenly announced that he was leaving Vince to his own devices and returning to Hollywood. The new single, *Brand New Cadillac*, had already been written off as a failure, future radio and television appearances were few and far between, and the gig-sheet was none too promising. "Things had not gone according to plan," says Rick Richards. "Vince and his manager had arrived in London thinking that they were going to clean up – but it didn't look as if that was ever going to happen. Joe had given it nine months or so and then thrown in the towel."

"I am confident there is a place for me over here," Taylor told *Melody Maker*. "I intend to fight all opposition and get right to the very top." This seemed rather unlikely in the short term, not least because his band had also done a bunk. Before he decamped, Joe Singer's last managerial act had been to put Licorice Locking and Brian Bennett out of the car, there and then, when they told him that they had decided to work with Marty Wilde instead. The others quit too: Joe Moretti replaced Denny Wright as guitarist with Johnny Duncan & the Blue Grass Boys and pianist Lou Brian reinvented himself as Perry Ford to begin a vain quest for solo recognition. With Les Vandyke, he would soon co-write Adam Faith's third hit *Someone Else's Baby*.

The beleaguered Taylor went out on a package tour with Chas McDevitt and Shirley Douglas, both acts backed by Leroy Powell & the Beatniks, before doing a deal with Tom Littlewood, who had graduated from doorman to manager of the 2Is, and was now managing singers too. Littlewood put him out on the road with two more of his acts, Keith Kelly and Dave Sutch (now calling himself Screaming Lord Sutch), and an all-purpose backing band held together by drummer Bobby Woodman – but Taylor was regarded as a marginal novelty rocker until he moved to Paris, where all his black-leather rock-god dreams and fantasies came true. "It was total madness from then on, right through the sixties," according to Woodman, who went with him.

Taylor's lack of success was predictable – he couldn't carry a tune in a bucket – but nobody could understand why, of all the 2Is talents, Tony Sheridan seemed to have missed the boat too. He had it all. In

January 1959, within a week of leaving Decca to head up the new Top Rank label, Dick Rowe proudly announced that Sheridan was to be his first signing. Jack Good, too, admired his confidence and flamboyance, booking him for six *Oh Boy!* shows. "I was the only guy in Britain playing lead guitar and singing too – like Buddy Holly," says Sheridan whose red source-of-wonder solid-bodied Grazioso, with its combination of pick-ups, push buttons and knobs, was the most advanced guitar available in the UK at the time.

He thinks that Tom Littlewood, with whom he had signed a management contract, might have soured the Top Rank deal by demanding too much money – after passing the audition, he heard no more from them – but he had only himself to blame for falling out with Jack Good. "He fired me for missing rehearsals," he admits. "I preferred to stay in bed with my girlfriend, a dancer from the Raymond Revuebar. She was the first bird I'd known intimately and I was in love with her in a big way. I was totally obsessed with music but I really got sidetracked there. At that point, I was freaking out, rebelling against my background, the conservatism of Norwich, discipline, anything I could think of! And my love for that girl seemed a good enough reason to miss rehearsals."

After a typhoon romance, Sheridan married Hazel, his femme fatale, on 18 May 1959 – just over a week after his final *Oh Boy!* appearance. He was three days shy of his nineteenth birthday.

He was back in action in time for Marty Wilde's month-long summer season at Blackpool Palace, singing a few songs as well as playing in the house band, alongside Cherry Wainer on organ, Don Storer on drums, Red Price on sax and Vince Cooze on double bass. After a slow autumn, he was added to the Gene Vincent/Eddie Cochran tour, running through to the final date on 16 April 1960, at Bristol Hippodrome.

"Red Reece and I were in the Beat Boys for that tour, backing Gene and whoever else didn't have a band," says Cooze, "but we also played in a Crickets-style trio with Tony." On some numbers, Georgie Fame would join them on piano. "Sheridan was not only a phenomenal guitarist but a great singer too," says Fame. "On that tour, he was doing *You'll Never Walk Alone* in his act – and I remember, during the week in Liverpool particularly, it used to bring the house down every night. That's where it started, and it spread from there."

The tour had barely got into gear when, on 3 February – 34 days into what would become known as the 'Permissive Sixties' – Larry Parnes put on his nanny hat and sent a personal letter to every singer and musician.

"I have had numerous complaints about the bad behaviour and foul language used by various musicians in my show," he wrote. "It is very difficult for me to pinpoint any one of you and say who exactly is responsible for this but I must severely caution all of you in view of these allegations. I do not want any more bad language used by anybody in the show and I do not want any more bad behaviour. You are to leave the stage as soon as you are told to. I want every one of you in the theatre one hour before curtain up and I do not want any of you to leave the theatre before the termination of the second show.

"I am strictly forbidding any drinking of alcohol during the hours of the show and no women are to be allowed backstage or in your dressing rooms unless they happen to be your mother, grandmother, sister or wife. Any person in breach of these regulations will be sacked instantly and if you leave the theatre during the show, I am leaving strict instructions with the stage manager not to allow you back into the theatre again.

"I am sorry to have to enforce such strict regulations on all of you because I am quite sure that it is only one or two of you who are responsible for this disgraceful behaviour. So now it is up to you to be on your best behaviour and not disgrace the name of the stars, the show or myself."

Of course, it was the stars of the show that were mainly to blame. This wasn't a vicar's tea party: this was rock 'n' roll! Gene Vincent had gone ballistic backstage at the Bradford Gaumont after hecklers had ruined his dramatic performance of *Over The Rainbow* and the theatre manager was clearly traumatised by his lack of self-control. Not only foul-mouthed and hedonistic, but pissed out of their brains much of the time, Vincent and Cochran were modern-day cowboys – incipient psychopath Gene was Billy the Kid, while Eddie was the cool gunfighter who came through every scrape unscathed, so everybody thought – and they were living life to the hilt, exemplary, if dangerous, role models who affected everyone on the tour.

On 4 June 1960, six weeks after Eddie Cochran's death, Tony Sheridan, Rick Richards and three of their 2Is mates took a train from

Liverpool Street to Harwich and a boat to Hamburg, where – as the Jets – they became the first British band to play Der Kaiserkeller and the Top Ten club. Many others would follow. "The St Pauli district of Hamburg was the most amazing place you could ever see; it made Saturday night in Soho look like a sleepy village fete," says Richards.

Sheridan never came home again.

Forty-one

At the start of 1959, for the second year running, Lonnie Donegan was dressed up like a cartoon Chinaman, playing Wishee Washee in *Aladdin* – this time at the Globe Theatre in panto-rich Stockton-on-Tees. Said the *NME*'s perceptive critic: "It seems very unlikely that one of his vocal offerings will ever reach the Top 20: *Does Your Chewing Gum Lose Its Flavour?*" Within weeks it was at number three and eventually took off to become Lonnie's biggest American hit, selling over a million copies. Four more singles reached the Top Twenty – *Fort Worth Jail, The Battle Of New Orleans, Sal's Got A Sugar Lip* and *San Miguel* – in a year which found him revelling in the luxuries of superstardom.

In May, he moved from his Wanstead semi into a £15,000 Scandinavian-style home ("built to Lonnie's own specification," it was claimed) at Woodford in Essex, on the edge of Epping Forest, and in August he bought a silver grey Lagonda, into which he packed his family for a well-earned motoring holiday in Europe. His wife Maureen was not only writing articles about 'my Lonnie' but was posing with him for the kind of magazines whose readership wanted to see photographs of them pushing the baby's pram down the street or making a cup of tea in their kitchen.

He was paid a record fee when he topped the bill on a fortnight of concerts at the Palace Theatre in Shaftesbury Avenue and got even more for his own television series *Putting On The Donegan*, transmitted at peak time on ITV every Monday for six weeks in summer and another six in winter. His act now embraced slapstick comedy, music hall, folk music, country music, Tin Pan Alley pop, blues, ballads, jazz, amusing anecdotes, anything else he felt like trying. Addicted to the spotlight, he never stopped working – although, in a sense, his work was now done. He was the magician of the age who had inspired all these kids to get guitars and learn how to play them. He had encouraged a generation to sing and to love music and, while he was at it, he had instilled an interest in Americana that no history or geography teacher ever could.

Although he was the founding father of British rock music, Lonnie was no longer an influence – but his flock had gone out with his message and become stars themselves, and there was a second wave, as yet unknown beyond Merseyside, who were even now completing their apprenticeships in the dance halls and cellar clubs of Liverpool.

Strangely, the Americans, a few years behind us in musical development, it now appeared, were enjoying the early stages of a skiffle boom – except that they called it folk music. Many of the songs were the same; the Kingston Trio's recording of *It Takes A Worried Man* was a Top 20 hit in October 1959. Jack Elliott would be able to go home and get some work.

Lonnie's career went up, down and sideways over the next few decades, but he was always the 'King of Skiffle' – and he was still the 'King of Skiffle', out on the road in the middle of a long nationwide tour in November 2002, when his "dodgy ticker", as he called it, finally gave out after 71 years of overuse. "He was performing right up until the day he died," says Joe Brown. "I saw him about three months earlier and he just tore the place up with his energy. He kept the standard up right until the end – and if anyone in British music should get the big accolades, it's him."

When Alexis Korner and Cyril Davies, now electrified and amped-up, were thrown out of the Roundhouse for making too much noise and had nowhere to go, Lonnie's old boss Chris Barber incorporated them into his act. This in the middle of the 'Trad' boom.

Riding into territory opened up by Barber's band, a posse of traddies spearheaded by Acker Bilk, Kenny Ball and Terry Lightfoot found enormous fad acceptance for their formulaic pop-jazz. That it was BBC Radio-friendly confirmed its vapidity. "The phrase 'dumbing down' was unknown then, but that's what was happening in some cases," says Barber. "The music was being presented as a package and had to conform to certain expectations. Some of the gimmicks were quite ridiculous: the Confederate Jazz Band, for instance, wore Confederate Army uniforms! Hang on a minute . . . New Orleans jazz, Black people, civil war . . . surely it was bad taste. It was rather like getting some Auschwitz pyjamas and making a fashion statement out of them."

Although the Barber band flew several miles above the herd, they were expected to play to formula when they appeared on the BBC radio programme *Trad Tavern*. This they were not prepared to do. "I insisted on having Alexis sing a couple of R&B numbers, as he did during our set," says Barber. "I had a lot of trouble with the producer, who felt it didn't represent what he understood to be 'trad' – but we got away with it for a while."

Not for long. When some higher-up sent a memo suggesting that Barber be given a series of his own, the producer of *Trad Tavern*, Terry Henebery, replied "I feel there is little to be gained by offering Chris Barber a series. His attitude towards radio is 'I play as I please'. This is acceptable for the occasional 'Jazz Club' outlet but for a regular weekly placing, it would be a bad thing. In any case, nine times out of ten, Mrs CB puts on a prima donna act, which doesn't exactly make for a smooth-running show – like ulcersville! Important also is the fact that there are now other bands of a comparable standard." Show me one.

Over the years, the Barber band would continue on their own sweet way, impervious to commercial constraints, developing as naturally as they felt. As partners in the Marquee Club, Chris and his manager Harold Pendleton would run the capital's premier showcase venue throughout the sixties and seventies, giving a stage to every worthwhile new band that came along, whatever their style. As a director of the annual National Jazz & Blues Festival, Barber would see all the unpleasant aspects of 'trad jazz' washed away by a tidal wave of young rhythm & blues bands – disciples of the man he had first brought to Britain, Muddy Waters.

On 17 March 1962, Alexis Korner, Cyril Davies, Long John Baldry and sundry friends would unveil their new electric band, Blues Incorporated, at a basement club in Ealing – a musical and social magnet whose influence would parallel that of the 2Is coffee bar five years earlier. Korner – now almost 34 years old, professorial, dapper, cheroots – became the catalyst in an R&B revolution which would see the rise of the Rolling Stones, Manfred Mann, John Mayall, the Animals, the Yardbirds, Rod Stewart, the Who, Cream, into the melting pot of psychedelia and beyond. In March 1963, the Stones would secure a residency at 10/11 Great Newport Street, in the cellar where Barber and Korner had first played together, 13 years earlier.

If 1959 was a year of consolidation for Lonnie Donegan and Chris Barber, it was the year that everything fell into place for Cliff Richard. His goldmine status was ratified when a squabble over rights erupted into the public glare. On successive weeks, in press advertisements, two rivals staked their claim. The first was inserted by George Ganjou: 'To Whom It May Concern. We George Ganjou Ltd of 26 Albemarle Street, London W1 wish it to be generally known that we are the sole and exclusive managers, agents and personal representatives of Cliff Richard and that no other person, persons or firms have any authority whatsoever to act on his behalf without our knowledge and written permission.'

The response, from Cliff himself, was swift. 'My father, Roger Webb, will continue to sign all documents on my behalf as he has done in the past and Tito Burns, my Personal Manager, will continue to act in this capacity as he has done in the past.' Ganjou and Burns would both be out of the picture before too long.

Despite sometimes feeling that he was being treated like a racehorse, Cliff rose above the business hassles and concentrated all his energy on his flourishing career. "I think back to the time, a year ago, when I worked in a factory," the teenager wrote in July 1959. "That seemed real; this seems unbelievable. I have to pinch myself to make sure I'm not dreaming and then I just say a prayer in gratitude for everything God has given me. I've got so much to thank Him for – and most of all for making it possible to give my family more security, so that mum doesn't have to go out to work again. Then I fall asleep once more, feeling really happy."

For Cliff, the first half of the year was relentless. Eight more *Oh Boy!* shows were interwoven with a long, draining, geographically torturous series of one-nighters on which he headlined over Wee Willie Harris, Johnny Duncan and Tony Crombie's Rockets. Two 20-minute sets each night and the rest of the time on the tour coach or in theatrical boarding houses. Fortunately, through luck and circumstance, he was now fronting the band of his dreams – Hank Marvin on lead guitar, Bruce Welch on rhythm guitar, Jet Harris on bass and Tony Meehan on drums – and there was nothing they enjoyed more than playing together. Two snappy singles, *Livin' Lovin' Doll* and *Mean Streak*, became moderate hits and when they broke for a summer holiday, the first Cliff could ever remember, they were feeling pretty optimistic.

Up until now, Hank Marvin had been playing an Antoria guitar, a solid-bodied Japanese electric, seemingly designed by someone who had only glimpsed a real electric guitar once and was trying to remember what it looked like – but compared with most guitars on the 2Is scene, it looked space-age and cool. Hank could get some interesting, fluid sounds from it, even though the fingerboard was bowed and he used to ruin his fingertips dealing with the high action.

For some time, he and the others had been discussing *Living Doll*, how it had been lost to the soundtrack of *Serious Charge*, how dissatisfied they were with the tempo and treatment – and they decided to remodel the song, slow it down to a comfortable, easy-loping sweet-beat, looking for a closer connection with the listener. The Hollywood heart-throb Ricky Nelson, by now Cliff's favourite singer, was the prime mover – not only in the re-styling of *Living Doll* but in the overall gentrification of his music. How to capture the same atmosphere and intimacy as Nelson and his band had created on such recent singles as *Don't Leave Me This Way*, *Someday*, *Lonesome Town* and *Never Be Anyone Else But You* was a subject Cliff and the boys would discuss at great length with their producer Norrie Paramor and his recording engineers.

In the hope of bringing what he called "a country feeling" to the session, Hank borrowed a guitar from his 2Is mate Tony Harvey, a mellow-toned Dutch-made Egmond, a single-cutaway semi-acoustic designed to look and hopefully sound like a Gretsch White Falcon. His dreamy, faraway Tex-Mex solo, coupled with Cliff's warm, secret-sharing vocal, made *Living Doll* the most relaxed, laid-back rock 'n' roll record any of his fans had heard. With no obvious influences, it not only began a uniquely English strand but also conferred unimaginable respectability on Cliff, smoothing out all the bumps in his reputation. All the barriers erected by the sneerers and scoffers, by the offended puritans, collapsed around him. He won them over, won everybody over, with that one record – which quickly bounded to number one.

The mood continued on *Travellin' Light* and *A Voice In The Wilderness*, which found Cliff singing, quite unashamedly, like a choir boy, inspired by "a voice from above". Whereas the core of his first album *Cliff* comprised a dozen of his favourite rockers, the songs he had been singing on *Oh Boy!* and on tour, his follow-up *Cliff Sings* was leavened with an even distribution of oldies. Eight songs, most of them from the 1930s, were embedded in panoramic settings devised by Paramor, who was obviously overjoyed to have found a singer he could develop and grow with at last. "A real pippin!" he called him.

By this time, Cliff had left home to move into his own flat in an exclusive block on Marylebone High Street – but the initial exhilaration soon wore thin when hangers-on began to treat it as a doss-house and knocking shop. "People whom I didn't consider to be my real friends were using it as their own," he complained in his first autobiography. Within a year, he had moved back to Cheshunt (suffering the ridicule of journalists who called him a 'mummy's boy') and very soon he would buy the family a new semi-detached suburban home in Winchmore Hill, complete with padlocked gates to deter fans – especially the more tenacious girls.

Many already longed to be his wife. Jet and Bruce had married during 1959 and Hank would soon follow. It's what everybody did. You found a girl, fell in love with her, swore to be true until the end of time and, in some cases (though not in any of theirs), it would all work out perfectly. Cliff sang about the process all the time – although when quizzed about his 'ideal girl', as he was continually, he fielded the question with assurances that he would not even consider marriage until he was at least 25. Very wise.

Also contracted to Columbia as a separate entity, the Drifters were on the way to becoming stars themselves, their personalities unfolding for all to see. Jet was deep and dangerous; Bruce was solid and dependable; Tony was neat and stylish; Hank was the bespectacled boffin who had discovered the secret formula, smiling his conspiratorial smile at the camera, knowing exactly what was going on. Even notes he played on Cliff's early hits *Mean Streak* and *Dynamite* would transmit a ten-year message through the Yardbirds into Led Zeppelin. In June 1959, the quartet put out their second single, *Jet Black* – immediately coming into conflict with a simultaneous release by another set of Drifters, a black vocal group from New York who had a six-year history in the American rhythm & blues market but who now had a fast-rising mainstream hit in *There Goes My Baby*. The solution was obvious: Cliff's group needed a new name fast – and it was Hank and Jet who suggested the Shadows. Cliff was able to employ a new signature tune for his Radio Luxembourg series, a modification of *Me And My Shadow*, which in 1927 had been an American hit for a band singer called Johnny Marvin. No relation.

When it became obvious that Hank needed to exchange his Antoria for an instrument to match his guitar-hero aspirations, his boss thoughtfully ordered up and paid for a top-of-the-range Fender. "I knew that James Burton played lead guitar, including the beautiful solos, on Ricky Nelson's records because he was credited on the album sleeves," says Marvin. "I had read somewhere that he played a Fender but, at that time, we hadn't seen any pictures – and I automatically assumed that it would be the same one that Buddy Holly played, the most expensive model in the catalogue. So that's the one we sent off for: the very latest flamingo-pink Stratocaster, with a solid contoured body, three pick-ups, a tremolo arm, and a maple fingerboard and neck. Because of some trade restriction, Fenders weren't available in Britain at the time, so we had to import it from the States – and unpacking it, seeing it for the first time, lifting this exquisite guitar out of its hand-made case was one of those glorious, heart-stopping moments you can never forget. It looked and sounded remarkable; when I first got it, boys would come up and ogle it, their mouths gaping, because they had never seen one up close before." Of course, it later transpired that James Burton played a Fender Telecaster, a rather more rudimentary model with a single pick-up and none of the 14-carat gold hardware – but Hank's Strat was to create and become the basis of the most distinctive rock sound of the early sixties. His first opportunity to flaunt it, if only in black and white, was in the coffee bar scenes of Cliff's latest movie.

Maybe it wasn't as expensive and universally popular as the Hollywood blockbuster *Rio Bravo*, starring Cliff's current favourite Ricky Nelson as John Wayne's sidekick, but *Expresso Bongo* was not only one of the more interesting British films of the year, it was also the best home-grown rock 'n' roll movie of the 1950s. Already up and running as a West End stage play by March 1958, it was a satire on the earliest days of the youth-music boom. Initially, Peter Sellers was lined up to play Johnny Jackson, a caricature Jewish manager, and Diane Cilento to play Maisie, his stripper girlfriend – but they dropped out and the roles were filled by Laurence Harvey, superb as a parodic amalgam of characters who have dotted the pages of this book, and Sylvia Syms, tantalising in black stockings and suspenders. "All those bald heads out there," she says as she comes off the stage, "it's like playing to an egg box." Glimpses of Soho nightlife, including doorway prostitutes and an abundance of bouncing bare breasts (nipples covered, of course), ensured another X certificate for Cliff, in his element as the naïve, manipulated singer Bongo Herbert.

After hyping Bongo into the charts by way of schmooze and crafty publicity stunts, Jackson is dispossessed when rivals discover that the onerous contract he cajoled the teenager into signing is null and void. He should also have obtained his parents' signatures – a mistake that Larry Parnes would never have made. Well, it was a spoof. Harvey, who was nominated for a BAFTA, then went off to Texas to star as Colonel Travis in *The Alamo* while Cliff, who played a lip-curling, mother-hating egotist unable to resist being seduced by a gaudy blonde twice his age, promised fans that his next picture would be altogether more wholesome. As indeed would be the rest of his career.

In amongst all the jokes and banter of *Expresso Bongo* was a spooky prediction: Johnny Jackson scammed his way onto Gilbert Harding's television show to tell viewers that "*A Voice In The Wilderness* will introduce a new era in the hit parade". It was a prediction that turned out to be as prophetic for Cliff as it was for Bongo Herbert. It was as if his two chart-toppers, *Living Doll* and *Travellin' Light*, together with the balmy *Voice In The Wilderness*, had lowered the safety curtain on rock 'n' roll, converting it into good clean harmless fun for all the family. The corner had been turned, with admirable though accidental precision, to coincide with the turn of the decade. Now shorn of threat or menace, 2Is culture was ready to shake hands with the establishment.

The Shadows' little dance helped, of course: everybody loved that. "We were working on the Johnny Otis song *Willie And The Hand Jive* towards the end of 1959, and that's when we started doing the dance steps," says Hank Marvin. "Up until that point, we had been a very basic rock 'n' roll act – every man for himself, jumping around, dropping to our knees, kicking our legs up, all the usual spontaneous moves, no organisation, just a chaotic, exciting show. That was what our audiences expected from us – but we started thinking that there must be a better way to present certain songs and we tried to work out a little routine. When Bruce and I had gone to Kilburn State to see Jerry Lee Lewis, one of the support acts was the Treniers, a very energetic show band who had all these different dance steps – and we took our inspiration from them. So, on *Willie And The Hand Jive*, when we did the backing vocals, one on either side of Cliff, we started moving around in unison, developing some rudimentary choreography. When we stuck it into the show, the reaction was fantastic – the roof almost came off! After that, we had to do it every time we played."

They saw out the year, the decade, in panto, *Babes In The Wood* – at Stockton-on-Tees, where else? For a couple of weeks, Cliff was sealed into his digs, chez Mrs Lewis at 34 Hartington Road. "We used to get this accumulation of young ladies at the window," says road manager Len Saxon. "It made us feel like goldfish in a bowl." When he ventured to the market, in an attempt to buy Christmas presents, Cliff found himself surrounded by fans. "Well, you shouldn't come out, should you?" one of them told him when he asked for a little space. Invasion of privacy came with the job; it was something he would have to get used to as he and his Shadows grew more successful and influential with each week that passed. Soon, every village hall, every ballroom, every school assembly room rang to the sounds of copy bands, all working their fingers off to keep up with the latest releases.

Lionel Bart, who seemed to have little interest in females beyond a songwriter's curiosity, was fortunate that the women's liberation movement hadn't got rolling when he wrote *Living Doll* – a celebration of hairy-chested male dominance over the subordinate species. Cliff sang it with open-hearted innocence. Those who doubted his girlfriend's qualities were invited to feel her hair, to reassure themselves, but any further examination was not on the agenda; he was going to lock her away in a trunk to prevent potential violation by rivals. This was the dream of many girls, to be possessed, to be called a 'doll' – one only needed to read the letters columns in *Valentine* to verify this – but, in a strange rearguard action, Bart later claimed to have written the song about a real toy doll, available for 10 shillings from an address in Grays Inn Road. Was he seriously trying to tell us that Cliff had been singing about a piece of moulded plastic with fluttering eyelashes and a delightful washable dress with matching panties?

1959 was a wonderful year for Lionel, the best. In February, Joan Littlewood's production of Frank Norman's play *Fings Ain't Wot They Used To Be*, with music and lyrics by Bart, opened to great acclaim at the Theatre Royal in Stratford East, running for a year before it was transferred to the Garrick in Charing Cross Road for another 897 performances. In the title song, Bart alluded to both Joan and Frank, an ex-jailbird and gambler: "Big hoods now are little hoods; gamblers now do Littlewoods."

In May, the brand new Mermaid Theatre in Puddle Dock was christened with *Lock Up Your Daughters*, adapted from Henry Fielding's 1730 play *Rape Upon Rape*. With music by Laurie Johnson and lyrics by Lionel Bart, it would run and run.

"By that point, although we still did the Tommy stuff together, my songwriting partnership with Mike Pratt wasn't running too smoothly," says Bart, "and I was writing more and more on my own. I was ambitious and wanted to do as much as I could, while Mike was often off on a jag, having a whale of a time, which was something I didn't really understand at the time. I understood it perfectly later on, when I was doing it myself – but back then, we were supposed to be working as a team and he was making every excuse not to work. I remember when we were putting songs together for *Tommy The Toreador* and he would be sitting there at the piano, smoking a joint, lost in dreams or laughing his head off about something. He just didn't seem to be concentrating and I think that was when I snapped. I shouted 'I'm sorry, but I can't work with someone who drinks and takes drugs!' It's hilarious when I think about it, because I eventually went off and made a far greater fool of myself."

But not quite yet. Sometime during the early part of 1959, at the sea-view house he often rented in Los Boliches, then a tiny village up the coast from Fuengirola, the workaholic Bart put the finishing touches to *Oliver*, the musical which would seal his reputation as a genius. It was less than three years earlier that he, Mike Pratt and Tommy Steele had created the first ever British rock 'n' roll record, *Rock With The Caveman*.

While Bart wrote his way to the stars and back (no safety net to catch him), Mike Pratt straightened out and became an actor, playing anything he was offered, from cameos in such television fluff as *Z Cars* and *Danger Man* to more challenging roles in Trevor Nunn-directed Royal Shakespeare Company productions. He left his most indelible mark playing Jeff Randall in the late sixties television series *Randall And Hopkirk (Deceased)*.

Tommy Steele continued to astound all his old cronies from the Gyre & Gimble with the intrepid bounds he made. Although he had stopped competing in the rock 'n' roll market by the end of the decade, he had been greatly responsible for its expansion. Not only had he set the ball rolling with his own records and stage shows, he had also effectively financed, through his prodigious earnings, Larry Parnes' entire stable of stars, allowing that area of the British scene to flourish and develop. But now he had other projects on his mind, new territory to explore. From the moment he first set eyes on him, John Kennedy had known that Tommy was a natural but, surely, no matter what visionary powers he might have possessed, he could never have dreamed that he would become one of the most versatile and accomplished artistes of his generation.

In a try-everything career, he (among many other diversions) played Tony Lumpkin alongside Judi Dench and Peggy Mount in Oliver Goldsmith's *She Stoops To Conquer* at the Old Vic; he starred in the smash hit musical *Half A Sixpence*, both in the West End and on Broadway (not to mention the movie); he was nominated for a Golden Globe in *The Happiest Millionaire*; he danced in shows with Fred Astaire and Gene Kelly; he took the leading role in Gilbert and Sullivan's operetta *Yeoman Of The Guard* at, appropriately, the Tower of London; he wrote and recorded an autobiographical album *My Life, My Song* with producer George Martin; he holds the record for the West End's longest running one-man show *An Evening With Tommy Steele*; he wrote a novel *The Final Run* and began work on the first instalment of his autobiography *Bermondsey Boy*; he composed a symphony *A Portrait Of Pablo* and conducted the London Symphony Orchestra performing it; he played squash for Surrey; he has topped the bill at the London Palladium more times than any other artiste; and he had one of his paintings *The Entertainer* accepted for a Royal Academy summer exhibition. Did anyone lead a fuller life during the last 50 years of the century?

Rock With The Caveman notwithstanding, Steele's most admired and lasting contribution to rock culture is the sculpture he created for the people of Liverpool in 1982: a bronze of Eleanor Rigby sitting on a bench in Stanley Street. Was there no activity in which this unassuming polymath could not excel? The most imaginative and spiritual statue in the city, it cost the citizens half a sixpence – a fee he has yet to collect.

In 1979, the Queen – a fan since the very beginning – awarded Tommy an OBE; there is still time to see him created Lord Steele of Bermondsey.

While Tommy became Britain's greatest all-round entertainer, Cliff Richard became our most successful pop singer ever, a chart fixture for half a century and a god to worshipful fans who know that he will never desert them, will never let them down, will always be there for them. Copycat turned innovator, always the gentleman, he would go on forever, doing what he did best. How has he managed to sustain? Over the years, since being launched off the top board by Jack Good, Harry Webb has become very good at being Cliff Richard.

In May 1959, *Melody Maker* had one of their periodic panic attacks: 'Stars and Theatre Staff Scared of Rock and Riot Shows' trembled their headline. "I have been in an audience during a rock show," said tuneful balladeer Joan Regan. "The mob hysteria is positively frightening." Although her own career was going into decline, she need not have worried about the population at large. A wave of decorum was about to sweep over the music business – prompted not only by a search for respectability but by the dictates of fashion.

The fifties should have ended on the last day of 1959 but, thanks to the war having taken five years out of the cycle, they continued on until 1963, when everything changed. During the intervening, anodyne, wilderness years, Cliff and his Shadows presided over a parade of chart newcomers, most of them entertainers rather than explorers. Gary Mills, Jess Conrad, Ricky Valance, Emile Ford & the Checkmates, Michael Cox, the Brook Brothers, Helen Shapiro, Eden Kane, Karl Denver, Danny Williams, Jimmy Justice, the Temperance Seven, Anthony Newley, Frank Ifield, the Allisons, John Leyton, every week another appeared, blown like tumbleweed up Charing Cross Road. Some made interesting records; most did not. Had the youth-music revolution merely been a flushing oil, to remove all the old dance-band and music hall fogies that had clogged the system, preparing the ground for pop blanderama? At times, it almost felt as if all Steve Race's fervent prayers had been answered, that his thin red line had held and that rock 'n' roll had laid down and died – but then, praise be!, the Beatles arrived to let everybody know that it had hardly been born. The last two tracks on their début album, *There's A Place* and *Twist And Shout*, were proof enough.

The media took to them immediately, little realising that they were wolves in mop-tops' clothing. Little did they realise it themselves, at the time. Towards the end of 1963, BBC radio interviewer Peter Woods asked George Harrison if he felt it could be possible for the Beatles to settle down to a life in show business. "Well, we're hoping to – not necessarily a life in show business but at least a couple more years," George told him. "I mean, if we do as well as Cliff and the Shadows have done up until now, we won't be moaning."

Before they went off to invade America, they and all these other north country groups came through the south of England, playing in ballrooms and clubs and dancehalls opened up by their predecessors, spreading the gospel of Carl Perkins and Chuck Berry and Buddy Holly and Little Richard and Larry Williams and it was all happening again, bigger and better than ever. By this time, the Stones had started rolling and *Ready Steady Go!* was on the air. Within a year, British rockers ruled the world: Americans bowed to our guys in reverence. England was swinging like a pendulum, ticking like a metronome. It was the greatest time to be alive; Britain was never a finer place to live.

Victor in the October 1964 general election, Harold Wilson, the first Labour Prime Minister for 13 years, arrived just in time to take all the credit. Ostentatiously, he hobnobbed with the stars, realising perhaps that rock music was already on its way to becoming one of Britain's greatest assets, one of Britain's greatest industries, one of Britain's greatest art-forms, one of Britain's greatest exports. Before the decade was out, the kid destined to become our first rock 'n' roll Prime Minister – born in the month that Bill Haley first reached the American chart, with *Crazy Man Crazy* – would be bent over his guitar, concentrating on the fingers of his left hand, trying to work out the chords of C, F and G.

Epilogue

I interviewed over 80 people for this book and – even though, in most cases, I just came and went with my tape-recorder – I felt a spiritual connection with all of them. Some seemed like older brothers and sisters, some like the schoolteachers I never had, some became good friends – none more so than Ian Samwell.

After writing a handful of hits for Cliff, he had become an independent record producer, responsible for the debut album by Georgie Fame & the Blue Flames *Rhythm And Blues At The Flamingo*, John Mayall's first single *Crawling Up A Hall*, and *What'cha Gonna Do About It* by the Small Faces, which he also co-wrote.

I first met him in 1970, when he was working as Artists' Liaison Manager at Warner Brothers and he arranged for me to interview the Grateful Dead and Don Everly for *Zigzag*, the magazine I was editing. We kept in touch, through the years in which he produced America (including their hit *Horse With No Name*), Elkie Brooks and Linda Lewis, among others.

By the early eighties, he was living in Sacramento, California, where he set himself up as a consultant in artist development, and I lost touch with him until I interviewed him for this book in 1995. After that, on the odd occasions that he managed to get across to England, we would meet for a pub lunch out near Newport Pagnell, where his closest family lived – he was always pining for decent fish and chips or bangers and mash, meals unavailable in his new world. "I love living in Sacramento, it's my kind of town," he would say, "but I love coming home to Britain." He was living what he called his 'second life'.

Sometime in late 1991, suddenly and unexpectedly overcome by breathlessness, he had collapsed and woken up in hospital, where he was diagnosed with idiopathic cardiomyopathy. If he didn't have a heart transplant, he would die, doctors told him – which was a bit of a bummer because he had allowed his medical insurance to lapse only six weeks earlier and the procedure was going to cost something in excess of a quarter of a million dollars.

"There was no way I was going to get that sort of bread together," said Samwell, "so I accepted that I was going to die. I was 54 years old and had enjoyed a wonderful life. I phoned up a few friends, including Robert Allen, my lawyer in London, to ask him if he could bring my will up to date, and then fell into a deep sleep in the hospital bed."

When he came to, fourteen and a half hours later, a hovering nurse came over. "Who are you?" she asked.

"Samwell, Ian Samwell," he replied, nodding towards the case notes hanging off the end of the bed.

"Yes, I know that," she said, "but *who are you?* The phone hasn't stopped ringing. All these people have been calling up with offers of money – Pink Floyd, Cliff Richard, Led Zeppelin . . . who are you?"

He was the guy who wrote *Move It*; that's who he was.

As soon as he had put the phone down, Robert Allen had got on to Jeff Dexter, the disc-jockey/producer/manager who was Ian's principal sidekick throughout the sixties and seventies, and Dexter phoned everyone he knew. A bank account was opened and cheques arrived from Cliff, David Gilmour, Derek Taylor, Terry the Pill, Peter Barnes, Tony Calder, Robert Greenfield, the Grateful Dead, David Geffen, Steve O'Rourke, John Paul Jones, Ian Knight, Malcolm Forrester, Billy Gaff, John McLaughlin, Brian Mason, many, many more. Sufficient funds were gathered for an operation at Sutter Memorial to replace his heart with that of a 19-year-old kid, who had died in a car wreck, and it pumped efficiently for another 11 years.

Ian Samwell eventually died on 13 March 2003, aged 66. Nicest guy you could ever meet. And he wrote *Move It*.

Chronology

For the benefit of trivia-scoopers, skimmers,
history pedants, statisticians and other interested parties
(though not internet parasites and thieves, if you don't mind),
here is a chronology detailing the advance of rock 'n' roll in Britain,
with other relevant or interesting bits and pieces thrown in.
All release dates and chart statistics refer to the UK.

1949
October
At their club in Cranford, members of the Crane River Jazz Band begin playing skiffle (though not under that name) between sets. Their repertoire is drawn from recordings by black blues singers, rural and urban. Early favourites include *Midnight Special* and *Take This Hammer* – both from the Leadbelly catalogue.
December
6 Leadbelly dies in Bellevue Hospital, New York, aged 60.
10 In New Orleans, Fats Domino records his first single *The Fat Man*.
17 BBC Television extends its coverage to the Midlands – the first area beyond London to benefit from the service.

1950
January
21 George Orwell dies of tuberculosis. *Nineteen Eighty-Four* had been published the previous June.
27 Eight nations, including Great Britain, set up the North Atlantic Treaty.
31 President Truman announces that he has ordered the US Atomic Energy Commission to produce a hydrogen bomb.
February
23 The Labour Party, under Clement Atlee, return to power after a general election but their majority of only six proves unworkable.
In Chicago, Muddy Waters records *Rollin' Stone* – which (in June) becomes the second release on the newly launched Chess label.
Senator Joseph McCarthy of Wisconsin, "the vilest demagogue in American history", launches a witch-hunt to root out and discredit Communists.

April

15 Police swoop on Club 11 (50 Carnaby Street) and arrest several musicians (including Ronnie Scott and Flash Winston) and five punters (including the actor Mario Fabrizi) for possession of Indian hemp (as cannabis was invariably described in legal circles).

25 Chris Barber's New Orleans Jazz Band make their début at the Empress Hall, Earls Court, as contestants in the First National Jazz Band Contest, staged by the NFJO.

27 In South Africa, the ruling National Party becomes synonymous with apartheid when the Group Areas Act imposes physical separation between races and enforces removal of black people living in white-only areas.

May

2 The government-imposed limit of five shillings on meals in restaurants and hotels, in force since June 1942, is removed.

21 BBC Television expands with the opening of new studios at Lime Grove in Shepherds Bush.

27 Petrol rationing, in force since September 1939, ends in Britain.

The first issue of the folk music magazine *Sing Out!* is published in New York.

June

27 Two days after troops from Soviet-dominated North Korea invade South Korea, President Truman orders US forces to retaliate. United Nations troops follow as the Korean War gains momentum.

July

11 Début of *Andy Pandy* on BBC Television.

16 Chris Barber's New Orleans Jazz Band open their weekly Sunday afternoon club at 11 Great Newport Street, under the temporary name of Lincoln Gardens. It runs until October.

The Weavers make their US chart début with the Leadbelly song *Goodnight Irene,* which holds the number one position for 13 weeks and becomes a standard on both sides of the Atlantic.

August

15 The birth of Princess Anne – a sister for Charles, who is now twenty-one months old.

30 Male teenagers groan as the Government announces an extension to National Service – from 18 months to two years.

September

Chris Barber's band plays the 100 Club for the first time.

November

11 Bertrand Russell, 78, is awarded the Nobel Prize for Literature.

Whirligig, presented by Humphrey Lestocq and a puppet called Mr Turnip, is BBC Television's first live children's programme. Jazz pianist Steve Race provides a regular musical interlude.

December

Frozen roads across the UK; worst driving conditions for years.

1951

January

1 After five localised pilot episodes, BBC Radio's serial *The Archers* is broadcast nationwide for the first time.

27 *Melody Maker* has an advertisement for 'The Tito Burns Hat' – as designed and worn by the man himself. It makes him look like a cross between Crocodile Dundee and Jimmy Hill. 19/11d. Save your money. A dance band accordionist, Tito will later become a wheel in rock management.

February

The Albemarle Jazz Band make their début at the White Hart in Southall.

March

19 A BOAC Stratocruiser flies from London to New York in 12 hours and 36 minutes – the fastest time recorded for a commercial aircraft.

April

10 In the budget, the price of petrol rises by 4d to 3/6d a gallon. Purchase tax on cars and home appliances is doubled from 33 per cent to 66 per cent. A single person's pension is increased by four shillings to 30 shillings a week.

Two modern jazz musicians, Lennie Bush and Johnny Rogers, are busted for possession of marijuana in Golden Square, round the corner from their Archer Street hang-outs. Rogers is fined £10 but Bush (great name for a toker), who has a previous conviction, gets three months in jail.

Nineteen-year old Rambling Jack Elliott befriends Woody Guthrie, moving into his house and learning to sing and play his songs.

Jack Kerouac writes *On The Road* in a three-week outpouring.

May

3 From the steps of St Paul's Cathedral, King George VI declares the Festival of Britain open. Most attention focuses on the South Bank

exhibition, particularly the Skylon and the Dome of Discovery, and the Pleasure Gardens at Battersea.

13 The London Studio at 11 Great Newport Street, off Charing Cross Road, is re-named Studio 51.

28 First edition of *The Goon Show* is broadcast on BBC Radio's Home Service.

July

13 The Queen and Princess Elizabeth lay the foundation stone for the National Theatre.

14 Princess Elizabeth attends a 13-band Festival of Britain jazz concert at the Royal Festival Hall – thus giving the royal nod to what was generally considered to be 'bordello music'. 7,000 punters applaud George Melly's spirited rendition of *Rock Island Line* and bid farewell to the original Crane River Jazz Band, who are playing together for the last time.

16 *What's My Line?* is broadcast for the first time on BBC Television.

Woody Guthrie learns he has the incurable Huntington's chorea, but discharges himself from hospital.

September

22 Big Bill Broonzy appears in Britain for the first time, playing two concerts at the Kingsway Hall in London.

October

25 In the general election, the Conservatives under Winston Churchill end five years of Labour government – a period which has seen wide scale nationalization of industry, the setting up of the National Health Service and the introduction of a comprehensive social security system. So begins 13 years of unbroken Tory rule.

26 Chris Barber's New Orleans Jazz Band cuts four titles for the Tempo label.

27 Ken Colyer plays his last gig with the Christie Brothers Stompers. A few days later, he re-enlists in the Merchant Navy with a view to reaching New Orleans.

November

Lyons Corner Houses raise the price of a cup of tea to 3d – up by a halfpenny.

Modern jazz trumpeter Hank Shaw is busted for possession of Indian hemp and fined £5.

A *New York Sunday Times* article officially launches the term 'Beat Generation'.

1952
January
29 The Chancellor of the Exchequer imposes tighter restrictions on hire purchase. Foreign travellers (except those on business) must restrict their expenditure to £25.
February
4 BBC Television begins broadcasting educational programmes for use in schools. Sales of television sets are already eclipsing those of radios.
6 After ailing with lung cancer for many years, King George VI dies from a coronary thrombosis, aged 56. His 25-year-old daughter Elizabeth accedes to the throne.
21 The Government announces the end of compulsory national identity cards.
Big Bill Broonzy makes his second UK visit, playing concerts in Sheffield, Edinburgh and London. The tour, promoted by the Wilcox brothers and the NFJO, loses £87.
March
28 The *Empire Windrush*, which transported the first wave of West Indian immigrants to Britain in June 1948, explodes and sinks in the Mediterranean.
April
The AIA Gallery in Lisle Street, Leicester Square, presents an exhibition of 'jazz paintings' by Russell Quaye.
May
2 Operating between London and Johannesburg, BOAC's Comet becomes the world's first commercial jet airliner.
June
2 On Whit Monday, Lonnie Donegan, George Melly and Beryl Bryden are featured vocalists on the Jazz Big Show at the Royal Albert Hall. Claimed to be 'the greatest programme ever staged in Great Britain', it features 18 acts, including the bands of Freddy Randall, Mick Mulligan and Sandy Brown, the Yorkshire Jazz Band and the Crane River Jazz Band.
28 Lonnie Donegan's Jazz Band open a Royal Festival Hall Concert headlined by Lonnie Johnson. Also on the bill are George Melly, Ron Simpson's Commodores, George Webb's Dixielanders, Ambrose Campbell's West Indians and Neva Raphaello. Accepted history, based on Donegan's rose-coloured recollections, is that he became

Lonnie Donegan rather than Tony Donegan on that very stage, on that very evening. The stuttering compère confused their names, calling him Lonnie Donegan and the American singer Tony Johnson. "The name stuck," claims Lonnie – but this wonderfully romantic story is arrant nonsense. He had already been calling himself Lonnie Donegan for over six months.

The Tempo label releases two singles by Chris Barber's New Orleans Jazz Band: *Camp Meeting Blues/Stomp Off, Let's Go* and *When Erasmus Plays His Old Kazoo/Misty Morning*.

July

2 The Lord Chief Justice declares that the banning of flogging and birching has contributed to the disturbing increase in juvenile crime.

August

16 Torrential rain causes serious flooding in Lynmouth, Devon – resulting in "the greatest natural disaster in Britain this century".

21 Birth of Clash leader Joe Strummer.

October

3 Britain becomes the third member of the perversely named Atomic Bomb Club, testing a device at Monte Bello Island, off the coast of Australia.

5 Britons are finally allowed to enjoy unlimited cuppas as controls are lifted on tea, which has been rationed since July 1940.

20 A state of emergency is declared in the colony of Kenya, where the Mau Mau threaten stability and British interests.

In French Indo China (Vietnam), the communist-inspired Viet Minh make steady headway in their offensive against the French, who are already benefiting from American arms and materials.

The average price of beer is 1/2d a pint; cigarettes are 2/7d for 20; milk is 6d a pint.

EMI release their first 45rpm single.

Big Bill Broonzy arrives on the *Queen Mary* for his third British tour, this one set for six weeks. He will share some concerts with Mahalia Jackson, on her first UK visit.

November

1 The US explodes the world's first hydrogen bomb at Eniwetok Atoll in the Marshall Islands, South Pacific. Horrific devastation introduces the phrase 'ultimate deterrent' to political language.

4 General Dwight D Eisenhower replaces Harry S. Truman to become the first Republican President of the United States since 1928.

14 The *NME* publishes Britain's first pop chart, showing comparative record sales for the week. Number one is *Here In My Heart* by Al Martino.

25 *The Mousetrap* opens at London's Ambassador's Theatre.

December

5 Thick smoke-laden fog, known as smog, shrouds London for four days, resulting in over 4,000 deaths.

15 *The Flowerpot Men* make their first appearance on BBC Television. The average weekly wage of a coal miner is £12.3.9d; of a farm labourer £5.13.0d. The mortgage rate is 2.5 per cent.

1953

January

1 Hank Williams dies in the back of his Cadillac, of heart failure induced by alcohol, morphine and other drugs, aged 29.

20 The inauguration of President Dwight Eisenhower; Richard Nixon is sworn in as Vice President.

31 Tempests and tidal surges cause widespread flooding on Britain's east coast, leaving over 300 dead.

Ken Colyer is arrested and imprisoned in New Orleans.

February

5 Sweet rationing ends.

March

5 After a 29-year rule, Russian Premier Joseph Stalin dies, aged 73.

Ken Colyer is deported to England, where he is embraced by Chris Barber's New Orleans Jazz Band – which now becomes Ken Colyer's Jazzmen.

April

3 On the first date of their Danish tour, Ken Colyer's Jazzmen play the Scala Restaurant in Copenhagen.

25 Ken Colyer's Jazzmen make their UK début at the London Jazz Club, 34 Bryanston Street, and take up Saturday and Sunday night residencies there.

May

2 As Blackpool beat Bolton Wanderers 4-3, 38-year-old Stanley Matthews finally wins his FA Cup Winners medal.

6 Future Prime Minister Tony Blair is born.

29 Mt Everest is conquered for the first time, by a British expedition led by Colonel John Hunt.

June

2 Queen Elizabeth II is crowned at Westminster Abbey. For the first time ever, more people watch television than listen to the radio. Traditional jazz bands play at Coronation street parties and on riverboat shuffles.

7 Tom Jones becomes a teenager.

The Volkswagen Beetle is introduced to Britain.

July

15 John Christie is hanged after being found guilty of several murders at 10 Rillington Place in west London.

27 The Korean War ends, dividing the country at the 38th Parallel. Over 25,000 US troops have died in the conflict and 710 British soldiers.

August

19 Led by Len Hutton, England's cricketers reclaim the Ashes from Australia, who have held them for the past 19 years.

29 White bread is available for the first time in 13 years.

First single by Bill Haley & his Comets to be released in UK is *Crazy Man Crazy/Whatcha Gonna Do*, which had taken them into the US pop chart for the first time. Decca persuade Lita Roza to cover *Crazy Man Crazy*, making her the first British artist to record a rock 'n' roll song.

September

21 BBC Radio transmits the first episode of *Journey Into Space*, with Andrew Faulds as Captain Jet Morgan and David Kossoff as Lemmy. Alto sax player Geoff Taylor, something of a bop sensation since his 'discovery' at the Robin's Nest in Hornchurch, where he was resident bandleader, forms an Earl Bostic style band.

October

9 John Lennon becomes a teenager.

14 Cliff Richard becomes a teenager.

Release of *Crying In The Chapel* by the Orioles, which – like their 1948 hit, *It's Too Soon To Know* – had crossed from the US R&B chart into the pop best sellers. Here, the song is covered by the stentorian balladeer Robert Earl.

November

9 The poet Dylan Thomas dies in New York at the age of 39.

11 First edition of *Panorama* is broadcast by BBC Television.

26 England's football team suffer a humiliating defeat, beaten 6-3 by Hungary.

Release of *Fractured/Pat-A-Cake* by Bill Haley & his Comets.

December

Among the handful of American rhythm & blues records issued here during 1953 are *Big Mamou/PlayGirl* by Smiley Lewis and *I Love My Baby/The Blues Came Rolling In* by Lowell Fulson.

During the year, eggs, bacon and sugar have come off the ration for the first time since the war, though butter is still rationed to three ounces per person per week.

1954

January

12 Long John Baldry becomes a teenager.

Pete Seeger starts a regular column in the American folk magazine *Sing Out!* under the heading Johnny Appleseed Jr – "dedicated to those who are using their guitars and their songs to plant the seeds of a better tomorrow".

February

The London-American label (a Decca Records offshoot) starts its magnificent HL 8000 series, the most valuable collection of treasure ever gathered under one logo, with *In The Mission Of St Augustine/ Write And Tell Me Why* by the Orioles (HL 8001). Also in the first batch is *Rose Mary/You Said You Love Me* – the first UK release by Fats Domino (HL 8007).

The Ministry of Health's advisory committee reports that a relationship between smoking and lung cancer "must be regarded as established".

March

1 Radioactive fallout following an American nuclear test at Bikini Atoll results in serious injury to both test personnel and the inhabitants of nearby islands.

April

2 BBC Television transmits the first episode of *The Grove Family* – Britain's first soap series.

8 President Eisenhower speaks of a 'domino theory', whereby communist expansion could become uncontrollable throughout the world. In August, he signs the Communist Control Act – effectively outlawing the Communist Party and its membership.

9 Johnnie Ray's cover of *Such A Night* enters the Top 20 for an eighteen-week run. Highest position, number one. An abysmal UK

version by Dennis Lotis, backed by the Johnston Brothers and the Ted Heath Orchestra, fails to make any impression, praise be. The original recording, by the Drifters, is not released here until the mid-sixties – and nor are any of the group's other 1953-5 classics, such as *Money Honey, Honey Love, Adorable* and *White Christmas*.

17 Billy Fury becomes a teenager.

18 Former army officer Lt-Col Nasser becomes Prime Minister and Military Governor of Egypt.

A proposal to raise the annual salaries of Members of Parliament from £1,000 to £1,500 is withdrawn after public fury.

May

1 The FA Cup Final is televised for the first time.

6 Britain's Roger Bannister becomes the first person to run a mile in under four minutes.

11 Eric Burdon becomes a teenager.

13 Joe Brown becomes a teenager.

17 The US Supreme Court rules that racial segregation in public schools is unconstitutional.

First issue of *Sing* is published. Eric Winter is Editor; John Hasted is Music Editor. The magazine, devoted to folk music, will continue for over 20 years.

On the last day of his British 'crusade', American evangelist Billy Graham addresses 180,000 in two rallies – at White City Stadium and Wembley Stadium.

June

1 The television licence fee is raised from £2 to £3 per year.

12 IRA men break into Gough Barracks, Armagh and steal weapons.

17 Rising from the ashes of the defunct *Sport & Show News*, the *Record Mirror* starts publishing from an office at 20 Rupert Street in Soho.

30 Britain experiences a total eclipse of the sun.

The *People*'s investigative reporter Duncan Webb names Archer Street, where musicians meet for employment, as 'the centre of the marijuana market'.

July

5 In Memphis, Sun Records owner Sam Phillips sees the future of popular music when Elvis Presley sings a supercharged version of *That's All Right* in his studio.

13 In Decca's London studio, Lonnie Donegan (guitar/vocals), Chris Barber (bass) and Beryl Bryden (washboard) join forces to record two

skiffle tracks, *Rock Island Line* and *John Henry*, for the Chris Barber Jazz Band album *New Orleans Joys*.

21 The Geneva Conference divides Indo China into North Vietnam and South Vietnam.

29 Publication of *The Fellowship Of The Ring* by J.R.R. Tolkien – the first part of his *Lord Of The Rings* trilogy.

It is revealed that in 1953, the United Kingdom received dollar aid from the United States to the tune of more than £110 million.

Release of the Crew Cuts' ersatz rock 'n' roll single *Sh-Boom*, which will reach number 12.

A current dance fad, the creep, is said to be "ruining ballroom dancing".

August

25 Lillian, the wife of Ross McManus, trumpeter and vocalist with the Arthur Rowberry Band, presents him with a son, to be christened Declan Patrick . . . and later to call himself Elvis Costello.

Britain's hottest pin-up film star, Diana Dors, pays a colossal £8,000 for a house in Maidenhead. It has a private cinema and three bathrooms – one with a sunken marble bath.

The Wolfenden Committee is set up to examine the law in relation to homosexual offences and prostitution.

September

Release of *Rock Around The Clock/Thirteen Women* by Bill Haley & his Comets and *Sh-Boom* by Bronx vocal group the Chords. The *NME*'s reviewer describes the latter as "the worst side I have listened to since I started writing in *NME* many months ago. If the folk on the other side of the Atlantic think this is great stuff, then I'm really sorry for them. It sounds as if it was recorded on amateur equipment in an old barn. I am happy to say that we do not make records this bad in the British Isles."

October

14 Future Rastafarian hero Emperor Haile Selassie of Ethiopia arrives in London for a state visit.

18 Ken Colyer opens his New Orleans Club, to be held every Monday evening at Studio 51.

28 Hank Marvin becomes a teenager.

Release of *Shake Rattle And Roll/ABC Boogie*, fourth UK single by Bill Haley & his Comets.

The Decca group of labels enters the 45 rpm singles market.

Jazz man Tubby Hayes is busted for possession of Indian hemp.

"I have no faith in the mambo as a future influence on popular music in Britain," says Reg Connelly, chairman of publishers Campbell Connelly.

Woolworth's announce plans to launch their own label, Embassy, featuring cover versions even less authentic than the major labels' cover versions. Their cut-price singles will retail at 3/9d, as opposed to the industry standard of 5/4d.

November

2 *Hancock's Half Hour* launched on BBC Radio.

2 Bruce Welch becomes a teenager.

19 Stan Freberg's frivolous send-up of *Sh-Boom* enters the Top 20 for a two-week run, reaching number 15.

24 Ken Colyer marries Delphine Fricker at Fulham Register Office.

Lonnie Donegan sings the title song of the movie *Passing Stranger*, released this month. Chris Barber's Jazz Band releases a single of *White Christmas/On A Christmas Day*. The latter, a Leadbelly song, features a vocal by Lonnie.

Release of Dennis Lotis' lamentable version of *Honey Love*, a US R&B hit by the Drifters.

Release of *Happy Days And Lonely Nights* by both Frankie Vaughan and Suzi Miller with the Johnston Brothers. These records are described as rock 'n' roll by some commentators, though the song is nothing more than a novelty item dating back to 1928. Suzi Miller is hyped as a rock 'n' roll singer but always seems more comfortable on novelty material like *Bimbo* and *Tennessee Wigwalk*.

December

2 Communist witch-hunter Senator Joe McCarthy is censured for unbecoming conduct by his Senate colleagues. He remains in office until 1956 but is increasingly less active.

17 Bill Haley's *Shake Rattle And Roll* starts a 14-week Top 20 run. Highest position, number 4.

Release of *What A Mouth* by the Two Bills From Bermondsey.

Worst Christmas record of the year: *When Santa Got Stuck In The Chimney* by Billy Cotton.

Popular Radio Luxembourg shows include *Perry Mason*, *Carroll Levis And His Discoveries*, *Double Your Money*, *Dan Dare* and *The Butlin's Beaver Club*.

The *Sunday Times* costs 4d, a bottle of Guinness is 1/3d.

During the year, sundry rhythm & blues records by Fats Domino, John Lee Hooker, the Spiders, T-Bone Walker, and others are released in UK to minimal interest.

Instances of juvenile crime dropped from 47,473 in 1951 to 34,829 in 1954. The total number of reported crimes for the year was 434,327. The bank rate is three per cent.

1955
January
7 Bill Haley's *Rock Around The Clock* enters the Top 20 for a two-week run. Highest position, number 17.

9 Belfast art teacher Ottilie Patterson makes her début as a member of Chris Barber's band at the Royal Festival Hall and stops the show dead with three numbers.

Decca releases albums by Chris Barber's Jazz Band and Ken Colyer's Jazzmen. Both contain skiffle tracks.

Release of *Dim Dim The Lights/Happy Baby* by Bill Haley & his Comets. Fails to chart.

Accordion virtuoso Tito Burns opens a West End theatrical agency, signing Canadian vocal trio the Three Deuces as his first act. Big-hearted Tito is forgoing his agent's percentage until they get established: "I know I'm going to get my money back, believe me." We believe you, Tito.

Soon to become a staunch opponent of rock 'n' roll, Jack Payne tells his own story – '30 Years In Showbiz' – in *John Bull* magazine. He objects to being called a disc jockey and invites a nobler job title. Suggestions include shellac spinner, spindle spinner, groove grinder, platter chatterer, wax wheeler, groove gremlin, music host, turntable twister, melody man, groove guy, platter spinner and needle nudger . . . but, much to his chagrin, the term disc jockey sticks.

A new Hofner Congress cello acoustic guitar costs 12 guineas.

Weekly sales of the *NME* now exceed 100,000, making it the world's biggest-selling music paper.

February
2 Graham Nash becomes a teenager.

8 Malenkov, Soviet Premier since the death of Stalin two years earlier, resigns. Marshall Bulganin is new leader. Foreign Secretary Molotov warns the US of Russia's strength, claiming superiority in nuclear weapons.

8 The South African government compulsorily moves African families from their homes in Johannesburg to a purpose built settlement 11 miles away. Jazz orchestra leader Johnny Dankworth turns down a lucrative tour because of the country's colour-bar policy. His decision follows Father Trevor Huddleston's plea, made in *The Observer*, for a cultural boycott of South Africa by musicians, dancers and other entertainers who consider racial segregation to be wrong.

15 The UK government announces a building programme for twelve nuclear power stations.

24 Paul Jones becomes a teenager.

28 Brian Jones becomes a teenager.

Release of *Earth Angel* by the Penguins. Sadly, the US white-market cover by the Crew Cuts will attract all UK airplay, obliterating the original.

A regular provider of Light Programme fodder, Malcolm Mitchell is the first guy in England to acquire a Fender Telecaster.

Dennis Lotis leaves the Ted Heath Orchestra to go solo. Another former Heath vocalist, Dickie Valentine, is booked to headline at the London Palladium – where he worked as a call boy 10 years earlier.

Ruby Murray is the first British girl to have three songs in the Top Ten: *Softly Softly*, *Heartbeat* and *Happy Days And Lonely Nights*.

Pye takes over the Polygon label.

March

12 Death of Charlie Parker.

31 Lonnie Donegan marries Maureen Tyler at St Luke's Church in Bow, east London.

Bill Haley cashes in on the mambo fad by releasing *Mambo Rock/Birth Of The Boogie*, which spends two weeks in the Top 20; highest position, number 14. Says *Record Mirror*: "His extrovert offerings lift the atmosphere with their loud, jolly and vulgar sounds."

Singer Ross McManus joins the Joe Loss Orchestra. Over the years, Loss will be responsible for some of the most anodyne Light Programme renderings of US hits ever heard. He has already been a bandleader for 25 years, having made his début at the Astoria, Charing Cross Road in 1930.

Bob Watson's Skiffle Group appears weekly at the Fox & Goose in Ealing, supporting resident traditional jazz band, the Southern Stompers.

Singer Dick James sets up his own music publishing business.

"Is radio a dying medium?" asks a *Melody Maker* headline. Apart from Radio Luxembourg, it's been dead for years – as any teenager could have told them.

Sixty per cent of *Picturegoer* magazine's readers name 29-year-old Tony Curtis as their favourite star. His hairstyle will become first choice for rock 'n' roll fans.

Marlon Brando counsels new-kid-in-town James Dean to give up motorcycling: "If you get in an accident, you're liable to slide off and lose half your face. That's all right in some other business, but as an actor you'll have trouble getting by without it."

Smart girls are advised to remove underarm hair with Veet. 'No cuts, no stubble. Keeps your skin hair-free longer and weakens re-growth.' 2/2d from chemists.

The Postmaster General imposes broadcasting regulations which restrict both BBC TV and soon-to-start ITV to 50 hours a week.

April

5 Sir Winston Churchill resigns as Prime Minister; Sir Anthony Eden succeeds him.

5 South Africa withdraws from UNESCO rather than modify racialist policies.

15 The Crew Cuts' vanilla version of *Earth Angel* enters the chart for a twenty-week run; highest position, number four.

18 Professor Albert Einstein dies, aged 76.

18 Drug firms begin marketing a poliomyelitis vaccine developed by Jonas Salk. Mass vaccination of schoolchildren is scheduled.

Marlon Brando's *The Wild One*, denied a release by the censor in 1953, is granted a temporary X certificate by Cambridge magistrates and shown for the first time in Britain, at the city's Rex Cinema. Says *Picturegoer*'s critic: "The film is nasty; it leaves a bitter taste in the mouth. I say it shouldn't have been made, never mind shown." However, teenage viewers report "nothing shocking or brutal. It could have had an A certificate."

Ronnie Aldrich & the Squadronaires re-launch as an rhythm & blues band but soon revert to conventional dance music.

After working as his assistant for five years, George Martin succeeds Oscar Preuss as head of EMI's Parlophone label.

George Melly gives a lecture at the ICA on 'Sexual Imagery in the Blues' – so graphic that some of the audience are shocked and upset.

Quizzed about rumours that he may quit Hollywood for politics, Ronald Reagan says "No! Not on your life! I wouldn't quit the movie business for anything."

American disc jockey Alan Freed grosses over $107,000 with a week of R&B shows at the Brooklyn Paramount Theatre, breaking the all-time house record and confirming the rising popularity of rhythm & blues and rock 'n' roll in the States.

May

2 BBC radio begins transmitting in VHF, acclaimed as vastly superior to the medium wave band, although relatively few listeners have radios and aerials capable of picking up the new signal.

11 First transmission of BBC television show *Off The Record* with Jack Payne. Guests include Alma Cogan, Max Bygraves, the Four Aces and George Shearing.

21 In Chicago, Chuck Berry cuts his first single, *Maybellene*.

26 A general election returns the Conservatives with an increased majority, endorsing Sir Anthony Eden's selection as Prime Minister.

Eighteen year old Edna Savage makes her TV début on Ernest Maxim's *Showcase*.

The Children and Young Persons (Harmful Publications) Act bans the distribution and sale of 'American horror comics, which glorify violence, brutality and gore'.

Gordon Langhorn (soon to become known as Don Lang) leaves the Ken Mackintosh Orchestra after four and a half years and joins vocal group the Nicholodeons.

Bob Miller & the Millermen, having been resident orchestra at Leeds Locarno and then Streatham Locarno, moves into the Astoria Ballroom on Charing Cross Road.

Film producer Sol Lesser signs up the eleventh guy to portray Tarzan on the silver screen – Gordon Scott, formerly a lifeguard at a Las Vegas swimming pool.

A letter to *Melody Maker* beseeches: "Stop being a poseur, Mr Melly." Fortunately, George takes not the blindest bit of notice.

June

18 Paul McCartney becomes a teenager.

Jimmy Young hits number one with his Light Programme version of *Unchained Melody*, beating out Al Hibbler (who, amazingly, reaches number 2) and Roy Hamilton. On his triumphant week, next to the chart in *NME*, is a picture of the star, above a message 'With grateful thanks to all who have helped', and a bible reference: Ecclesiastes 9, verse 11. Oh, hit us with that humility, Jimmy!

Melody Maker publishes a comprehensive article on the rhythm & blues boom sweeping America. They quote Peter Potter, a popular disc jockey on Los Angeles radio station KLAC, as saying: "All rhythm & blues records are dirty and as bad for kids as dope."

A poll reveals that the most popular stars on BBC Television are Peter Cushing, Eamonn Andrews, Benny Hill, Gilbert Harding, Arthur Askey, and Armand & Michaela Denis.

July

9 BBC Television broadcasts the first episode of *Dixon Of Dock Green* and 20 days later unveils *This Is Your Life*.

15 The McGuire Sisters processed cover of *Sincerely* enters the chart for a four-week run; highest position, number 14. The original, by the Moonglows, finds no UK release until 1965.

18 A summit meeting brings together President Eisenhower, Prime Minister Eden, Premier Bulganin and French Premier Faure. No important agreements are reached but international tension is relaxed.

Exploiting his somewhat dated back catalogue, London release not only old singles by Bill Haley & His Comets, but also a long player, *Live It Up* – the first rock 'n' roll album to be released in Britain. Meanwhile, Brunswick issues his latest single *Razzle Dazzle/Two Hound Dogs*, which fails to chart.

Newspapers are full of scare stories about 'the Teddy boy menace'.

Harrow County Grammar School pupils Tony Kohn and Colin Stroud go to the Soho Fair to busk in the street. There they meet Ken Johnson and Tony Maitland and nip into an Old Compton Street coffee bar called Orlando's. As the Ghouls, the earliest independent teenage skiffle group working in the West End, they take up residency there for the next 18 months.

August

2 The government takes action to control urban sprawl by establishing 'green belts' around towns and cities.

With sales of *Cara Mia* exceeding a million, David Whitfield becomes the third British artist to win a gold record. Only three years earlier, he was working as a building labourer in Hull. The only other British artists to receive a gold disc are Vera Lynn (for *Auf Weidersehn*) and Eddie Calvert (for *Oh Mein Papa*).

Unemployment in Britain drops below one per cent.

September

1 Bob Watson and Cyril Davies start the West End's first weekly skiffle club (every Thursday evening), featuring their own group and guest artists. Its home is the first floor of the Roundhouse pub in Wardour Street. Admission is two shillings.

4 Kenneth Kendall is the first in-vision newsreader on BBC Television.

14 In New Orleans, Little Richard records *Tutti Frutti*.

18 US astronomers report that an area of Mars has turned a bluey-green colour, leading to widespread speculation about the possibility of extraterrestrial life forms.

19 The Crew Cuts start their UK tour at Liverpool Empire. They sing duff versions of R&B numbers before going into hat-and-cane routines for *Shine On Harvest Moon* and *Me And My Girl*.

22 Commercial television (ITV) starts broadcasting in the London area and viewers see advertisements for the first time. Says actors' newspaper *The Stage*: "Some feel that while the novelty lasts, television may keep people at home and thus reduce attendance at theatres." The annual television licence fee is still £3.

26 Britain and USA are linked by a submarine telephone cable.

30 Death of James Dean, killed in a collision en route to a sports car race in Salinas, California. His speed at the point of impact was estimated at 85 mph.

Release of *Ain't That A Shame* by Pat Boone (his first UK single) and *Ain't That A Shame* by Fats Domino. Consecutive catalogue numbers on the London American label, but white takes black in two moves: BBC approval, into the charts. Pat enjoys a nine-week Top 20 run; highest position, number 7. Fats fails to chart – but wins tortoise and hare race when rock intelligentsia praises his work and mocks Pat's.

Saxophonist Red Price leaves Ronnie Aldrich & the Squadronaires; Rex Morris leaves the Vic Lewis Orchestra.

October

10 Release of movie *East Of Eden*, featuring James Dean in his first starring role.

14 Ken Colyer's Skiffle Group is the first to issue a single: *Take This Hammer/Down By The Riverside*. As authentic as anyone in Britain, he is destined to remain a purist/cult favourite, mainly because of dull delivery, lack of image and refusal to compromise.

17 UK Release of the juvenile delinquency movie *Blackboard Jungle*, featuring Bill Haley's *Rock Around The Clock* over the credits.

26 Prime Minister Ngo Dinh Diem proclaims South Vietnam a republic and declares himself President.

28 Birth of Microsoft founder Bill Gates.

The title of Faron Young's UK début encapsulates the James Dean/ rock 'n' roll ethic: *Live Fast, Love Hard, Die Young.* Along similar lines is the Leiber & Stoller-written *Black Denim Trousers And Motor Cycle Boots* by the Cheers.

Teenagers are now becoming a lucrative market, a fact acknowledged by the *Daily Sketch*, which now devotes a weekly page, 'Teenage Sketch', to the twixt twelve and twenty set. It features fashions, disc reviews, slimming advice and such scintillating articles as 'The Women In My Life' by Johnnie Ray, 'Are You The Girl We Are Looking For To Become A Model?' and 'He Makes Up The Stars – Now He Will Show You'.

Mary Quant and Alexander Plunkett-Green open their fashion shop Bazaar on the King's Road in Chelsea.

The British Musicians' Union and the American Federation of Musicians agree to lift their mutual ban on musicians playing on the other side of the Atlantic. For the first time since 1935, UK audiences will be able to see American bands – good news for rock 'n' roll fans.

November

10 The author becomes a teenager.

11 Two tracks off Chris Barber's year old album *New Orleans Joys* are paired for release under the name of vocalist Lonnie Donegan: *Rock Island Line/John Henry*

25 Reactivated by *Blackboard Jungle*, Bill Haley's *Rock Around The Clock* tops the charts - staying there for three weeks before being dislodged by Dickie Valentine's *Christmas Alphabet*.

Voted the year's Most Promising Country & Western Artist in America's annual disc jockey poll, Elvis Presley leaves the independent Memphis-based Sun label and signs with RCA.

In his *Melody Maker* column, Jack Payne asks "Are We Heading For A Dance Band Slump?" Are we ever, Jack!

A purchase tax hike raises the cost of a single to 5/7d.

In the newspapers, there are no advertisements for guitars yet – but plenty for things like Edmundo Ros Maracas (still the best for that authentic Latin American tone), Galanti & Gaudini Accordions, and the Famous Gold Lacquered Ambassador Trumpet – yours for a deposit of only 36/-.

December

1 On a bus in Montgomery, Alabama, black seamstress Rosa Parks refuses to give up her seat to a white man and is arrested for violating the city's racial segregation laws. Baptist minister Martin Luther King Jr subsequently leads a bus boycott – later seen as the first step towards the nationwide Civil Rights Movement. The US eventually becomes a democracy a decade later.

7 Clement Attlee resigns as leader of the Labour party and is succeeded by Hugh Gaitskill.

Ruby Murray moves into an exclusive flat overlooking Regents Park, paying an extortionate £15-a-week rent.

Release of Bill Haley's *Rock-A-Beatin' Boogie/Burn That Candle*, which soon begins a nine-week Top 20 run; highest position, number 4. Says the *NME* reviewer: "It's simply terrific; rocks from the word go, and there is some brilliant saxophone playing of the unconventional type."

Pye Nixa releases the latest Chris Barber album, *Echoes Of Harlem*.

During the year . . .

. . . work starts on the world's first nuclear power station at Calder Hall in Cumberland – later known as Windscale and Sellafield. What do you know? Rock music in Britain is as old as nuclear power and Independent Television.

Elvis Presley, the Platters, Little Richard, Chuck Berry and Bo Diddley are all having records released in the States but none are issued here.

Rock Hudson comments on his recent marriage to Phyllis Gates: "Take it from me, finding a wife wasn't easy. I'm the sort of guy who likes to squeeze a toothpaste tube in the middle." I think we know what you're getting at, Rock.

Most popular television shows include *The Grove Family*, *The Appleyards*, *Animal Vegetable Or Mineral*, *Fabian Of The Yard*, *What's My Line?*, *Double Your Money*, *Dixon Of Dock Green*, *Zoo Quest*, *Sunday Night At The London Palladium*, and the imported *I Love Lucy*. The latest comedy duo pairs Bill Maynard and Terry Scott.

Many leading singers – including Alma Cogan, Lita Roza, Dickie Valentine and Dennis Lotis – choose Frank Sinatra's *Learning The Blues* as their favourite single of the year.

Among the first companies to suss out the financial potential of merchandising, Starpic Ltd advertises souvenirs of stars. Hottest sellers this year are brooches (at 2/11d each, post free) or photo-identity bracelets (4/11d) of Jeff Chandler, Johnnie Ray, Tony Curtis, Dickie Valentine, David Whitfield and Doris Day.

During the year, booming trade conditions see US companies manufacturing eight million cars, thus achieving the remarkable output level of one new vehicle for every 20 citizens. The UK car industry increases output by 16 per cent, thanks to continuing prosperity in the home market.

Convictions for dangerous drug offences of all kinds dropped to 172 (as opposed to 219 in 1954). Of these, 120 were for marijuana or hashish. Over 72 per cent of offenders were 'coloured persons'. Not one teenager was convicted.

Throughout the year, *Melody Maker* refuses even to mention rock 'n' roll. The words appear only in the occasional small-ad for a novelty dance contest.

1956
January
6 Bill Haley's *Rock Around The Clock* regains the number one position; stays there for a fortnight.

10 In Nashville, Elvis Presley records his first sides for RCA.

10 Europe's largest blast furnace is fired at Margam, near Port Talbot, South Wales. Britain is still a leading contender in world industry.

28 In the US, Elvis Presley appears on national television for the first time.

31 Birth of John Lydon, later known as Johnny Rotten.

Richard Attenborough writes a record review column for the *News Of The World*; Michael Winner writes for the *NME*.

Rock Island Line by Lonnie Donegan enters the UK chart the same week as similar Americana-rooted songs *The Ballad Of Davy Crockett* and *Sixteen Tons*. The record is regarded as a novelty, and skiffle a transient fad, but Lonnie's zestful personality soon wins the hearts of punters young and old.

Ronnie Scott and Tony Crombie break up their big jazz-orientated dance bands and, with the best players from each, combine to form a new Ronnie Scott Orchestra.

February

1 The coldest day since 1895.

16 The UK Bank Rate rises to 4½ per cent – the highest since 1932.

17 Five months after transmissions began in London, the ITV network expands into the Midlands.

25 At the Communist Party Congress in Moscow, Nikita Khrushchev leads a bitter attack on Stalin's leadership and rule.

25 George Harrison becomes a teenager.

A survey confirms that beer consumption has fallen every year since the war, while wine grows in popularity.

March

5 Release of seminal teen movie *Rebel Without A Cause*, which, like *Blackboard Jungle*, is given an X certificate. Its stars, James Dean, Natalie Wood and Sal Mineo, will all die dramatically.

9 Trouble in the Empire: Archbishop Makarios is deported from Cyprus to the Seychelles.

10 Recording 1,132 mph, a British Fairey Delta 2, piloted by L.P. Twiss, becomes the first plane to take the air speed record beyond 1,000 mph.

12 Statistics reveal that UK citizens' expenditure on tobacco has reached an all-time high of £880 million – in spite of research linking smoking with lung cancer.

25 Ewan MacColl is inspired to write an evergreen when he sees Peggy Seeger's face for the first time ever.

Decca, who have already lost Lonnie Donegan, release a second single under his name: *Diggin' My Potatoes/Bury My Body*. Owing to questionable lyrics, it receives no airplay and fails to chart.

The Bob Watson/Cyril Davies Roundhouse skiffle club is now billed as 'the firstest and bestest' in *Melody Maker*'s small-ads column.

Unable to find an audience, the Ronnie Scott/Tony Crombie Orchestra disbands after only three months.

April

3 Opening night of London's second skiffle club, every Tuesday at 44 Gerrard Street, with John Hasted's Skiffle and Folksong Group.

7 Having previously published only sheet music sales, *Melody Maker* begins printing a weekly list of best-selling discs.

11 For the first time, Elvis Presley has the best-selling single in America, *Heartbreak Hotel*. During the year, three more Presley discs will reach number one.

16 London's third skiffle club opens its doors at the Princess Louise, a pub in High Holborn. Residents: Russell Quaye's City Ramblers.

22 'Rebel' Ray Hunter and Paul Lincoln, Australian wrestlers, take over the lease on the 2Is Coffee Bar at 59 Old Compton Street, Soho – named after the previous owners, Freddie and Sammy Irani, who move to 47 Frith Street and open a nightclub, the Cote D'Azur (in premises later more famous for housing Ronnie Scott's Jazz Club).

Ted Heath's Orchestra, the first UK musicians to tour the States in a generation, report back in *Melody Maker*: "The general public down here in the south aren't very interested in jazz – it's all hillbilly music."

Ex-Ted Heath Orchestra vocalist Kathy Lloyd becomes the first artiste to record in the Capitol Tower, the new stack-of-45s shaped office of Capitol Records in Hollywood.

The Musicians' Union instructs members not to accept engagements in South Africa or Rhodesia if they involve the segregation of audiences by colour.

With his début on Pye Nixa, *Lost John/Stewball*, Lonnie Donegan reaches number 2.

May

3 The ITV network expands further as Granada begins broadcasting in the north of England.

4 The real thing for a change! Trad jazz fans rejoice as Louis Armstrong & his All Stars open their 17-day UK tour at the Empress Hall, Earls Court. Extraordinarily, the MU exchange band is Freddy Randall's lacklustre outfit, who later this month will have the sublime pleasure of touring the States with Bill Haley & his Comets, the Platters, the Colts, the Flamingos, LaVern Baker, and the Red Prysock Band.

8 Theatre's equivalent of the rock 'n' roll era starts when John Osborne's *Look Back In Anger* opens at the Royal Court Theatre in Sloane Square. Heading the cast are Kenneth Haigh, Alan Bates and Mary Ure.

16 The first of two more British nuclear tests, again at Monte Bello Islands.

18 Presented by Gus Goodwin, Radio Luxembourg's new weekly show *Jamboree* (8 until 10 on Saturday nights) features rock 'n' roll. From the New Year, it will include a specially recorded half-hour of Alan Freed, playing his current R&B favourites.

19 His British fans would get used to rumours of an impending tour by Elvis. The first of many was spread by *Melody Maker*: "Elvis Presley, young country & western star whose *Heartbreak Hotel* has passed the million mark, is rumoured for British appearances after he ends his film for Paramount." In vain we waited – but we stopped holding our breath.

20 The Americans explode the first hydrogen bomb to be dropped from the air – over Namu Island in the Bikini atoll.

22 The world's first nuclear power station, at Calder Hall (Sellafield) in Cumberland, goes into operation. It will be officially opened by the Queen on 17 October.

24 The first Eurovision Song Contest.

Lonnie Donegan confirms that he has left Chris Barber's Jazz Band for a solo career. He flies to USA, where *Rock Island Line* is a Top 10 hit, and stays until July.

June

8 The coldest summer day this century.

23 In *Melody Maker*, Jack Payne asks "Should we surrender to the teenagers?" Sorry mate, but you have no option.

26 Georgie Fame becomes a teenager.

The Goons reach the chart with *I'm Walking Backwards For Christmas*. Two novel jazz records also hit during the summer: *Bad Penny Blues* by Humphrey Lyttelton and *Experiments With Mice* by Johnny Dankworth.

July

6 BBC Television launches *Hancock's Half Hour*.

10 The House of Lords stifles a bill to abolish hanging.

13 *Be Bop A Lula* by Gene Vincent & the Blue Caps nudges into the chart as the first wave of rock 'n' roll fanatics discover another hero.

14 Three coffee bar strummers – Wally Whyton, Johnny Booker and Jean Van Den Bosch – stumble into the 2Is Coffee Bar at 59 Old Compton Street and ask if they can sing. As the core of the Vipers, they become regular performers and quickly transform the cellar into a goldmine.

19 The US and the UK inform President Nasser of Egypt that no funds are available to help finance the Aswan Dam.

20 The Bill Haley, Alan Freed movie *Rock Around The Clock* opens in London. Inspired, jazz drummer Tony Crombie forms a rock 'n' roll group, the Rockets.

26 President Nasser seizes control of the Suez Canal, under a decree nationalising the Suez Canal Company.

26 Mick Jagger becomes a teenager.

26 Sixty miles off Nantucket Island, Massachusetts, the Italian liner *Andrea Doria* sinks after collision with the Swedish liner *Stockholm*, with a loss off 50 lives. Among the 1,700 survivors is songwriter Mike Stoller, whose partner Jerry Leiber meets him at the quayside to tell him that their composition *Hound Dog* is about to be released as Elvis Presley's next single.

30 The City Ramblers host the Princess Louise skiffle club for the last time before setting off on a European odyssey. Nancy Whiskey, who has been a regular guest, takes over as resident singer.

As wage restraint is being urged in other sectors of the community, MPs' annual salary of £1,000 is not increased.

Lonnie Donegan's EP *Skiffle Session* reaches number 20 on the singles chart.

August

2 With *My Prayer*, the Platters become the first black act to top the US pop charts.

19 Lonnie Donegan, freshly returned from the States, unveils his new Skiffle Group at Blackpool Palace. Says Lonnie, as he takes delivery of his new Daimler Super-Sports Drop-Head Coupé, "I haven't gone commercial . . . it's just that my act has become commercial".

27 Provincial release of *Rock Around The Clock* provokes widespread consternation. Police are called to quell trouble at many cinemas.

September

1 Starting today, Studio 51 becomes Ken Colyer's Jazz Club for five nights a week.

6 From today, Thursday nights at Studio 51 will be devoted to rock 'n' roll. Leon Bell's Hi-Fi Four are regular performers. By November, they will have changed their name to Leon Bell & the Bell Cats.

10 Tony Crombie & the Rockets start their bill-topping variety tour at the Theatre Royal, Portsmouth.

19 In the jet-powered speedboat *Bluebird*, Donald Campbell sets up a new world water speed record of 225 mph on Coniston Water.

27 Promoted by Rik Gunnell, Club Haley starts at the Tavistock Restaurant Ballroom in London's Charing Cross Road, every Thursday. Rory Blackwell's Rock 'n' Rollers play opening night. The Vipers back their mate Tommy Hicks for an audition at the 2Is

Coffee Bar. Within the month, he is playing at Al Burnett's Stork Room in Swallow Street (off Piccadilly), under the name of Tommy Steele – on his way to becoming Britain's first rock 'n' roll star.

Lonnie Donegan reaches number 7 with *Bring A Little Water, Sylvie/ Dead Or Alive* and starts a 14-week bill-topping variety tour, in theatres across the country.

American ethno-musicologist/folklorist Alan Lomax gets in on the act with a Decca single, *Hard Case* – written by Ewan MacColl.

October

10 Chris Barber's Jazz Band record *Petite Fleur*, which will become a million-selling single in 1959. At the console, recording engineer Joe Meek ensures optimum sound.

12 Release of Tommy Steele's first single: *Rock With The Caveman*.

15 Steele makes his television début on Jack Payne's BBC show *Off The Record*.

19 Tony Crombie & the Rockets reach the charts (number 25) with their first single, *Teach You To Rock/Shortnin' Bread*.

24 Russian troops intervene after insurrection in Hungary. Their brutality is condemned by the United Nations, who vainly call for a Soviet withdrawal. Recently elected Hungarian Prime Minister Nagy is arrested, deported and executed.

31 Anglo-French planes begin bombing raids on Egypt, prior to invasion by paratroops who ultimately regain control of the Suez Canal, nationalised by Egypt's President Nasser three months earlier.

After a talent-spotting expedition to the 2Is Coffee Bar, Parlophone A&R man George Martin signs the Vipers Skiffle Group.

The People is serialising Bill Haley's life story; the *Daily Sketch* is doing the same for Elvis Presley.

Former jazz-band vocalists Art Baxter and Bobby Breen both form rock 'n' roll bands.

November

1 Premium Bonds launched; the Lord Mayor of London buys the first one.

4 Wimbledon Palais introduces a weekly rock 'n' roll night. The first band is Rory Blackwell's Rock 'n' Rollers.

5 Backed by the Steelmen, Tommy Steele starts his first provincial tour at Sunderland Empire.

6 General Dwight Eisenhower is re-elected President of the United States, beating Adlai Stevenson by a huge majority.

9 The 2Is Coffee Bar starts a weekend skiffle and rock 'n' roll club at 44 Gerrard Street in Soho. Headlining the opening night are the Vipers Skiffle Group.

10 The Big Ben Accordion Band releases *Rock 'n' Roll Number One* as the music-biz starts to cash in on the new music.

23 Shell-shocked after the Suez crisis, Prime Minister Sir Anthony Eden leaves London for three weeks of recuperation in Jamaica.

The Vipers' first single is *Pick A Bale Of Cotton/Ain't You Glad*.

Ray Bush & the Avon Cities Skiffle Group, a trad-jazz spin-off group from Bristol, release an EP on the Tempo label. Though capable and quick off the mark, they never reach the first division.

Decca launch their new signing, former London bus driver Matt Monro (allegedly discovered by Winifred Atwell), with a cover of the Five Keys' *Out Of Sight, Out Of Mind*.

Gracie Fields is reported to be doing a rock 'n' roll spoof in her act.

December

16 Studio 51 starts hosting rock 'n' roll on Sunday afternoons.

18 The Vipers infiltrate the trad-jazz world, supporting Terry Lightfoot at the 100 Club every Tuesday until April.

18 Keith Richards becomes a teenager.

21 Lonnie Donegan becomes the first UK act to reach the singles chart with an album! *The Lonnie Donegan Showcase* makes number 26. Skiffle is legitimised as West End theatrical impresarios respond to public demand. Lonnie Donegan headlines at the Prince of Wales Theatre for three weeks.

Jazzers turned rock 'n' rollers Art Baxter & his Sinners release their first single, *Jungle Rock*.

Diana Dors and her husband Dennis Hamilton split up. Says Hamilton: "I wish we could go back five years. We didn't have a bean, couldn't even afford anything more than a bun at a snack bar. But we were happy."

Television's most popular comedians are Dave King and Benny Hill. The year's most innovative show, ITV's *Son Of Fred*, scripted by Spike Milligan and starring Peter Sellers, is cancelled after one series.

1957

January

1 ITV premières its first teen-orientated weekly music show *Cool For Cats*.

9 Sir Anthony Eden resigns as Prime Minister and is succeeded by Harold Macmillan.

9 Jimmy Page becomes a teenager.

10 Opening night of the Razzle Dazzle club, the latest Thursday night rock 'n' roll scene at Studio 51.

11 Tommy Steele tops the UK chart with *Singing The Blues*.

16 The Cavern Club opens at 10 Mathew Street in Liverpool.

21 UK release of first Elvis Presley movie *Love Me Tender*.

21 The Chas McDevitt Skiffle Group, featuring Nancy Whiskey, headline the week-long 'Skiffle Show of 1957' at the Metropolitan Theatre, Edgware Road – to coincide with the release of their first single, *Freight Train/The Cotton Song*. Catchy and novel, it will eventually reach number 5 in Britain and number 40 in the States.

25 Simultaneous with the release of a second Bill Haley movie *Don't Knock The Rock*, Decca announces that Haley's *Rock Around The Clock* is the first record to sell a million copies in Britain.

Soon to enter the repertoire of a million provincial skiffle groups, *Don't You Rock Me Daddy-O* is the new single by the Vipers (who reach number 10), Lonnie Donegan (number 4) and Bob Cort (nowhere).

The Royal Festival Hall is the setting for the most ambitious skiffle concert so far – with the Vipers, Ken Colyer and Bob Cort.

February

Bandleaders Eric Delaney and Teddy Foster introduce skiffle in a desperate attempt to forestall their decline in popularity.

4 Tommy Steele begins a week at the Chiswick Empire – during which time he will meet his future wife Ann Donoughue and impress BBC television producer Jack Good, who wants to sign him for a 13-week run in the *6.5 Special* (though his bosses only allow six).

4 The unlikely combination of busty blonde songstress Yana and the Vipers share top billing at the Prince of Wales Theatre for two weeks. The bill is completed by various singers, jugglers, animal acts and comedians, including the youthful Des O'Connor.

5 Bill Haley & his Comets arrive for their much-heralded UK tour, which opens in London at the Dominion Theatre in Tottenham Court Road the following day.

7 The skiffle backlash starts! "The music is unsuitable," says Swansea Council, rejecting a booking for Lonnie Donegan to play at Brangwyn Hall. Other corporations adopt a similar stance.

8 Jazz drummer Phil Seamen, found to be in possession of heroin, is arrested at Southampton as he is about the board the *Queen Elizabeth* for an American tour.

16 BBC Television begins a weekly 55-minute show mixing pop, skiffle, jazz, comedy and teen-orientated topics . . . *6.5 Special.*

24 Filming starts on *The Tommy Steele Story.*

Two Chris Barber band members/Donegan replacements – Johnny Duncan and Dickie Bishop – strike out as solo acts. As skiffle gathers momentum nationally, Barber perversely drops it altogether.

March

1 Cyril Davies and Alexis Korner re-name their club the Blues and Barrelhouse, still held every week at the Roundhouse in Wardour Street.

8 The Suez Canal reopens after the removal of obstructions placed by Egyptian forces.

9 The Vipers appear on *6.5 Special* – alongside Big Bill Broonzy and Humphrey Lyttelton's Jazz Band.

10 UK release of Jayne Mansfield rock 'n' roll movie *The Girl Can't Help It.*

12 Opening date of the Platters' two-month UK tour.

18 Frankie Lymon & the Teenagers start their UK tour.

22 Prime Minister Macmillan meets President Eisenhower in Bermuda to seal a deal whereby the US will provide Britain with guided missiles.

25 Six countries unite to form the Common Market (EEC): France, West Germany, Italy, Belgium, Netherlands and Luxembourg. Great Britain is conspicuously absent.

29 Lonnie Donegan starts his US tour at Madison Square Garden.

31 Although Larry Parnes is later given credit for creating the all-teenage rock 'n' roll package show, the idea is formulated and test-flown by 2Is coffee bar owner Paul Lincoln at Romford Odeon, where he launches his discovery Terry Dene.

Released in versions by the Vipers (number 10), Dickie Bishop & his Sidekicks, and Lonnie Donegan (who only takes two weeks to reach number 1), *Cumberland Gap* becomes an overnight skiffle standard.

Dim-witted pundits predict that a new nationwide craze is about to replace rock 'n' roll and skiffle . . . calypso music!

The 2Is Coffee Bar is now London's prime teenage haunt, packed solid every night. New resident skiffle groups are the Cotton Pickers,

Les Hobeaux and the East Siders, though the Vipers still play on Wednesday, Thursday and Friday until touring commitments take precedence.

April

4 A Government White Paper confirms that 'call-up' (conscription) will be scrapped in 1960 and that the last National Serviceman will leave the Armed Forces by the end of 1962.

13 The Skiffle Cellar, London's first seven-nights-a-week skiffle club, opens at 49 Greek Street in Soho – operated by Russell Quaye and featuring his City Ramblers as resident group. Within seven weeks, the club has a thousand fully paid-up members.

19 First single by Johnny Duncan & his Blue Grass Boys is *Ella Speed/Kaw Liga*.

22 On Easter Monday, another big skiffle bash at the Royal Festival Hall: Johnny Duncan & his Bluegrass Boys, Chas McDevitt and Nancy Whiskey, Dickie Bishop, Bob Cort and Ray Bush.

27 Already billed as 'Decca's sensational new star', Terry Dene makes his début on *6.5 Special*.

Ron Goodwin & his Orchestra join the fray with *Skiffling Strings*.

Jimmy Jackson attempts to combine two current crazes with his single *California Zephyr* – released under the banner of 'Rock 'n' Skiffle'. He makes little commercial headway.

The Vampires win the first of many National Skiffle Contests (this one at the Empire Rooms, Leicester Square) and are barely heard of again.

Calypso fad declared a dead duck.

May

3 Bob Cort records a version of *6.5 Special*, which supplants the Don Lang original as the television show's theme music.

7 Adam Faith's skiffle group the Worried Men make their West End début at the Skiffle Cellar.

16 Freddie Bell & the Bellboys, an American band popular in the casinos of Las Vegas and Reno, start a UK tour with Tommy Steele & the Steelmen, who quickly overshadow them to claim top billing.

17 The new Chas McDevitt/Nancy Whiskey single is *Greenback Dollar*.

30 *The Tommy Steele Story* premieres at London's Rialto Cinema.

31 First single by Terry Dene is *A White Sport Coat/The Man In The Phone Booth*, on Decca.

Local magistrates ban the Vipers from appearing at the King's Hall, Belle Vue – and BBC Radio bans their song, *Maggie May*, on grounds of taste.

Orchestra leader Geraldo claims "skiffle is piffle".

The latest fashion accessories, originated by Teddy boys but adopted by schoolboys, are fluorescent socks – available in pastel pink, lime green, yellow and orange at 9/6d a pair.

June

1 BBC Radio broadcasts the first of a new weekly Saturday morning series, *Skiffle Club*. Guests are Johnny Duncan & his Blue Grass Boys and the Pete Curtis Folk & Blues Quintet. Originally scheduled for a three-month trial run, it keeps going and evolves.

1 The '2Is Rock Across The Channel' ferry bash, going to Calais and back, is the brainchild of 2Is owner Paul Lincoln and promoter Rik Gunnell. Terry Dene is the biggest name on board, but Tommy Steele's brother Colin Hicks, making his début, is hailed as a future star.

9 An all-star skiffle package at the Royal Albert Hall features Lonnie Donegan, Chas McDevitt, Bob Cort and the Avon Cities Group.

21 Ray Davies becomes a teenager.

23 Another 'Rock Across The Channel' ferry trip, organised by former 2Is coffee bar owners Sammy and Freddy Irani, features Chas McDevitt's Skiffle Group and Rory Blackwell's Blackjacks.

24 Release of the Vipers' single *Streamline Train*, which will reach number 23 to become their third and last hit. Along with Jim Dale and a full variety bill, they embark on a nationwide tour which will include local skiffle contests at each venue.

24 Terry Dene starts his first variety tour, headlining at Middlesbrough Empire.

24 Jeff Beck becomes a teenager.

28 Release of Johnny Duncan's single *Last Train To San Fernando*, which will reach number 2.

30 The Chas McDevitt Skiffle Group with Nancy Whiskey appear on Ed Sullivan's television show, along with another act new to the US charts, the Everly Brothers.

Recorded at the London Palladium (on 9 May), Lonnie Donegan's new single *Gambling Man/Putting On The Style* is a sure-fire number one. He tops an all-skiffle bonanza at the Royal Albert Hall before embarking on a month at the London Hippodrome. Not only the

'King of Skiffle', Lonnie is now one of the biggest show-biz names in Britain.

July

6 Paul McCartney is introduced to John Lennon, whose skiffle group the Quarry Men are playing a garden fête in Walton, Liverpool.

6 American tennis star Althea Gibson is the first 'coloured' player to win a title at Wimbledon.

12 Release of Terry Dene's second single *Start Movin'/Green Corn*.

14 The Minister of Transport outlines plans to introduce an annual compulsory road-worthiness test on all cars over 10 years old.

20 At a Tory rally in Bedford, Prime Minister Harold Macmillan tells fellow Conservatives that "most of our people have never had it so good".

29 Larry Page makes his variety début, topping the bill at Reading Palace. His first single *Cool Shake/Start Movin'* has recently been issued by EMI Columbia.

The City Ramblers travel to Moscow for the sixth International Youth Festival.

The UK film industry notes a 10 per cent drop in cinema attendance over the past year, attributing it to the growing influence of television.

After complaints from impoverished stars and allegations that some clubs have been making illegal payments to players, the Football League magnanimously agrees to raise footballers' legal wages by two pounds to £17 per week. Meanwhile, the Welsh international John Charles makes headlines by leaving Leeds United to sign with Juventus of Turin for the unimaginable transfer fee of £65,000.

August

Chas McDevitt unveils his new girl singer Shirley Douglas.

Already signed to Philips, Marty Wilde débuts on the *6.5 Special*.

5 American rock 'n' roll star Charlie Gracie plays two weeks at the London Hippodrome.

5 Tony Crombie disbands his Rockets. Singer Clyde Ray joins Jan Ralfini's dance band at Fountainbridge Palais in Edinburgh.

7 The Quarry Men skiffle group play the Cavern Club in Liverpool for the first time.

31 Nancy Whiskey leaves the Chas McDevitt Skiffle Group to resume her solo career.

Terry Dene starts filming for *The Golden Disc* at Walton Studios.

September

1 The Most Brothers make their début at the Commodore Ballroom at Ryde on the Isle of Wight. On the same bill are Les Hobeaux, making their first appearance since turning professional.

1 Housewarming party at the swish new Hicks family residence in Ravensbourne Park, Catford, purchased by Tommy.

4 Sir John Wolfenden's report on Homosexual Offences and Prostitution is published.

5 Jack Kerouac's novel *On The Road* is published in the US.

22 Paul Lincoln presents another all-teenage package show at the Trocadero, Elephant & Castle. "It was rock 'n' roll and skiffle non-stop without relief, and it was what the audience wanted," said one newspaper, congratulating Lincoln on "his faith in the teenage movement." "Eliminated completely were the uselessly dated variety acts that still clutter up and spoil so many shows." The vaudeville era was coming to an end, it seemed; a sad prospect for so many music-hall acts.

October

1 The Royal Mail raises inland letter postage to 3d.

4 Release of a new Donegan single, *My Dixie Darling* – sourced from a recording by the Carter Family.

4 Terry Dene's third single is *Teenage Dream/Come And Get It*.

4 Russia takes an early lead in the space race, launching the sputnik satellite.

7 UK Release of Elvis Presley's second movie, *Loving You*.

11 Larry Page's second single, described by EMI as 'the most sensational record of the year', is a cover of the Crickets' US hit *That'll Be The Day*.

12 Little Richard throws four diamond rings (valued at $8,000) into Sydney's Hunter River following the last date of his Australian tour – and horrifies fans by renouncing music in favour of a spiritual life. "If you want to live for the Lord," he tells reporters, "you can't rock 'n' roll too. God doesn't like it."

12 Radioactive material escapes from the Windscale atomic power station at Sellafield. "There is no danger," a spokesman assures the press.

14 A 'Skiffle Jamboree' at the Royal Albert Hall features Johnny Duncan & his Blue Grass Boys, Bob Cort, the Cotton Pickers and the Eden Streeters.

18 Lennon and McCartney play their first public gig together when the Quarry Men appear at the Conservative Club in Norris Green, Liverpool.

25 Already well known for almost a year, Bob Cort finally turns professional, leaving his advertising agency job.

A year after he started in the business, Tommy Steele is voted top British Musical Personality by *NME* readers. Hoping to emulate his brother, Colin Hicks signs with Pye Nixa.

Paul Lincoln, 2Is coffee bar owner, signs up his fourth act of the year (after Terry Dene, Les Hobeaux and the Most Brothers), Wee Willie Harris – whose gimmick is cerise-coloured hair.

The final of the 'All England Skiffle Contest' at Tottenham Royal is won by the John Henry Skiffle Group – fronted by 16-year-old John Deighton, later to become Chris Farlowe. Chas McDevitt and Shirley Douglas present him with a cheque for £25.

November

3 The Russians launch a second satellite, this one containing a husky dog, the first living creature in space.

4 Marty Wilde starts his first variety tour at Sunderland Empire. The Most Brothers, just signed by Decca, are also on the bill.

8 Decca record an album, *Rockin' At The 2Is*.

10 Tim Rice becomes a teenager.

15 Release of Johnny Duncan's third and last hit *Footprints In The Snow*.

16 The *6.5 Special* is broadcast live from the 2Is Coffee Bar.

18 To cap a triumphant first year in show business, Tommy Steele plays the Royal Variety Performance at the London Palladium.

25 At Twickenham Studios, production begins on *The 6.5 Special* movie, starring Avril Leslie and Diane Todd.

Dennis Main-Wilson, new co-producer of *6.5 Special*, admits he is "an off-duty Mozart fan".

A touring version of *6.5 Special* features Don Lang & his Frantic Five, Ronnie Aldrich & the Squadronaires, Chris Barber's Jazz Band, Sheila Buxton, Mike and Bernie Winters and the John Barry Seven.

First single by Colin Hicks is *Wild Eyes And Tender Lips/Empty Arm Blues*.

The *NME* reports that success has allowed Terry Dene to buy a house for his parents in Camberwell – with a separate bedroom for Terry.

Latest skiffle group to hit the Soho scene are the Spacemen from Wanstead, featuring Joe Brown on guitar.

Bob Cort publishes a book: *Making The Most Of Skiffle*.

December

5 The Lord Chancellor announces that the Government will not be accepting the Wolfenden Committee's recommendation to legalise homosexuality between consenting adults.

6 The fourth single (in seven months) from Terry Dene is *Lucky Lucky Bobby*.

6 US prestige falters as their first satellite-carrying rocket rises only four feet before bursting into flames at Cape Canaveral.

18 Production starts at the first atomic power plant in the States – Three Mile Island in Pennsylvania.

20 First single by the Most Brothers is *Whistle Bait/I'm Coming Home*.

25 The Queen's Christmas message is televised for the first time.

27 First single by Wee Willie Harris is *Rockin' At The 2Is*, on Decca.

The *NME* describes Jackie Wilson's vocal on *Reet Petite* as a "strange collection of noises ranging from gargling to an outboard motor".

Tommy Steele stars in *Goldilocks And The Three Bears*, the annual pantomime at the Royal Court Theatre in Liverpool.

US star Paul Anka plays UK dates, supported by the John Barry Seven, Bob Cort and Billie Anthony.

Adam Faith leaves the Worried Men Skiffle Group to go solo.

The *Daily Mirror* costs 2d, 20 Senior Service are 3/11d, best bitter is 1/3d a pint, a large white loaf is a shilling.

1958

January

1 The European Common Market comes into being; Britain is not included.

10 Rod Stewart becomes a teenager.

25 The Musicians' Union complains that during the past year amateur skifflers have undermined their members' livelihoods.

31 'Is skiffle dying? No, but it's changing,' concludes the *NME*.

In their début game, the Show Biz Soccer XI beats the *Daily Sketch* by 5-1. Lonnie Donegan scores a goal.

The Vipers release a single *No Other Baby/Baby, Why* and an album *Coffee Bar Session*. Johnny Duncan's first album is *Tennessee Songbag*.

Producer Jack Good leaves the BBC for ITV.

February

6 Eight Manchester United players are among 21 dead when a BEA Elizabethan airliner crashes during take-off at Munich airport.

21 Magistrates at Gloucester fine Terry Dene for causing wilful damage while drunk and disorderly.

23 US rock movie *Disc Jockey Jamboree*, featuring Jerry Lee Lewis, Carl Perkins and Charlie Gracie goes on general release, as does Elvis Presley's third film, *Jailhouse Rock*.

Latest recruit to *6.5 Special*, 15-year-old Scot Jackie Dennis is tipped for stardom.

NME's singles reviewer Keith Fordyce pans the doo-wop classic *Get A Job* by the Silhouettes, calling it one of the worst rock 'n' roll discs ever. "It opens with a fair imitation of hens clucking," he writes, "but is monotonous, meaningless, miserable mumble jumble."

March

1 Buddy Holly & the Crickets begin a 25-date UK tour, supported by Gary Miller, the Tanner Sisters and Des O'Connor.

1 The Lyceum Ballroom starts lunchtime record hops from Tuesday to Friday, as well as Monday evening disc sessions. Strict dress code for males: jacket and tie essential, no jeans allowed.

9 Alexis Korner, the Vipers, and the bands of Humphrey Lyttelton, Chris Barber, Johnny Dankworth are among those playing a benefit concert at the London Coliseum, to raise money for Big Bill Broonzy who is undergoing an operation for throat cancer in Chicago.

14 A second Broonzy benefit is held at the Dominion Theatre, with Chris Barber, Lonnie Donegan, Ken Colyer and their bands.

14 The Most Brothers go up against Marvin Rainwater with their second single *Whole Lotta Woman*.

16 Fats Domino stars in the latest rock movie *The Big Beat*.

21 Release of *Dynamo* by Les Hobeaux.

24 Elvis joins the US Army, becoming Private Presley 53310761.

27 Nikita Khrushchev replaces Marshall Bulganin as the Russian premier.

30 Tommy Steele's second movie *The Duke Wore Jeans* goes on general release.

30 Eric Clapton becomes a teenager.

Larry Parnes signs Grantham teenager Vince Eager.

Chas McDevitt opens his own coffee bar, the Freight Train, in Berwick Street, Soho.

April

2 *San Francisco Chronicle* columnist Herb Caen coins the word 'beatnik' to describe followers of the Beat Generation.

4 Release of *Grand Coolie Dam/Nobody Loves Like An Irishman* by Lonnie Donegan. The BBC bans the B-side for mentioning the Koran.

4 The first Campaign for Nuclear Disarmament march, from London to Aldermaston.

5 Charlie Gracie arrives for a second UK tour.

6 Release of *Violent Playground*, a juvenile delinquent movie set in Liverpool – with Freddie Starr playing a young hooligan.

12 Jim Dale replaces Pete Murray as a compère on the *6.5 Special*.

13 *The 6.5 Special* movie goes on general release.

14 *He's Got The Whole World In His Hands* by UK child star Laurie London (recorded when he was 13) reaches number one in the US charts.

14 Ritchie Blackmore becomes a teenager.

19 The National Jazz Federation opens a new West End venue, the Marquee at 165 Oxford Street.

20 Terry Dene's movie, *The Golden Disc*, released today.

22 Sonny Terry and Brownie McGhee begin their first UK tour at Birmingham Town Hall, guests of Chris Barber's Jazz Band. While here, they cut three albums with producer Denis Preston.

26 "Now is the time to ban these horror discs," is *Melody Maker*'s headline. Steve Race is hot under the collar about the "scabrous disc" *Dinner With Drac* by John Zacherle.

27 A new Lonnie Donegan single: *Sally Don't You Grieve/Betty Betty Betty*.

30 On a goodwill tour of Latin America, Vice President Nixon is stoned, spat upon and booed in Lima, Peru. Days later, troops are flown to the Caribbean when mobs attack him in Caracas.

Marvin Rainwater plays UK dates and television shows. Under his influence, Brian Rankin changes his name to Hank Marvin.

The Drifters play the 2Is Coffee Bar; Harry Webb changes his name to Cliff Richard.

May

1 Tommy Steele is mauled by over-enthusiastic fans at Caird Hall, Dundee, and is laid up for six weeks.

3 First gig by re-named Cliff Richard & the Drifters is at the Regal Ballroom, Ripley.

7 Colin Hicks & the Cabin Boys go to Italy – the first rock 'n' roll group to tour there.

19 Pete Townshend becomes a teenager.

24 Jerry Lee Lewis opens his UK tour at the Regal in Edmonton. After two more dates, he is sent home in disgrace. At the root of the indignation is the discovery of his 13-year-old wife, Myra.

24 Bert Weedon's *Play In A Day*, an indispensable tutor for any budding guitarist, is published by Chappell & Co for five shillings.

25 Paul Weller born.

As the popularity of skiffle dwindles, the Skiffle Cellar in Soho modifies it name to the Cellar.

The BBC bans Jack Scott's single *My True Love*, which begins "I prayed to the Lord".

Publication of *Tommy Steele* by John Kennedy – the first rock biography, the birth of a new literary genre.

Latest hopeful is Barry Barnett, a 19 year old from Crouch End.

Following the success of *Tom Hark* by Elias & his Zigzag Jive Flutes, A&R man Reg Warburton predicts a national craze for Kwela music. "It shouldn't take long to learn to play those wooden penny whistles," he says.

June

1 The Clean Air Act comes into force, restricting chimney emissions.

9 The Queen opens Gatwick, London's second airport.

11 Tommy Steele announces his engagement to Ann Donoughue.

14 In *Melody Maker*, Steve Race bids farewell to rock 'n' roll, which he believes is now dead. "Good riddance," he writes, in an article which provides the inspiration for *Move It*.

15 First trial edition of Jack Good's new television show *Oh Boy!* The second is transmitted two weeks later.

20 Release of *Endless Sleep* by Marty Wilde – his first hit.

25 The Minister of Labour answers questions on Jerry Lee Lewis in the House of Commons.

On its first anniversary, BBC Radio's *Skiffle Club* features Al Meek & his Rio Ranch Boys and the Soho Skiffle Group. Compère is Brian Matthew.

After only one year, Larry Parnes drops Colin Hicks from his roster.

Westminster Electronics introduce their new guitar amplifier: 10 watts of power, five valves, a 10-inch speaker. A luxury-styled two-colour cabinet features treble and bass tone controls. It costs £19.10.0.

Pops Go Stereo by Marion Ryan is Britain's first stereo record. Pye's cheapest stereo record player costs 60 guineas.

July

8 Terry Dene and Edna Savage marry at Marylebone Register Office.

10 First parking meters in London.

11 Larry Page, the 'Teenage Rage', marries teenager Ann Ward at Caxton Hall, Westminster.

12 Hank Marvin and Bruce Welch make their television début on *6.5 Special*, as members of the Five Chesternuts.

14 A military *coup d'état* in Iraq sees revolutionaries assassinate King Faisal and burn down the British embassy in Baghdad. Local radio announces that the Iraqi people have been liberated from the corrupt influence of western imperialism.

24 Cliff Richard & the Drifters record their first single, *Move It*, at EMI's Abbey Road studio.

26 Nine-year-old Prince Charles, heir to the throne, is created Prince of Wales.

27 The third and last single by the Most Brothers is *Dottie/Don't Go Home*. Also out today is *Got A Match?/No Chemise Please* by Wee Willie Harris.

27 Traffic is brought to a standstill in the centre of Poole, Dorset, as crowds throng to see England football captain Billy Wright marry Joy, the eldest of the Beverley Sisters.

August

8 Release of the Five Chesternuts single *Teenage Love*.

9 Cliff Richard quits his day job.

15 Big Bill Broonzy succumbs to cancer, aged 65.

29 Release of first single by Cliff Richard & the Drifters: *Schoolboy Crush/Move It*.

31 Thirteen are arrested during race riots in the Notting Hill area of London. Also serious race riots in Nottingham this month.

31 Van Morrison becomes a teenager.

September

8 Under orders from Jack Good, Cliff Richard drops his guitar and shaves off his sideburns. In his review of Cliff's début single, *Melody Maker*'s Laurie Henshaw talks of "a tortured vocal pattern that seems to be the vogue these days".

13 Start of Saturday night television series *Oh Boy!* Marty Wilde and Cliff Richard are stars of the first show.

20 Tommy Steele is the first rock 'n' roller to be immortalised in wax at Madame Tussaud's.

26 Bryan Ferry becomes a teenager.

29 A new entry in the *Billboard* singles chart, *Tom Dooley* by the Kingston Trio sows the seeds of a US folk music boom.

The three finalists in Stanley Dale's interminable National Skiffle Contest are said to be the Woodlanders from Plymouth, the Saxons from Barnsley and the Double Three from Bury St Edmunds – but no winner is ever announced.

Latest resident bands on *6.5 Special* are Tony Osborne's Brass Hats and Tito Burns' 6-5ers.

October

1 Thrust on to the stage by Larry Parnes, Ronnie Wycherley makes an impromptu appearance on Marty Wilde's 'Extravaganza' package show at Birkenhead Essoldo. Parnes takes him to London, where he will launch him as Billy Fury.

4 The BBC's Light Programme renames and updates *Skiffle Club*, which today becomes *Saturday Club*. First edition features Terry Dene, Johnny Duncan & his Blue Grass Boys, the City Ramblers and Humphrey Lyttelton. Compère is still Brian Matthew.

4 A British BOAC Comet is the first scheduled jet airliner to cross the Atlantic.

5 The Kalin Twins/Cliff Richard tour opens at the Victoria Hall in Hanley.

6 Unemployment in Britain reaches 476,000 – the highest figure for a decade.

10 Release of Vince Eager's first single *No More/Five Days Five Days*.

11 First edition of *Grandstand* broadcast by BBC Television.

16 BBC transmits the first edition of *Blue Peter*, originally planned for a seven-week run.

18 Muddy Waters makes his UK début at Newcastle City Hall, the guest of Chris Barber's Jazz Band.

20 New single by the Vipers *Summertime Blues* seals their fate.

22 For the first time in its thousand-year history, women are allowed to sit in the House of Lords.

In the annual *NME* readers' poll, Frankie Vaughan is voted Outstanding Musical Personality over Lonnie Donegan and Favourite Male Singer over Marty Wilde. Cliff Richard is the Favourite New Singer; Marty Wilde is runner-up.

November

11 Release of second single by Cliff Richard & the Drifters: *High Class Baby/My Feet Hit The Ground*.

14 Release of *Tom Dooley* by Lonnie Donegan.

14 Recently incorporated into the Drifters, Hank Marvin, Bruce Welch and Jet Harris record with Cliff Richard for the first time. Still playing drums is original member Terry Smart – though his days are numbered.

28 *Hoots Mon*, by *Oh Boy!* residents Lord Rockingham's XI, tops the chart.

The publication of *Skiffle*, a book by Brian Bird, comes a little too late . . . the craze is all but over.

December

7 The first stretch of motorway opens in Britain: the Preston bypass.

21 General de Gaulle is elected President of France.

22 First episode of *Quatermass And The Pit* on BBC Television.

24 As Will Scarlet in *Babes In The Wood*, Marty Wilde starts a month of pantomime at Stockton Hippodrome – while Lonnie Donegan stars in *Aladdin* at Stockton Globe.

27 The final edition of *6.5 Special* is broadcast after a run of almost two years. *Oh Boy!* has made it look antiquated.

Vince Taylor & his Playboys make their début on *Oh Boy!*

NME describes Cliff Richard's "violent hip-swinging" as "indecent . . . vulgar . . . the most crude exhibitionism ever seen on British TV".

The National Register of Births reveals that the most popular names are currently John, Richard and David; Jane, Elizabeth and Mary.

During the year, UK sales of 45 rpm singles eclipse those of 78s.

1959

January

1 The latest element of American culture to be imported into Britain is the bowling alley. Every town feels the need for one.

3 *Dig This* is the new BBC replacement for *6.5 Special*. Riddled with fogies, it stands little chance of survival.

8 Britain agrees to recognise the new Cuban government installed by the revolutionary leader Dr Fidel Castro. Ousted president General Fulgenico Batista seeks refuge in the Dominican Republic.

12 Henry Cooper defeats Brian London to become the new British and Empire heavyweight boxing champion.

16 Release of Billy Fury's first single, *Maybe Tomorrow*.

22 Terry Dene reports to Winchester Barracks to start his National Service.

30 The Top Rank label is launched. First release is *Little Drummer Boy* by the Harry Simeone Chorale – but the label will soon rival London-American for quality US product.

February

1 Cliff Richard & the Drifters headline over Vince Taylor, Cuddly Dudley and other regulars as the *Oh Boy!* package show takes to the road.

3 Buddy Holly, the Big Bopper and Ritchie Valens are killed in a plane crash, soon after take-off from Mason City Airport, Iowa.

6 Marty Wilde goes into the studio to record a cover of Ritchie Valens' US hit *Donna*.

7 Release of *Fury Unleashed* (known as *Hot Rod Gang* in the States), a movie featuring Gene Vincent & the Blue Caps, with an uncredited appearance by Eddie Cochran.

9 Chris Barber's Jazz Band sail for New York and their first US tour.

13 The entry of Chris Barber's *Petite Fleur* into the UK chart marks the official start of the 'Trad-Jazz Boom'.

17 The Stratford Royal unveils a new, groundbreaking musical: *Fings Ain't Wot They Used To Be* – with words and music by Lionel Bart.

21 Gerry Dorsey appears on *Oh Boy!* but makes little impact. Eight years later, as Engelbert Humperdinck, he will top the charts with *Release Me* and *The Last Waltz*.

26 Sighs of relief all round as it is announced that men born after 1 October 1939 are to be spared call-up to National Service. Those born before will serve.

28 Larry Parnes' latest discovery Dickie Pride makes his début on *Oh Boy!* He has already been signed by the Columbia label's A&R manager Norrie Paramor.

March

11 *Sing Little Birdie* by Pearl Carr & Teddy Johnson takes second place in the Eurovision Song Contest – beaten by the entry from Holland.

12 Hawaii becomes America's 50th state, following Alaska which joined the USA on 3 January this year.

16 BBC Television's *Panorama* profiles Larry Parnes and his stable of colts.

17 The BMC/Austin Mini is launched.

18 EMI discontinues the production of 78 rpm records.

26 Terry Dene is discharged from the Army as unsuitable for military service.

28 BBC Television's *Dig This* gets the chop after a run of only 13 weeks.

30 Ten thousand CND protesters congregate in Trafalgar Square, following a march from Aldermaston.

31 The Dalai Lama evades Chinese troops to reach sanctuary at the India-Tibet frontier.

Souvenir Press publishes *Protest*, the first anthology to include selections from the US Beat Generation writers and our own 'Angry Young Men'.

April

4 *Drumbeat*, with Adam Faith and Vince Eager, débuts on BBC Television. Marginally better than its predecessor *Dig This*, it will survive only until August.

5 Chas McDevitt marries Shirley Douglas at St Patrick's Church in Soho.

7 In the annual budget, the standard rate of income tax is reduced by 9d to 38.75 per cent. The price of a pint of beer is reduced by 2d. A cut in purchase tax sees the price of a single reduced to six shillings.

8 NASA tells Congress they will have a man on the moon within a decade. The first seven space travellers, to be known as astronauts, are selected.

8 The first picture of the world from outer space is transmitted from US satellite *Explorer 6* and broadcast on television.

11 On his ITV show *Spectacular*, Hughie Green presents Chris Barber with a gold disc to mark one million-plus sales for *Petite Fleur*.

16 Marty Wilde is declared unfit for Army service on the basis of 'fallen arches and severe corns'. He celebrates by having his cream and black Austin Healey sprayed powder blue.

27 The Labour Party promises to cease all nuclear tests if voted into power in the next UK general election.

27 Liu Shao-Chi succeeds Mao Tse-Tung as Chairman of the Chinese People's Republic.

28 Cliff Richard & the Drifters record their seminal *Living Doll*.

The Decca label signs Jack Good as its first independent rock 'n' roll record producer.

The Cellar in Greek Street, formerly the Skiffle Cellar, closes.

May

2 Luton Town FC ruin their best-ever decade by losing the Cup Final to Nottingham Forest 2-1.

8 Conway Twitty arrives in London for media appearances, including two *Oh Boy!* shows.

8 Making their début at Dartford, on a Marty Wilde package show, are the Viscounts – formerly members of Morton Fraser's Harmonica Gang. One of the trio, Gordon Mills, will later become a multi-millionaire managing Tom Jones and Engelbert Humperdinck.

11 The British government agrees to supply aircraft, tanks and other weapons to Iraq.

12 Larry Parnes' latest discovery Duffy Power records his first single for Fontana.

14 Première of *Serious Charge*, Cliff Richard's movie début. He buys a £4,000 house in Winchmore Hill for his parents.

22 Release of Marty Wilde's latest single *A Teenager In Love*.

28 Première of the movie *Look Back In Anger*, featuring Chris Barber's Jazz Band in a cameo role.

28 Opening of the Mermaid, the first new theatre to be built in the City of London for 250 years. Lionel Bart writes the lyrics for their first production, *Lock Up Your Daughters*.

29 Start of Lonnie Donegan series on ATV.

30 Last edition of *Oh Boy!* transmitted.

June

1 BBC airs the first edition of *Juke Box Jury*, chaired by David Jacobs.

5 In Hibbing, Minnesota, Robert Zimmerman graduates from high school. He starts at the University of Minneapolis in September and is singing under the name of Bob Dylan in local coffee houses before the end of the year.

6 At the 2Is, Rory Blackwell sets a new non-stop drumming record of 28 hours, 3 minutes and 8 seconds. "With a masseur at my side, I feel I could have carried on for four days and nights," he boasts.

17 Liberace is awarded £8,000 damages after it was decided that the *Daily Mirror* columnist Cassandra had libelled him in an article on 26 September 1956. Among other things, he had described the pianist as "fruit-flavoured".

23 Rock 'n' roll is a feature of Manchester's first Royal Variety Performance, at the Palace Theatre before the Queen Mother and

Princess Margaret. Cliff Richard, Marty Wilde and the *Oh Boy!* cast perform alongside Liberace.

24 'The Adoration of the Magi' by Rubens is sold at Sotheby's for £275,000 – the highest price ever paid for a painting.

July

16 The Street Offences Act comes into law, making it 'an offence for a common prostitute to loiter or solicit in a public place'.

16 Latest Larry Parnes discovery Sally Kelly makes her début at Blackpool Palace.

17 Death of Billie Holiday, aged 44.

22 Marty Wilde starts his own series on Radio Luxembourg: 13 weekly shows of 15 minutes each.

24 Post codes are introduced in Britain, initially in the Norwich area.

31 A market research paper *The Teenage Consumer* reveals the spending habits of the working-class young, who now have more disposable income than ever before. Much of their money is spent on dressing up to impress others of a similar age.

Adam Faith is contracted to make his movie début in *Beat Girl*.

August

12 Former Vipers frontman Wally Whyton replaces Rolf Harris as host of the ITV children's programme, *Small Time*.

23 Jack Good spots and signs up Joe Brown, who is playing in the backing group on a package show at Southend Odeon.

27 A Polaris missile is fired at sea, indicating that intercontinental ballistic missiles need no longer be land based. A submarine capable of carrying 16 missiles is launched on 30 December.

29 The Quarry Men play at the opening of Mona Best's Casbah Coffee Club in West Derby, Liverpool.

September

3 *Absolute Beginners* by Colin MacInnes is published.

12 ITV unveils producer Jack Good's latest pop music series *Boy Meets Girls*, with Marty Wilde as resident star and anchor man. Joe Brown emerges as a witty cockney guitarist.

13 Première of *Jet Storm*, featuring Marty Wilde in an acting role, at the Regal Cinema in Old Kent Road.

14 Due to the growing success of American vocal group the Drifters, Cliff Richard's backing band become the Shadows.

18 Release of Marty Wilde's first album *Wilde About Marty*.

19 Johnny Cash guests on *Boy Meets Girls*.

20 The Humphrey Lyttelton Club is no more . . . 100 Oxford Street reopens tonight as Jazzshows Jazz Club.

28 At the invitation of Jack Good, American songwriting duo Doc Pomus and Mort Shuman arrive in London to write songs for British acts.

October

3 Celebrating its first birthday, BBC Light Programme's *Saturday Club* presents Vince Eager and the John Barry Seven.

4 Pete Seeger plays a memorable concert at St Pancras Town Hall, recorded for a live album.

8 In the UK general election, the Conservatives under Harold Macmillan are returned to power for a third term, with an increased majority. Their slogan: 'Peace and Prosperity'.

9 In the annual *NME* poll, Cliff Richard is voted favourite male singer over nearest rival Marty Wilde.

14 Movie star Errol Flynn dies of a heart attack, aged 50 – leaving a generation of schoolboys to speculate on whether he actually did have a 17-inch prick.

26 A Soviet rocket photographs the dark side of the moon for the first time.

30 Opening night of Ronnie Scott's Jazz Club, housed in the freshly decorated basement of 39 Gerrard Street.

November

2 Transport Minister Ernest Marples opens the first 72-mile stretch of the M1 motorway, allowing the bike boys of Luton's Spanish Doll coffee bar to test the speed of their machines.

5 Recording engineer Joe Meek leaves Lansdowne Studio with plans to set up on his own.

12 Chris Barber marries Ottilie Patterson. Pat Halcox is best man.

15 Seemingly destined for obscurity, Johnny & the Moondogs fail to win acclaim in the north-west final of the Carroll Levis 'Search For A Star' contest. Within a year, they will have undergone a transitional period as the Silver Beatles and emerged from a Hamburg residency as the Beatles, the hottest band on Merseyside.

18 Première of Tommy Steele's latest film, *Tommy The Toreador*.

19 The New York District Attorney's office, investigating allegations of 'payola', serves subpoenas on several record labels and music publishers, demanding to see their books. DJ Alan Freed, fired by station WABC, becomes the most famous victim and scapegoat.

27 Première of *Expresso Bongo*, starring Cliff Richard and Laurence Harvey.

December

2 Marty Wilde marries Joyce Baker of the Vernons Girls. At the wedding, Joe Brown asks out his future wife Vicki Haseman, another Vernons Girl, for the first time.

5 Rescued from oblivion by Jack Good, Gene Vincent arrives in London to start phase two of his career. During the month, he appears on *Boy Meets Girls* and makes his UK stage début at the Tooting Granada.

30 Official crime statistics reveal that, during the year, 164 people have been convicted for possession of cannabis (Indian hemp) and of these, '100 were Africans, Asians or West Indians'.

30 Since 1956, due mainly to the spread of television, cinema attendance is down by 50 per cent.

31 New words and phrases added to dictionaries during the year include polypropylene, hovercraft, unilateralism, nuclear club, muzak, nymphet and the establishment.

31 The UK population stands at 51,681,000. As we make our New Year resolutions, we all wonder what the sixties will bring. Will the new decade be as exciting as the old one?

The Top 20 UK Singles

released during the 1950s, in order of appearance.

Selected for various reasons . . . their influence, their stepping-stone importance, a guitar solo, a drum sound, an intuitive performance – maybe just because I like them.

1 Rock Island Line – Lonnie Donegan
Decca F 10647; December 1955

2 Rock With The Caveman – Tommy Steele
Decca F 10795; October 1956

3 Freight Train – Chas McDevitt Skiffle Group with Nancy Whiskey
Oriole CB 1352; January 1957

4 Don't You Rock Me Daddy-O – The Vipers Skiffle Group
Parlophone R 4261; January 1957

5 No Other Baby – Dickie Bishop & his Sidekicks
Decca F 10869; January 1957

6 Cumberland Gap – Lonnie Donegan
Pye 7N 15087; March 1957

7 Gamblin' Man – Lonnie Donegan
Pye 7N 15093; May 1957

8 Last Train To San Fernando – Johnny Duncan & his Blue Grass Boys
Columbia DB 3959; June 1957

9 Rockin' At The 2Is – Wee Willie Harris
Decca F 10970; December 1957

10 Endless Sleep – Marty Wilde
Philips PB 835; July 1958

11 Teenage Love – The Five Chesternuts
Columbia DB 4165; August 1958

12 Move It – Cliff Richard & the Drifters
Columbia DB 4178; August 1958

13 Hoots Mon – Lord Rockingham's XI
Decca F 11059; October 1958

14 Maybe Tomorrow/Gonna Type A Letter – Billy Fury
Decca F 11102; January 1959

15 Danny – Marty Wilde
Philips PB 926; May 1959

16 Brand New Cadillac – Vince Taylor & the Playboys
Parlophone R 4539; May 1959

17 Please Don't Touch – Johnny Kidd & the Pirates
HMV POP 615; May 1959

18 Living Doll/Apron Strings – Cliff Richard & the Drifters
Columbia DB 4306; July 1959

19 Travellin' Light/Dynamite – Cliff Richard & the Shadows
Columbia DB 4351; October 1959

20 What Do You Want – Adam Faith
Parlophone R 4591; November 1959

Index

ABOUT THE AUTHOR

"He dresses like a country squire who's having trouble meeting the servants' wages bill and talks like a village publican with a mouth full of rice pudding."

Pete Silverton, *Sounds*

Pete Frame was born in Luton, Bedfordshire in 1942. He was on course to become a Chartered Surveyor but his career path was bent out of shape during the late 1960s when, as an emotional response to the heady times, he "dropped out to do his own thing", to write about rock music – a passion since his schooldays.

During the 1970s, economic necessity forced him to endure spells with two record companies, Charisma and Stiff; to work in various clandestine operations involving the spotting, managing and publicising of talent; and to pay further dues in the employ of two local authorities, a building firm and a brewery. Since 1979, however, he has managed to scratch a living off his pen, contributing to NME, *Melody Maker*, *Rolling Stone*, *The Times* and *Zigzag* – a pioneering rock magazine which he founded and edited for several years.

He has researched and written many documentaries for BBC Radio, including *30 Years Of Rock*, *The Story Of Atlantic*, *The Paul Simon Songbook*, *Signs Of The Times* and *Mavericks*. He and producer Kevin Howlett won Sony Awards for their Buddy Holly tribute *Not Fade Away* (1989) and their celebration of Leonard Cohen's work *Tower Of Song* (1995). Further programmes on Elvis Presley and Frank Zappa took silver and bronze, respectively. He was awarded a Gold Badge of Merit by the British Academy of Songwriters Composers and Authors in October 1995 – an event which found him sharing the stage with the unlikely company of Rolf Harris, Albert Lee and Larry Adler.

His handwritten *Rock Family Trees*, for which he is probably best known, have been used in the packaging of recordings by Jeff Beck, the Byrds, Eric Clapton, Crosby Stills & Nash, Fairport Convention, Iron Maiden, Talking Heads, Paul McCartney, Rod Stewart, and many more. Omnibus Press has published four anthologies of these genealogical charts, judged by *Rolling Stone* magazine to be "so elegantly organised as to defy description". The originals have been exhibited in various art galleries and some are on permanent display at the Museum of Liverpool Life.

BBC Television have broadcast two six-part television series based on *Rock Family Trees*, plus further programmes based on his Monty Python genealogy and his Manchester United family trees, *The United Years*, which were also published in book form by Andre Deutsch.

He is currently living in the Highlands of Scotland, exploring new territory as ever.

ABOUT THE TYPEFACE

This book was set in Benbow (not to be confused with the more familiar Bembo), a recutting of a typeface long thought to have been originated by Pieter Gallizowski, a practising typefounder in Luxembourg during the years 1668–1687. However, it has been conclusively demonstrated that the font was actually the work of Thomas Rapp (1650–1712), a Dutchman who learned his trade in Utrecht, under the influential Flemish master Dirk Faes. The type was subsequently adapted and modified by the Worcestershire gun engraver and toolmaker William Caslon (1692–1766), whose graceful styles became fashionable across Europe during the eighteenth century. The name was given to this typeface as a tribute to Caslon's second cousin Admiral John Benbow, who had received fatal injuries during a skirmish with French forces off the West Indies in 1702.